Insights in Banking Analytics and Regulatory Compliance Using AI

Sudhir Rana
Gulf Medical University, UAE

Shalini Aggarwal
Chandigarh University, India

Sharneet Singh Jagirdar
Chandigarh University, India

Sanjeev Jain
Chandigarh University, India

IGI Global
Scientific Publishing
Publishing Tomorrow's Research Today

Vice President of Editorial Melissa Wagner
Director of Acquisitions Mikaela Felty
Director of Book Development Jocelynn Hessler
Production Manager Mike Brehm
Cover Design Phillip Shickler

Published in the United States of America by
IGI Global Scientific Publishing
701 East Chocolate Avenue
Hershey, PA, 17033, USA
Tel: 717-533-8845
Fax: 717-533-7115
Website: https://www.igi-global.com E-mail: cust@igi-global.com

Library of Congress Cataloging-in-Publication Data

Names: Rana, Sudhir, editor.
Title: Insights in banking analytics and regulatory compliance using AI / [edited by] Sudhir Rana, Shalini Aggarwal, Sharneet Jagirdar, Sanjeev Jain.
Description: Hershey, PA : IGI Global Scientific Publishing, [2025] | Includes bibliographical references and index. | Summary: "In order for organizations to stay competitive, organizations will have to implement the changes to their processes and embed the wave of AI, and which role in particular helps organizations implement change?"-- Provided by publisher.
Identifiers: LCCN 2024055695 (print) | LCCN 2024055696 (ebook) | ISBN 9798337302096 (hardcover) | ISBN 9798337302102 (paperback) | ISBN 9798337302119 (ebook)
Subjects: LCSH: Banks and banking--Technological innovations. | Artificial intelligence--Financial applications. | Artificial intelligence.
Classification: LCC HG1709 .I539 2025 (print) | LCC HG1709 (ebook)
LC record available at https://lccn.loc.gov/2024055695
LC ebook record available at https://lccn.loc.gov/2024055696

British Cataloguing in Publication Data
A Cataloguing in Publication record for this book is available from the British Library.

Table of Contents

Detailed Table of Contents

This chapter aims to comprehend consumer perception towards Artificial Intelligence and Robotic Process Automation in the Indian Banking sector. This study focuses on consumers' awareness level and usability of Artificial Intelligence and RPA toward various banking services. The study will explore the scope of artificial intelligence (AI) and RPA implementation in the Indian banking sector for consumer satisfaction. Exploratory-cum-descriptive research design techniques were used to analyze the data with one sixty respondents collected from NCR through cluster sampling. The semi-structured questionnaire was framed based on the Likert scale. Descriptive, Exploratory Factor Analysis, t-test, ANOVA, correlation, and regression statistical techniques have been used to analyze the data. This study gives insights into the Indian banking industry to understand the behaviour of consumers regarding the accessibility and usage of Artificial Intelligence and RPA.

This study identifies key variables influencing the risk of failure in Indonesia's Conventional and Sharia Rural Banks (BPR and BPRS) and proposes strategies to mitigate these risks. Using the Analytical Network Process (ANP) method, the study engaged 11 respondents, including banking practitioners from Conventional and Islamic Commercial Banks, Rural Banks, Islamic Rural Banks, and academics. Data were analyzed with Super Decision software and Excel. Results reveal four critical variables: 1) macroeconomic, 2) microprudential, 3) macroprudential, and 4) bank internal variables. The welfare aspect of macroeconomic variables emerged as the most significant, followed by the liquidity indicator in microprudential variables and the internal resilience indicator in macroprudential variables. These findings guide strategies to enhance banking performance and reduce failure risks. Regulators and the government should prioritize macroeconomic welfare indicators to strengthen the banking system and address factors contributing to BPR and BPRS failures.

Preface

Sudhir Rana, Shalini Aggarwal, Sharneet Jagirdar, Sanjeev Jain, Editors
April 2025

In an era marked by rapid digital transformation and evolving regulatory landscapes, the financial sector is undergoing seismic shifts. The confluence of Artificial Intelligence (AI), machine learning, blockchain technology, and other fintech innovations is reshaping how financial institutions operate, comply with regulations, and serve increasingly tech-savvy consumers. *Insights in Banking Analytics and Regulatory Compliance Using AI* seeks to explore these multifaceted changes through a collection of forward-thinking research contributions that blend empirical analysis, theoretical frameworks, and technological foresight.

This edited volume brings together global scholars and practitioners who provide deep insights into the intersections of AI, financial inclusion, regulatory compliance, sustainability, and consumer behavior. It aims to serve as a foundational resource for academics, industry professionals, policymakers, and students alike, offering not only theoretical explorations but also practical tools and frameworks to understand the challenges and opportunities within the evolving financial services ecosystem.

The book is divided into 17 chapters, each addressing a specific aspect of innovation and compliance in financial services, particularly through the lens of AI and digital transformation. Below is a chapter-wise overview of the volume.

CHAPTER OVERVIEW

Chapter 1 sets the tone with a review of corporate governance and corporate social responsibility (CSR) in the energy sector, emphasizing sustainability and the strategic role of governance in addressing climate and regulatory challenges.

Chapter 2 delves into the bibliometric analysis of AI-driven innovations in banking compliance, offering a data-rich perspective on trends, emerging technologies, and thematic evolution from 2007 to 2024.

Chapter 3 presents empirical research on the financial structure of firms in the Indian automobile sector, highlighting capital structure determinants and testing competing financial theories post the 2008 financial crisis.

Chapter 4 explores AI's role in transforming the retail sector, particularly in enhancing customer experience and operational efficiency, with quantitative validation through Structural Equation Modelling (SEM).

Chapter 5 introduces the concept of *Composable Banking*, a modern, API-led model that enables banks to build agile, customer-centric financial solutions rapidly and cost-effectively.

Chapter 6 investigates consumer perceptions of AI and Robotic Process Automation (RPA) in the Indian banking sector, using quantitative tools to analyze awareness, trust, and usability in the NCR region.

Chapter 7 examines risk indicators in Indonesia's rural banking systems (both conventional and Sharia), identifying macroeconomic and prudential factors influencing bank failures through the Analytical Network Process (ANP).

Chapter 8 explores how fintech can bridge the financial gap for unbanked and underbanked populations, analyzing global case studies and fintech innovations such as mobile wallets and blockchain-based solutions.

Chapter 9 focuses on the development and future prospects of green bonds in India, highlighting regulatory frameworks, market challenges, and strategic recommendations for expanding sustainable finance.

Chapter 10 builds on the theme of fintech and financial inclusion, emphasizing cooperative strategies across sectors to scale impact, while showcasing use-cases across decentralized platforms and mobile-based banking.

Chapter 11 discusses *Neobanks* and their disruptive potential across global financial landscapes, analyzing growth trends and challenges in digital-only banking models.

Chapter 12 shifts the lens to hybrid learning environments, exploring how self-efficacy and technological readiness influence student satisfaction—an important study relevant for institutions adopting AI-enabled learning platforms.

Chapter 13 introduces an Explainable AI (XAI) framework tailored for regulatory audits in banking, integrating mathematical models that balance AI performance with compliance transparency across major audit categories.

Chapter 14 investigates the strategic role of machine learning in financial services, from fraud detection to customer personalization, while highlighting the importance of integrating blockchain and addressing ethical concerns.

Chapter 15 takes a broader ethical stance, presenting a framework that integrates sustainability, responsible analytics, and ethical AI, urging a holistic approach to technological innovation.

Chapter 16 dives into blockchain and DeFi's transformative potential in Indian financial services, addressing regulatory readiness, scalability challenges, and opportunities for decentralized finance models.

Chapter 17 concludes with a case study from Pakistan, examining how liquidity influences return on average equity (ROAE) and overall bank performance using extensive panel data analysis.

This compilation not only reflects the ongoing evolution in financial services but also underscores the need for an interdisciplinary, inclusive, and ethically grounded approach to innovation. It is our hope that this volume inspires further research and collaborative dialogue across sectors as we navigate a future where finance and technology are more intertwined than ever.

Chapter 1
A Review of Trends, Challenges, and Best Practices in CSR and Corporate Governance for Sustainability Within the Energy Sector

Suzan Dsouza
https://orcid.org/0000-0002-6274-6110
College of Business Administration, American University of the Middle East, Kuwait

ABSTRACT

Corporate governance and CSR are essential for sustainability in the energy sector. This review investigates trends, challenges, and best practices in governance and CSR for sustainability in this industry. It highlights the role of governance frameworks in shaping CSR strategies, emphasizing board oversight and stakeholder involvement. The review also addresses the responsibility of energy companies in mitigating environmental issues like climate change through CSR and transparent reporting. It analyzes industry challenges, including regulatory hurdles, stakeholder demands, and the dichotomy between short-term gains and long-term sustainability. The necessity for strong governance and effective CSR initiatives is emphasized to navigate these complexities and uphold social legitimacy. Best practices in governance and CSR are examined, advocating for the integration of sustainability into business strategies.

1. INTRODUCTION

The energy sector remains a cornerstone of modern economies, powering industries, transportation, and daily human activities. Its vast influence, however, comes with significant challenges that span environmental degradation, socio-economic disparities, and complex governance issues. In recent decades, Corporate Governance and Corporate Social Responsibility (CSR) have emerged as pivotal frameworks not only to address these challenges but also to steer the energy industry toward a more sustainable future. As global demand for energy continues to rise amid growing concerns over climate change and resource depletion, the role of effective governance and responsible corporate practices becomes increasingly

DOI: 10.4018/979-8-3373-0209-6.ch001

critical (Dudin, et al., 2019; Litvinenko, 2020).Corporate governance is defined as the set of processes, customs, policies, and laws that affect the way a corporation is directed, administered, or controlled. It encompasses the relationships between a company's management, its board of directors, its shareholders, and other stakeholders. Effective governance is fundamental for ensuring accountability, transparency, and ethical decision-making at all levels of the organization (Larcker and Tayan, 2020; Puni and Anlesinya, 2020; Solomon, 2020). On the other hand, CSR refers to the business practices that involve initiatives that benefit society. CSR goes beyond regulatory compliance by incorporating social and environmental concerns in business operations and interactions with stakeholders (Aluchna and Roszkowska-Menkes, 2019; Fatima and Elbanna, 2023; Nave and Ferreira, 2019).

This chapter provides an extensive review of current trends, challenges, and best practices in corporate governance and CSR within the energy sector. It explores the historical development of these concepts, analyzes contemporary methodologies, and discusses how both frameworks intersect to support sustainable business practices. Through detailed examination, this chapter underscores the importance of integrating ethical business practices into operational strategies, ensuring that energy companies not only meet immediate market and regulatory demands but also build long-term resilience and societal trust. The narrative is further enriched with critical insights into how regulatory changes and technological advancements are reshaping the sector. As global energy demands intensify and environmental challenges become more pronounced, companies within the sector are compelled to reassess traditional business models. Increasingly, they are embracing holistic approaches that account for both profit and societal welfare. This chapter lays the foundation for understanding the evolving role of CSR and corporate governance in promoting sustainable practices, offering a comprehensive view that is both theoretically robust and practically applicable.

2. REVIEW OF LITERATURE

The scholarly discussion on corporate governance and CSR in the energy sector has evolved significantly over recent decades. Researchers and practitioners have examined these topics from multiple perspectives economic, environmental, social, and regulatory. This section synthesizes key themes from the literature and is structured into several sub-sections to provide clarity on the evolution, contemporary developments, challenges, and best practices associated with these frameworks.

2.1 Evolution of Corporate Social Responsibility in the Energy Sector

Corporate Social Responsibility in the energy sector has undergone profound changes over time. In its nascent stages, CSR was often associated with isolated philanthropic activities and community engagement projects. Early energy companies, primarily focused on resource extraction, recognized the need to maintain positive relations with local communities. However, these early engagements were limited in scope and often did not address the broader social and environmental impacts of operations. The modern concept of CSR began to take shape during the mid-20th century, spurred by rising public awareness about environmental degradation and social inequality. This period witnessed a gradual shift in the energy sector, as companies started to adopt more formalized CSR initiatives. The increasing public scrutiny and heightened media attention in the latter half of the 20th century further accelerated this transformation. By the late 20th century, energy companies were increasingly held accountable not only for their economic performance but also for their impact on society and the environment (Agudelo, Johannsdottir and Davidsdottir, 2020; Olanipekun et al., 2020; Suska, 2021).

In recent years, CSR has evolved into a strategic imperative rather than a peripheral activity. This evolution is characterized by:

- **A Broader Scope of Initiatives:** Modern CSR in the energy sector now includes comprehensive environmental management systems, community development projects, and initiatives aimed at mitigating climate change.
- **Integration with Business Strategy:** CSR is increasingly integrated into the core business strategies of energy companies. It is no longer viewed solely as a tool for public relations but as a mechanism for risk management, innovation, and long-term value creation.
- **Stakeholder-Centric Approaches:** With the proliferation of digital communication channels, stakeholders have become more empowered, and their expectations more diverse. This shift has led companies to adopt more inclusive CSR practices that emphasize dialogue and partnership with local communities, regulatory bodies, and non-governmental organizations.

The historical progression of CSR illustrates a transition from reactive measures to proactive strategies that align business objectives with societal needs. Energy companies are now expected to demonstrate a commitment to reducing environmental impacts, fostering social equity, and ensuring economic benefits are shared across all stakeholder groups.

2.2 Developments in Corporate Governance

Parallel to the evolution of CSR, corporate governance in the energy sector has also experienced significant changes. Traditional governance models that focused primarily on shareholder interests are being redefined to incorporate broader stakeholder perspectives. Recent developments include the incorporation of Environmental, Social, and Governance (ESG) factors into board-level decision-making processes.

Key developments in corporate governance include:

2.2.1 Emphasis on Long-Term Value Creation

In contrast to short-term profit maximization, modern corporate governance frameworks prioritize long-term value creation. Boards are increasingly tasked with overseeing strategies that balance immediate financial returns with sustainable growth, innovation, and risk management. This shift is driven by the recognition that sustainable business practices ultimately lead to more resilient and competitive organizations.

2.2.2 Integration of ESG Factors

Environmental, Social, and Governance (ESG) considerations have become central to the governance discourse. Investors and regulatory bodies are increasingly demanding transparency regarding how companies manage ESG risks and opportunities. The adoption of frameworks such as the Global Reporting Initiative (GRI), Sustainability Accounting Standards Board (SASB), and the Task Force on Climate-related Financial Disclosures (TCFD) has standardized ESG reporting. Companies now disclose detailed reports on their sustainability performance, environmental impact, and governance practices (Crifo, Escrig-Olmedo, and Mottis, 2019; Dicuonzo, et al., 2022; Neri, 2021).

2.2.3 Enhancing Board Diversity and Expertise

Modern governance practices emphasize the importance of board diversity not only in terms of gender and ethnicity but also in professional expertise and experience. A diversified board can provide multifaceted insights and more robust risk management, as different perspectives contribute to more informed and balanced decision-making. Research indicates that diverse boards are more effective in monitoring and guiding corporate strategy, particularly in sectors facing rapid technological changes and evolving regulatory environments (El-Bassiouny and El-Bassiouny, 2019; Fernández-Temprano and Tejerina-Gaite, 2020; Sarhan, Ntim and Al-Najjar, 2019).

2.2.4 Digital Transformation and Governance Challenges

The advent of digital technologies has transformed how companies operate and manage risk. In the energy sector, digitalization has introduced challenges such as cybersecurity threats and data privacy issues, requiring boards to develop a deeper understanding of technology's implications. The rapid pace of digital change means that governance frameworks must be agile and responsive to emerging risks and opportunities. The COVID-19 pandemic further underscored the importance of digital resilience and robust risk management practices (Brennan, Subramaniam, and Van Staden, 2019; Flyverbom, Deibert, and Matten, 2019; Manita, et al., 2020).

2.3 Current CSR Initiatives in the Energy Sector

The contemporary CSR landscape within the energy sector is marked by ambitious initiatives that aim to balance economic performance with social and environmental responsibilities. Companies are investing heavily in renewable energy projects, energy efficiency measures, and technological innovations to reduce carbon footprints. Simultaneously, there is an increasing focus on community engagement, capacity building, and the protection of human rights.

2.3.1 Environmental Initiatives

Energy companies are actively implementing projects to minimize their environmental impact. These initiatives include:

- **Investment in Renewable Energy:** Shifting from fossil fuels to renewable sources such as wind, solar, and hydroelectric power.
- **Energy Efficiency Programs:** Implementing technologies and processes that improve operational efficiency and reduce energy consumption.
- **Carbon Emission Reduction:** Adopting strategies aimed at reducing greenhouse gas emissions, including carbon capture and storage technologies.

These initiatives are not only critical for mitigating climate change but also serve as a strategic driver for innovation and cost reduction in the long run.

2.3.2 Social and Community Development Projects

Beyond environmental concerns, CSR initiatives also target social issues. Energy companies engage in community development by:

- **Supporting Local Infrastructure:** Building schools, hospitals, and community centers to improve local quality of life.
- **Empowering Local Communities:** Investing in education and vocational training programs to enhance skills and employment opportunities.
- **Ensuring Indigenous Rights:** Developing policies that respect and protect the rights of indigenous and vulnerable populations impacted by energy projects.

Such initiatives help companies maintain social licenses to operate and foster positive relationships with the communities in which they function.

2.3.3 Transparency and Stakeholder Reporting

Transparency in CSR practices has become a benchmark for accountability. Companies now employ standardized metrics and key performance indicators (KPIs) to monitor and report their CSR activities. This detailed reporting, often aligned with international standards such as GRI and SASB, builds stakeholder trust and demonstrates a commitment to continuous improvement. Energy companies that provide clear, consistent, and transparent CSR reports are better positioned to attract investment and enhance their public image.

2.4 Challenges and Barriers

Despite significant progress in the fields of corporate governance and CSR, the energy sector continues to grapple with multiple challenges. These challenges arise from a complex interplay of regulatory, economic, technological, and societal factors.

2.4.1 Regulatory Inconsistencies and Compliance Burdens

One of the foremost challenges is the inconsistency of regulatory frameworks across different jurisdictions. Multinational energy companies often face divergent legal requirements, which complicates compliance and increases operational costs. The dynamic nature of these regulations demands continuous adaptation and significant resource allocation, particularly from smaller firms with limited capacity.

2.4.2 Balancing Profit with Sustainability

There is an inherent tension between the short-term pressures to maximize profits and the long-term investments required for sustainable practices. Energy companies frequently face difficult decisions when allocating resources between immediate financial returns and investments in environmental and social initiatives. This balance is further complicated by the unpredictable nature of energy markets and fluctuating commodity prices.

2.4.3 Technological and Cybersecurity Challenges

The rapid pace of technological change in the digital era brings with it both opportunities and risks. While digital transformation can enhance efficiency and innovation, it also introduces new vulnerabilities, particularly in the realm of cybersecurity. Energy companies must invest in robust digital infrastructure and develop advanced risk management protocols to safeguard against cyber threats that could disrupt operations and compromise sensitive data.

2.4.4 Heightened Stakeholder Expectations

In today's interconnected world, stakeholders from local communities to international investors demand greater transparency and accountability. The rise of social media and digital communication has empowered stakeholders, enabling them to voice concerns and mobilize public opinion rapidly. This increased scrutiny forces companies to engage in proactive dialogue and to continually adapt their strategies to meet evolving expectations.

3. RESEARCH METHODOLOGY

This section outlines the comprehensive methodological approach adopted in this study. The research aims to explore the intricate interplay between corporate governance and CSR within the energy sector, and to assess how these frameworks contribute to sustainability. Detailed descriptions of data collection, analytical techniques, and validation processes are provided, along with a clear statement of the study's objective.

3.1 Objective of the Study

The primary objective of this study is to investigate the trends, challenges, and best practices associated with corporate governance and CSR in the energy sector. More specifically, the study aims to:

- **Examine the historical evolution** of CSR and corporate governance practices in response to changing regulatory, social, and environmental landscapes.
- **Identify and analyze contemporary challenges** faced by energy companies as they strive to integrate sustainability into their strategic frameworks.
- **Assess the effectiveness of current CSR initiatives and governance methodologies** in promoting long-term sustainability and value creation.

- **Propose actionable recommendations** for industry stakeholders, including corporations, policymakers, and community groups, to enhance governance frameworks and CSR practices in light of emerging trends and best practices.

By achieving these objectives, the study seeks to contribute to the broader discourse on sustainable business practices and to provide practical insights that can guide future policy and corporate strategy in the energy sector.

3.2 Methodological Approach

To address the research objectives, a comprehensive qualitative research design was employed. The approach combines a systematic review of academic literature with in-depth case study analyses. This multi-method strategy enables a robust understanding of both theoretical frameworks and practical applications.

3.2.1 Data Collection

Data were gathered from a diverse array of sources to capture the full spectrum of insights on corporate governance and CSR. These sources include:

- **Academic Journals and Conference Proceedings:** A rigorous review of peer-reviewed articles and conference papers was conducted. The selection focused on publications that address historical trends, contemporary challenges, and future directions in corporate governance and CSR. Key studies that were included in this review include works by Agudelo, Johannsdottir and Davidsdottir (2020) and analyses on ESG reporting frameworks by Crifo, Escrig-Olmedo, and Mottis (2019).
- **Industry Reports and Regulatory Documents:** These documents provided critical insights into the practical challenges faced by energy companies. They also shed light on the impact of regulatory changes on corporate practices and how these organizations adjust to new requirements.
- **Case Studies of Leading Energy Companies:** Detailed case studies of companies known for their exemplary CSR and governance practices such as Unilever, Patagonia, Microsoft, Novartis, and Tesla were analyzed. These cases highlight the strategic importance of aligning business operations with sustainability goals and illustrate the diverse approaches taken by companies across different geographies and markets.

3.2.2 Data Analysis

The collected data were subjected to thematic analysis to identify recurring patterns, trends, and key issues. The analysis was guided by the following focal points:

- **Evolutionary Trends:** Mapping the historical progression of CSR and corporate governance, with particular attention to shifts in stakeholder expectations and regulatory environments.

- **Challenges and Barriers:** Identifying specific obstacles ranging from regulatory inconsistencies to technological vulnerabilities that hinder the effective integration of CSR and governance frameworks.
- **Best Practices and Innovations:** Evaluating strategic approaches that have successfully merged CSR initiatives with corporate governance structures, leading to improved sustainability outcomes.

The analysis involved synthesizing findings across multiple sources to draw robust conclusions that are applicable to both academic and practical contexts.

3.2.3 Validation of Findings

To ensure the reliability and validity of the findings, the study employed cross-referencing techniques across multiple data sources. This triangulation process allowed for the confirmation of key insights and the identification of converging evidence from both theoretical literature and real-world case studies. Such an approach not only strengthens the credibility of the recommendations but also ensures that the study's conclusions are grounded in a comprehensive understanding of the challenges and opportunities facing the energy sector.

4. IMPLICATIONS AND CONCLUSION

The insights derived from the review of literature and research methodology have far-reaching implications for the energy sector. In this final section, we discuss how effective corporate governance and CSR practices contribute to sustainable development, enhance stakeholder trust, and foster innovation. The discussion is supported by real-world examples and concludes with strategic recommendations for future practice.

4.1 Implications for the Energy Sector

The energy sector is at a critical juncture as it faces unprecedented environmental challenges, fluctuating market conditions, and evolving regulatory landscapes. The implications of robust corporate governance and well-integrated CSR initiatives are significant and multifaceted:

4.1.1 Driving Long-Term Sustainability

Energy companies that embed sustainable practices within their corporate governance frameworks are better positioned to navigate market uncertainties and regulatory pressures. By focusing on long-term value creation rather than short-term profit maximization, these organizations can build resilience and adapt to changing environmental and social conditions. This approach not only mitigates risks such as those associated with volatile energy prices and regulatory non-compliance but also creates opportunities for innovation and growth.

4.1.2 Enhancing Stakeholder Trust and Engagement

Transparent governance practices and comprehensive CSR reporting have a profound impact on stakeholder relationships. Enhanced stakeholder engagement builds trust, ensuring that companies maintain their social license to operate. The active involvement of local communities, investors, regulatory bodies, and other interested parties fosters an environment of accountability. As stakeholders increasingly demand ethical and sustainable practices, companies that proactively address these concerns are more likely to secure long-term support and positive public sentiment.

4.1.3 Fostering Technological and Digital Innovation

The integration of digital technologies into corporate governance processes has opened new avenues for managing risks and optimizing performance. As energy companies invest in digital transformation initiatives, they are better able to monitor real-time operational data, anticipate potential disruptions, and implement proactive risk management strategies. However, this technological shift also requires robust cybersecurity measures and data governance frameworks to safeguard sensitive information. The dual focus on technological innovation and risk mitigation ensures that energy companies remain competitive in an increasingly digital world.

4.1.4 Promoting Environmental and Social Justice

By embracing CSR initiatives that emphasize environmental stewardship and social equity, energy companies can play a pivotal role in advancing broader societal goals. Initiatives aimed at reducing carbon emissions, transitioning to renewable energy sources, and supporting community development not only contribute to environmental conservation but also promote social justice. In regions where energy production has historically led to adverse social outcomes, a commitment to CSR can help redress past inequities and build a more inclusive future.

4.2 Conclusion

The comprehensive review presented in this chapter highlights the dynamic interplay between corporate governance and CSR within the energy sector. Both frameworks are evolving to meet the challenges of a rapidly changing global landscape. Key trends such as the integration of ESG factors, the drive toward long-term sustainability, and the increasing emphasis on stakeholder engagement are reshaping how energy companies operate.

The study demonstrates that effective corporate governance and CSR are not mutually exclusive but are complementary strategies that, when integrated, provide a powerful tool for addressing the multifaceted challenges of today's energy landscape. Energy companies that invest in robust governance structures, transparent reporting, and proactive CSR initiatives are better equipped to navigate regulatory complexities, manage technological disruptions, and meet the evolving expectations of their stakeholders.

The findings of this research underscore the need for continued investment in innovative governance frameworks and CSR practices. Recommendations for industry stakeholders include:

- **Strengthening Board Diversity and Expertise:** Ensuring that boards are composed of members with diverse backgrounds and expertise to provide comprehensive oversight.
- **Enhancing Transparency through Standardized Reporting:** Adopting internationally recognized reporting frameworks to improve accountability and build stakeholder trust.
- **Prioritizing Long-Term Sustainability:** Balancing short-term financial objectives with long-term investments in environmental and social initiatives.
- **Leveraging Digital Technologies:** Embracing digital transformation to enhance operational efficiency while maintaining robust cybersecurity measures.
- **Fostering Collaborative Partnerships:** Engaging with local communities, government agencies, and non-governmental organizations to co-create solutions that address environmental and social challenges.

In summary, the convergence of corporate governance and CSR practices represents a promising pathway toward a more resilient, ethical, and sustainable energy sector. As global energy demands evolve and new challenges emerge, the continued integration of these frameworks will be critical for ensuring that energy companies remain agile, innovative, and accountable. Through a committed approach to sustainability, the energy sector can not only meet its immediate operational challenges but also contribute to the long-term well-being of society and the environment.

The insights presented in this chapter provide a robust foundation for both academic inquiry and practical implementation. As the sector navigates the complexities of the 21st century, the principles of effective governance and responsible corporate behavior will remain central to its success. By aligning business objectives with societal needs, energy companies can foster positive change, secure stakeholder trust, and drive sustainable economic development.

REFERENCES

Adams, D., Adams, K., Ullah, S., & Ullah, F. (2019). Globalisation, governance, accountability and the natural resource 'curse': Implications for socio-economic growth of oil-rich developing countries. *Resources Policy*, *61*, 128–140. DOI: 10.1016/j.resourpol.2019.02.009

Agudelo, M. A. L., Johannsdottir, L., & Davidsdottir, B. (2020). Drivers that motivate energy companies to be responsible. A systematic literature review of Corporate Social Responsibility in the energy sector. *Journal of Cleaner Production*, *247*, 119094. DOI: 10.1016/j.jclepro.2019.119094

Alshbili, I., Elamer, A. A., & Beddewela, E. (2020). Ownership types, corporate governance and corporate social responsibility disclosures: Empirical evidence from a developing country. *Accounting Research Journal*, *33*(1), 148–166. DOI: 10.1108/ARJ-03-2018-0060

Aluchna, M., & Roszkowska-Menkes, M. (2019). Integrating corporate social responsibility and corporate governance at the company level. Towards a conceptual model. *The Engineering Economist*, *30*(3), 349–361. DOI: 10.5755/j01.ee.30.3.17511

Blazquez, J., Dale, S., Jefferiss, P., Heffron, R. J., Herbertson, J., West, R., & Hegland, J. (2020). Decarbonization pathways for oil and gas. In *Oxford Energy Forum (Vol. 121, pp. 1-40).*

Blondeel, M., & Bradshaw, M. (2022). Managing transition risk: Toward an interdisciplinary understanding of strategies in the oil industry. *Energy Research & Social Science*, *91*, 102696. DOI: 10.1016/j.erss.2022.102696

Brennan, N. M., Subramaniam, N., & Van Staden, C. J. (2019). Corporate governance implications of disruptive technology: An overview. *The British Accounting Review*, *51*(6), 100860. DOI: 10.1016/j.bar.2019.100860

Chowdhury, R. H., Choi, S., Ennis, S., and Chung, D. (2019). Which dimension of corporate social responsibility is a value driver in the oil and gas industry? *Canadian Journal of Administrative Sciences/ Revue Canadienne des Sciences de l'Administration, 36*(2), 260-272.

Crifo, P., Escrig-Olmedo, E., & Mottis, N. (2019). Corporate governance as a key driver of corporate sustainability in France: The role of board members and investor relations. *Journal of Business Ethics*, *159*(4), 1127–1146. DOI: 10.1007/s10551-018-3866-6

Dicuonzo, G., Donofrio, F., Iannuzzi, A. P., & Dell'Atti, V. (2022). The integration of sustainability in corporate governance systems: An innovative framework applied to the European systematically important banks. *International Journal of Disclosure and Governance*, *19*(3), 249–263. DOI: 10.1057/s41310-021-00140-2

Dudin, M. N., Frolova, E. E., Protopopova, O. V., Mamedov, O., & Odintsov, S. V. (2019). Study of innovative technologies in the energy industry: Nontraditional and renewable energy sources. *Entrepreneurship and Sustainability Issues*, *6*(4), 1704–1713. DOI: 10.9770/jesi.2019.6.4(11)

El-Bassiouny, D., & El-Bassiouny, N. (2019). Diversity, corporate governance and CSR reporting: A comparative analysis between top-listed firms in Egypt, Germany and the USA. *Management of Environmental Quality*, *30*(1), 116–136. DOI: 10.1108/MEQ-12-2017-0150

Fatima, T., & Elbanna, S. (2023). Corporate social responsibility (CSR) implementation: A review and a research agenda towards an integrative framework. *Journal of Business Ethics*, *183*(1), 105–121. DOI: 10.1007/s10551-022-05047-8 PMID: 35125567

Fernández-Temprano, M. A., & Tejerina-Gaite, F. (2020). Types of director, board diversity and firm performance. *Corporate Governance (Bradford)*, *20*(2), 324–342. DOI: 10.1108/CG-03-2019-0096

Flyverbom, M., Deibert, R., & Matten, D. (2019). The governance of digital technology, big data, and the internet: New roles and responsibilities for business. *Business & Society*, *58*(1), 3–19. DOI: 10.1177/0007650317727540

Klein, P. G., Mahoney, J. T., McGahan, A. M., & Pitelis, C. N. (2019). Organizational governance adaptation: Who is in, who is out, and who gets what. *Academy of Management Review*, *44*(1), 6–27. DOI: 10.5465/amr.2014.0459

Koolwal, N., & Khandelwal, S. (2019, February). Corporate social responsibility (CSR) implementation in oil and gas industry: Challenges and solutions. In *Proceedings of International Conference on Sustainable Computing in Science, Technology and Management (SUSCOM), Amity University Rajasthan, Jaipur-India*. DOI: 10.2139/ssrn.3358059

Larcker, D., & Tayan, B. (2020). *Corporate governance matters*. FT Press.

Litvinenko, V. (2020). The role of hydrocarbons in the global energy agenda: The focus on liquefied natural gas. *Resources*, *9*(5), 59. DOI: 10.3390/resources9050059

Manita, R., Elommal, N., Baudier, P., & Hikkerova, L. (2020). The digital transformation of external audit and its impact on corporate governance. *Technological Forecasting and Social Change*, *150*, 119751. DOI: 10.1016/j.techfore.2019.119751

Manning, B., Braam, G., & Reimsbach, D. (2019). Corporate governance and sustainable business conduct—Effects of board monitoring effectiveness and stakeholder engagement on corporate sustainability performance and disclosure choices. *Corporate Social Responsibility and Environmental Management*, *26*(2), 351–366. DOI: 10.1002/csr.1687

Martiskainen, M., Axon, S., Sovacool, B. K., Sareen, S., Del Rio, D. F., & Axon, K. (2020). Contextualizing climate justice activism: Knowledge, emotions, motivations, and actions among climate strikers in six cities. *Global Environmental Change*, *65*, 102180. DOI: 10.1016/j.gloenvcha.2020.102180

Nave, A., & Ferreira, J. (2019). Corporate social responsibility strategies: Past research and future challenges. *Corporate Social Responsibility and Environmental Management*, *26*(4), 885–901. DOI: 10.1002/csr.1729

Neri, S. (2021). Environmental, Social and Governance (ESG) and Integrated Reporting. In *Global Challenges to CSR and Sustainable Development: Root Causes and Evidence from Case Studies*, 293-302.

Oguejiofor, B. B., Omotosho, A., Abioye, K. M., Alabi, A. M., Oguntoyinbo, F. N., Daraojimba, A. I., & Daraojimba, C. (2023). A review on data-driven regulatory compliance in Nigeria. *International Journal of Applied Research in Social Sciences*, *5*(8), 231–243. DOI: 10.51594/ijarss.v5i8.571

Olanipekun, A. O., Oshodi, O. S., Darko, A., & Omotayo, T. (2020). The state of corporate social responsibility practice in the construction sector. *Smart and Sustainable Built Environment*, *9*(2), 91–111. DOI: 10.1108/SASBE-11-2018-0056

Park, J., Cuervo-Cazurra, A., & Montiel, I. (2023). The evolution of sustainability concerns over business activities: from local to cross-national to global. In *Research Handbook on International Corporate Social Responsibility* (pp. 7–24). Edward Elgar Publishing. DOI: 10.4337/9781802207040.00007

Popescu, C. R. G. (2019). Corporate social responsibility, corporate governance and business performance: Limits and challenges imposed by the implementation of directive 2013/34/EU in Romania. *Sustainability (Basel)*, *11*(19), 5146. DOI: 10.3390/su11195146

Puni, A., & Anlesinya, A. (2020). Corporate governance mechanisms and firm performance in a developing country. *International Journal of Law and Management*, *62*(2), 147–169. DOI: 10.1108/IJLMA-03-2019-0076

Sarhan, A. A., Ntim, C. G., & Al-Najjar, B. (2019). Board diversity, corporate governance, corporate performance, and executive pay. *International Journal of Finance & Economics*, *24*(2), 761–786. DOI: 10.1002/ijfe.1690

Schoenmaker, D. (2020). The impact economy: Balancing profit and impact. In *The Impact Economy: Balancing Profit and Impact*, Working Paper, 4.

Shah, S. Q. A., Lai, F. W., Shad, M. K., & Jan, A. A. (2022). Developing a green governance framework for the performance enhancement of the oil and gas industry. *Sustainability (Basel)*, *14*(7), 3735. DOI: 10.3390/su14073735

Solomon, J. (2020). *Corporate governance and accountability*. John Wiley and Sons.

Suska, M. (2021). Environmental Corporate Social Responsibility (ECSR) on the Example of Polish Champion Oil, Gas and Mining Companies. *Sustainability (Basel)*, *13*(11), 6179. DOI: 10.3390/su13116179

Sze, J. (2020). *Environmental justice in a moment of danger* (Vol. 11). University of California Press.

Chapter 2
AI-Driven Innovations in Banking Analytics and Regulatory Compliance:
A Bibliometric Perspective

Sharneet Singh Jagirdar
https://orcid.org/0000-0001-5716-6368
Chandigarh University, India

Pradeep Kumar Gupta
https://orcid.org/0000-0001-5680-4612
Thapar Institute of Engineering and Technology, India

Sanjeev Jain
https://orcid.org/0009-0005-0905-6304
Chandigarh University, India

Gagan Vibhu
Chandigarh University, India

Manish Sharma
https://orcid.org/0009-0007-9022-2019
Chandigarh University, India

ABSTRACT

The rapid growth of Artificial Intelligence (AI) is reshaping the financial industry, enhancing risk management, fraud detection, compliance automation, and decision-making. This bibliometric study explores AI-driven innovations in banking analytics and regulatory compliance, focusing on emerging themes, contributors, and research trends. Using the Scopus database, relevant studies from 2007–2024 were analyzed with tools like Biblioshiny to map co-occurrence networks, thematic evolution, and citation patterns. Results highlight financial systems, data analytics, machine learning, and ethical AI as dominant themes, while uncovering gaps in cross-market integration and the potential of technologies like quantum computing and blockchain. This study offers critical insights for academics, practitioners, and

DOI: 10.4018/979-8-3373-0209-6.ch002

policymakers to foster sustainable and ethical financial innovations.

1. INTRODUCTION

AI (Artificial Intelligence) has had a revolutionary impact across a variety of sectors, of which the financial sector is the most affected. AI tools like machine learning, data analytics, as well as automation have resulted in enhanced financial operations in terms of risk management, decision making and prediction. Despite its increasing complexity, the financial market will be both beneficial and disadvantageous when AI is incorporated due to factors that include; regulatory compliance issues among others like ethical concerns.

For the past few years many different types of businesses in finance (Jagirdar & Gupta, 2023) have been utilizing various programs based on AI for example tracing it back to fraud detection systems which are part and parcel of every bank's everyday life today or applications such as algorithmic trading or stress test preparations within SI banks globally too." Once these advances have been made then what becomes difficult are issues surrounding transparency (making something clearer), accountability (being responsible for what you do) or even fairness including determining appropriate regulatory frameworks that regulate their usage_pattern. This has also created issues of data privacy and security, along with the possibility of AI contributing to systemic risks if not properly managed.

This paper does a bibliometric analysis of the state of current research on AI in financial technologies, key themes being: compliance automation (RegTech), risk management, fraud detection, AI-driven stress testing, and the ethical implications of AI in financial decision-making. This study aims to provide a comprehensive overview of how AI is shaping the financial sector by analyzing research trends, leading authors, institutions, and emerging topics and identifying gaps in the literature that require further exploration. It aims to contribute to the fast-growing body of knowledge about AI in finance and offers useful insights for researchers, practitioners, and policymakers seeking to find a route through the ever-changing financial technology landscape.

2. OBJECTIVES OF THE CHAPTER

This paper is an attempt at doing a comprehensive bibliometric analysis on the use of Artificial Intelligence in finance. It takes a focused theme of RegTech and the use of AI for risk management, fraud detection, AI-based stress testing, and ethical considerations. The investigation is aimed at helping to reveal major trends in the AI research, determine who the top contributors are from among authors, institutions, and journals associated with this field, as well as establish upcoming issues within academic writing on artificial intelligence. Such directions should result into recognizing leading research areas, comprehending finance's AI evolution, and predicting the future of financial operations using artificial intelligence.

What is more, the paper looks into the implications of these changes and examines academic and industry's implications within the study. It opens up some insights into potentially missing parts of the body of existing literature and introduces directions for further research work. It is also directed at exploring challenges associated with taking in and implementing AI in a financial institution in terms of regulatory compliance, ethical questions, and risk management. The research would thus contribute to a better understanding of the intersection between AI and finance.

3. LITERATURE REVIEW

Academic publication has been constantly rising across all scientific fields leading to publications increasing with around 250% every decade since 190 (Thelwall & Sud, 2022). This unbridles growth makes a good literature review necessary for systematic and synthesizing existing knowledge, gap identification and theory building (Alegre et al., 2023; Rousseau et al., 2008). Amidst such boom the use bibliometric analysis has become a significant tool for researchers in understanding the research domains through identification of key contributions, influential authors, prominent journals and thematic shifts (Zupic & Čater, 2015; Donthu et al., 2021).

Although bibliometric methods initially began as simple citation analyses, they have evolved into more sophisticated ones like co-citation analysis, bibliographical coupling, and co-words analysis (Zupic & Čater, 2015). For instance, co-citation analysis traces intellectual lineage by linking work frequently cited together whereas bibliographic coupling connects recent studies based on common references (Donthu et al., 2021). These methods help researchers systematically organize vast and fragmented academic output, overcoming the challenge of mapping knowledge in growing research domains (Fan et al., 2022).

Bibliometric methods have become a backbone of knowledge mapping. They rely more on establishing the quantitative basis for finding the relevant literature or hub papers within a knowledge network (Zupic & Čater, 2015). These analyses have helped in determining research clusters and measuring the impact of the journal or author as well as tracing thematic development trends over time (Donthu et al., 2021). For example, citation analysis highlights the most influential works in a field, while co-word analysis detects emerging themes (Fan et al., 2022; Breslin & Gatrell, 2023).

Bibliometric methods add to conventional literature reviews, in terms of replicability and clarity for scholars. Research in the field of Management exists in the form of detailed syntheses termed as "miners" or expansive explorations called "prospectors" (Breslin & Gatrell, 2023). Through integrating these dimensions, bibliometric analysis serves not only the present state, but it also hints at the potential futures (Paul & Criado, 2020).

Bibliometric analysis serves the past, present, and future by considering all these dimensions. The integration of bibliometric methods in overview research can help in generating new theoretical understandings. Bibliometric analyses stimulate academic community to move on from well-worn theories and methodologies, thereby fostering innovation through varied angles (Alegre et al., 2023). The increased use of the methodology in such areas as finance, technology and environmental studies is a growing evidence of the adoption of fresh frameworks by scholars (Kunisch et al., 2023). For instance, Fan et al. (2022) have argued that the application of bibliometric analysis could reveal less-studied areas, thereby increasing the depth of understanding about systemic gaps.

Even though bibliometric analysis has various advantages, it becomes even more useful when applied in combination with qualitative methods such as SLRs. According to Zupic and Čater (2015), bibliometric methods, alone, cannot have the depth required for theorization. However, they allow the identification of meaningful gaps and proposing novel theoretical contributions when combined with qualitative approaches. Integration also supports the principles of open science since researchers increasingly rely on non-proprietary tools, such as VOSviewer, to visualize bibliometric data (van Eck & Waltman, 2010; UNESCO, 2022).

Today's bibliometric analysis has dramatically reshaped college studies because it has given us vibrant instruments to locate, blend together and propel forward various fields of cognition: evolution in this part of human learning might be seen from here.

4. RESEARCH METHODOLOGY

This study will make use of bibliometric analysis to systematically review literature in the application of AI to banking analytics and regulatory compliance. Bibliometric methods have been widely recognized as providing systematic literature reviews, hence the added transparency and rigor to results (Lim & Zhang, 2022; Paul et al., 2021). Specifically, this study employs the three-stage Scientific Procedures and Rationales for Systematic Literature Review (SPAR4SLR) framework, which entails gathering, synthesizing, and appraising data (Alonso-Garcia et al., 2021).

The gathering stage (Jagirdar & Gupta, 2024) describes the process of how relevant research papers are selected and retrieved for analysis. To identify appropriate documents, this study seeks to address key research questions such as conducting a network analysis of authors, institutions, and countries; examining the main growth trends and trajectories in AI-driven banking analytics and compliance; analyzing annual scientific production; and identifying the most frequently used keywords related to themes like compliance automation, fraud detection, risk management, stress testing, and ethical considerations in AI. In this study, we also examine other dimensions of textual data such as using textual content vectors from paragraph embeddings for machine learning (ML) models with a focus on banking analytics as well as sampling various article databases like EconLit to consider their impacts.

Otherwise, it would be impossible to determine accurate frequencies of banks leveraging artificial intelligence (AI) technology worldwide or specific measures taken by each one of them towards this direction. Several reasons justify the focus:. First, journal articles have strong peer review, often stronger than other types of publication, such as conference proceedings and book chapters (Paul et al., 2021). Second, Scopus allows for quick download and processing of bibliometric data (Donthu, Kumar, Mukherjee et al., 2021). Third, Scopus covers all titles extensively as it indexes more than 26,400 titles from over 5,000 publishers (Fahimnia et al., 2015; Andersen, 2021). These criteria ensure the use of quality and relevant literature for bibliometric analysis on AI and banking.

The study's search period was up to June 2023, and bibliometric data were retrieved from Scopus database in addition to the full text of journal publications. The selection of papers was based on the use of specific keywords constructed through vast discussions and reviews of previous expert evaluations in the artificial intelligence applications in banking analytics and regulatory compliance. The keywords used in the search were: (TITLE-ABS-KEY ("artificial intelligence" OR "AI" OR "machine learning" OR "ML" OR "deep learning")) AND ("banking analytics" OR "financial compliance" OR "financial regulation" OR "RegTech" OR "FinTech")) AND ("fraud detection" OR "risk management" OR "stress testing" OR "compliance automation" OR "AML" OR "KYC")).

This Boolean search has produced 164 articles, all of which were manually reviewed at a later stage. The few most significant publications on that specifically addressed goals the investigation had been left out for in-depth analysis. The methodology advocated by Donthu, Kumar, Mukherjee, et al. (2021) as well as by Paul et al. (2021) is followed in searching and choosing, aiming at integrating all relevant secondary sources that might contain valuable information on best practices among other things.

4.1 Organizing the Data

The prime aim of categorizing phase is to categorize and prepare articles ahead of assessment. This study employs the refine results filter for Scopus in order to refine the articles retrieved from the database (Lopes et al., 2021; Makrides et al., 2021). Articles are filtered based on specific criteria, including document type ("articles" and "reviews"), source type ("journals"), and language ("English"). The thematic relevance of papers to topics such as "Compliance Automation," "Fraud Detection," "Risk Management," "AI-Driven Stress Testing," and "Explainability and Ethics in AI" was also considered during the filtering process.

Only articles in English were considered, and other types of non-English publication were excluded. Few notes and editorials were also considered based on relevance criteria (Mukherjee et al., 2022). Topics unrelated to banking analytics and regulatory compliance, such as engineering or medicine, were excluded at the discretion of the authors. Non-journal documents are also excluded because they often lack the rigorous peer-review scrutiny that journals go through. These inclusion and exclusion methods are consistent with those outlined in the methodologies by Paul et al. (2021) as well as (Donthu et al., 2021) and they was used in identifying the final set of 164 articles at this stage.

4.2 Assessing the Data

SPAR4SLR approach has the final stage of reviewing and analyzing data for meaningful insights. For this research, it uses various bibliometric analytical techniques (White & Borgholthaus, 2022) to appraise a set of 164 papers about AI applications in banking analytics and regulatory compliance. Bibliometric analysis is a quantitative and statistical method used to objectively assess a body of literature from specific research area (Donthu et al., 2021).

In comparison with systematic or critical review approaches, bibliometric analysis gives more objective results, not susceptible to subjective bias as that is common with qualitative approaches. Traditional approaches are likely to focus on a small set of documents (tens to hundreds) and use qualitative techniques such as thematic and content analysis (Paul et al., 2021; Andersen, 2021; Donthu et al., 2021). On the other hand, methods of bibliometric analysis with approaches like bibliographic coupling and co-word analysis shed light on the intellectual structure within the field (Donthu, Kumar, Mukherjee, et al., 2021).

This study utilized the Biblioshiny package, which is an open-source tool operating within the R environment, for scientific mapping and bibliometric analysis (Aria & Cuccurullo, 2017; Thomas & Gupta, 2022).

There are limitations that the study acknowledges. These include possible gaps in what is covered due to certain restrictions within the databases and keyword selections made. It finally suggests avenues for more studies concerning the use of banking analytics as well as regulatory compliance within AI contexts.

5. RESULTS

Table 1. Descriptive analysis:

Description	Results
MAIN INFORMATION ABOUT DATA	
Timespan	2007:2024
Sources (Journals, Books, etc)	129
Documents	164
Annual Growth Rate %	26.98
Document Average Age	1.93
Average citations per doc	10.15
References	6837
DOCUMENT CONTENTS	
Keywords Plus (ID)	703
Author's Keywords (DE)	522
AUTHORS	
Authors	462
Authors of single-authored docs	30
AUTHORS COLLABORATION	
Single-authored docs	38
Co-Authors per Doc	3.04
International co-authorships %	23.78
DOCUMENT TYPES	
Article	70
Book	9
book chapter	17
conference paper	56
conference review	3
Review	9

The bibliometric data (Table 1) reveals significant insights into the evolving landscape of AI in banking analytics and regulatory compliance. The period of 2007-2024 is the recent but rapid development of this field, with an annual growth rate of 26.98%, which means that AI in banking is a dynamic and expanding area. This growth is reflected in the low average age of documents (1.93 years), showing that most of the research is cutting-edge and addresses current challenges in the financial sector. Research on this topic is widely distributed across various academic outlets namely publications, books and conference papers as evidenced by the 164 documents retrieved from 129 sources. The average citation count per document of 10.15 indicates that these studies are influential and make substantive contributions to academic discourse.

A myriad of issues has been covered from AI-driven compliance automation to fraud detection, risk management, AI ethics and others. The diversity of research in the field is also evident in terms of document types e.g., 70 articles; 56 conference papers with lesser contributions in books or book chapters. The content-wise dataset has an abundance of keywords represented by 703 Keywords Plus as well as 522 Author's Keywords which show how diverse the themes under discussion are. This implies that though peer-reviewed articles are dominant, conferences also play a significant role in disseminating the latest developments.

This research is very much global since there are 462 authors with a relatively high proportion of international co-authorship, which constitutes 23.78% of all authors. Every document in average is written with 3.04 co-authors; it, thus, portrays a collaborative feature of AI and banking-related research work. The fact that 38 single-authored papers exist also means that, while scholars working alone have also contributed significantly to this area of study, their collaborative research has tended to be more influential. The growth in publications and citations, the diversity of document types, and the global collaboration reflect the high relevance and expanding interest in this area. Moreover, the large number of keywords and the collaboration metrics point to the interdisciplinary and international nature of the research, emphasizing the need for ongoing studies and reviews to synthesize these developments and identify future research directions.

5.1 Co-occurrence Network Analysis:

Figure 1. Co-occurrence Network (abstract)

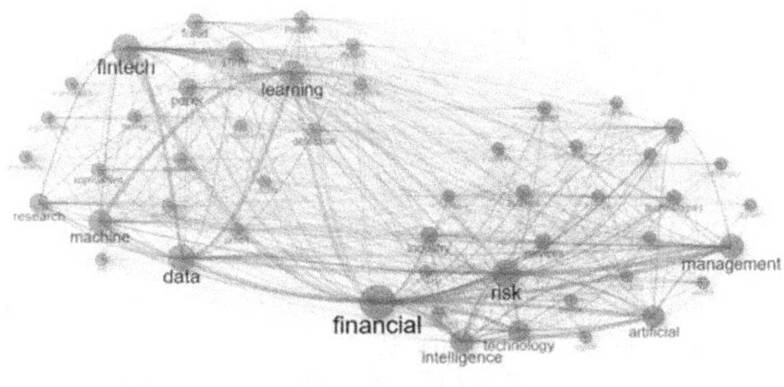

Figure 2. Co-occurrence Network - density (abstract)

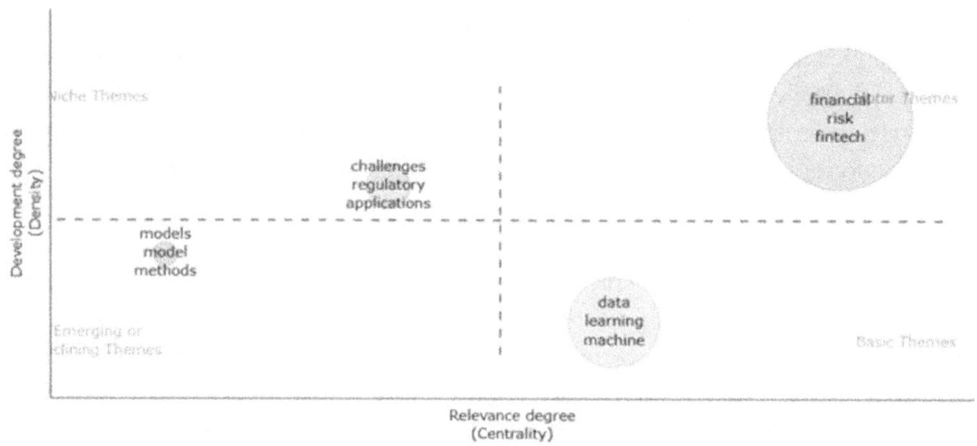

Figure 3. Co-occurrence Network – degree plot (abstract)

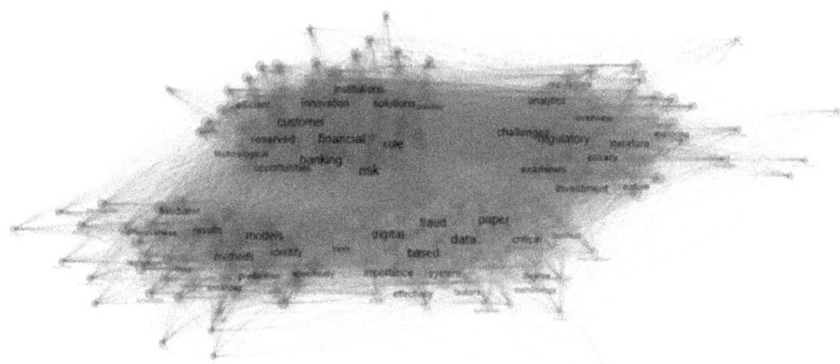

After performing bibliometric analysis on abstracts (Figure 1 refers to Co-occurrence Network, Figure 2 includes Co-occurrence Network – Density, Figure 3 includes Co-occurrence Network – Degree Plot), it becomes evident that the crux of Artificial Intelligence, banking, and regulatory compliance are significantly important. The abstracts are dominated by terms such as "financial," "risk," "AI," "management" which form the basis of the research terrain. To grasp how AI has been incorporated in financial sectors or for risk management and decision-making processes as well as these most critical words. Higher betweenness centrality values were found for "financial" (1.934) and "risk" (1.216) indicating their function as bridges between many other topics studied within this manuscript suggesting their significance in the broader academe discourse Additionally their closeness centralities were more similar among each other amounting to roughly .02 which shows that these terms integrate well into broader research community indicating their general nature.

In terms of importance on the network, the words “financial” and “risk” receive highest PageRank values of .047 and .038 respectively; affirming their pivotal contribution in setting research directions within AI-driven banking context. Other words such as “technology” and “banking” also make it to our top list again pointing at technology advancement and its application in banking sector as core subject for research. The second cluster is characterized by words such as “fintech,” “data,” “learning,” and “machine,” indicating the growing trend of technical sides of AI, for instance, machine-learning models, data analytics, and how they are used in the fintech industry. This is an indication of an increasing preference for more complex data-oriented approaches among financial professionals.

Furthermore, the regulatory as well as compliance dimensions remain crucial with words like “regulatory”, “compliance”, as well as “challenges” featuring prominently throughout the document analysis process. This indicates an agreement by scholars that in order to maintain regulatory compliance in the finance domain, AI plays a central role. Additionally, “Regtech”, “impact”, and “potential” as references indicate that AI's role in regulatory technology is being taken seriously, as researchers are looking into how it can change financial systems and compliance practices. Lastly, “fraud”, “detection”, and “models” are the concepts that show the attention placed on AI-driven fraud detection and risk assessment, further showing the importance of the applications in banking and finance.

In conclusion, analysis of abstracts shows that, though foundational concepts like risk management and AI are at the forefront of research, newer trends like fintech, machine learning, and fraud detection are on the rise. The results point toward the fact that the incorporation of AI in banking, especially in the aspects of regulatory compliance (RegTech) and fraud detection, remains a prime area of interest. This is valuable guidance for future research that accentuates the necessity for a thorough comprehension of how AI can be employed in handling problems facing current financial environments.

5.2 Bibliographic Coupling & Citation Analysis:

Figure 4. Clustering by coupling map

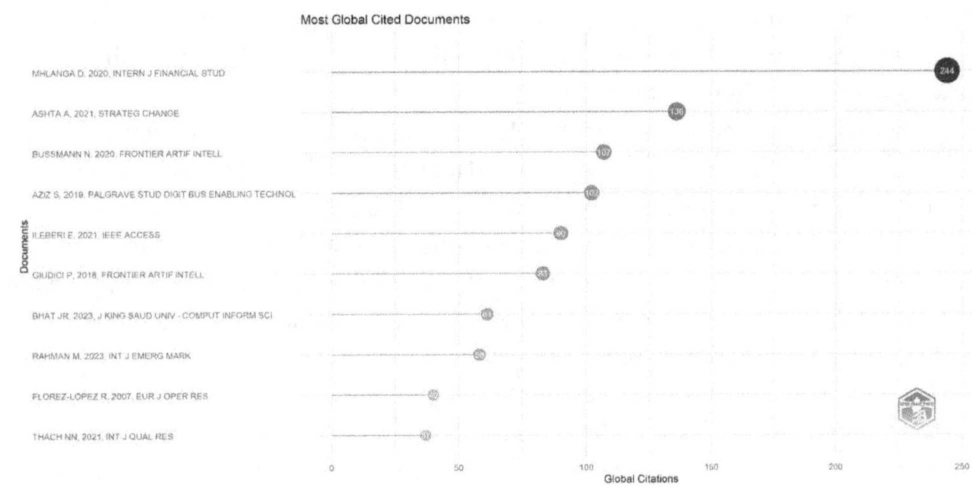

The association between measured citations and cluster labelling (Figure 4) based on abstract terms within research papers showed vital insights on the extent to which these papers are visible and impactful in their respective fields. When focusing on the first group that includes papers published in varied journals such as Heliyon (2024), International Journal of Financial Studies (2020), or even Strategic Change (2021), it is to be noted that the number of citations tends to strongly fluctuate. To give an example, not all papers are looked at similarly with some appearing more in isolation compared to other papers; for instance if one examines the work of Mhlanga D (2020), it has 244 times more reference than that of Ali G (2024). This demonstrates high citation rate against niche works; these may be concentrated areas under which specific studies can be found e.g., ICT in banking or AI in financial risk management. Also, every article in Cluster 1 falls under similar thematic areas including but not limited to fintech, risk management or AI. Mid-level citation on the topic however varies from one paper to another. One can infer from the provided information that everything is related in this cluster i.e., these journals focus mostly on patterns involving artificial intelligence or finance.

Cluster two includes articles published in other journals such as IEEE Access 2021 and Expert Systems Applications 2024 which are less cited generally suggesting that while research themes are still pertinent—usually revolving around AI, financial innovation including decision making—the influence of citations in totality might be subjected to specific limitations depending on among other things, how readily understandable the articles are, the exact subject under investigation or its freshness within the sphere of academia. Notably, there are papers in this group with citation scores of 90, like Ileberi E (2021), and 35 like Stojanović B (2021); hence, it is evident that some of the works found in the cluster have solidified stronger academic influence. Cluster 2 having varied citation scores and foundational papers for a wider acceptance and use among other fields like AI-based financial strategies as well as risk management suggests that these are emerging fields in which certain papers serve as bases for their adaptation by other disciplines.

In conclusion, it is evident from the clustering of citations that the degree of influence of an article according to citations is not always commensurate with how new or unique its subject matter might be. The citation levels might be varied differently within clusters and might relate to factors such as a journal's impact factor or the niche focus of a research study or even broader factors such as relevance to either the academic or practical financial technology and risk management world in general. The patterns identified give an understanding of how some topics, such as AI integration into finance, are gaining increased traction, while others may take more time to achieve high recognition and influence, no matter how academically rigorous they are.

The linkage between abstract terms and the cluster labeling based on the citation scores provides keen observations on the academic relevance and influence of different areas of research in finance, fintech, and banking. With the global citation score of 3.991 and centrality of 0.624, first-cluster topics with terms including financial, fintech, or risk are obviously at the center of discourse. Indeed, research into these topics-related to fintech and management of financial risks-is seen as highly visible and with great influence over the sphere. This has to do with the citation impact, reflecting the relevance and importance of these topics in both theoretical and applied research.

The second cluster is for the financial, data and learning topics, and at a moderate citation score has centrality of 0.585 and impact of 2.322; there's a sense in this case that these topics are receiving a lot of interest; they have not gained even remotely the same recognition the topic in Cluster 1 have. This might describe work at the nexus point between data analytics and/or machine learning and finance research where there is growing interest by how advanced technologies can be adopted to model and decide. Yet, the work appears just emerging.

Cluster3withafocusonabstracttermandhasnegligiblecitation impact with a centrality of .092and an impact of 2.417. It is plausible to assert that the low citation score for this cluster could be an indication of theoretical essence of the study which has not reached appreciable heights in influencing scholarship arena. Put differently, this is a probable indication that this particular cluster represents such early-stage or general concepts which have never been elaborately explored or applied:

Cluster 4: Banking, banks, and digital. This cluster's centrality value is very high as it stands at .989 though it lacks any significant citations so far; therefore, despite its principal role within banking discourse, it has not attracted much scholarly attention. This probably stems from its novelty or specificity necessitating further research efforts to raise awareness of it among academicians. Generally speaking, fintech and risk management emerge as strong areas exhibiting relative concentration. As such, upcoming themes such as data driven financial technologies are gaining momentum while these theoretical arguments may not be so rampant in social science literature but they have a bright future as they increase their popularity among other scholars.

Figure 5. Thematic map

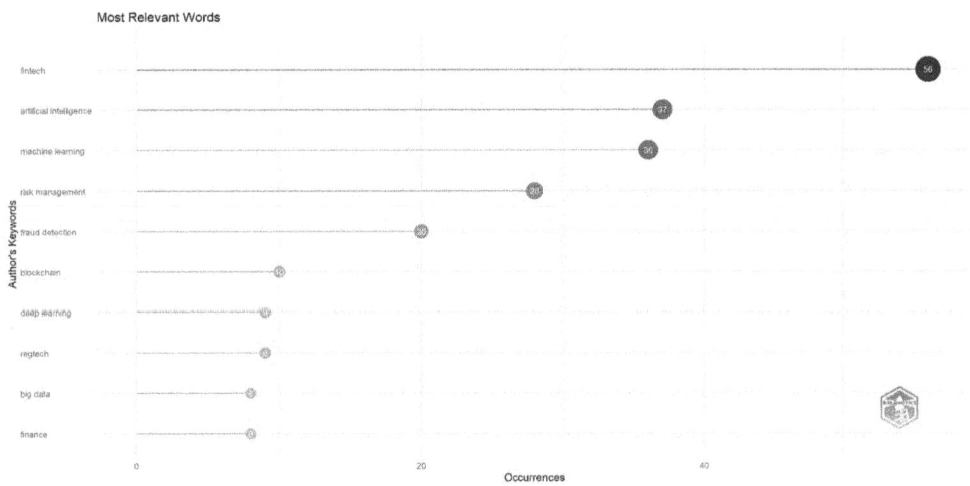

A myriad of financial, tech, as well as regulatory terminologies are presented in the dataset illustrating the fluid and multi-faceted nature of the financial landscape (Figure 5). Commonly discussed in relation to the financial sector are words like financial, fintech, risk, data. It is an indication of their importance that these words occur in various research papers or reports. For example, ai, management, technology, fraud, research, intelligence are also frequently used showing how Artificial Intelligence (AI) and technology are increasingly impacting on financial services, risk management and fraud detection.

Accordingly, words like risk, compliance, fraud detection, regulation and fraud remain paramount in the fight against financial crimes, automation of compliance processes (RegTech) and the management of all sorts of risks. Furthermore, the dominance of blockchain, AML, lending, investment, technology among other words reflects the emphasis that is put by this sector on technological innovations and regulatory frameworks that aid in carrying out financial transactions and making investments.

Terms with high centrality values such as regtech (179.326), AML (340.461), lending (134.983), and financing (313.186) are considered very important in the financial ecosystem. These terms can also constitute core elements of nowadays' business practices and they may be found in all business and financial regulations govern the business environment. For example, the frequent use in financial institutions of such terms as customer, business, service, development, and security is reflective of efforts made to enhance service delivery as well as improved operational efficiency and ensure regulatory compliance within finance industry.

The analysis also hails some of the current concepts like cybersecurity, innovation, and automation, leading to an indication that the industry is constantly progressing towards using advanced technologies and streamlining operations, reducing associated risks, and enhancing total efficiency. Additionally, terms representing research methodology, such as framework, analysis, impact, and approach, indicate a great emphasis on evidence-based research and analytical methods in addressing any financial challenge.

Overall, these results confirm that the financial sector has experienced a tremendous transformation as technology and regulatory forces create pressures and constant demands for better risk management and fraud prevention techniques.

Figure 6. Thematic map – network

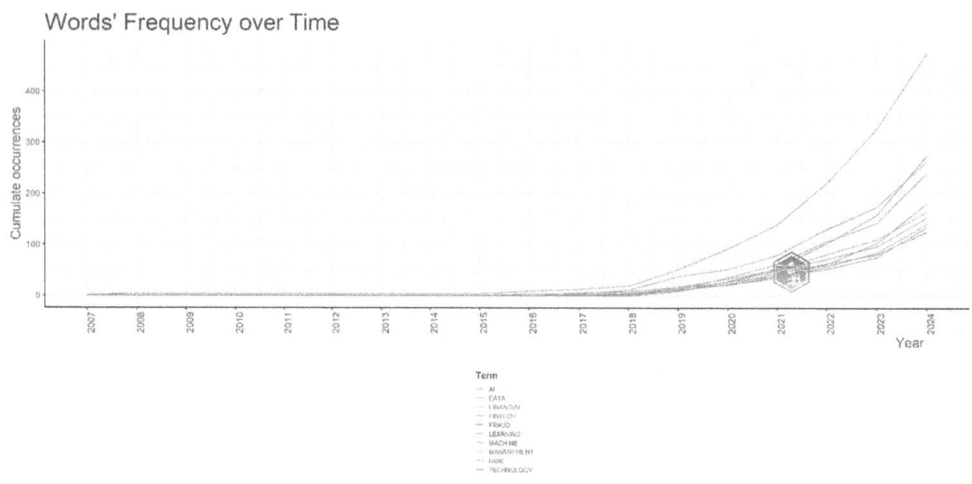

A large network dataset is provided (Figure 6) and indicates important clusters within this network that have contributed to the transformation of the financial sector, with specific insights gained through various centrality and frequency measures.

With high values for both centrality and frequency, the financial cluster is the most central and frequent cluster; it has a Callon Centrality score of 40.365 and a Cluster Frequency score of 416. The group of nodes comprising this cluster is made up of core concepts which are regarded as indispensable for contemporary finance including but not limited to risk management, fintech, compliance as well as investment strategies. Such high centrality would be a very important node in this network since it appears frequently in conversations about the overall financial space.

This has a moderate centrality value at 23.892 ranking second on centrality measures (Rank Centrality: 2), but its density is exceptionally high at 31.938. That means, even though learning, especially topics connected to AI and finance, is less frequent than any financial themes, it's always connected to understanding modern financial systems. Discussions in the learning cluster may likely involve education, skill development, and knowledge transfer-issues that are important to adaptation in changing financial technologies.

Market cluster has the highest rank in frequency, at 588 (Cluster Frequency), but a lower centrality score, at 19.853 (Callon Centrality). This indicates that even though market-related topics such as market trends, investments, and trading are prevalent, they are less central to the greater financial and technological contexts. Ranking the cluster based on density and frequency highlights the fact that financial markets take precedence, albeit without strong linkages to other major components within finance.

Summarily, insights extracted showed financial terms dominate in both frequency and centrality; however learning and market are also crucial, where learning indicating rising attention towards education and skills required in adapting financial technologies while market-related words showing constant changes in the dynamics of markets.

Figure 7. Thematic evolution map – abstract

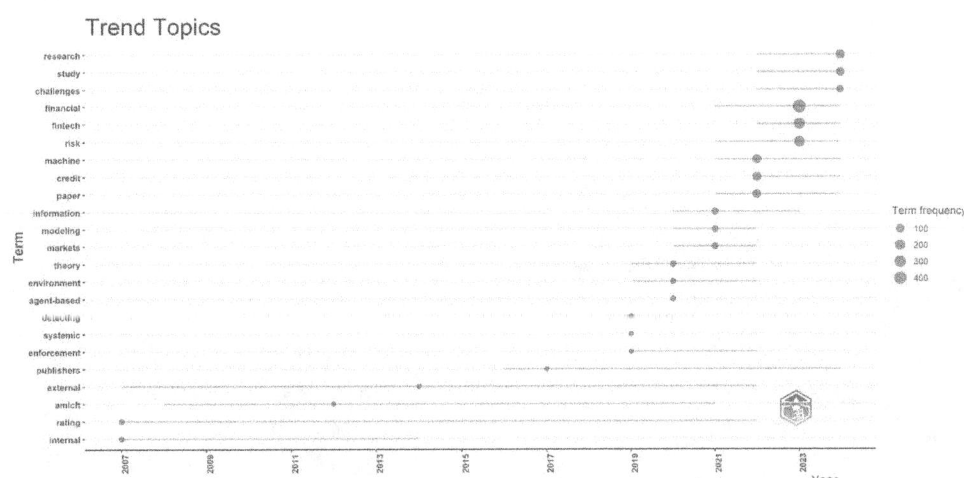

The data (Figure 7) shows the dramatic evolution of financial research from 2007 to 2024, with significant trends there. The connection of the words "financial" and "challenges" relates to an increased concern towards regulatory issues, compliance, and governance, and a lot of this can happen through technologies like regtech and automation. Despite a lower inclusion index, terms related to regulations and industry impacts suggest that these challenges are a key area of exploration. The relationship between "financial" and "data" shows the growing importance of data-driven approaches in financial decision-making, with an emphasis on machine learning, fraud detection, and risk management. This trend towards data analytics is seen in the high frequency of terms like "fraud," "data," and "banks," showing that financial institutions are now increasingly dependent on advanced data systems to deal with risks and improve operational efficiency.

The combination of "financial" and "financial" also shows that the themes of risk management, fintech, and artificial intelligence continue to expand. Research focuses on how these technologies are changing the financial sector, with terms like "AI," "fintech," and "regulation" signifying a strong focus on innovation, cybersecurity, and the new regulatory concerns that arise. The term "financial" and "models" relates to predictive models and machine learning in economic analysis, investment strategies, and financial risk management but is less focused on those models than on other topics.

The co-occurrence of "model" and "challenges" reveals that while financial modeling itself forms the heart of research, problems exist in the deployment of such models into actual settings. Complexity and scalability and similar issues continue to dictate how financial models develop themselves. The final association that has come up with the terms "techniques" and "financial" establishes an important area of optimizing analytics applications within finance. Increased practical, globally deployable solutions form the center for most work in finance recently. Similarly, the relationship between "techniques" and "models" indicates that financial models must be refined with more advanced techniques like algorithms and machine learning for accuracy, performance, and risk prediction.

Overall, the findings are indicative of a trend towards more sophisticated data-driven approaches in finance, where AI, machine learning, and advanced analytics continue to be integrated into financial services. While regulatory challenges are still substantial, technological innovation is gradually helping overcome these challenges, thus suggesting that the financial research and practice landscape is changing very fast.

Figure 8. Thematic evolution map – time slice 1

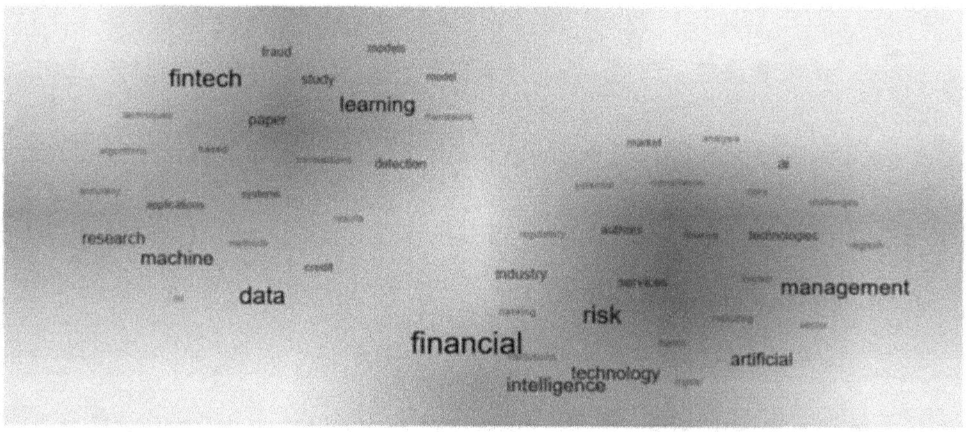

The data (Figure 8) presents an analysis of terms in the financial domain, with each word assigned various centrality measures that indicate its relative importance in the context. Words such as "regtech," "lending," "scoring," and "corporate" were the most prominent according to centrality measures, even of betweenness centrality measures, which points toward highly bridging words on this topic in the literature. Centrality values relate to the word position toward connecting broader topics. The world "AI" occurs crucial with high betweenness centrality. It is indicative of AI's great influence in financial systems including but not limited to financial technologies like machine learning, fintech as well as fraud detection. Its pagerank centrality speaks to its influence throughout the network. The word "AI" appears crucial with high betweenness centrality, suggesting it is pivotal in financial contexts, especially in technologies like machine learning, fintech, and fraud detection. Other regulatory terms such as "compliance," "regulation," and "regulatory" also represent critical functions, reflective of the trend on compliance automations within the financial segments due to the fact that "RegTech" puts an importance on that. In addition, the talk can be seen to manifest newly identified trends such as online banking, growth in data utilization specifically in assessing financial risks with the help of AI and machine learning techniques. Notably, the use of various terms like "technology", "applications" and "systems" occurs where financial services intersect with technical innovations. Conversely, terms such as 'data", "analysis", and "research" underscore how data-driven this era of modern finance has become.Altogether, this analysis looks into how technology, AI and regulatory frameworks transform financial systems with a strong emphasis on predictive models, compliance and risk management.

Figure 9. Thematic evolution network – time slice 1

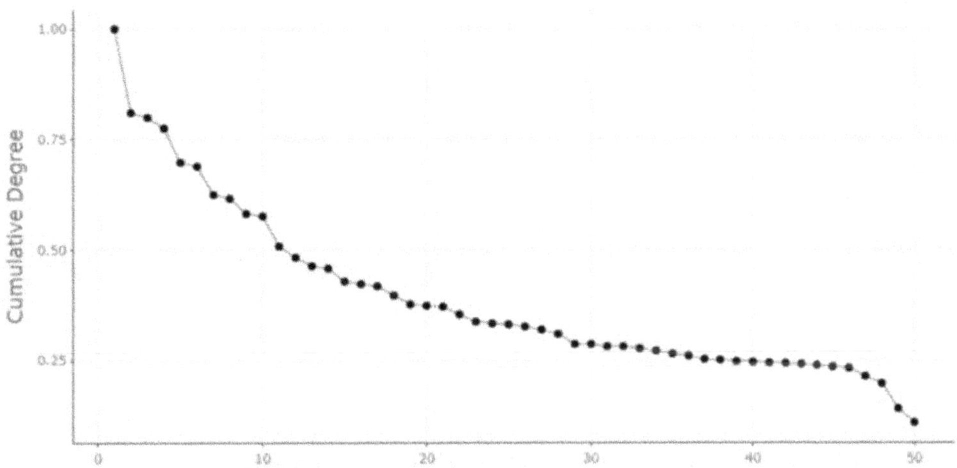

The abstract cluster data analysis (Figure 9) points to three clusters with strong patterns of influence and connectivity, which are the financial, techniques, and model clusters. The financial cluster appears to be the most central and densely connected cluster in the network with the highest Callon Centrality at 64.757 and Callon Density at 102.655, which indicates that financial topics are highly influential and strongly related within the larger landscape of research. In addition, the financial cluster has a 3rd rank in both RankCentrality and RankDensity, meaning that it is very important and cohesive in the general dataset, with a high Cluster Frequency of 2691, meaning that the research focuses widely on financial themes.

The techniques cluster, although important, has a lower Callon Centrality (30.735) and Callon Density (61.375) than the financial cluster, meaning that it has a more moderate level of influence and interconnection. It holds the highest RankCentrality value, which is 1. This indicates that topics associated with techniques are much appreciated within the research community. Having a rank density of 2 means the terms are related to techniques but not strongly - bound as they are in finance (or financial cluster). The Cluster Frequency was at 392 which implies that compared to the financial cluster, this techniques cluster is not often seen in this dataset.

In terms of centrality, the middle cluster model has Callon Centrality of 31.772 and Callon Density of 49.884 while falling between the other two. From these statistics it can be seen that there is some level of influence by the model cluster but the words do not show high links amongst themselves. The cluster ranks 2nd in RankCentrality and 1st in RankDensity, indicating a relatively high level of internal cohesion. With a Cluster Frequency of 491, the model cluster is more frequently mentioned than the techniques cluster but less so than the financial cluster, reflecting its moderate importance in the research network.

In summary, the financial cluster is the most dominant and interconnected, with techniques and models holding important, yet less central, positions in the overall dataset.

Figure 10. Thematic evolution map – time slice 2

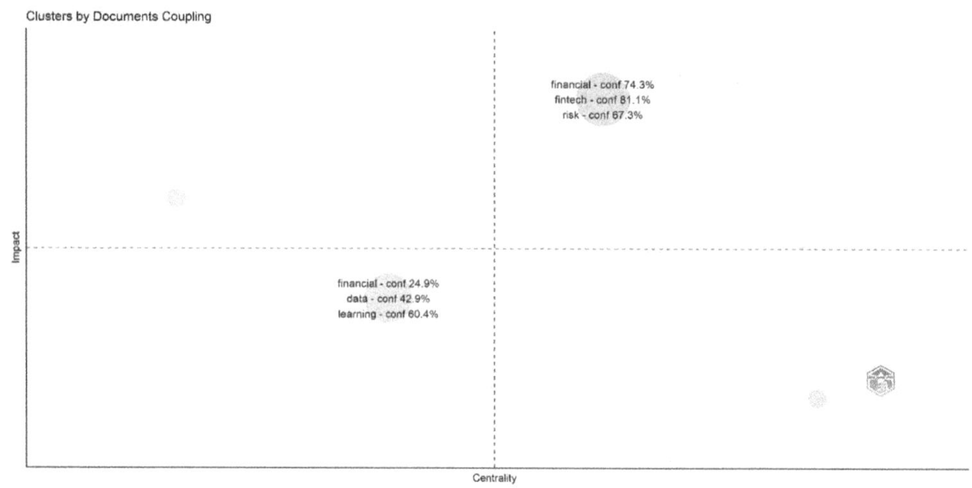

The key terms (Figure 10) and concepts of the challenges and advancements in financial models relate to fraud detection, regulatory compliance, and the use of AI technologies. The cluster "models" The use of algorithms, accuracy, prediction and performance as basic components of machine learning; is based on predictive analytics when it comes to fraud detection and financial decision-making. The centrality measures are betweenness, closeness and PageRank also show the importance of words like "algorithm," "prediction" and "fraudulent" which are important roles that these words play in the network of financial technologies.

The "challenges" cluster includes terms such as "regulatory," "compliance" or "frameworks" showing how much overlap exists between financial systems themselves as well as their regulation or legislative context. Important terms like "finance," "impact," "applications" and "benefits" help to highlight the industry impact, among others, whereas "governance," "ethics" and "privacy" are the ones that reflect increasing attention to ethical considerations in financial modeling and AI applications.

The "data" cluster emphasizes data and machine learning within financial systems in today's world—fraud, learning, detection and transaction represent massive datasets as well as sophisticated algorithms that underpin effective decision-making processes within economic environments particularly when dealing with stock markets. The "financial" cluster indicates how AI, fintech and blockchain technologies are increasingly influencing financial services sector with 'fintech,' 'AI,' 'technology' and 'blockchain' serving as reference points for integration of these technologies into banking systems.

The "data" and "financial" clusters are centrally positioned by the network centrality measures, highlighting that technological advances are interrelated with core functions of financial markets. In general, the analysis outlines the transformation taking place in financial institutions due to AI and machine learning by exploring opportunities and challenges related to fraud detection; regulatory compliance; and financial decision-making.

Figure 11. Thematic evolution network – time slice 2

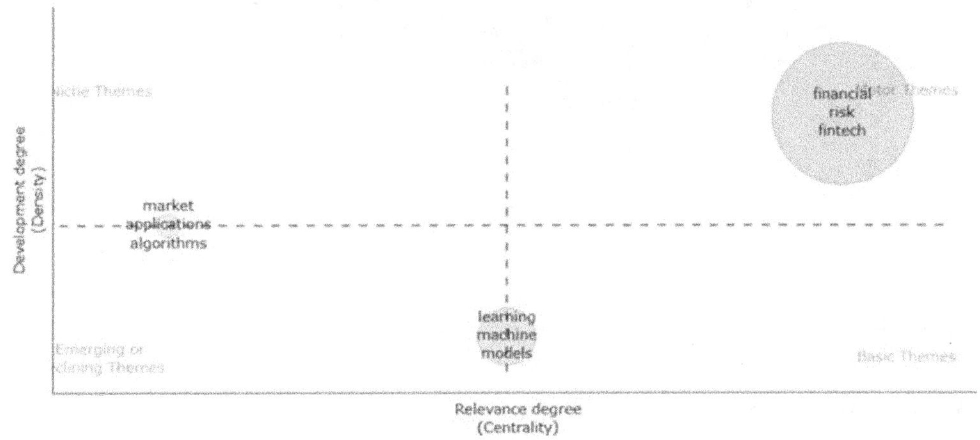

Figure 11 cluster analysis provides crucial insights into the connections between terms in the context of financial modeling and AI. The models cluster, with a Callon Centrality of 48.987 and Cluster Frequency of 315, is fundamental but ranks lower in terms of overall influence. Its high Callon Density of 87.497 indicates that the terms within this cluster are closely connected. The challenges cluster, with Callon Centrality as 66.237 is more influential, ranking at the second centrality place and third in density by reflecting the importance of addressing regulatory, governance, and ethical challenges in financial modelling. It is also highly interlinked, as indicated by Callon Density as 101.638. The data cluster has the highest Cluster Frequency at 599 and is most important in financial technologies but only slightly lower in Callon Density (67.042), indicating that data-driven concepts are a little more spread out compared to other terms. The financial cluster has the highest Callon Centrality of 133.364 which is why it is considered an important player in the debates on how AI coupled with blockchain, fintech are changing finance. In addition to 109.79 Callon Density, which shows there exists certain related concepts it is composed with, most underlining statement is made that finance remains a central theme amidst numerous developments around financial technologies' (FTs) landscape aspects such as banks' Internet policies vis-à-vis digital currency integration as well as merchant online payment solutions versus traditional card systems like VISA or MasterCard Worldwide among others even though there must be changes made sooner than later so commercial banks does not go bankrupt due to inability pay back their debts incurred during monetary crises like that one occurred in Asia in 1997. This discussion about financial systems' current dominance over the talk fails to consider the future path the industry will take because equally significant are issues about regulating entities' actions regarding it and appropriate utilization of predictive models. Refer Figure 12 for most globally cited documents.

Figure 12. Most global cited documents

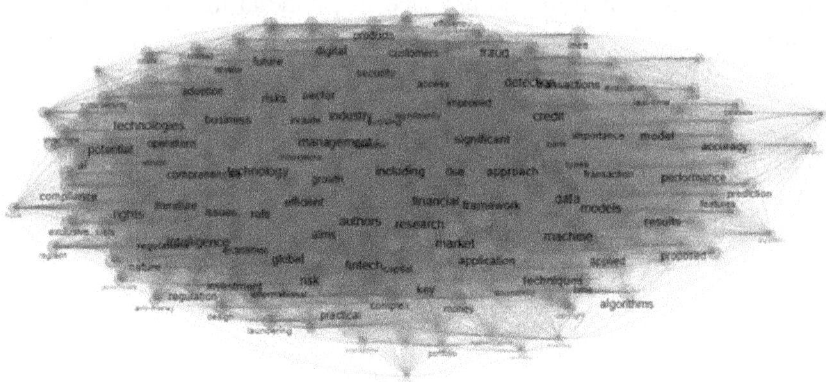

5.3 Text Mining

Figure 13. Most relevant words

Analysis of keywords related to AI in financial applications (Figure 13) reveals a significant trend in the use of various technologies. This article discusses common themes in various related sectors such as risk; finance; fraud detection among others. The study found out that fintech appeared 56 times while artificial intelligence and machine learning were mentioned 37 and 36 times respectively. This implies that there is a significant focus on incorporating AI into finance (html). Other prevalent subjects were risk management with 28 references made unto it; likewise, fraud detection came up 20 times together blockchain made 10 appearances indicating an industry concern for safety, adherence to regulations and novelty. Other niche topics such as deep learning (9 mentions), regtech (9 mentions), and big data (8 mentions) demonstrate an increasing relevance of advanced analytics in the financial industry. Credit scoring, portfolio management, liquidity risk, and financial fraud are some of the other terms related to financial operations, which have 5 instances each. These examples show the applicability of AI in risk analysis, decision-making, and financial strategy. Emerging trends in AI include explainable AI, neural networks, and reinforcement learning, indicating a shift towards enhancing transparency and model interpretability in the financial industry. Additional terms such as anti-money laundering, compliance, and cybersecurity imply that there are still attempts to make regulatory frameworks stronger and safeguard financial operations from any harm or danger. The representation of evolution in the fintech sphere can also be seen through different terms like digital banking, cryptocurrencies, peer-to-peer lending as well as insurance (though their frequency is lower), signaling the proliferation of AI applications in multiple financial sectors. This data shows that there is an increase in blending AI into risk management with financial technology to reshape contemporary finance.

Figure 14. Word's frequency over time

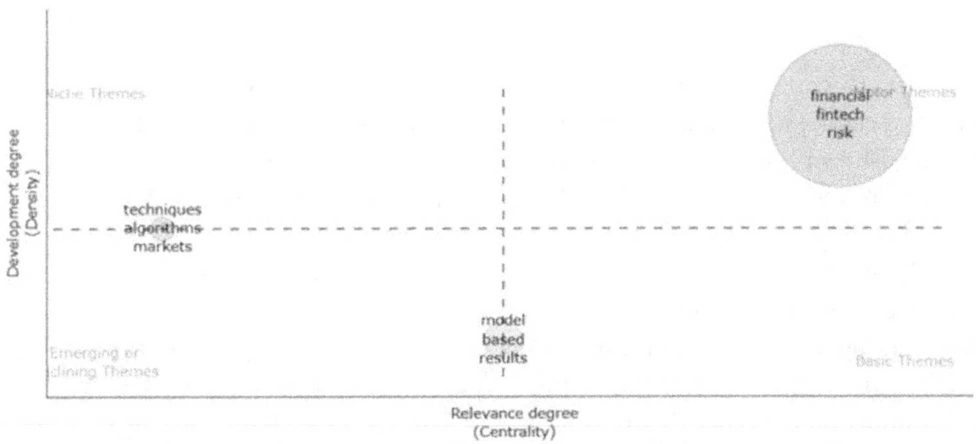

From 2017 till now, when it comes to finance, technology as well as risk management coming together in one place we are clear. Taken from Figure 14, these data forecasts a strong uptrend at an intersection where financial services meet technological advancements side by side with managing risks associated with them especially 2017 onwards. Terms like Financial, Fintech and Risk have seen their usage rate increase drastically as well as being frequent whereas about financial experienced 476 cases in 2024 that is very high compared to previous years Defined trends speak about direction that has to do with this integration of advanced risk mitigation strategies through financial technologies. AI-related terms, especially AI and Machine Learning, have seen the most dramatic rise, particularly from 2020, underscoring the expanding role of artificial intelligence in shaping financial strategies and mitigating risks. Risk has increasingly gained importance and reflects increased interest in financial stability and fraud prevention. Data and technology jargons have gradually become so popular since they are indicating more data analytics and new technologies reliance in financial sector. Activity was minimal in the early years between 2007 and 2012 which shows the initial stage in AI and fintech uptake. Nevertheless, from 2019, this trend has significantly gained acceleration and is driven by the introduction of machine learning and AI in managing financial operations to enhance compliance and prevent fraud. Overall, the data demonstrates how technological advancements, in particular AI, have completely transformed finance and have turned risk management, data analytics, and fraud prevention at its core.

Figure 15. Trend topics

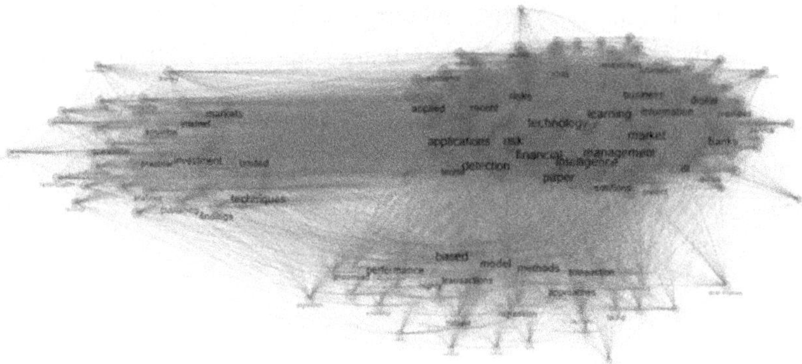

Frequency data (Figure 15) shows a significant emphasis on emerging trends and concepts in Finance and Technology sectors, particularly from 2019 onwards. The words Finance, Risk, Machine, Credit and Fintech have shown high frequencies over this period; in the year 2024 'frequency' reached an all time high of 476 for the word finance alone. These are arguably the main financial markets, Risk management strategies as well as Fintech innovations. Machine and Credit are also notable from 432 and 299 respectively indicating an increasing need for Machine Learning solutions as well as Credit Risk Analysis within Financial Operations

It appears that models, markets, data and research have been gaining popularity since 202 suggesting that decision making is increasingly being guided by data driven approaches linked to financial modelling. Introduction of Agent Based Modeling in 202 shows growing interest in Simulation based Techniques for Market studies.

The appearance of terms such as theory, environment, challenges, study, and research suggests that there is an academic and theoretical focus on the changing dynamics of finance and technology. These terms are concentrated around the years 2019–2024, signaling an era of deep exploration of the challenges, theoretical frameworks, and research directions in financial analytics.

Interestingly, terms like internal, external, amlcft (anti-money laundering and combating the financing of terrorism), and enforcement indicate some activity between 2007 and 2022; therefore, it is clear that issues on the regulatory and compliance front persist.

Overall, the results indicate a trend toward more complex methods, including machine learning and agent-based models, where innovation is taking place at the intersection of financial services, risk management, and compliance with an increased focus on research and data modeling. The growth in fintech and credit terms supports the trend of the finance sector undergoing digital transformation while credit risk assessment becomes progressively more relevant.

6. DISCUSSION

6.1 Key Findings

This bibliometric analysis reveals several critical insights into the evolving role of Artificial Intelligence (AI) in financial technologies. The study points out the major talking points as well as gives a description of the patterns with the high Callon Centrality and Callon Density showing how essential this particular sector is over others when we talk about its importance on AI related areas including risk management, stock trading or even forecasting in relation to finance. Data was the other major theme that emerged. Its high Cluster Frequency reflected that big data analytics, machine learning models, and predictive algorithms are gaining importance in the dynamics of financial markets. Both the challenges and models clusters further stress the need for innovative financial models to confront emerging challenges such as regulatory hurdles, market volatility, and ethical concerns in AI deployment.

Regarding research outputs, the study highlights the growing importance of challenges in AI. Issues with regulation and ethics become the dominant area of concern in financial technology research. It also suggests gaps in literature that deal with cross-market integration and the application of emerging technologies such as quantum computing and blockchain in finance.

6.2 Implications for Research

The findings do seem to point to AI expanding its scope in the financial systems. There would then be the need to cope with challenges in the fields of compliance automation, transparency with AI, and generally meeting ethical standards. Increased interest in how AI models and data practically apply themselves to financial operations calls for even more empirical studies to prove the hypothesis. The literature mirrors a shift toward regulatory compliance (RegTech) and the integration of AI in fraud detection and stress testing, areas that hold significant promise for future development.

This study highlights the necessity of integrating a variety of fields such as Artificial Intelligence, Law & Ethics; and Finance so as to guarantee responsible implementation as well efficiency of technological advances (Manhart and Mayer-Schönberger 2019). To maintain relevance of financial innovations within the rapidly changing marketplace, future studies would do well to concentrate on AI at connection points with emerging technologies within the financial services industry given its highly dynamic nature.

6.3 Limitations

This research has some limitations that need to be considered. Since the Scopus database does not include all output from every discipline it might have restricted the selection of papers in this review. In addition, some relevant works could have been excluded based on keyword selection even if they do not explicitly mention them during search terms definition but still contribute to the subject matter. Changes in time show kinds of things happening now like new developments which may not be included yet in any provided datasets.

Additionally, while on one hand drawing trends from general analysis, it might be important to realize that such things as specific internal subjects still remain uncovered if not looked at from an interdisciplinary perspective. Since the AI and financial technologies change so rapidly, the literature is constantly evolving, and future studies could refine these findings by incorporating newer data.

6.4 Future Directions

There are several directions for future research to be conducted based on this analysis. First, the ethical considerations of AI in financial markets should be further explored, especially regarding the transparency, accountability, and fairness of decisions. With the development of regulatory frameworks for AI, more studies regarding the impact of AI regulations (RegTech) and ethical models would be useful.

Another promising research area is the analysis of the position of xenon computing combined with blockchain in finance. Both are relatively new but are believed to have great potential in areas such as detection of fraud, real-time trade and data defense that would need more research efforts.

Finally, research on AI adoption across markets and cross-border financial systemsis another promising domain. This theme could open up furtherto discuss how AI-powered tools can be used for facilitating cross-market risk management; predictive analytics; and compliant automation, especially with relation to global financial stability.

7. CONCLUSION

This bibliometric analysis aimed to explore the evolving role of AI in financial technologies, focusing on key themes such as risk management, compliance automation, fraud detection, and AI-driven stress testing. Using data from the Scopus database, the study examined dominant research trends, leading authors, and institutional contributions, offering a comprehensive overview of the current state of research in this field.

7.1 Contributions to the Field

The study would contribute to the understanding of the intersection between AI and finance by identifying dominant research areas, emerging trends, and potential gaps in the literature. In this regard, it gives prominence to financial systems, which are at the forefront of data-driven technologies transforming financial markets. Additionally, the study offers valuable insights into the challenges that may arise from AI, specifically in terms of regulation, transparency, and ethical issues.

7.2 Practical Implications

For practitioners, policymakers, and researchers, this analysis has very important implications on the leverage of AI in financial services, particularly in aspects like risk management and compliance. The challenges that regulatory mechanisms pose and the ethical dimensions surrounding the use of AI demand an ongoing conversation and research process to ensure sustainable and responsible growth in the financial technology sector. Understanding these trends and challenges will help industry stakeholders better navigate the rapidly evolving landscape of AI and finance.

REFERENCES

Alegre, J., Callahan, J., & Iszatt-White, M. (2023). Innovative conceptual contributions—Raising the game for theory-driven reviews. *International Journal of Management Reviews, 25*(2), 233–239. DOI: 10.1111/ijmr.12333

Alonso-Garcia, J., Pablo-Martí, F., & Nunez-Barriopedro, E. (2021). Omnichannel Management in a B2B context: Concept, research agenda and bibliometric review. *International Journal of Industrial Engineering and Management, 12*(1), 37–48. DOI: 10.24867/IJIEM-2021-1-275

Andersen, N. (2021). Mapping the expatriate literature: A bibliometric review of the field from 1998 to 2017 and identification of current research fronts. *International Journal of Human Resource Management, 32*(22), 4687–4724. DOI: 10.1080/09585192.2019.1661267

Aria, M., & Cuccurullo, C. (2017). bibliometrix: An R-tool for comprehensive science mapping analysis. *Journal of Informetrics, 11*(4), 959–975. DOI: 10.1016/j.joi.2017.08.007

Breslin, D., & Gatrell, C. (2023). Theorizing through literature reviews: The miner-prospector continuum. *Organizational Research Methods, 26*(1), 139–167. DOI: 10.1177/1094428120943288

Donthu, N., Kumar, S., Mukherjee, D., Pandey, N., & Lim, W. M. (2021). How to conduct a bibliometric analysis: An overview and guidelines. *Journal of Business Research, 133*, 285–296. DOI: 10.1016/j.jbusres.2021.04.070

Fahimnia, B., Sarkis, J., & Davarzani, H. (2015). Green supply chain management: A review and bibliometric analysis. *International Journal of Production Economics, 162*, 101–114. DOI: 10.1016/j.ijpe.2015.01.003

Fan, D., Breslin, D., Callahan, J. L., & Iszatt-White, M. (2022). Advancing literature review methodology through rigour, generativity, scope and transparency. *International Journal of Management Reviews, 24*(2), 171–180. DOI: 10.1111/ijmr.12291

Jagirdar, S. S., & Gupta, P. K. (2023). Value and contrarian investment strategies: Evidence from Indian stock market. *Journal of Risk and Financial Management, 16*(2), 113. DOI: 10.3390/jrfm16020113

Jagirdar, S. S., & Gupta, P. K. (2024). Charting the financial odyssey: A literature review on history and evolution of investment strategies in the stock market (1900–2022). *China Accounting and Finance Review, 26*(3), 277–307. DOI: 10.1108/CAFR-10-2023-0124

Kunisch, S., Denyer, D., Bartunek, J. M., Menz, M., & Cardinal, L. B. (2023). Review research as scientific inquiry. *Organizational Research Methods, 26*(1), 3–45. DOI: 10.1177/10944281221127292

Lim, J. S., & Zhang, J. (2022). Adoption of AI-driven personalization in digital news platforms: An integrative model of technology acceptance and perceived contingency. *Technology in Society, 69*, 1–10. DOI: 10.1016/j.techsoc.2022.101965

Lopes, J. M., Sousa, A., Calçada, E., & Oliveira, J. (2021). A citation and co-citation bibliometric analysis of omnichannel marketing research. *Management Review Quarterly*, 1-34

Makrides, A., Kvasova, O., Thrassou, A., Hadjielias, E., & Ferraris, A. (2021). Consumer cosmopolitanism in international marketing research: A systematic review and future research agenda. *International Marketing Review*. Advance online publication. DOI: 10.1108/IMR-12-2020-0304

Mukherjee, D., Lim, W. M., Kumar, S., & Donthu, N. (2022). Guidelines for advancing theory and practice through bibliometric research. *Journal of Business Research, 148*, 101–115. DOI: 10.1016/j.jbusres.2022.04.042

Paul, J., & Criado, A. R. (2020). The art of writing literature review: What do we know and what do we need to know? *International Business Review, 29*(4), 101717. DOI: 10.1016/j.ibusrev.2020.101717

Paul, J., Lim, W. M., O'Cass, A., Hao, A. W., & Bresciani, S. (2021). Scientific Procedures and Rationales for Systematic Literature Reviews (SPAR-4-SLR). *International Journal of Consumer Studies, 45*(4), O1–O16. DOI: 10.1111/ijcs.12695

Rousseau, D. M., Manning, J., & Denyer, D. (2008). 11 Evidence in management and organizational science: Assembling the field's full weight of scientific knowledge through syntheses. *The Academy of Management Annals, 2*(1), 475–515. DOI: 10.5465/19416520802211651

Thelwall, M., & Sud, P. (2022). Scopus 1900–2020: Growth in articles, abstracts, countries, fields, and journals. *Quantitative Science Studies, 3*(1), 37–50. DOI: 10.1162/qss_a_00177

Thomas, A., & Gupta, V. (2022). Tacit knowledge in organizations: Bibliometrics and a framework-based systematic review of antecedents, outcomes, theories, methods and future directions. *Journal of Knowledge Management, 26*(4), 1014–1041. DOI: 10.1108/JKM-01-2021-0026

UNESCO. (2022) UNESCO recommendation on open science. Available from: DOI: 10.54677/MNMH8546

Van Eck, N., & Waltman, L. (2010). Software survey: VOSviewer, a computer program for bibliometric mapping. *scientometrics, 84*(2), 523-538.

White, J. V., & Borgholthaus, C. J. (2022). Who's in charge here? A bibliometric analysis of upper echelons research. *Journal of Business Research, 139*, 1012–1025. DOI: 10.1016/j.jbusres.2021.10.028

Zupic, I., & Čater, T. (2015). Bibliometric methods in management and organization. *Organizational Research Methods, 18*(3), 429–472. DOI: 10.1177/1094428114562629

Chapter 3
An Empirical and Inclusive Evidence of the Financial Structure and Value of Firm

Madhu Ruhil
Institute of Information Technology and Management, India

Aarti Suryavanshi
https://orcid.org/0000-0001-5022-3032
Manav Rachna International Institute of Research and Studies, India

Latika Malhotra
Institute of Information Technology and Management, India

Sonam Arora
Institute of Information Technology and Management, New Delhi, India

ABSTRACT

This paper investigates the impact of financial structure determinants on capital structure in the Indian automobile sector, focusing on the post-financial crisis period of 2008-09. The paper presents a descriptive and empirical study using panel data from 11 prominent automobile companies on BSE/NSE. The study covers ten years following the financial crisis of 2008-09, specifically from 2009-10 to 2018-19. This study employed correlation analysis and panel data regression models to identify the determinants of capital structure in the Indian automobile industry. The study identified five key factors that influence the optimal capital structure in the Indian automobile industry: Size, Tangibility, Growth, Debt Service Capacity, and Liquidity. Additionally, this study aims to determine which of the two competing theories, namely the Trade-off theory and the Pecking Order theory, provides a better explanation for the factors determining the capital structure of the Indian automobile sector.

DOI: 10.4018/979-8-3373-0209-6.ch003

1. INTRODUCTION

The capital structure is an imperative managerial decision. In today's scenario, managers are confronted with the most appropriate financing mix that would eventually benefit their shareholders' wealth. Hampton (1992); Vijayalakshmi, and Manoharan (2014), also suggested that a firm should concentrate on designing an optimum financial structure to achieve its fundamental objective, i.e., maximization of firm value. Therefore, financial managers must cultivate an appropriate capital mix that is most beneficial for the organization. Such capital structure can be developed by considering the various aspects that impact the composition of financial sources configuring the funding policies of a firm. Several factors influence the investment structure decisions of a company, and such bearing of particular factors changes over time. Hence, financial executives must frequently comprehend each factor's approach to their company's financial policies to design an ideal capital structure. Following the conventional beliefs from the various model such as net income, net operating income, and modigliani and miller approach of capital structure, many contemporary theories have developed that predicted the relationship of several determinants with the corporation's investment structure choices in detail. The two of these modern theories- *Trade-off and Pecking Order* Theory are said to be competitors of each other (Ambadkar, 2010).

The trade-off theory aligns with the conventional thought of Kraus and Litzenberger (1973), suggesting that the financial composition of a company is decided with the level of debt and equity in the mix to achieve equilibrium between the leverage tax shield benefits, agency costs and financial distress. Whereas the pecking-order approach proposed that a corporation follow a particular sequence of funding its assets, i.e., a firm prefers to first use its internally generated funds like retained earnings as a prime source; however, if the investment is higher than available funds, it would seek funds through debt and lastly, as a last resort, resort funds through fresh equity. The two theories have predicted the associations of factors like size, profitability, tangibility, volatility, growth, liquidity, and dividend with the capital structure. Ever since these two competing modern approaches emerged, the financial system and its contributing factors have been a significant consideration among economic researchers. Several studies have tried to identify the determining factors of financial construct and the applicability of these theories to such determinants in various sectors across countries. However, previous studies contradictory and mixed results documentation further necessitated comprehensive research on the capital composition determinants.

The projections of these contemporary approaches are applicable in most industries across countries (Tripathi, 2018). However, every economy and industry are different from one another, and their capital structure may differ amongst countries (Song and Philippatos, 2004; Hall et al., 2004), as well as industries (Bhattacharjee, 2010; Dawood, and El-Hennawi, 2011; Garima Dalal, 2013). Thus, the present research intends to identify the pertinency of these approaches (Trade-off Approach and Pecking Order Approach) on the financial composition factors of the automobile industry in India. Being a capital-intensive industry, it requires sizeable investment and consequently necessitates its financial executives to carefully design the capital structure after comprehending the factors determining its financial structure.

The study comprehensively works on the research question: Which of the theories above holds more relevance in the association of contributing factors with the capital structure of the automobile industry in India? Therefore, the present research aims to undertake a diverse examination to enquire the determinants influencing the capital mix and to trace the practicability of these theories on the relationship of identified elements of capital structure in the Indian automobile manufacturing industry. For this purpose, the decade from 2009-10 to 2018-19 has been taken as it represents the period, post the financial crisis 2008-09 and before the COVID outbreak 2019-20, to avoid manipulating results due to any of the stated causes.

2. LITERATURE REVIEW

The relevance of determinants of financial structure emerged from the Modigliani and Miller (1958) approach, which asserted that a concern's worth is separate from its capital mix composition in the absence of taxes. The assumption of the non-existence of taxes was strongly criticized and consequently resulted in the subsequent research of Modigliani and Miller in 1963, concluding a favourable impact of leverage tax shield, one of the capital structure's determining factors, on the firm's value. Ever since then, there has been continual debate on identifying the determining factors of the ideal financial building that ultimately enhances the worth of shareholders, and numerous modern theories have developed that predicted the affiliation of various determining components with the financial assembly decisions of a company in detail.

According to the arguments of Kraus and Litzenberger (1973), the ideal level of leverage and equity can be attained by bringing logrolling amid the debt tax-cover perks and financial blues and agency charges as the large chunk of edge in the financial structure of a firm will boost the financial dejection costs that eventually will offset the advantage enjoyed because of the credit tax-shield. Moreover, the vigorous rendition of the trade-off theory proposed by Fischer et al.,(1989) suggests an elastic capital structure in which the upper boundaries and the lower boundaries for raising the debt can be fixed, and within these boundaries, restructuring the debt of the firm and equity can be attempted to stabilize its capital structure. Quite a reverse, Gordon Donaldson (1961), proposed the pecking order theory, which doesn't predict any favourable financial structure but suggests a specific financing sequence of financing the firm investments. It recommends using internally generated funds first; if it requires further funds, it would seek funds through the debt and, as a final recourse, through fresh equity. Another theory that Majluf and Myers (1984), regarded as the modified pecking order theory recognizes the presence of asymmetrical facts, signaling theory, financial distress cost and the firm's sticky dividend policies. They recognized the reasoning behind the sequential financing strategy by stating that the firms keep a check on their debt levels and retain them within the caution limits to reserve their borrowing capacity, referred to as financial slack, to use it when they need additional funds, and to avoid financing through any risky securities issuance. Both theories projected the associations in factors like size, profitability, tangibility, volatility, growth, liquidity, and dividend with the capital structure. Since these two competing modern theories emerged, the debate on capital determinants has intensified, and numerous contributions have been made. Several authors have tried to test the relationship of various factors on the financial mix structure, but the results documented were contradictory and mixed, as discussed below:

2.1 Size

The role of size on leverage is unclear and vague. Some of the empirical research studies show that Size possesses a positive relation with leverage and supports the trade-off approach, which prognosticates a reverse association between size and the likelihood of bankruptcy and, thus, an affirmative association between size and leverage (Lee Remmers et al.,1974; Huang and Song 2002; Rajan and Zingales 1995; Buferna et al., 2005; Song 2005; Ambadkar 2010; R. Deepa 2011; Mukherjee and Mahakud 2012).

Whereas other studies show a negative relation supporting the pecking order theory that facilitates the prediction of more prominent firms exhibiting a growing preference for internal funds about debt (Titman and Wessel's 1988; Chen 2003; Purohit and Khanna 2012; Tripathi 2018). Test the bearing of size on debt ratios, the study assumes the hypothesis mentioned below:

H_1: There is a substantial bearing of size on the leverage ratios of the automobile industry in India.

2.2 Profitability

The Static trade-off approach shows a converse association between distress cost and profitability and, therefore, exhibits an affirmative affiliation with leverage. Peterson and Rajan, (1994); Singh, (1995); Pandey, (2004); Buferna, et al., (2005); Deepa, (2011), supported the static trade-off approach by confirming an affirmative relationship between them. Whereas Kakani,(1999); Booth, et al., (2001); Bahudri, (2002); Chen, (2003); Bevan, and Denbolt (2004); Mallikarjunappa, and Carmelita, (2007); Chakraborty, (2010); Ambadkar, (2010); Tripathi, (2018) confirmed the estimations of pecking order approach indicating a firm's preference to use residual profits initially, subsequently debt and after that equity to finance its projects, and hence show the existence of inverse relation of profitability with leverage. On the grounds of this literature, the following hypothesis is posited:

H_2: There is a substantial bearing of profitability the leverage ratios of the automobile industry in India.

2.3 Tangibility

Creditors demand high-interest rates and set strict terms & conditions for firms having less assets to use as collateral. To avoid these severe conditions, firms may opt for equity in place of debt financing (Ambadkar, 2010). The trade-off theory also suggests that a high ratio of tangible assets reduces the cost of debt and increases the debt capacity of a firm (Rajan and Zingales, 1995; Tripathi, 2018). Kakani, (1999) and Song, (2005) found that tangibility positively relates to total debt and long-term debts. Still, the former found a substantial and later negative relation with short run debt. The pecking order approach suggests that due to agency cost, a firm with less tangibility may opt for a higher level of debt as it serves to curb managers' tendency to spend the organizational cash on their perquisites by reducing the availability of free cash for wasteful expenses (De Angelo and Masulis, 1980; Kunt & Maksimovic, 1994; Mallikarjunappa and Carmelita, 2007; Deepa, 2011). In contrast, some empirical results showed an insignificant association between the trade-off and pecking order approach (Titman and Wessel,1988; Bhaduri, 2002). Test the bearing of tangibility on debt ratios, the study posited the below-mentioned hypothesis:

H_3: There is a substantial bearing of tangibility on the leverage ratios of the automobile industry in India.

2.4 Volatility

As per the trade-off and pecking order approach, company with variable earnings opt lower debt portion to avoid the possibility of bankruptcy and suggest an inverse association among the volatility and its leverage. The pecking order approach also states that a firm with high volatility in earnings accumulates its cash during years with good returns to avoid under-investment problems in the forthcoming period (Myers, 1977; Bhat 1980; Mittal and Singla, 1992; Kakani, 1999; Pandey, 2001; Gonenc, 2005). Huang and Song, (2002); Ambadkar, (2010), discovered a positive relation between the debt and volatility indicating that company with volatile income incline to borrow more debt. Some studies like Titman and Wessel, (1988); Baral, (2004); Deepa, (2011), highlighted insignificant associations between the firm's leverage and variations in its income. On the grounds of this literature the following hypothesis is developed:

H_4: There is a substantial bearing of volatility on the leverage ratios of the automobile industry in India.

2.5 Growth

As stated in the trade-off approach, growth has an inverse relationship with leverage because growth opportunities possess high risk and return relationships, leading to higher bankruptcy costs and avoiding raising funds via debt financing. Similarly, the pecking order approach advices a positive relationship by reasoning that higher the growth means a more requirements for finance and hence requires raising funds from debt sources. Kakani, (1999); Bevan and Danbolt, (2000); Pandey, (2001); Baral, (2004); Deepa, (2011), supported the pecking order theory and found a significant positive relationship with all the debt ratios. In comparison, Titman and Wessel, (1988), stated a inverse association among the growth of the compnay and influence with the reasoning that growth opportunities cannot be collateralized to raise funds and do not generate instant income. Ambadkar, (2010), stated that to avoid agency costs, a growing firm may issue short-period debt rather than long-period debt. Bhat, (1980); Song, (2005); Tripathi, (2018), found that growth rate has no significant relationship with leverage. Test the bearing of growth on debt ratios, the study assumes the following hypothesis:

H_5: There is a substantial bearing of growth on the leverage ratios of the automobile industry in India.

2.6 Non-Debt Tax Shield (NDTS)

Masuils and DeAngelo (1980), claimed that since the tax cover is available on debt and NDTS, firms may decide on a lower proportion of debt in their financial mix to avoid the probability of insolvency and further cost of debt capital from an additional unit of debt. With the same argument, the Trade-off approach also suggests an adverse association between NDTS and leverage. Tripathi, (2018), supported the theory and found an inverse relationship. Kakani, (1999); Huang and Song, (2002); Song, (2005), found NDTS positively impact on short term debt and an adverse impact on long-period debt ratios. Ambadkar, (2010), established that NDTS is adversely related to short term debt and completely associated to long tem and total debt. Titman and Wessel's, (1988); Mallikarjunappa and Carmelita, (2007); Deepa, (2011), found an insignificant relation between the two. Hence, the following hypothesis is posited by the study:

H_6: There is a substantial bearing of NDTS on the leverage ratios of the automobile industry in India.

2.7 Debt Service Capacity (DSC)

The DSC is applied to ascertain the capacity of a company to atone for its fixed payments on its outstanding debt. It informs lenders whether the firm can bear the interest expenses even if its profits significantly fall in any upcoming year. The higher the DSC ratio, the more debt a firm can have in its capital structure. Therefore, a positive relationship between DSC and leverage (Bhat,1980; Mittal and Singla, 1992; Tripathi, 2018). Whereas Mallikarjunappa and Carmelita, (2007) found a negative relationship between them, stating that firms might like to avoid financial distress involved in debt financing. Baral, (2004) and Ambadkar, (2010) found a statistically insignificant relationship between DSC and leverage. Test the bearing of debt service capacity on debt ratios, the study assumes the following hypothesis:

H_7: There is a substantial bearing of debt service capacity on the leverage ratios of the automobile industry in India.

2.8 Uniqueness

Bhaduri (2002), indicated that companies with exclusively distinct products find it hard to borrow due to their restrictive use of finance and less tactile assets and deduced an inverse association between uniqueness and leverage. Wessel and Titman's, (1988), gave a model that links a company's liquidation choice to its bankruptcy position. They argued that the clientele, employees, and traders of companies that churn out distinctive products undoubtedly grieve proportionately high costs at the time of liquidation because their employees and suppliers have only job-specific skills. Their clients may find it strenuous to find substitutes for their distinctive products. Therefore, this uniqueness and distinction is presumed to be adversely related to a firm's debt ratios. The trade-off approach also predicts an inverse relation between identity and a firm's leverage (Ambadkar, 2010; Tripathi, 2018). Kakani, (1999), also found an affirmative association between uniqueness and the firms' short-period debt and total debt. Mallikarjunappa and Carmelita, (2007), indicated a weak positive relation of uniqueness with leverage. On the grounds of these literatures the hypothesis given below is developed:

H8: There is a substantial bearing of uniqueness on the leverage ratios of the automobile industry in India.

2.9 Liquidity

Liquidity is the amount that is readily available for investment and spending. According to the pecking order hypothesis, businesses with more substantial financial assets might utilize them as an alternative internally reserve for capital to borrow, resulting in smaller amounts of debt and pointing to a possible inverse link between liquidity and leverage. The trade-off theory shows a positive relationship, as firms with higher Liquidity demonstrate their capability to placate the short-term liabilities and, thus, increase the debt-issuing capacity of that firm supported the pecking order theory and posited a negative relation between the two. (Mallikarjunappa and Carmelita, 2007; Ambadkar, 2010). Zuhaib, (2015) found a puzzling relationship and confirmed the pertinence of trade-off and pecking order theories due to the positive connection of liquidity with total debt and negative with long term and short term debt. Hence, the following hypothesis is posited by the study:

H9: There is a substantial bearing of liquidity on the leverage ratios of the automobile industry in India.

2.10 Dividend

The dividend is that part of earnings which is paid to the shareholders. The larger the dividend amount, the lesser will be left as retained earnings to finance the future investments; in this case, firms will go for debt issue to arrange funds for their future investments. It has also been suggested by the pecking order approach and indicated the affirming association between dividends and debt. Whereas the trade-off approach suggested an inverse relation between them, reasoning that the dividend payout can be higher only when the firm adopts a lower level of leverage in its capital structure, subsequently has to pay a lower cost of debt and saves a larger part of the earnings that are to be dispersed as a dividend. Ambadkar, (2010) and Zuhaib, (2015) also found that dividend payouts possess a statistically significant inverse relationship with different leverage ratios. But Tong and Green, (2005), supported the pecking order approach and found an affirmative association between dividends paid and a firm's debt. On the grounds of this literature, the following hypothesis is posited:

H10: There is a substantial bearing of dividends on the leverage ratios of the automobile industry in India.

3. RESEARCH METHODOLOGY

The paper presents a descriptive and empirical study using panel data from 11 prominent automobile companies operating under the Bombay Stock Exchange or National Stock Exchange for a 10-year financial period from 2009-10 to 2018-19 collected from the PROWESS database sustained by the CMIE. The study executed the panel data regression analysis on ten factors of capital mix as predictor variables and four leverage ratios as predicting variables, as summarized in Table 2, carefully chosen through an intensive literature review.

Table 1 presents the compendium of projections of the trade-off approach and the pecking order approach concerning the association between leverage and the above-mentioned financial structure determinants.

Table 1. summary of relationship predictions of pecking order and trade-off approaches amid determinants and leverage.

S. No.	Determinant of Capital Structure	Pecking Order Approach Prediction	Trade-off Approach Prediction
1	Size	-ve	+ve
2	Profitability	-ve	+ve
3	Tangibility	-ve	+ve
4	Volatility	-ve	-ve
5	Growth	+ve	-ve
6	Non-debt Tax Shield	No Prediction	-ve
7	Debt Service Capacity	No Prediction	No Prediction
8	Uniqueness	No Prediction	-ve
9	Liquidity	-ve	+ve
10	Dividend	+ve	-ve

To assess the effect of those, as mentioned earlier, on financial structure from the micro perspective, it is necessary to investigate the bearing of determinants on the most significant constituents of financial structure. Conventionally, long-term debt has been considered a prominent capital structure component. The long-term debt-to-equity proportion is the most acceptable measure of financial structure to express the relationship between debt funds and equity funds. Most of the researchers have adopted the ratio described above to represent the financing strategies of the companies and therefore, following Titman and Wessels, (1988); Mittal and Singla, (1992); Kakani, (1999); Garg and Shekhar, (2002); Bhattacharjee, (2010); Ambadkar, (2010); Deepa, (2011); Rasoolpur, (2012); Kavitha, (2014); Sofat and Singh, (2017); Tripathi, (2018), this study as well adopted LTD/NW ratio as one of the measures of financial structure. Many researchers like Rajan and Zingales, (1995); Bevan and Danbolt, (2000); Drobetz and Fix, (2005); Ambadkar, (2010); Ali,(2011); Tongkong, (2012); Anshu and Kapil, (2014); Bhattacharjee et al., (2015); Bazaz, (2015); Jagannathan, (2017); Merve, (2018); Kaur etal., (2020); Ghayas et al., (2020) studied the combined influence of short-term and long-term debt ratios on company value. Following their work, this study also adopted two total debt ratios, i.e., TD/TA and TD/NW. As a result, the present study undertakes four ratios to represent the capital structure of the industry, i.e., Long-Term Debt / Total Asset (LTD/TA), Long-Term Debt / Net Worth (LTD/NW), Total Debt / Total Assets (TD/TA) and Total Debt / Net Worth (TD/NW).

Table 2. Table representing the summary of variables.

S. No.	Dependent Variables	Independent Variables			
		Determinant of Capital Structure	**Acronyms**	**Measurement**	**Researchers followed the Measurement**
1	LTD/TA, LTD/ NW, TD/TA, and TD/NW	Size	SIZE	Natural Log of Sales	Bhat (1980), Titman & Wessel's (1988), Bevan & Danbolt (2000), Booth et.al (2001), Manos & Green (2001), Pandey (2001), Huang & Song (2002), Drobetz & Fix (2005), Baral (2004), Song (2005), Mallikarjunappa T and Carmelita Goveas (2007), Ambadkar (2010), R. Deepa (2011), Tripathi (2018)
2		Profitability	PROF	PBITDA / TA	Tripathi (2018)
3		Tangibility	TANG	Net Fixed Assets / Net Total Assets	Bevan & Danbolt (2000), Pandey (2001), Huang & Song (2002), Drobetz & Fix (2005), Gupta (2004), Song (2005), Bufermaet.al (2005), Mallikarjunappa T and Carmelita Goveas (2007), Ambadkar (2010), Tripathi (2018)
4		Volatility	VOL	SD of PBITDA / TA	R. Deepa (2011)
5		Growth	GROW	Year-on-Year Growth in Sales	Mallikarjunappa T and Carmelita Goveas (2007), Tripathi (2018)
6		Non-debt Tax Shield	NDTS	Dep & Amort / TA	Mallikarjunappa T and Carmelita Goveas (2007), Chakraborty (2010) and R. Deepa (2011)
7		Debt Service Capacity	DSC	PBITDA / Interest Expense	-
8		Uniqueness	UNIQ	R&D Expenditure / Net Sales	Titman & Wessel's (1988), Bhaduri (2002), Song (2005), Ruplai S. Ambadkar (2010)
9		Liquidity	LIQ	CA / CL	Mallikarjunappa T and Carmelita Goveas (2007), Ambadkar (2010), Rasoolpur (2012), Zuhaib A. Bazaz (2015)
10		Dividend	DIV	Equity Dividends / PAT	Bhat (1980), Baral (2004) and Ambadkar (2010)

The mathematical panel data regression models to empirically inspect the impact of selected factors on the leverage measures of the selected automobile companies are as follows:

(i) Pooled Ordinary Least Square (POLS) or Panel Least Square Model:

$$LEV_{it} = \beta_0 + \beta_1 SIZE_{it} + \beta_2 PROF_{it} + \beta_3 TANG_{it} + \beta_4 VOL_{it} + \beta_5 GROW_{it} + \beta_6 NDTS_{it} + \beta_7 DSC_{it} + \beta_8 UNIQ_{it} + \beta_9 LIQ_{it} + \beta_{10} DIV_{it} + \epsilon_{it}$$

(ii) Fixed Effect Model (FEM):

$$LEV_{it} = \beta_{0i} + \beta_1 SIZE_{it} + \beta_2 PROF_{it} + \beta_3 TANG_{it} + \beta_4 VOL_{it} + \beta_5 GROW_{it} + \beta_6 NDTS_{it} + \beta_7 DSC_{it} + \beta_8 UNIQ_{it} + \beta_9 LIQ_{it} + \beta_{10} DIV_{it} + \gamma_2 D_{2_{it}} + \gamma_3 D_{3_{it}} + \gamma_4 D_{4_{it}} + \dots\dots\dots\dots + \gamma_{11} D_{11_{it}} + \epsilon_{it}$$

(iii) Random Effect Model (REM):

$$LEV_{it} = \beta_0 + \beta_1 SIZE_{it} + \beta_2 PROF_{it} + \beta_3 TANG_{it} + \beta_4 VOL_{it} + \beta_5 GROW_{it}$$
$$+ \beta_6 NDTS_{it} + \beta_7 DSC_{it} + \beta_8 UNIQ_{it} + \beta_9 LIQ_{it} + \beta_{10} DIV_{it} + \omega_{it}$$

Here,

- o LEV = The value of the Dependent variable (Leverage or Debt Ratios), i.e., LTD/TA, LTD/NW, TD/TA and TD/NW
- o B_0 = Constant term across sample companies.
- o B_{0i} = Constant term of each sample company.
- o $\beta_1, \beta_2, \beta_3, \ldots \beta_n$ = Coefficients of the independent variables.
- o SIZE, PROF, TANG, VOL, GROW, NDTS, DSC, UNIQ, LIQ and DIV are the independent variables that predict LEV's value.
- o = Coefficients for individual companies (e.g., $_2$ for Atul Auto Ltd., $_3$ for Bajaj Auto Ltd. and so on)
- o $D_2, D_3, D_4, \ldots$, and D_{11} are dummy variables for the second, third, fourth, ... till eleventh sample company. D_1 is not taken since having it will cause perfect multicollinearity.
- o ε_{it} = e being the error value for individual i at time t.
- o ω_{it} = Composite error (Individual specific error + Model specific error)

4. RESULTS AND INTERPRETATION

The study took on the empirical investigation of panel data to recognize the bearing of financial structure determinants on the leverage ratios of automobile corporations over the duration of this study. The correlation results found a negative affirmation of profitability, debt service capacity and liquidity, whereas a positive affirmation of tangibility and uniqueness with all the leverage ratios at a 5% significance level. However, there is statistically no significant correlation of size, volatility, growth and non-debt tax shield with leverage ratios. Lastly, the dividend is significantly correlated with only TD/TA.

Table 3 indicates the results of panel data regression analysis for selected capital structure factors on long periods and total debt ratios (capital mix) for the sample automobile companies in India. Regression models' sturdiness is confirmed through the lowest score of the selected information criterion, specifically the Akaike Information Criterion (AIC). The models' durbin-watson statistic values between from 1.2 to 1.9, close to 2. It seems the data are auto-correlated, which could be due to some specification error. The validity of the models for examining the association amongst the elements of the capital mix and leverage ratios was proven with their F-statistics values significant at the 5% level. The Adjusted R-square values of all the models disclosed a better predictive capacity as they range from 60% to 90% of the fluctuation in the leverage ratios of the industry.

4.1 Panel Data Regression Analysis Results on LTD/TA Ratio

In Model 1, the pooled regression model shows a significant F-statistics value of 27.96, validating the model for the present study, and its adjusted R-square value indicates that the model can explain almost 71% variation in the LTD/TA ratio. The results reveal that size, tangibility and uniqueness have a significant negative impact at a 5% level on the leverage ratio, and uniqueness owns a higher coefficient value of 2.35. Further, debt service capacity and non-debt tax cover adversely impact long-term debt ratios as their t-statistics are -3.379 and -4.415, respectively. It shows that automobile companies with high debt service capacity and non-debt tax shield borrow less long-term debt funds to finance their total assets.

Since the Chow test and Hausman test results show significant cross-section chi-square value, the study selects the fixed effect model to study the relationship between the determinant of capital structure and LTD/TA ratio, whose results are shown in Model 2. The model gives a significant F-statistic value of 31.06 at a 5% level, leading to the model's validity. The results state a better predictive capacity of the model with its adjusted R-square value of 0.847. Like the pooled regression model, FEM also found a significant positive impact of tangibility and a negative impact of debt service capacity on the LTD/TA ratio. Unlike the previous model, FEM shows a substantially negative size effect on the leverage ratio. It led to rejecting null hypotheses and accepting the alternate hypotheses H_1, H_3 and H_7, confirming that size, tangibility and debt service capacity significantly impact the LTD/TA ratio.

4.2 Panel Data Regression Analysis Results on LTD/NW Ratio:

In Model 3, the F-statistics value of 23.207 of the pooled regression model is significant at the 5% level and shows the model's validity. The adjusted R-square of the model indicates that the selected determinants of capital structure can explain 67% of changes in the LTD/NW ratio. As per its results, non-debt tax shield, debt service capacity and liquidity indicate a significant negative impact at a 5% level on the debt-equity ratio. On the other hand, the model presents a significant positive effect of size, tangibility and uniqueness with LTD/NW ratio, and the latter with the highest coefficient value of 7.740, stating that as the expenditure on research and development increases, the automobile company seeks more funds from long-term debt sources.

In the model selection process, the Chow and Hausman tests show significant cross-section chi-square values. Therefore, the study accepts the fixed effect model 4, for studying the impact of the determinant of capital structure on the LTD/NW ratio. This model has a significant F-statistic value of 25.40 at a 5% level, showing the model's validity. Its results also disclosed the significant positive impact of tangibility on the LTD/NW ratio with a high coefficient value of 1.404. However, FEM results contradict the pooled regression result of size by showing its significantly negative impact on LTD/NW, implying that the large automobile companies use more of their shareholders' funds and raise less long-term borrowing. The debt service capacity also significantly negatively impacts the ratio, as shown by its t-statistic value of -2.306. Based on the FEM results, the study rejects the null hypotheses that size, tangibility and debt service capacity have no impact on the LTD/NW ratio and accepts the alternate hypotheses H_1, H_3 and H_7 for the same.

4.3 Panel Data Regression Analysis Results on TD/TA Ratio:

Model 5 indicates the results of panel data regression analysis of independent variables on TD/TA and found valid from the significant F-statistics value of 21.649 at the 5% level. Its adjusted R-square value shows that the selected determinants of capital structure can explain almost 65% of changes in the TB/TA ratio. Its results show that debt service capacity and liquidity have a significant negative impact. Tangibility discloses a significant positive effect on the total debt to total asset ratio, indicating that automobile companies with more collateralized assets raise more debt funds.

Due to the significant cross-section chi-square value of the Chow test and the Hausman test, the study accepted the fixed effect model 6, to represent the relationship of the determinant of capital structure with the TD/TA ratio. The model has a significant F-statistic value of 25.046 and has a better predictive capacity of 81%, as shown by its adjusted R-square value. The FEM results indicate a significant positive impact on growth and a significant adverse effect on liquidity. Further, like the pooled regression model 5, the FEM results also show a significant positive impact of tangibility on the TD/TA ratio. It led the study to reject the null hypotheses and accept the alternate hypotheses (H_3, H_5 and H_9) that tangibility, growth and liquidity significantly impact the TD/TA ratio.

4.4 Panel Data Regression Analysis Results on TD/NW Ratio:

In model 7, panel data regression analysis' result of each independent variable on the TD/NW ratio demonstrates a significant value of F-statistics, i.e., 17.344. It can explain 60% of the TD/NW ratio's variation. The results disclose that debt service capacity and liquidity significantly negatively impact the said ratio, showing that automobile companies with large PBITDA and current assets depend less on long-term and short-term debt funds.

Since the Chow test and Hausman test results show significant F-statistics and cross-section chi-square value, the study rejects both the pooled regression model and random effect model and selects the fixed effect model 8, to study the relationship between the determinant of capital structure and TD/NW ratio. The FEM gives a significant F-statistic value of 17.344 and has a better predictive capacity of 77%. Like the pooled regression model, FEM also found a significant negative impact of debt service capacity and liquidity on the TD/NW ratio. Unlike the previous model, FEM shows a significant positive effect of tangibility and growth on the debt ratio. It led the study to reject null hypotheses and accept the H_3, H_5, H_7 and H_9 hypotheses.

Table 3. Representing regressions results of determinants on various measures of capital structure

Debt Ratios	LTD/TA		LTD/NW		TD/TA		TD/NW	
	Model 1	**Model 2**	**Model 3**	**Model 4**	**Model 5**	**Model 6**	**Model 7**	**Model 8**
Determinants	**Pooled Reg Model**	**Fixed Effect Model**	**Pooled Reg Model**	**Fixed Effect Model**	**Pooled Reg Model**	**Fixed Effect Model**	**Pooled Reg Model**	**Fixed Effect Model**
Size	**0.017 (3.920) ****	**-0.031 (-2.278) ****	**0.044 (3.047) ****	**-0.093 (-2.022) ****	**0.006 (0.871)**	**-0.035 (-1.559)**	**0.023 (0.709)**	**-0.116 (-1.112)**
Profitability	0.052 (0.626)	0.054 (0.759)	0.169 (0.608)	0.097 (0.401)	0.046 (0.334)	0.152 (1.285)	0.011 (0.018)	0.193 (0.350)
Tangibility	0.370 (4.821) **	0.561 (6.362) **	1.012 (3.944) **	1.404 (4.668) **	0.285 (2.234) **	0.545 (3.709) **	0.916 (1.587)	1.873 (2.744) **
Volatility	-0.049 (-0.487)	-0.058 (-0.687)	-0.138 (-0.412)	-0.209 (-0.728)	-0.052 (-0.310)	-0.050 (-0.360)	-0.334 (-0.444)	-0.416 (-0.640)
Growth	0.053 (1.737)	0.000 (0.017)	0.172 (1.704)	0.019 (0.210)	0.098 (1.936)	0.120 (2.672) **	0.344 (1.508)	0.464 (2.225) **
Non-debt Tax Shield	-1.225 (-3.379) **	-0.407 (-1.232)	-3.206 (-2.646) **	-1.713 (-1.519)	-0.661 (-1.098)	0.214 (0.389)	-3.156 (-1.158)	-2.257 (-0.882)
Debt Service Capacity	-0.023 (-4.415) **	-0.012 (-2.072) **	-0.068 (-3.978) **	-0.045 (-2.306) **	-0.036 (-4.193) **	-0.016 (-1.793)	-0.150 (-3.879) **	-0.103 (-2.327) **
Uniqueness	2.351 (3.454) **	-0.067 (-0.097)	7.740 (3.403) **	-0.264 (-0.112)	0.766 (0.677)	-0.911 (-0.793)	3.817 (0.746)	-4.035 (-0.755)
Liquidity	-0.020 (-1.938)	-0.004 (-0.451)	-0.075 (-2.144) **	-0.019 (-0.673)	-0.091 (-5.257) **	-0.051 (-3.676) **	-0.339 (-4.319) **	-0.182 (-2.839) **
Dividend	0.014 (1.113)	-0.004 (-0.477)	0.045 (1.105)	-0.049 (-1.418)	0.032 (1.576)	0.009 (0.517)	0.130 (1.422)	-0.034 (-0.434)
R-square	**0.739**	**0.875**	**0.701**	**0.851**	**0.686**	**0.849**	**0.637**	**0.815**
Adjusted R-Square	**0.712**	**0.847**	**0.671**	**0.817**	**0.655**	**0.815**	**0.600**	**0.774**
F Statistics	**27.96****	**31.06****	**23.207****	**25.400****	**21.649****	**25.046****	**17.344****	**19.665****
AIC	**-2.925**	**-3.479**	**-0.512**	**-1.026**	**-1.909**	**-2.460**	**1.109**	**0.613**
SIC/BIC	**-2.655**	**-2.964**	**-0.242**	**-0.511**	**-1.639**	**-1.944**	**1.379**	**1.128**
HQC	**-2.816**	**-3.270**	**-0.402**	**-0.817**	**-1.799**	**-2.250**	**1.218**	**0.822**
Durbin Watson	**1.751**	**1.922**	**1.649**	**1.830**	**1.236**	**1.570**	**1.356**	**1.640**
Chow Test	**9.672****		**8.952****		**9.612****		**8.626****	
Hausman Test	**96.72****		**89.522****		**96.116****		**86.264****	

**Significant at 5% level

5. FINDINGS AND DISCUSSION

This empirical study inspected the bearing of financial structure determinants on the leverage ratios of automobile concerns post the financial crisis period of 2008-09, i.e., from 2009-10 to 2018-19. For the analysis purpose, the study used a panel data regression model with ten determinants of capital structure, i.e., SIZE, PROF, TANG, VOL, GROW, NDTS, DSC, UNIQ, LIQ and DIV and four leverage ratios, i.e., LTD/TA, LTD/NW, TD/TA, and TD/NW.

According to the panel data regression results of the fixed effect models, being selected as the better model to represent the relationship between the determinant of capital structure with debt ratios, it is established that tangibility has a substantial affirmative influence on all the debt ratios, showing consistency (Rajan and Zingales, 1995; Basu et al., 2013; Akinyomi et al.,2013; Handoo et al., 2014; Kavitha, 2014; Bhattacharjee et al., 2015; Zuhaib 2015; Sofat and Singh 2017; Merve, 2018; Ghayas, et al.,2020; Kaur, et al.,2020). It also confirms the prediction of the trade-off theory, showing that an increase in automobile companies' sales and fixed assets increases their long-term and overall debts. Highlights that automobile companies, having large fixed assets to use as collateral securities, raise more long-term debt to fund their additional sales.

Further, a significant negative impact of debt service capacity on LTD/TA, LTD/NW and TD/NW ratios shows that when the automobile companies have increasing PBITDA to pay off their fixed payment obligations, they prefer taking less debt. It may be because automobile companies prefer to spend their profits internal funds on future investment opportunities rather than attracting lenders to handle debts (Mallikarjunappa and Carmelita, 2007; Basu and Rajeev, 2013; Handoo, et al.,2014; Sofat and Singh, 2017).

Similarly, size has shown a significant negative impact on LTD/TA and LTD/NW but not on total debt ratios. It may be due to the presence of short-term debt. It indicates that size as a determinant does not significantly influence short-term debts, but it substantially impacts the long-term debt of the automobile industry in India. It corroborates the prediction of the pecking order theory that large automobile companies add more retained earnings and rely more on internal funds rather than long-term debt funds to finance their total assets and support the results (Handoo, et al.,2014; Zuhaib, 2015; Sofat and Singh, 2017; Tripathi, 2018).

The FEM results evidence the prediction of pecking order theory by indicating a significant positive impact of growth on total debt ratios, i.e., TD/TA and TD/NW. Due to the inclusion of short-term debt, growth exhibits insignificant bearing on long-term debt. Suggests that automobile firms with mounting sales raise more short-term debts against shareholders' funds to finance their operations. The results supporting the findings of (Ali, 2011; Ali and Hossain, 2011; Tongkong, 2012; Handoo et al., 2014; Nelson, et.al., 2015). Quite the reverse, liquidity manifested a significant negative impact on TD/TA and TD/NW ratios, suggesting that the automobile firms with large liquid assets have less requirement of raising additional funds from short-term debt because of insignificant influence on long-term leverage ratios, as they can finance their operations through their available working capital. Again, it manifested the prediction of the pecking order theory and supported the results (Ambadkar, 2010; Ali and Hossain, 2011; Merve, 2018; Kaur, et al.,2020; Ghayas, et al., 2020).

Table 4. Epilogue of panel data analysis results on debt ratios and theories implications

Debt Ratios	Long-Term Debt to Total Asset		Long-Term Debt to Net Worth		Total Debt to Total Assets		Total Debt to Net Worth	
Determinants	**Significance Result**	**Theory Implication**	**Significance Result**	**Theory Implication**	**Significance Result**	**Theory Implication**	**Significance Result**	**Theory Implication**
Size	Significant (-ve)	Pecking Order Theory	Significant (-ve)	Pecking Order Theory	X	—	X	—
Profitability	X	—	X	—	X	—	X	—
Tangibility	Significant (+ve)	Trade-off Theory	Significant (+ve)	Trade-off Theory	Significant (+ve)	Trade-off Theory	Significant (+ve)	Trade-off Theory
Volatility	X	—	X	—	X	—	X	—
Growth	X	—	X	—	Significant (+ve)	Pecking Order Theory	Significant (+ve)	Pecking Order Theory
Non-debt Tax Shield	X	—	X	—	X	—	X	—
Debt Service Capacity	Significant (-ve)	No Prediction	Significant (-ve)	No Prediction	X	—	Significant (-ve)	No Prediction
Uniqueness	X	—	X	—	X	—	X	—
Liquidity	X	—	X	—	Significant (-ve)	Pecking Order Theory	Significant (-ve)	Pecking Order Theory
Dividend	X	—	X	—	X	—	X	—

Table 4 presents a summary result of the panel data regression using the fixed effect model and implications of the predictions of theories regarding the relationship between various debt ratios and capital structure determinants of the Indian automobile industry.

6. MANAGERIAL IMPLICATION

The study has significant managerial contributions to the Indian automobile companies. It is a fresh effort to comprehend the bearing of financial structure determinants on various leverage measures on the worth of companies in the automobile sector of India with a more detailed evaluation. It inspected the influence of ten factors on indicators of capital mix construction. These indicators represent the different categories of debt ratios: long-period and total debt ratios.

The study will lead the way for the finance executives of automobile companies to frame their ideal capital structure as it is grounded on the recent figures and studied the post-recession period from 2009-10 to 2018-19. This study scrutinizes the impression of determinants on the financial mix of the automobile sector. It will act as a directory to the managers that shows the significance of considering the size, tangibility, growth, debt service capacity and liquidity factors before framing their debt policies, as they possess a significant bearing on the capital mix of the industry.

Further, the research also tracks the applicability of the predictions of two contending theories, namely the trade-off approach and the pecking order approach, on the financing pattern and elements of capital mix of the automobile sector in India. Corporate financial executives can consider the suggested theory's implications while making financing decisions.

Investors can also comprehend the influence of various factors on automobile manufacturers' financial mix decisions. This way, they will be cautious about their investments in the sector and make decisions for further investments based on the riskiness of the segment. The study can also be presented to any financial institution by firms for better understanding of their capital mix, to inspect the bearing of financial structure measures on the business value, and to assess the sanctioning of debt amount further.

7. CONCLUSION

The present study used panel data regression analysis models to identify the bearing of financial structure determinants on its measures in automobile associations for 10 years after the financial recession of 2008-09. For this examination, the study selected ten determinants, i.e., SIZE, PROF, TANG, VOL, GROW, NDTS, DSC, UNIQ, LIQ and DIV, and four indicators of capital structure, which comprised two long-term debt ratios, i.e., LTD/TA and LTD/NW, and two total debt ratios, i.e., TD/TA and TD/NW.

The study, based on the detailed investigation of the effects of these elements on the indicators of financial structure, concluded that size, tangibility, growth, debt service capacity and liquidity have significant importance in the financial structure decision of the automobile manufacturing sector in India. Tangibility was found to influence all the capital structure decisions of the industry positively and confirmed the implication of the trade-off approach. At the same time, size evidenced the applicability of the pecking order theory by revealing a negative impression of the long-term debt policies of the industry. Growth and liquidity disclosed a significant impression on the industry's total debt ratios, showing influence on the TD/TA and TD/NW ratios. The affirming impact of growth and the adverse effect of liquidity reiterate the appropriateness of the pecking order theory on the automobile industry in India. None of these theories have predicted debt service capacity's relation with leverage. In contrast, the present study found a noteworthy negative influence on three capital structure indicators except TD/TA debt ratios in the automobile industry in India. Therefore, it is recommended that the sector exercise caution when determining its capital structure composition, particularly regarding debt service coverage.

The present research is restricted to examining microeconomic components as the factors of the financial structure of automobile manufacturing companies in India. Further research can be done by investigating the influence of macroeconomic determinants like inflation rate, GDP, exchange rate, forex reserves, financial markets' efficiency, and India's political and legal environment. The capital structure has an added comprehensive picture of the automobile industry in India.

8. LIMITATION

This research is grounded on the secondary data collected from the database of CMIE (Centre for Monitoring Indian Economy) PROWESS. The quality of the study purely hinges on the accuracy and reliability of secondary data, and the drawbacks of the formation in the database will also apply to the data analysis. Secondly, the paper scrutinizes capital structure determinants of leading automobile manufacturing establishments operating under BSE /NSE on the data collection date; other companies in the automobile sector, like the Auto Ancillary sector, are not considered. Further, the sample firms chosen were restricted to eleven automobile corporations due to restrictions such as lack of continuous listing, negative net worth in some years, and inaccessibility of data relating to those organizations in the prowess database. Lastly, the study is confined to only ten years, from 2009-10 to 2018-19.

REFERENCES

Akinyomi, O. J., & Olagunju, A. (2013). Determinants of capital structure in Nigeria.

Ali, I. (2011). Determinants of Capital Structure: Empirical Evidence from Pakistan. SSRN Electronic Journal. DOI: 10.2139/ssrn.1977024

Alipour, M., Mohammadi, M. F. S., & Derakhshan, H. (2015). Determinants of capital structure: An empirical study of firms in Iran. *International Journal of Law and Management*, *57*(1), 53–83. DOI: 10.1108/IJLMA-01-2013-0004

Ambadkar, S. Rupali, (2010), Determinants of Capital Structure – A Study of FDI Companies in India, The Maharaja Sayajirao University of Baroda's thesis, retrieved from https://shodhganga.inflibnet.ac.in/handle/10603/59571

Hossain, F., & Ali, A. (2012). Impact of firm specific factors on capital structure decision: An empirical study of Bangladeshi Companies. *International Journal of Business Research and Management*, *3*(4), 163–182.

Baral, K. J. (2004). Determinants of capital structure: A case study of listed companies of Nepal. *Journal of Nepalese Business Studies*, *7*(1), 1–13.

Basu, K., & Rajeev, M. (2013), "Determinants of capital structure of Indian corporate sector: Evidence of regulatory impact," Working Papers 306, Institute for Social and Economic Change, Bangalore.

Bevan, A. A., & Danbolt, J. Dynamics in the Determinants of Capital Structure in the UK (May 2000). Capital Structure Dynamics Working Paper No. 2000-9, Available at SSRN: https://ssrn.com/abstract=233551 or DOI: 10.2139/ssrn.233551

Bhattacharjee, B. J. (2010). Determinants of capital structure of Indian industries. The Indian Journal of Commerce, Vol. 63, Issue No. 3, Pp 14-25.

Bhattacharjee, A., & Dash, M. (2015). Determinants of capital structure in the Indian sugar sector. *Sky Journal of Business Administration and Management*, *3*(6), 63–69.

Booth, L., Aivazian, V., Demirguc-Kunt, A., & Maksimovic, V. (2001). Capital Structures in Developing Countries. *The Journal of Finance*, *56*(1), 87–130. DOI: 10.1111/0022-1082.00320

Buferna, F. M., Bangassa, K., & Hodgkinson, L. (2005), Determinants of Capital Structure: Evidence from Libya, WP2005/08, ISSN:1744-0718.

Cevheroglu-Acar, M. (2018). Determinants of Capital Structure: Empirical Evidence from Turkey. *Journal of Management and Sustainability*, *8*(1), 31. DOI: 10.5539/jms.v8n1p31

Chadha, S., & Sharma, A. K. (2015), Determinants of capital structure: An empirical evaluation from India, Journal of Advances in Management Research, Vol.12, Issue No.1, Pp 3-14.

Chakraborty, I. (2010). Capital structure in an emerging stock market: The case of India. Research in International Business and Finance, Vol. 24, Issue No.3, Pp 295-314. ISSN 0275-5319, DOI: 10.1016/j.ribaf.2010.02.001

Garima Dalal (2013), Capital Structure Decisions, Journal of Business Management Social Sciences Research (JBM&SSR) ISSN No: 2319-5614.

DeAngelo, H., & Masulis, R. W. (1980). Optimal Capital Structure Under Corporate and Personal Taxation. *Journal of Financial Economics*, *8*(1), 3–29. DOI: 10.1016/0304-405X(80)90019-7

Deepa, R. (2011), A Study on the Determinants of Capital Structure and Profitability with Special Reference to Food Industry in India, Pondicherry University's thesis, retrieved from https://shodhganga.inflibnet.ac.in/handle/10603/5253

Drobetz, W., & Fix, R. (2005). What are the Determinants of the Capital Structure? Evidence from Switzerland, Swiss Journal of Economics and Statistics (SJES) [SSES]. *Swiss Society of Economics and Statistics*, *141*(I), 71–113.

Ghayas, A., & Khan, T. (2020). A Study on the Determinants of Capital Structure: Evidence from India. *The IUP Journal of Applied Finance.*, *26*, 47–59.

Gonenc, H. (2005). comparison of debt financing between international and domestic firms: Evidence from Turkey, Germany and UK. *International Journal of Managerial Finance*, *1*(1), 49–68. DOI: 10.1108/17439130510584883

Hall, G., Hutchinson, P., & Michaelas, N. (2004). Determinants of the capital structures of European SMEs. *Journal of Business Finance & Accounting*, *31*(5-6), 711–728. DOI: 10.1111/j.0306-686X.2004.00554.x

Hampton, J. J. (1992). *Financial decision making: concepts, problems and cases*. Prentice-Hall of India.

Handoo, A., & Sharma, K. (2014). A study on determinants of capital structure in India. IIMB Management Review. Volume 26. Issue 3. Pp 170-182, ISSN 0970-3896, DOI: 10.1016/j.iimb.2014.07.009

Huang, G., & Song, F. (2002). The Determinants of Capital Structure: Evidence from China. *China Economic Review*, *17*(1), 14–36. DOI: 10.1016/j.chieco.2005.02.007

Jagannathan, U., & Narayanarao, S. (2017), The Nature and Determinants of Capital Structure in Indian Service Firms (November 1, 2017). Indian Journal of Finance, Available at SSRN: https://ssrn.com/abstract=3078393 DOI: 10.17010/ijf/2017/v11i11/119340

Jean, C. J. (2003). Determinants of capital structure of Chinese-listed companies. *Journal of Business Research*, *57*, 1341–1351.

Kaur, R., Chattopadhyay, A. K., & Rakshit, D. (2020). Determinants of Capital Structure with Reference to Select Indian Companies: A Panel Data Regression Analysis. Asia-Pacific Journal of Management Research and Innovation, 2319510X2091345. DOI: 10.1177/2319510X20913454

Kavitha, S. (2014), Determinants of Corporate Capital Structure among Selected Manufacturing Industries in India, Avinashilingam Institute for Home Scienceand Higher Education for Women Thesis, Retrieved from, https://shodhganga.inflibnet.ac.in/handle/10603/40672

Kraus, A., & Litzenberger, R. H. (1973). A State-Preference Model of Optimal Financial Leverage. *The Journal of Finance*, *28*(4), 911–922.

Mallikarjunappa T and Carmelita Goveas (2007), “Factors determining the capital structure of pharmaceutical companies in India,” The ICFAI journal of applied finance, Vol.13 (11), Pp.56-72.

Mukherjee, S., & Mahakud, J. (2012). Are trade-off and pecking order theories of capital structure mutually exclusive?: Evidence from Indian manufacturing companies. *Journal of Management Research, 12*(1), 41–55.

Myers, S. C. (1984). The capital structure puzzle. *The Journal of Finance, 39*(3), 574–592. DOI: 10.1111/j.1540-6261.1984.tb03646.x

Pandey, I.M. (2004). Capital structure, Profitability and market structure: Evidence from Malaysia, Asia Pacific Journal of Economics and Business, Vol.8, Issue No.2, Pp 78-91.

Patnaik, R., Patra, S. K., Mahapatra, D. M., & Baral, S. K. (2022). *Adoption and Challenges Underlying OTT Platform in India during Pandemic: A Critical Study of Socio-Economic and Technological Issues.* FIIB Business Review., DOI: 10.1177/23197145221101676

Purohit, H., & Khanna, S. (2012). Determinants of Capital Structure in Indian Manufacturing Sector. *Asia-Pacific Journal of Management Research and Innovation, 8*(3), 265–269. DOI: 10.1177/2319510X1200800306

Rajan, R., & Zingales, L. (1995). What do we know about capital structure? Some evidence from international data. *The Journal of Finance, 50*(5), 1421–1460. DOI: 10.1111/j.1540-6261.1995.tb05184.x

Ram, K. K. (1999). The Determinants of Capital Structure- An Econometric Analysis. *Finance India, XIII*(1), 51–69.

Rasoolpur, G. S. (2012). An empirical analysis of capital Structure determinants: Evidence from the Indian corporate sector. International Journal of Management & Information Technology, Vol. 1, Issue No.3, Pp 1-12.

Remmers, L., Stonehill, A., Wright, R., & Beekhuisen, T. (1974). Industry and Size as Debt Ratio Determinants in Manufacturing Internationally. *Financial Management, 3*(2), 24–32. DOI: 10.2307/3665286

Saumitra, B. N. (2002). Determinants of Corporate Borrowings: Some Evidence from the Indian Corporate Sector. *Journal of Economics and Finance, 26*(2), 200–215. DOI: 10.1007/BF02755986

Singh, A. (1995), Corporate financial patterns in industrializing economies, International Finance Corporation Technical Paper 2.

Sofat, R., & Singh, S. (2017). Determinants of capital structure: An empirical study of manufacturing firms in India. *International Journal of Law and Management, 59*(6), 1029–1045. DOI: 10.1108/IJLMA-05-2016-0051

Song, J., & Philippatos, G. (2004). Have we resolved some critical issues related to international capital structure? Empirical evidence from the 30 OECD countries. Working Paper, University of Tennessee

Tongkong, S. (2012). Key factors influencing capital structure decision and its speed of adjustment of Thai listed real estate companies. *Procedia: Social and Behavioral Sciences, 40*, 716–720.

Titman, S., & Wessels, R. (1988). The determinants of capital structure choice. *The Journal of Finance*, *43*(1), 1–19.

Tong, G., & Green, C. J. (2005), "Pecking Order or Trade-Off Hypothesis? Evidence on the Capital Structure of Chinese Companies", Journal of Applied Economics, Vol 37, Issue 19, Pp.2179-2189, ISSN 0003-6846.

Tripathi, V. D. K. (2018), An Analysis of Capital Structure of Leading Automobile Companies in India, Gujarat University's thesis, retrieved from https://shodhganga.inflibnet.ac.in/handle/10603/208737

Vergas, N., Cerqueira, A., & Brandão, E. (2015), "The determinants of the capital structure of listed on stock market non-financial firms: Evidence for Portugal", FEP-UP, School of Economics and Management, University of Porto, Retrieved from https://wps.fep.up.pt/wps/wp555.pdf

Vijayalakshmi, D., & Manoharan, P. (2014). Corporate Leverage and its Impact on Profitability and Shareholder Value Creation in the Indian Textile Sector. *Indian Journal of Finance*, *8*(12), 21. Advance online publication. DOI: 10.17010/ijf/2014/v8i12/71689

Yadav, N., Singh, A. B., & Tandon, P. (2023). Volatility Spillover Effects between Indian Stock Market and Global Stock Markets: A DCC-GARCH Model. *FIIB Business Review*, *0*(0), 23197145221141186. Advance online publication. DOI: 10.1177/23197145221141186

Chapter 4
Artificial Intelligence in Retail: Transforming Customer Experience and Business Operations

Souvik Banerjee
https://orcid.org/0000-0001-9988-8887
Management Development Institute, Murshidabad, India

Abhijit Pandit
https://orcid.org/0000-0003-2122-3468
Management Development Institute, Murshidabad, India

ABSTRACT

Artificial Intelligence (AI) is revolutionizing the retail industry by enabling personalized customer experiences, optimizing operations, and enhancing customer service. This study investigates the impact of AI on retail operations through Structural Equation Modelling (SEM), focusing on five key variables: AI recommendation effectiveness, operational efficiency, customer service, consumer trust, and business performance. The research employs both quantitative and qualitative methods to provide insights into the benefits and challenges of AI in retail. The findings emphasize AI's dual role in driving business success and addressing ethical concerns, offering a balanced perspective for retailers and policymakers.

1. INTRODUCTION

Artificial Intelligence (AI) has become a revolutionary influence in the retail industry, altering conventional business practices and reshaping the consumer experience. Retailers are utilising AI-driven technology to augment personalisation, optimise operational efficiency, and meet the changing needs of contemporary consumers. These breakthroughs have established AI as a fundamental element of innovation in a competitive, rapidly evolving marketplace (Chen, Zhang, & Huang, 2020; Grewal, Roggeveen, & Nordfält, 2021).

The emergence of AI in retail is notably seen in the widespread adoption of recommendation systems. These systems evaluate consumer preferences, purchase histories, and behavioural patterns to provide tailored product recommendations, hence enhancing customer satisfaction and sales conversion rates (Tan, He, and Xu (2019) and Ransbotham, Kiron, Gerbert, and Reeves (2020)). Smith and Anderson's

DOI: 10.4018/979-8-3373-0209-6.ch004

(2022) research indicates that more than 80% of consumers favour organisations that provide customised recommendations, emphasising the significance of personalisation in the digital era.

Operational efficiency is a crucial domain in which AI has significantly advanced. AI-driven demand forecasting systems have allowed merchants to enhance inventory management, decrease stockouts, and lower excess inventory expenses (Huang & Rust, 2020). These solutions employ machine learning algorithms to examine past sales data, seasonal trends, and external variables like as weather conditions or economic indicators, yielding enhanced predictive accuracy and optimised supply chain procedures (Meyer & Schwager, 2021; Li, Sun, & Zhao, 2020).

Furthermore, AI-driven customer care solutions, such as chatbots and virtual assistants, have revolutionised the manner in which merchants interact with their clientele. These technologies deliver real-time assistance, address enquiries, and facilitate decision-making, so enhancing the purchasing experience and alleviating the workload of human customer service teams (Grewal et al., 2021; Zhu, Li, & Wang, 2021). Research conducted by McCarthy and Wright (2021) indicates that AI-driven customer care has resulted in a 35% decrease in customer assistance expenses for prominent retail firms.

Nonetheless, the use of AI into retail presents certain challenges. Ethical issues related to data protection, algorithmic prejudice, and the risk of dehumanising customer interactions continue to pose substantial obstacles to mainstream adoption (Zhu et al., 2021; Kaplan & Haenlein, 2019). Algorithmic bias in AI-driven recommendation systems has prompted enquiries on fair access to services and products (Li et al., 2020). Moreover, consumer confidence in AI technologies is significantly affected by views of transparency and data security (Smith et al., 2020).

The ramifications of AI implementation surpass operational advantages and client contentment, incorporating strategic gains in market competitiveness. Retailers who successfully incorporate AI into their operations are more adept at adapting to fluctuating market conditions, predicting customer trends, and providing enhanced services (Ransbotham et al., 2020; Manyika et al., 2017). These competencies are vital for survival in an industry increasingly characterised by innovation and adaptation.

This study examines the revolutionary capabilities of AI in retail, emphasising its applications in personalisation, operational efficiency, and customer engagement. The report examines the ethical dilemmas related to AI adoption, providing guidance for retailers on how to manage these complications to optimise the advantages of AI integration.

This chapter is organised to systematically examine the complex processes of AI adoption in retail. The section on Literature Review, examines prior academic and industry research across five thematic domains: AI in personalisation, operational efficiency, customer service, ethical implications, and strategic outcomes, thereby establishing a conceptual foundation for the study. Subsequently, Research Methodology delineates the research design, sampling methodologies, data collection tools and the operationalisation of latent constructs including AI Recommendation Effectiveness (ARE), Operational Efficiency (OE), Customer Service Effectiveness (CSE), Consumer Trust (CT), and Business Performance (BP). This section delineates the hypotheses and describes the Structural Equation Modelling (SEM) framework employed for empirical validation.

The section on Results delineates the descriptive statistics, distribution visualisations (violin plots) and SEM results, encompassing model fit indices, factor loadings and path coefficients. The results experimentally confirm the proposed correlations among the constructs, indicating that AI-driven improvements in customisation, operations and customer service positively affect consumer trust, which significantly influences corporate performance.

The Discussion section analyses the conclusions concerning theoretical implications and practical realities. It emphasises the intermediary function of trust in converting AI capabilities into concrete business results and examines how merchants may strategically navigate AI ethics and consumer perceptions to realise its complete potential.

Conclusion consolidates the principal discoveries and offers pragmatic recommendations for merchants and governments. It emphasises that although AI possesses transformative potential, its successful implementation must be accompanied by a dedication to ethical integrity, transparency, and customer focus to secure a lasting competitive edge in the digital era.

This comprehensive chapter assesses the present state of AI in retail and presents a verified paradigm for comprehending its determinants and effects, facilitating informed decision-making and future study.

2. LITERATURE REVIEW

The significant impact of Artificial Intelligence (AI) in retail has been thoroughly examined in terms of customer personalisation, operational efficiency, and ethical implications. This part offers an extensive analysis of the current literature, emphasising the uses of AI and its ramifications for the retail industry.

2.1. AI in Personalization

Personalisation has emerged as a fundamental element of contemporary retail tactics, with AI-driven solutions facilitating tailored purchasing experiences for consumers. Recommendation systems utilise machine learning algorithms to analyse customer data, forecast preferences, and propose products. Research conducted by Chen, Zhang, and Huang (2020) illustrates that AI-driven recommendations markedly improve customer satisfaction and purchasing behaviour. Grewal, Roggeveen, and Nordfält (2021) contend that personalised recommendations enhance loyalty by fostering a perception of uniqueness and value among consumers.

The efficacy of AI in personalisation include targeted marketing. Li, Sun, and Zhao (2020) assert that AI systems examine behavioural patterns and demographic data to create customised marketing efforts, leading to increased engagement rates. Research conducted by Smith and Anderson (2022) indicates that more than 70% of consumers favour firms that provide personalised experiences, underscoring the strategic significance of AI in enhancing customer retention.

2.2. AI in Operational Efficiency

Operational efficiency is a crucial domain in which AI has exhibited significant potential. AI's capacity to properly predict demand has transformed inventory management. Tan, He, and Xu (2019) examine the utilisation of AI-driven demand forecasting systems that leverage past sales data, seasonal trends, and external variables, including economic fluctuations, to enhance inventory management. These techniques mitigate the risks of overstocking and stockouts, resulting in substantial cost reductions and enhanced profitability.

Artificial intelligence improves supply chain management by delivering real-time insights into logistics and inventory movements. Manyika et al. (2017) assert that AI-driven solutions empower retailers to anticipate delays and adjust to interruptions, hence facilitating seamless operations. Meyer and Schwager (2021) assert that these tools enhance operational agility, enabling merchants to swiftly adapt to fluctuating market conditions.

2.3. AI in Customer Service

Artificial intelligence has revolutionised customer service with chatbots and virtual assistants, providing immediate assistance and addressing client enquiries. Huang and Rust (2020) emphasise the efficacy of AI-driven technologies in diminishing response times and improving customer satisfaction. Research conducted by McCarthy and Wright (2021) demonstrates that chatbots can manage up to 80% of standard enquiries, allowing human personnel to concentrate on intricate matters.

Nonetheless, over dependence on AI in customer service prompts apprehensions regarding the possible erosion of human interaction. Zhu, Li, and Wang (2021) contend that although AI enhances productivity, it may also estrange clients who prioritise personalised relationships with human representatives. The equilibrium between automation and human interaction is essential for sustaining client loyalty.

2.4. Ethical Concerns in AI Adoption

The incorporation of AI in retail presents ethical dilemmas, especially concerning data privacy and algorithmic prejudice. Kaplan and Haenlein (2019) examine the dangers posed by data breaches, emphasising the necessity for strong cybersecurity protocols. Smith et al. (2020) assert that consumer trust in AI technologies is significantly affected by transparency and ethical standards.

Algorithmic bias represents a significant concern, as research by Zhu et al. (2021) demonstrates that biassed algorithms can sustain discriminatory practices in pricing and marketing. Ransbotham et al. (2020) assert that mitigating these biases necessitates enhanced accountability and regulatory supervision.

2.5. Strategic Implications of AI in Retail

The strategic benefits of AI implementation surpass mere operational improvements. Chen et al. (2020) demonstrates that shops utilising AI are more adept at predicting consumer trends and providing enhanced services. Grewal et al. (2021) contend that AI empowers retailers to sustain a competitive advantage in a progressively digitised marketplace.

Nevertheless, the enduring consequences of AI implementation necessitate additional investigation. Manyika et al. (2017) emphasise the risk of workforce displacement due to technology supplanting conventional positions. This highlights the necessity for reskilling programs to guarantee that employees maintain relevance in an AI-driven economy.

3. RESEARCH METHODOLOGY

3.1. Population

The study's target population consists of people working in AI-driven organisations in India, including managers, business owners, and staff. These experts provide substantial insights into the impact of AI on business models and employment dynamics across several sectors, including manufacturing, retail, and services.

3.2. Sampling Technique

The study used a purposive sampling technique. This non-probability technique was chosen to ensure that participants have relevant experience and exposure to AI applications within their organisations. This methodology ensures that the collected data is relevant and substantial for assessing the impacts of AI.

3.3. Sample Size

The research encompassed a sample size of 100 individuals. The choice sought to reconcile analytical rigour with the practicality of data collection, guaranteeing sufficient data for Structural Equation Modelling (SEM) analysis while maintaining statistical integrity.

3.4. Data Collection Techniques

The data was collected using a standardised survey questionnaire distributed to the selected participants. The study comprised enquiries designed to evaluate many aspects of AI's impact, including operational efficiency, innovation, and employment dynamics. Demographic data, encompassing gender, years of experience, and industry type, was collected to examine moderating effects.

3.5. Latent Constructs and Indicators

Table 1. Constructs and indicators

Code	Description
ARE: AI Recommendation Effectiveness	
ARE_Effectiveness	Effectiveness of AI Recommendations
ARE_Usefulness	Usefulness of AI Recommendations
ARE_Personalization	Personalization Level of AI Recommendations
OE: Operational Efficiency	
OE_Inventory_Management	Efficiency in Inventory Management
OE_Demand_Forecasting	Accuracy of Demand Forecasting
OE_Supply_Chain_Operations	Improvement in Supply Chain Operations

continued on following page

Table 1. Continued

Code	Description
CSE: Customer Service Effectiveness	
CSE_Responsiveness	Responsiveness of AI-based Customer Service
CSE_Helpfulness	Helpfulness of AI in Resolving Queries
CSE_Satisfaction	Overall Satisfaction with AI Customer Support
CT: Consumer Trust	
CT_Data_Privacy	Perception of Data Privacy
CT_Transparency	Transparency in AI Decisions
CT_Fairness	Fairness in AI-based Pricing or Targeting
BP: Business Performance	
BP_Sales_Growth	Improvement in Sales Growth
BP_Cost_Savings	Cost Savings Due to AI
BP_Overall_Satisfaction	Overall Satisfaction with Business Outcomes from AI

3.6. Data Analysis Tools

A comprehensive script in R is utilized for conducting Structural Equation Modelling (SEM) using the lavaan package. It imports dataset, ensures necessary packages like lavaan and semPlot are installed and loaded and sets up the environment for SEM analysis and visualization.

The SEM model is delineated with an emphasis on several latent components and their associated indicators. The constructs comprise AI Recommendation Effectiveness (ARE), Operational Efficiency (OE), Customer Service Effectiveness (CSE), Consumer Trust (CT), and Business Performance (BP). Each concept is assessed by distinct indicators. ARE is designed according to its efficacy, utility, and customisation. Likewise, OE integrates efficiency in inventory management, precision in demand forecasting, and enhancement in supply chain operations. CSE evaluates timeliness, assistance, and happiness with AI-driven customer service. CT embodies perceptions regarding data protection, openness, and equity, whereas BP emphasises revenue expansion, cost reduction, and overall contentment resulting from AI activities.

The model delineates the structural links among these constructs. CT is posited to rely on ARE and CSE, suggesting that trust in AI is affected by its recommendation proficiency and customer service efficiency. Business performance (BP) is asserted to rely on both operational efficiency and consumer trust. The model is calibrated to the data via the sem() function from the lavaan package, and comprehensive results, encompassing fit indices, parameter estimates, and standardised coefficients, are obtained to assess the model's validity and explanatory capacity.

The code visualises the SEM results with the semPlot package, with the semPaths() method generating a tree layout diagram that illustrates the linkages between constructs and their indicators. The edge labels in the diagram denote standardised path coefficients, facilitating model interpretation.

The underlying structures and their corresponding indications are essential for comprehending the framework. For ARE, indicators encompass the efficacy, utility, and degree of personalisation of AI suggestions. Operational efficiency is assessed via enhancements in inventory management, demand forecasting, and supply chain operations. CSE highlights the significance of AI in enhancing response, assistance, and overall customer pleasure. CT encompasses trust characteristics such as data privacy, transparency, and equity in AI-driven choices. Finally, BP assesses company outcomes including revenue growth, cost reductions, and overall satisfaction with AI-driven efforts.

This R script methodically models and assesses the relationship between AI-driven functionality, consumer trust, and business performance utilising a rigorous SEM approach. The amalgamation of theoretical notions and practical indicators establishes a systematic framework for evaluating the influence of AI in retail settings.

3.7. Research Hypotheses:

The following research hypotheses can be formulated to align with the structural relationships being tested:

H_1: AI Recommendation Effectiveness positively influences Consumer Trust.

This hypothesis examines whether the effectiveness, usefulness, and personalization of AI recommendations enhance consumers' trust in the AI systems.

H_2: Customer Service Effectiveness positively influences Consumer Trust.

This hypothesis evaluates whether responsiveness, helpfulness, and overall satisfaction with AI-based customer service contribute to building consumer trust.

H_3: Operational Efficiency positively influences Business Performance.

This hypothesis tests whether improvements in inventory management, demand forecasting, and supply chain operations driven by AI lead to enhanced business outcomes such as sales growth, cost savings, and overall satisfaction.

H_4: Consumer Trust positively influences Business Performance.

This hypothesis investigates whether trust in AI, as reflected by perceptions of data privacy, transparency, and fairness, translates into improved business performance.

These hypotheses directly reflect the relationships specified in the structural model, where CT is regressed on ARE and CSE, and BP is regressed on OE and CT. The hypotheses test the causal links between latent constructs based on their respective indicators.

4. RESULTS

Figure 1. Descriptive statistics

Variable	Mean	Std. Error of Mean	Std. Deviation	Shapiro-Wilk	P-value (Shapiro-Wilk)
ARE_Effectiveness	4.060	0.083	0.827	0.830	< .001
ARE_Usefulness	3.980	0.070	0.696	0.819	< .001
ARE_Personalization	3.910	0.074	0.740	0.838	< .001
OE_Inventory_Management	3.930	0.081	0.807	0.842	< .001
OE_Demand_Forecasting	3.920	0.077	0.774	0.843	< .001
OE_Supply_Chain_Operations	3.780	0.072	0.719	0.828	< .001
CSE_Responsiveness	3.980	0.082	0.816	0.847	< .001
CSE_Helpfulness	4.070	0.077	0.769	0.828	< .001
CSE_Satisfaction	3.970	0.070	0.703	0.822	< .001
CT_Data_Privacy	3.810	0.077	0.775	0.840	< .001
CT_Transparency	3.960	0.072	0.724	0.830	< .001
CT_Fairness	3.830	0.079	0.792	0.843	< .001
BP_Sales_Growth	4.130	0.076	0.761	0.821	< .001
BP_Cost_Savings	4.000	0.078	0.778	0.840	< .001
BP_Overall_Satisfaction	4.120	0.074	0.742	0.804	< .001

Figure 1 presents descriptive statistics that summarize the principal variables in the study, emphasizing central tendency, variability, and normalcy measures. The variables denote the indicators of latent components associated with AI Recommendation Effectiveness (ARE), Operational Efficiency (OE), Customer Service Effectiveness (CSE), Consumer Trust (CT), and Business Performance (BP).

The average values for the majority of variables fall between 3.78 and 4.13, indicating that respondents typically assessed the efficacy of AI-based tools and their results favourably on a 5-point scale. For example, BP_Sales_Growth exhibits the highest mean of 4.13, signifying that respondents recognise substantial enhancement in sales growth attributable to AI. Likewise, CSE_Helpfulness and BP_Overall_Satisfaction received elevated scores, indicating substantial satisfaction with AI-driven services and business results. OE_Supply_Chain_Operations has a mean of 3.78, suggesting a marginally lower perceived enhancement in this domain relative to other metrics.

The standard errors of the mean (Std. Error of Mean) are consistently minimal, ranging from 0.070 to 0.083, signifying that the sample means are dependable and exhibit little variability. The standard deviations range from 0.696 to 0.827, indicating a substantial dispersion of answers within the sample.

The Shapiro-Wilk test results and associated p-values (< .001) demonstrate that none of the variables conform to a normal distribution at the 0.05 significance threshold. The Shapiro-Wilk statistic values, ranging from 0.804 to 0.847, are below 1, hence reinforcing the departures from normalcy. The non-normality indicates that advanced statistical methods, including structural equation modelling (SEM), which can withstand deviations from normality assumptions, are suitable for analysing this dataset.

The descriptive statistics indicate favourable assessments of AI's impact across all constructs, substantial response variability, and non-normal distributions for all variables. These results establish a fundamental comprehension of the dataset, paving the way for more profound studies via SEM.

Figure 2. Box plots

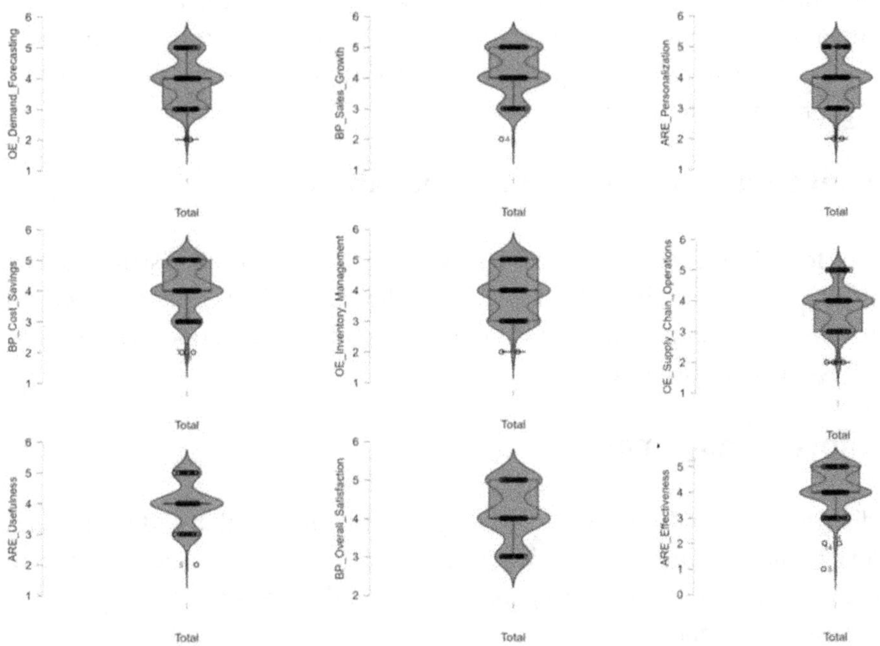

The violin plots in the images offer a comprehensive visualisation of the distribution, dispersion, and central tendencies of the many indicators employed in the study. These plots integrate boxplot components (depicting medians, interquartile ranges, and possible outliers) with kernel density estimations, providing an extensive overview of the data distributions.

4.1. ARE_Personalization

The violin plot for ARE_Personalization indicates a concentrated aggregation of results near the median, implying that respondents consistently rated the personalisation of AI suggestions highly. The minimal tails at both ends signify a narrow range of lower and higher ratings, whereas the majority of responses are concentrated closely around the central number.

4.2. ARE_Effectiveness

The distribution of ARE_Effectiveness displays a marginally wider spread, with a clearly delineated density centred around the median. The tails signify a minor segment of outliers who assessed the efficacy as either lower or greater than the central tendency. The clustering around the median indicates a predominantly favourable opinion of AI suggestion efficacy.

4.3. ARE_Usefulness

The ARE_Usefulness graphic demonstrates a closely grouped distribution with a comparatively narrower range than the other indicators in this category. The elevated concentration at the central values indicates robust consensus among respondents concerning the efficacy of AI advice, with a limited number of outliers present in the extremes.

4.4. Operational Excellence Demand Forecasting

The violin plot for OE_Demand_Forecasting exhibits a symmetrical distribution with a moderate dispersion, signifying consistency in replies concerning the accuracy of demand forecasting. The density is centred towards the centre, indicating a predominantly positive perception, whilst a few outliers in the lower range imply slight dissatisfaction.

4.5. OE Inventory Management

The answer distribution for OE_Inventory_Management resembles that of demand forecasting, exhibiting a central density that signifies favourable ratings. The tails indicate a marginal increase in response variability, whereas the core clustering persists robustly, underscoring the observed enhancements in inventory management efficiency.

4.6. OE_Supply_Chain_Operations

The violin plot for OE_Supply_Chain_Operations illustrates a marginally wider distribution relative to other operational efficiency measures. The density near the median is significant, indicating positive perceptions, whereas the wider tails reveal greater variability in ratings for this particular operational domain.

The violin plots visually depict the distributions of metrics for two constructs: Customer Service Effectiveness (CSE) and Consumer Trust (CT). These graphs indicate trends in the replies, including the central tendency, variability, and presence of outliers.

4.7. Customer Service Efficacy (CSE)

CSE Responsiveness: The distribution of CSE_Responsiveness is closely concentrated around the median, signifying strong consensus among respondents about the effectiveness of AI-driven customer service. The density surrounding the centre value is considerable, with only a few outliers present, indicating little deviations from the core trend.

CSE_Helpfulness: This metric has a comparable trend to CSE_Responsiveness, characterised by a pronounced central concentration and limited dispersion. Participants consistently evaluated the efficacy of AI in addressing enquiries favourably, with a few exceptions marginally diverging from the overall pattern.

The distribution of CSE_Satisfaction answers is rather wider than that of other CSE measures, however the core density remains significant. This signifies overall contentment with AI-driven customer service, accompanied by considerable unpredictability as indicated by the tails.

Consumer Trust (CT) CT_Data_Privacy: The violin plot for CT_Data_Privacy demonstrates a wider range in contrast to the CSE indicators, with a significant dispersion around the core values. The predominant responses are favourable; nonetheless, the diversity suggests divergent views on data privacy in AI systems.

The distribution of CT_Transparency is notably narrow, indicating a high level of consensus among respondents about the transparency of AI systems. The density surrounding the median indicates a favourable assessment, with minimal outliers detected.

CT_Fairness exhibits a little wider distribution than CT_Transparency, however the core clustering is still apparent. This indicates that although judgements of justice in AI-driven decisions are predominantly favourable, there exists diversity across responders.

The violin plots illustrate the distribution of responses for the Business Performance (BP) indicators: BP_Sales_Growth, BP_Cost_Savings, and BP_Overall_Satisfaction. These plots integrate components of boxplots and kernel density estimations, offering insights into central tendency, variability, and distribution shape for each statistic.

4.8. BP_Sales_Expansion

The distribution of BP_Sales_Growth is centred around the median, exhibiting a reasonably compact cluster, indicating that the majority of respondents judged sales growth attributed to AI favourably. The distribution of responses exhibits significant variability, with some outliers at the lower end. This suggests that although sales growth is typically regarded as advantageous, a minor segment of respondents encountered less favourable results.

4.9. BP_Cost_Efficiencies

The violin plot for BP_Cost_Savings demonstrates a narrow concentration of responses around the mean, indicating robust consensus among respondents regarding the beneficial effect of AI on cost savings. The density surrounding the median is significant, with few outliers present. This indicates that the cost-saving advantages of AI are generally constant and positively regarded.

4.10. Overall Satisfaction of BP

The distribution of BP_Overall_Satisfaction exhibits greater breadth than the other indicators, signifying increased variety in perceptions of overall satisfaction with AI-driven business outcomes. Nevertheless, the density is focused around a high median value, indicating that respondents predominantly perceive the overall influence of AI positively. The symmetrical tails indicate a balanced distribution of replies, with few outliers.

Figure 3. Structural equation model fit indices

Index	Value
Comparative Fit Index (CFI)	0.973
T-size CFI	0.965
Tucker-Lewis Index (TLI)	0.965
Bentler-Bonett Non-normed Fit Index (NNFI)	0.965
Bentler-Bonett Normed Fit Index (NFI)	0.967
Parsimony Normed Fit Index (PNFI)	0.764
Bollen's Relative Fit Index (RFI)	0.958
Bollen's Incremental Fit Index (IFI)	0.973
Relative Noncentrality Index (RNI)	0.973

Note. T-size CFI is computed for $\alpha = 0.05$. The T-size equivalents of the conventional CFI cut-off values (poor < 0.90 < fair < 0.95 < close) are poor < 0.807 < fair < 0.878 < close for model: Model 1.

The fit indices offered deliver a thorough assessment of the structural model's goodness-of-fit. These indices demonstrate the degree of alignment between the suggested model and the observed data, evaluated in relation to established cut-off values and benchmarks.

The Comparative Fit Index (CFI) is 0.973, above the standard criterion of 0.95 for an adequate fit. This indicates that the model exhibits a strong alignment with the data, reflecting significant correspondence between the proposed model and the observed data structure. Correspondingly, the T-size CFI, calculated for $\alpha = 0.05$, is 0.965, which is within the "close" range of the model-specific cut-off values. This further substantiates the model's robustness and reliability.

The Tucker-Lewis Index (TLI), or Non-Normed Fit Index (NNFI), is 0.965, indicating an excellent fit. Similar to the CFI, values exceeding 0.95 are deemed suggestive of a well-fitting model, which is corroborated in this instance. The Bentler-Bonett Non-Normed Fit Index (NNFI) and Normed Fit Index (NFI) exhibit comparable strength at 0.965 and 0.967, respectively, substantiating the assertion that the model is congruent with the data.

The Parsimony Normed Fit score (PNFI) is somewhat reduced to 0.764, as this score accounts for model complexity. Although PNFI values are often lower than those of other indices, the present value is acceptable and indicates that the model achieves an equitable balance between fit and parsimony without excessive complexity.

Additional indices, including Bollen's Relative match Index (RFI) and Incremental Fit Index (IFI), achieve remarkable scores of 0.958 and 0.973, respectively, surpassing the suggested threshold of 0.90 for an adequate match. The Relative Noncentrality Index (RNI) of 0.973 signifies an exceptional fit, further validating the model's robustness.

The fit indices jointly demonstrate that the structural model attains an exceptional fit to the observed data. The elevated values of CFI, TLI, NFI, RFI, IFI, and RNI, all beyond the 0.95 criterion, indicate that the model successfully represents the relationships across constructs and is appropriately aligned with the dataset. Although the PNFI is marginally reduced due to its parsimony correction, it yet indicates a satisfactory level of model complexity. The fit indices confirm the structural equation model as a dependable and resilient foundation for comprehending the proposed linkages.

Figure 4. Parameter estimates-factor loadings

Latent	Indicator	Estimate	Std. Error	z-value	p
ARE	ARE_Effectiveness	1.000	0.000		
	ARE_Usefulness	0.894	0.041	21.761	< .001
	ARE_Personalization	1.120	0.042	26.707	< .001
BP	BP_Sales_Growth	1.000	0.000		
	BP_Cost_Savings	0.944	0.029	32.245	< .001
	BP_Overall_Satisfaction	1.064	0.032	33.752	< .001
CSE	CSE_Responsiveness	1.000	0.000		
	CSE_Helpfulness	0.948	0.032	29.299	< .001
	CSE_Satisfaction	1.015	0.032	31.378	< .001
CT	CT_Data_Privacy	1.000	0.000		
	CT_Transparency	0.942	0.033	28.828	< .001
	CT_Fairness	0.838	0.032	25.802	< .001
OE	OE_Inventory_Management	1.000	0.000		
	OE_Demand_Forecasting	0.935	0.035	26.889	< .001
	OE_Supply_Chain_Operations	0.963	0.035	27.729	< .001

The parameter estimates for factor loadings indicate the degree to which the observed indicators accurately reflect their corresponding latent components. Each loading signifies the intensity of the relationship between a latent variable and its observed indicator, with elevated loadings denoting stronger relationships. The statistical significance of these loadings is assessed using z-values and p-values.

For the latent construct AI Recommendation Effectiveness (ARE), the factor loading for ARE_Effectiveness is established at 1.000 as a reference point. The additional indicators, ARE_Usefulness (0.894) and ARE_Personalization (1.120), exhibit robust and statistically significant loadings ($p < .001$), with z-values of 21.761 and 26.707, respectively. These findings indicate that utility and personalisation are significantly associated with the efficacy of AI recommendations.

Within the Business Performance (BP) construct, BP_Sales_Growth functions as the benchmark indicator with a loading of 1.000. The loadings for BP_Cost_Savings (0.944) and BP_Overall_Satisfaction (1.064) are comparably robust and statistically significant, with z-values of 32.245 and 33.752 ($p < .001$). This signifies that cost savings and general satisfaction are essential metrics of corporate performance and effectively embody the latent construct.

The reference indicator for Customer Service Effectiveness (CSE) is CSE_Responsiveness, which has a loading of 1.000. CSE_Helpfulness (0.948) and CSE_Satisfaction (1.015) demonstrate robust and substantial loadings, with z-values of 29.299 and 31.378 ($p < .001$). The findings indicate that helpfulness and satisfaction are essential elements of effective AI-driven customer service.

For Consumer Trust (CT), CT_Data_Privacy serves as the reference indication with a loading of 1.000. The loadings for CT_Transparency (0.942) and CT_Fairness (0.838) are statistically significant, with z-values of 28.828 and 25.802 ($p < .001$). The findings show that views of openness and fairness, while marginally less correlated than data privacy, significantly contribute to customer trust.

Ultimately, for Operational Efficiency (OE), OE_Inventory_Management serves as the reference indicator with a loading of 1.000. The other indicators, OE_Demand_Forecasting (0.935) and OE_Supply_Chain_Operations (0.963), exhibit robust and significant loadings, with z-values of 26.889 and 27.729 ($p < .001$). These findings underscore that enhancements in demand forecasting and supply chain operations are critical aspects of operational efficiency.

All factor loadings are statistically significant, with p-values below 0.001, demonstrating that each observed indicator accurately represents its corresponding latent construct. The significant loadings across all constructs validate the measurement model, confirming the strength of the postulated links between latent variables and their indicators. These results establish a robust basis for the structural equation modelling framework.

Figure 5. Structural equation modeling

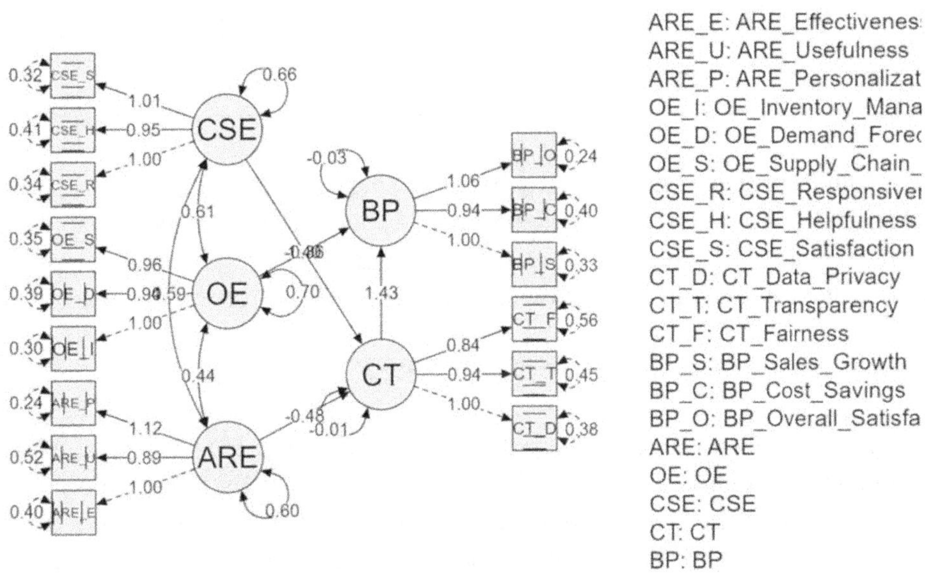

Table 2. Interrelations among latent constructs

Code	Description
ARE: AI Recommendation Effectiveness	
ARE_Effectiveness	Effectiveness of AI Recommendations
ARE_Usefulness	Usefulness of AI Recommendations
ARE_Personalization	Personalization Level of AI Recommendations
OE: Operational Efficiency	
OE_Inventory_Management	Efficiency in Inventory Management
OE_Demand_Forecasting	Accuracy of Demand Forecasting
OE_Supply_Chain_Operations	Improvement in Supply Chain Operations
CSE: Customer Service Effectiveness	
CSE_Responsiveness	Responsiveness of AI-based Customer Service
CSE_Helpfulness	Helpfulness of AI in Resolving Queries
CSE_Satisfaction	Overall Satisfaction with AI Customer Support
CT: Consumer Trust	
CT_Data_Privacy	Perception of Data Privacy
CT_Transparency	Transparency in AI Decisions
CT_Fairness	Fairness in AI-based Pricing or Targeting
BP: Business Performance	

continued on following page

Table 2. Continued

Code	Description
BP_Sales_Growth	Improvement in Sales Growth
BP_Cost_Savings	Cost Savings Due to AI
BP_Overall_Satisfaction	Overall Satisfaction with Business Outcomes from AI

The structural model presents a detailed visualization of the interrelations among the latent constructs: AI Recommendation Effectiveness (ARE), Operational Efficiency (OE), Customer Service Effectiveness (CSE), Consumer Trust (CT), and Business Performance (BP). The factor loadings, path coefficients, and correlations indicate the intensity of these relationships and their respective markers.

4.11. AI Recommendation Effectiveness (ARE)

The latent construct ARE is assessed using three indicators: ARE_Effectiveness, ARE_Usefulness, and ARE_Personalization, exhibiting standardized factor loadings of 1.00, 0.89, and 1.12, respectively. The loadings demonstrate that personalization exhibits the most robust correlation with the concept, closely succeeded by effectiveness and usefulness. The construct ARE directly affecting Consumer Trust (CT) with a path coefficient of 0.44, indicating that AI recommendation systems play a substantial role in fostering trust in AI systems.

4.12. Operational Efficiency (OE)

Operational Efficiency (OE) is quantified by OE_Inventory_Management, OE_Demand_Forecasting, and OE_Supply_Chain_Operations, exhibiting standardized factor loadings of 1.00, 0.90, and 0.96, respectively. The elevated loadings signify robust correlations, with inventory management acting as the benchmark indication. OE significantly enhances Consumer Trust (CT) (path coefficient = 0.70) and indirectly affects Business Performance (BP) via CT. This underscores the essential function of operational enhancements in augmenting both trust and performance results.

4.13. Customer Service Effectiveness(CSE)

The latent construct CSE is characterized by CSE_Responsiveness, CSE_Helpfulness, and CSE_Satisfaction, with factor loadings of 1.00, 0.95, and 1.01, respectively. The significant loadings underscore the relevance of all three measures in delineating effective AI-driven customer service. CSE positively influences CT (path coefficient = 0.61), highlighting that efficient AI-driven customer service substantially enhances consumer trust.

Consumer Trust (CT) is characterized by CT_Data_Privacy, CT_Transparency, and CT_Fairness, with factor loadings of 1.00, 0.94, and 0.84, respectively. Although all variables are significantly correlated with CT, data privacy stands out as the paramount element. CT directly impacts Business Performance (BP) (path coefficient = 1.43), establishing it as the most significant predictor of performance outcomes in the model. This highlights the essential role of trust in facilitating economic success, especially in AI-driven systems.

4.14. Business Performance (BP)

BP is quantified by BP_Sales_Growth, BP_Cost_Savings, and BP_Overall_Satisfaction, exhibiting standardized factor loadings of 1.00, 0.94, and 1.06, respectively. Overall satisfaction is the most significantly correlated measure, succeeded by sales growth and cost reduction. BP is indirectly affected by ARE, OE, and CSE via CT, underscoring the mediating function of trust in enhancing business results.

4.15. Comprehensive Model Insights

The structural model emphasizes the interrelation of the latent components. ARE, OE, and CSE directly contribute to CT, which acts as a crucial mediating variable affecting BP. The elevated path coefficient between CT and BP (1.43) indicates that trust is the most significant determinant of business performance. The robust factor loadings for all indicators substantiate the measurement model and affirm the significance of each indicator in delineating its corresponding construct. This model offers compelling proof of how AI-driven capabilities in recommendations, operations, and customer service augment trust and, consequently, business performance.

5. DISCUSSION

The descriptive statistics offer a thorough summary of the dataset, emphasising the central tendencies, variability, and distribution traits of the indicators for the constructs of AI Recommendation Effectiveness (ARE), Operational Efficiency (OE), Customer Service Effectiveness (CSE), Consumer Trust (CT), and Business Performance (BP). The average values for all variables indicate that respondents predominantly view AI's influence on these areas favourably, with most averages ranging from 3.78 to 4.13 on a 5-point scale. This suggests that, on average, respondents hold a positive view on the efficacy, utility, and customisation of AI systems, along with their impact on operational enhancements, customer service, trust, and corporate performance.

The standard deviations, spanning from 0.696 to 0.827, indicate moderate variability across the responses, with certain indicators, such as ARE_Usefulness and BP_Overall_Satisfaction, demonstrating reduced variability. This indicates a greater consensus among responders about these metrics. In contrast, indicators such as OE_Supply_Chain_Operations and CT_Data_Privacy exhibit greater variability, suggesting a wider range of perspectives or experiences concerning these facets of AI. The standard errors of the mean, ranging from 0.070 to 0.083, are minimal, showing the precision of the mean estimations and the reliability of the responses in the sample.

The Shapiro-Wilk test findings for normality demonstrate that all indicators significantly depart from a normal distribution, with p-values under 0.001 for all variables. The Shapiro-Wilk statistics, ranging from 0.804 to 0.847, further substantiate non-normal distributions among the indicators. This divergence from normalcy indicates the existence of skewness or kurtosis in the data, which must be considered in the statistical studies. The non-normality highlights the necessity of employing robust statistical techniques, such as Structural Equation Modelling (SEM), which adeptly manage departures from normality.

The descriptive data indicate a predominantly favourable view of respondents on AI's influence in multiple areas. The elevated means and moderate standard deviations indicate a predominantly positive and stable assessment of AI systems, with certain metrics exhibiting increased variability, probably attributable to variations in implementation or personal expectations. Non-normal distributions, although significant, are common in survey data and can be managed by suitable analytical methods. These findings establish a robust basis for subsequent research and interpretation within the structural equation modelling paradigm.

The aggregate analysis of the violin plots for the indicators of AI Recommendation Effectiveness (ARE), Operational Efficiency (OE), Customer Service Effectiveness (CSE), Consumer Trust (CT), and Business Performance (BP) yields a thorough comprehension of respondents' perceptions regarding the role and influence of AI across various facets of business and customer interactions.

The violin plots indicate a uniform pattern of elevated central tendency across all dimensions, with the majority of answers aggregating around positive values (means near 4 on a 5-point scale). This clustering indicates a robust consensus among respondents concerning the beneficial effects of AI on recommendation efficacy, operational efficiency, customer service, trust, and corporate performance. Specific variables, like BP_Overall_Satisfaction, CSE_Helpfulness, and ARE_Effectiveness, exhibit pronounced clustering, suggesting that respondents perceive AI as consistently effective in these domains.

Although the general opinion is favourable, many indicators exhibit variability. Constructs such as CT_Data_Privacy, OE_Supply_Chain_Operations, and BP_Overall_Satisfaction demonstrate wider variances, indicating a diversity of experiences or perspectives among respondents. This diversity may be ascribed to disparities in organisational implementation or individual anticipations of AI systems. The existence of outliers in indicators such as ARE_Personalization, CSE_Responsiveness, and BP_Sales_Growth indicates that, although the overall perception is positive, certain respondents possess less favourable experiences or expectations for specific facets of AI.

Each concept offers distinct insights. The metrics for AI Recommendation Effectiveness (ARE) demonstrate positive clustering, highlighting that AI-generated suggestions are typically regarded as effective and personalised, exhibiting little heterogeneity in personalisation. Operational Efficiency (OE) metrics reflect robust positive opinions; nevertheless, supply chain operations demonstrate marginally greater variability, indicating possible areas for enhancement. Customer Service Effectiveness (CSE) measures exhibit significant concordance and favourable aggregation, indicating robust satisfaction with AI-enhanced customer service. Consumer Trust (CT) exhibits greater variety in measures such as data privacy, indicating divergent attitudes of AI's handling of sensitive information while upholding fairness and openness. company Performance (BP) measures, such as sales growth, cost savings, and overall satisfaction, exhibit persistent positive clustering, highlighting the recognised advantages of AI in improving company KPIs.

The violin plots together indicate that respondents perceive AI's function in recommendation systems, operational procedures, customer service, trust-building, and company success favourably. The pronounced central clustering of replies, along with moderate fluctuation and few outliers, indicates a robust overall acceptance of AI systems. Nevertheless, particular domains like as supply chain operations and data privacy may necessitate further focus to reconcile the discrepancies in perceptions and integrate these elements with the overall favourable experiences. These results establish a solid basis for corroborating the structural model and pinpointing actionable areas for improving AI implementations.

Structural equation modelling (SEM) analysis offers a robust framework for elucidating the interrelationships among the latent constructs: AI Recommendation Effectiveness (ARE), Operational Efficiency (OE), Customer Service Effectiveness (CSE), Consumer Trust (CT), and Business Performance (BP). The model combines theoretical frameworks and practical data, underpinned by rigorous statistical analysis, to demonstrate how AI capabilities affect trust and commercial results.

The latent constructs are effectively represented by their observed indicators, with all factor loadings being statistically significant and demonstrating robust connections. ARE is characterised by its efficacy, utility, and customisation, with customisation being the most significant indicator. Likewise, OE encompasses enhancements in inventory management, demand forecasting, and supply chain operations, whereas CSE denotes responsiveness, assistance, and satisfaction with AI-driven customer care. CT is characterised by data privacy, openness, and fairness, with data privacy being especially crucial, whereas BP is assessed through sales growth, cost savings, and overall satisfaction, with satisfaction exhibiting the most significant correlation.

The model fit indices, such as the Comparative Fit Index (CFI), Tucker-Lewis Index (TLI), and Incremental Fit Index (IFI), constantly surpass the 0.95 threshold, signifying an exceptional fit between the proposed model and the observed data. This robust alignment reinforces the legitimacy of the proposed linkages. The descriptive statistics indicate a predominantly favourable perception of AI systems across all constructs, characterised by elevated mean values and moderate variability, hence reinforcing the robustness of the SEM framework.

The structural model emphasises critical pathways among the constructions. ARE, OE, and CSE all exert a favourable influence on CT, with operational efficiency and customer service effectiveness demonstrating particularly significant effects. CT appears as the most pivotal construct, exerting a significant direct influence on BP. This signifies that trust serves as a crucial intermediary, converting AI-enabled skills into concrete commercial results. The mediating function of CT highlights the necessity of addressing customer apprehensions regarding data protection, transparency, and equity to bolster trust and improve business success.

The SEM study offers a definitive and evidence-based comprehension of the influence of AI systems on corporate performance. Enhancing recommendation efficacy, operational efficiency, and customer service effectiveness enables organisations to cultivate consumer trust, a crucial catalyst for increased sales, cost reductions, and overall pleasure. This report provides concrete recommendations for utilising AI to meet strategic corporate goals, while underscoring the importance of upholding openness, justice, and data protection.

6. IMPLICATIONS OF THE STUDY

The study presents various relevant implications spanning theoretical, practical, strategic and policy dimensions. From a theoretical perspective, it greatly contributes to the academic conversation on AI in retail by providing a validated Structural Equation Modelling (SEM) paradigm. This model empirically proves the connection between AI functionalities—such as suggestion efficacy, operational efficiency and customer service effectiveness—and their impact on consumer trust and business performance. In doing so, the research underlines the mediating function of consumer trust, presenting it not only consequently but as a vital conduit via which AI capabilities influence business results. This discovery extends current theories on technology acceptance and customer behaviour by incorporating trust as a core element that bridges technological utility with strategic business results. Additionally, the study stands at the intersection of disciplines such as service marketing, behavioural science, and technology ethics, showing that successful AI integration in retail requires more than technical excellence—it demands an appreciation for the human and ethical dimensions of AI adoption.

On the practical level, the findings make a compelling case for merchants to prioritize individualised experiences. The results reveal that personalization has the largest influence on AI suggestion effectiveness, which in turn plays a crucial role in gaining customer trust. As such, investment in adaptive, machine-learning-based recommendation engines should be regarded crucial for sustaining loyalty and long-term engagement. Operational efficiency appears as another crucial domain, with evidence pointing to the value of AI in enhancing inventory management, demand forecasting, and supply chain responsiveness. These capabilities not only expedite internal procedures but also enhance consumer confidence by ensuring dependability and punctuality in service delivery.

Customer service, too, is witnessing a shift led by AI technology such as chatbots and virtual assistants. These tools boost response and address queries swiftly, contributing to overall satisfaction. However, the study also underlines the significance of balancing technology with the human touch. While AI can handle routine questions, keeping some level of human involvement is vital for sustaining emotional bonds and long-term loyalty. Ethical governance plays a vital role in reinforcing this trust. As consumers become more aware of how their data is used and how AI decisions are made, transparency, fairness, and data security become central to a successful AI strategy. Retailers must embed ethical considerations into their AI deployment practices to maintain and strengthen consumer trust.

Strategically, the findings elevate consumer trust from a passive perception to a vital business asset. It becomes clear that trust is not merely a reaction to AI, but a driver of performance outcomes such as increased sales, cost savings, and overall satisfaction. This understanding urges business leaders to treat trust-building as a strategic objective. It also points to the need for thoughtful AI implementation that integrates personalization, operational efficiency, and customer service without losing sight of the human aspect. Furthermore, organizations that successfully adopt AI in an ethical and transparent manner are likely to enjoy a competitive advantage. Their readiness and agility in leveraging AI for customer satisfaction and operational excellence will allow them to respond more effectively to dynamic market conditions. This also brings to light the need for internal transformation, where companies invest in reskilling their workforce to adapt to AI-driven environments. By equipping employees with the right capabilities, retailers can ensure inclusive growth that aligns technological advancement with human development.

The study also underscores the necessity for a supportive policy environment. The ethical concerns surrounding AI, particularly in areas like data privacy, algorithmic bias, and transparency, highlight the urgency for regulatory frameworks that can guide responsible AI use in retail. Policymakers have an important role to play in setting standards for accountability, fairness, and consumer protection. In addition to regulation, governments can actively encourage ethical AI adoption through incentives such as tax benefits or grants, particularly for companies that demonstrate commitment to ethical practices and workforce development.

Finally, the research lays the groundwork for future exploration. While the model offers a comprehensive view of AI's impact in the Indian retail context, it invites replication in other cultural and geographic settings to understand how perceptions of AI vary across populations. Longitudinal studies could provide insights into the evolving nature of AI's influence over time, particularly in terms of how trust is built and maintained. There is also some scope to expand the model by incorporating employee perspectives, which would allow for a more holistic understanding of AI's organizational impact. Overall, this study not only confirms AI's transformative potential in retail but also charts a roadmap for its ethical and effective implementation, positioning trust as the central mechanism for translating AI capabilities into sustainable business success.

7. CONCLUSION

This study's findings underscore the significant influence of Artificial Intelligence (AI) in revolutionising the retail sector by improving consumer experiences and streamlining business procedures. This research employs Structural Equation Modelling (SEM) to elucidate the evidence-based relationships among AI Recommendation Effectiveness (ARE), Operational Efficiency (OE), and Customer Service Effectiveness (CSE) in fostering Consumer Trust (CT), which subsequently enhances Business Performance (BP). These structures offer a comprehensive framework for assessing the dual function of AI in achieving operational excellence and cultivating significant customer relationships, both essential for sustained success in the intensely competitive retail industry.

The effectiveness of AI recommendations (ARE) is crucial for bolstering customer trust. The effectiveness, utility, and personalisation of AI recommendations are significantly correlated with trust, with personalisation being the most impactful element. This indicates that customers increasingly appreciate AI systems that offer personalised and pertinent recommendations, hence enhancing their trust in the retailer's capacity to comprehend and satisfy their unique preferences. The results underscore that merchants should invest in advanced recommendation systems driven by sophisticated machine learning algorithms to enhance customer loyalty and confidence.

Operational Efficiency (OE) enhances trust by optimising inventory management, demand forecasting, and supply chain operations. These innovations not only optimise processes but also yield concrete benefits, including diminished stockouts, reduced excess inventory, and enhanced responsiveness to market dynamics. The research indicates that Organisational Excellence (OE) substantially enhances Consumer Trust (CT) and indirectly affects Business Performance (BP). Retailers who utilise AI to enhance operational procedures are more effectively positioned to establish confidence by showcasing reliability and efficiency in the delivery of goods and services.

Customer Service Effectiveness (CSE) is a vital determinant of trust, with responsiveness, helpfulness, and overall customer satisfaction identified as major markers. AI-powered solutions, like chatbots, virtual assistants, and automated customer assistance systems, have transformed retail consumer engagement. By delivering real-time support and efficiently addressing enquiries, these platforms improve customer experiences while reducing the burden on human service workers. The study emphasises the necessity of equilibrating automation with personalised interactions to sustain consumer loyalty and happiness, especially in contexts where human touchpoints are still esteemed.

Consumer Trust (CT) serves as the fundamental mediator inside the structural model, linking AI-enabled capabilities to Business Performance (BP). The study emphasises that trust is not just a result but also an essential facilitator of economic success. The elevated path coefficient between CT and BP underscores the critical role of trust in shaping essential performance indicators, including sales growth, cost efficiency, and overall satisfaction. Furthermore, the findings indicate that trust is significantly affected by perceptions of data privacy, transparency, and fairness, which are critical ethical factors in the implementation of AI. Retailers must prioritise these factors to address concerns over algorithmic bias, data security, and ethical transparency, hence assuring ongoing consumer confidence in their AI-driven projects.

Business Performance (BP), as the result in the structural model, signifies the concrete advantages of incorporating AI into retail operations. Metrics such as revenue growth, cost reduction, and general satisfaction illustrate the substantial beneficial effect of AI-enabled capabilities. Overall satisfaction is recognised as the most significant factor influencing BP, highlighting the necessity of providing a comprehensive and cohesive client experience. The research indicates that ARE, OE, and CSE indirectly affect BP via CT, with their collective influence underscoring the interrelated dynamics of AI-enhanced advancements in retail.

Notwithstanding the generally favourable results, the study also highlights areas necessitating additional focus. Certain variables, like data privacy and supply chain operations, demonstrate diversity in answers, indicating that customer perceptions and organisational deployment of AI are not consistently favourable. These inequalities underscore the necessity for retailers to tackle difficulties, like guaranteeing ethical transparency, reducing algorithmic bias, and improving the uniformity of AI solutions across all operational areas.

This research illustrates the transformative capacity of AI in retail, highlighting its capability to enhance operational efficiency, improve consumer experiences, and elevate corporate performance concurrently. By cultivating consumer trust, AI empowers merchants to attain strategic objectives, including enhanced revenue, diminished costs, and elevated customer pleasure. Nonetheless, the ethical ramifications of AI implementation, especially regarding transparency, equity, and data privacy, must remain a central issue to guarantee enduring success. Retailers must implement a balanced strategy that harnesses AI's technological potential while simultaneously confronting its ethical and operational concerns. Policymakers also contribute by creating regulatory frameworks that foster accountability and equity in AI systems.

The comprehensive study provides practical recommendations for retailers, highlighting the necessity of investing in sophisticated AI technology while upholding a customer-focused and ethical framework. It underscores the necessity for ongoing investigation into topics such as algorithmic equity, consumer behaviour, and the enduring effects of AI on labour dynamics and market competitiveness. By tackling these difficulties and leveraging AI's promise, merchants can attain a durable and competitive advantage in an increasingly digital world.

REFERENCES

Chen, L., Zhang, Y., & Huang, R. (2020). The impact of AI-driven recommendation systems on retail: A customer perspective. *Journal of Retailing and Consumer Services*, *55*, 102109. DOI: 10.1016/j.jretconser.2020.102109

Grewal, D., Roggeveen, A. L., & Nordfält, J. (2021). AI in retail: A strategic review and research agenda. *Journal of Retailing*, *97*(1), 6–22. DOI: 10.1016/j.jretai.2021.02.004

Huang, M. H., & Rust, R. T. (2020). Engaged to a robot? The role of AI in service. *Journal of Service Research*, *23*(2), 155–168. DOI: 10.1177/1094670517752459

Kaplan, A., & Haenlein, M. (2019). Siri, Siri, in my hand: Who's the fairest in the land? *Business Horizons*, *62*(1), 15–25. DOI: 10.1016/j.bushor.2018.08.004

Li, R., Sun, F., & Zhao, J. (2020). Ethical implications of AI in retail. *Computers in Human Behavior*, *124*, 106909. DOI: 10.1016/j.chb.2020.106909

Manyika, J., Lund, S., Chui, M., Bughin, J., Woetzel, J., Batra, P., & Sanghvi, S. (2017). *What the future of work will mean for jobs, skills, and wages*. McKinsey Global Institute. https://www.mckinsey.com/featured-insights/future-of-work/what-the-future-of-work-will-mean-for-jobs-skills-and-wages

McCarthy, J., & Wright, P. (2021). The role of AI in customer service. *Journal of Service Management*, *31*(4), 789–808. DOI: 10.1108/JSM-2020-0187

Meyer, C., & Schwager, A. (2021). How AI is reshaping customer service in retail. *Journal of Retailing and Marketing*, *92*(4), 42–53. DOI: 10.1007/s10729-021-09541-9

Ransbotham, S., Kiron, D., Gerbert, P., & Reeves, M. (2020). Artificial intelligence in business gets real. *MIT Sloan Management Review*. https://sloanreview.mit.edu/article/artificial-intelligence-in-business-gets-real

Smith, K., & Anderson, J. (2022). Consumer preferences for AI-driven personalization. *Retail Analytics Quarterly*, *15*(2), 32–45. DOI: 10.1016/raq.2022.103245

Smith, K., Johnson, P., & Lee, D. (2020). Transparency and trust in AI: Consumer perspectives in digital environments. *Journal of Business Ethics*, *164*(3), 605–623. DOI: 10.1007/s10551-018-4067-3

Tan, Y., He, M., & Xu, Z. (2019). AI applications in retail: From inventory management to demand forecasting. *Operations Research Perspectives*, *7*, 100127. DOI: 10.1016/j.orp.2019.100127

Zhu, L., Li, X., & Wang, Y. (2021). Algorithmic bias in AI-driven retail systems: Implications for ethical AI adoption. *Computers in Human Behavior*, *124*, 106909. DOI: 10.1016/j.chb.2021.106909

Chapter 5
Composable Banking

Shweta Harish
https://orcid.org/0009-0005-8098-2407
Putra Business School, Malaysia

ABSTRACT

Improving the market competitiveness and profitability for traditional banks by prioritizing customer's preference is the biggest issues experienced by FI's across the globe. Innovation is helping traditional banks to survive and develop in the emerging technology environment to compete with Neo Banks. Leading to innovation of new banking products and processes that can provide enhanced customer experience and improve banks' efficiency and profitability. Banking innovation and its implementation is a potential way for FI's to enhance their development capability and performance. Composable banking(CB) is leading with an API backed technology model to build customized products and processes with high speed and low IT cost. It is designed to delivered financial services based on the rapid and flexible assembly of independent, best for purpose systems. This chapter will explain the working model of CB, the request-response cycle of APIs, it's pros and cons, list of early adopters & third-party service providers, new insights, trends into management of traditional banks.

1 INTRODUCTION

The word "Bank" is derived from the Italian word Banco or the French Banque, which means a bench or currency exchange table. Traditional Banks provide the financial services necessary for businesses and consumers to do their business as they provide a means of holding and exchanging financial assets, intermediating savings for investment in productivity through lending to businesses and consumers, enabling risk sharing. In today's competitive world, apart from these traditional banks, we have digital banks and Neo Banks. These banks have different working models with the key difference is in their operating cost, adaptability to technology innovations, usage of customer data to make swift changes basis customer's preferences. This has increased the banking competition many folds. Leading to innovation of new banking products, processes, technology, and marketing that can provide its customers with an enhanced banking experience and improve banks' efficiency and profitability.

There is existing evidence which suggests that the biggest barrier is the impersonalisation which is impacting the customers to fully adopt the digital financial services and hence, encouraging banks to implement customized measures to promote the ongoing development of digital financial services

DOI: 10.4018/979-8-3373-0209-6.ch005

(Dimitrova et at., 2022). Similarly, Makudza, 2021 did provide the evidence that there is a positive association between customer experience management and customer loyalty which can be beneficial for financial institutions to gain competitive advantage. These digital finance offerings also lead to the rise of FinTech companies offering services in Africa and supported small and medium businesses and entrepreneurs in their different stages of growth (Sanga, Aziakpono, 2024).

A recent study by Omal (2024) highlighted the critical role of organizational digital transformation in driving continuous technological progress, supported by eight successful and four unsuccessful case studies. The successful examples include Amazon's retail transformation, GE's industrial IoT shift, Starbucks' enhanced digital experience, Tesla's electric revolution, Ford, McDonald's, Volkswagen's European electric initiative, and Alibaba's e-commerce dominance in Asia. These cases provide valuable insights into the strategies, adaptations, and innovations that helped these organizations transition from traditional models to leaders in digital excellence. On the other hand, the four unsuccessful case studies—Blockbuster, Kodak, Nokia, and Toys "R" Us—offer lessons in the challenges and complexities faced by organizations in their quest for digital success. Overall, the study emphasizes that customer-centric digitalization and technological innovation are key to organizational transformation, enhancing customer experience and loyalty.

Like any other industry, the key to success in the new banking era is also "customer preference's". We can relate this to food analogy where Traditional Banks used to offer the standard meal menu all days of the week with limited choices. Here, diners would walk-in, see the menu and order from the available list. As compared to digital banks, where diners can see the review, rating, menu, chef's specialty etc digitally and book the table to dine in. Whereas Neo banks are the example of cloud kitchens providing composable options where customers can choose what they want to eat veggies, toppings, calories, protein portions, ingredients preference etc and then the chef would right away prepare those preferred meals for the consumers and get it delivered at their doorstep. As a fourth industrial revolution scenario, the focus on customer participation is essential to reinforce customer's relevance in shaping firm's offering. Therefore, combine use of technological offerings and product customization are best works for firms in meeting customer's demand and for organizational growth (Naeem & Di Maria, 2022).

Traditional banks are facing many challenges with the continuous changes in customer's behavior and their banking expectations. This includes their online banking platform, customer service delivery, personalized products, methods of banking etc. All the traditional banks are looking at solving these issues with the help of evolving technology and its adoption. However, banks are still facing below issues on this transitional journey to meet customer's expectations and remain competitive:

- Upgrade of Legacy systems
- Transition to the latest technology infrastructure
- Adoption of digitalization
- How and where to use Artificial Intelligence (AI)
- Remain compliant.
- Be Future Ready

A Composable Business is a dynamic and adaptable organization that constructs and modifies its services, processes, and resources like modular building blocks or Lego pieces. These components can be arranged, rearranged, or discarded as needed. This approach allows businesses to break down large, outdated applications into separate parts that can be designed, scaled, and maintained independently.

Similarly, composable banking is the banking model where banks make use API's and build customer preferred products and services with high speed at low IT cost.

Strategic partnerships between banks and fintechs for digital innovation offer advantages for both parties. Banks benefit by accessing rapid innovation without directly participating in its development, while fintechs gain the resources and expertise needed to scale within the heavily regulated financial industry (Klus et al., 2019). This collaboration aims to provide financial services through the quick and flexible integration of independent, best-in-class systems. It places engines at the heart of the financial architecture, enabling the selection of features that can be easily added to a range of connected services using APIs, which are compatible with all cloud architectures.

In this paper, we will provide the pros and cons of composable banking along with the list of banks who are the early adopters of composable banking. In addition to this, we will also provide the details of service providers and their offerings.

Innovation is recognized as a key aspect of entrepreneurial self-efficacy (Yeh et al., 2021) and has become increasingly vital in the banking sector. Banks operate in a dynamic and unpredictable environment where factors like customer preferences, loyalty, product-service technologies, and competition frequently change (Kim et al., 2024). Innovation, especially when supported by customization and co-creation, is viewed as a crucial factor for long-term success in today's competitive markets (Stojcic et al., 2024). Investing in innovation based on customer needs is essential for gaining a competitive edge, whether for startups or established firms (Sreenivasan & Suresh, 2024). Research confirms that innovation is a significant source of competitive advantage for businesses (Ke et al., 2023). According to Baffour & Appiah et al. (2024), banks must actively seek new opportunities and embrace innovation to maintain stable performance. Innovative businesses can more quickly address market challenges by adopting digital technologies in three phases: Stretching (where digital technologies become central), Streamlining (extensive use of digital technologies), and Synergizing (ongoing integration of digital technologies) (Mancuso et al., 2025). Furthermore, the COVID-19 pandemic accelerated business transformation through entrepreneurial innovation (Sahi et al., 2023a; Santos et al., 2023).

Previous research has established a positive connection between innovation and firm performance (Cho & Pucik, 2005; Gunday et al., 2011). Studies have shown that different types of innovation significantly impact firm performance in areas such as return on investment, market share, competitiveness, and customer value (Neely et al., 2001). Technological innovations can include new products, services, production processes, and organizational structures (Frame & White, 2004). Research on the adoption of intelligent technology solutions by banks has primarily focused on improvements like back-end system upgrades, including artificial intelligence, big data, and blockchain (Lu et al., 2019). Many of these technological products are self-service options designed to meet customer preferences and choices. Composable banking is one such model that can greatly assist traditional banks in staying competitive by allowing them to build customer-preferred banking products using APIs.

2 LITERATURE REVIEW

Digital transformation has had a profound impact on financial services, reshaping both society and industry as one of the most significant trends. A study by Thottoli et al. (2023) offers a bibliometric analysis of 299 peer-reviewed research articles published over the past 22 years on digital transformation in financial services. The study explores the effects of digital transformation on the financial sector, examines applied technologies, and provides valuable insights into this ongoing transformation. The Traditional Banking System is well-managed, well-regulated and recognized worldwide for their strength and resiliency. Economies heavily rely on stable banks for their citizen's banking needs which includes mortgage to buy home, saving for retirements as well as business funding. The existing banking model includes a national banking system where several large, medium or small domestic retails banks competes as well as with foreign banks operating globally. All these banks are federally regulated by their respective countries under the various Bank Act.

There is considerable global research highlighting the direct relationship between innovation and organizational performance. For instance, a study on the banking sector in Ghana found a significant positive relationship between innovation dimensions and firm performance, emphasizing the importance of selecting the right types of innovation to enhance a bank's performance by meeting customer needs (YuSheng & Ibrahim, 2020). Similarly, a study by Hornuf et al. (2025) on mobile fintech adoption in Sub-Saharan Africa explored the factors driving the adoption of mobile fintech services, with ease of use and usefulness being key perceptions for mobile money, mobile banking, electronic wallets, and internet banking. Islamic banking in Jordan gained financial success from 2017 to 2021 by optimizing fintech services like internet banking, crowd funding, mobile banking, and automated teller machines (Alghadi, 2024). Artificial Intelligence is reshaping future across all the industries like healthcare, transportation, banking and education. The revolutionary potential of AI is investigated for its implications, applications, challenges, and opportunities (Rawas, 2024). An intersectional literature review explores the use of artificial intelligence to enhance customer experience across sectors like tourism, banking, and e-commerce. This includes the use of conversational agents such as chatbots, voicebots, and machine learning prediction models to improve customer interactions. In the banking sector, the use of artificial neural networks to identify people's faces in smart banking systems is gaining momentum, particularly for verifying the rightful owners in mobile banking applications (Nosrati et al., 2024). Another study on improving financial advisory services with GenAI found that personalized investment suggestions, human-like empathy, and the continuous improvement of GenAI's recommendations positively affect consumer perceptions of its authenticity, which in turn influences their responses to GenAI-based financial advisory solutions (Yang & Lee, 2024).

There are many more existing studies which provides the insights on how technology innovation is leading and changing the banking industry. The traditional banking industry faces significant competition from various sectors, including banks, trust companies, life insurance companies, finance companies, federal and provincial credit unions, cooperative banks, financial agencies, and fintech companies. Consumers have a wide array of options from both domestic and foreign banks, along with a broad range of financial products and services, such as bank accounts, credit cards, loans, and investments. This creates intense competition for banks, compelling them to develop unique products and services that stand out and become the preferred choice for consumers' banking needs.

While it's complicated for the traditional banks to upgrade their technology but it's much faster and easier for the non- banks to build customer preferred products and services since these non-banks do not have legacy bundle to deal with. As per Grigorescu et al., 2023 wherein statistical data was taken from Eurostat 2023 and the time series was considered from 2004 to 2022 shows that the changes in the procedural-fiscal-financial sphere are the ones that fully reflect two principles underlying the tax evolution: digitalization and simplification. Additionally, even regulators have made it easier for the non-banks to provide customers with the financial products and services which is more user friendly and promotes business and economy. These non-banks are having access to latest technology, cloud infrastructure, business mindset which makes them first choice for the consumers especially millennials who are super comfortable with technology applications. Meanwhile, traditional banks spending a lot more on their existing high cost infrastructure and it's maintenance while trying to build and optimize technological innovations but success looks far behind. To gain customer's preference and remain competitive in the financial industry, traditional banks are seeking composable solutions which can be the best model like plug and play to build customer preferred products at high speed with low cost. This gives technology companies a brand-new horizon to come up with composable banking solutions.

Composable Banking is a platform which allows combination of pre-built technology backed business solutions which can be customized on need basis using API's. This integration works efficiently to perform any specific function while still optimizing the large legacy core systems. This way composable banking can be a new outlook for traditional banks to leverage technology-based innovations to build customer preferred products and services with more flexibility and higher efficiencies at much lower cost. Furthermore, banks can easily collaborate with third-party vendors or FinTech's to build customized banking products and services using APIs. This model is a win-win model for everyone as banks can get faster technology innovated customized banking solutions at low cost, third-party vendors can use their resources to build these solutions and can get benefit of bank's reputation and existing regulatory framework (Frederik et al., 2019) and lastly, customers find it much easier and prefer this solution through their primary banks.

2.1 Composable Banking Platform – Working Model

Digital platforms have achieved significant success across many industries, particularly in the banking sector. With the rise of open banking, banks in emerging markets are receiving support from investors to implement digital platforms that leverage the capabilities of third-party developers. A study by Schreieck, Huang et al. (2024), which surveyed 165 banks globally, highlights how APIs have made the digital journey smoother, improving customer service and creating new revenue models by enabling data-driven business intelligence and fostering industry-wide collaboration. Additionally, interfaces play a crucial role in integrating external sources of innovation and structuring ecosystems. Web APIs are increasingly used to offer or sell services, becoming an important revenue source. Pujadas, Valderrama, and Venters (2024) provided evidence of an ecosystem where decentralized interfaces support decentralized governance, fostering both cooperative and competitive relationships. Web APIs also enable the integration of capabilities from various organizations to co-produce services and products by connecting their information systems (Pujadas et al., 2024).

With reference to the Figure 1, these APIs are a three-tier architecture which consists of client, server, and databases independently. Usually, a client is web browser or mobile application user who requests information. Server tier will have the actual business logic and the information is requested by client to server is based on the different protocols. The server will pull the data from the connected databases tier. The system and logic of protocol-dependent requests are the APIs itself. These APIs are the foundation of composable solutions which helps with industry level collaboration by identifying new streams of revenue generation at low cost.

Figure 1. API working model – request & response cycle

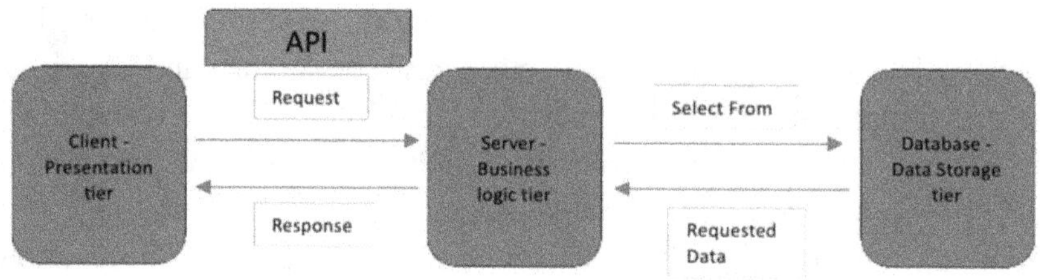

Composable banking is a kind of open system which primarily relies on open API's offered by vendors which can allow application software to link up easily and efficiently. These open API's gives banks an unlimited choice of modules and vendors to work with. This way banks can operate and optimize technology backed solutions on their existing technology infrastructure by integrating different systems, services and third-party providers. This allows faster collaboration, exchange of data between multiple partners for enhanced products and services which improves digital experience for the end users. Hence, API's play an important role in composable banking solutions which allows banks to leverage technology innovation which can be easily reused, repurposed, and replaced basis customers evolving needs and the market offerings. There are already many existing success stories of value generation through API driven business models.

A well-known single case study in the travel industry, Amadeus Corporation, conducted by Heshmatisafa & Seppanen (2023), identified six distinct values generated by exposing digital assets to API consumers through API-driven business models of self-service platforms: commercialization, ecosystem, big data, market and marketplace, entrepreneurship, and R&D. This shows that APIs have already proven successful across industries in driving low-cost business models, whether in the digital space or within marketplaces. Therefore, it is reasonable to conclude that banking is evolving to meet customers' needs, choices, and preferences. Technology plays a vital role in helping service providers transition from traditional banking to future platform banking, which is likely to rely on composable banking solutions supported by third-party service providers.

Figure 2. Traditional compared to platform banking

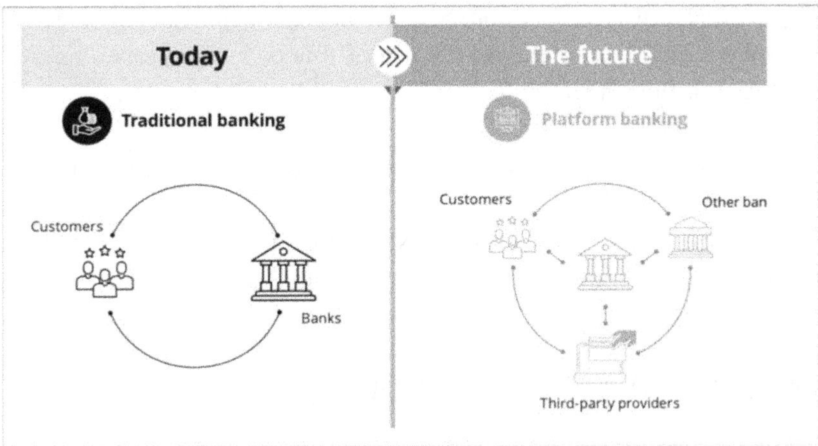

3 RESEARCH METHODOLOGY

With this paper, the intent is to provide the concept how composable banking can positively impact the organization performance in bank when the focus is on growth. Additionally, how our traditional banks can strategically take benefit of composable banking and it's direct and indirect challenges and considerations for the organizations. Technology plays a crucial role in reducing operating costs, enhancing process reliability by eliminating intermediaries, and minimizing manual processes to improve efficiency and productivity (Vedapradha & Ravi, 2021). A firm's ability to balance innovation with quality is an intangible resource essential for sustaining growth, increasing profitability, and creating superior market value. These factors contribute to long-term competitiveness (Cho & Pucik, 2005). Heshmatisafa and Seppanen (2023) expanded on the concept of a firm's extended digital resources as a tool to create and capture opportunities, emphasizing the importance of digital assets in fostering an open ecosystem that stays relevant and generates various business values.

This paper makes three key contributions: First, it introduces the concept and working model of Composable Banking, outlining its benefits and considerations. Second, it provides a list of current service providers, their offerings, early adopters, and the key challenges they face. Third, it explores future trends and opportunities in Composable Banking. Additionally, the paper briefly discusses APIs and their operational cycle, highlighting the critical role APIs play in helping banks build composable banking solutions tailored to customer preferences.

This study is significant considering this will provide the theoretical and practical approach to the banks while optimizing existing research work. The goal is to evaluate Composable banking, it's working model, benefits, considerations and challenges. In future, this will help the industry to align innovation management with composable banking and its strategies to set the achievable goals to improve the organization performance.

3.1 Research Objectives

This paper will provide an overview of composable banking which can be used as the starting point by traditional banks. We would like to extend the use of this paper in the banking field with the main objectives of this research article are:

- To provide comprehensive review, working model, pros and cons, challenges and considerations of Composable Banking
- To provide list of market leaders, their offerings, and list of early adopters of Composable Banking.
- Finally, future trends and opportunities for Composable Banking in the banking industry.

4 DATA ANALYSIS AND INTERPRETATION

4.1 Composable Banking v/s Embedded Banking

Many people often confuse Composable Banking with Embedded Banking, as both are related to FinTech solutions, but they differ in focus. Embedded Banking primarily deals with the front-end and customer experience, offering financial solutions alongside the purchase of goods and services. A good example is Uber, where the customer books a ride, and the financial transaction is seamlessly processed in the background, focusing on enhancing the customer experience.

In contrast, Composable Banking refers to the back-end processes, where services are consumed digitally and are driven by the developer experience, primarily benefiting financial institutions. In this model, both digital banks and non-banks can offer financial services by providing financial products. Composable Banking acts as a prerequisite and enabler for Embedded Finance, helping organizations integrate financial solutions into their services. For instance, in Europe, Composable Banking typically involves a collection of third-party providers working together to create solutions that challenge traditional banking systems. In North America, it helps traditional banks access newer technologies and overcome legacy technology challenges.

An important distinction is that Embedded Banking typically involves organizations that are not necessarily regulated, while Composable Banking solutions are generally subject to regulatory oversight worldwide (Fintech Global, Jan 2023).

4.2 Drivers of Composable Banking

As per the blog by Head of Banking Practices, Dennis Joosten at EPAM, below the primary key drivers of Composable banking which is a mix of technological advancements and stringent global regulatory demands:

- **Global Regulatory Demands:** In the post-credit-crisis era, there has been decisive shift towards the simplification of banking products spurred by the need to avoid the pitfalls of past complexities and to meet the heightened regulatory standards of transparency and consumer protection. This is giving way to innovate financial products which are both simpler and modular.

- **Consumers Expectations:** Role of customer feedback is certainly shaping the financial industry like any other industry. Meeting customer expectation is paramount to remain competitive and profitable for all the financial institutions is the biggest challenge. Hence, composable solutions fosters a more agile and responsive banking environment, crucial for adapting to the rapidly evolving financial landscape and customer expectations.
- **Embracing cloud services:** Unlike the traditional legacy technology, cloud services are more scalable and innovative. This transition is pivotal for a clean architecture, facilitating compliance and ensuring that banking services can be efficiently audited and adapted without the encumbrances of legacy systems.
- **FinTech Partnerships:** Banks can easily leverage FinTech partnerships, using APIs to create technology landscape needed instead of building it from scratch. This way banks can focus on their primary business function and enhance digital experience, customer experience at low cost and high speed.
- **Revolutionizing Banking Operations:** The integration of Generative AI (Gen AI) is revolutionizing banking operations by allowing automation of banking processes, using voice modules, co-pilot etc to deliver services which are customer centric and compliant with regulations.

4.3 Regulatory Compliance with Composable Banking

The history of banks goes back hundreds of years, and they have evolved significantly over the years, and so does the rules and regulations that govern these banks. Regulatory compliance in financial sector started out with the need of it, the need for stability, the need for protecting customers, as well as a response to many financial crises and economic changes. Twenty years ago, no one would have thought about how to regulate cryptocurrency for example, but today, the existence of crypto necessitates the need for such regulations across the globe.

Similarly, with composable banking solutions, banks must also focus on meeting essential elements and key aspects such as legal requirements set by governmental and international bodies like the Federal Reserve and the Basel Committee. In addition, customer protection and financial stability are critical priorities. Banks must uphold laws that protect customers from fraud, discrimination, and unfair practices. They also need to ensure they maintain adequate capital and liquidity, as well as implement proper reporting mechanisms to prevent systemic risks and ensure the overall stability of the financial system.

Globally, different regions are adopting varied approaches to open banking and the use of APIs. While some countries like India and Japan are encouraging data sharing through non-compulsory measures, others like the EU, Hong Kong, and Australia have implemented more regulatory-driven frameworks. The EU's PSD3 and PSR are significant in shaping its payments sector, while the US is moving towards a regulator-supported market-led approach. Although Europe pioneered open APIs, jurisdictions worldwide are customising their strategies, sometimes extending beyond financial services. Despite progress, further efforts are needed to raise consumer awareness and establish secure, cross-industry data sharing ecosystems. Ultimately, open APIs are seen as the future, requiring firms and regulators to prioritise data protection and adapt their strategies to a changing landscape where customer data control is paramount.

4.4 Considerations for Composable Banking

Everything comes with a cost and so as all the technology innovations. There can be strategic and non-strategic considerations. Under Strategic considerations for traditional banks, it can be huge shift in the overall strategy, knowing that the return on investment would be medium to long-term goal. Bank's strategic alignment with the short-term & long-term organizational goals is the first step which is internal to the initiating bank. Hence, the overall bank's strategy should consider having to manage competition, formal and informal collaborations, establish relationships with small companies and start-up's, integrate an open API driven model, create synergic relationship with existing customers, and create strategy to attract new customers for the banks. These considerations need research and analysis to set the strategic roadmap with tangible and achievable milestones.

However, the non-strategic consideration is specific to Composable Banking Model itself. Composable banking works with Open API's efficiently but there are many considerations that banks needs evaluate before implementing.

- Firstly, its existing enterprise architecture and cloud maturity. Composable solutions are built using integration of multiple components and systems which means this would need resilient architecture with right governance to manage the platform by doing current state assessment.
- Similarly, composable solutions are cloud native and if the organization is not cloud matured then it needs to be addressed through proper planning and investments.
- Apart from this, composable solutions would involve strong data management including use of existing data storage from multiple systems, data privacy and data governance so banks must consider its current state of enterprise architecture, cloud maturity and data management before building the roadmap and investing in composable banking solutions.

As per Sopra banking, there are below six essential topics for banks, when deploying a composable banking solution:

1. **Adopting flexible and scalable technologies**: To increase agility, retail banks can focus on personalized customer service, improve time-to-market, offering real time products and services, efficient management of end-to-end lifecycle of accounts, loans and other banking products.
2. **Collaboration:** Banks can collaborate with other FinTechs to expand their products, enhancing digital experience, ensuring cyber security etc. which is essential for composable banking.
3. **Flexibility in built:** Focusing on small wins, making sure to invest basis business priorities and to limit the cost to optimize the transformation programs.
4. **Continuous transformation in run:** Using the right cost models for transformations and upgrades like choosing to pay as you go instead of making long term cost decisions. Also, using financial optimization models to review the current usage and ways to reduce the unnecessary expenses.
5. **Control & Reduce Risk**: To mitigate financial, security, and regulatory compliance risks, it is essential for banks to implement a resilient and upgradeable IT platform with sustainable architecture. Prioritizing cybersecurity is critical, as financial institutions must address and protect against cyber threats that could compromise sensitive data or disrupt operations. Additionally, ensuring that the system is adaptable and can be upgraded to meet evolving security standards and regulatory require-

ments is key to reducing risks associated with regulatory non-compliance, data breaches, and other financial risks.

6. **Enhance Data Assets**: To improve performance, banks must enhance their data assets by adopting a global data architecture that supports data ownership and effective analysis using AI tools. This involves consolidating data across all touchpoints to provide a comprehensive view of the customer and operations. Key use cases should include customer insights, satisfaction, the effectiveness of bank offerings, operational efficiency, and regulatory compliance. By leveraging advanced analytics and AI, banks can unlock actionable insights that drive decision-making and support continuous improvements across all aspects of their business.

Overall, banks need to follow a strategic approach, do the current state assessment of their technology infrastructure, build or re-build policy and process framework, use the data to evaluate customer's preference, conduct proposal requests for third-party or FinTech's collaboration, ensure proper controls to reduce the risk, follow the industry, company & country regulatory requirements, do proof of concepts for initial testing, start with small wins, follow the Plan-Do-Check-Act Model.

4.5 Implementation Strategy

Composable banking represents a significant evolution in the financial industry. It enables banks to utilize modular and flexible architectures to better respond to market dynamics, improve customer experiences, and streamline operations. This approach allows for the rapid adaptation of services to meet changing market demands and customer expectations, thereby improving operation efficiency, fostering continuous innovation, and improving overall responsiveness.

Aligning composable banking strategies with the institution's overarching business goals and customer-centric objectives is vital. This ensures that banks can fully capitalize on the benefits of composable banking, such as improved customer experiences, quicker time-to-market for new services, and amplified regulatory compliance.

By following these steps as phased strategy, banks can harness the full potential of composable banking, positioning themselves at the forefront of financial innovation and effectively meeting the continuously evolving demands of their customers.

- **Identifying and Defining Composable Capability blocks:** To effectively implement composable banking, start by identifying and defining the key capability blocks that will form the modular components of your banking infrastructure. This process begins with a thorough assessment of current systems to understand existing capabilities and areas for improvement.
- **Localizing change and achieving functional grouping:** Implementing localized changes involves updating isolated modules rather than overhauling the entire system simultaneously. This strategy reduces risk and disruption, making managing updates and testing phases easier. Localized changes allow for more targeted improvements, enabling banks to address specific issues without affecting the broader system. Hence, Isolated testing and deployment, incremental rollouts, alignment with business processes by focusing on customer centric design is essential for strategic achievement.
- **Ensuring Seamless Integration and Interoperability:** Seamless integration and interoperability are critical for the success of a composable banking strategy. Ensuring all components commu-

nicate effectively and integrate smoothly with third-party services is essential for maintaining a cohesive and efficient system. This includes adopted an API first approach and using standardized protocols to ensure compatibility and interoperability.

- **Continuous Testing and Monitoring:** Continuous testing is vital for identifying and resolving issues early in the development process. This proactive strategy enhances the reliability and performance of composable components. Automated testing includes early issue identification and maintaining the integrity with real-time monitoring are the best industry wide accepted approaches for continuous testing and monitoring.
- **Investing in scalable and secure infrastructure:** Making enterprise-wide decisions to Investing in scalable infrastructure is critical to supporting the dynamic nature of composable banking. This ensures that resources can be allocated efficiently based on demand for scalability and cost efficiency. Apart from this, security, and compliance for data protection with best integration practices to ensure regulatory and compliance requirements will be successfully fulfilled.

4.6 Service Providers and Their Offerings

Table 1. A list of few service providers, their offerings, early adopters, and Unique Selling Proposition (USP)

Service Provider	Offerings	Early Adopters	USP
i2cinc	Unified banking and payments platform	Shore United Bank, Banco Do Brasil, Credit Sesame, Credijusto, Bright Services	Configurability and Flexibility, Global Scalability, Speed to Market, Reliability
Unit Finance	Embedded Platform	Thread, AngelList, The Coterie, Invoice2go	API, Client Dashboard, Bank Oversight Dashboard, End-Users banking apps
Spora	Banking Software	Arion Bank, BGFI Bank, Bank of Africa, Attijariwafa Bank, ADIB, Charity Bank, ING, IDB, Mansa Bank, Standard Bank, The co-operative Bank, Sparda bank, Siemens Financial Services	Banking operations, customer engagement and enterprise management services
Mambu	Cloud banking platform with composable approach	ABN Amro, Recognise Bank, N26, Tyme Bank, uala, Tnex, Western Union	Banking as-a-service, Islamic Banking, Embedded Finance, Buy now pay later
Finastra	Open Platform, BaaS	Seatle Bank, First Citizen Bank, Commonwealth Bank, Yoma Bank	Drive route to growth, Marketplace Model, Proven Solutions
i-exceed	Appzillon digital Banking Platform	Barclays, Bank of America, Citi Bank, Al Masraf, TSB, NBF, Seciete Generale, Rothschild & co	Microservices- based, API-Driven, AI/ML, workflows, Notification Hub, Cloud Native, Headless, Rule Engine, Entitlements, Secutiry Control
Thought works	Services and Solutions	Saxo Bank, TBC Bank, Shenzhen Rural Commercial Bank, Xapo Bank, Shanghai Huarui Bank	Data & AI, Generative AI, Digital Transformation, Data Platform Modernization

Sources: Author's own work using Service provider's website

4.7 Global Use Cases of Composable Banking

- Western Union which has presence in 200 countries and territories and deals in over 130 currencies adopted the cloud by collaborating with Mambu to accelerate their financial services by building products that can be scalable and cloud agnostic.
- Another example of delivering value is the collaboration of Capgemini, IBM and Temenos who are the key financial industry leaders bringing unmatched expertise. As composable banking empowers financial institutions to focus on growth and innovation, Temenos can offer a roadmap for sustainable and scalable transformation while Capgemini and IBM will ensure a seamless transition by focusing on middle and back-office functions.
- Collaboration of Mambu and Fourthline to help financial institutions to provide their customers with streamlined onboarding journey with a blend of AI-driven checks and human expertise which can digitally verify users' real identities, with ease and speed.
- When full-service non-bank lender Bluestone was developing a new digital lending platform, it intentionally focused on modularity and decoupling to establish an exceptionally efficient, fast, and flexible foundation for its services. Collaborating with AWS and Thoughtworks, Bluestone built its platform using numerous bespoke business capabilities, including an innovative solution that replaced the traditional CRM. This approach allowed Bluestone to create a highly adaptable and scalable system that could quickly respond to evolving customer needs and market demands.

4.8 Key Challenges of Composable Banking

The benefits of composable banking are significant but it does come with its on challenges and implications. While we have listed few considerations for the banks as prerequisite but there can be still many implications that are equally important to navigate during implementation.

- **Complexity:** Every technology comes with its own complexities, and it would need the sound development with testing before implementation. Providing customized products and services may sound attractive to the customers but it can be really complicated to manage its development and operational maintenance. This customization can lead to the orchestration of multiple services into the overall banking model which can further bring operational inefficiencies if not executed properly.
- **Security and Compliance:** Banks would need to adhere to the strict security and compliance policies for meeting all the privacy and regulatory requirements while implementing composable solutions. Considering there will be significant engagement with vendors, fintech's through API's, it will be very crucial for banks to adhere to the best practices by implementing strict controls and validations.
- **Third-Party Partnerships:** Composable solution will have the major dependency on third-party partnerships which includes Saas (Software as a service) offerings and FinTech's offerings. Choosing the right partner to fill the technology gap is biggest challenge and hence, robust vendor onboarding models to be designs and implemented to adhere to the requirements and regulations.
- **Policy and Processes:** Banks would have to build or re-build policies and processes to end to end life cycle of composable banking solutions. This will help banks to mitigate the risks and reduce the complaints.

- **Transition Journey:** Transition from traditional legacy banking to the latest technology driven banking would need a super strong strategic vision and roadmap. Banks would need to do some proof of concepts for these newer products and services in the initial phase to mitigate the overall investment risk. Additionally, not one size for all which means it will be an iterative process at every stage. Hence, strategic alignment and implementation can be really complicated but crucial for the successful transition.
- **Key Performance Metrics:** Setting the key performance metrics to set the target and to monitor the performance is very crucial and can be complicated too. However, for the success of any new business model, it's quint essential that the performance is measure and return on investment is tracked.
- **Lack of skilled professionals:** The rapid evolution of composable applications has gained the interest in the businesses and hence, hiring of subject matter experts in this field. As this concept is gaining momentum, hiring, and training can be challenging for the organizations.

5 DISCUSSION AND RECOMMENDATIONS

As the financial services industry is continuously evolving, this study provides an overview and insights of Composable Banking which can be one solution wherein traditional banks gets benefit with low cost & fast innovation, customer's get customized banking solutions and Fintech's can gain trust & credibility using technology by collaborating with banks. The findings from Frederik et al., 2019, also showed that banks are focusing on rapid innovation by pursuing outsourcing while Fintech's sought to benefit from bank's resources and reputation. Firms that foster a supportive innovation culture and employ staff with an innovative mindset are more likely to explore profitable and competitive ideas, transforming them into successful business strategies for long-term growth and profitability (YuSheng & Ibrahim, 2020). Additionally, digital transformation enhances customer experiences by meeting their increasing expectations for personalization, seamlessness, and responsiveness. Technology-driven, data-focused banks can offer these tailored experiences through intuitive interfaces and timely responses, fostering customer loyalty and satisfaction (Ellitan, 2020). Moreover, innovation encourages a culture of creativity and experimentation within organizations, enabling firms that embrace technological advancements to develop novel products, services, and business models. By staying agile and adaptable to market changes, these firms can gain a competitive advantage and solidify their position in any industry (Minchin, 2021).

The relationship between customer experience management and customer loyalty was statistically analyzed by Makudza, 2021, which concluded that customers experience management explains customers loyalty by 67.9% which is significant enough to be useful to lock-in customers, to reduce attrition and churning as well as to promote loyalty behavior.

Globalization and the digitalization of business processes have intensified the pressure on companies to innovate. Now more than ever, maintaining market position and competitive advantage is closely tied to adopting innovative business models. This has driven companies to engage with actors in the innovation ecosystem, which serve as invaluable sources of information on market trends and customer preferences, helping businesses create customized products and services. Baffour et al. (2024) highlighted that AI technology innovation in banking and finance significantly impacts a bank's return on assets, suggesting that increased innovation in the sector improves financial performance. This impact extends beyond just

AI; it is more broadly related to technology innovations that can be leveraged in various ways, including through models like Composable Banking.

This study is supported by Stojcic et al. (2024), who shed new light on the innovation process by highlighting the influential role of customization and co-creation at different stages of the process. Most importantly, their research demonstrated that the impact of user engagement is significantly stronger when it involves mutual knowledge sharing, compared to scenarios where the information flow is unidirectional. This emphasizes the value of collaborative, two-way interactions in driving innovation and achieving better outcomes. This can be related to the Composable Banking Solutions wherein banks are collaborating with Fintech's or third-party service providers to build customized banking solutions by focusing on customization and co-creation based on customer's preferences. Composable Solutions approach is the nucleus to guarantee that era innovation is aligned with business price, averting the high-priced problem of overspending/unnecessary spending, and bucketing investments in keeping with categories that assist run the business, grow the business, and rework the business. Composable solutions that is driven by business cost offers the area of balancing threat against predicted returns, comparing the overall performance and making use of the present systems, analyzing, and assessing opportunity and trade-offs, and eliminating waste ensuing in full-size efficiencies and cost financial savings.

As the technology continues to evolve in financial industry, composable banking is likely to play a significant role in this journey.

- **Banking-as-a-service platforms:** With increased competition and heavy technology upgrades, banks and FinTech's are likely to offer wider range of customized products and services and composable banking can make it all possible just with right strategical technology investments and implementation.
- **Use of Artificial Intelligence and Machine Learning:** AI and ML can easily help banks to innovate customized products leveraging data and analytics. It will be much faster to develop innovative financial solutions that can evolve at lower cost with high efficiency.
- **API adoption:** API integration and interoperability between banks and third-party vendors or FinTech's will foster seamless innovation and revenue generation.
- **Higher competition:** All this will lead to much higher competition in providing fast, easy, safe and cost-effective banking to the customers.
- **Banks need to have it all:** To remain competitive & to maintain customer primacy, banks cannot neglect anything. Customers would expect to have products and services to meet their needs and choices and hence, it will evolve around which bank can make it happen efficiently.

5.1 Future Trends and Opportunities

For the purpose of showing the trends and opportunities, we looked at two survey's. First Survey which was conducted by The Motley Foot Ascent's 2024 Digital Banking Trends and Consumer Priorities to learn what consumers value in bank on 2000 consumers from banks, credit unions and online-only banks, there were interesting findings which showed that 76% respondents are likely to switch their banks to meet their needs and priorities as compared to 52% in 2020 with millennials leading with high percentage of population to switch the banks if needs are not fulfilled, (Figure 3). This is indeed a noticeable number and hence, financial industry must prepare in advance to know the customer's priorities, preferences, and choices to remain competitive and profitable in the industry. Below is the snapshot of the percentage across generations:

Figure 3. Percent likely to switch banks if another one better meets their priorities

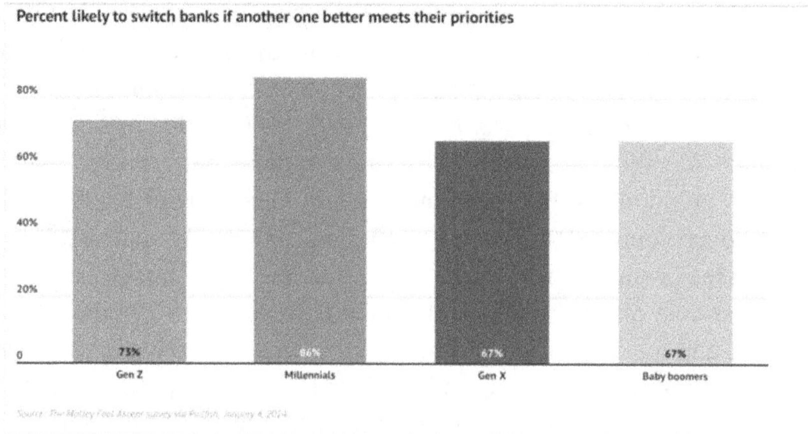

Similarly, the second survey (Figure 4) by MarketsandMarkets forecasts the composable applications market size to grow from an estimated USD 5.2 billion in 2023 to USD 11.8 billion by 2028, at a CAGR of 17.5%. This significant growth spans various sectors, including Platform and Services, and industries such as BFSI, Retail & eCommerce, Government, Healthcare & Life Sciences, Manufacturing, IT & ITeS, and Energy & Utilities, across regions like North America, Europe, APAC, and RoW. This promising market forecast gives us confidence that composable banking solutions could play a key role in the future of banking. According to the survey, the main factors driving market growth include the increasing demand for rapid customization and scalability. However, a lack of skilled professionals or trainers among developers is expected to pose a challenge to this growth.

Figure 4. Global forecast survey

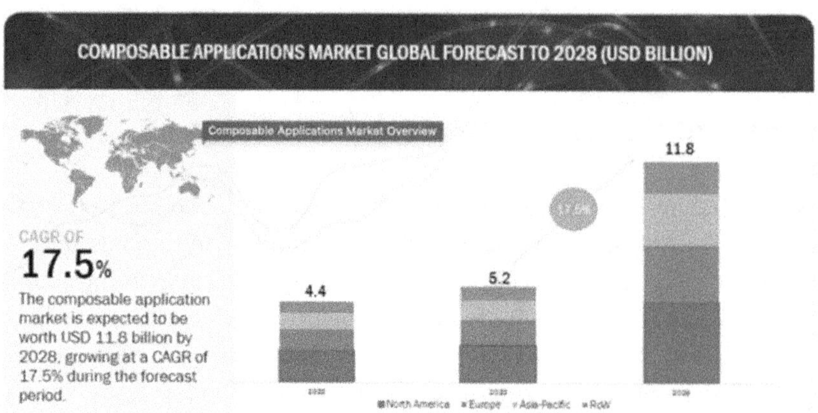

5.2 Future Research Avenues

Every study has its limitations, and ours is no exception. Future research should take a long-term approach, examining composable banking solutions more holistically by developing policies, change management strategies, and implementation frameworks. Our study did not allow us to analyze different categories of banks based on their size, geographic locations, existing banking models, and customer bases. Additionally, in less advanced innovation systems, the limited knowledge of users about innovation trends and requirements is recognized as a limitation in the literature (Mitrega et al., 2020; Zamborsky et al., 2023). Furthermore, we believe that our research has only partially explored the working model and opportunities of APIs. Separate research is needed to examine the complexities and value derived from APIs, particularly with regard to public and private endpoints, as well as the deployment of APIs. As technologies evolve and companies adopt innovative solutions for strategic purposes, further research is essential to explore the competitive dynamics of emerging digital technologies within the realm of strategic management.

5.3 Conclusion

Composable banking is presented as a necessary evolution for traditional banks struggling with outdated IT infrastructure. This research highlights the **inefficiencies of maintaining legacy systems**, where developers dedicate a minority of their time to innovation. **Adopting a composable approach**, characterised by a modern digital core, cloud-native infrastructure, a platform mindset, modular architecture, and real-time data, is advocated. This shift is portrayed as a pathway to **increased speed, agility, and improved customer focus**, overcoming the limitations of point solutions.

5.4 Limitations of the Study

Acknowledging potential limitations, such as this paper will not cover how to transition to the composable banking to improve the organization performance which can be driven by sustainable value. This is another area which needs a separate research and focus. This Study focuses only on the composable banking overview without any sponsorship from service providers or any of the banks. Details shared in the paper are basis the industry information available on their website.

5.5 Practical Implications of the Study

We believe that this research has only partly revealed the list of service providers, implications, and opportunities of API-driven composable banking solutions. As technology evolves and banks embrace innovation solutions for strategic reasons, more research is needed to explore the competitive dynamics of emerging technology driven banking solutions. From a practical perspective, our findings highlight several ways in which banks can make use of considerations, challenges, and insights gained through customization to develop, digitalize, and commercialize banking products and services to gain the competitive edge and improve overall organizational performance. Composable banking has potential to lead to tailored offerings that meet the needs for every user in a peculiar way. Our study provides details of various service providers who can collaborate with banks to co-create composable banking solutions.

5.6 Policy & Managerial Implications of the Study

From a policy standpoint, potential areas for intervention could involve creating policies and best practices for composable banking solutions. This would cover aspects such as obtaining customer consent, ensuring data privacy and security, aligning with regulatory standards, and managing third-party vendors. Another key area requiring attention is the creation of platforms that enable interaction and collaboration between banks, third-party service providers, and customers. These platforms could also provide valuable insights for both academic research and practical solutions to meet current banking needs.

From a management viewpoint, the paper emphasizes the central role of customer needs in the innovation process. Banks must focus on ensuring high service reliability by offering enhanced customer care, swift solutions, comprehensive financial information, trustworthy services, minimized risks, rapid resolution of complaints, and low-cost, convenient options for customers (Kim et al., 2024). To stay competitive, banks should nurture long-term customer relationships, leveraging customer insights to customize products over time. This can be achieved by utilizing APIs through third-party service providers at low cost and high speed. Establishing dedicated teams, platforms, and processes to gather and incorporate customer feedback at various stages is crucial. Product customization and co-creation require a flexible approach to development, which necessitates change management within the organization to prepare for, adapt to, and iterate based on evolving customer needs and expectations. Additionally, given the challenges banks face—such as rising customer expectations, increasing acquisition costs, heightened competition, and rapidly advancing technology—they must engage in open innovation ecosystems. Strategic partnerships with FinTechs and other tech companies can help optimize operational costs, boost revenue, and develop new channels offering flexible, innovative, and convenient products and services, enhancing the customer banking experience.

Furthermore, engaging with a wide range of customers, including private companies, individuals, and public institutions, will help develop a comprehensive understanding of market needs and preferences. This could involve organizing workshops and focus groups, which will require considerable time, effort, and financial investment.

REFERENCES

Alghadi, M. Y. (2024). The influence of some fintech service on the performance of Islamic bank in Jordan. *International Journal of Data and Network Science*, *8*(1), 393–400. DOI: 10.5267/j.ijdns.2023.9.015

Baffour Gyau, E., Appiah, M., Gyamfi, B. A., Achie, T., & Naeem, M. A. (2024). Transforming banking: Examining the role of AI technology innovation in boosting banks financial performance. *International Review of Financial Analysis*, *96*, 103700. Advance online publication. DOI: 10.1016/j.irfa.2024.103700

Briones de Araluze, G., & Cassinello Plaza, N. (2023). The relevance of initial trust and social influence in the intention to use open banking-based services: An empirical study. *SAGE Open*, *13*(3), 21582440231187607. Advance online publication. DOI: 10.1177/21582440231187607

Cho, H. J., & Pucik, V. (2005). Relationship between innovativeness, quality, growth, profitability, and market value. *Strategic Management Journal*, *26*(6), 555–575. DOI: 10.1002/smj.461

Dimitrova, I., Öhman, P., & Yazdanfar, D. (2022). Barriers to bank customers' intention to fully adopt digital payment methods. *International Journal of Quality and Service Sciences*, *14*(5), 16–36. DOI: 10.1108/IJQSS-03-2021-0045

Ellitan, L. (2020). The information technology industrial revolution and its role in building business strategy of global retail. *Jurnal Manajemen Maranatha*, *19*(2), 151–158. DOI: 10.28932/jmm.v19i2.2408

Frederik Klus, M., Stefan Lohwasser, T., Holotiuk, F., Moormann, J., Frederik, M., & Stefan, T. (2019). Strategic alliances between banks and fintechs for digital innovation: Motives to collaborate and types of interaction. *The Journal of Entrepreneurial Finance*, *21*(1).

Grigorescu, A., Oprisan, O., Lincaru, C., & Pirciog, C. S. (2023). E-banking convergence and the adopter's behavior changing across EU countries. *SAGE Open*, *13*(4), 21582440231220455. Advance online publication. DOI: 10.1177/21582440231220455

Gunday, G., Ulusoy, G., Kilic, K., & Alpkan, L. (2011). Effects of innovation types on firm performance. *International Journal of Production Economics*, *133*(2), 662–676. DOI: 10.1016/j.ijpe.2011.05.014

Heshmatisafa, S., & Seppänen, M. (2023). Exploring API-driven business models: Lessons learned from Amadeus's digital transformation. *Digital Business*, *3*(1), 100055. Advance online publication. DOI: 10.1016/j.digbus.2023.100055

Hornuf, L., Safari, K., & Voshaar, J. (2025). Mobile fintech adoption in Sub-Saharan Africa: A systematic literature review and meta-analysis. *Research in International Business and Finance*, *73*, 102529. Advance online publication. DOI: 10.1016/j.ribaf.2024.102529

Kaur, J., Syan, A. S., Kaur, S., & Sharma, R. R. (2022). *Understanding the factors influencing actual usage of payments banks: An empirical investigation using the extended information systems success model.* FIIB Business Review., DOI: 10.1177/23197145221099095

Jayawarsa, A. K., Saputra, K. A. K., Jayanti, L. G. P. S. E., Kawisana, P. G. W. P., & Aryawan, G. (2021). WITHDRAWN: A comprehensive overview on intelligent mechanical systems and its applications of mobile banking technology.

Kim, L., Jindabot, T., & Yeo, S. F. (2024). Understanding customer loyalty in banking industry: A systematic review and meta-analysis. *Heliyon*, *10*(17), e36619. Advance online publication. DOI: 10.1016/j.heliyon.2024.e36619 PMID: 39281651

Liu, D., Fang, H., Tang, Y., Mohd Isa, S., & Tang, J. (2023). Intelligent technology solutions and banking efficiency: The impacts of institutional innovation and consumer participation. *SAGE Open*, *13*(2), 21582440231184205. Advance online publication. DOI: 10.1177/21582440231184205

Lu, Z., Wan, X., Yang, J., Wu, J., Zhang, C., Hung, P. C. K., & Huang, S.-C. (2019). BIS: A novel blockchain-based bank-tax interaction system in smart city. *2019 IEEE Intl Conf on Dependable, Autonomic and Secure Computing, Intl Conf on Pervasive Intelligence and Computing, Intl Conf on Cloud and Big Data Computing, Intl Conf on Cyber Science and Technology Congress (DASC/PiCom/CBDCom/CyberSciTech)*, 1008–1014. https://doi.org/DOI: 10.1109/DASC/PiCom/CBDCom/CyberSciTech.2019.00183

Makudza, F. (2021). Augmenting customer loyalty through customer experience management in the banking industry. *Journal of Asian Business and Economic Studies*, *28*(3), 191–203. DOI: 10.1108/JABES-01-2020-0007

Mancuso, I., Petruzzelli, A. M., Panniello, U., & Vaia, G. (2025). Business model innovation in the banking sector: How digital technologies transform innovation drivers in value mechanisms innovations. *Journal of Engineering and Technology Management - JET-M, 75*. https://doi.org/DOI: 10.1016/j.jengtecman.2024.101858

Manzoor, A. (2023). Antecedents to following brands on Facebook and Instagram with moderating role of user experience. *FIIB Business Review*, *0*(0). Advance online publication. DOI: 10.1177/23197145221151010

Minchin, T. J. (2021). 'The factory of the future' Historical continuity and labor rights at Tesla. *Labor History*, *62*(4), 434–453. DOI: 10.1080/0023656X.2021.1940115

Mitrega, M., Spacil, V., & Pfajfar, G. (2021). Co-creating value in post-communists contexts: Capability perspective. *Journal of Services Marketing*, *35*(2), 169–181. DOI: 10.1108/JSM-03-2019-0114

Naeem, H. M., & di Maria, E. (2020). Customer participation in new product development: An Industry 4.0 perspective. *European Journal of Innovation Management*, *25*(6), 637–655. DOI: 10.1108/EJIM-01-2021-0036

Nosrati, L., Bidgoli, A. M., & Javadi, H. H. S. (2024). Identifying people's faces in smart banking systems using artificial neural networks. *International Journal of Computational Intelligence Systems*, *17*(1), 9. Advance online publication. DOI: 10.1007/s44196-023-00383-7

Omol, E. J. (2024). Organizational digital transformation: From evolution to future trends. In *Digital Transformation and Society* (Vol. 3, Issue 3, pp. 240–256). Emerald Publishing. https://doi.org/DOI: 10.1108/DTS-08-2023-0061

Patnaik, R., Patra, S. K., Mahapatra, D. M., & Baral, S. K. (2022). *Adoption and challenges underlying OTT platform in India during pandemic: A critical study of socio-economic and technological issues*. FIIB Business Review., DOI: 10.1177/23197145221101676

Peruchini, M., da Silva, G. M., & Teixeira, J. M. (2024). Between artificial intelligence and customer experience: A literature review on the intersection. *Discover Artificial Intelligence*, *4*(1), 4. Advance online publication. DOI: 10.1007/s44163-024-00105-8

Pujadas, R., Valderrama, E., & Venters, W. (2024). The value and structuring role of web APIs in digital innovation ecosystems: The case of the online travel ecosystem. *Research Policy*, *53*(2), 104931. Advance online publication. DOI: 10.1016/j.respol.2023.104931

Ravi, H. (2021). Innovation in banking: Fusion of artificial intelligence and blockchain. *Asia Pacific Journal of Innovation and Entrepreneurship*, *15*(1), 51–61.

Rangaswamy, E., Nawaz, N., Mohamed, S. B. S., & Joy, G. V. (2024). A study on entrepreneurial innovation among entities in Singapore. *Journal of Innovation and Entrepreneurship*, *13*(1), 10. Advance online publication. DOI: 10.1186/s13731-024-00362-y

Rawas, S. (2024). AI: The future of humanity. In *Discover Artificial Intelligence* (Vol. 4, Issue 1). Springer Nature. https://doi.org/DOI: 10.1007/s44163-024-00118-3

Sahi, G. K., Modi, P., & Mantok, S. (2023). New product innovations in times of crisis: How did women entrepreneurs survive the COVID-19 crisis? *Industrial Marketing Management*, *111*, 19–29. DOI: 10.1016/j.indmarman.2023.03.004

Sanga, B., & Aziakpono, M. (2024). FinTech developments and their heterogeneous effect on digital finance for SMEs and entrepreneurship: Evidence from 47 African countries. *Journal of Entrepreneurship in Emerging Economies*. https://doi.org/DOI: 10.1108/JEEE-09-2023-0379

Santos, S. C., Liguori, E. W., & Garvey, E. (2023). How digitalization reinvented entrepreneurial resilience during COVID-19. *Technological Forecasting and Social Change*, *189*, 122398. Advance online publication. DOI: 10.1016/j.techfore.2023.122398 PMID: 36778643

Schreieck, M., Huang, Y., Kupfer, A., & Krcmar, H. (2024). The effect of digital platform strategies on firm value in the banking industry. *Journal of Management Information Systems*, *41*(2), 394–421. DOI: 10.1080/07421222.2024.2340825 PMID: 38974483

Shahid, S., Islam, J. U., Malik, S., & Hasan, U. (2022). Examining consumer experience in using m-banking apps: A study of its antecedents and outcomes. *Journal of Retailing and Consumer Services*, *65*, 102870. Advance online publication. DOI: 10.1016/j.jretconser.2021.102870

Sreenivasan, A., & Suresh, M. (2024). A comparative analysis of lean start-up and design thinking and its integration. *Asia Pacific Journal of Innovation and Entrepreneurship*, *18*(2), 172–194. DOI: 10.1108/APJIE-09-2023-0181

Stojčić, N., Dabić, M., & Kraus, S. (2024). Customisation and co-creation revisited: Do user types and engagement strategies matter for product innovation success? *Technovation*, *134*, 103045. Advance online publication. DOI: 10.1016/j.technovation.2024.103045

Thottoli, M. M., Islam, M. A., Yusof, M. F., Hassan, M. S., & Hassan, M. A. (2023). Embracing digital transformation in financial services: From past to future. *SAGE Open*, *13*(4), 21582440231214590. Advance online publication. DOI: 10.1177/21582440231214590

Wu, D., Zhang, H., Feng, Y., & Dong, Z. (2024). MITU: Locating relevant tutorial fragments of APIs with multi-source API knowledge. *Journal of Systems and Software*, *112296*. Advance online publication. DOI: 10.1016/j.jss.2024.112296

Yang, Q., & Lee, Y. C. (2024). Enhancing financial advisory services with GenAI: Consumer perceptions and attitudes through service-dominant logic and artificial intelligence device use acceptance perspectives. *Journal of Risk and Financial Management*, *17*(10), 470. Advance online publication. DOI: 10.3390/jrfm17100470

Yeh, C. H., Lin, H. H., Wang, Y. M., Wang, Y. S., & Lo, C. W. (2021). Investigating the relationships between entrepreneurial education and self-efficacy and performance in the context of internet entrepreneurship. *International Journal of Management Education*, *19*(3), 100565. Advance online publication. DOI: 10.1016/j.ijme.2021.100565

Zámborský, P., Ingršt, I., & Bhandari, K. R. (2023). Knowledge creation capability under different innovation-investment motives abroad: The knowledge-based view of international innovation management. *Technovation*, *127*, 102829. Advance online publication. DOI: 10.1016/j.technovation.2023.102829

Chapter 6

Consumer Perceptions Towards Artificial Intelligence and Robotic Process Automation in the Indian Banking Sector With Reference to NCR

Pawan Kumar
https://orcid.org/0000-0003-2059-9818
SRM University, India

Jyoti Bhoj
https://orcid.org/0000-0002-9687-4217
Amity University, Noida, India

Sushma Sharma
SRM University, India

ABSTRACT

This chapter aims to comprehend consumer perception towards Artificial Intelligence and Robotic Process Automation in the Indian Banking sector. This study focuses on consumers' awareness level and usability of Artificial Intelligence and RPA toward various banking services. The study will explore the scope of artificial intelligence (AI) and RPA implementation in the Indian banking sector for consumer satisfaction. Exploratory-cum-descriptive research design techniques were used to analyze the data with one sixty respondents collected from NCR through cluster sampling. The semi-structured questionnaire was framed based on the Likert scale. Descriptive, Exploratory Factor Analysis, t-test, ANOVA, correlation, and regression statistical techniques have been used to analyze the data. This study gives insights into the Indian banking industry to understand the behaviour of consumers regarding the accessibility and usage of Artificial Intelligence and RPA.

DOI: 10.4018/979-8-3373-0209-6.ch006

1. INTRODUCTION

There is a growing trend of consumers' shifting perceptions towards AI and RPA technologies in the banking sector. These technologies are being recognized for their ability to streamline and expedite customer requests, minimize errors, and enhance the overall efficiency of banking operations. By leveraging AI and RPA, banks can provide personalized recommendations, tailored products, and targeted marketing strategies, thereby enriching the customer experience and effectively addressing individual needs. The use of mobile services (m-services) triggers an effective response, which in turn predicts post-adoption behaviors related to coping strategies. In this study, researchers examined consumer satisfaction with current m-services and their interest in using such services as an affective outcome. Additionally, they investigated the subsequent coping responses associated with m-services use (Bagozzi, 1992).

Artificial Intelligence (AI) stands at the forefront of the global technological revolution (Alzaidi, 2018). Its potential to transform banking operations is met with enthusiasm, as it can make human-like decisions while avoiding errors. Although AI adoption varies across sectors, the banking industry has shown moderate acceptance and adoption of this technology. Jewandah (2018) also acknowledges the changing business landscape due to technology. While the Indian banking sector gradually embraces AI, it remains a manpower-intensive field. However, recognizing the need to reduce costs and eliminate redundant tasks, Indian banks explore AI's power to enhance processes and customer service. The paper delves into AI applications in the banking sector, particularly within India's top banks (Maček et al. 2020).

Mobile banking enables people to conveniently check the status of their fixed deposits (Harrison, 2000). Through mobile banking, individuals can also access credit card statements, loan statements, and other account-related information. For instance, insurance policy management, checking the status of cheques, and stopping cheque payments can all be done via mobile banking. Furthermore, Mohr (2001) highlighted that checking account balances is a straightforward process using mobile banking. Users can check their account balance anytime and anywhere by entering the personal identification number (PIN) provided by the bank during account setup. In a study by Baruah (2020), the adoption of Artificial Intelligence (AI) and Machine Learning (ML) in data analytics and customer service has created opportunities for personalized and faster customer experiences, improved insights, and streamlined back-end workflows. Notably, over 36 percent of large financial institutions are already investing in these technologies, with nearly 70 percent planning to do so in the near future. Among leading Indian commercial banks—such as State Bank of India (SBI), HDFC, ICICI, and Axis—various successful AI applications have been introduced (Pramod, 2021).

Consumer awareness and understanding of AI and RPA in the banking sector are pivotal to their adoption and acceptance. Research suggests that while awareness is growing, a comprehensive understanding of these technologies remains limited among consumers (Kumar & Gupta, 2024). This lack of understanding can lead to concerns regarding data privacy, security, and job displacement. Accessibility and usability of AI and RPA-powered banking services are crucial for enhancing consumer experience. Banks in India have made significant strides in deploying AI-powered chatbots and virtual assistants to provide round-the-clock customer support. However, challenges such as language barriers and technical glitches can hinder their effectiveness (Bhuvana et al., 2016).

The integration of AI and RPA has led to significant improvements in various banking processes, including loan processing, fraud detection, and customer service. These technologies have streamlined operations, reduced costs, and enhanced efficiency. However, concerns about potential job losses and dehumanization of banking services persist (Alzaidi, 2018). Consumer satisfaction with AI and RPA-powered banking services is a complex issue. While these technologies offer convenience and speed, they may also lead to impersonal interactions and a lack of human touch. Striking a balance between technological innovation and human empathy is crucial for maintaining customer satisfaction (Kumar & Gupta, 2024).

Further, the study is categorised as follows: related work is discussed in the review of literature section. The Sampling, methodology, and results are discussed in the research methodology, result analysis and interpretation Sections, respectively. Finally, the conclusion policy recommendations and future research direction are presented respectively.

2. REVIEW OF LITERATURE

AI, often referred to as machine intelligence, simulates human intelligence in machines. It represents the intellect exhibited by machines, distinct from the natural knowledge demonstrated by humans. In the finance sector, AI extends beyond chatbots and has significantly impacted various industries, including banking. This research sheds light on AI's role in modern banking, its revolutionary changes, and its impact on human manpower. It serves as a preview of the current AI applications in the banking domain (Kaur et al., 2020). In the era of rapid technological change, banks are increasingly turning to Artificial Intelligence (AI) for growth and enhanced customer satisfaction. While AI adoption varies across sectors, the banking industry has shown a moderate interest in integrating this technology (Husain, 2022). This research paper provides an overview of AI applications in Indian banking, emphasizing its benefits, current implementations, and future prospects. As the banking landscape evolves, AI is becoming the "new normal." By leveraging AI, banks can enhance efficiency, improve customer experiences, and stay competitive. Both employees and customers stand to benefit from its implementation, leading to increased profits and better engagement (Sachdeva and Sivakumar, 2022).

In the current technological landscape, artificial intelligence (AI) offers a multitude of features that aim to augment human intelligence with machine-based capabilities. The banking sector, too, is undergoing a transformation, moving away from traditional systems (Jaiwani and Gopalkrishnan, 2022). AI contributes to error-free business operations and provides several advantages, including enhanced risk management, streamlined wealth management, efficient fraud detection, improved lending processes, and even more effective insurance underwriting and claims handling. As AI continues to evolve, it has the potential to revolutionize the banking industry, transitioning it from paper-based practices to more agile and digitally empowered solutions (Hepsiba and Yamuna, 2022). The convergence of artificial intelligence (AI) and blockchain technology holds immense promise for the financial sector. AI algorithms enhance risk management, fraud detection, and decision-making, while blockchain fosters transparency, security, and efficiency through its decentralized ledger system. However, addressing scalability, privacy, security, and regulatory challenges is essential for successful implementation (Addula et al., 2024).

Garg & Jain (2023) examined the impact of facilitators and inhibitors on bankers' behaviors and perceptions regarding AI applications, using an extended UTAUT model that included risk, perceived complexity, and technological anxiety. Data was collected from 108 bankers in Delhi/NCR through a structured questionnaire assessing seven factors: performance expectancy, effort expectancy, social influence, risk, technological anxiety, perceived complexity, and behavioural intention. Statistical analysis, including reliability tests, KMO and Bartlett's test, exploratory factor analysis, regression, and ANOVA, was conducted. Results indicated that social influence and risk significantly affected bankers' intention to adopt AI, with demographic factors such as age, education, gender, and bank type also influencing perceptions. Saraswat et al. (2024) explored that Robotic Process Automation (RPA) significantly contributed to organizational success by improving process accuracy, reducing errors, and enhancing overall performance. Data collected from 1,020 respondents in the Indian corporate sector through a Google Docs questionnaire highlighted the positive impact of RPA on accounting, cost management, and customer service. The findings confirmed that the adoption of RPA not only streamlined business processes but also enhanced employee experience and reporting accuracy. Overall, RPA proved to be a valuable tool for firms seeking to improve operational efficiency and achieve greater organizational success.

Sharma & Choubey (2024) described that information technology (IT) has significantly transformed the Indian banking sector, improving service quality, data management, and security, especially post-pandemic. While IT has contributed to infrastructural development and enhanced consumer awareness, challenges such as consumer trust, employee training, and connectivity issues remain. Primary data collected from forty bankers across ten public and private banks revealed that AI, robotics, blockchain, and IT-driven core banking solutions are key future trends in the sector. Despite the progress, the research emphasized the need for continued efforts to address technical and awareness-related issues to ensure a secure and efficient banking ecosystem. Another study by Sharma & Choubey (2021) concluded that Information Technology (IT) has had a significant impact on the Indian banking sector, driving improvements in data management, security, safety, and service quality. Banks, by investing heavily in IT, aimed to enhance their performance, but the effectiveness of these investments varied based on the implementation and use of technology. The findings highlighted the critical role of IT in enabling economic growth and improving banking services, though challenges remain in its full implementation.

Arjun et al. (2021) concluded that the banking industry's reliance on intelligent systems for operational and marketing performance is critical, yet a knowledge gap exists in the adoption of these technologies by management. A review of prior work from 1970 to 2020 on intelligent decision support models revealed key outcomes for technology, employees, customers, and organizations in service ecosystems. The research also highlighted managerial perceptions of technology's impact on work and discussed the potential of advancements like big data, IoT, and VR to further enhance the sector. The chatbot-enabled mobile banking (m-banking) significantly impacts elderly users' attitudes towards banking, customer loyalty, and usage frequency, particularly in emerging markets like India. By testing a conceptual model using structural equation modeling and multi-group analysis, the research found that perceived intelligence, ease of use, and anthropomorphism of chatbots positively influenced elderly users' attitudes towards m-banking. The post-adoption phase showed that chatbot-enabled m-banking led to higher bank loyalty compared to chatbot-disabled m-banking. These findings provide valuable theoretical and practical insights for banks and developers targeting elderly consumers, offering guidance on product design, communication, and customer lifecycle management (Pathria et al., 2022).

Kumar & Gupta (2023) highlighted that the increasing adoption of AI technology in the Indian banking sector has both positive and negative implications. While AI has enhanced consumer experiences by providing seamless, 24/7 access to banking services such as digital money transfers and e-banking, it has also posed challenges for the financial sector. Data collected from 187 customers in Delhi, across public and private sector banks, revealed that AI has improved customer relationships by offering more personalized services. However, the study also highlighted the associated costs and challenges, indicating a need for balanced integration of AI to optimize benefits while managing risks. The background of the study suggests that there is a growing trend of consumers' shifting perceptions towards AI and RPA technologies in the banking sector. These technologies are being recognized for their ability to streamline and expedite customer requests, minimize errors, and enhance the overall efficiency of banking operations. By leveraging AI and RPA, banks can provide personalized recommendations, tailored products, and targeted marketing strategies, thereby enriching the customer experience and effectively addressing individual needs.

The study provides valuable insights into consumer perceptions of AI and RPA in the Indian banking sector, several research gaps remain that warrant further investigation. There is a need for deeper exploration into the specific barriers to AI and RPA adoption from the consumer's perspective. While this study highlights general consumer awareness and usability, more granular research is required to identify factors such as age, education level, and socio-economic status that may influence perceptions and acceptance of these technologies. Furthermore, the impact of AI and RPA on different demographic groups, such as rural versus urban populations, remains underexplored. Another key gap is the long-term impact of AI and RPA on customer satisfaction and loyalty in banking services. Most studies, including this one, focus on immediate or short-term perceptions, but there is limited research on how sustained exposure to these technologies influences customer behavior, trust, and overall satisfaction over time. Additionally, while the current study assesses the awareness and usability of AI and RPA, more research is needed on the ethical implications of their use in banking, particularly regarding data privacy, algorithmic transparency, and fairness. Lastly, research into the specific operational challenges banks face during the implementation of AI and RPA, particularly in the Indian context, is sparse and warrants further exploration to guide effective policy formulation.

3. RESEARCH METHODOLOGY

The present chapter includes the research design, research objectives, hypotheses tested, sample design, data collection instrument, and statistical techniques of the study.

3.1 Research Design

The Exploratory-cum-descriptive research design techniques were used to analyze the data. The two hundred respondents' data has been collected from NCR through cluster sampling technique with 160 found to be fit for further analysis. The semi-structured questionnaire was framed based on the Semantic Likert scale technique. Descriptive, Exploratory Factor Analysis, t-test, ANOVA, correlation, and regression statistical techniques have been used to analyze the data with SPSS Software.

3.2 Objectives

1. To comprehend consumers' perception towards Artificial Intelligence and Robotic Process Automation in the Indian Banking sector.
2. To know the consumers' awareness level, accessibility, and usability of Artificial Intelligence and RPA toward various banking services.
3. To find the usage of Artificial Intelligence and RPA in the Indian banking sector.
4. To explore the impact on consumers' satisfaction from the implementation of Artificial Intelligence and RPA in the Indian banking sector.

3.3 Hypotheses

Table 1 presents the hypotheses, which will test whether consumer perceptions, opinions, and satisfaction towards AI and RPA in Indian banks vary across different demographic factors.

Table 1. Hypotheses on perceptions, opinions, and satisfaction towards AI and RPA

$H0_1$	**There is no significant difference in consumers' perception towards AI and RPA in Indian Banks across demographic factors-** **• Gender ($H0_{1a}$),** **• Education ($H0_{1b}$),** **• Year of transactions ($H0_{1c}$),** **• Region ($H0_{1d}$), and** **• Annual Income ($H0_{1e}$).**
$H0_2$	There is no significant difference in consumers' opinion towards the usage of AI and RPA applications in Indian Banks across demographic factors- • Gender (**$H0_{2a}$**), • Education (**$H0_{2b}$**), • Year of transactions (**$H0_{2c}$**), • Region (**$H0_{2d}$**), and • Annual Income (**$H0_{2e}$**).
$H0_3$:	There is no significant difference in consumers' satisfaction from AI and RPA in Indian Banks across demographic factors- • Gender (**$H0_{3a}$**), • Education (**$H0_{3b}$**), • Year of transactions (**$H0_{3c}$**), • Region (**$H0_{3d}$**), and • Annual Income (**$H0_{3e}$**).

Source: Compiled by researcher

4. RESULT AND INTERPRETATION

The research tool utilized in this research is a structured survey designed to gather opinions and preferences from individuals regarding Robotic Process Automation (RPA) and Artificial Intelligence (AI) in Indian Banks, specifically from a customer perspective. The survey comprises four sections. The first section deals with Demographic Profile. This section collects basic demographic information about the respondents, such as age, gender, occupation, etc. This information helps in analyzing responses based on different demographic segments. Section B, Awareness About AI and RPA in Banks which aims to gauge the respondents' awareness levels regarding AI and RPA technologies as applied in the banking sector. Questions include inquiries about familiarity with terms, understanding of applications, and awareness of existing implementations. Applications of AI and RPA in Banks is Section C concerned with, this section seeks to understand respondents' opinions and preferences regarding the various applications of AI and RPA within banking operations. Questions may explore perceptions of efficiency, convenience, and potential benefits or concerns related to these technologies.

The last section deals with Effect on Customer Satisfaction This section focuses on gathering respondents' opinions and preferences regarding the impact of AI and RPA implementation on customer satisfaction in banking services. Questions may explore perceived improvements or challenges in customer experience resulting from the adoption of these technologies. The survey is structured to facilitate systematic data collection and analysis, providing insights into respondents' perceptions and preferences regarding AI and RPA in Indian banking from a customer perspective.

4.1 Demographic Profile of the Consumers

The demographic characteristics of the respondent revealed in Table 2 with seventy percentage male and thirty percent female participants. Based on representation based on education eighteen percent of respondents are 12th pass, fifty-seven percent are undergraduate, sixteen percent are post graduate and seven percent have above post graduate. Only ten percent of the respondents are transacting for more than 15 years, 15 percent for between 10 to 15 years with the majority of them transacting for 1 to 5 years. Location wise forty four percent are from Delhi, forty percent from Sonepat, 9.5 percent from Gurugram, Noida 5.6 percent, and Gaziabad 0.6 percentage. Annual Income revealed that most of our respondents are in the category of earning bracket of 1.25 lakh to 5 lakh INR. The second largest category is of respondents earning upto 1.25 lakh INR, only 11.3 percent are earning above 30 lakh INR and 8.8 percent between 5 lakh to 30 lakh INR.

Table 2. Demographic profile of the consumers (N=160)

Sr. No.	Demographics	Sub Demographics	Frequency	Percentage
1.	**Gender**	Male	48	70
		Female	112	30
2.	**Education Level**	12th	29	18.1
		Under-Graduate	92	57.5
		Post Graduate	27	16.9
		Above Post Graduate	12	7.5
3.	**Years of Transaction**	1-5 Years	106	66.3
		5-10 Years	13	8.1
		10 -15Years	24	15.0
		More than 15 Years	17	10.6
4.	**Region**	Delhi	71	44.4
		Ghaziabad	1	.6
		Gurugram	15	9.4
		Noida	9	5.6
		Sonepat	64	40.0
5.	**Annual Income**	1.25 Lakhs	47	29.4
		1.25 – 5 Lakhs	81	50.6
		5 – 30 Lakhs	14	8.8
		More than 30 Lakhs	18	11.3

Source: Compiled by researcher

4.2 Exploratory Factor Analysis

Table 3 shows Kaiser Meyer Olkin measure of sampling adequacy tests the suitability of data for factor analysis. The Kaiser-Meyer-Olkin (KMO) Measure of Sampling Adequacy is a statistical tool indicating the extent of variance in your variables attributable to underlying factors. High KMO values (close to 1.0) generally suggest the potential usefulness of factor analysis with your dataset. Conversely, if the value falls below 0.50, the outcomes of factor analysis are likely to be less informative. The calculation employed IBM SPSS 19.0 statistical analysis software, specifically utilizing the factor analysis function and selecting the correlation matrix option for descriptors as KMO and Bartlett's Test of sphericity. Varimax rotation method was chosen, with other settings remaining as the default options. Previous research has proposed that a KMO exceeding 0.5 is suitable for factor analysis, while values surpassing 0.8 are highly suitable. From looking at the table we understand that the KMO measure is 0.892 which is between 0.8 to 1 which corresponds to an adequate data (Li et al. 2020).

Table 3. Exploratory factor analysis

KMO and Bartlett's Test		
Kaiser-Meyer-Olkin Measure of Sampling Adequacy.		**.892**
Bartlett's Test of Sphericity	Approx. Chi-Square	738.997
	df	28
	Sig.	.000

Source: Compiled by researcher.

Bartlett's test of Sphericity serves to evaluate the null hypothesis that the correlation matrix is an identity matrix. Such an identity correlation matrix suggests that variables are unrelated, rendering them unsuitable for factor analysis. Significance in this statistical test, typically indicated by a p-value below 0.05, indicates rejection of the null hypothesis, affirming that the correlation matrix is not an identity matrix, as depicted in the table below. Thus as per table two with a significance value below 0.05 we can proceed with the factor analysis.

4.3 Consumers' Awareness Regarding RPA and AI in Indian Banks

Table 4 corresponds to the awareness w.r.t use of RPA and AI enabled services in their respective banks. RPA has resulted in Automates repetitive loan processing tasks, such as data entry, document verification, and communication with borrowers. On other hand AI assists in credit risk assessment by analyzing historical data, predicting default probabilities, and optimizing loan terms. RPA monitors transaction logs, detects anomalies, and generates alerts for suspicious activities. AI Enhances fraud detection by learning patterns from historical data and identifying unusual behaviour. Loans are RPA an AI anabled was accepted by 40 percent of the respondents whereas 60 percent show negative response to it. A high percentage of respondents with 63.125 percentile were aware about banking transaction alert. 58.75 percentile showed negative response to credit processing by RPA and AI enabled services. RPA and AI Streamlines credit application processing, including data validation, credit score calculation, and decision-making. Predicts creditworthiness based on customer profiles, financial history, and market trends.

Table 4. Consumers' awareness regarding RPA and AI in Indian Banks

Sr. No.	Description	NO		YES	
		TOTAL	PERCENTAGE	TOTAL	PERCENTAGE
1.	Loans	96	60	64	40
2.	Banking transactions alert	59	36.875	101	63.125
3.	Credit Processing	66	41.25	94	58.75
4.	Customer Service	45	28.125	115	71.875
5.	KYC	52	32.5	108	67.5
6.	Fraud Detection	66	41.25	94	58.75
7.	Account Payable	59	36.875	101	63.125
8.	Report automation	73	45.625	87	54.375
9.	Cash collection and deposits	60	37.5	100	62.5
10.	Underwriter Support	89	55.625	71	44.375
11.	Other processes	71	44.375	89	55.625

Source: Compiled by researcher

Banks are using RPA and AI enabled services to provide a better customer experience with Automates responses to common queries, updates customer records, AI Powers chatbots and virtual assistants, providing personalized support resolving complex issues. and schedules follow-up calls. This is also reflected by our data with seventy-one percent agreeing to it. Sixty-seven percent also believed that KYC is automated in their banks which Collects and validates customer information, performs background checks, and maintains compliance records. For fraud detention, 58 percent is aware of the automated fraud detention system applicable in their banks to flag suspicious transactions, investigate discrepancies, and generate reports for further analysis. Sixty-three and fifty four percent of respondents are aware of the use of RPA and AI in account payable (Extracts relevant data from invoices, validates accuracy, and predicts cash flow requirements and report automation (Generates routine reports, compiles data from multiple sources, and distributes them to stakeholders). Sixty-two percentage agreed about cash collection and deposit being automated. Fifty percent were unaware of automated underwriting services. RPA assists underwriters by automating data extraction, risk assessment, and policy compliance checks. AI evaluates complex risk factors, predicts claim outcomes, and recommends policy adjustments.

4.4 ANOVA Statistics of Consumers' Preference Regarding RPA and AI

Table 5 presents the results of a series of one-way ANOVA tests examining the relationships between demographic variables (education, year of transaction, region, annual income) and three test variables (awareness of RPA and AI, usage of RPA and AI application, customer satisfaction from RPA and AI).

Table 5. ANOVA statistics of Consumers' preference regarding RPA and AI

Test variables	Demographic variables	Levene's	Sig.	F value	Sig.
Awareness of RPA and AI	Education	5.905	**.000**	20.647	**.000***
	Year of Transaction	5.081	.001	21.633	.000*
	Region	5.592	**.000**	18.164	.000*
	Annual Income	6.749	**.000**	21.094	.000*
Usage of RPA and AI Application	Education	9.048	.000	18.241	.000*
	Year of Transaction	5.498	.000	18.468	.000*
	Region	5.014	.001	16.573	.000*
	Annual Income	7.593	.000	18.682	.000*
Customer Satisfaction from RPA and AI	Education	6.881	.000	21.097	.000*
	Year of Transaction	4.894	0.001	22.525	.000*
	Region	5.318	.000	18.266	.000*
	Annual Income	6.062	.000	21.650	.000*

Source: Compiled by researcher *the significant difference at the 0.05 level.

For each test variable, Levene's test for homogeneity of variances is conducted across different levels of the demographic variables. The Levene's test assesses whether the variances of the groups are equal. The Sig. column provides the significance level associated with Levene's test. Following Levene's test, one-way ANOVA tests are performed to evaluate whether there are statistically significant differences in the means of the test variable across different levels of each demographic variable. The F value column represents the test statistic for the ANOVA test, and the "Sig." column provides the associated significance level.

4.5 Independent T-test on Consumers' Preference Regarding RPA and AI

Table 6 shows that the independent t-test is commonly used in research settings to compare the means of experimental and control groups or to compare the means of two distinct populations. It's a powerful tool for evaluating whether an intervention or treatment has had a significant effect on a particular outcome. The means of awareness for female and male groups are close.

Table 6. Independent t-test on consumers' preference regarding RPA and AI

Variables	Mean		SD		Levene's test for equality of variances		t-test for equality of means		Mean difference
	Female	Male	Female	Male	F	Sig.	t-value	Sig(2-tailed)	
Awareness of RPA and AI	3.6065	3.6369	.80514	.94716	3.990	.047	158	.846	-.03042
Usage of RPA and AI Application	3.5964	3.5123	.85023	.96911	1.790	.183	158	.603	.08408
Customer Satisfaction	3.4896	3.5971	.76745	.94704	4.343	.039	158	.488	-.10751

Source: Compiled by researcher

The Levene's test indicates unequal variances between the groups with F = 3.990 and p = 0.047 (significant). However, the independent t-test does not show a significant difference between the means, suggesting that there's no statistically significant difference in awareness between females and males with t = 0.846 and p = 0.398 (not significant). The means of usage for female and male groups are also close. Levene's test indicates no significant difference in variances with F = 1.790 and p = 0.183 (not significant). The independent t-test confirms there's no statistically significant difference in usage between females and males with t = 0.603 and p = 0.548 (not significant). The means of customer satisfaction for female and male groups are again close. Levene's test indicates unequal variances with F = 4.343 and p = 0.039 which is significant. However, the independent t-test does not show a significant difference between the means with t = 0.488 and p = 0.626 (not significant), suggesting that there's no statistically significant difference in customer satisfaction between females and males.

4.6 Acceptance and Rejection of Hypothesis

Table 7 shows that the hypotheses test whether consumer perceptions, opinions, and satisfaction towards AI and RPA in Indian banks vary across demographic factors. The results show that gender does not significantly affect these aspects, as most gender-related hypotheses are accepted. However, education, year of transactions, region, and annual income show significant differences, as their hypotheses are rejected. This indicates that consumers' backgrounds—especially their education level, experience with banking, location, and income—play a crucial role in shaping their views and satisfaction regarding AI and RPA technologies in banking. Banks should tailor AI/RPA strategies considering these demographic variations for better customer engagement.

Table 7. Acceptance and rejection of hypothesis

Hypothesis	Accept	Reject
HO_{1a} There is no significant difference in consumers' perception towards AI and RPA in Indian Banks across gender	Yes	No
HO_{1b} There is no significant difference in consumers' perception towards AI and RPA in Indian Banks across Education	No	Yes
HO_{1c} There is no significant difference in consumers' perception towards AI and RPA in Indian Banks across Year of transactions	No	Yes
HO_{1d} There is no significant difference in consumers' perception towards AI and RPA in Indian Banks across Region	No	Yes
HO_{1e} There is no significant difference in consumers' perception towards AI and RPA in Indian Banks across Annual Income (HO_{1e}).	No	Yes
HO_{2a} There is no significant difference in consumers' opinion towards the usage of AI and RPA applications in Indian Banks across Gender	Yes	No
HO_{2b} There is no significant difference in consumers' opinion towards the usage of AI and RPA applications in Indian Banks Education	No	Yes
HO_{2c} There is no significant difference in consumers' opinion towards the usage of AI and RPA applications in Indian Banks across Year of transactions	No	Yes
HO_{2d} There is no significant difference in consumers' opinion towards the usage of AI and RPA applications in Indian Banks across Region	No	Yes

continued on following page

Table 7. Continued

Hypothesis	Accept	Reject
HO_{2e} There is no significant difference in consumers' opinion towards the usage of AI and RPA applications across Annual Income	No	Yes
HO_{3a} There is no significant difference in consumers' satisfaction from AI and RPA in Indian Banks across Gender	Yes	No
HO_{3b} There is no significant difference in consumers' satisfaction from AI and RPA in Indian Banks across Education	No	Yes
HO_{3c} There is no significant difference in consumers' satisfaction from AI and RPA in Indian Banks across Year of transactions	No	Yes
HO_{3d} There is no significant difference in consumers' satisfaction from AI and RPA in Indian Banks across Region	No	Yes
HO_{3e} There is no significant difference in consumers' satisfaction from AI and RPA in Indian Banks across Annual Income	No	Yes

Source: Compiled by researcher

4.7 Consumer Education and Digital Literacy in the Indian Banking Sector

The growing digitisation of India's banking industry has revolutionised financial services, increasing their accessibility and efficiency. However, this transition emphasises the crucial importance of consumer education and digital literacy in ensuring that all sectors of the population can successfully and safely interact with digital banking systems (Muduli & Choudhury, 2024). According to a survey by the Merchant Payments Alliance of India (MPAI) and the National Institute of Bank Management (NIBM), just 38% of rural consumers in India engage in digital transactions, which is lower than in countries such as Brazil (50%) and the United States (78%). Unreliable internet access, limited digital proficiency, and socio-cultural limitations for women all contribute to this inequality (Garg et al., 2024; Schuetz & Venkatesh, 2020).

The need of digital literacy is especially apparent in rural regions, where traditional banking infrastructure is frequently restricted. Initiatives such as the Pradhan Mantri Gramin Digital Saksharta Abhiyan (PMGDISHA) aim to educate six crore rural families about computers, internet usage, and access to different digital services. Despite these attempts, obstacles continue. In response to these problems, financial institutions are increasingly using AI to improve client interactions and simplify procedures. For example, the Commonwealth Bank has integrated AI into its processes, resulting in more efficient customer service and enhanced fraud detection procedures. While such improvements hold promise, a concurrent emphasis on teaching customers about these technologies is required to establish confidence and promote their successful usage (Pahari et al., 2023).

5 DISCUSSION

Individuals with different education levels may have varying levels of exposure, understanding, or skepticism toward AI and RPA technologies. The evolution of technology over time may influence consumers' perceptions, with those experiencing recent transactions having different attitudes compared to those from earlier years. Regional disparities in infrastructure, access to information, or cultural factors may shape consumers' attitudes toward AI and RPA (Vijai et al., 2020). An additional critical evaluation of AI's impact beyond consumer perception will support in understanding its broader implications, including ethical concerns, financial stability and operational efficiency. Socioeconomic status can influence exposure to technology, with higher-income individuals potentially having greater access or familiarity with AI and RPA. Hence, the adoption of AI and RPA in India's banking sector, customer trust, digital literacy and cultural perception impact acceptance, while regulatory framework and financial inclusion policies shape implementation. Balancing compliance and ethical considerations is considerations is significant for ensuring for technology adoption in banking sector.

Overall, these results suggest that demographic factors play a significant role in shaping consumers' perceptions, usage, and satisfaction regarding AI and RPA in the context of Indian Banks. Understanding these factors can inform targeted strategies for the implementation and adoption of these technologies (Rashed et al., 2021). The study has failed to reject the null hypothesis based on demographic factor gender with a p-value greater than 0.5 percent on the perception and usage scale but with regards to satisfaction level null hypothesis is accepted. There is no significant difference in the satisfaction level of males and females. Taking education as a demographic factor p-value is less than 5 percent indicating rejection of the null hypothesis on the three scales. The same result is also derived when we undertake demographic factors such as years of transaction, region, and annual income (Oshri and Plugge, 2022; Zhou, 2021).

China has effectively improved rural banking by using public-private partnerships and AI integration. China's Rural Taobao program, supported by Alibaba and local governments, has considerably expanded e-commerce usage in remote rural regions, illustrating the efficacy of integrating technology with localised initiatives (Prakash, 2023). In contrast, India's rural banking industry has distinct problems, such as low levels of digital literacy and limited infrastructure. The use of artificial intelligence (AI) into banking has the potential to transform financial services in rural India by tackling long-standing issues such restricted access to banking facilities and financial illiteracy. Fintech technologies such as digital payments, microfinance, and digital banking have helped to close the financial inclusion gap in these sectors (Pahari et al., 2023; Roy, 2025). To solve these issues, a holistic strategy is necessary, which includes installing privacy-enhancing technology, incorporating AI into regulatory frameworks, and tailoring digital financial literacy initiatives. Such measures can assist lessen the hazards associated with AI deployment while also promoting trust among rural customers. By learning from global benchmarks and adjusting methods to the local environment, India may successfully negotiate the hurdles of AI adoption in rural banking, resulting in increased financial inclusion and economic development (Rashmi & Nirmal, 2021).

The use of Artificial Intelligence (AI) in the Indian banking sector has improved operational efficiency and customer service. However, this integration carries issues such as data privacy problems, algorithmic biases, and cybersecurity vulnerabilities (Subudhi, 2019; Bhattacharya & Sinha, 2022). To solve these difficulties, it is critical to create strong AI risk management systems. Internationally, frameworks such as the European Union's Artificial Intelligence Act and Singapore's Model AI Governance Framework prioritise risk-based methods, categorising AI applications based on possible effect and establishing associated regulatory criteria. These frameworks emphasise the significance of accountability, transparency, and ongoing monitoring in AI systems. In the Indian context, the Reserve Bank of India (RBI) has recognised the importance of such structures. The RBI Governor has emphasised the possible systemic dangers presented by a significant reliance on artificial intelligence. He emphasised that failures or disruptions in these systems might spread across the financial sector, emphasising the importance of banks implementing proper risk mitigation strategies (Roy, 2025). Establishing procedures for data quality, privacy, and security to prevent unauthorised access and assure regulatory compliance. Implementing steps to detect and reduce biases in AI models, ensuring that judgements are transparent and egalitarian. By implementing these components, Indian banks may capitalise on AI's promise while mitigating related risks, promoting customer and regulator trust (Kumar & Gupta, 2023; Talreja et al., 2023).

6 CONCLUSION

This study has contributed in the development of three scales i.e., perception scale, usage scale and consumer satisfaction scale with respect to AI and RPA in banking. Figure one shows awareness data among consumers of the NCR region with respect to RPA and AI highlighting growing awareness among consumers of AI and RPA-enabled services in the banking sector. Today's technological advances are changing consumers' demands at an accelerated pace. New technologies can not only handle a growing number of repetitive and manual tasks but also perform increasingly sophisticated kinds of knowledge-based work. In the Indian banking sector, the assimilation of Artificial Intelligence (AI) and Robotic Process Automation (RPA) has catalysed a transformative paradigm shift. AI, employing advanced algorithms, augments decision-making with predictive analytics, enhancing customer satisfaction through personalized insights. Concurrently, RPA streamlines operations by automating repetitive tasks, thereby bolstering operational efficiency, and reducing errors. This synergy of AI and RPA engenders a potent cocktail of innovation. It is propelling Indian banks toward unprecedented levels of competitiveness, resilience, and service quality, ultimately redefining the contours of the industry landscape.

7 POLICY RECOMMENDATIONS

The European Union's Ethics Guidelines for Trustworthy AI emphasise values such as human agency and supervision, technical robustness, privacy, and responsibility (Schuetz & Venkatesh, 2020; Talreja et al., 2023). Similarly, the OECD's AI Principles encourage equitable growth, sustainable development, and well-being while emphasising openness and explainability. India can create explicit rules that specify permissible AI techniques and ensure compliance with ethical norms and human rights. Implement systems for continuous assessment and adaption of AI policy in order to stay up with technical advances and new dangers. By incorporating these global best practices, India may create a creative, ethical, and resilient AI ecosystem in banking (Rashmi & Nirmal, 2021; Bhattacharya & Sinha, 2022). Moreover, strengthening policy recommendations with international best practices will offer a comparative perspective, ensuring that the Indian banking sector aligns with the global standards for AI governance and Implementations in data security, workforce up-skilling, cybersecurity, consumer trust. AI scam prevention as perceived in the U.K and US, should be directed to reinforce cyber security. Hence, banks must implement consumer awareness program to build trust, safeguarding transparency in AI driven services.

The study on consumer perception of AI and RPA in the Indian banking sector transmits significant policy implications for both regulatory authorities and banking institutions. The policymakers should focus on creating a regulatory framework that encourages the adoption of AI and RPA while ensuring consumer protection. Clear guidelines are needed to address data privacy, transparency, and security concerns, ensuring that banks implement these technologies ethically and in a manner that prioritizes customer rights. Regulations should mandate robust data protection measures and the transparent use of consumer data, which will build trust and alleviate fears surrounding AI and RPA deployment.

There is a need for government initiatives to foster digital literacy among consumers, especially in understanding the role of AI and RPA in banking services. This can be achieved through public awareness campaigns and training programs that demystify these technologies, improving customer acceptance. The banking sector should be encouraged to adopt a consumer-centric approach when deploying AI and RPA solutions. Banks should focus on enhancing user experience by ensuring these technologies are accessible, intuitive, and responsive to diverse customer needs. Policymakers should consider providing incentives for banks that implement AI and RPA solutions that significantly improve customer satisfaction and service delivery, driving innovation in the sector.

8 FUTURE RESEARCH DIRECTION

The impact of artificial intelligence on consumer-facing financial services is widely established, it also has a substantial impact on internal operations and strategic decision-making. AI-powered analytics help banks better analyse credit risk, optimise asset management, and improve fraud detection procedures (Rashmi & Nirmal, 2021). For example, AI systems may analyse complicated information to detect patterns suggestive of fraudulent activity, so increasing the bank's risk posture. However, relying on AI creates issues. AI integration requires significant investment in technological infrastructure and personnel acquisition, which might be prohibitively expensive for smaller financial institutions. As a result, a complete assessment of AI's influence on banking must take into account these several dimensions, combining technical advancement with ethical issues and human capital development (Kumar & Gupta, 2023).

Future research in the Indian banking sector should examine the long-term effects of artificial intelligence (AI) and robotic process automation (RPA) on customer behaviour, loyalty, and trust. Additionally, studies should address ethical issues such as data privacy, transparency, and algorithmic bias, especially as these technologies become more prevalent. Comparative research could investigate the adoption and impact of AI and RPA in urban versus rural areas, focusing on the unique challenges faced in each region. Moreover, understanding the barriers to AI and RPA implementation in banks including organizational resistance, infrastructure limitations, and regulatory hurdles would provide valuable insights for effective policy-making and smoother integration of these technologies. A multifaceted study exploring the intricate interplay of demographic, cultural, and socioeconomic factors in shaping consumer perceptions is essential. Finally, an in-depth investigation into the effectiveness of banks' communication strategies for educating consumers about these technologies can reveal insights to enhance awareness campaigns.

REFERENCES

Addula, S. R., Meduri, K., Nadella, G. S., & Gonaygunta, H. (2024). AI, and Blockchain in Finance: Opportunities and Challenges for the Banking Sector. *International Journal of Advanced Research in Computer and Communication Engineering*, *13*(2), 184–190. DOI: 10.17148/IJARCCE.2024.13231

Alzaidi, A. A. (2018). Impact of artificial intelligence on performance of banking industry in Middle East. *International Journal of Computer Science and Network Security*, *18*(10), 140–148.

Alzaidi, A. A. (2018). Impact of use of big data in decision making in banking sector of Saudi Arabia. *International Journal of Computer Science and Network Security*, *18*(12), 72–80.

Arjun, R., Abhisek, K., & Suprabha, K. R. (2021). Developing banking intelligence in emerging markets: Systematic review and agenda. *International Journal of Information Management Data Insights*, *1*(2), 1–11.

Bagozzi, R. P. (1992). The self-regulation of attitudes, intentions, and behavior. *Social Psychology Quarterly*, *55*(2), 178–204. DOI: 10.2307/2786945

Baruah, A. (2020). *AI applications in the Top 4 Indian Banks*. EMERJ.

Bhattacharya, C., & Sinha, M. (2022). The role of artificial intelligence in banking for leveraging customer experience. Australasian Accounting, Business and Finance Journal, 16(5).

Bhuvana, M., Thirumagal, P. G., & Vasantha, S. (2016). Big data analytics-a leveraging technology for Indian commercial banks. *Indian Journal of Science and Technology*, *9*(32), 98643. DOI: 10.17485/ijst/2016/v9i32/98643

Garg, N., & Jain, N. (2023). An Empirical Analysis on Facilitators and Inhibitors of Bankers' Intention to Use Artificial Intelligence Applications in Delhi/NCR. *International Management Review*, *19*(2), 64–94.

Garg, P., Srivastava, T., Goel, A., & Gupta, N. (2024). Accelerating Financial Inclusion in Developing Economies (India) Through Digital Financial Technology. In AI-Driven Decentralized Finance and the Future of Finance (pp. 201-224). IGI Global.

Harrison, T. (2000). *Financial services marketing*. Prentice Hall.

Hepsiba, M. M. S., & Yamuna, S. M. (2022). Thriving With Artificial Intelligence In Banking Industry. *GEDRAG & ORGANISATIE REVIEW*, *35*(2), 194–199.

Husain, A. R. A. M., Hamdan, A., & Fadhul, S. M. (2022). The impact of artificial intelligence on the banking industry performance. *Future of organizations and work after the 4th industrial revolution: The role of artificial intelligence, big data, automation, and robotics*, 145-156.

Jaiwani, M., & Gopalkrishnan, S. (2022). Adoption of RPA and AI to Enhance the Productivity of Employees and Overall Efficiency of Indian Private Banks: An Inquiry. *In 2022 International Seminar on Application for Technology of Information and Communication (iSemantic)* (pp. 191-197). IEEE.

Jewandah, S. (2018). How artificial intelligence is changing the banking sector–A case study of top four commercial Indian banks. International Journal of Management. *Technology And Engineering, 8*(7), 525–530.

Kaur, D. N., Sahdev, S. L., Sharma, D. M., & Siddiqui, L. (2020). Banking 4.0:'the influence of artificial intelligence on the banking industry & how ai is changing the face of modern day banks'. *International Journal of Management, 11*(6). Advance online publication. DOI: 10.34218/IJM.11.6.2020.049

Kumar, J., & Gupta, S. S. (2023). Impact of artificial intelligence towards customer relationship in Indian banking industry. *Gyan Manag. J, 17*(1), 105–115. DOI: 10.48165/gmj.2022.17.1.12

Kumar, J., & Gupta, S. S. (2023). Impact of Artificial Intelligence towards customer relationship in Indian banking industry. *Gyan Management Journal, 17*(1), 105–115. DOI: 10.48165/gmj.2022.17.1.12

Li, N., Huang, J., & Feng, Y. (2020). Construction and confirmatory factor analysis of the core cognitive ability index system of ship C2 system operators. *PLoS One, 15*(8), e0237339. DOI: 10.1371/journal.pone.0237339 PMID: 32833969

Maček, A., Murg, M., & Čič, Ž. V. (2020). How robotic process automation is revolutionizing the banking sector. In *Managing customer experiences in an omnichannel world: Melody of online and offline environments in the customer journey* (pp. 271–286). Emerald Publishing Limited. DOI: 10.1108/978-1-80043-388-520201020

Mohr, P. (2001). The governors and deputy governors of the South African Reserve Bank 1921-2001. *South African Journal of Economic History*, 16(1_2), 101-138.

Muduli, A., & Choudhury, A. (2024). Digital technology adoption, workforce agility and digital technology outcomes in the context of the banking industry of India. Journal of Science and Technology Policy Management.

Oshri, I., & Plugge, A. (2022). Introducing RPA and automation in the financial sector: Lessons from KAS Bank. *Journal of Information Technology Teaching Cases, 12*(1), 88–95. DOI: 10.1177/2043886921994828

Pahari, S., Polisetty, A., Sharma, S., Jha, R., & Chakraborty, D. (2023). Adoption of AI in the banking industry: A case study on Indian banks. *Indian Journal of Marketing, 53*(3), 26–41. DOI: 10.17010/ijom/2023/v53/i3/172654

Pathria, M., Saini, R., & Manchanda, M. (2022). Examining Consumer Attitude towards AI-powered M-banking Chatbots: A Study on Elderly Users in an Emerging Market. *Bank Parikrama, XLVII*(3 & 4), 74–108.

Prakash, B. K. (2023). Adoption, Applications and Challenges of Artificial Intelligence in Indian Banking Sector. *Journal of Management and Entrepreneurship, 17*(2).

Pramod, D. (2021). Robotic process automation for industry: Adoption status, benefits, challenges and research agenda. *Benchmarking, 29*(5), 1562–1586. DOI: 10.1108/BIJ-01-2021-0033

Rashed, A., Alchuban, M., Hamdan, A., & Alareeni, B. (2021). The Impact of Robotic Process Automation (RPA) Technology in Banking Sector in Bahrain. *InInternational Conference on Business and Technology(pp.* 273-281*).* Cham*:* Springer International Publishing.

Rashmi, R., & Nirmal, R. V. (2021). A study on the implementation and the impact of artificial intelligence in banking processes. *Asian Journal of Management, 12*(1), 47–54.

Roy, S. (2025). AI Adoption and Central Banks in Emerging Markets: Challenges and Strategies. Available at *SSRN* 5121231. DOI: 10.2139/ssrn.5121231

Sachdeva, K., & Sivakumar, P. (2022). Performance of commercial banks in India: A non-parametric Malmquist index-based DEA approach. *International Journal of Business and Globalisation, 32*(4), 392–413. DOI: 10.1504/IJBG.2022.128175

Saraswat, P., Chouhan, V., & Goswami, S. (2024). Application of Robotic Process Automation (RPA) in Accounting: A Study of User's Perception At Delhi-NCR and Gujarat. *Finance India, 38*(3), 589.

Schuetz, S., & Venkatesh, V. (2020). Blockchain, adoption, and financial inclusion in India: Research opportunities. *International Journal of Information Management, 52*, 101936. DOI: 10.1016/j.ijinfomgt.2019.04.009

Sharma, M., & Choubey, A. (2024). Impact of information technology on Indian banking sector. *Journal of Financial Services Marketing, 29*(4), 1609–1622. DOI: 10.1057/s41264-024-00287-3

Sharma, M., & Choubey, A. A. (2021). Qualitative Study on Role of Information Technology in Indian Banking Sector. *AIMA Journal of Management & Research, 15*(3/4), 1–24.

Subudhi, S. (2019). Banking on artificial intelligence: Opportunities & challenges for banks in India. *International Journal of Research in Commerce, Economics and Management, 9*(7).

Talreja, P., Shrivastava, A., Mishra, A., & Gupta, N. (2023). A Critical Study of ICT Oriented Innovations based on Artificial Intelligence (AI) Applications towards BFSI Sector. In 2023 IEEE International Conference on ICT in Business Industry & Government (ICTBIG) (pp. 1-5). IEEE.

Vijai, C., Suriyalakshmi, S. M., & Elayaraja, M. (2020). The future of robotic process automation (RPA) in the banking sector for better customer experience. *Shanlax International Journal of Commerce, 8*(2), 61–65. DOI: 10.34293/commerce.v8i2.1709

Wahab, A. (2024). Impact of Artificial Intelligence on Indian Banking Sector-A Study of Banks. [IRJAEM]. *International Research Journal on Advanced Engineering and Management, 2*(05), 1261–1268.

Zhou, S. (2021). Research on Banking Process Optimization Based on RPA in Financial Sharing Mode. [). IOP Publishing.]. *Journal of Physics: Conference Series, 1865*(2), 022069. DOI: 10.1088/1742-6596/1865/2/022069

KEY TERMS AND DEFINITIONS

Artificial Intelligence (AI): Artificial Intelligence is the simulation of human intelligence in machines designed to think, learn, and perform tasks that typically require human cognition. It involves technologies like machine learning, natural language processing, and computer vision, enabling systems to analyze data, recognize patterns, and make decisions autonomously.

Robotic Process Automation (RPA): Robotic Process Automation is a technology that uses software robots or "bots" to automate repetitive, rule-based tasks in business processes. It mimics human actions to perform tasks such as data entry, processing transactions, and managing workflows, improving efficiency, accuracy, and reducing operational costs in various industries.

Perception: Perception is the process by which individuals interpret and make sense of sensory information from their environment. It involves organizing, identifying, and interpreting data through the senses to form an understanding or awareness of objects, events, or concepts. Perception is influenced by experiences, beliefs, and cognitive biases.

Indian Banking Sector: The Indian Banking Sector refers to the network of financial institutions in India, including commercial banks, regional rural banks, cooperative banks, and development banks. It provides services like savings and loans, payment systems, and investment products, playing a key role in economic development, financial inclusion, and national growth.

National Capital Region (NCR): The National Capital Region is a metropolitan area centered around Delhi, India, encompassing parts of neighboring states such as Haryana, Uttar Pradesh, and Rajasthan. It includes Delhi and surrounding districts, aiming to promote balanced regional development and ease congestion in the capital by fostering economic growth and infrastructure.

Chapter 7
Determining the Most Important Indicators Affecting the Failure Risk of Conventional and Sharia Rural Banks

Lina Nugraha Rani
Universitas Airlangga, Indonesia

Eko Fajar Cahyono
Universitas Airlangga, Indonesia

Mohammad Irfan
https://orcid.org/0000-0002-4956-1170
Christ University, Bengaluru, India

Sylva Alif Rusmita
Universitas Airlangga, Indonesia

ABSTRACT

This study identifies key variables influencing the risk of failure in Indonesia's Conventional and Sharia Rural Banks (BPR and BPRS) and proposes strategies to mitigate these risks. Using the Analytical Network Process (ANP) method, the study engaged 11 respondents, including banking practitioners from Conventional and Islamic Commercial Banks, Rural Banks, Islamic Rural Banks, and academics. Data were analyzed with Super Decision software and Excel. Results reveal four critical variables: 1) macroeconomic, 2) microprudential, 3) macroprudential, and 4) bank internal variables. The welfare aspect of macroeconomic variables emerged as the most significant, followed by the liquidity indicator in microprudential variables and the internal resilience indicator in macroprudential variables. These findings guide strategies to enhance banking performance and reduce failure risks. Regulators and the government should prioritize macroeconomic welfare indicators to strengthen the banking system and address factors contributing to BPR and BPRS failures.

DOI: 10.4018/979-8-3373-0209-6.ch007

1. INTRODUCTION

Indonesia's economic development cannot be separated from the hands of the government, financial sector institutions and business actors. The government as a policy maker is expected to provide a conducive climate for the business world, so that financial institutions, both banking and non-banking as well as business actors in the field, are able to take advantage of these policies and carry out business activities smoothly, which in turn can encourage the acceleration of domestic economic development. According to (Wulandari, et al 2020) this economic growth is an indicator that shows the success and failure of government policies and economic development in a country.

(Harianto and Nuryantono, 2008) explained that the Rural Bank (BPR) is a financial institution that was formed to serve the needs of financial services (banking) for the economically weak community, especially small businesses in Indonesia. The impact of the existence of Rural Bank on small businesses is considered important for increasing micro and small business financing because small businesses as a sector that plays an important role in the Indonesian economy require capital injections from outside parties in this case are financial institutions. The large role of small businesses is shown by their contribution to national production, the number of business units and entrepreneurs, as well as the absorption of labour in micro, small and medium enterprises (MSMEs). From this statement, it can be said indirectly that Rural Bank has a role in improving the Indonesian economy.

Hidajat (2020), Rural Bank is a financial institution that is close to the community. Locations are scattered throughout the village and in places not served by other financial institutions. For most rural communities, Rural Banks are preferred over commercial banks because of the ease and speed of service.

Rural Bank (conventional) or Sharia Rural Bank have a great opportunity to improve their operations caused by the growth of public trust in banking, this is supported by Indonesian Deposit Insurance Company (LPS) in 2020, through a press release Number: PRESS-42 /SEKL/2020 states that progress in the banking system in Indonesia is marked by much of the corporate funds moved to smaller banks. Third Party Funds (DPK) or deposits above 5 billion rupiah are seen starting to move from BUKU IV banks to BUKU I, BUKU II, and BUKU III banks. According to him, with many business entities moving their funds to smaller banks, it shows an increase in trust in banks.

Based on the LPS press release in February 2021, it shows that there are 22 Rural Bank and Sharia Rural Banks that are included in the list of liquidation processes. From 2006 to 2021 the first quarter of the total number of banks included in the list of banks were liquidated as many as 111 banks. A total of 100 banks are Rural Banks and Sharia Rural Banks, and the remaining 1 are Commercial Banks.

The results of the study (Miskak, 2019) show that the cause of the failure of a Rural Bank or Sharia Rural Bank is that the bank cannot meet the minimum capital adequacy ratio (CAR) because of the losses it suffers. Bank losses are caused by fraud by owners, management, and employees. Losses are recognized in the financial statements after being discovered by Central Bank of Indonesia (BI) or Financial Services Authority (OJK). In the research of Anggraeni, et al (2020) found that banking failure is positively related to cost inefficiency, debt to equity ratio, inflation rate, but negatively related to profitability.

In Rustiarini, et al. (2016) stated that there were several factors that led to the revocation of the Rural Bank business license, but the OJK and the Indonesian Rural Bank Association (Perbarindo) stated that the revocation of the license was not due to the inability of the Rural Bank to compete, but due to fraud committed by the management or owner of the microbank.

Based on the literature presented about the factors as indicators that influence the failure of Rural Banks, both conventional and Islamic, this study aims to determine the most important indicators that affect the risk of failure of Conventional and Sharia Rural Banks. The method used in this research is the Analytic Network Process (ANP), which collects the opinions of experts who understand the operations of conventional and Islamic Rural Banks to provide a ranking of indicators that are used as references in strategies to reduce the risk of failure of Conventional and Sharia Rural Banks.

2. LITERATURE REVIEW

2.1. Bank Failure

Bank failure is a condition where the bank is unable to meet its short-term obligations or liquidity. Bank failures can trigger a banking crisis as happened in supermarkets in the United States in 2007. The banking crisis was followed by bank runs or massive withdrawals of funds by customers which further added to the big impact on bank failures, especially in meeting liquidity. Massive withdrawals of funds cause a decrease in customer confidence in banking institutions and can have a contagious effect or spread downwards. History has proven that banking crises have always been accompanied by panic or panic as well as banking crises that occurred before the 1st World War. Banking institutions are very vulnerable to risk so they must be able to manage their liquidity and mercure mismatches. The occurrence of bank runs is triggered by economic fundamental conditions such as economic contraction, interest rate volatility, exchange rate volatility, declining asset values, uncertainty in the financial sector, a weak economy, bad credit and other things (Simorangkir, 2011).

2.2. Bank Failure Risk Indicator

Banking is an important institution for a country that acts as intermediary related to financial transactions as stated in the Republic of Indonesia Law Number 10 of 1998. Banking has a main function in collecting funds in the form of deposits from the public and redistributing them in the form of credit or financing. The role of banking is very important in terms of increasing economic growth in a country. Banking is very open to risks related to managed financial service transactions. Therefore, banks must be able to plan risks properly in order to be efficient and to continue to achieve optimal profits. Banking is also faced with a very important risk, namely systemic risk that greatly affects the stability of the state financial system due to several reasons, such as moral hazard problems, problems related to asymmetric information later and the condition of financial intermediation productivity. Systemic risk can cause banks to fail and can even affect one bank to another. This is because the banking industry is interconnected with each other. Based on the crisis that has been experienced by Indonesia, it is very important to pay attention to systemic risks that can result in bank defaults (Ayomi and Hermanto, 2013).

Based on the events of the Global financial crisis in the United States in 2008 also illustrates that the failure of a bank can potentially become a financial crisis if it is not handled immediately. This is because institutions in the banking industry are interconnected with each other. According to Ayomi and Hermanto (2013) there are four sources of bank failure, namely:

1. Excessive bank credit expansion.

2. Information asymmetry results in the inability of depositors to accurately value bank assets, especially when the bank's economic condition worsens.
3. The shock starts from outside the banking system, regardless of the financial condition of the bank, which causes savers to change their liquidity preferences or causes a reduction in bank reserves.
4. Institutional and legal restrictions that weaken banks and lead to bankruptcy.

Bank failure can be concluded to be influenced by several indicators from macroeconomic, macroprudential, microprudential, and internal bank.

2.3. Macroeconomics

The macroeconomic environment has a fairly strong influence on the banking sector. As stated by Festić and Bekő (2008) that exposure to macroeconomic risk factors is a source of systemic risk that affects the performance of the banking sector which is expressed as the ratio of non-performing loans to total loans. Banking sector outcomes are also determined by the macroeconomic environment, which affects the values of external indicators such as credit relative to GDP, net foreign currency position relative to capital, geographic distribution of loans relative to total credit, and foreign currency loans relative to total credit.

Chirwa and Odhiambo (2016) state that in developing countries, the determinants of macroeconomic growth include foreign direct investment, fiscal policy, investment, trade, monetary policy, natural resources, reforms and geographical, regional, political factors and so on. According to Sudarmono, et al (2011), higher economic growth helps offset increased risk taking and instability in less competitive markets.

Oliveria, et al (2015) found that the CAMEL indicator played a consistent role both during the broadest period of analysis and, more specifically, the period of financial instability crises. Furthermore, during the financial crisis, management quality factors have a significant impact, such as the emergence of capital growth indicators, the latter being a vehicle to finance losses and maintain credibility.

Fazio et al (2018) find that, while banks in Inflation Targeting countries with high-quality institutions do not benefit significantly from this policy "the credibility paradox", banks in countries with average quality institutions seem to benefit. Furthermore, according to estimates, inflation targeting and financial stability are negatively related in countries with low levels of institutional quality, which is consistent with the fact that governments must have at least the public's confidence to undertake effective economic policies. This inverse U-shaped relationship between inflation and financial stability as a function of institutional quality reflects two opposing views on this topic in the literature.

Umar, et al (2014) found two opposing points of view. As a result, inflation has a negative impact on the performance of the banking sector, and its abundance effect is very harmful to the economy as a whole. Inflation affects the purchasing power and exchange rate regime of banks, the opportunity cost of holding currency in the future, worsens lending policies, disrupts business plans, and the performance of banks' equity holdings. While the other side of the argument argues that inflation improves bank performance as long as banks can anticipate future inflation and adjust interest rates to generate higher income than costs, resulting in higher profits and performance as a result of interest rate adjustments.

Mirna (2019) states that anti-capacity tax policies, the role of automatic stabilizers, tax incentives that encourage or some types of financing, and the impact of tax relief on systemic risk, especially those aimed at real estate. The role of fiscal policy during periods of strong capital inflows is also described from a financial stability perspective, followed by an overview of the fiscal and quasi-fiscal costs of financial instability. The particular problem of the different time horizons of economic policy makers, which is usually tied to the electoral cycle in terms of fiscal policy and thus negatively affects its counter-cyclical capacity.

According to McDonald and Johnson (2012), the global financial crisis was not caused by the worldwide tax system, but the possibility that several elements contributed to chaos that was greater in magnitude and duration than required. Similarities to financial regulations accused of contributing to the crisis. The tax system, in particular, favors debt financing, housing investment, and assets with capital gains. It also encourages people to avoid transaction taxes and take advantage of tax losses. As a result, the tax system encourages people to take risks they would not normally take, increasing the overall vulnerability of the economy to financial shocks.

Eichler and Sobanski (2016) investigated the impact of national politics on Eurozone Bank default risk as measured by the stock market-based distance to default. They find that national election cycles, government power, and ideological alignment of government parties all have a significant impact on bank stability in eurozone member countries. Furthermore, we show that the impact of national politics on bank default risk is more pronounced for large and small banks.

According to Brown and Dinc (2005), political problems play an important role in delaying government intervention in bank failure. Failing banks are much less likely to be taken over by the government or have their licenses revoked before an election than after.

Brei, et al (2019), they constructed a panel of quarterly banking data and historical hurricane losses for islands in the Eastern Caribbean to investigate the econometric impact of these natural disasters on the banking industry. Their findings suggest that, after the storm, banks face negative deposit draws and funding shocks, which they respond to by reducing the supply of loans and attracting liquid assets. The default on loans and bank capital shows no signs of deterioration. As a result, the withdrawal and use of deposits, rather than credit expansion, appears to play an important role in the region's post-hurricane funding recovery. This emphasizes the importance of an active GWM policy. Based on research by Noth and Schwer (2018), property damage due to weather-related natural disasters significantly weakens the stability of banks operating in the affected areas, as evidenced by lower core zs, higher probability of default, higher ratio of non-performing assets. higher, higher foreclosure ratios, lower returns on assets, and lower bank equity ratios. The effect is economically significant, implying that insurance payments and public assistance programs do not adequately protect bank borrowers from financial distress. They also find that the negative effect on bank stability fades after a few years if no further disasters occur during that time.

2.4. Macroprudential

Based on Bank Indonesia (2021) that macroprudential policy is a policy aimed at maintaining overall financial system stability through limiting systemic risk. Systemic risk is the potential for instability due to contagion in part or all of the financial system due to the interaction of size, business complexity, interconnection between institutions and/or financial markets (interconnectedness), as well as behavioral tendencies that excessive amount of financial actors or institutions to follow the economic cycle (procyclicality).

Macroprudential policies are implemented to strengthen microprudential regulation and supervision in the interest of financial stability. Indonesia's macroprudential policies aim to (i) mitigate systemic risk; (ii) promote balanced and healthy intermediary functions; and (iii) improving efficiency and access to the financial system. This last objective is specifically designed to encourage the development of the financial system, especially in terms of financial deepening and inclusion (Warjiyo, 2017).

Macroprudential is a preventive policy implemented by the government to encourage banks to be more assertive and prudent as providers of public financing. This is done because banks are financial institutions that are prone to decline if they do not have a strong system of resilience.

The instruments contained in macroprudential policies have a significant impact on the health of banking performance, and these policies become a barometer of whether a bank is in a safe or dangerous failure stage (Kiemo, et al. 2021). One of the most emphasized in macroprudential policies is the procurement of financing or capital or loans, because their values will affect NPF and NPL, so a policy is needed to strengthen capital or public financing so that there is no default experienced by the community and will harm the banking sector and the economy. country, in other words the economic crisis (Cahyono and Rani, 2018).

The economic crisis will increase the risk of systemic bankruptcy, resulting in a high probability of default due to a lack of confidence in macroprudential regulatory policies (Chatelain and Ralf, 2012). As a result, the Central Bank of Kenya has shown in research (Kiemo, Kamau, et al. 2021) that macroprudential policies dampen the banking credit market and cause domestic leakage, so it is necessary to record steps that must be carried out more effectively and efficiently.

According to Morgan et al. (2019), macroprudential policies have become an increasingly important part of the regulatory and supervisory framework since the early 2000s. Similarly, the housing market has been at the center of the debate on preventing systemic financial risks. The loan-to-value ratio (LTV) is a macroprudential tool used to limit the creation of mortgage loans. This paper is unique in that it investigates the impact of LTV on mortgage lending moderation using a large sample of more than 4000 banks from 46 countries. According to their analysis, mortgage lending has been successfully restricted in countries with LTV policies. The two most important factors influencing the effectiveness of LTV are loan size and non-performing loans. When nonlinear analysis is taken into account, the effect of the mean LTV can be quite large; however, with large banks and banks with bad credit, it becomes less effective. Our findings suggest that the addition of other macroprudential tools, particularly for large banks, may have a complementary effect for LTV.

According to Purwono, et al (2020), the recent subprime mortgage crisis shows the importance of monitoring housing price bubbles. Bank Indonesia (BI), Indonesia's central bank, responded to the recent crisis by launching Loan-to-Value (LTV) for housing loans. However, research on strategies to prevent business failure due to the housing price bubble and its consequences in Indonesia is very limited. In their paper, they will forecast Indonesia's housing bubble to provide more context for the property business strategy. Using data from the Indonesian property price index. They determine LTV policies change the conditions of the price bubble and, as a result, strategies to prevent firm failure. According to their paper's findings, miscalculations in LTV can lead to a housing price boom rather than acting as a counter-cyclical buffer. However, the recent LTV changes were effective in reducing housing price misalignment, so companies can respond with confidence in future housing price stability.

Santosa, et al (2020) stated that the correlation between the Bank Indonesia (BI) rate as the reference interest rate and the productive interest rate showed a positive and significant impact on bank capital. Their findings indicate that an increase in the BI rate will increase the ROA and efficiency of Sharia banking because an increase in profit sharing and an increase in the BI rate will reduce the capital of Islamic banking. An increase in inflation will trigger an increase in the BI rate which will have a negative impact on CAR.

Yunita (2020) stated, similar to the Federal Reserve's policy, Bank Indonesia's policy of lowering the benchmark interest rate had an impact on the performance of the Indonesian Islamic banking industry throughout the pandemic. Based on monthly data from the Financial Services Authority's report on Sharia Banking Statistics, the Sharia Banking Industry Ratio from November 2019 to February 2020 showed various fluctuations, especially a decline in performance between December 2019 to January to February 2020. It is estimated as the impact of national and international financial sector conditions during pandemic in the first quarter of 2020.

According to Alper et al (2017), an increase in reserve requirements is associated with a decrease in bank liquidity (and thus a decrease in bank lending (dashed line). In the early stages of the quantitative tightening cycle, a decrease in bank liquidity is associated with relatively stable bank lending, most likely due to the contractual nature of bank loans, which are slower to adjust.As a result, banks reduce their liquid assets to finance their loans before adjusting their loan books.

Tovar Escribano and Martin (2012) conducted an empirical study of the relevance and usefulness of the reserve requirement and other macroprudential instruments in a sample of Latin American countries. Their investigation revealed that authorities in Brazil, Colombia, and Peru have actively used the reserve requirement as a tool to "lean against the wind," increasing the Reserve Requirement during the upside phase of the cycle to contain excessive credit growth and the associated buildup of vulnerabilities and lowering it during the downside phase to relieve pressure. liquidity. Both before and after the global financial crisis, the active management of Statutory Reserves was evident.

According to Kalatie, et al (2015), the proposed countercyclical capital buffer (CCB) of the Basel Committee on Banking Supervision aims to reduce excessive and pro-cyclical credit explosions in the financial system. The CCB extends a key component of traditional banking regulations, the minimum capital requirement, which requires banks to keep at least a certain amount of loss-absorbing capital on hand. The idea is to increase banks' capital requirements when credit cycle vulnerabilities increase, such as when there are signs of excessive credit growth or a credit-driven asset price boom.

Tente, et al. agree Countercyclical Capital Buffer (CCB) is a new macroprudential tool. CCB is a surcharge on the general equity of a Tier 1 capital 2 bank, the amount of which varies depending on the credit cycle. If aggregate domestic credit growth is excessive, the supervisory authority may set a positive CCB rate. Once credit growth returns to normal or the bank suffers losses, the CCB rate can be lowered to zero. As a result, CCB provides banks with additional capital buffer in times of trouble. This will strengthen the resilience of the banking system throughout the credit cycle.

Zulkhibri and Sakti (2018) state that the banking procyclicality system is associated with low or too high risk, which strengthens the cyclical behavior of banking institutions and the real economic sector. Many scholars say that the procyclicality of the banking sector is one of the main causes of financial instability in the economy. The procyclicality of the banking sector can exacerbate fluctuations in the business cycle and have a negative impact on financial stability. The interaction of the financial sector and the real economy tends to amplify the magnitude of the business cycle. Simple descriptions rarely capture the behavior of financial systems in real life, as these systems are distinguished by their complexity. In most cases, the asset price trajectory will be erratic and volatile.

According to Anathasouglhu (2014), due to procyclicality, banks usually finance risky investments with a slightly positive or even negative net present value during an upswing, while they do the opposite during a downturn. So, instead of compensating for changes in economic activity during the cycle, the banking system intensifies them.

Cheng et al (2020) investigated the impact of bank contagion in China. This paper estimates the interbank bilateral lending matrix using the maximum entropy method using data from 111 Chinese banks from 2013 to 2016. The estimated matrix is used to model the effect of credit and liquidity shocks on the Chinese banking system. However, according to the simulation results, in the extraordinary stress scenario, the contagion caused by liquidity shocks is significantly stronger than the effect of credit shocks, indicating the importance of liquidity in the banking system. The contagion effect caused by credit shock did not vary significantly over the sample period. However, the contagion effect of the liquidity shock was significantly reduced, which could be attributed to the contraction of the interbank business as a result of tighter interbank business supervision. The simulation results also identify the most important and vulnerable banking system nodes. Their findings also show that the risk contagion risk faced by Chinese banks varies across banking network structures.

David Ricardo, an English political economist, coined the term "contagion" in 1797. He attributed it to the feeling of panic that led to the suspension of convertibility, as well as the unfounded fear of shy community members. Le Bon, a French sociologist, wrote in 1895 that the ideas, emotions, and opinions that fuel a crowd are as powerful as germs. Prior to 1995, the term "contagion" was rarely used in articles describing the impact of the Mexican crisis on other Latin American countries. Contagion, as a medical concept, refers to the manifestation or transmission of a virus throughout the body, followed by the transmission of the disease to others by passing from virus to disease. Only after the Thai crisis occurred, when the currency was devalued and affected other Asian countries, financial markets around the world suffered. These events piqued the interest of researchers, and in the early 2000s, academic papers began to appear in an attempt to study how to measure, understand, predict, and prevent international financial contagion (Nica, 2020). Given the global credit crisis and the damage caused to financial institutions, the study of contagion in the financial system is particularly timely. Contagion is the spread of defaults through a network of financial institutions, each of which adds to the burden on other components of the system (Nica, 2020).

2.5. Microprudential

Microprudential policies measure, assess and address risks by looking at the soundness of individual banks (as economic actors) and the performance of each financial institution. With the soundness of banks and good performance of financial institutions, it will have a good impact on financial system stability (Silalahi, 2018).

Microprudential policy is a policy in supervising and protecting individual financial institutions from systematic risks and preventing other risks from arising (Financial Stability Review, 2014). Specifically for the banking sector, Article 7 (Law no. 21 of 2011 concerning the Financial Services Authority) also regulates microprudential supervision of the sector where the explanation in Article 7 states that microprudential regulation includes regulation and supervision of institutional, health, and prudential matters. caution, and bank checks. (OJK. 2019)

According to Isnaini and Bimo (2019) Internal financial conditions, one of which is to strengthen capital, considering the role of capital is very important to maintain public trust and capital also plays a role in buffering risk. Sharia Rural Bank must at least meet the Minimum Capital Requirement (KPMM) ratio that has been set by the regulator as the initial foundation to build trust from the public. Besides improving internal conditions, Sharia Rural Bank must also be sensitive to macroeconomic conditions. This is important because the performance of a Sharia Rural Bank is determined by the economic conditions of the area in which the bank operates. Banks located in areas with a high level of competition and good regional economic conditions determine their performance differently from banks located in areas with low levels of competition and low economic conditions.

2.6. Internal Bank

The role of banks in the economy is critical, even though they are the first institutions to suffer casualties when the economy recedes into crisis. (Anggraeni et al, 2020). In 2017 banks in Indonesia controlled a share of assets of 69.75% of the entire financial institution system (Bank Indonesia, 2018). In carrying out this function, the banking sector has exposure to various kinds of risks (Damayanti, 2020).

On the results of research Windriya (2014). Internal factors are proxied by bank characteristics which are measured using financial ratios. Indicates that internal banking has a major role in the sustainability of business activities in the banking industry.

In the banking industry, internal control can be defined as stated in SE No. 5/22/DPNP concerning Guidelines for Internal Control System Standards for Commercial Banks. The circular states that internal control is a supervisory mechanism established by bank management on an ongoing basis (on going basis) in order to maintain and secure bank assets, ensure the availability of more accurate reports, improve compliance with applicable regulations, reduce financial impact. losses, irregularities including fraud, and violations of prudential aspects, as well as increasing organizational effectiveness and increasing cost efficiency.

3. METODE PENELITIAN

This research is a qualitative research using Analytical Network Process (ANP) analysis which is the development of an analytical hierarchical process (Saaty and Vargas, 2006). ANP is a comprehensive analysis of decision making by considering qualitative and quantitative matters. This is a qualitative approach that is non-parametric and non-Bayesian. This research went through several stages. The first stage is the model construction stage to identify, analyze and structure the complexity of the problem into an appropriate ANP network, which consists of a literature review and focus group discussion (FGD) with practitioners, academics, associations and regulators. Second, the preparation of the ANP model framework is done by making relevant questionnaires and pairwise comparisons. Third, the authors calculated the geometric mean and rater agreement. The results of filling out the questionnaire are processed using Super Decision software to obtain conclusions and priorities on the most important indicator aspects that affect the risk of bank failure. The respondent's data is then processed through Super Decision and Microsoft Excel to achieve quantification results, calculation of appraiser agreement and geometric mean. Appraiser agreement is a measure that shows the level of conformity of the respondent (R1-Rn) to a problem in one cluster. The tool used to measure rater agreement is Kendall's Coefficient of Concordance (W; 0 < W < 1), where W = 1 indicates a perfect match. Geometric average is a type of average calculation that shows a certain trend or value (Ascarya, 2005). The stages of the ANP research method are shown in Figure 1.

Figure 1. Research stages

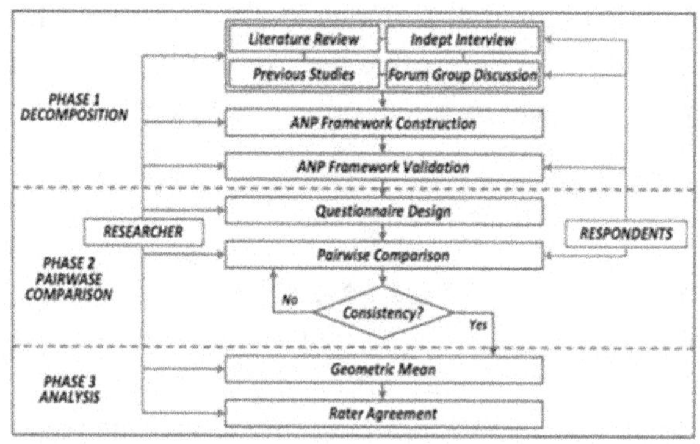

Source: (Ascarya, 2010)

The data used are primary data obtained through FGDs, in-depth interviews and ANP questionnaires. The selection of respondents using purposive sampling method where valid respondents in the ANP are people who master or are experts in their fields, which in this study are experts in the fields of banking and finance. Therefore, the respondents selected in this survey are banking/finance practitioners in Indonesia.

In the process of selecting respondents, the research was conducted by considering the respondents' understanding of the risk factors for bank failure in the banking industry in Indonesia. The number of respondents in this study consisted of 11 respondents. Eleven people are banking/finance practitioners and experts with competency considerations, academics who have an interest in finance and banking, and are members of banking association organizations in Indonesia.

In general, there are 4 (four) variables used in the study to determine the most important variables that affect the risk of failure of conventiona and sharia rural banks, namely: (1) Macroeconomics, (2) Macroprudential, (3) Microeconomics, and (4) Internal Banks. Each variable consists of several indicators, and each indicator consists of indicator components. The basis for determining the variables, indicators and component indicators is the result of studies from previous research conducted by the research team. According to the ANP stages in Figure 3.1.

4. RESULTS AND DISCUSSION

Determination of variables, indicators and component indicators obtained through the model validation process with a phase 1 questionnaire and measured the importance and priority levels with a phase 2 questionnaire conducted by respondents in accordance with the ANP stages in Figure 3.1. The following is a table of the results of the data processed using super decision.

Table 1. Processed data

Criteria	Summary
Internal Bank	0.146
Macroeconomics	0.350
Macroprudential	0.230
Microprudential	0.274
Internal Bank	
1. Banking Operations	**0.289**
1a. Growth in Number of Financial Institutions	0.320
1b. Rural Bank / Sharia Rural Bank Human Resource Capability	0.295
1c. Brand Image	0.253
2. Pricing Bank	**0.298**
2a Total TPF	0.238
2b. Central Bank Credit at rural bank or sharia rural bank	0.281
2c. rural bank Interest Rate or sharia rural bank Profit Sharing	0.272
2d. Stock price	0.231
3. Financial Technology	**0.282**
3a. Operational Technology of rural bank / sharia rural bank	0.236
3b. Digitizing Bank Operations	0.248
3c. Competition between Banks	0.191
4. Bank Risk Management	**0.302**
4a. Lack of Credit or Financing Guarantee Facilities	0.282
4b. Internal Audit for Fraud	0.245
4c. Good Corporate Governance	0.248
Macroeconomics	
1. Welfare Aspect	**0.362**
1a. High Unemployment Rate	0.318
1b. Labor Wage Rate	0.336
1c. Gini Ratio Gap	0.345
2.Economic Performance	**0.354**
2a. Economic growth	0.342
2b. Economy Crysis	0.343
2c. Aggregate Capital Ratio (Capital Accumulated)	0.315
3. Economic Dynamics	**0.284**
3a. Inflation Volatility	0.197
3b. Interest Rate Volatility	0.192
3c. Fiscal Policy on Tax	0.179
3d. Regional Politics	0.196
3e. Natural disasters	0.236

continued on following page

Table 1. Continued

Criteria	Summary
Macroprudential	
1. Bank Internal Resilience	**0.563**
1a. Difficulty Accessing Money Market	0.256
1b. Loan to Value	0.315
1c. BI Rate	0.218
1d. Statutory Reserve Requirement	0.211
2. Systemic Risk	**0.438**
2a. Countercyclical Buffer (CCB)	0.344
2b. Procyclicality	0.313
2c. Contagion Effect	0.343
Microprudential	
1. Liquidity	**0.342**
1a. Bank Liquidity Loan Amount	0.219
1b. Liquidity Ratio	0.289
1c. Liquid Liabilities	0.225
1d. LDR rural bank or FDR sharia rural bank	0.266
2. Asset Quality	**0.251**
2a. NPL rural bank or NPF sharia rural bank	0.212
2b. Credit Rating	0.163
2c. Minimum Capital Requirement (KPMM)	0.205
2d. Allowance for Impairment Losses (CKPN)	0.201
2e. Maximum Lending Limit (BMPK)	0.219
3. Solvency	**0.219**
3a. DER (Debt to Equity Ratio)	0.306
3b. Expense to Income Ratio	0.318
3c. Sharia Compliance for BPRS	0.375
4. Profitability	**0.188**
4a. Return on Assets (RoA)	0.365
4b. Return on Equity (RoE)	0.322
4c. Profit Margin	0.313

Based on the output results of ANP data processing using the Super Decision 2.10 application (which is shown in table 1), from the perspective of the criteria related to the most important variables that affect the risk of conventional/sharia rural bank failure in the opinion of banking practitioners, both macroeconomic, macroprudential, microprudential and internal bank variables . Of the four criteria, the ranking of the weight values that are considered important and priorities are as follows:

1. The first rank is the macroeconomic variable with a weighted value of 0.35.
2. The second rank is the macroprudential variable with a weighted value of 0.27.

3. The third rank is the macroprudential variable with a weighted value of 0.23.
4. The fourth rank is the value of the bank's internal variables by obtaining a weighted value of 0.170.

4.1. Macroeconomic Variables

In the macroprudential variable, there are 3 (three) indicators, namely:

1) Welfare Aspect indicators have 4 (four) indicator components, namely High Unemployment Rate, Labor Wage Level, Gini Ratio Gap.
2) Economic Performance Indicators Has 4 (four) indicator components, namely: Economic Growth, Economic Crisis, Aggregate Capital Ratio (Capital Accumulation), and
3) Economic Dynamics indicator which has 5 (five) indicator components, namely Inflation Volatility, Interest Rate Volatility, Fiscal Policy on Taxes, Regional Politics, Natural Disasters.

4.2 Macroprudential Variables

In the macroprudential variable, there are 2 (two) indicators, namely:

1) Bank Internal Resilience Indicator with indicator components: Difficulty Accessing Money Market, Loan to Value, BI Rate and Statutory Reserves,m,
2) Systemic Risk Indicator with component indicators: Contagion Effect, Procyclicality, Countercyclical Buffer (CCB) in it,

4.3 Microprudential Variables

In the microprudential variable there are 4 (four) indicators, namely:

1) Liquidity indicator with indicator components: Total Bank Liquidity Loans, Liquidity Ratio, Liquid Liabilities, LDR rural bank or FDR sharia rural bank,
2) Asset Quality Indicator component indicators: BPR NPL or BPRS NPF, Credit Rating, Minimum Capital Requirement (KPMM), Allowance for Impairment Losses (CKPN), Maximum Lending Limit (BMPK),
3) Solvency Indicator with indicator components: DER (Debt to Capital Ratio), BOPO (Expense to Income Ratio), Sharia Compliance for sharia rural bank, and
4) Profitability Indicators Indicator Components: Return on Assets (RoA), Return on Equity (RoE) and Profit Margin

4.4 Variabel Internal Bank

In the bank's internal variables there are 4 (four) indicators as follows:

1) Banking Operational Indicators with Indicator Components: Growth in the Number of Financial Institutions, Human Resources Capability of conventional / sharia rural bank, Brand Image,

2) Bank Pricing Indicator with indicator components: Total TPF, Central Bank Credit at r rural bank or sharia rural bank, rural bank Interest Rate or sharia rural bank Profit Sharing, Share Price,
3) Financial Technology Indicators With Indicator Components: Rural Bank / Sharia Rural Bank Bank Operational Technology, Digitalization of Bank Operations, Competition Between Banks, and lastly from the aspect of
4) Bank Risk Management Indicators With Indicator Components: Lack of Credit or Financing Guarantee Facilities, Internal Audit for Fraud, Good Corporate Governance)

5. ANALYSIS AND DISCUSSION

5.1 Macroeconomics

In this study, macroeconomics is the indicator that has the largest eigenvalue with a value of 0.35, with the highest sub-indicator on the aspect of inequality in which there is the Gini Ratio Index as the variable that has the highest value. Heryanah's research (2017) on income inequality shows that the results show that in general the level of income inequality in Indonesia within a period of 5 years is included in the category of moderate inequality and shows an increasing trend in 10 years.

This is in line with Prastowo's research (2018) which states that financial inclusion in Islamic banking has a significant negative relationship with the Gini Index. Financial inclusion in Islamic banking contributes to reducing income inequality in Indonesia. Arno's research (2018) states that the failure of a bank is a threat that can occur at any time if the bank is not able to fulfill its obligations on time when customers withdraw funds. So it can be concluded that the Gini ratio index has a role in maintaining equality in the welfare aspect, if the index is high it can be assumed that poverty is getting higher and will further add to the list of risks from banking failure because people have the risk of failing to make payments to the bank. So that it can be understood that macroeconomics is the most important indicator that affects the risk of bank failure, because the Gini Index is an indicator that measures the risk of bank failure.

5.2 Microprudential

In this study, microprudential is the second indicator that has the largest eigenvalue with a value of 0.274, with the highest sub-indicator on bank internal resilience which includes Loan to Value (LTV) in conventional banks and Financing to Value (FTV) in Sharia banks as variables that has the highest value.

In the research of Wenten and Nadi (2021) showed that the results of the t-test (partial testing) for the LTV/FTV policy variable showed that the LTV/FTV variable had a significant and significant effect on the dependent variable of KPR Supply. Mortgage is one of the existing financing in the banking sector whose value per contract is quite large, so the LTV policy on mortgage financing is important in mitigating the risk of bank failure. In Syaputra and Tohirin's research (2019), it shows that the FTV variable has a positive and significant effect on the confidence level of (5%) and implies that there is a positive and significant influence between the financing to value (FTV) variable on home ownership financing in Islamic banks. This means that the existence of the FTV policy has increasingly encouraged banks to provide more financing to the community, one of which is home ownership financing by considering the regulations related to policies issued by the government through Bank Indonesia. Thus, it can be said that an increase in the provision of financing to the public will also increase the risk of bank failure.

Therefore, the microprudential indicator is crucial because the microprudential policy here is very important in mitigating the risk of bank failure, if the regulator and government fail to determine microprudential policies, it will have an effect on increasing the risk of failure with a large number of failed loans or financing.

5.3 Macroprudential

Banks in carrying out their operations certainly cannot be separated from various kinds of risks. Bank business risk is uncertainty about a result that is expected or expected to be received. In this study, macroprudential is the third indicator that has the largest eigenvalue with a value of 0.23, with the highest sub-indicator on liquidity resilience in which there is a liquidity ratio as the variable that has the highest value.

In the research of Margaretha and Aditya (2013), it is stated that a low level of liquidity can also cause a bank to receive a penalty from the regulator, in this case Bank Indonesia. Today, liquidity risk has become a challenge in the modern banking world. Liquidity indicates a bank's ability to meet transaction needs when a customer makes a withdrawal, if the bank cannot meet the customer's needs, it means that the bank is experiencing liquidity risk. This is in line with Yoel's research (2016) which states that macroprudential policies that have been implemented in Indonesia such as the CAR and Statutory Reserves have been quite effective in reducing the credit cycle. So that in determining macroprudential policy in mitigating the risk of bank failure, one of them uses the liquidity ratio instrument, which measures how the bank is able to meet its liquidity obligations.

5.4 Internal Bank

In this study, Internal Bank is the fourth indicator that has an eigenvalue equivalent to a value of 0.146, with the highest sub-indicator on risk management which includes Good Corporate Governance (GCG) as the variable that has the highest value.

Lopa et al.'s research (2019) concluded that Good Corporate Governance (GCG) has a negative and significant effect on banking risk. Second, Good Corporate Governance has a positive and significant impact on banking performance. Third, Banking Risk has a negative and significant impact on banking performance. Fourth, Good Corporate Governance has a positive and significant direct influence on banking performance. So that GCG has an important role in the Bank's Internal to be able to have a good performance in an effort to mitigate the risk of bank failure. This is in line with Setiawaty's research (2016) which states that the results of the study show that there is a direct and indirect influence of GCG on banking performance through risk management.

6. CONCLUSION

6.1. Conclusion

The results showed that the aspects/variables that were considered very priority and most important according to the top ranking were 1) macroeconomic variables with a weighted value of 0.35, 2) prudential micro variables with a weighted value of 0.7, 3) prudential macro variables with a weighted value of 0.23, and 4) Bank Internal variables with a weighted value with a weighted value of 0.15. Furthermore, the results of the study indicate which indicator components are considered the most important for the risk of failure of Rural Bank and Sharia Rural Bank. The indicator component of the Welfare Aspect on macroeconomic variables is the most important with a weighted value of 0.36. The component of the Liquidity indicator in the microprudential variable is the most important with a weighted value of 0.34. In addition, the Bank's Internal Resilience indicator on the macroprudential variable becomes very important with a weighted value of 0.56. Component Bank internal variable indicator component of Bank Risk Management indicator has a weighted value of 0.33.

6.2. Policy Recommendations

To the Government and Regulators

1. Issue and establish policies in the context of mitigating the risk of failure of Rural Bank and Sharia Rural Bank by taking into account microprudential factors, the main thing being the resilience of banks, especially the regulation of Loan to Value. The policy must reflect reward and punishment for Rural Bank in managing Loan to Value.
2. Issue and establish policies in the context of mitigating the risk of failure of Rural Bank and Sharia Rural Bank by taking into account microprudential factors primarily by maintaining good economic growth and reducing growth rates.
3. Issue and establish policies in the context of mitigating the risk of failure of Rural Bank and Sharia Rural Bank by taking into account macroprudential factors, mainly by establishing a Countercyclical Buffer (CCB) as a buffer for financial system stability. The policy must reflect rewards and punishments for Sharia Rural Banks in compliance with implementing Countercyclical Buffers (CCB).
4. Issue and establish policies in order to mitigate the risk of Rural Bank and Sharia Rural Bank failure by paying attention to improving the quality of Rural Bank and Sharia Rural Bank human resources by providing massive and continuous scholarships and training.
5. Issue and establish policies to support capacity building in the implementation of digitalization of Bank Operations at Rural Bank and Sharia Rural Banks by providing accessible tools in synergy with Conventional and Sharia Commercial Banks
6. Issue and establish policies to support capacity building in the implementation of Good Corporate Governance for Rural Bank and Sharia Rural Bank by organizing training for Rural Bank and Sharia Rural Bank staff.

REFERENCES

Alam, S., & Umar, F. (2019). PENGARUH GOOD COORPORATE GOVERNANCE, RISIKO PERBANKAN TERHADAP KINERJA PERBANKAN PADA BANK UMUM SWASTA DEVISA.

Alper, K., Binici, M., Demiralp, S., Kara, H., & Özlü, P. (2018). Reserve requirements, liquidity risk, and bank lending behavior. *Journal ofMoney, Credit and Banking*, *50*(4), 817–827. DOI: 10.1111/jmcb.12475

Anggraeni, A. (2020). dkk. 2020. Prediction Models for Bank Failure: ASEAN Countries. *JurnalEkonomi Malaysia*, *54*(2), 41–51.

Arno, A. K. (2018). Failure Bank dan Resiko Sistemik Perbankan (Sebuah Konsep Penanganan). Journal Of Institution And Sharia Fiance, 1.

Ascarya, P. (2011). The persistence of low profit and loss sharing financing in Islamic banking: The case of Indonesia. Review of Indonesian Economic and Business Studies, 1.

Athanasoglou, P. P., Daniilidis, I., & Delis, M. D. (2014). Bank procyclicality and output: Issues and policies. *Journal of Economics and Business*, *72*, 58–83. DOI: 10.1016/j.jeconbus.2013.10.003

Ayomi, S., &Hermanto, B. (2013). Mengukur Risiko Sistemik Dan Keterkaitan Finansial Perbankan Di Indonesia. *Buletin Ekonomi Moneter dan Perbankan, 16*(2), 103-125.

Bank Indonesia (BI). (2021). Kebijakan Makroprudensial. https://www.bi.go.id/id/fungsi-utama/stabilitas -sistem-keuangan/ikhtisar/Default.aspx#floating-2 (diakses pada 13 juli 2021)

Brei, M., Mohan, P., & Strobl, E. (2019). The impact of natural disasters on the banking sector: Evidence from hurricane strikes in the Caribbean. *The Quarterly Review of Economics and Finance*, *72*, 232–239. DOI: 10.1016/j.qref.2018.12.004

Brown, C. O., & Dinc, I. S. (2005). The politics of bank failures: Evidence from emerging markets. *The Quarterly Journal of Economics*, *120*(4), 1413–1444. DOI: 10.1162/003355305775097506

Chirwa, T. G., & Odhiambo, N. M. (2016). Macroeconomic determinants of economic growth: A review of international literature. The South East European Journal of Economics and Business, 11(2).

Dumičić, M. (2019). Linkages Between Fiscal Policy and Financial (In) Stability. *Journal of central banking theory and practice, 8*(1), 97-109.

Eichler, S., & Sobański, K. (2016). National politics and bank default risk in the eurozone. *Journal of Financial Stability*, *26*, 247–256. DOI: 10.1016/j.jfs.2016.07.008

Fatahullah, F. (2019). Eksistensi Wakaf Dengan Uang Dalam Sistem Hukum Indonesia. *Jatiswara*, *34*(2), 117–130. DOI: 10.29303/jtsw.v34i2.202

Fazio, D. M., Silva, T. C., Tabak, B. M., & Cajueiro, D. O. (2018). Inflation targeting and financial stability: Does the quality of institutions matter? *Economic Modelling*, *71*, 1–15. DOI: 10.1016/j.econmod.2017.09.011

Heryanah, H. (2017). Kesenjangan Pendapatan Di Indonesia: Berdasarkan Susenas 2008, 2011 Dan 2013. *Jurnal BPPK: Badan Pendidikan Dan Pelatihan Keuangan*, *10*(2), 43–58.

Hidajat, T. (2020). Rural banks fraud: A story from Indonesia. *Journal of Financial Crime*, *27*(3), 933–943. DOI: 10.1108/JFC-01-2020-0010

Kalatie, S., Laakkonen, H., & Tölö, E. (2015). Indicators used in setting the countercyclical capital buffer. Bank of Finland Research Discussion Paper(8).

Kara, G., & Vojtech, C. M. (2020). Bank Failures, Capital Buffers, and Exposure to the Housing Market Bubble. Capital Buffers, and Exposure to the Housing Market Bubble (July 20, 2020).

Lee, M.-C. (2010). The analytic hierarchy and the network process in multicriteria decision making: Performance evaluation and selecting key performance indicators based on ANP model. Convergence and Hybrid Information Technologies, 426.

Lembaga Penjamin Simpanan (LPS). 2020. Banyak Dana Korporasi Berpindah Ke bank-bank kecil, LPS ;Tanda Meningkatnya Kepercayaan Pada Sistem Perbankan. Siaran Pers Nomor: PRESS-42 /SEKL/2020

Lembaga Penjamin Simpanan (LPS). 2020. Kondisi Perbankan Stabil, Tidak Ada Bank Umum Yang Ditangani LPS. Siaran Pers Nomor: 35/X/2020

LPS. (2020). Lembaga Penjamin Simpanan - Banyak dana korporasi berpindah ke bank-bank kecil, LPS; Tanda meningkatnya kepercayaan pada sistem perbankan - Siaran Pers [Press release]. Retrieved from https://lps.go.id/web/guest/siaran-pers/-/asset_publisher/1T0a/content/banyak-dana-koorporasi-berpindah-ke-bank-bank-kecil-lps-tanda-meningkatnya-kepercayaan-pada-sistem-perbankan?inheritRedirect=false&redirect=https%3A%2F%2Flps.go.id%2Fweb%2Fguest%2Fsiaran-pers%3Fp_p_id%3D101_INSTANCE_1T0a%26p_p_lifecycle%3D0%26p_p_state%3Dnormal%26p_p_mode%3Dview%26p_p_col_id%3Dcolumn-2%26p_p_col_count%3D1

Margaretha, F., & Aditya, K. (2013). Pengaruh Resiko Likuiditas Terhadap Profitabilitas Bank Konvensional di Indonesia. *Journal of Accounting and Investment*, *14*(2), 96–105.

McDonald, J., & Johnson, S. M. (2010). Tax Policies To Improve The Stability Of Financial Markets. *Bank Of Italy Occasional Paper*.

Miskak, S. (2020). Kegagalan Analisis Laporan Keuangan Dalam Memprediksi Kebangkrutan BPR/BPRS di Indonesia. *Kajian Ekonomi Dan Keuangan*, *3*(3), 161–181.

Morgan, P. J., Regis, P. J., & Salike, N. (2019). LTV policy as a macroprudential tool and its effects on residential mortgage loans. *Journal of Financial Intermediation*, *37*, 89–103. DOI: 10.1016/j.jfi.2018.10.001

Noth, F., &Schüwer, U. (2018). Natural disaster and bank stability: Evidence from the US financial system.

Nugrohowati, R. N. I., & Bimo, S. (2019). Analisis pengaruh faktor internal bank dan eksternal terhadap Non-Performing Financing (NPF) pada Bank Perkreditan Rakyat Syariah di Indonesia. Jurnal Ekonomi & Keuangan Islam, 42-49.

Olilingo, F. Z., & Putra, A. H. P. K. (2020). How Indonesia economics works: Correlation analysis of macroeconomics in 2010-2019. *The Journal of Asian Finance, Economics and Business*, *7*(8), 117–130. DOI: 10.13106/jafeb.2020.vol7.no8.117

Oliveira, A., Martins, F. V., & Brandao, E. (2015). Bank failure and the financial crisis: An econometric analysis of US banks. *Available atSSRN* 2698881. DOI: 10.2139/ssrn.2698881

Otoritas Jasa Keuangan (OJK). (2019). *Buku I – OJK dan Pengawasan Makroprudensial.* Otoritas Jasa Keuangan.

Prastowo, P. (2018). Analisis regional keuangan inklusi perbankan syariah terhadap ketimpangan pendapatan di Indonesia. Jurnal Ekonomi & Keuangan Islam, 51-57.

Purwono, R., & Dimayanti, A. U. R. (2020). The effect of internal banking and macroeconomic variables on systemic risk. Polish Journal of Management Studies, 21.

Rustiarini, N. W., Suryandari, N. N. A., & Nova, I. K. S. (2016). Red flags and fraud prevention on rural banks. BuletinEkonomiMoneter dan Perbankan, 19(2), 177-206.

Rusydiana, A. S. (2016). Analisismasalahpengembanganperbankan syariah di Indonesia: Aplikasi Metode analytic network process. Esensi: Jurnal Bisnis dan Manajemen, 6(2), 237-246.

Rusydiana, A. S., & Devi, A. (2018). Elaborating cash waqf development in Indonesia using analytic network. International Journal of Islamic Business and Economics (IJIBEC), 1-13.

Rusydiana, A. S., Rani, L. N., & Hasib, F. F. (2019). Manakah indikator terpenting stabilitas sistem keuangan?: Perspektif makroprudensial. Jurnal Ekonomi dan Pembangunan, 27(1), 25-42.

Santosa, P. W., Setianingrum, A., & Huda, N. (2020). The Relationship of Macro-risk Indicators, Internal Factors, and Risk Profile of Islamic Banking in Indonesia. *ETIKONOMI*, *19*(2), 221–236. DOI: 10.15408/etk.v19i2.15528

Setiawaty, A. (2016). Pengaruh mekanisme good corporate governance terhadap kinerja perbankan dengan manajemen risiko sebagai variabel intervening. Kinerja. *Jurnal Ekonomi Dan Manajemen*, *13*(1), 13–24.

Silalahi, E. S. B. (2018). *Analisis Keterkaitan Kebijakan Mikroprudensial Dengan Kebijakan Makroprudensial Di Indonesia. Fakultas Ekonomi dan Bisnis*. Universitas Brawijaya Malang.

Simorangkir, I. (2011). Penyebab Bank Runs di Indonesia: Bad Luck atau Fundamental?.Buletin Ekonomi Moneter dan Perbankan, 14(1), 51-78.

Sipahi, S., & Timor, M. (2010). The analytic hierarchy process and analytic network process: An overview of applications. *Management Decision*, *48*(5), 775–808. DOI: 10.1108/00251741011043920

Siregar, P. A., Supitriyani, S., Parinduri, L., Astuti, A., Azwar, K., Simarmata, H. M. P., . . . Sudarmanto, E. (2021). Bank dan Lembaga Keuangan Lainnya: Yayasan Kita Menulis.

Syaputra, A. A., & Tohirin, A. (2019). Pengaruh kebijakan Financing to Value dan faktor ekonomi terhadap pembiayaan pemilikan rumah di bank syariah. In *Proceeding of Conference on Islamic Management, Accounting, and Economics* (pp. 190-199).

Tente, N., Stein, I., Silbermann, L., & Deckers, T. (2015). *The countercyclical capital buffer in Germany. Analytical framework for the assessment of an appropriate domestic buffer rate*. Deutsche Bundesbank.

Warjiyo, P. (2017). Indonesia: The Macroprudential Framework and the Central Bank's Policy Mix. BIS Paper, (94n).

Wenten, I. K., & Nadi, L. (2021). ANALISIS PENGARUH KEBIJAKAN LOAN TO VALUE, NON PERFORMING LOAN, LOAN TO DEPOSIT RATIO DAN SUKU BUNGA KREDIT TERHADAP SUPPLY KREDIT KEPEMILIKAN RUMAH PADA BANK TABUNGAN NEGARA. Jurnal Riset Akuntansi dan Keuangan, 9(1).

Yoel, E. M. T. (2016). Pengaruh kebijakan makroprudensial terhadap siklus kredit: Sebuah studi atas penggunaan instrumen CAR dan GWM perbankan Indonesia 2006-2013. *Bina Ekonomi*, *20*(1), 77–96.

Yunita, P. (2020). The Future of Indonesia Islamic Banking Industry: Bankruptcy Analyzing the Second Wave of Global Financial Crisis. [IJIEF]. *International Journal of Islamic Economics and Finance*, *3*(2), 199–226. DOI: 10.18196/ijief.3227

Yusron, M. (2020). Kondisi Perbankan Stabil, Tidak Ada Bank Umum Yang Ditangani LPS [Press release]. Retrieved from https://lps.go.id/web/guest/siaran-pers/-/asset_publisher/1T0a/content/banyak-dana-koorporasi-berpindah-ke-bank-bank-kecil-lps-tanda-meningkatnya-kepercayaan-pada-sistem-perbankan?inheritRedirect=false&redirect=https%3A%2F%2Flps.go.id%2Fweb%2Fguest%2Fsiaran-pers%3Fp_p_id%3D101_INSTANCE_1T0a%26p_p_lifecycle%3D0%26p_p_state%3Dnormal%26p_p_mode%3Dview%26p_p_col_id%3Dcolumn-2%26p_p_col_count%3D1

Chapter 8
Financial Inclusion and Access: Leveraging Fintech for Unbanked and Underbanked

Ram Singh
https://orcid.org/0000-0002-6565-3091
Symbiosis University of Applied Sciences, Indore, India

Divya Bisht
https://orcid.org/0009-0005-4888-0582
Government Degree College, Kunjwani, India

Jyotirmoy Banerjee
Amity University, Bengaluru, India

Rashi Garg
https://orcid.org/0009-0009-5297-3422
Institute of Management Studies, Noida, India

Prashant Kumar
https://orcid.org/0009-0006-0760-268X
Study Hall College, University of Lucknow, India

Deepika Verma
RCU Government PG College, Uttarkashi, India

ABSTRACT

Focusing on innovative resources and platforms that empower the underbanked and unbanked, this chapter considers the potential of fintech to promote financial inclusion. The aim of this chapter is to explore the ways that fintech can enhance financial inclusion by addressing the unique challenges that marginalized individuals face. It will explore various fintech applications that have the potential to transform financial services access in underserved markets, such as digital wallets, peer-to-peer lending, mobile banking, and blockchain technology. The chapter also seeks to assess how these technologies impact literacy, affordability, and financial inclusion. Methodologically, this chapter offers a systematic review of the state of the literature, case studies of international efforts in fintech, and data analysis to better understand how financial technologies may expand financial access. Some details on financial institutions will be combined with industry professionals to give comprehensive knowledge about the current fintech ecosystem.

DOI: 10.4018/979-8-3373-0209-6.ch008

1. INTRODUCTION

Financial inclusion is critical to achieving fair economic growth and access to timely, affordable and appropriately sized financial products and services for all, especially the underbanked and unbanked. Despite significant advancements, the challenge of financial exclusion is still a very real concern. According to the Global Findex Database (Kunt et al., 2021), 24% of adults worldwide did not have a bank account in 2021, disproportionately represented among women, rural areas, and the poor. Apart from limiting options for economic engagement and resilience against financial shocks, this exclusion further prolongs poverty. Due to their limited access to mainstream financial systems, the underbanked turn to alternative methods such as payday lenders or pawnshops to provide and retrieve financial services, while the unbanked do not have access to conventional financial institutions (Cámara & Tuesta, 2014). Some of the major setbacks to financial inclusion include lack of an official identity, low financial knowledge, a subpar physical banking infrastructure, and poor transaction costs (Chakrabarty, 2012). For those who do try to engage with finance, especially in rural areas, socio-cultural barriers to financial participation and geographic isolation compound these challenges, since most unbanked people are lower-income people living in rural areas (Singh, R. & Singh, V. P., 2025).

1.1 Financial Inclusion and Access:

The Financial inclusion is the process of ensuring that individuals and businesses, regardless of net worth or location, have access to valuable financial services. This includes payment systems, banking, credit, savings, and insurance. Financial access is a key enabler of economic empowerment, poverty reduction, and sustainable development, because it allows individuals and small businesses to invest in their own futures, manage risks, and build financial resilience. Yet despite the importance of financial inclusion, it remains a global problem. According to the World Bank's Global Findex Database, about 1.4 billion adults remained account less in 2021, 70 percent of whom were in low- and middle-income countries (Demirgüç-Kunt et al., 2021). Women, rural populations, and low-income individuals are among the groups disproportionately excluded from financial systems due to hurdles such as low financial literacy, high transaction costs, lack of identity, and limited access to traditional banking infrastructure. Fintech innovations are particularly disrupting the way these divides are being bridged. Fintech has employed digital platforms, mobile technologies, and data analytics to deliver financial services to previously underserved segments of the population. This wields changes like blockchain technology, mobile wallets, and digital payment systems that have made financial transactions more affordable and accessible. Biometric authentication and AI-based credit assessment (who's creditworthy) have enabled further access by solving the identification and creditworthiness problems, respectively.

1.2 Fintech in Advancing Financial Inclusion:

Financial technology, or fintech, is one powerful tool to narrow the gap between exclusion and inclusion in the financial world. Fintech is revolutionizing how financial services are designed, delivered, and made available either through emerging technologies such as blockchain, digital payment platforms, mobile money, and artificial intelligence. More than half of all adults in Kenya are integrated into the financial ecosystem at a modest cost through mobile money services such as M-Pesa, revolutionizing financial inclusion in the country by enabling safe and fairly priced transactions without requiring the traditional banking infrastructure (Jack & Suri, 2014). Technological advancements and government initiatives have led to the meteoric rise of the fintech sector in India. In January 2023 the Pradhan Mantri Jan Dhan Yojana (PMJDY), a financial inclusion programme, had opened more than 490 million bank accounts and most of these accounts were linked with mobile payment systems and integrated with Aadhaar for biometric authentication (RBI, 2023). In addition, the NPCI has launched the Unified Payments Interface (UPI) which allows seamless digital payments. Even semi-urban and rural areas were embracing UPI, with over 12 billion transactions on UPI monthly as of 2023 (NPCI, 2023)

1.3 Barriers Through Fintech:

Fintech is a solution which is revolutionizing financial inclusion, as it is addressing the major barrier with creative solutions. Biometric authentication systems, such as India's Aadhaar, have enabled the unbanked (or those without traditional identifying credentials) to get financial services by bridging the identity gap. AI-enabled credit scoring also fosters financial inclusion by extending credit to individuals who otherwise would not qualify for credit using traditional models (Ozili, 2020) by using alternative sources of data to ascertain creditworthiness (such as utility bill payments and mobile phone use). In addition, mobile money services and digital payment platforms greatly reduce transaction costs, decreasing the cost of financial services for bottom of the income pyramid segments. Fintech is also expanding geographic reach that brings financial services to rural and remote locations through agent networks and mobile applications to eliminate the requirement for physical banking infrastructure. Together, these trends create a financial ecosystem that is more accessible and inclusive.

1.4 Challenges in Leveraging Fintech:

Fintech is extremely powerful in promoting financial inclusion, but it does have challenges. The digital gap, a dynamic that manifests itself through contrasting degrees of smartphone uptake and internet access, continues to be a significant challenge — particularly in low-income countries. This leaves the fintech provider and consumer alike with uncertainty as regulatory frameworks often struggle to keep pace with the rapid evolution of technology (Arner et al., 2017). Also, due to data security and privacy concerns, vulnerable groups that may not know about digital protection measures could fall victim to scams.

1.5 Towards Inclusive Fintech Solutions:

This type of collaborative approach is necessary for fintech to achieve its goal of universal inclusion. Industry, financial institutions, and government must work together to establish regulatory frameworks that reasonably balance consumer protection with innovation. Interfaces in native languages or simplified, streamlined user interfaces are examples of how tailored solutions can meet the demands of different customer groups. Additionally, for fintech systems to be used fairly in the long run, it is vital to popularize digital literacy and trust in them. Encouraging digital literacy and building confidence in fintech systems are vital for these procedures to be adopted by all of society, not just the elite, in the long run.

1.6 Leveraging Fintech for Unbanked and Underbanked:

Fintech, a revolutionary product, provides relief to the unbanked and underbanked individuals suffering from various factors, such as lack of access to formal financial institutions or expensive alternative economic services. Innovative solutions that are enabled by technology make financial services more affordable, accessible, and convenient. A biometric authentication system such as India's Aadhaar system is a world-changing invention that allows people without traditional identity to securely access banking and other financial services. Furthermore, algorithms utilize alternative data, including cash flow, utility payment history, and mobile phone usage, to assess the creditworthiness of potential clients, thereby facilitating the provision of credit to individuals who do not conform to the traditional credit profile (Ozili, 2020). Digital payment platforms, such as peer-to-peer payment systems or mobile wallets, have drastically reduced transaction costs, allowing efficient and cost-effective transactions catering to low-income groups. By bypassing the need for an actual banking infrastructure, fintech also avoids regional limitations. Mobile applications and agent networks that provide financial services to rural and remote areas have opened up the formal financial ecosystem to underserved demographics. And blockchain, adding even more security and transparency, makes unbanked people feel safer while making digital transactions. These events have had an especially pronounced impact in countries like India, where government initiatives such as the Pradhan Mantri Jan Dhan Yojana (PMJDY) and the Unified Payments Interface (UPI) have integrated fintech solutions to empower millions. Good examples around the world, including Kenya's M-Pesa, demonstrate how fintech transforms lives by providing the poor with access to useful financial instruments. Fintech continues to advance, leveraging these technologies to navigate the gentle balance between financial exclusion and inclusion.

2. REVIEW OF LITERATURE

According to Kunt et al. (2021) There are 1.4 billion adults all over the world who are affected by the financial exclusion, and the most affected ones are the low-income groups, women, and the people from rural areas. They said that digital financial services such as online banking and mobile wallets are vital for overcoming traditional hurdles such as high transaction fees and geographic limitations. The study highlighted the potential of digital payments to enhance resilience and economic engagement, thereby reducing reliance on informal mechanisms. M-Pesa as a revolutionary mobile money platform was discussed by Jack & Suri (2014). They noted that M-Pesa had provided unbanked people with a safe and convenient way to access, transfer, and store cash. This one invention brought over half of Kenya's adult population into the banking system, reducing poverty and providing an increase in economic resilience. Key challenges to financial inclusion: Chakrabarty (2012) highlighted low literacy, lack of identity, and non-existence of banking infrastructure in rural areas as major roadblocks in the way of financial inclusion. He advocated for mobile platforms and biometric authentication to give disenfranchised individuals access to financial services. Cámara and Tuesta (2014) proposed a multidimensional index to measure financial inclusion in access, use, and quality of financial services. They argued that fintech has the potential to improve all of these quality dimensions by reducing the cost of, increasing the accessibility to, and improving the operation of services.

Ozili (2020) explored different AI uses to bridge the credit gap, highlighting how fintech platforms can assess creditworthiness for individuals who are not represented in traditional systems through alternative credit data, including utility payments, social media activity, and mobile phone usage. India's Aadhaar initiative has been instrumental in addressing identity challenges, and it has helped millions gain access to formal financial services. As per the Reserve Bank of India (2023), Aadhaar-linked accounts have reduced fraud and ensured that the benefits reach the right people, which is a prime example of how biometrics can help increase financial access. Arner et al. conducted a study on how regulatory sandboxes contributed to fintech innovation in 2017. They argued that for these solutions to scale, such frameworks must hit the right balance between protecting consumers and enabling experimentation. Through evidence from Kenya (Suri and Jack 2016), they demonstrated that mobile money led to an expansion of households' income and improvements in their financial stability. According to the report, increased access to mobile platforms for financial inclusion allows people to better manage risks and diversify income sources. UPI recorded over 12 billion monthly transactions in 2023 (National Payments Corporation of India, 2023). This rapid adoption demonstrates the potential for various fintech solutions to expand, ensuring accessibility for various demographics and bringing financial inclusion to India. Ghosh (2017) discussed how financial literacy is useful in helping increase adoption of fintech. Visual aids, as well as user-friendly interfaces in the native languages of rural populations, may yield better comprehension and acceptance of some digital financial instruments, he emphasized. The term bottom of the pyramid was introduced by Prahalad and Hammond (2002) through the lens of developing scalable, affordable fintech solutions. They demonstrated how such strategies can empower low-income populations and establish sustainable business opportunities.

For example, Burgess and Pande (2005) showed how rural banking initiatives in India improved agricultural production and lowered poverty. By overcoming physical barriers, fintech solutions such as agent networks and mobile banking could improve these outcomes, they argued. Cull et al. (2014) investigated the possible benefits for microfinance institutions of adopting fintech. They said digital platforms help increase outreach and operational efficiency and lower transaction costs for users and providers. As Beck et al. ascertain, economic growth and financial inclusion are strongly correlated. Beck et al. (2007) noted that inclusive institutions enable marginalized groups to invest in education, obtain loans, and operate their own businesses. According to Ratha et al. (2011), the cost of remittances has come down significantly due to fintech platforms such as mobile money and blockchain-based solutions, enabling even low-income households to pay for them. Rhyne and Otero (2006) focused on fintech as a key component of increasing the reach of microfinance. Digital solutions offer various repayment options, lower administrative expenses, and better loan monitoring, they argue.

According to Bhagat and Reddy (2019), in developing nations, a lack of digital literacy, infrastructure, and regulatory inequalities can also hinder the adoption of fintech. But to tackle these challenges, they drilled into the importance of public-private collaboration. Blockchain has the ability to create a secure and transparent digital ledger strategy, construct beliefs among unbanked individuals, and allow problem-free cross-border transactions (KPMG, 2020). Sahay et al. (2015) analyzed the ways that macroeconomic stability influences investment in human capital, reduces income inequality, and promotes savings in the context of financial inclusion. Kumar and Bhattacharya (2020) emphasized the need for women-specific fintech solutions targeted at rural areas to combat mobility issues, socio-cultural determinants, and digital illiteracy. In a 2016 estimate, the McKinsey Global Institute claimed that fintech innovations could add

$3.7 trillion to the world economy, largely by uplifting the underbanked and unbanked. Mohapatra et al. emphasized the significance of agent networks in connecting international remittances with the final stage of financial services. (2019). Such networks combined with digital platforms have helped improve access in rural areas significantly. Chattopadhyay (2019) highlighted the imperative for a clear regulatory framework to foster fintech developments. He argued that while policy clarity fosters innovation in the financial inclusion space, it also ensures consumer protection.

According to GPFI (2020), partnerships between government, private companies, and development organizations are vital for bringing fintech solutions to underserved areas. Mehrotra and Yetman (2015) found that financial inclusion facilitates savings and risk management, which strengthens household resilience in economic crises. As stated by Findex (2018), fintech has significantly contributed to the substantial rise of financial inclusion globally in the last decade. Some of the relevant elements that have been previously found to drive the adoption of fintech are digital literacy. Data show that usage and confidence in digital financial tools can be significantly improved by community-based training initiatives (Bhagat & Reddy, 2019). New types of microinsurance solutions targeted at low-income groups have become available through fintech platforms that manage risks like crop failures and medical issues (Cull et al., 2014). Emerging fintech applications for the youth demographic, along with a new technology-based financial consumer society, have enhanced financial literacy, gamified saving platforms, and improved saving habits (KPMG, 2020). The entry of fintech players has enhanced financial inclusion for underprivileged groups and increased the adoption of sustainable practices by incorporating environmental, social, and governance (ESG) factors (McKinsey Global Institute, 2016).

2.1 Research Gap

Despite the remarkable progress accomplished in utilizing fintech to sample financial inclusion, several research gaps exist. Despite studies illustrating the revolutionary potential of such platforms (refer to Jack & Suri, 2014), little research exists on the long-standing socioeconomic impact of mobile money platforms, including M-Pesa (Jack & Suri, 2014) and biometric authentication (Chakrabarty, 2012), on underprivileged communities, particularly in rural and low-income settings. Also, there are issues about the accuracy, fairness, and scalability of AI-powered credit scoring (Ozili, 2020) and nontraditional data sources, even though they have the potential to fill the credit gap. In addition, the regulatory implications of a blockchain-powered financial inclusion framework are largely unknown (KPMG, 2020), especially in aging countries suffering from weak financial infrastructure. Further, there is very limited comprehensive research that studies the intersection of gender, digital literacy, and fintech adoption (Kumar & Bhattacharya, 2020). Such research could lead to the development of more inclusive financial products. Finally, while fintech is widely recognized for reducing transaction costs (Suri & Jack, 2016), less is known about its impact on overall macroeconomic stability and resilience, particularly in the context of post-crisis recovery scenarios. These gaps indicate that in terms of fintech for financial inclusion to meaningfully advance, policy and practice require building out from more nuanced, context-specific research.

3. OBJECTIVES AND METHODOLOGY

With an emphasis on cutting-edge resources and platforms that enable the underbanked and unbanked, this chapter examines how fintech might be used to advance financial inclusion. This chapter's goal is to investigate how fintech can improve financial inclusion by tackling the particular difficulties marginalized people confront. It will examine a number of fintech models that could revolutionize underserved markets' access to financial services, including digital wallets, peer-to-peer lending, mobile banking, and blockchain technology. The chapter also attempts to evaluate how these technologies affect literacy, affordability, and financial accessibility. In order to assess how well fintech solutions enhance financial access, this chapter's methodology consists of a comprehensive examination of the body of existing literature, case studies from international fintech efforts, and data analysis. A thorough understanding of the present fintech ecosystem will be provided by combining information from financial institutions and insights from industry professionals.

4. FINTECH AND FINANCIAL INCLUSION

Fintech has emerged as a powerful tool in the push for financial inclusion, particularly in regions where large segments of the citizenry remain unbanked. Fintech helps with providing financial services to underserved populations who would not have access to traditional financial services due to their location, lack of government issued identification or good credit history made possible through the use of digital technologies. Mobile money systems, such as M-Pesa in Kenya, have changed the game in financial inclusion (Jack & Suri, 2014) by removing the need for physical bank branches and enabling users to transfer, receive, and save money through a single cell phone. Millions of people without formal identification documents are now able to use fundamental banking services such as opening bank accounts and obtaining loans due to biometric authentication systems (for example, India has put in place the Aadhaar programme) (Chakrabarty, 2012). In addition, AI-powered credit scoring systems, which utilise alternative data, such as utility bill payment or mobile phone usage (Ozili, 2020), have also extended credit to individuals who had been previously excluded from formal financial systems due to the absence of conventional credit histories. This reduces the reliance on traditional scores, which often exclude excluded groups, and enables lenders to evaluate creditworthiness in a more inclusive and scalable manner.) Moreover, especially in the realm of cross-border transfers, fintech has driven down transaction costs dramatically, making financial services more affordable for low income individuals (Suri & Jack, 2016). Platforms like WorldRemit and PayPal have greatly reduced the cost of remittances (Ratha et al., 2011), and in doing so, have given people in developing nations much easier access to financial resources. The expansion of fintech is also solving geographical barriers that have made accessing financial services difficult, particularly in rural and remote areas. Digital payment systems and mobile banking applications allow financial institutions to serve underprivileged individuals without the necessity of developing an extensive physical infrastructure (Arner et al., 2017). Through these developments, it has immensely impacted women empowerment, financial inclusion, supporting small businesses, and contributing to economic growth.

4.1 Role of Fintech in Financial Inclusion

4.1.1 Mobile Money Platforms and Access to Financial Services:

One of the most potential fintech advancements in terms of financial inclusion is the advent of mobile money platforms. In countries like Kenya, M-Pesa has transformed the way that people, particularly those living in rural or underserved communities, access financial services. M-Pesa enables users to send, receive, and store money through their phones, all without needing a physical banking infrastructure or conventional bank account. This technology has broadened financial inclusion tremendously, providing consumers with an easy and accessible mechanism that facilitates the management of their funds in a cost-effective manner (Jack & Suri, 2014). M-Pesa's success was a demonstration of mobile money's potential to overcome geographical barriers and improve financial inclusion of underbanked population in developing economies.

4.1.2 AI-Driven Credit Scoring for Unbanked Populations:

One of the critical challenges that has been addressed by fintech is providing lending access to those who do not have a bank account or credit history. Many underserved individuals lack access to loans only because they do not possess official financial records, especially in developing countries. Fintech firms are addressing this issue by assessing creditworthiness through alternative data streams. AI-powered credit scoring algorithms provide access to people who were previously denied financial services based on traditional credit scoring models (Ozili, 2020); the new models utilize information such as social media activity, energy bill payments, and mobile phone usage. Some businesses, like Tala and Branch, for example, use smartphone data to assess credit risk and extend microloans to individuals in regions with minimal formal credit infrastructure.

4.1.3 Digital Financial Education and Literacy:

In addition, fintech is being a game-changer of financial literacy, especially deprived sections of society. Most low-income people don't know how to invest, get loans and manage money. Fintech digital platforms have begun to provide educational materials to promote financial literacy. These platforms often include educational resources, money management tools, and personalized advice to help users make informed choices. This has most benefited women and rural people, who typically have limited access to formal financial literacy interventions (Kumar & Bhattacharya, 2020). Fintech helps consumers to make better loan, investment, and savings decisions by making financial education widely accessible on digital channels.

4.1.4 Blockchain and Digital Payments for Reducing Transaction Costs:

Another area where fintech is helping is by reducing the cost of financial transactions. Cross-border remittances are often a lifeline for families in developing nations, but they are usually expensive on account of long transmission times and steep transaction fees. Blockchain technology and digital remittance providers such as Transfer Wise (now Wise) and Western Union's mobile platform have made it cheaper for people to send and receive payments abroad. These prevent high transaction fees for the low-income migrants, as the digital currencies and blockchain technology make it possible to transfer internationally fast, securely and inexpensively (Ratha et al., 2011). This is critical for those who rely on remittances for their livelihood because it ensures that more of the money can be sent to the intended recipient (Singh, R., et. al. (2025).

4.1.5 Expansion of Financial Services through Digital Infrastructure:

One of the biggest challenges that has historically made it difficult to access banking services is geographic constraints, but fintech is addressing this issue as well. Mobile banking, digital payments, and agent networks can enable the offering of basic financial services even in rural and remote locations with few traditional bank branches. Fintech platforms can therefore access people in the most remote areas across the globe and do not need a lot of physical infrastructure. This matters more in places without physical banks are unreachable owing to poor road systems or high operating costs. Through the use of digital banking services, fintech allows individuals to easily open bank accounts, take loans and purchase insurance products (Arner et al., 2017).

4.1.6 Financial Inclusion for Women and Vulnerable Groups:

Fintech is critical to empower underrepresented groups, particularly women. Providing financial services to women especially in developing countries can be more challenging due to various reasons including cultural barriers, lack of legal identity and low financial literacy. Examples of fintech solutions are peer-to-peer lending, microfinance platforms, and mobile banking, which make it easier for women to have a say in their financial decisions and access to resources they require, Kumar and Bhattacharya (2020) state that Fintech improves economic equality and inclusion by offering a digital platform that helps to remove financial barriers between genders. (Kumar & Bhattacharya, 2020).

5. INNOVATIVE TOOLS & PLATFORMS: UNBANKED & UNDERBANKED

In order Innovative tools and platforms are essential to enable underbanked and unbanked populations to utilize the financial services that were once out of reach. It employs technology to reduce barriers to financial inclusion, such as exclusion from formal financial systems, absence of formal identification, and distance from financial services. The following are some of the notable innovations:

5.1 Mobile Money Platforms:

Mobile money has completely changed the financial situation of millions of people in countless nations, especially those developing ones, who are unbanked. Platforms like GCash in the Philippines and M-Pesa in Kenya have created a simple, effective way for users to transfer, receive and retain money using their mobile phones. Because these platforms do not need a traditional bank account, everyone who have been excluded from the official financial system can use them. Mobile money also facilitates savings, credit, and insurance, in addition to being a general system for delivering financial services (via mobile devices) (Jack & Suri, 2014). This innovation has benefited a particular group of people, those who live in rural or isolation areas and are generally unable to access financial institutions.

5.2 Blockchain and Cryptocurrency:

Cryptocurrency and blockchain technology are changing the pathway to financial inclusion by providing an alternative to traditional banking systems. By removing intermediaries for users, these technologies enable peer-to-peer transactions among users thus reducing transaction costs and cost of cross-border payments. People in countries with fragile or unstable economies are also gaining from being able to access financial services without needing to rely on traditional banking infrastructure thanks to cryptocurrencies like Bitcoin and Ethereum Blockchain platforms such as Stellar and Ripple aim at reducing the cost of cross-border remittance and making it easy for migrant workers to send money home (Narula, 2020).

5.3 Peer-to-Peer (P2P) Lending Platforms:

Peer-to-peer (P2P) lending platforms have gained popularity as an alternative to traditional bank loans over time. These platforms offer lower interest rates by cutting out the middleman and linking borrowers directly with private lenders. This will particularly be of benefit to the underbanked, as many of them don't have collateral or a credit history that makes it difficult for them to obtain a loan from a traditional financial institution. (Aker et al., 2016)

5.4 AI and Alternative Credit Scoring:

AI-enabled credit rating systems are upending traditional due diligence, allowing underbanked groups to gain access to credit. Many people in the unbanked population do not have existing credit histories, which traditional credit vetting methodologies rely on. Fintech companies are assessing consumers' creditworthiness through the use of alternative data such as utility bill payments, social media activity and mobile phone usage. Using smartphone data, Tala and Branch are allowing microloans to be made to these new borrowers that would never be approved in the traditional lending system (Ozili, 2020). Thanks to this, a large segment of the population who were previously underserved by formal credit markets is being served with credit.

5.5 Biometric Authentication:

In specific regions where individuals do not have legitimate identification documents, technologies for biometric authentication including finger print recognition and facial scanning are helping to overcome challenges in identification. Aadhaar in India is a great example of such a system, where a biometric identity number is generated for 1.2 billion people. It enables people to apply for loans, open bank accounts, and access government services even in the absence of official documentation (Chakrabarty, 2012). Likewise, financial institutions deploy biometric technologies for secure access to financial services, thereby enhancing accessibility as well as security.

5.6 Digital Wallets:

Use of digital wallets is gaining ground among unbanked and underbanked individuals, both domestically and internationally. These systems allow individuals to use their cellphones to conveniently transfer money, conduct transactions and hold funds online. Digital wallets have been particularly useful in markets lacking traditional banking services because they allow users to manage their money electronically without needing a real bank account. Moreover, digital wallets provide a secure way to handle money and often are associated with other financial technology products including mobile payments and peer-to-peer loans (Suri & Jack, 2016).

5.7 Microinsurance Platforms:

Microinsurance has emerged as an important tool for providing low-income and underserved segments with affordable insurance access. Through digital platforms, fintech companies offer insurance coverage with lower premiums and simplified claim processes. Bima and MicroEnsure are two providers of microinsurance to low-income communities in countries including Bangladesh, Tanzania, and Kenya. These platforms use mobile phones to distribute insurance products and process claims, enabling people who may not have otherwise have had enough money or connections to engage with traditional insurance providers (Karlan et al., 2014).

5.8 Digital Savings Programs:

Digital savings programs such as Kiva and M-Shwari in Kenya, the underbanked can access loans based on savings, and secure their savings in a safe place. By means of these services, consumers can set aside small amounts of cash using their smartphones, making money off their savings. Banks provide their customers with a history of savings so they are able to lend to the unbanked to establish a cycle of credit and saving Digital savings programs help people cope with crises and improve their financial security by helping people build financial resilience (Suri & Jack, 2016).

5.9 Fintech-Enabled Financial Literacy Tools:

Financial literacy remains a significant barrier to financial inclusion for many marginalized populations. Fintech companies have developed digital tools to elevate financial literacy by offering personalized financial advice, budgeting tools and easy-to-understand educational materials. Sites like Mint and Money Dashboard provide users with details about their spending habits, help them plan budgets and offer tips on how to manage their money. By improving financial literacy, these platforms allow users to make the best use of available financial services and make better informed financial decisions (Kumar & Bhattacharya, 2020). Revolutionary fintech solutions and platforms are breaking new ground in financial inclusion by addressing the unique challenges faced by underbanked and unbanked populations. The changes addressed both processes of money lending, loaning, cashless services, that incorporate blockchain technology and biometrics identification systems, mobile money platforms with AI-based credit scoring mechanisms that aid millions in accessing their desired financial services, thus providing them with the opportunity of minimum transactions of cash with maximum services available to elevate the overall structure of their financial well-being.

6. CHALLENGES FOR MARGINALIZED COMMUNITIES IN FINTECH AND FINANCIAL INCLUSION

Fintech services and financial inclusion is often hard to access among marginalized groups including low-income people, women, people living in rural areas and ethnic minority members. While fintech has massive potential to address these barriers, it faces some hurdles of its own. Here are some of the primary barriers underserved populations face to accessing fintech and financial inclusion:

6.1 Digital Divide and Lack of Access to Technology:

One of the biggest problems lower-income individuals and communities face is the digital divide, or the disparity between those who have access to technology and those who do not. Many people in rural or less developed places do not have reliable access to a computer, a smartphone, and the internet, which are also required to use fintech services such as online lending, digital payments, and mobile banking. If these groups do not have access to these devices, they are essentially shut out of the digital financial ecosystem, forcing them to rely on conventional financial services that are often more difficult to access (van der Zwan et al., 2020).

6.2 Limited Financial Literacy:

Financial literacy is one of the largest hurdles to financial inclusion, particularly for underbanked communities. Many in these communities are not equipped with the information and skills to navigate digital payments or navigate fintech platforms or even understand concepts like credit or insurance or savings. Women are the more vulnerable group to financial exclusion due to poor financial literacy rates observed in many of the developing nations (Kumar & Bhattacharya, 2020)

6.3 Lack of Trust in Digital Financial Services:

Trust is another major obstacle to using fintech services for underprivileged populations. In some areas where people are not used to digital banking, or have previously been a victim of fraud or exploitation by financial entities, there is likely to be a pronounced distrust of digital financial services. They are worried about fraud, scams and the security of personal information, and are therefore reluctant to use digital wallets, online lending platforms or mobile money. This is especially true for low income or rural communities, who can be more vulnerable to financial exploitation (Finlay, 2017).

6.4 Exclusion Due to Lack of Formal Identification:

In rural or underdeveloped areas, many marginalized people do not have any documents of their identification to register them in the fintech services or for generating a bank account. Elsewhere, such systems are not widespread or efficient, as in the case of countries like India, which has adopted the Aadhaar system to use biometric identification to facilitate access to services. Their exclusion from formal identification systems (Chakrabarty, 2012) limits marginalized populations' access to fintech platforms and their rhythm in the dance of the digital economy.

6.5 Gender Barriers:

Gender inequality is one of the main reasons why financial inclusion is still lagging especially when it comes to women in less developed countries. In many places in the world, women are financially excluded because of social rules, lack of mobility, and lower levels of education and financial literacy. Despite the availability of fintech products, women are often unable to take advantage of digital financial solutions because they do not have control of home finances.

6.6 Inadequate Legal and Regulatory Framework:

The lack of a comprehensive legal and regulatory framework for fintech can also be troublesome in the context of underserved populations. Fintech companies can operate in a gray area with no clearly defined laws and regulations, which can expose customers to abuse. In many developing countries, rules regulating online lending, mobile money, and other fintech products are still in their early days, which can create confusion and prevent underserved segments of society from benefiting fully from fintech solutions. This issue is further exacerbated by the absence of consumer protection laws, which makes it harder for individuals to recover from potential fraud or losses (Arner et al., 2017).

6.7 High Costs and Hidden Fees:

Although Fintech is often marketed as a low-cost option compared with traditional banking, it may still come with hidden or other fees that are disproportionately burdensome on the low-income. For example, they might charge high fees for cash-out services or for sending money to that person in a rural area, even as they lower transaction costs. These expenses may sap the meager earnings of marginalized people, undercutting the overall benefit of fintech services. Moreover, price structures on digital platforms can be complicated and people with low financial literacy may find it difficult to understand (Rai & Choudhary, 2018).

6.8 Cultural and Linguistic Barriers:

Linguistic and cultural aspects play an significant role in the acceptance and use of fintech services in most underprivileged divisions. Often, fintech platforms adopt a one-size-fits-all approach that may not take account of the linguistic, cultural and personal preferences of different segments. Digital financial systems, for instance, may be inapplicable to local norms, such as a preference for cash transactions or social lending practices; in addition, they may not exist in local languages. These barriers can leave people who could otherwise benefit from fintech services feeling left behind (Kunt et al., 2018).

6.9 Limited Credit History:

Many members of marginalized populations having lack of credit histories, making it difficult for them to obtain loans or other financial goods. People without bank accounts or credit histories don't qualify for traditional credit scoring models, which derive a person's creditworthiness from their financial history with formal institutions. Whereas fintech companies have begun to assess creditworthiness based on alternative data such as utility bill payments or mobile phone usage, such methods are still not common, and many find themselves excluded from financial services for that reason (Ozili, 2020).

6.10 Geographical Barriers:

Underprivileged groups living in remote rural regions face significant obstacles to adopting financial technology platforms due to deficiencies in infrastructure and internet access. Electricity, too, is limited. While mobile phones are widespread, the lack of physical access points like agent offices and kiosks concentrated in cities further disadvantages those residing in the countryside. Even where mobile money is readily available, efficient use may be impeded by inadequate utilities and poor connectivity (Patnaik, R., et. al. 2022).

7. FINTECH: FINANCIAL ACCESSIBILITY, AFFORDABILITY, & LITERACY

Fintech has revolutionized financial literacy, affordability, and accessibility by providing innovative solutions to historically underserved groups. Its impact on these three aspects can be understood in various ways, facilitating improved money management and greater financial inclusion.

7.1 Impact on Financial Accessibility:

Fintech, which offers digital alternatives to traditional banking, has been essential in improving financial accessibility. Due to economic, geographical, infrastructure or political constraints, many individuals and communities have faced barriers preventing participation in mainstream financial systems. However, the emergence of peer-to-peer lending platforms, digital wallets accessible via smartphones and computers, and online banking options without need for physical branches have eliminated such obstacles. As a consequence, populations previously cut off from conventional banking now gain access to a diversity of important financial services including but not limited to insurance, savings accounts, and loans (Narain, 2019). Moreover, in areas lacking extensive organized banking infrastructure, digital tools enabling money transfer, bill payment, and savings via mobile phones or internet have become indispensable for handling financial needs without the requirement of a standard bank account (Suri & Jack, 2016).

7.2 Impact on Financial Affordability:

Additionally, fintech has served to make financial services more financially feasible, especially for individuals with more modest means. Traditional banking frequently imposed outrageous charges for access to loans, ATM withdrawals, and account maintenance, rendering financial services unaffordable for underserved populations. Meanwhile, fintech platforms generally offer lower transaction costs and reduced prices for services such as lending, payments, and money transfers. Millions have been able to safely send and receive funds without incurring exorbitant fees thanks to mobile money services like M-Pesa in Kenya, which provide reasonably priced remittance options (Aker & Mbiti, 2010). The credit gap for marginalized groups is also increasingly addressed through the emergence of microloan platforms, allowing those with brief credit histories to secure small loans at reasonable interest levels (Ozili, 2020).

By lowering the expense of financial services, fintech serves to make them more cost effective for those previously unable to access them due to excessive charges.

7.3 Impact on Financial Literacy:

By providing instructional materials and tools that assist people in understanding and managing their finances, fintech platforms have also helped to increase financial literacy. To assist consumers in making smarter financial decisions, a few fintech platforms offer personalized recommendations and tailored financial advice based on individual circumstances and objectives. To help users better grasp personal finance management, some applications include sophisticated yet simple to use features including investment advice customized to risk tolerance, real-time cost tracking with spend categorization and alerts, as well as comprehensive yet straightforward budgeting tools. Furthermore, users can learn about savings vehicles, loan options, insurance products, and alternative investment strategies in an engaging and relatable way through interactive digital financial education modules frequently integrated into fintech platforms. People with little prior financial knowledge, who might otherwise have struggled to comprehend intricate financial instruments, have found these resources to be remarkably illuminating according to studies (Demirgüç-Kunt et al., 2018). Additionally, by enabling ongoing monitoring and analytics of current spending patterns, past saving habits, and future budget targets, fintech has promoted heightened financial mindfulness and enhanced people's capacity to make prudent fiscal decisions according to research (Duflo et al., 2013). Fintech has had a revolutionary impact on financial understanding, affordability, and access to services, especially benefiting those residing in under-resourced or marginalized communities. Fintech has reduced the expense of transactions and financial offerings, bridged gaps to financial services, and furnished customers with helpful tools for self-paced financial learning through inventive digital remedies. In addition to advancing financial inclusion, these advancements provide people augmented influence over their financial destiny. To fully realize fintech's potential for furthering financial participation and optimizing monetary outcomes, however, pressing issues including digital proficiency, data privacy concerns, and regulatory hurdles still need to be addressed.

8. FINDINGS AND SUGGESTIONS

8.1 Findings

8.1.1 Increased Access to Financial Services:

There are various obstacles such as geographical isolation, lack of infrastructure, and costly fees inhibited widespread financial access. Particularly for remote and rural locales, innovative platforms such as M-Pesa have effectively provided banking alternatives to the unbanked and underserved through cellular networks. Individuals lacking traditional accounts can now employ mobile devices to engage an array of monetary handles, including accruing savings, exchanging and receiving funds, and facilitating purchases (Aker & Mbiti, 2010).

8.1.2 Reduction in Transaction Costs:

Fintech's primary advantages involves diminished expenses correlated with money transfers, remittances, and other financial undertakings. Thanks to digital payment systems and mobile banking options, the outlays pertaining to such activities have noticeably dwindled. This has enabled those with limited incomes to obtain previously unattainable services because of exorbitant levies imposed by remittance agencies or conventional banking institutions (Narain, 2019). Moreover, owing to its capacity to reduce costs, fintech has further expanded inclusion for underserved groups.

8.1.3 Improved Financial Literacy:

Financial technology applications offering instruction on budgeting, saving strategies, and money management have certainly helped further financial literacy for some, their impact remains limited. A variety of digital platforms provide customized counsel to clients, sharing tips and budgeting tools aimed at efficient funds oversight. However, their influence on improved financial decision making through enabling expense and savings tracking remains minimal, as many folks, notably in underdeveloped rural areas where educational resources are scarce, continue struggling with financial acumen (Mishra, V., & Singh, J. 2022).

8.1.4 Gender and Social Barriers:

Gender and community barriers persist in accessing financial technologies, especially oppressively in less developed nations. Significant impediments stem from cultural norms insufficiently addressed, lacking digital proficiency, and constrained access to mobile devices and internet connectivity. Women may lack autonomy over household finances, constricting their capability to utilize available financial technologies even where offered. Moreover, the monetary marginalization of these populations is exacerbated by issues including sparse credit histories and lack of official identification, cementing financial exclusion.

8.1.5 Regulatory and Infrastructure Challenges:

Even fintech shows great promise to transform our financial system, many countries continue developing regulatory frameworks to support such innovation. In locations where consumer laws offer insufficient protection, customers remain at risk of fraud or exploitation since legal guidelines fail to fully address new technologies. Furthermore, the potential of fintech solutions often goes unrealized in some areas due to a lack of basic infrastructure. Dependable internet access, most notably in rural communities, forms the lifeblood through which these services flow. However, the digital divide stubbornly persists in many regions worldwide. Consequently, those living on the wrong side of this gap find themselves unable to access or benefit from the emerging financial technologies rapidly being adopted elsewhere (Arner et al., 2017).

8.2 Suggestions

8.2.1 Invest in Digital Infrastructure and Connectivity:

Investing in digital infrastructure is crucial to maximizing the opportunities of fintech, particularly in remote and isolated areas. For underprivileged groups to fully benefit from fintech services, improved internet access, mobile network coverage, and affordable smartphones are essential. Governments and private businesses must work together to close the digital divide and increase access to fintech solutions (Kumra, R., & Arora, S. 2022).

8.2.2 Enhance Financial Literacy Programs:

Financial literacy remains an important issue requiring improvement, especially among underserved communities. More knowledge of digital banking tools can be promoted through specially designed educational initiatives tailored to the specific needs of groups like women and rural populations. Using mobile platforms and apps, fintech companies and non-profits can collaborate to develop and apply financial literacy programs offering comprehensible and accessible resources to enhance financial decision making. (Demirgüç-Kunt et al., 2018).

8.2.3 Regulatory Frameworks for Consumer Protection:

Thorough regulatory frameworks for consumer protection, competition encouragement, and fraud prevention must be established by governments. Precise regulations for mobile money, digital payments, and digital lending in addition to transparency assurance systems are needed. According to Arner et al. (2017), regulatory certainty will also boost customer confidence and trust in fintech services, allowing for broader adoption among underserved areas.

8.2.4 Address Gender-Specific Barriers:

Gender-specific barriers preventing women's to access fintech deserve special attention. Initiatives like women's smartphone and mobile device access, digital literacy encouragement for women, and customized financial services for women can significantly reduce gender inequality in financial inclusion. Fintech platforms should also incorporate tools empowering women financially and catering to their unique needs, such as healthcare financing and family budget management. (Kumar & Bhattacharya, 2020).

8.2.5 Use of Alternative Credit Scoring Models:

Fintech companies should use alternative credit scoring techniques beyond conventional credit histories to ensure more inclusive participation. Alternative data like social networks, utility payments, and mobile phone use help estimate creditworthiness for those without official records, opening up insurance and loans otherwise inaccessible under traditional models in underserved areas.(Ozili, 2020).

8.2.6 Collaboration with Local Communities:

Companies must work with local communities to understand specific needs and preferences, boosting fintech solution relevance and effectiveness. Collaborating with community leaders and organizations can foster confidence and ensure cultural relevance and convenience, promoting greater adoption among marginalized populations and overcoming aversion to digital financial technologies. (Van der Zwan et al., 2020).

9. CONCLUSION AND DIRECTION FOR FUTURE RESEARCH

9.1 Conclusion:

Fintech has empowered underprivileged populations by increasing access to financial services, lowering transaction costs, and enhancing financial literacy through digital platforms like mobile money, peer-to-peer lending, and alternative credit scoring. Notwithstanding these developments, there are still issues, namely with regard to internet infrastructure, gender inequality, legal frameworks, and financial literacy. In order for fintech to fully realize its potential in promoting financial inclusion, these obstacles must be removed. Fintech solutions must be specifically designed to meet the requirements of marginalized groups, such as low-income individuals, women, and rural communities, if they are to have a significant impact. Furthermore, to guarantee the sustainability and inclusivity of fintech technologies, strong regulatory frameworks, consumer protection policies, and enhanced digital infrastructure are essential.

9.2 Direction for Future Research:

While the role of fintech in promoting financial inclusion is becoming clearer, there are several areas that require further exploration:

9.2.1 Impact of Fintech on Financial Behavior:

The effect of using fintech solutions on the financial behavior or decision-making process of individuals belonging to the underbanked and unbanked groups should be a topic to be explored by further researches. Understanding how these tools influence credit usage, saving patterns, and overall financial health will help clarify how effectively fintech persuades individuals to change their financial behaviors.

9.2.2 Gender and Socioeconomic Barriers:

Future research can investigate multidimensionality of gender and income or another dimensions of technology adoption because socioeconomic and gender barriers still limit access to fintech services. To drive inclusive growth, research needs to be conducted on how fintech can be better designed to meet the specific needs women and underserved populations.

9.2.3 Regulatory and Legal Frameworks:

Strong regulatory and legal frameworks have to emerge in the fintech industry to ensure consumer safety, promote fair competition, and prevent fraudulent activities. Future research can investigate whether, and how, international norms for fintech regulation can be established, and how adoption rates and customer trust are impacted in other nations by their regulatory approach to the industry.

9.2.4 Sustainability of Fintech Solutions:

Investigate the long-term sustainability of the Fintech solutions especially for the developing countries How viable are business models based on mobile money and microlending platforms in the light of economic obstacles such as inflation or political unrest? Moreover, conducting more research into the environmental effects of fintech would be good, because the rapid growth of the industry could have unexpected ecological consequences.

9.2.5 Digital Financial Literacy:

Future research can study the effectiveness of fintech-facilitated financial education efforts in the context of digital literacy's impact on effective use of fintech solutions. Research could focus on developing targeted digital literacy initiatives for specific populations, and measuring the outcomes on financial inclusion.

REFERENCES

Aker, J. C., Boumnijel, R., McClelland, A., & Tierney, N. (2016). Payment mechanisms and mobile money adoption in Niger. *Journal of Development Economics, 118*, 148–159. DOI: 10.1016/j.jdeveco.2015.12.003

Aker, J. C., & Mbiti, I. M. (2010). Mobile phones and economic development in Africa. *The Journal of Economic Perspectives, 24*(3), 207–232. DOI: 10.1257/jep.24.3.207

Arner, D. W., Barberis, J., & Buckley, R. P. (2017). FinTech, regtech, and the reconceptualization of financial regulation. *Northwestern Journal of International Law & Business, 37*(3), 371-413. https://scholarlycommons.law.northwestern.edu/njilb/vol37/iss3/2

Beck, T., Demirgüç-Kunt, A., & Levine, R. (2007). Finance, inequality, and the poor. *Journal of Economic Growth, 12*(1), 27–49. DOI: 10.1007/s10887-007-9010-6

Bhagat, C., & Reddy, S. (2019). Overcoming digital literacy barriers in fintech adoption. *International Journal of Financial Studies, 7*(3), 45–58. DOI: 10.3390/ijfs7030045

Burgess, R., & Pande, R. (2005). Do rural banks matter? Evidence from the Indian social banking experiment. *The American Economic Review, 95*(3), 780–795. DOI: 10.1257/0002828054201242

Cámara, N., & Tuesta, D. (2014). Measuring financial inclusion: A multidimensional index. *BBVA Research Working Paper*, No. 14/26. Retrieved from https://www.bbvaresearch.com

Chakrabarty, K. C. (2012). Financial inclusion: Issues in measurement and analysis. *Reserve Bank of India Bulletin*, May 2012, 75-81. Retrieved from https://www.rbi.org.in

Chattopadhyay, S. (2019). Regulatory sandboxes for financial inclusion. *Economic and Political Weekly, 54*(32), 32–37. https://www.epw.in/

Cull, R., Demirgüç-Kunt, A., & Morduch, J. (2014). Banks and microfinance: Institutions, stability, and growth. *World Bank Policy Research Working Paper No. 7136.* https://doi.org/DOI: 10.1596/1813-9450-7136

Demirgüç-Kunt, A., Klapper, L., Singer, D., Ansar, S., & Hess, J. (2021). *The Global Findex Database 2021: Financial Inclusion, Digital Payments, and Resilience in the Age of COVID-19.* World Bank. https://doi.org/DOI: 10.1596/978-1-4648-1751-1

Demirgüç-Kunt, A., Klapper, L. F., Singer, D., & Van Oudheusden, P. (2018). *The Global Findex Database 2017: Measuring financial inclusion and the fintech revolution.* World Bank., DOI: 10.1596/978-1-4648-1259-0

Duflo, E., Kremer, M., & Robinson, J. (2013). Nudging in education. *Brookings Papers on Economic Activity, 2013*(2), 1–56. https://www.brookings.edu/bpea-articles/nudging-in-education/

Finlay, R. (2017). Building trust in fintech: Solutions for overcoming digital finance's barriers. *Journal of Financial Services Marketing, 22*(1), 39–52. DOI: 10.1057/s41264-017-0032-0

Ghosh, S. (2017). How financial literacy and awareness drive fintech adoption. *Economic and Political Weekly, 52*(9), 23–26. https://www.epw.in/

Global Partnership for Financial Inclusion (GPFI). (2020). *Fintech for financial inclusion: A framework for digital financial services*. https://www.gpfi.org/publications

Jack, W., & Suri, T. (2014). Risk sharing and transactions costs: Evidence from Kenya's mobile money revolution. *The American Economic Review, 104*(1), 183–223. DOI: 10.1257/aer.104.1.183

Karlan, D., Ratan, A. L., & Zinman, J. (2014). Savings by and for the poor: A research review and agenda. *Review of Income and Wealth, 60*(1), 36–78. DOI: 10.1111/roiw.12101 PMID: 25792764

KPMG. (2020). The future of blockchain in financial inclusion. *KPMG Insights*. https://home.kpmg/xx/en/home/insights.html

Kumar, R., & Bhattacharya, P. (2020). Gender-sensitive fintech innovations for rural women. *Journal of Gender Studies, 29*(4), 510–523. DOI: 10.1080/09589236.2020.1744611

Kumra, R., & Arora, S. (2022). Digital Sensory Marketing Factors Affecting Customers' Intentions to Continue Organic Online Purchases during COVID in India. *FIIB Business Review, 0*(0), 23197145221105674. Advance online publication. DOI: 10.1177/23197145221105674

McKinsey Global Institute. (2016). Digital finance for all: Powering inclusive growth in emerging economies. https://www.mckinsey.com/mgi

Mehrotra, A., & Yetman, J. (2015). Financial inclusion and optimal monetary policy. *Bank for International Settlements Working Paper No. 482*. https://doi.org/DOI: 10.2139/ssrn.2582911

Mishra, V., & Singh, J. (2022). *Health Technology Assessment of Telemedicine Interventions in Diabetes Management: Evidence from UAE*. FIIB Business Review., DOI: 10.1177/23197145221130651

Mohapatra, S., Plaza, S., & Ratha, D. (2019). *Remittance markets in Africa: Prospects and challenges*. World Bank Publications., DOI: 10.1596/978-0-8213-8256-6

Narain, R. (2019). Financial inclusion through fintech: A study of financial access in India. *Indian Journal of Economics and Development, 7*(4), 448–457. DOI: 10.5958/2322-0430.2019.00072.1

Narula, R. (2020). Blockchain and the future of financial inclusion. *Journal of International Business and Economy, 21*(2), 113–126. DOI: 10.5102/jibe.2020.01.07

National Payments Corporation of India (NPCI). (2023). UPI monthly report. Retrieved from https://www.npci.org.in

Ozili, P. K. (2020). Financial inclusion and fintech during COVID-19 crisis: Policy solutions. *Journal of Financial Regulation and Compliance, 28*(4), 565–573. DOI: 10.1108/JFRC-06-2020-0046

Ozili, P. K. (2020). Financial inclusion research around the world: A review. *The Forum for Social Economics, 49*(4), 457–478. DOI: 10.1080/07360932.2020.1715238

Patnaik, R., Patra, S. K., Mahapatra, D. M., & Baral, S. K. (2022). *Adoption and Challenges Underlying OTT Platform in India during Pandemic: A Critical Study of Socio-Economic and Technological Issues*. FIIB Business Review., DOI: 10.1177/23197145221101676

Prahalad, C. K., & Hammond, A. (2002). Serving the world's poor, profitably. *Harvard Business Review*, *80*(9), 48–57. https://hbr.org/2002/09/serving-the-worlds-poor-profitably PMID: 12227146

Rai, S., & Choudhary, M. (2018). Fintech in India: Role of financial inclusion in driving economic growth. *International Journal of Economics and Financial Issues*, *8*(6), 59–66. https://www.econjournals.com/index.php/ijefi/article/view/7032

Ratha, D., Mohapatra, S., & Plaza, S. (2011). *Leveraging migration for Africa: Remittances, skills, and investments*. World Bank., DOI: 10.1596/978-0-8213-8257-8

Reserve Bank of India. (2023). Annual Report 2022-2023. https://www.rbi.org.in/Scripts/AnnualReportPublications.aspx

Rhyne, E., & Otero, M. (2006). Microfinance through the next decade: Visioning the who, what, where, when and how. *Accion International Report*. https://www.accion.org/resource/microfinance-through-the-next-decade

Sahay, R., Čihák, M., N'Diaye, P., & Barajas, A. (2015). *Financial inclusion: Can it meet multiple macroeconomic goals?* IMF Staff Discussion Notes., DOI: 10.5089/9781513542683.006

Singh, R., & Singh, V. P. (2025). Global Mobility and Economic Incentives in Prenatal Tourism. In, Exploration of Prenatal Tourism and Birthright Citizenship (pp. 77-104). IGI Global Scientific Publishing. https://doi.org/ Available on: https://www.igi-global.com/gateway/chapter/365545DOI: 10.4018/979-8-3693-8206-6.ch005

Singh, R., Singh, V. P., Rabby, F., Bansal, R., & Gupta, N. K. (2025). The Road to Sustainable Tourism: Financial Mechanisms for Green Project Development. In B. Sousa, L. Arantes, & S. Bhartiya (Eds.), Regenerative Tourism for Social Development (pp. 235-254). IGI Global Scientific Publishing. Available on: https://doi.org/DOI: 10.4018/979-8-3373-0235-5.ch010

Suri, T., & Jack, W. (2016). The long-run poverty and gender impacts of mobile money. *Science*, *354*(6317), 1288–1292. DOI: 10.1126/science.aah5309 PMID: 27940873

Van der Zwan, N., Gersonius, B., & Tilmans, P. (2020). Barriers to financial inclusion: A socio-economic perspective. *The Journal of Development Studies*, *56*(9), 1683–1700. DOI: 10.1080/00220388.2019.1643388

Chapter 9
Green Bonds Development in the Indian Markets

Farhat Aziz Lone
https://orcid.org/0009-0002-8566-5230
Chandigarh University, India

Shalini Aggarwal
https://orcid.org/0000-0002-7357-9880
Chandigarh University, India

Manisha Paliwal
https://orcid.org/0000-0002-4439-4457
Sri Balaji University, India

ABSTRACT

Green bonds are an emerging financial instrument that offers potential to attract private investors. These fixed-income debt securities provide interest over a set period, after which the principal is repaid. The objective of the paper is to understand the types of the green bonds; Regulation to Issue Green Bonds in India; Role and Importance of Green Bonds in India; Benefits of Investing in Green Bonds; Challenges for the Green Bonds Market in India; Measures for Expanding the Green Bonds Market in India. To address the challenges of the Indian green bonds market and facilitate growth, recommendations include (a) establishing taxonomy and standardizing reporting and disclosures, (b) introducing fiscal and policy levers, (c) implementing awareness-building measures, and (d) adopting innovative issuance strategies.

1. INTRODUCTION

India's vulnerability to climate change and its push for 'green growth' is reinforced by its commitment to net-zero emissions by 2070 and a 45% reduction in emissions intensity by 2030 (Government of India, 2022). Achieving these goals demands significant financial backing, with an estimated USD 12.7 trillion needed by 2050, which amounts to about USD 470 billion annually (BloombergNEF, 2023).

DOI: 10.4018/979-8-3373-0209-6.ch009

This immense sum requires private sector involvement and institutional investment, as public funds alone will not suffice.

Green bonds, an emerging financial instrument, offer potential to attract private investors. These fixed-income debt securities provide interest over a set period, after which the principal is repaid. Unlike traditional bonds, green bonds allocate proceeds specifically for financing or refinancing environmentally sustainable projects (Agarwal & Singh, 2018). Since the first 'climate awareness bond' issued by the European Investment Bank in 2007, the green bond market has grown exponentially, reaching a cumulative global issuance of USD 2.334 trillion by 2023, with USD 420.6 billion issued in 2023 alone. However, these bonds still hold a limited share in India's bond market.

Green bonds refer to a kind of climate financing monetary tool that tackles environmental and climate-related concerns. Being an emerging economy, India has the potential to attract a significant amount of foreign direct investment (FDI) into its economy through the use of green bonds (Weber & Saravade, 2020). A novel financial instrument well-known as a green bond is one method that can be utilized in the process of luring increased FDI (Climate Bond Initiative, 2018). Over a period of time, the number of green bond issuances has increased steadily, and it appears that both formal regulation from organisations like India's Securities and Exchange Board

In India, green bond issuances, valued at around USD 21 billion as of February 2023 (World Bank, 2023), represent just 3.8% of the total domestic corporate bonds, which exceed USD 500 billion (The Economic Times, 2023). With increasing Corporate Social Responsibility (CSR) funds directed toward green projects, private investment in climate financing appears more promising. The nascent stage of India's green bond market presents an opportunity to drive its growth through strategic market and policy interventions, following global trends. Additionally, as clean energy and infrastructure investments require 'patient capital' with long-term returns, green bonds can become highly attractive to institutional investors, such as pension funds, insurance companies, and mutual funds (Weber & Sarvade, 2019). Table 1 present the different types of bonds issued to protect the environment

Table 1. Different type of bonds issued to protect the environment

S.No	different bonds issued to protect environment	Purpose
1	Climate Change Bonds	These bonds are issued to finance projects aimed at mitigating climate change, such as renewable energy and energy efficiency initiatives.
2	Renewable Energy Bonds	These bonds are issued to finance projects that generate and utilize renewable energy sources, such as wind, solar, and hydroelectric power.
3	Energy Efficiency Bonds	These bonds are issued to finance projects aimed at increasing energy efficiency and reducing energy consumption, such as building retrofits and upgrades to equipment and appliances.
4	Social or Sustainable Development Bonds	These bonds are issued to finance projects that promote sustainable development, including initiatives that create jobs, reduce poverty, and improve public health. Examples include affordable housing, education, and healthcare projects.
5	Green Infrastructure Bonds	These bonds are issued to finance projects that promote green infrastructure, including initiatives that protect natural resources and ecosystems. Examples include urban green spaces, reforestation, and water conservation projects.
6	Natural Resources Bonds	These bonds are issued to finance projects that promote the conservation and sustainable use of natural resources. Examples include sustainable forestry management, reforestation, rehabilitation of mined areas, and the development of clean energy initiatives.

continued on following page

Table 1. Continued

S.No	different bonds issued to protect environment	Purpose
7	Project-linked bonds	These bonds are linked to specific projects, such as the construction of a wind farm or the development of a public transportation system. E.g. light rail or bus rapid transit system.
8	Asset-linked bonds	These bonds are linked to a portfolio of assets such as a group of wind turbines, a fleet of electric buses, electric vehicle charging stations or construction of a green building.
9	Corporate green bonds	These bonds are issued by companies to finance their own green projects or to refinance existing projects. For e.g. Bonds issued by a major car manufacturer to finance the development and production of electric vehicles (EVs) and related infrastructure.
10	Sovereign Green bonds	These bonds are issued by National Government to finance green projects such as renewable energy, sustainable infrastructure and climate change adaptation.
11	Green bond funds	These are funds that invest in a diversified portfolio of green bonds, enabling investors to gain exposure to the green bond market without having to buy individual bonds. Examples include fund that invests primarily in bonds issued by companies in the renewable energy sector such as solar and wind power companies.

Source: Kumar & Kundalia. (2023).

2. HISTORY OF GREEN BONDS ISSUANCES IN INDIA

India has long shown potential for green financing. As early as 2016, the Climate Bonds Initiative reported that India held around USD 15.7 billion in unlabeled climate-aligned bonds, used for low-carbon transport and renewable energy projects (Climate Bonds Initiative, 2017). Officially, India entered the green bond market in 2015 when YES Bank issued the first green bond, with a 10-year maturity, to finance renewable energy projects (Agarwal & Singh, 2018). Since then, various banks and corporates, including IDBI Bank, EXIM Bank, ReNew Power, Axis Bank, PNB Housing Finance, IREDA, NTPC, and Greenko have entered the market. Many of these issuances are listed on international exchanges like the London Stock Exchange and the Singapore Exchange. The private sector has driven green bond issuance in India, accounting for 84% of the total share (World Bank, 2023), highlighting limited public sector involvement and slow overall market growth.

Figure 1 illustrates the share of green bond issuances from various Indian entities. Notably, most green bond financing in India has been concentrated in the energy sector, indicating a focus on clean energy while leaving other sectors relatively underfunded, despite regulatory allowances for broader applications.

Figure 1. Green Bond issuances in India by type of issuer

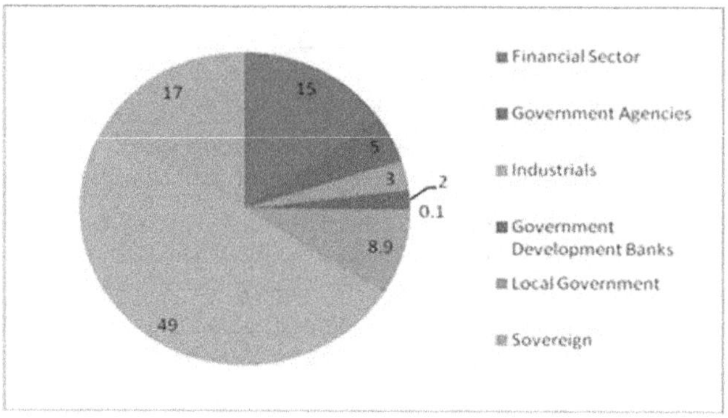

Table 2 the diverse sectors that could benefit from green bond financing, highlighting the untapped potential for expanding sustainable investments beyond energy.

Table 2. Issuance of green bonds in India

Issuer	Milestone	Year	Amount
YES Bank	First green bond issuance in India	2015	USD 260 million
Greenko	First high-yield green bond issuance in India. Greenko is also the highest cumulative issuer of green bonds in India.	2016	USD 500 million
NTPC	Issuance of a corporate green 'Masala' bond	2016	INR 2000 crores (USD 300 million)
Ghaziabad Municipal Corporation	First local civic body in India to issue a green bond (The Hindu Business Line, 2021).	2021	USD 20 million
Indore Municipal Corporation	First city to enlist municipal green bonds on the National Stock Exchange's (NSE) debt securities platform (Vats, 2023).	2023	USD 87 million
Government of India	First sovereign bond in two tranches of 5 and 10 year tenors	2023	USD 1 billion

Source: Singh and Shrivastava (2024)

2.1 Policy Overview and Sustainable Finance

The development of policy supporting the sustainable finance creates a necessary framework for the growth of green bond market in India. There is a need to align the domestic policies with the international standards and best practices, greater degree of transparency and standardization, the policy and regulatory reforms have been framed in 2020 in India. The ministry of finance (MOF)set up sustainable finance task force to develop four pillars of action outlined in sustainable finance roadmap:

Pillar one: Indian taxonomy of sustainable activities
Pillar two: Reporting and disclosure
Pillar three: Financial policy and regulation
Pillar four: Ecosystem development

The set of recommendations and an action plan under each pillar, with a report published in 2022. Actions under each pillar may further be prioritized keeping in view the targets of 2030 set for the country by the govt of India at COP26 meeting. The RBI has join the network set the targets for greening the financial system (NGFS) and the MOF represents the India as founding member at the international platform for sustainable finance (IPSF). The Indian GSS debt market is showing growth and momentum. The major attributes to the Indian debt market have five key themes influencing the market development in 2022:

1. The Union budget of 2022 included the announcement of domestically issued green bonds using conventional methods. The sovereign green bond market will likely encourage both public and private sector in domestic market and relatively immediate impact in the market. The policy framework will create the necessary platform for market development. The domestic policies should be in line with the international standards and Indian financial system are also exploring the assessment, disclosure and mitigation of risks related to ESG factors. The various risks associated with climate driven physical and transition are not adequately disclosed both financial and non-financial entities are not disclosed.
2. The government has not yet announced the distinct green stimulus or green recovery programme, towards policy decisions. The main example includes National Hydrogen Policy which includes roadmap for using hydrogen as an energy source for central and state level policy announcements for most of the GSS deals originating from India have been in offshore markets. The MOFs Sustainable task force is likely to strengthen the domestic market further however the effects may only materialize in medium to long term issuance of green bonds.
3. The utilization scale of the renewable energy sector is expected to continue its dominance among UoP categories based on the auction mechanism of assets and support from the banking community while there is action from other sectors described above, the large scale renewable energy sector is expected to dominate the market in next three to five years . hybrid and EV market sporadic but emphasis is on sustainable agriculture on which the 60% of population rely and enhances income of the farmers. the MOF has announced the intent to join the sovereign green bond club in 2022. The Indian sovereign green bond is intended to raise the profile of the India as a green finance hub and encourage the development of policy and local infrastructure and attract both public and private capital to the market. Climate bond initiative report on sovereign green social sustainability bond survey describes the challenges and benefits faced by sovereign issuers entering the market
4. The solar energy like solar rooftop and EVs will remain the next best thing and prospects in Indian market and are expected to benefit from future green bonds. The medium-term bonds are likely to capitalize on declining storage costs with the application across the commercial, industrial and residential segments.
5. In past interest rates movements have influenced the GSS issuance volumes. the expectation of higher interest rates could lead to lower volumes in the near term across not only thematic but overall debt issuance.

The important role of pension and insurance funds in financing the green bonds in India. These sources of funds have potential to become the source of funding for sustainable initiatives. There is growing concern over the environment, social, governance (ESG) issues and sustainability however there is room for improvement in banking sector where there is gaps in accommodating the sustainability factors and risk management. The biggest challenges in banking sector and other financial institution is the management of data and categorizing loans on the basis of ESG and their requirements. Moreover, the banking institutions and financial institutions are trading carefully in order to avoid green washing, but the regulatory reforms and precise definition to the green and sustainable reforms.(Wu, Y. and Tian, Y. (2022). Transition financing is the other important factors that banks are uncertain about their regulatory reforms. The SEBI and RBI are taking proactive steps towards including the regulations regarding the ESG and green finance. There is absence of overall well-defined framework for sustainable finance in India unlike the well-defined structure in western countries. Climate related information is becoming the crucial factor for banks and financial institutions, due to the fact that banks focus on short term assets duration and emphasis is laid on understanding climate risk especially unpredictable physical risk. But due to the unpredictable climate related events like extreme weather conditions and addressing physical risk is concern. The international investors are taking keen interest in information regarding the banks having climate risk related policies and other ESG related activities. There is hurdle in the way that interpreting physical risk data of banks and creating common database for insurance as well.

The climate finance and sustainability policies put a challenge for that purpose banks must include sector specialists and their framework. Who can assess the various pros and cons of sectors and their impact and moreover climate scientists are being hired to assess the associated data in order to navigate the complex gap between the information and their impact on climate finance and sustainability? The banks should align their strategies with India's international commitments to Paris and SDGs reduce funding in high emission sectors and actively invest in low emission sectors like renewable energy projects, it is about bringing a cultural shift within financial institution fostering an environment, sustainability and climate action being an integral part of the financial system of India.

3. OBJECTIVE OF THE PAPER

The objective of the paper is to understand the types of the green bonds; Regulation to Issue Green Bonds in India; Role and Importance of Green Bonds in India; Benefits of Investing in Green Bonds; Challenges for the Green Bonds Market in India; Measures for Expanding the Green Bonds Market in India.

4. RESEARCH METHODOLOGY

Regulation to Issue Green Bonds in India

The global green bond market is guided by the 'Green Bond Principles' (GBP) set by the International Capital Market Association (ICMA) and supported by the Climate Bond Initiative (CBI). CBI classifies bonds into certified green, CBI-labelled, and unaligned bonds. CBI-labelled bonds require at least 95% of proceeds to finance green assets with detailed disclosure (Tomfort, 2023). National regulations, such as those in France, China, and India, also define the market. In India, the Securities and Exchange Board of India (SEBI) regulates green bonds. The regulator issued guidelines in 2017 and enhanced them in 2023 to align with the GBP and include blue and yellow bonds (The Economic Times, 2023).The Government of India has established the Sovereign Green Bonds Framework to streamline the selection and monitoring of projects funded by sovereign green bonds (Climate Bonds Initiative, 2023) SEBI's framework requires green bond issuers to disclose the environmental objectives of their issuances, procedures for tracking proceeds, and details on the projects financed by the green debt securities (Raju et al., 2022; Kumar, 2022). It also outlines the categories under which funds can be raised as green debt securities. A "green debt security" complies with SEBI (Issue and Listing of Non-Convertible Securities) Regulations, 2021, and is issued to raise funds for projects or assets in the following categories:

1. Renewable and sustainable energy sources, including wind, solar, and bioenergy.
2. Clean transportation, such as public transport and mass transit.
3. Sustainable water management practices, including water recycling and access to clean drinking water.
4. Climate change adaptation
5. Energy efficiency, encompassing green and energy-efficient construction.
6. Effective waste disposal, including recycling and waste-to-energy practices.
7. Sustainable land use, including reforestation and sustainable agriculture.
8. Biodiversity conservation, along with any additional categories that SEBI may notify.

Table 3: Role and importance of green bonds in India

Sr No.	Particulars	Details
1	Climate change	India, being highly vulnerable to climate change impacts such as rising sea levels, extreme weather events, and crop failures, can benefit from green bonds to finance projects that mitigate these effects and promote sustainable development.
2	Renewable energy	India aims to increase its renewable energy capacity to 175 GW by 2022, and green bonds can play a crucial role in financing this transition to cleaner energy sources.
3	Infrastructure	India is expanding its infrastructure, and green bonds can help ensure that this development is sustainable and environmentally responsible.
4	Job creation	Investing in green projects can create jobs in sectors such as renewable energy, energy efficiency, and sustainable transportation.
5	Access to finance	Green bonds can offer an additional funding source for government agencies, Indian companies, and municipal corporations, seeking to finance environmentally beneficial projects.
6	Attracting foreign investment	Green bonds can attract foreign investment from investors interested in environmentally responsible projects.
7	Improving Global Rating	Issuing green bonds demonstrates a country's commitment to sustainable development, positively impacting its credit rating. This can facilitate access to capital markets and secure lower interest rates on its debt.

Source: Kumar & Kundalia. (2023).

5. BENEFITS OF INVESTING IN GREEN BONDS

Green bonds enable investors to support environmental initiatives, appealing particularly to those motivated to combat climate change (Aggarwal et al., 2021). While retail investors may find individual green bonds expensive, there are options available for investing in green bond baskets. Increased demand for these bonds typically leads to lower interest rates, which reduces corporate borrowing costs. The resulting savings can be distributed as dividends or reinvested, thereby enhancing profitability. Additionally, some issuers utilize the proceeds from green bonds to reduce carbon emissions and restore water ecosystems. Notably, the credit ratings of green bonds generally align with those of other financial instruments issued by the same entity (Mzoughi et al., 2024).

5.1 Challenges for the Green Bonds Market in India

Despite promising prospects, green bond issuance in India has progressed slowly in recent years. The Indian bond market remains in a nascent stage, with a lower sovereign credit rating (BBB-) forcing corporates to offer higher coupon rates on green bonds compared to international standards (Arif et al., 2021; Kumar, 2022). Historically, Indian green bonds have averaged coupon rates of 2.75-6% for USD-denominated issuances and 7.5-10% for INR-denominated issuances.

This disparity results from the currency risk associated with the Indian rupee, including higher hedging costs due to volatility and low liquidity in the secondary market (Kumar et al., 2019). For example, the two tranches of sovereign green bonds issued by the Indian government in 2023 initially benefited from a 'greenium,' indicating strong domestic investor demand and lower financing costs (Climate Bonds Initiative, 2023). However, a lack of trading activity and resulting illiquidity has diminished this advantage (Acharya, 2023; Lone et al., 2024). The volatility of returns due to exchange rate fluctuations and market illiquidity have impacted demand among foreign investors, especially when considering the currency hedging costs associated with green bonds (Kumar, 2022; Weber & Sarvade, 2019).

Awareness gaps regarding Indian green bonds in the international market have further discouraged foreign investment. Interested investors often face challenges such as limited investment pipelines, insufficient data availability, and a lack of green bond indices, listings, and ratings for Indian green bonds (Azhgaliyeva et al., 2020; Lone et al., 2024). Additionally, the lack of standardized methodologies and reporting in India contributes to insufficient data and raises concerns about potential greenwashing. Without a common taxonomy for 'green,' determining which assets qualify for financing through the green bond market remains ambiguous (Agarwal & Singh, 2018). The effectiveness of a green bond largely depends on the nature of the projects it funds, making standardization of assessment procedures challenging and requiring careful consideration.

In early-developing bond markets like India, fiscal incentives are essential for reducing issuance costs and investment risks. However, India lacks such incentives, including tax rebates for green bond investors and subsidies for issuers (Rathee & Aggarwal, 2023). As a result, investors do not benefit from green bonds compared to traditional bonds, while issuers face discouraging additional costs associated with green bond issuance, such as third-party verification and reporting (Ling & Wang, 2024).

Regressive domestic regulations have hindered investment growth in the green bonds market. For example, the Insurance Act in India restricts investments to assets with a minimum AA credit rating, preventing insurance companies from financing many green infrastructure and energy projects (Arif et al., 2021). In contrast, the Pension Fund Regulatory and Development Authority (PFRDA) recently permitted pension funds to invest in sovereign green bonds. Such regulatory changes are essential for allowing institutional investors to diversify their portfolios and for directing retail investments toward profitable green assets (Ojha, 2023). Moreover, to stimulate institutional investment in green bonds, the issuance size must be sufficient. Currently, there is a mismatch between the size of small green projects, like rooftop solar and energy efficiency initiatives, and the large issuance sizes that institutional investors prefer (Agarwal & Singh, 2018; Tomfort, 2023). Consequently, both the nature and size of green projects have impeded the effective use of green bonds in India.

Currently, only the energy and banking sectors have actively participated in the green bonds market, while other sectors have approached it with caution (Abhilash et al., 2023). This concentration of issuances in renewables and energy has limited their appeal to a broader investor base. Individual issuances have also encountered project-specific risks, including poor asset quality and inadequate financial management and reporting (Kumar, 2022). To foster the growth of the green bonds market in India, it is essential to address several key challenges: the absence of a common taxonomy, regulatory bottlenecks, lack of fiscal incentives, and the characteristics of current issuances.

6. MEASURES FOR EXPANDING THE GREEN BONDS MARKET IN INDIA

Policy opportunities to increase the growth of the green bonds market in India arise from three aspects: (1) developing the market through necessary regulations and support structures for issuers, (2) building awareness among investors, and (3) implementing policy and fiscal incentives for engagement with the green bonds market (Ling & Wang, 2024). To address the challenges of the Indian green bonds market and facilitate growth, recommendations include (a) establishing a taxonomy and standardizing reporting and disclosures, (b) introducing fiscal and policy levers, (c) implementing awareness-building measures, and (d) adopting innovative issuance strategies (Lim, 2024).

6.1 Taxonomy and Standardization

Establishing strong frameworks for a green taxonomy and defining reporting mandates is essential for ensuring transparency and addressing greenwashing concerns in India's green bonds market (Rathee & Aggarwal, 2022a). A green taxonomy is central to developing any green financial product, and strengthening reporting frameworks should focus on two aspects: (1) addressing the unique requirements of the domestic market and (2) aligning with international standards. Disparities between international and domestic standards can hinder cross-border investments. A well-defined green taxonomy and enforced reporting mandates will also enhance awareness of the green bonds market by providing clear signals regarding green bond issuances on listings and exchanges, allowing investors to assess risks effectively (Mzoughi et al., 2024). Ultimately, these measures will promote harmonization within the regulatory environment for both issuers and investors (Kuang et al., 2024).

6.2 Fiscal and Policy Levers

To promote the growth of green bonds in India, it's essential to create cost and investment advantages for issuers and investors (Arshad et al., 2023). Given the early stage of India's bond market development, these advantages should be introduced through fiscal and policy interventions.

(a) Fiscal Levers – Issuance of green bonds can be stimulated by subsidizing their issuance costs, particularly the expenses associated with third-party verification. To encourage firms to issue green bonds, it is essential to offset this additional cost through fiscal measures. Exploring a green bond fund or grant scheme, similar to those implemented by countries like Singapore and Malaysia, could be beneficial for the Indian market. Subsidies could either cover a portion of the issuance costs or the expenses for obtaining external certification (Giri et al., 2024). Covering these certification costs can significantly enhance the supply of green bonds in India, as cost-effective external certifications are a major barrier to smooth issuance.

(b) Policy Levers – The issuance of green bonds can be boosted through policy measures such as credit enhancement, which includes providing guarantees or partial credit funds. In India's green bonds market, where credit ratings are generally low, such enhancements can mitigate risks associated with new technologies and sectors, ultimately improving the credit ratings of issuances (Chen et al., 2024). A notable example is ReNew Power's 2016 green bond issue, which was jointly guaranteed by the Asian Development Bank (ADB) and the India Infrastructure Finance Company Ltd. (IIFCL). This guarantee improved its credit rating from BBB to AA+, leading to oversubscription (Agarwal & Singh, 2018). Additionally, credit enhancement is crucial for attracting institutional investments, as these investors often have restrictions based on bond credit ratings. By providing guarantees and risk coverage, the credit ratings of several green bond issuances could improve, unlocking the potential for greater institutional investment. Credit enhancement is generally provided by public sector entities or financial institutions.

6.3 Awareness Building Measures

For green bonds to effectively serve as a dynamic financial instrument, transparency and clear discernibility among investors are essential to maintain their price advantage in capital raising (Lim, 2024). Therefore, building awareness is crucial for the development of the green bonds market. Exchanges can act as vital intermediaries between issuers and investors, facilitating transparency for green bonds. To enhance visibility and trading of green bonds in India, exchanges need to be empowered and equipped adequately (Rathee & Aggarwal, 2022b). This is particularly important to address potential secondary market inactivity and resulting illiquidity, which can cause these bonds to lose their greenium (Kuang et al., 2024).

6.4 Innovative Issuance Strategies

To address the challenge of small project sizes in India's green initiatives, innovative issuance strategies must be implemented (Giri et al., 2024). One effective approach is securitization, which can mitigate the risks associated with small projects by improving their credit ratings and ensuring consistent aggregated income flows. This strategy enables smaller projects to collectively achieve a scale that attracts institutional investors. Asset-based securitization (ABS) is a well-established practice in markets like Canada, the U.S., the EU, and Australia, where it raises capital by aggregating multiple small projects and leveraging cash flows from reliable assets rather than relying solely on credit ratings (Kharb et al., 2024).

In India green bonds were first traded in the year February 2015, after that it has shown tremendous growth. India ranks third in terms of funds raised through GBs while ass emerging economies raised only US$ 22.1 billion between 2015 to 2022 and requires around US$200 billion per year till 2030 to achieve sustainability targets announced at COP-26 as estimated by the Council on Energy, Environment, and Water (CEEW) for energy finance. To reach this target fund per year, India needs to attract domestic retail investors along with institutional investors in domestic and foreign markets

7. CONCLUSION

India faces challenges in mobilizing private investments through green bonds, including low credit ratings, small issuance sizes, inconsistent regulations, awareness gaps, lack of fiscal incentives, and currency volatility (Chen et al., 2024). To overcome these issues, regulatory adaptations and fiscal incentives should be complemented by internationally backed credit enhancement structures and collaboration efforts. Additionally, innovative strategies are needed to scale green projects and attract institutional investors, whose long-term capital is crucial for financing emerging green technologies (Arshad et al., 2023).

REFERENCES

Abhilash, S., Shenoy, S. S., Shetty, D. K., Lobo, L. S., & N, S. K. (2023). Green bond as an innovative financial instrument in the Indian financial market: Insights from systematic literature review approach. *SAGE Open*, *13*(2), 21582440231178783. Advance online publication. DOI: 10.1177/21582440231178783

Acharya, N. (2023, October 11). India looks to boost domestic green bond market with longer-dated deal. Responsible Investor. https://www.responsible-investor.com/india-looks-to-boost-domestic-greenbond-market-with-longer-dated-deal/

Agarwal, S., & Singh, T. (2018). Unlocking The Green Bond Potential in India. TERI. https://www.teriin.org/projects/nfa/files/Green-Bond-Working-Paper.pdf

Aggarwal, S., Garg, V., & Pathak, S. (2021). Green Bonds: A Catalyst for Sustainable Development. *Journal of Contemporary Issues in Business and Government*, *27*(1), 2633–2651. https://cibg.org.au/article_9378.html

Arif, M., Naeem, M. A., Farid, S., Nepal, R., & Jamasb, T. (2021). Diversifier or more? Hedge and safe haven properties of green bonds during COVID-19. SSRN *Electronic Journal*. DOI: 10.2139/ssrn.3782126

Arshad, A., Shahzad, F., Rehman, I. U., & Sergi, B. S. (2023). A systematic literature review of block-chain technology and environmental sustainability: Status quo and future research. *International Review of Economics & Finance*, *88*, 1602–1622. DOI: 10.1016/j.iref.2023.07.044

Azhgaliyeva, D., Kapoor, A., & Liu, Y. (2020). Green bonds for financing renewable energy and energy efficiency in South-East Asia: A review of policies. *Journal of Sustainable Finance & Investment*, *10*(2), 113–140. DOI: 10.1080/20430795.2019.1704160

Bloomberg, N. E. F. (2023). *New Energy Outlook India* accessed on 2 October, 2024 from https://assets.bbhub.io/professional/sites/24/BNEF_New-Energy-Outlook-India-2023.pdf

Chen, J., Meng, W., Chen, Y., & Zhou, W. (2024). To be an eco-and tech-friendly society: Impact research of green finance on AI innovation. *Journal of Cleaner Production*, *466*, 142900. DOI: 10.1016/j.jclepro.2024.142900

Climate Bonds Initiative. (2017). Green Bonds Highlights accessed on 2 October, 2024 from https://www.climatebonds.net/files/files/2016%20GB%20Market%20Roundup

Climate Bonds Initiative. (2023). *India's debut in the sovereign green bond market: First deal landed a greenium!*https://www.climatebonds.net/2023/03/india%E2%80%99s-debut-sovereign-greenbond-market-first-deal-landed-greenium

Giri, G., Nivedhitha, K. S., & Manohar, H. L. (2024). Can blockchain enabled green bond issuance lead to intent to invest? A moderated mediation model. *Applied Economics*, *56*(18), 2191–2208. DOI: 10.1080/00036846.2023.2186360

Government of India. (2022). *India's Updated First Nationally Determined Contribution Under Paris Agreement (2021-2030)*. UNFCCC. https://unfccc.int/sites/default/files/NDC/2022-08/India%20Updated%20 First% 20 Nationally %20Determined%20Contrib.pdf

Kharb, R., Suneja, V., Aggarwal, S., Singh, P., Shahzzad, U., Saini, N., & Kumar, D. (2024). The Relationship between investment determinants and environmental sustainability: Evidence through meta-analysis. *The Quarterly Review of Economics and Finance, 94*(April), 267–280. DOI: 10.1016/j.qref.2024.02.001

Kuang, M., Kuang, D., Rasool, Z., Saleem, H. M. N., & Ullah, M. I. (2024). *From bytes to sustainability: Asymmetric nexus between industrial artificial intelligence and green finance in advanced industrial AI nations*. Borsa Istanbul Review.

Kumar, N., Vaze, P., & Kidney, S. (2019). Moving from Growth to Development: Financing Green Investment in India. ORF. https://www.orfonline.org/wp-content/uploads/2019/02/pg-98-115.pdf

Kumar, S. (2022). Critical Assessment Of Green Financing Initiatives In Emerging Market: A Review Of India's Green Bond Issuances. *Academy of Marketing Studies Journal, 26*(5).

Kumar, S., & Kundalia, L. (2023). Green Bonds - Role and scope in India's financial and fiscal landscape The Journal of Indian Institute of Banking & Finance accessed on 1 October, 2024 from https://www .iibf.org.in/documents/BankQuest/6.%20.pdf

Lim, T. (2024). Environmental, social, and governance (ESG) and artificial intelligence in finance: State-of-the-art and research takeaways. *Artificial Intelligence Review, 57*(4), 76. DOI: 10.1007/s10462-024-10708-3

Ling, X., & Wang, H. (2024). Green Behavior Strategies in the Green Credit Market: Analysis of the Impacts of Enterprises' Greenwashing and Blockchain Technology. *Sustainability (Basel), 16*(11), 4858. DOI: 10.3390/su16114858

Lone, F., Aggarwal, S., & Gupta, S. (2024). Green Bonds Sustainable Development and Economic Benefits for Investors and Pharmaceutical Companies. IGI Global. https://www.igi-global.com/gateway/chapter/353812

Lone, F., Aggarwal, S. & Jain, S. (2024). Retail Investors' Perception towards Green Bonds in Advancing Sustainability: Evidence from India. accepted for publication in Asia pacific Financial markets

Mzoughi, H., Amar, A. B., Guesmi, K., & Benkraiem, R. (2024). Blockchain markets, green finance investments, and environmental impacts. *Research in International Business and Finance, 69*, 102249. DOI: 10.1016/j.ribaf.2024.102249

Ojha, S. (2023, July 21). *Pension funds to invest in green bonds: How it will impact retail investors?* Mint. https://www.livemint.com/money/personal-finance/pension-funds-to-invest-in-sovereign-greenbonds -sgrbs-how-it-will-impact-retail-investors-11689920200494.html

Raju, P., Joshi, J., & Nannapaneni, P. (2022, September 19). *Green Bonds - Environmental Law - India*. Mondaq. https://www.mondaq.com/india/environmental-law/1231314/green-bonds

Rathee, P. (2023, January 09). Governing Behaviours of Impact Investors in India: A Path to Balance Double Bottom Line. *Global Business Review*, 09721509221141200. Advance online publication. DOI: 10.1177/09721509221141200

Rathee, P., & Aggarwal, S. (2022a). Understanding Impact Investment Intention Using the Extended Theory of Planned Behaviour. *Global Business Review*, 09721509221115001. Advance online publication. DOI: 10.1177/09721509221115001

Rathee, P., & Aggarwal, S. (2022b). Investors' Preference for Creating Impact:(A study to understand impact investors' preference while making investment in India). *Vision (Basel)*, •••, 09722629221131110.

Singh, U. V., & Shrivastava, M. K. (2024). Accelerating the Growth of Green Bonds in India. New Delhi:The Energy and Resources Institute accessed on 1 October, 2024 from https://teriin.org/sites/default/files/files/Accelerating_the_Growth_of_Green_Bonds_Policy_Brief.pdf

The Economic Times. (2023, February 10). *India's green bond issuances just 3.8 PC of overall domestic corporatebond market: Report.*https://economictimes.indiatimes.com/markets/bonds/indias-green-bondissuances-just-3-8-pc-of-overall-domestic-corporate-bond-market-report/articleshow/97806148.Cms

Tomfort, A. (2023). Making Green Bonds Greener: Proposals to Increase the Efficiency of Green Bonds. *Journal of Applied Finance & Banking*, *13*(1), 5. DOI: 10.47260/jafb/1315

Weber, O., & Saravade, V. (2019). Green Bonds: Current Development and Their Future. DOI: 10.13140/RG.2.2.10059.82722

World Bank. (2023). *India incorporates green bonds into its climate finance strategy*. https://blogs.worldbank.org/climatechange/india-incorporates-green-bonds-its-climate-finance-strategy

Chapter 10
Harnessing Fintech for Financial Inclusion:
Bridging the Gap for the Unbanked and Underbanked

Sulagna Das
https://orcid.org/0000-0003-4683-453X
JIS University, India

Moupiya Mallick
https://orcid.org/0000-0002-5773-1520
JIS University, India

Tanaya Das
https://orcid.org/0000-0001-5601-2295
JIS University, India

ABSTRACT

Financial inclusion is crucial for economic growth and poverty alleviation. Fintech, combining technologies like blockchain, mobile banking, AI, machine learning, and decentralized finance, offers accessible, affordable, and customized financial solutions. These services enable quick, affordable transactions, peer-to-peer lending, and microfinance platforms. A cooperative strategy involving governments, fintech businesses, public-private partnerships, and conventional banks is needed to scale fintech services while maintaining regulatory compliance and transparency. Fintech solutions utilize advanced technologies like blockchain, mobile banking, AI, machine learning, and decentralized finance to offer scalable, affordable services. These include quick transactions, peer-to-peer lending, and microfinance platforms. A cooperative strategy involving governments, fintech businesses, and banks is needed to scale fintech services while maintaining regulatory compliance.

DOI: 10.4018/979-8-3373-0209-6.ch010

1. INTRODUCTION TO FINANCIAL INCLUSION

The worldwide idea of financial inclusion empowers individuals and fosters economic development. It entails offering timely, reasonably priced, and adequate financial services and products, including credit facilities, insurance, savings accounts, and payment methods. In order to reduce financial inequities, fintech is essential. Access to these services, however, needs to be made sustainable and morally. Because it enables individuals to save, invest, and get credit, financial inclusion is essential for economic growth and promotes job creation and entrepreneurship. As a result, ensuring sustainable and moral access to financial services is crucial. It helps in:

- *Promoting Economic Growth:* By providing small and medium-sized businesses (SMEs) with easily available funding, it stimulates local economies.
- *Reducing Inequality:* Women, low-income households, and rural communities are among the marginalized groups whose quality of life is improved by having access to financial services. It lessens dependency on unofficial loan channels, which are frequently linked to exorbitant interest rates and unethical behavior. (Nobanee et al., 2024)
- *Building Resilience:* By providing savings and insurance products, financial inclusion assists households in managing risks including natural catastrophes, medical emergencies, and job loss.

1.1. Global Landscape: The State of Financial Inclusion

Financial exclusion is still a problem worldwide, despite tremendous advancements. Perspectives on the present status of financial inclusion point to both successes and shortcomings are given below:

Unbanked Population: 1.4 billion adults globally do not have access to any official financial institution, according to the World Bank's 2021 Global Findex study. Most of these are found in low- and middle-income nations, especially in South Asia, Latin America, and Sub-Saharan Africa. (Dar et al., 2024)

- *Gender Gap:* A sizable percentage of those who are financially excluded are women. The gender disparity in account ownership remains at around 7 percentage points in many emerging nations.
- *Rural vs. Metropolitan Divide:* Due to a lack of financial knowledge, cultural barriers, and inadequate infrastructure, rural communities have less access to financial services than urban centers.

1.1.1. Regional Insights:

- Sub-Saharan Africa: Significant advancements have been made in this region, with mobile money accounts promoting financial inclusion. In 2011, just 12 percent of adults had mobile money accounts; today, over 33 percent do.
- South Asia: More than 80% of individuals already possess an account thanks to government programs like India's Pradhan Mantri Jan Dhan Yojana (PMJDY). However, a lack of financial understanding keeps a lot of accounts dormant.
- Developed economies: Even in developed economies, there are still issues with financial inclusion. As of 2021, 5.4 percent of American households (about 7 million) lacked a bank account, sometimes as a result of exorbitant costs or a lack of confidence in financial institutions.

The present challenges faced are:

- *Infrastructure:* In remote locations, there is a lack of physical banking infrastructure.
- *Cultural Barriers:* Social constraints and gender conventions that prevent women from accessing financial resources.
- *Digital Divide:* The adoption of digital financial services is hampered in rural and underserved areas by limited access to cellphones and the internet.

Role of Fintech in Financial Inclusion: In the fight against financial exclusion, financial technology, or fintech, has become a revolutionary tool. Fintech businesses offer easily accessible, reasonably priced, and effective financial solutions by utilizing cutting-edge technologies. The key contribution of Fintech is explained below:

- *Accessibility:* Mobile banking solutions make it possible for even the most distant communities to access financial services via cellphones. By doing away with the requirement for traditional bank accounts, digital wallets such as M-Pesa (Kenya) and bKash (Bangladesh) provide simpler and more inclusive transactions. (Shi et al., 2024)
- *Affordability:* Fintech uses digital infrastructure and removes middlemen to lower transaction costs. For instance, migrant workers and their families benefit from low-cost cross-border remittance systems like Ripple, which are powered by blockchain technology.
- *Innovation in Credit:* AI-powered credit scoring examines other data sources (such as utility bills and cellphone usage) to provide loans to those without official credit histories. Microloans totaling billions of dollars have been distributed throughout Asia and Africa by companies such as Tala and Branch.
- *Financial Literacy and Awareness:* To help users make wise financial decisions, fintech applications utilize gamified learning modules to teach them about investing, saving, and budgeting techniques.

Financial inclusion is crucial for economic growth, and fintech has helped fill gaps in traditional financial institutions through digital payments, blockchain, AI, and mobile technologies. However, governments, private companies, and civil society must collaborate to overcome challenges like digital literacy, infrastructural deficiencies, and regulatory barriers for universal financial inclusion.

2. OBJECTIVES OF THE STUDY:

- The study aims to explore the role of fintech in enhancing financial inclusion for unbanked and underbanked populations. The specific objectives are:
- To analyze the impact of fintech innovations such as digital payments, mobile banking, and blockchain on financial inclusion.
- To identify the key barriers preventing unbanked and underbanked individuals from accessing formal financial services.
- To evaluate the effectiveness of fintech solutions in improving access to banking, credit, and financial literacy.

- To assess the role of government regulations and policies in supporting fintech-driven financial inclusion.
- To provide strategic recommendations for fintech firms, financial institutions, and policymakers to enhance financial accessibility.

3. RESEARCH METHODOLOGY:

This study uses a qualitative research methodology to examine fintech's role in promoting financial inclusion among unbanked and underbanked populations. It analyzes fintech innovations, identifies barriers, and evaluates regulatory implications. Secondary data sources, including academic articles, industry reports, and financial inclusion indices, provide a comprehensive understanding of fintech's role in expanding financial services, especially in emerging economies. Case studies highlight best practices and scalable models. The study uses semi-structured interviews with fintech experts, banking professionals, policymakers, and financial regulators to understand fintech solutions' effectiveness, adoption challenges, and regulatory landscape. Thematic analysis identifies trends and obstacles in leveraging fintech for financial inclusion. Despite limitations like regional adoption differences and data availability constraints, the research aims to provide strategic recommendations for fintech firms and policymakers.

4. DATA ANALYSIS AND INTERPRETATION:

4.1. Challenges Faced by the Unbanked and Underbanked:

Accessing financial services presents a number of difficulties for the underbanked and unbanked communities. These difficulties are complex and include institutional, financial, and geographic obstacles.

4.1.1 Barriers to Access:

Rural or remote areas often lack access to banking services due to geographical isolation or lack of formal identification. This leads to individuals relying on informal financial systems like local money lenders or community savings groups, which can be less secure and more expensive. Additionally, many lack necessary identification documents for opening a bank account. This lack of financial literacy also hinders effective use of banking services, such as interest rates, credit, and digital tools.(Ozili, 2021)

- *Geographic Isolation:* Geographic isolation is a significant obstacle to financial inclusion, particularly in rural or remote areas. Traditional banks are more profitable in urban centers, but in rural areas, branch establishments may not be feasible due to financial constraints. Traveling long distances is time-consuming and expensive, leading to reliance on informal financial networks. While mobile banking and agents exist, technological and infrastructure gaps hinder widespread adoption. Additionally, rural areas often lack reliable internet connectivity, exacerbating their exclusion.
- *Lack of Formal Identification:* Formal identification is a major issue for marginalized groups, especially the unbanked, in many countries. Banks require government-issued IDs, proof of address,

and biometric data for account opening. However, millions lack these due to bureaucratic inefficiencies, poverty, or lack of awareness. This leads to reliance on informal systems. Governments and financial institutions can explore innovative methods like biometric data-based digital ID systems or "Know Your Customer" processes to lower ID requirements.(Shabir & Ali, 2022)

- *Inadequate Financial Literacy:* Financial literacy is a major obstacle to financial inclusion, as many people lack understanding of basic financial concepts like savings, interest rates, and budgeting. This mistrust, particularly among marginalized communities, is exacerbated by historical instances of exploitation or discrimination. Financial education programs, delivered through schools, community centers, or digital platforms, can empower individuals to engage with the financial system. Banks, microfinance institutions, and fintech companies can also play a crucial role in making financial services more transparent and accessible.

4.1.2. Economic Inequalities:

Traditional banking services are often unaffordable for low-income households due to high fees and minimum balance requirements. Without stable income or savings, they are discouraged from using these systems. Additionally, many unbanked or underbanked individuals lack a formal credit history, making it difficult for them to secure loans for education, business, or personal needs.

- *Poverty and Income Disparities:* Poverty and income inequality contribute to financial exclusion, as banks often cater to those who can afford them. This cycle perpetuates poverty, making it harder for the poor to escape poverty. They often lack access to essential financial tools, leading to reliance on informal lenders with high interest rates or unfair terms. To address this, low-cost banking options, social safety nets, and financial service subsidies could be implemented by governments.
- *Lack of Credit History and Collateral*: Unbanked and underbanked individuals often lack access to credit due to their lack of a formal credit history. Traditional banks use credit scores and collateral to determine loan eligibility, but many have never participated in the system. This lack of access hinders financial resilience, investment, and economic advancement, exacerbating poverty and preventing social mobility. Alternative credit scoring methods and peer-to-peer lending platforms are emerging as alternatives.

4.1.3. High Costs:

Traditional banks face challenges for the unbanked, including high transaction fees, minimum balance requirements, and lack of affordable alternatives. These fees, including monthly maintenance, withdrawal, and ATM usage, can be prohibitive for individuals with limited funds. Additionally, institutions often impose minimum balance requirements to avoid maintenance fees, making it difficult for low- or inconsistent-income individuals to maintain a balance. Despite advancements in digital and mobile banking, these alternatives still require access to technology and internet services, making them less accessible for lower-income groups.(Thottoli, 2024)

- *Transaction Fees and Banking Costs:* Traditional banking services often charge high fees, disproportionately affecting low-income individuals. These fees make it financially unsustainable for unbanked and underbanked individuals to open and maintain accounts. Fintech companies are offering low-fee or fee-free digital banking services like mobile wallets like PayPal and Venmo, while banks can introduce lower-cost services like fee-free basic accounts and fee waivers for certain transaction types.

- *Minimum Balance Requirements:* Traditional banks often require customers to maintain a minimum balance to avoid fees, which is often difficult for low-income individuals due to inconsistent income. This discourages them from opening accounts and reliance on cash or informal financial systems, which can be risky and costly. Some banks and fintech companies are now offering "no-minimum-balance" accounts, designed specifically for low-income individuals, allowing them to manage their money without the added burden of maintaining a certain balance.

To access and benefit from traditional financial services, unbanked and underbanked individuals must overcome structural barriers. A multifaceted strategy includes improving financial literacy, reducing costs, increasing accessibility, and developing inclusive financial products. Mobile banking technology could be a significant step towards enabling these traditionally excluded groups to access and benefit from financial inclusion.(Arora & Madan, 2023) Underbanked and unbanked individuals face challenges due to institutional, social, and economic factors. To address these issues, systemic changes in financial institutions, regulations, and technology are needed. A more inclusive financial system can be achieved by reducing obstacles and creating affordable, creative financial services.

4.1.4. Transition: Connecting Challenges to the Role of Technology:

Technology is transforming underserved populations' economic challenges into opportunities for inclusion and growth by bridging access, affordability, and trust gaps through digital tools, artificial intelligence, and innovative platforms.

- ***Breaking Geographical Barriers***: Mobile banking and agent networks allow individuals to access banking services through smartphones and local retail outlets. For instance, mobile money platforms like M-Pesa have revolutionized financial access in rural Africa by enabling secure and instant transactions without physical bank branches.
- ***Reducing Costs of Financial Services:*** Blockchain and peer-to-peer payment platforms minimize costs by eliminating intermediaries. Apps like Venmo and Revolut enable users to transfer money at lower costs compared to traditional wire transfers.
- ***Enabling Credit Access Without Traditional Histories***: AI and big data analytics assess creditworthiness using alternative data sources, such as mobile phone usage, utility payments, and e-commerce activity. Companies like Tala and Branch use these methods to provide microloans to underserved populations.
- ***Improving Financial Literacy and Trust***: Gamified educational apps and interactive platforms enhance understanding of financial concepts. For example, apps like Khan Academy's financial literacy tools make learning accessible, while user-friendly interfaces in fintech apps build trust by simplifying complex processes.
- ***Enhancing Security and Reducing Fraud***: AI-driven fraud detection systems and biometric authentication enhance security, ensuring safe transactions. For instance, facial recognition and fingerprint scanning reduce risks in mobile banking and e-wallet platforms.

Technology is not merely a tool for improving efficiency—it is a bridge that connects underserved populations to opportunities that were previously out of reach. By addressing specific challenges with tailored solutions, technology drives financial inclusion, economic participation, and empowerment on a global scale.

4.2. Role of Financial Education in Enhancing Fintech Adoption

Financial education is crucial for fintech adoption, enabling informed decision-making, trust building, and maximizing benefits of digital platforms, despite limited understanding of financial concepts and digital tools. The text below highlights the significant contributions of financial education.

- *Building Confidence in Digital Platforms:* Financial literacy programs can help individuals, particularly in underserved communities, understand the operation of fintech platforms, their security features, and avoid scams, thereby increasing trust and confidence.
- *Improving Adoption Rates:* Fintech tools' complexity can deter users, but simplified training programs and tutorials from fintech companies can make them accessible to those with limited technical knowledge
- *Enhancing Decision-Making Skills*: Fintech users may misuse services without proper financial knowledge, leading to debt or instability. Programs focusing on budgeting, saving, and responsible borrowing can guide healthier financial habits.(Susan et al., 2023)
- *Addressing Generational and Cultural Barriers:* Targeted education programs addressing cultural norms and promoting fintech benefits can encourage broader adoption, especially among older generations and traditional financial practices.
- *Enabling Financial Independence:* Programs promoting digital literacy and financial empowerment, such as Global Money Week, help marginalized groups like women access financial education and resources, fostering financial independence and inclusion.(Okello Candiya Bongomin et al., 2024)

4.2.1. Integrating Financial Education with Fintech:

- *Gamification and Interactive Learning*: Fintech platforms can enhance financial education by incorporating gamified tools like Duolingo, which can simplify complex topics into manageable lessons.
- *Partnerships Between Fintech and Education Providers*: Fintech companies, schools, and NGOs can enhance financial education through partnerships like Visa's Financial Literacy Program, which trains users in digital financial tools.
- *Localized Content Delivery*: Financial education should be delivered in local languages and contexts to cater to diverse audiences and address regional challenges like mobile penetration and cultural norms. (Hidayat-ur-Rehman, 2024)

Financial education is not just complementary to fintech adoption; it is foundational. By equipping individuals with the knowledge and skills needed to navigate digital financial systems, these programs amplify the reach and impact of fintech, driving greater financial inclusion and economic resilience.

4.3. Enhancing Depth of Analysis with Theoretical Context

To provide a stronger academic foundation, integrating theories such as the Diffusion of Innovation Theory (Rogers, 1962) and the Technology Acceptance Model (TAM) (Davis, 1989) can deepen the analysis of how financial literacy and fintech adoption intersect to promote financial inclusion. These frameworks offer insights into user behavior, adoption patterns, and the factors influencing the integration of technology in underserved communities.

4.3.1. Diffusion of Innovation Theory:

The Diffusion of Innovation (DOI) Theory explains how, why, and at what rate innovations spread through specific populations or social systems. This framework is particularly relevant to understanding fintech adoption and the role of financial literacy.

Application to Fintech Adoption:

- *Innovators & Early Adopters:* Financially literate people are more likely to be early adopters of fintech solutions because they see the relative benefits (such as reduced costs and convenience) and fit in with their needs.
- *Early and Late Majority:* By bridging the knowledge gap, financial education can assist the majority in overcoming the perceived risks and complexity of fintech.
- *Laggards:* The skepticism or resistance frequently observed in this group can be addressed through targeted education and trust-building techniques, especially in communities with low financial literacy or digital penetration. (Patnaik, et.al., 2022)

Case: M-Pesa in Kenya serves as a classic example of DOI in action. Early adopters highlighted the benefits of mobile money transfers, and word-of-mouth diffusion, coupled with financial education campaigns, accelerated adoption among the majority.

4.3.2. Technology Acceptance Model (TAM):

According to TAM, a person's intention to use technology is influenced by two main factors: perceived usefulness (PU) and perceived ease of use (PEOU). These views are directly influenced by financial literacy, which shapes users' assessments and adoption of fintech.

Application to Financial Education and Fintech:

- *Perceived Usefulness (PU):* Programs for financial literacy improve knowledge of how fintech solutions address particular needs, like granting access to credit, cutting expenses, or saving time.
- *Perceived Ease of Use (PEOU):* Fintech tools are made simpler through training programmes, which allay users' fears of complexity and make technology more approachable.
- *External Variables:* Localized financial education programmes are necessary because cultural norms, trust in digital systems, and demographic factors also affect PU and PEOU.

Case: The rapid adoption of digital wallets like Paytm in India highlights the role of perceived usefulness (cashless payments during demonetization) and ease of use (user-friendly apps), supported by extensive educational campaigns.

4.3.3 Financial Inclusion Theories:

- *Access-Usage Framework:* Access (the availability of financial services) and usage can be used to analyze financial inclusion (active and sustained participation in the financial system). Financial education concentrates on usage by helping people comprehend and have faith in these services, whereas fintech deals with access through digital platforms.
- *Poverty Alleviation Theories:* According to the Capabilities Approach (Sen, 1999), financial inclusion increases people's economic capabilities, thereby empowering them. Fintech is enhanced by financial literacy, which gives users the skills they need to use these tools efficiently and promotes long-term economic empowerment. (Ozili, 2020)

4.3.4. Combining Theories to Promote Fintech Adoption and Financial Literacy:

- *Diffusion of Innovation Meets TAM:* By enhancing potential adopters' perceptions of fintech's utility and usability, financial literacy quickens its spread. For instance, educational initiatives aimed at early adopters have the potential to spread, inspiring the majority to follow suit.
- *Adoption Category-Based Localized Strategies:* By using DOI, financial literacy campaigns can be customized for various adopter groups (e.g., innovators vs. laggards), guaranteeing that the messages are understood by a wide range of demographics.
- *Creating Long-Term Financial Habits:* By integrating the Capabilities Approach into financial literacy programmes, users are not only exposed to fintech but are also given the tools they need to continue using it, which enhances their long-term financial health.

Incorporating theoretical frameworks such as the Diffusion of Innovation Theory, Technology Acceptance Model, and financial inclusion paradigms provides a richer context for analyzing the interplay between financial literacy and fintech adoption. These theories underscore the importance of addressing psychological, social, and cultural factors to maximize the impact of technology on financial inclusion.

4.4. Fintech Innovations Promoting Financial Inclusion

Fintech innovations that support financial inclusion dive into the systemic problems that fintech seeks to solve in addition to examining how these technologies offer concrete answers to persistent obstacles to financial access. We can better grasp fintech's revolutionary potential in closing the inclusion gap by looking at the convergence of technology, financial services, and socioeconomic variables. The four main categories of digital wallets and payments, microfinance platforms, savings and investment platforms, and embedded finance are further examined below.

4.4.1. Digital Wallets and Payments: Transforming Financial Accessibility:

People who don't have access to traditional banking may now make payments, save money, and transfer money thanks to digital wallets and payment systems like Paytm, M-Pesa, and Venmo. Through the use of mobile devices, these platforms have proven essential in advancing financial inclusion for those without bank accounts. (Naili et al., 2023)

a) *The Role of Digital Wallets*: M-Pesa in Kenya and Paytm in India are two prominent instances of platforms that have drastically changed how customers obtain financial services. By allowing more than 40 million individuals to access financial services like mobile money transfers, utility payments, and even insurance—all through their mobile phones—M-Pesa, for example, has extended financial inclusion to Kenya's rural and underprivileged communities. This change eliminates the requirement for actual bank branches, enabling access to financial services in areas with limited or nonexistent traditional banking infrastructure.
   - *Impact on Financial Inclusion*: Digital wallets provide financial services to individuals in remote areas and low-income areas, reducing reliance on cash and enabling secure, trackable transactions. They also offer financial security by moving financial activities online, protecting users from theft or loss of cash. Users can engage in savings programs, access microloans, and invest, broadening their financial capabilities. Digital wallets also reduce transaction costs, as they typically offer lower fees for low-value transactions or cross-border payments, making them more affordable for low-income users.
   - *Challenges*: Digital wallets, despite their potential, rely heavily on smartphone access and reliable internet connections, which can be challenging in rural or economically disadvantaged areas. Low smartphone penetration and limited digital literacy can hinder their adoption. Additionally, regulatory frameworks around digital wallets and mobile money services are still evolving, creating uncertainty and increasing the risk of fraud. Trust in digital platforms remains an issue for those unfamiliar with online transactions, further limiting the adoption of these services.

4.4.2. Microfinance Platforms: Providing Financial Services Without Collateral:

Microfinance platforms have long been essential to financial inclusion because they give people and companies access to financing that they would not otherwise have because they lack collateral, credit histories, or other requirements that banks frequently apply. Online platforms, which provide low-income consumers and small business owners with digital microloans, crowdfunding, and financing options, have expedited this shift. (Ozili et al., 2023)

a) *Online Microfinance Platforms:* Platforms like Kiva, Funding Circle, and Branch International let people to borrow modest sums of money without requiring physical collateral or conventional credit checks, democratizing access to finance. These systems frequently evaluate a borrower's creditworthiness using alternative data, such utility payments, social connections, or mobile phone activities. For instance, Branch International in Africa provides modest, short-term loans to people without official credit records using data analytics and machine learning algorithms.

- *Impact on Financial Inclusion*: Microfinance platforms offer low-income individuals and small businesses access to credit that is not available through traditional banking systems, enabling them to expand their businesses, improve living conditions, and invest in education and healthcare. These loans also encourage entrepreneurs to start or scale businesses, promoting job creation and local economic development, particularly in rural or isolated communities.
- *Challenges:* Microfinance provides capital access but also poses risks, particularly in unstable economic conditions. High interest rates, unsustainable loan terms, and lack of regulation can lead to debt traps. The proliferation of microfinance platforms increases the risk of over-indebtedness, and lack of financial literacy can create a debt cycle.

4.4.3. *Savings and Investment Platforms: Empowering Low-Income Populations to Build Wealth:*

Platforms for investments and savings are essential to assisting marginalized communities in gradually increasing their wealth. These platforms use technology to facilitate low-barrier investment possibilities and micro savings, which promote wealth growth and financial responsibility.

a) *Micro-Savings and Investment Platforms*: Automatic savings systems have been established by platforms such as Acorns, Chime, and GoSave, enabling users to gradually save tiny sums of money. These platforms frequently move the difference into investment funds or savings accounts after rounding transactions to the closest dollar. Users may easily start investing without needing to pay huge quantities of money up front thanks to Acorns, which invests leftover change from their purchases into diverse portfolios. (Thomas et al., 2023)
   - *Impact on Financial Inclusion*: Micro-savings platforms help individuals develop gradual savings habits, managing financial volatility and preparing for emergencies. They provide access to investment, reducing barriers to entry and democratizing wealth-building tools for underserved populations. They also offer financial education resources, helping individuals make better financial decisions and understand their money's function. Overall, micro-savings platforms contribute to diverse and resilient wealth accumulation.
   - *Challenges:* Financial platforms like Chime, which require internet access, smartphones, and bank accounts, may not be accessible to low-income users in remote areas or without formal banking relationships. High transaction costs and lack of financial literacy may also reduce savings rates and hinder effective investment management.

4.4.4. Embedded Finance: Integrating Financial Services into Non-Financial Platforms:

Embedded finance refers to the integration of financial services into non-financial digital platforms such as e-commerce, agriculture, and even healthcare, enabling users to access credit, payments, insurance, and investment opportunities directly through the platform they are already using.

a) *Embedded Finance in E-Commerce and Agriculture:* E-commerce platforms like Amazon Pay, Alipay, and Shopify Payments integrate financial services into their payment ecosystems, enabling users to buy goods, services, access credit, and insurance products. In the agricultural sector, fintech solutions like FarmDrive and M-Farm provide farmers with crop insurance, loans, and market pricing information without requiring them to visit a traditional bank.
    - *Impact on Financial Inclusion*: Embedded finance offers seamless financial services, allowing individuals to access them in their existing transactions, such as online purchases or agricultural management. This makes financial services more accessible and cost-efficient, as it reduces overhead costs. Embedded finance platforms also promote financial participation, allowing people to buy products on credit or access emergency loans without a formal bank account, thereby enabling underserved populations to engage in commerce and investment. (Elsaid, 2023)
    - *Challenges*: The success of embedded finance relies on a robust digital infrastructure, which may be lacking in rural or economically disadvantaged areas. It also necessitates a basic level of digital literacy, as users may struggle to navigate digital platforms or understand financial products effectively.

Fintech has significantly enhanced financial inclusion by providing low-cost, efficient solutions to underserved populations. However, challenges like digital literacy, regulatory uncertainty, the digital divide, and privacy concerns persist. To maximize fintech's benefits, policymakers, financial institutions, and technology providers must collaborate on inclusive policies, infrastructure improvements, and financial education programs. The goal is to ensure effective, responsible, and sustainable use of financial services for long-term empowerment.

4.5 Fintech as A Catalyst for Financial Inclusion

Fintech is a technology that promotes financial inclusion by removing obstacles and transforming the financial system. It offers scalable, equitable, and sustainable solutions to global financial exclusion. Fintech enhances accessibility, gender inclusion, economic empowerment, and efficiency, supporting social justice, empowering marginalized populations, and promoting inclusive economic growth.

4.5.1. Enhanced Accessibility: Reaching Remote and Underserved Communities:

Fintech's fundamental advantage is its capacity to offer financial services in areas where conventional banking models have fallen short or are still scarce. Fintech can provide services to people in underserved, rural, or distant areas by utilizing technology; many of these individuals would not otherwise have access to fundamental financial goods.

- *Mobile Banking: Breaking Geographic Barriers:* M-Pesa, Alipay, and Paytm have made significant strides in making financial services accessible in remote and underserved areas, particularly in Sub-Saharan Africa. Mobile money has enabled millions of unbanked individuals in Kenya to access the formal financial system through their mobile phones, allowing them to transfer money, save, borrow, and buy insurance without needing to visit a physical bank branch. Fintech bypasses the need for physical infrastructure by providing services directly on mobile devices or via the internet, significantly lowering the cost of reaching underserved populations. In rural Africa, the cost of building a brick-and-mortar bank branch is prohibitively high, but mobile money services are relatively inexpensive to deploy, enabling millions of people to access financial services on their phones. Fintech services tailored to informal workers, such as microloans and savings plans, provide access to essential financial products, allowing them to build financial stability, save for future needs, and access capital for business expansion. (Mushtaq et al., 2023)

- *Overcoming Identity Barriers:* Underserved populations, especially in rural areas, face a significant challenge in accessing banking services due to the lack of formal identification. Fintech platforms have addressed this by offering alternative identity verification methods, such as mobile money platforms that use SIM card registration as a unique identifier. This system not only provides a more inclusive solution but also helps build a digital identity, opening up opportunities for financial services. (Kaur, et.al., 2022) Fintech platforms also use alternative credit scoring methods, such as mobile usage patterns, payment history, and social network data, to assess creditworthiness and offer services based on individuals' actual behavior, rather than their lack of formal documentation or a traditional credit score.

4.5.2. Economic Empowerment: Enabling Access to Credit, Savings, and Economic Growth:

Fintech plays a pivotal role in enabling economic empowerment by providing access to credit, savings tools, and investment opportunities, especially for those who have historically been excluded from these essential financial services.

- *Access to Credit and Microloans*: Fintech platforms like Tala, Branch, and LendUp provide microloans to millions of low-income individuals and small businesses without collateral or formal income. These platforms use mobile data to assess creditworthiness, allowing individuals to be deemed "uncreditworthy" by traditional financial institutions. This leads to economic empowerment, as microloans enable small businesses to purchase inventory, expand operations, and hire employees, contributing to job creation and local economic growth. Fintech services also provide quick access to small loans or emergency funding.
- *Savings and Investment:* Micro-savings and micro-investing platforms like Acorns, Chime, and GoSave have revolutionized the way low-income individuals approach savings and wealth-building. These platforms enable users to save small amounts regularly or invest spare change into diversified portfolios, democratizing access to savings and investment opportunities previously unattainable for these communities. These platforms also contribute to economic empowerment by providing financial resilience, teaching financial discipline, and promoting wealth creation. By allowing users to invest modest sums, fintech opens up wealth-building opportunities previously restricted to the wealthy, allowing users to access returns on investment, closing the wealth gap and promoting long-term economic mobility. (Jha & Dangwal, 2024)

4.5.3. Improved Efficiency: Reducing Transaction Costs and Time through Digitization:

One of the most significant advantages of fintech is the efficiency it brings to the financial system by reducing transaction costs, eliminating unnecessary intermediaries, and enabling faster financial transactions. This efficiency leads to better service for underserved communities and fosters greater economic activity.

- *Reducing Transaction Costs:* Traditional banking systems often charge high transaction fees, particularly for cross-border payments or remittances. The World Bank estimates that the global average remittance fee is over 7%, which is particularly high for low-income individuals. Fintech solutions like Wise and Revolute have significantly reduced international money transfer costs, offering cheaper and faster alternatives. This lower cost makes it more affordable for low-income users to send money, make payments, or purchase goods and services. The digitization of financial services also speeds up transaction processing, reducing waiting times for payments to clear or money transfers. This rapid access to funds improves liquidity and allows businesses to operate more efficiently, especially for small enterprises relying on quick payments to maintain cash flow. (Shen et al., 2024)
- *Automation and Streamlining of Processes:* Fintech solutions automate traditional financial processes like loan approval, credit scoring, and payments, eliminating paperwork and human error. This leads to quicker and more accurate financial services. Automation saves time for users and providers, reducing physical visits and operational costs. Financial institutions can reach a larger audience with fewer resources. Digitization of financial services allows fintech companies to scale offerings quickly, reaching a larger population with less infrastructure investment, especially in countries with large unbanked populations where traditional banking systems may struggle.

4.5.4. Gender Inclusion: Empowering Women Through Access to Financial Tools:

Fintech plays a critical role in promoting gender inclusion by providing women with the financial tools and services they need to achieve economic independence and empowerment.

- *Tailored Financial Products for Women:* Fintech has developed products for women, such as microloans, savings accounts, and insurance, to address their unique financial needs. Services like She Leads Africa and Women's World Banking provide these services to women entrepreneurs, overcoming challenges like gender bias in lending, unpaid labor, and income inequality. These platforms also offer financial control and independence, reducing reliance on male family members in developing countries, empowering women with greater control over their personal finances.
- *Financial Literacy for Women:* Fintech platforms offer financial products and financial literacy education for women, focusing on savings, investing, and budgeting. These programs help women navigate financial challenges and build confidence. Financial literacy programs promote long-term economic security and well-being, enabling them to manage household finances, save for future goals, and invest in education or businesses. This positively impacts gender inclusion by

building confidence and equipping women with the necessary skills for financial success. (Anarfo et al., 2019)

Fintech has significantly impacted financial inclusion by overcoming historical and systemic barriers, enabling access to essential financial services through mobile banking, microloans, digital payments, and tailored financial products. However, challenges like digital literacy, internet connectivity, and regulatory frameworks need to be addressed for fintech to continue promoting inclusive growth and empowering underserved populations, particularly women, low-income individuals, and those in remote areas. By addressing these challenges, fintech can continue to promote sustainable growth and economic participation.

4.6. Environmental Sustainability in Fintech Operations

The rapid growth of fintech, while transformative, has significant ecological implications. Key among these is the environmental impact of resource-intensive technologies, such as blockchain. As fintech expands, it is critical to balance innovation with sustainability to minimize its ecological footprint.

4.6.1. Ecological Impact of Fintech Operations:

- *Blockchain Energy Consumption*: Blockchain technologies, like Bitcoin, consume significant amounts of electricity due to their decentralized nature, which necessitates high computational power for transaction validation and network security, potentially consuming entire countries' energy consumption.
- *Data Centers and Cloud Services:* Fintech platforms heavily rely on data centers for real-time processing, storage, and analytics, generating significant carbon emissions due to energy consumption and cooling systems, driven by the increasing volume of transactions and AI-driven processes.

4.6.2. Sustainable Practices for Fintech Operations:

- *Adopting Energy-Efficient Blockchain Protocols*: Ethereum's transition to Proof-of-Stake (PoS) has significantly reduced energy consumption by over 99%, and layer-2 solutions are being explored to process transactions off-chain, reducing the load on primary networks.
- *Greening Data Centers*: Utilize renewable energy sources and advanced cooling technologies to optimize data centers, while utilizing green cloud computing services from providers like Google Cloud and AWS.
- *Carbon Offset Initiatives*: Fintech companies can offset their emissions by investing in carbon offset programs and providing customers with carbon-neutral payment solutions to encourage eco-friendly behaviors.
- *Encouraging Digital Financial Literacy:* The goal is to promote paperless banking to minimize waste and encourage the adoption of eco-friendly digital solutions.

4.6.3 Emerging Risks in Fintech: Algorithmic Bias in AI-Driven Credit Scoring

AI-driven credit scoring systems, crucial for financial inclusion, pose new risks like algorithmic bias, where models unintentionally disadvantage specific demographic groups due to data or design flaws. The key risks and solution to mitigate algorithmic bias are discussed under. AI models may be biased due to historical data, which may reflect systemic biases like racial, gender, or socioeconomic disparities. Lack of model transparency can obscure biased outcomes, and discriminatory practices can lead to legal challenges and erode public trust in fintech systems. Therefore, it is crucial to ensure transparency and avoid bias in AI models. The solutions to mitigate algorithmic bias are. To improve AI model accuracy, use representative datasets and regularly audit them for potential biases. Implement Explainable AI (XAI) techniques to make AI models more transparent and interpretable. Conduct regular bias audits to detect and mitigate bias. Embrace ethical design principles, such as the Fairness Through Awareness principle, to minimize disparate impacts. Adhere to guidelines like GDPR's "right to explanation" and emerging AI regulations to ensure transparency and accountability. Implement user feedback loops to address errors or biases in real-time. These measures ensure fairness, transparency, and accountability in AI systems. Fintech's growth brings both environmental challenges and ethical risks. By adopting sustainable practices, such as greener technologies and carbon offset initiatives, the industry can minimize its ecological footprint. Simultaneously, addressing algorithmic bias through better data practices, transparency, and regulation ensures that AI-driven solutions remain fair and inclusive. Balancing innovation with responsibility is key to building a fintech ecosystem that is both sustainable and equitable.

4.6.4. Addressing Challenges and Limitations in Fintech

Fintech faces challenges such as cybersecurity threats, especially in low-literacy regions, and regulatory hurdles. These issues can hinder the growth of the sector. Cybersecurity concerns include phishing and fraud risks, as users in these regions are more vulnerable to such attacks. Fraudsters exploit trust and lack of understanding of digital platforms to gain unauthorized access. Weak authentication practices, such as basic passwords or PINs, are common, and lack of digital literacy can exacerbate these risks. Addressing these challenges is crucial for a resilient, inclusive, and globally scalable fintech ecosystem.

- *Fintech Solutions:* Fintech companies are implementing various security measures to enhance their services. These include Two-Factor Authentication (2FA) and biometric security, which are widely used by platforms like Paytm and EcoCash. They also partner with local organizations to deliver cybersecurity awareness campaigns in local languages, such as Safaricom in Kenya. AI-powered fraud detection is also being used, with models like Zest AI detecting anomalies in real-time. Additionally, fintech apps are designed with simplified user interfaces for low-literacy users.
- *Challenges in Fintech Adoption:* Fintech regulations vary across jurisdictions, complicating cross-border operations. Small fintech firms face high compliance costs, such as anti-money laundering and KYC protocols. Strong data protection laws like GDPR in Europe require careful data management, while weak privacy laws create uncertainty and risk. Additionally, obtaining licenses for digital payments or lending can be time-consuming and costly, delaying market entry in some countries.
- *Best Practices to Overcome Regulatory Challenges:* Fintech companies should collaborate with regulators to create policies that balance innovation and risk management. Regulatory sandboxes

in the UK, Singapore, and India allow firms to test solutions under supervision, fostering innovation while ensuring compliance. Global standards initiatives like the Global Financial Innovation Network (GFIN) aim to create a unified regulatory framework for fintech, reducing compliance complexity. Fintech firms can use RegTech solutions to automate compliance processes, such as real-time transaction monitoring for AML purposes. Privacy-by-design principles ensure user data protection, building trust in regions with stringent data privacy laws. Governments can simplify licensing and registration for fintech startups, as seen in Rwanda's fintech-friendly regulatory environment.

4.6.5. Case Studies of Regulatory Challenges and Resolutions

India's fintech adoption faced challenges due to RBI regulations requiring stringent KYC processes. Digital KYC alternatives like Aadhaar-based eKYC provided a secure solution. Europe faced GDPR compliance issues, but firms adopted robust encryption and anonymization techniques. Nigeria's Central Bank introduced guidelines for mobile money operators, promoting competition and innovation. These solutions helped fintech companies navigate regulatory uncertainty, maintain operational efficiency, and promote innovation in the mobile money market. Addressing cybersecurity concerns and navigating regulatory hurdles are essential for the sustainable growth of fintech. By adopting robust security measures, fostering digital literacy, and collaborating with regulators, fintech platforms can build trust, enhance user safety, and drive innovation. A proactive and inclusive approach ensures that the benefits of fintech are accessible to all, regardless of geographic or economic barriers.

4.7. Challenges in Leveraging Fintech for Financial Inclusion

Fintech has the potential to significantly improve financial inclusion, but a number of obstacles currently stand in the way of its full potential, particularly in developing nations and among marginalized communities. These difficulties include regulatory and security issues as well as limitations in infrastructure and technology. For fintech solutions to be equitable, sustainable, and successful in advancing financial inclusion for all, these obstacles must be removed.

4.7.1. Digital Divide: The Gap in Access to Technology Due to Lack of Infrastructure and Affordability:

The digital divide is a gap between those with easy access to modern information and communication technology (ICT) and those without, influenced by factors like geographic location, income levels, and infrastructure availability. In rural and underserved areas, large populations lack access to the internet, smartphones, and basic telecommunications infrastructure. Challenges include limited access to devices and connectivity, high costs of data and technology, and geographic isolation. To address this, companies can focus on providing affordable smartphones and data packages for low-income populations, partnering with telecom providers to offer subsidized services. Fintech providers are also developing solutions that allow people to conduct financial transactions without constant internet connection, using technologies like SMS-based systems or USSD codes. Infrastructure development is also crucial, as governments and private companies must invest in strengthening digital infrastructure, including broadband internet and mobile networks, in rural and underserved areas. By addressing these challenges, the digital divide can be bridged and improved for all.

Cybersecurity Risks: Concerns Over Fraud, Data Breaches, and Identity Theft:

The rise of fintech platforms has raised concerns about cybersecurity threats, including fraud, data breaches, and identity theft. These risks can have severe consequences for individuals and organizations, as digital financial services handle sensitive personal data. Unbanked and underserved individuals often lack knowledge to identify and avoid financial scams or phishing attacks. Data breaches, especially in low-income markets, make fintech platforms attractive targets for hackers. Lack of trust in fintech platforms can discourage adoption. To address these challenges, fintech companies should invest in stronger security protocols, user education on digital security practices, and develop and enforce clear cybersecurity standards to protect users and foster innovation in the fintech space.

4.7.2. Regulatory Hurdles: Compliance Issues with Varying Global and Local Regulations:

Fintech companies face significant challenges in navigating the regulatory landscape due to diverse regulations across different countries and regions. These regulations can hinder the scalability of fintech solutions, especially in cross-border operations. The complexity of these regulations can be costly and time-consuming, especially in emerging markets. Legal and tax compliance can be challenging, especially in digital financial services. Cross-border challenges arise when fintech platforms expand internationally, as they often face difficulties dealing with data privacy, payments, and taxes. Solutions include global regulatory frameworks, regulatory sandboxes, and regulatory technology (RegTech), which can help establish global standards for fintech and foster innovation.(Anarfo et al., 2019)

4.7.3. Sustainability of Fintech Models: Ensuring Long-Term Viability and Scalability:

Fintech innovations, often based on venture capital or subsidies, face challenges in transitioning to a financially sustainable model that can serve underserved populations in the long term. These include profitability vs. accessibility, scalability issues, funding and investment, and securing long-term funding. Fintech companies often offer services at low or no cost, straining profitability. Scaling fintech services requires significant capital investment in technology, customer support, and marketing. Securing long-term funding is a challenge, as investors may demand high returns, putting pressure on companies to prioritize short-term profits over long-term sustainability and social impact. Solutions include diversifying revenue streams, partnering with businesses, and focusing on sustainable lending practices. By addressing these challenges, fintech platforms can continue to grow and serve underserved populations in the long term.

Fintech offers significant opportunities for financial inclusion, but challenges must be addressed to fully realize its potential. These include overcoming the digital divide, securing cybersecurity, navigating regulatory hurdles, and ensuring business model sustainability. Collaboration between governments, private companies, and regulatory bodies is crucial for fintech innovations to thrive and serve underserved populations. (Manzoor, 2023)

4.8. Regulatory and Policy Frameworks: Essential for Promoting Fintech and Financial Inclusion

The legal and policy landscape is crucial in determining how fintech develops and guaranteeing its capacity to advance financial inclusion. To provide a flexible and encouraging environment that promotes innovation while safeguarding consumers and maintaining financial stability, governments, international organizations, and commercial parties must collaborate. Good regulations and laws foster confidence, direct the growth of fintech, and establish the prerequisites for scalable solutions that assist marginalized communities.

4.8.1. Role of Governments: Policies and Initiatives to Encourage Fintech Adoption for Financial Inclusion:

Governments play a crucial role in enabling fintech's role in financial inclusion by adopting policies and initiatives that impact its ability to serve underserved populations. Key areas of government role include creating clear and flexible regulatory frameworks, incentivizing fintech innovation through tax breaks, grants, and funding, investing in digital infrastructure, promoting financial literacy and education, and implementing consumer protection regulations. Regulatory clarity and flexibility are essential for fintech firms to operate confidently and expand their services, while incentives like tax breaks, grants, and funding can reduce initial costs. Investment in digital infrastructure is essential for widespread use in rural and remote areas. Governments must also implement regulations to safeguard consumers from fraud, privacy violations, and abusive lending practices.(Hong et al., 2024)

4.8.2. Public-Private Partnerships: Collaboration Between Fintech Companies, Governments, and NGOs to Reach Underserved Populations:

Public-private partnerships (PPPs) are crucial in addressing financial exclusion by utilizing fintech solutions. These partnerships can build infrastructure, provide services, and create a holistic financial inclusion ecosystem. Key areas of collaboration include infrastructure development, expanding financial products, digital identity solutions, and social impact. Governments can partner with telecom companies, internet service providers, and fintech firms to provide low-cost mobile phones, internet coverage, and payment systems in rural areas. Fintech companies can create products catering to underserved populations, such as microloans, insurance products, and small savings accounts. Governments and NGOs can create standardized digital identities for customers, enabling fintech companies to onboard customers and provide services like credit scoring and loan disbursement. These collaborations help millions of underserved individuals access financial services.

4.8.3. Global Standards: The Role of International Organizations in Promoting Inclusive Fintech Practices:

International organizations like the World Bank, IMF, and UN are crucial in setting global standards for financial inclusion and fintech adoption. Their influence ensures that fintech grows sustainably and inclusively worldwide. Key areas of influence include developing global standards, harmonizing regulations across countries, providing technical assistance to developing countries, and promoting cross-border fintech solutions. The World Bank and IMF have developed frameworks and guidelines for financial inclusion, providing recommendations on regulations, infrastructure needs, and consumer protection. They also provide technical assistance to developing countries to build fintech regulatory capacity, including training regulators, cybersecurity guidance, and digital infrastructure development. Examples of global standards and initiatives include the G20's Financial Inclusion Agenda and the World Bank's ID4D Initiative. (Alfawareh & Al-Kofahi, 2024)

Governments, public-private partnerships, and international organizations play a crucial role in fostering an ecosystem for fintech to achieve financial inclusion. Governments must establish clear regulations, incentives, and infrastructure support, while public-private partnerships can reach underserved communities and provide tailored financial solutions. Global organizations offer frameworks to ensure inclusive, secure, and sustainable fintech use, making financial inclusion a reality for billions of underserved people worldwide.

4.9. Tailoring Recommendations to Stakeholders

The recommendations are tailored for academics, policymakers, and practitioners, who are crucial in shaping the future of fintech and addressing its challenges.

- *For Academics: Research Directions*: Academics can significantly contribute to the fintech industry by examining its long-term socio-economic impact, including income equality, healthcare access, education, and wealth distribution. A longitudinal study on mobile banking services in rural areas could reveal how digital financial services drive economic mobility and poverty alleviation. Behavioral insights on fintech adoption, especially in underbanked and low-literacy populations, can be gained using the Technology Acceptance Model (TAM). Additionally, exploring the impact of AI and blockchain on financial decision-making, particularly in lending and payments, can contribute to more equitable algorithms. (Tyagi, 2024)
- *For Policymakers: Specific Initiatives*: Policymakers must foster a supportive environment for fintech innovation while ensuring consumer protection, fairness, and financial stability. This can be achieved through public-private partnerships (PPPs), regulatory sandboxes, and inclusive digital infrastructure. PPPs involve collaborations between fintech firms, traditional financial institutions, and government agencies to tailor services to diverse populations. Regulatory sandboxes allow fintech startups to test products in controlled environments, identifying regulatory gaps and fostering innovation. The UK's Financial Conduct Authority has established a regulatory sandbox to facilitate fintech innovation while ensuring regulatory compliance. Investing in digital infrastructure ensures affordable internet and smartphones for all citizens, including low-income and rural populations.
- *For Practitioners: Strategies for User-Centric and Scalable Fintech Solutions*: Fintech companies are focusing on creating user-friendly, low-cost solutions for underbanked or low-literate users. They aim to create intuitive platforms with low entry barriers, ensuring even those with limited technological literacy can access and use services effectively. Fintech solutions should be optimized for mobile and offline capabilities, reaching underserved populations with limited internet connectivity. Scalable technologies like cloud-based platforms and blockchain can offer low-cost services while ensuring data security and transparency. Ripple, a blockchain-based payment system, facilitates low-cost, cross-border payments. Fintech products should be scalable and efficient,

minimizing operational costs. Financial literacy resources should be integrated into the application, empowering users to make informed financial decisions. (Unsal & Ozkan, 2024)

The fintech ecosystem thrives when all stakeholders—academics, policymakers, and practitioners—work collaboratively. Academics can offer insights that deepen our understanding of fintech's long-term effects, policymakers can foster an enabling environment through regulatory support, and practitioners can design user-friendly, scalable solutions that meet the needs of diverse populations. By tailoring recommendations to each group, we can ensure that fintech becomes a powerful tool for financial inclusion and socio-economic progress.

4.10. Future Prospects of Fintech in Financial Inclusion

Fintech's future in promoting financial inclusion is promising due to technological advancements, local needs understanding, and sustainable growth. It can offer personalized, affordable, and inclusive financial services to underserved populations globally, but careful planning is needed to prevent new inequalities. (Thomas et al., 2023)

4.10.1. Technological Advancements: The Potential of Emerging Technologies

- *Artificial Intelligence (AI):* Artificial Intelligence (AI) is expected to revolutionize financial services by making them more accessible, personalized, and efficient. AI can improve credit scoring by using alternative data sources like payment histories, social media activity, and mobile data. This can help individuals without traditional credit histories access loans and create alternative credit models that better reflect their financial behavior. AI-powered chatbots and virtual assistants can provide personalized financial advice to those with limited financial literacy, making financial decision-making more accessible. AI can also be used for fraud detection and risk management, ensuring greater security and reducing the likelihood of financial fraud. AI algorithms are already integrated into mobile apps, providing personalized financial recommendations, predictive analytics, and notifications to help users manage their money more effectively.
- *Blockchain:* Blockchain technology enables the creation of Decentralized Finance (DeFi) platforms that eliminate the need for traditional intermediaries like banks, making financial services more transparent, secure, and accessible. This is particularly beneficial for regions with poor or unreliable banking infrastructure, providing a trustworthy, borderless alternative for lending, insurance, and payments. Blockchain can also reduce costs associated with cross-border payments and remittances, benefiting underserved communities. Blockchain-based solutions bypass traditional intermediaries, allowing faster, cheaper, and more secure cross-border transfers. Smart contracts built on blockchain platforms automate loan agreements, insurance payouts, and other financial transactions, opening up opportunities for micro-insurance and micro-lending for underserved populations. Blockchain also enables tokenization of assets, making investment opportunities more accessible for individuals.
- *5G Technology:* 5G technology will improve mobile connectivity, enabling faster, reliable, and secure access to fintech services. This will be particularly beneficial in underserved and rural areas where stable internet is a barrier. Additionally, 5G will enable IoT-integrated financial products, allowing real-time data integration from connected devices. For instance, IoT-enabled micro-

insurance products could provide affordable solutions to underserved populations by adjusting premiums based on data from vehicles, health, or homes. Overall, 5G technology will significantly improve the accessibility of digital financial services.

4.10.2. Customization and Localization: Tailoring Fintech Solutions to Specific Regional and Cultural Contexts

Fintech solutions must be customized and localized to effectively address financial exclusion, as one-size-fits-all approaches often fail to cater to the unique needs of different regions, cultures, and socio-economic groups.

- *Cultural and Regional Sensitivity:* Fintech solutions should be available in multiple languages and use culturally appropriate communication methods, making them more inclusive and understandable in regions with diverse linguistic and cultural backgrounds. For instance, WhatsApp-based banking has been successful in markets like India, where the messaging app is widely used and supports multiple languages. Fintech companies must also understand cultural nuances and financial behaviors to create solutions that cater to the local context. For instance, in African countries, fintech solutions can integrate informal savings systems with digital platforms, allowing users to save in a trusted environment while benefiting from the digital economy. Additionally, fintech solutions should be mobile-first, operating seamlessly on low-cost smartphones, offering lightweight apps, and utilizing SMS-based services to ensure accessibility even in regions with limited high-end devices and internet connections. (Dar et al., 2024)
- *Financial Inclusion for Specific Groups:* Fintech platforms can enhance financial inclusion for marginalized groups, particularly women and youth. Women-focused micro-loans, savings plans, and insurance can empower them, while youth-focused services like student loans and savings accounts promote financial independence and responsibility among younger populations. These products can help overcome socio-cultural barriers and promote financial inclusion in developing economies.

4.10.3. Sustainable Growth: Ensuring Fintech Evolves Without Creating New Inequalities

Fintech can enhance financial inclusion, but it's crucial not to create new inequalities. Long-term strategies are needed to ensure fintech's sustainability and inclusivity.

- *Addressing the Digital Divide:* Fintech services should be accessible to all, regardless of socio-economic status, through infrastructure investment and affordable internet access. Governments and private companies should collaborate to build networks in underserved regions and provide affordable smartphones and internet services. Fintech companies should design sustainable business models that cater to all populations, including low-income groups. Offering no-fee accounts, small savings plans, and micro-insurance can help individuals with limited income participate in the financial system without excessive costs. Providing small loans and low-cost services is crucial for maintaining financial inclusivity. (Nobanee et al., 2024)

- *Balancing Profit and Social Impact:* Fintech companies must prioritize ethical use of data, data privacy, and security measures to protect users from exploitation, fraud, and identity theft. Regulatory oversight is crucial for maintaining trust in the fintech ecosystem. To have lasting impact, companies should adopt scalable, sustainable business models that promote financial inclusion and profitability. These models should prioritize long-term impact over short-term gains, focusing on low-cost models, digital platforms, and partnerships with local actors. These strategies will ensure fair distribution of fintech's benefits.

Fintech's future in financial inclusion is promising due to emerging technologies, regional customization, and sustainability commitment. AI, blockchain, and 5G can create personalized financial services and a more inclusive global economy. However, development should be guided by equity, affordability, and responsibility to avoid exacerbating inequalities. The future of financial inclusion depends on a balance between innovation, localization, and sustainable growth, ensuring fintech benefits are accessible to all.

5. CONCLUSION: FINTECH'S ROLE IN TRANSFORMING FINANCIAL INCLUSION GLOBALLY:

Fintech has significantly impacted financial inclusion by introducing technologies like mobile money, blockchain, AI, and 5G, enabling access to savings, loans, payments, and insurance products for previously excluded populations. This has been particularly significant in developing countries, where innovations like mobile payments, cryptocurrency, and peer-to-peer lending have increased economic participation. The integration of digital infrastructure, such as India Stack and M-Pesa in Africa, demonstrates how fintech can thrive in underserved environments. AI-driven solutions for personalized financial services, alternative credit scoring, and real-time transactions cater to the unique needs of various populations, including women, small-scale entrepreneurs, and those in remote areas. However, achieving inclusive growth requires a multi-stakeholder approach, including governments, the private sector, and non-profit organizations. Governments should introduce regulatory frameworks that support innovation and consumer protection, while private sector companies and financial institutions should continue innovating and creating affordable, scalable, and accessible solutions. Non-profit organizations can reach marginalized communities, provide education, and build trust in fintech solutions. To continue its transformative journey, fintech should invest in infrastructure, encourage innovation, build partnerships, foster digital literacy, and address data security.

REFERENCES

Alfawareh, F. S., & Al-Kofahi, M. (2024). Analysis of global research trends on FinTech: A bibliometric study. *Journal of Internet and Digital Economics*, *4*(1), 30–49. DOI: 10.1108/JIDE-06-2023-0014

Anarfo, E. B., Abor, J. Y., Osei, K. A., & Gyeke-Dako, A. (2019). Financial inclusion and financial sector development in Sub-Saharan Africa: A panel VAR approach. *International Journal of Managerial Finance*, *15*(4), 444–463. DOI: 10.1108/IJMF-07-2018-0205

Arora, S., & Madan, P. (2023). Conceptual Framework Depicting the Drivers for the Fintech Growth: An Outlook for India. In *Contemporary Studies of Risks in Emerging Technology, Part A* (pp. 197–220). Emerald Publishing Limited. DOI: 10.1108/978-1-80455-562-020231014

Dar, B. I., Badwan, N., & Kumar, J. (2024). Investigating the role of Fintech innovations and green finance toward sustainable economic development: A bibliometric analysis. *International Journal of Islamic and Middle Eastern Finance and Management*, *17*(6), 1175–1195. DOI: 10.1108/IMEFM-01-2024-0018

Elsaid, H. M. (2023). A review of literature directions regarding the impact of fintech firms on the banking industry. *Qualitative Research in Financial Markets*, *15*(5), 693–711. DOI: 10.1108/QRFM-10-2020-0197

Hidayat-ur-Rehman, I. (2024). The role of financial literacy in enhancing firm's sustainable performance through Fintech adoption: A moderated mediation analysis. *International Journal of Innovation Science*. Advance online publication. DOI: 10.1108/IJIS-03-2024-0056

Hong, J., Wang, N., & Zhou, T. (2024). The effects of FinTech adoption on bank loan spreads. *Managerial Finance*. Advance online publication. DOI: 10.1108/MF-03-2024-0238

Jha, S., & Dangwal, R. C. (2024). Fintech services and financial inclusion: a systematic literature review of developing nations. *Journal of Science and Technology Policy Management*. DOI: 10.1108/JSTPM-03-2023-0034

Kaur, J., Syan, A. S., Kaur, S., & Sharma, R. R. (2022). *Understanding the Factors Influencing Actual Usage of Payments Banks: An Empirical Investigation Using the Extended Information Systems Success Model*. FIIB Business Review., DOI: 10.1177/23197145221099095

Manzoor, A. (2023). Antecedents to Following Brands on Facebook and Instagram with Moderating Role of User Experience. *FIIB Business Review*, *0*(0). Advance online publication. DOI: 10.1177/23197145221151010

Mushtaq, R., Dastane, O., Rafiq, M., & Başar, B. D. (2023). Women financial inclusion research: A bibliometric and network analysis. *International Journal of Social Economics*, *50*(8), 1169–1185. DOI: 10.1108/IJSE-06-2022-0438

Naili, M., Jabbouri, I., & Helmi, I. (2023). Financial inclusion and the financial and economic development: Review of the literature, evidence gaps and the road ahead. *Qualitative Market Research*, *26*(5), 632–662. DOI: 10.1108/QMR-02-2023-0017

Nobanee, H., Ellili, N. O. D., Chakraborty, D., & Shanti, H. Z. (2024). Mapping the fintech revolution: How technology is transforming credit risk management. *Global Knowledge, Memory and Communication*. Advance online publication. DOI: 10.1108/GKMC-12-2023-0492

Okello Candiya Bongomin, G., Akol Malinga, C., Manzi Amani, A., & Balinda, R. (2024). Recalibrating the scope of financial inclusion through financial technologies in the digital age: The role of digital literacy as a moderator in rural Uganda. *Information Technology & People*. Advance online publication. DOI: 10.1108/ITP-09-2022-0732

Ozili, P. K. (2020). Theories of Financial Inclusion. In *Uncertainty and Challenges in Contemporary Economic Behaviour* (pp. 89–115). Emerald Publishing Limited., DOI: 10.1108/978-1-80043-095-220201008

Ozili, P. K. (2021). Financial inclusion research around the world: A review. *The Forum for Social Economics*, *50*(4), 457–479. DOI: 10.1080/07360932.2020.1715238

Ozili, P. K., Ademiju, A., & Rachid, S. (2023). Impact of financial inclusion on economic growth: Review of existing literature and directions for future research. *International Journal of Social Economics*, *50*(8), 1105–1122. DOI: 10.1108/IJSE-05-2022-0339

Patnaik, R., Patra, S. K., Mahapatra, D. M., & Baral, S. K. (2024). Adoption and challenges underlying OTT platform in India during pandemic: A critical study of socio-economic and technological issues. *FIIB Business Review*, *13*(3), 356–363.

Shabir, S., & Ali, J. (2022). Determinants of financial inclusion across gender in Saudi Arabia: Evidence from the World Bank's Global Financial Inclusion survey. *International Journal of Social Economics*, *49*(5), 780–800. DOI: 10.1108/IJSE-07-2021-0384

Shen, Y., Agyekum, F., Reddy, K., & Wallace, D. (2024). The welfare impact of financial inclusion: A research agenda. *Journal of Accounting Literature*. Advance online publication. DOI: 10.1108/JAL-10-2023-0190

Shi, W., Ali, M., & Leong, C.-M. (2024). Dynamics of personal financial management: A bibliometric and systematic review on financial literacy, financial capability and financial behavior. *International Journal of Bank Marketing*. Advance online publication. DOI: 10.1108/IJBM-06-2023-0359

Susan, M., Winarto, J., & Gunawan, I. (2023). *Financial Literacy of Micro, Small, and Medium Enterprises: Empirical Study During the Pandemic Period* (pp. 113–122). DOI: 10.1108/S1571-038620230000031014

Thomas, N. M., Mendiratta, P., & Kashiramka, S. (2023). FinTech credit: Uncovering knowledge base, intellectual structure and research front. *International Journal of Bank Marketing*, *41*(7), 1769–1802. DOI: 10.1108/IJBM-01-2023-0039

Thottoli, M. M. (2024). The tactician role of FinTech in the accounting and auditing field: A bibliometric analysis. *Qualitative Research in Financial Markets*, *16*(2), 213–238. DOI: 10.1108/QRFM-11-2021-0196

Tyagi, A. (2024). Risk Management in Fintech. In *The Emerald Handbook of Fintech* (pp. 157–175). Emerald Publishing Limited., DOI: 10.1108/978-1-83753-608-520241015

Unsal, O., & Ozkan, B. (2024). Technologies and Emerging Trends Shaping Fintech. In *The Emerald Handbook of Fintech* (pp. 399–418). Emerald Publishing Limited., DOI: 10.1108/978-1-83753-608-520241046

Chapter 11
Neobanks:
Revolutionizing the Financial Landscape and Redefining Banking Paradigms

Sulagna Das
https://orcid.org/0000-0003-4683-453X
JIS University, India

Shitikanth Kumar Tripathi
https://orcid.org/0009-0006-5271-7312
Eminent College of Management and Technology, India

ABSTRACT

Neobanks, digital-only banks, use advanced technology to offer cost-effective, customer-focused financial services. They operate on agile platforms, offering competitive pricing, fee-free accounts, and improved savings returns. Despite challenges like regulatory compliance and cybersecurity risks, they have prompted increased digital transformation efforts.The study examines the geographical dynamics of neobanks expansion, focusing on North America, Europe, and emerging countries like Asia and Africa. Neobanks have the potential to influence a more technologically advanced, competitive, and inclusive global financial environment as they develop and expand.

1. INTRODUCTION

Neo Banks are Digitally equipped advanced new era banks which operates round the clock throughout the year without having any brick-mortar kind traditional bank. With the advent of Neo Banks, traditional banking system is getting stern competition and challenges in almost all sphere of banking system. Neo Banks are also termed as "Challenger Banks". Neo Banks are specialized in catering to tech savvy customers as the boon of the banking is based on AI.(Nur Aliftiani et al., 2024) Generally, in Indian financial system Neo Banks could be categorized in three verticals

a) A Digital subsidiary: YONO is the digital subsidiary of full flagged commercial bank, State Bank of India.

DOI: 10.4018/979-8-3373-0209-6.ch011

b) Front- end neo bank: Since Front End bank does not have banking license to operate so it banks on traditional banks or NBFC for providing services, ex. Jupiter, Fi Money which works as a partner of Federal Bank. Instant Pay has partnered with ICICI Bank, Axis Bank, Yes Bank, IndusInd Bank.
c) Full stacked digital banks: Full stacked Digital banks are like any other commercial banks which provide all banking services including loan disbursal and taking deposits. (Shanti et al., 2024)

Invasion of Neo Banks in Indian Financial System has given some impetus to analyze it's SWOC, i.e. Strengths, weaknesses, opportunities and Challenges.

- S1) First and the foremost strength is its accessibility throughout the year and round the clock which plays pivotal role to change the banking paradigm.
- S2) Since it provides only online services so it is cost effective.
- S3) Stretch of services are from Money transfer, bill payments, savings account facility, loan disbursal to wealth management.(Monis & Pai, 2023)
- S4) Real time settlement with convenience.

Neo banks, encounter fundamental weaknesses that challenge their growth and stability, which have been listed below:

- W1) Awareness in rural areas as majority of netizens from tier 2 and tier 3 cities are not aware of the concept of Neo Bank
- W2) Trustworthy, Conventional commercial banks are so deeply rooted in Indian Financial system that it will take some time to shift the notion of the customers towards Neo Bank's functionality and concept. (Dey, 2022)

Commercial Bank Customers of late prefer to have printed passbook for their financial transactions despite having soft copy of transactions history. No commercial banks are removing automatic printing machines from their setup.

- O1) Neo Banks can superimpose entire banking system primarily in urban India and secondarily into rural area.
- O2) Neo banks can extend its tentacles in subsidiary banking products like Mutual Fund, Life Insurance, General Insurance and in Govt. Bonds.(Banga et al., 2023)

Neo banks, though offer advanced and user-centric financial services through digital platforms. However, despite their growing popularity, they face several challenges:

- C1) Neo Banks are facing prime challenge in getting the license from statutory regulatory body, not all Neo banks are allowed to in full flagged commercial banks which lead to their dependence on the partner banks or NBFC.(Jaglan, 2021)
- C2) Data encryption, Data authentication, Data protection, AML, Cyber-attack, Technology transference, Technology upgradation are going to be the big challenges in this vertical.

Indian post payment Banks abbreviated as IPPB, a department under the Ministry of communication, GOI. It has over 9 crore customers till March 2024, which had started its operation in the year 2018. In addition to the conventional services provided by any commercial banks, IPPB provides services like Unified payment interface (UPI), Immediate payment service (IPS), National Electronic Fund Transfer (NEFT), Real -time gross settlement (RTGS), Bharat Bill pay (BPP), Direct Benefit Transfer (DBT) and the most important rampantly used in rural India specifically is Adhar Enabled Payment Services (AEPS). DBT (Direct Transfer benefit) like PM Jan Dhan Yojana has been introduced by Govt. of India which also comes under the purview of Neo banking System where subsidies by Govt. of India are credited directly to beneficiaries account to mitigate the leakage, duplicity and delay and to increase transparency of transactions. (Vidya, 2023) A big question pertains that can Neo bank get its full flagged potential and sustenance without tapping its rural customers where only 36.6% of total population reside in Urban India?

2. OBJECTIVES OF THE STUDY

- The study aims to explore the role of neobanks in transforming the financial sector and redefining traditional banking practices. The specific objectives are:
- To analyze the evolution and growth of neobanks and their impact on the financial industry.
- To examine the key features, technological advancements, and innovative business models adopted by neobanks.
- To identify the challenges faced by neobanks, including regulatory concerns, cybersecurity risks, and customer trust issues.
- To assess the competitive landscape and how neobanks differentiate themselves from traditional banks and fintech firms.
- To evaluate the role of neobanks in promoting financial inclusion, particularly among underserved and unbanked populations.
- To provide strategic recommendations for the sustainable growth and adoption of neobanking solutions.

3. RESEARCH METHODOLOGY

This study adopts a qualitative research approach to examine how neobanks are transforming the financial landscape. A descriptive and exploratory methodology is used to analyze neobanks' business models, technological innovations, regulatory challenges, and market impact. The research is based on secondary data analysis, drawing insights from academic papers, industry reports, regulatory guidelines, and case studies of leading neobanks. These sources provide a comprehensive understanding of market trends, customer adoption patterns, and operational strategies. A thematic analysis is applied to identify key trends such as customer-centric innovations, compliance challenges, cybersecurity risks, and financial inclusion efforts. The study acknowledges limitations, including regulatory variations and rapidly evolving fintech developments, but aims to provide a well-rounded perspective on neobanks' role in reshaping modern banking.

4. DATA ANALYSIS AND INTERPRETATION

4.1. The Evolution Of Neo Banks

Neo banks, also known as digital-only banks, have emerged as transformative players in the financial services sector, challenging traditional banking paradigms. (Bhargava, 2023) Their rise has been shaped by technological advancements, changing consumer needs, and evolving regulatory landscapes.

4.1.1. Early Foundations (1990s–2000s): The Dawn of Internet Banking

In the 1990s, traditional banks introduced online banking for essential services like fund transfers and account management. Fintech companies explored digital innovations to streamline payments and lending, laying the groundwork for fully digital banking systems. As internet adoption increased, customers sought more accessible and efficient financial services.

4.1.2. The Emergence of Neo Banks (2010s): Transition to Digital-Only Models

Neo banks like Simple and Moven have revolutionized the banking industry with their app-based, branchless banking. European banks like N26 and Revolute have also gained momentum with features like multi-currency wallets, zero-fee transactions, and real-time financial tracking. Regulatory advancements like e-money and challenger bank licenses have facilitated the rise of these fully digital institutions. (Garg & Sahu, 2024) Key advantages include cost savings, real-time insights, intuitive digital interfaces, and simplified on boarding processes.

4.1.3. Global Growth and Innovation (2015–2020): Expanding Horizons

Neo banks like Nubank and Uala have entered emerging markets, providing accessible financial solutions to previously excluded populations. They integrate technology like AI and Big Data, enhancing customer experiences through personalization and predictive analytics, and partnering with fintech entities for enhanced service diversity and reach. (Bhatnagr & Rajesh, 2024)

4.1.4. Pandemic-Driven Acceleration (2020–2022): A Digital Leap Forward

The COVID-19 pandemic accelerated the adoption of contactless and remote banking solutions, leading to significant venture capital growth for Neo banks and solidifying mobile banking dominance as the primary financial channel for convenience and real-time capabilities.(Surya Gifari et al., 2023)

4.1.5. Maturity and Competition (2022–2024): Facing New Realities

Neo banks like Revolut expanded globally, while traditional banks intensified digital transformation. Tech giants like Apple and Google entered financial services, leveraging their ecosystems. Policymakers introduced operational guidelines addressing data privacy, anti-money laundering, and consumer protection.(Naresh Sardar Vallabhbhai Patel et al., 2022)

Key Milestones: In 2009, Simple introduced the neo banking model in the USA, gained global traction with multi-currency wallets, became the largest independent digital bank in 2020, and UK-based neo banks achieved profitability milestones in 2023.The journey of neo banks highlights a fundamental shift in the global financial landscape, driven by innovation, customer-centricity, and regulatory evolution. From their inception as challengers to becoming essential players in the financial ecosystem, neo banks continue to redefine banking with cutting-edge technology and tailored services.(Alaeddine Ziouache, 2023) Their ongoing development represents both the opportunities and challenges of the digital age.

4.2. Comparison Between Traditional and Neo Banking

Neo banks have transformed the financial services industry by transforming from traditional banks to digital-first alternatives. They use advanced technologies to reshape customer interactions, offering a comprehensive comparison across key dimensions.

- ***Accessibility and Convenience:*** Traditional banking relies on physical branches, limiting access to rural areas and requiring lengthy, paperwork-intensive processes. Neo banking offers 24/7 accessibility through mobile apps or web platforms, streamlined account setup, and paperless transactions, catering to tech-savvy users and providing seamless, on-the-go financial services.
- ***Cost Efficiency:*** Traditional banking involves high operational expenses and fees for services, while neo banking eliminates physical infrastructure and overhead costs, offering low-cost or fee-free services, making it attractive to cost-conscious customers who prefer low-cost or fee-free options.
- ***Technology Integration:*** Traditional banking involves upgrading to digital solutions, but is limited by legacy systems. Online banking and mobile apps supplement branch-based operations. Neo banking, built on advanced technology, integrates AI, blockchain, and machine learning, offering real-time analytics and AI-driven financial advice.(V & B, 2023)
- ***Customer Experience:*** Traditional banking involves in-person interactions to build trust and personal relationships with bank representatives, but often involves bureaucratic processes and slower query resolution. Neo Banking focuses on user-centric designs and instant support through chatbots and online help centres, but lacks face-to-face personal connection for some customers.
- ***Product Offerings:*** Traditional Banking offers a variety of financial products like savings, loans, investments, and insurance, excelling in handling complex instruments and catering to large corporate needs. Neo Banking focuses on simplified, niche products for individuals or small businesses, but may not offer extensive service range in areas like wealth management or corporate financing.
- ***Trust and Security:*** Traditional banking, backed by decades of service and strict regulatory compliance, provides deposit insurance. Newer entrants, despite advanced encryption and cybersecu-

rity measures, face scepticism about long-term reliability and stability due to concerns over data breaches and fraud.

- ***Regulatory Framework:*** Traditional banking operates within established regulatory frameworks, ensuring consumer protection and stability. Neo banking operates under emerging licensing models like e-money or payment institution licenses, facing evolving regulatory environments and challenges in data privacy and anti-money laundering compliance.
- ***Inclusivity:*** Traditional banking, with a strong urban presence, struggles to reach unbanked or underbanked populations due to infrastructure limitations. Neo Banking, designed to promote financial inclusion, offers low-cost, mobile-first solutions, particularly in emerging markets with high smartphone penetration.

Traditional banks provide reliability and services, while neo banks offer innovative approaches that cater to modern consumer expectations and technological advancements. Coexisting both models is crucial for a more inclusive, efficient, and customer-centric financial landscape.

4.3. Disruption of Traditional Banking

The conventional banking industry has seen a significant transformation due to the rise of technology-driven financial services including fintech platforms and neo banks. The financial environment is changing as a result of this disruption, forcing long-standing institutions to adapt or face obsolescence. The main places where conventional banking has been affected are listed below:

4.3.1. Transition to Digital Banking

- *Demand for Digital Solutions:* Due to ease and round-the-clock accessibility, customers are choosing online and mobile banking over in-person branch visits.
- *Emergence of Digital-Only Banks:* Neo banks have challenged established models by introducing customer-centric services including quick account setup, real-time financial data, and cheap costs.
- *Branch Decline:* As a result of the move to digital platforms, fewer branches are being used, which has led to closures and a review of their functions.

4.3.2. Advancements in Technology

- *AI and Automation:* Neo banks outperform traditional banks in speed and accuracy by using AI to provide individualized services, improve fraud protection, and expedite customer care.
- *Blockchain Solutions:* By enabling safe and transparent transactions, blockchain technology lessens reliance on middlemen and revolutionizes traditional financial procedures.
- *Cloud Computing:* While traditional banks struggle to adapt antiquated systems, Neo banks use scalable cloud-based infrastructures to spur innovation.

4.3.3. Evolving Customer Expectations

- *Personalization:* Neo banks use sophisticated analytics and AI-driven insights to provide the customized financial solutions that customers increasingly want.

- *Smooth Interfaces:* Neo banks establish new standards for the customer experience by emphasizing intuitive designs and user-friendly apps.
- *Speed of Service:* In contrast to traditional banks' sluggish procedures, Neo banks are excellent at offering quick fixes, such immediate loan approvals.

4.3.4. Cost and Operational Efficiency

- *High Overheads:* Because of their vast branch networks, sizable workforces, and physical infrastructure, traditional banks have high overhead expenses.
- *Lean Models:* By doing away with physical branches and automating procedures, Neo banks are able to operate with much lower overheads, saving clients' money.

4.3.5. Innovation in Product Offerings

- *Niche Services:* Neo banks focus on providing focused services that traditional banks frequently ignore, such microloans, multi-currency accounts, and expenditure management software.
- *Flexible Solutions:* Digital wallets and real-time spending analytics are features that meet the demands of contemporary consumers.
- *Collaborative Ecosystems:* Neo banks collaborate with insurers, investment platforms, and payment processors to build integrated service ecosystems that compete with more established products. (Sharma, 2024)

4.3.6. Advancing Financial Inclusion

- *Reaching Underserved Populations:* Neo banks give financial inclusion a priority by providing unbanked and underbanked populations with affordable, mobile-first solutions.
- *Global Accessibility:* Neo banks have effectively entered developing nations, providing financial services that are frequently unavailable through regular banks.

4.3.7. Regulatory and Competitive Challenges

- *Regulatory Barriers:* Innovation is frequently slowed by the complicated, highly regulated settings in which traditional banks operate. Despite being more flexible and having less stringent regulatory frameworks, Neobanks must contend with changing compliance requirements.
- *Increasing Competition:* Tech behemoths like Apple, Google, and Amazon are stepping into the financial services market and using their platforms to take on conventional banks head-to-head.

4.3.8. Pandemic-Induced Transformation

- *Accelerated Digital Shift:* Contactless and remote banking solutions became widely used as a result of the COVID-19 epidemic, which further reduced the need for conventional banking techniques.
- *More Funding:* During the epidemic, neo banks and fintechs were able to acquire sizeable investments, which fuelled their quick development and expansion.

- *Emphasis on Mobile-First Solutions:* Consumers have adopted mobile applications as their main financial transaction interface, placing a premium on accessibility and ease of use.

4.3.9 Challenges for Traditional Banks

- *Legacy Infrastructure:* Modernizing antiquated systems to rival Neobanks' technologically advanced business strategies.
- *Cultural Resistance:* Getting beyond internal obstacles to implementing creative, flexible methods.
- *Maintaining Trust:* Younger consumers are lured to neo-banks' ease and contemporary characteristics, even if conventional banks are still seen as reliable establishments.
- *Revenue Pressures:* Traditional banks are being forced to re-evaluate their charge structures because to the low-cost models of neo banks.

Traditional banks have been forced to reconsider their operations, strategies, and approaches to consumer interaction as a result of the disruption brought about by fintechs and neo banks. Traditional banks must adopt digital transformation and customer-first strategies to be competitive, even if they still have advantages like trust, regulatory stability, and extensive service offerings. Both models will probably coexist in the banking industry in the future, with neo banks expanding their offerings to accommodate a greater variety of financial demands and conventional banks using cutting-edge procedures.

4.4. Regulatory And Compliance Challenges in Case of Neo Banking and Traditional Banking

Traditional banks and neo banks have different regulatory and compliance concerns because of their different business structures. While traditional banks are subject to established frameworks, neo banks are negotiating changing regulations in a financial environment that is becoming more and more digital. Below is a summary of the regulatory and compliance issues that both parties must deal with:

4.4.1. Regulatory Frameworks and Licensing

Traditional Banking

- *Well-Established Regulations:* Central banks and financial authorities supervise traditional banks' operations under extensive and well-established regulatory frameworks. They must uphold capital reserves, follow liquidity guidelines, and guarantee financial reporting is transparent. (Monis & Pai, 2023b)
- *Strict Licensing Requirements:* In order to maintain financial stability and consumer protection, traditional banks must comply to stringent licensing requirements set out by national banking legislation. These requirements include frequent audits and compliance criteria.
- *International Regulation:* Traditional banks operating internationally are required to adhere to cross-border norms and regulations, such as Know Your Customer (KYC) guidelines, anti-money laundering (AML) laws, and combatting the financing of terrorism (CFT) laws.

Neo Banking

- *Non-Conventional Licensing:* Neo banks frequently function under alternative licenses, such as those for e-money or payment institutions, which enable them to offer services like savings and payments without having access to the full range of banking operations that traditional banks provide (e.g., large-scale lending).
- *Changing Regulatory Environment:* Neo Bank regulations are still developing. There are defined regulations for digital-only banks in some areas (like the UK and the EU), but there aren't always clear norms, which leaves neo banks vulnerable to ambiguity.
- *Regulatory Arbitrage:* Neo banks may occasionally profit from laxer laws in particular areas, which raises questions about regulatory irregularities and makes cross-border compliance difficult.

4.4.2. Consumer Protection and Data Privacy

Traditional Banking

- *Consumer Protection Procedures:* Long-standing client ties and well-established consumer protection procedures are advantages of traditional banks. These consist of fraud prevention strategies, deposit insurance, and adherence to data privacy laws such as the Consumer Financial Protection Bureau and the General Data Protection Regulation (GDPR) (CFPB).
- *Cybersecurity Risks:* Because of their extensive, centralized infrastructure, traditional banks are vulnerable to serious cybersecurity threats. To reduce these risks, they must adhere to stringent regulatory scrutiny and security standards. (Shabu & Ramankutty, 2022)

Neo Banking

- *Emphasis on Data Security:* Neo banks rely significantly on client data because they are fully digital. They have to abide by a number of data protection regulations, including as the California Consumer Privacy Act (CCPA) and the General Data Protection Regulation (GDPR), which frequently call for sophisticated encryption and frequent audits.
- *Compliance and Data Residency:* Neo banks that operate internationally can struggle to satisfy different data residency regulations, which might clash with cloud services' worldwide reach.
- *Issues with cybersecurity:* Neo banks are sometimes viewed as being more susceptible to data breaches because they are new to the market. Given their very limited operational history, any breach might undermine customer trust.

4.4.3. Anti-Money Laundering (AML) and Know Your Customer (KYC)

Traditional Banking

- *Strong AML/KYC Systems:* To stop fraud and money laundering, traditional banks have well-established AML and KYC procedures. They have mechanisms in place to keep thorough client identity records, track transactions, and identify questionable activities.
- *Anti-Money Laundering:* Comprehensive AML laws, such as the Fourth Anti-Money Laundering Directive of the EU and the Bank Secrecy Act (BSA) of the United States, apply to traditional banks. Noncompliance carries severe penalties.

Neo Banking

- *Difficulties with KYC/AML Compliance:* Neo banks are digital-first, which makes it harder to put in place efficient KYC and AML procedures. Even if they rely on digital verification technologies like video ID checks and face recognition, fraud may still be possible.
- *Cross-Border Regulatory Obstacles:* Neo banks that conduct business in several countries have to modify their KYC and AML procedures to conform to regional rules, which can vary greatly.
- *Creative Fraud Prevention:* Neo banks are still under a lot of regulatory pressure to follow worldwide AML requirements, even though they use cutting-edge technologies like artificial intelligence (AI) for real-time fraud detection.

4.4.4. Financial Stability and Risk Management

Traditional Banking

- *Capital and Liquidity Regulations:* To make sure they can survive economic downturns; traditional banks must pass stringent stress tests and meet capital adequacy standards set by laws like Basel III. These frameworks aid in safeguarding the larger financial system as well as customers.
- *Systemic Risk:* Traditional banks are integral to the global financial system and are under constant regulatory scrutiny to prevent systemic risks that could trigger a financial crisis.

Neo Banking

- *Limited Physical Assets:* Neo banks, which are frequently exclusively online, are unable to adequately control credit risk since they do not have the physical infrastructure that traditional banks may use as collateral for loans.
- *Operational Risk Exposure:* Neo banks are more vulnerable to risks including system failures, cyberattacks, and fraud because of their reliance on digital platforms and technology, which can cause disruptions to their business operations.
- *Less Thorough Stress Testing:* Neo banks might not go through the same stress testing as traditional banks since they usually function under less strict regulatory frameworks, which might expose them to unanticipated risks. (Mall et al., 2024)

4.4.5. Compliance Costs

Traditional Banking

- *High Compliance Burden:* Because of laws pertaining to capital adequacy, data security, and AML/KYC, traditional banks must pay hefty compliance fees. These expenses may be transferred to clients, raising operating and service rates.
- *Investment in Old Systems:* Updating legacy systems to comply with contemporary regulatory norms also comes at a considerable cost to traditional banks.

Neo Banking

- *Increased Compliance Expenses:* Neo banks frequently incur more compliance costs as new market entrants, particularly when they grow into new areas with different rules. To comply with

KYC/AML and data protection laws, they must spend money on compliance software, AI technologies, and specialized staff.

- *Uncertain Regulatory Environment:* Long-term uncertainty brought about by the changing regulatory frameworks for neo-banks makes it challenging to prepare for compliance and raises the possibility of unanticipated expenses.

Despite facing enormous regulatory problems, conventional and neo banks take quite different approaches to compliance. Conventional banks frequently struggle with inflexible systems while navigating well-established regulatory frameworks that guarantee financial stability. Neo banks, on the other hand, must fast innovate while maintaining compliance in more flexible yet fragmented regulatory regimes. Clear and flexible regulatory frameworks are essential for the success of neo banks, as is worldwide uniformity in crucial areas like data protection and anti-money laundering. Both models will keep changing, and cooperation between financial firms and regulators is essential to creating a financial environment that is inventive, inclusive, and stable.

4.5. Profitability And Sustainability Challenges of Neo Banks

Neo banks, or digital-only banks, have revolutionized the financial sector by offering seamless, tech-driven banking experiences. However, despite their rapid growth and customer appeal, these banks face significant profitability and sustainability challenges.

4.5.1. Profitability Challenges:

a. *Exorbitant Expenses for Acquiring Customers:* To attract new clients, Neo banks frequently use aggressive marketing techniques, referral schemes, and alluring incentives. Digital banks must constantly invest in customer acquisition, which affects profitability, in contrast to traditional banks with established clientele.
b. *Limited revenue streams and low margins:* The low-cost, low-fee business model used by many neo banks makes it challenging to create steady revenue. They find it difficult to keep healthy profit margins in the absence of traditional banking services like lending, wealth management, and investment offerings.
c. *Reliance on Collaborations:* The majority of nonbanks function through joint ventures with conventional banks or financial institutions and lack banking licenses. Their profitability is further strained by this reliance, which also subjects them to revenue-sharing arrangements and restricts their control over core banking operations.
d. *Costs of Regulation and Compliance:* Neo banks still have to pay for regulatory and compliance costs even though they do not have to pay the exorbitant fees associated with physical branches. Operational costs are raised by complying with changing cybersecurity, anti-money laundering (AML), and financial regulations.
e. *The Challenge of Profitable Scaling:* It takes a large investment in infrastructure, compliance, and customer service to expand internationally or even domestically. Maintaining cost-effective operations while scaling effectively is the challenge.

4.5.2. Sustainability Challenges

a. *Loyalty and Customer Retention:* Customer loyalty may be brittle because many neobanks provide free or inexpensive services. If better offers come up, users might move to rival banks or traditional banks, which would make long-term viability uncertain.
b. *Data privacy and cyber security risks:* Neo banks are particularly vulnerable to cyberattacks because they are entirely digital organizations. It is essential but expensive to ensure strong security frameworks, fraud prevention techniques, and data protection policies. Any security lapse has the potential to seriously harm their brand and clientele.
c. *Market volatility and economic downturns:* Neo banks are especially susceptible to downturns in the economy. Digital banks that depend on interchange or transaction fees may find it difficult to survive economic downturns when consumer spending falls, in contrast to traditional banks that have a variety of revenue streams.
d. *Limited Selection of Products:* Traditional banks generate steady income streams through a wide range of financial products, such as loans, mortgages, and investment services. However, a lot of neo banks only offer basic banking services, which restricts their capacity to make steady, long-term income.
e. *Uncertainty in Regulation:* Globally, governments and financial authorities are still establishing regulations pertaining to online banking. Any modifications to capital requirements, data privacy laws, or fintech regulations may present unanticipated difficulties for nonbanks.

4.5.3 Path to Profitability and Sustainability:

Neo banks need to diversify their revenue sources by offering investment services, subscription-based premium accounts, or lending in order to overcome these obstacles.

- Boost client loyalty with tailored offerings, financial insights powered by AI, and first-rate user experiences.
- Invest in state-of-the-art cybersecurity solutions to safeguard client information and stop fraud.
- Increase operational efficiency by utilising scalable digital infrastructure, partnerships, and automation.
- To maintain compliance and long-term stability, adjust to changing regulations by collaborating closely with legislators.

Neo banks can use technology, data-driven decision-making, and customer-centric innovations to transform banking in spite of these obstacles. However, diversification, strategic growth, and regulatory flexibility are necessary to achieve sustainable profitability.

4.6. Key Features and Services of Neobanks and Factors Driving the Growth of Neobanks

4.6.1. Key Features and Services:

Neobanks, also known as digital-only or challenger banks, provide a wide range of services that differentiate them from traditional banking institutions. These banks leverage modern technology to offer efficient, customer-focused banking experiences. Below are the primary features and services offered by Neobanks:

4.6.1.1. Digital-Only Banking

- *No Physical Branches:* Neobanks operate solely in the digital space, removing the need for physical branches. This allows them to lower operational costs and pass the savings on to customers in the form of competitive pricing and services.
- *Mobile-First Approach:* Neobanks prioritize mobile apps and online platforms for services like account management and payments. Customers can access their accounts anytime, anywhere, via smartphones or web applications. (Singh et al., 2017)

4.6.1.2. Effortless Account Opening

- *Instant, Paperless Registration:* Neobanks enable quick and easy account openings with minimal documentation, all done online without needing to visit a branch.
- *Digital Verification:* Neobanks use technologies such as biometric scans, document uploads, and facial recognition for compliance with KYC (Know Your Customer) regulations.

4.6.1.3. Affordable and Low Fees

- *Zero or Low Fees:* Neobanks typically offer fee-free or low-cost services, such as no minimum balance requirements, free account maintenance, and affordable transfers, both locally and internationally.
- *Clear Pricing:* Unlike traditional banks that may have hidden fees, Neobanks provide clear, upfront pricing and low-cost options for various financial products and services.

4.6.1.4. Real-Time Financial Management

- *Expense Tracking:* Neobanks provide real-time tracking of spending and categorize expenses to help customers manage their finances more effectively.
- *Personalized Financial Advice:* Many Neobanks use AI to offer tailored financial suggestions, including product recommendations and savings tips, based on individual spending habits.

4.6.1.5. Payments and Transfers

- *Easy Payments:* Neobanks allow users to make payments via mobile apps, debit/credit cards, and third-party payment systems like Google Pay and Apple Pay.
- *International Transfers:* Many Neobanks offer affordable, fast international money transfers with low conversion fees, making them ideal for individuals and businesses with global transactions.

4.6.1.6. Lending and Credit

- *Fast Loans and Credit Lines:* Some Neobanks provide personal loans and credit lines based on data-driven assessments, offering faster approval times than traditional banks.
- *Buy Now, Pay Later:* Certain Neobanks offer "buy now, pay later" (BNPL) services, giving customers flexibility when making purchases. (Chauhan et al., 2021)

4.6.1.7. Investments and Wealth Management

- *Savings and Investment Products:* Neobanks offer competitive interest rates on savings accounts and investment opportunities in stocks, ETFs, and other assets, either directly or through partnerships with third-party platforms.
- *Automated Investing:* Some Neobanks feature robo-advisory services, using algorithms to recommend investment portfolios based on customer risk preferences.

4.6.1.8. Integration with Third-Party Fintech Services

- *Fintech Partnerships:* Neobanks often collaborate with other fintech companies to enhance their offerings, integrating services like budgeting tools, cryptocurrency exchanges, and insurance products into their platforms.

4.6.2. Factors Driving the Growth of Neobanks:

Several factors contribute to the rapid growth of Neobanks, including technological advances, changing consumer behaviour, and evolving regulatory landscapes:

4.6.2.1. Technological Progress

- *Fintech Advancements:* The growth of fintech has allowed Neobanks to harness advanced technologies such as AI, machine learning, blockchain, and big data for personalized services, risk management, and fraud detection.
- *Cloud and API Integration:* Neobanks rely on cloud computing and open banking APIs, which facilitate easy integration with other financial services, reducing the need for costly physical infrastructure and enabling scalability.
- *Widespread Mobile Use:* With smartphones becoming ubiquitous, Neobanks can capitalize on the mobile-first trend, offering services on the go with user-friendly apps and interfaces.

4.6.2.2. Consumer Demand for Convenience and Efficiency

- *Convenience:* As consumers increasingly demand fast, accessible, and 24/7 banking solutions, Neobanks cater to this need with mobile-first, paperless services that are easy to use.
- *User-Focused Design:* Neobanks place a strong emphasis on user experience, offering intuitive interfaces and real-time information, which appeals to tech-savvy customers.

4.6.2.3. Cost-Effectiveness and Transparent Pricing

- *Lower Fees and Competitive Rates:* Neobanks are able to offer lower fees and more transparent pricing compared to traditional banks, thanks to their lack of physical branches and smaller staff.

- *Appealing to the Underserved:* Neobanks attract underserved populations, including the unbanked, by offering affordable banking solutions that provide access to financial services at a fraction of the cost of traditional banks. (Elia et al., 2023)

4.6.2.4. Promoting Financial Inclusion

- *Access to Unbanked Populations:* Neobanks are especially effective at reaching underserved communities in emerging markets, where physical banking infrastructure is limited. By leveraging mobile technology, they help provide financial services to those without access to traditional banking.
- *Global Reach:* Neobanks offer cross-border services, making banking accessible to a global customer base, particularly those who require low-cost international transactions.

4.6.2.5. Regulatory Support and Evolution

- *Regulatory Flexibility:* In regions like Europe and Asia, favourable regulations have created an environment conducive to the growth of digital banks, with challenger bank licenses and e-money regulations providing a clear operational framework.
- *Open Banking Regulations:* Open banking regulations in places like the EU and the UK have accelerated neo-banks' growth by promoting data sharing and integration with third-party fintech services.

4.6.2.6. Shifting Consumer Preferences

- *Digital-First Services:* Younger generations, particularly millennials and Gen Z, are more inclined to adopt digital-first banking solutions. Their preference for managing finances via mobile apps and digital interfaces has benefited neo-banks.
- *Alternative Financing Models:* Consumers are moving away from traditional banks and increasingly adopting alternative financial services like peer-to-peer lending, crowdfunding, and digital credit, all of which neo-banks offer.

4.6.2.7. Competitive Pressure on Traditional Banks

- *Disrupting Traditional Models:* Neobanks are disrupting traditional banking by challenging established institutions burdened with legacy systems and high operational costs. This has forced traditional banks to innovate and improve their digital services.
- *Collaborations with Neobanks:* In response to competition, many traditional banks are partnering with or acquiring neo-banks to enter the digital-first market and expand their digital offerings. (Nguyen et al., 2022)

Neo Banks would Target primarily two segments of customers, students and millennials, the reason behind this is students of this era are generally tech savvy, go getter with prompt result, they would prefer to disburse the loan amount with the help of technology and in hassle freeway. Millennials look for secured and real time settlement of their transactions. (Arun, et al, 2023). All thirty-six Neo Banks operating in Indian financial system are vying hard to acquire customers to create a niche in financial system catering to their demand. Neo banks are growing at the rate of 43% CAGR. The rapid rise of neo-banks is driven by a combination of technological advancements, changing consumer demands, cost-efficiency, and supportive regulatory environments. By offering personalized, affordable, and user-friendly services, neo-banks are reshaping the financial landscape. The details of the thirty-six banks are as follows in Figure 1:

Figure 1. Details of Neo-Banks in India

S.No.	Name	Founding year	CEO	Headquarters
1	Fino payments bank	2017	Rishi Gupta	Mumbai
2	IPPB	2018	J. Venkatramu	New Delhi
3	Paytm payments bank	2015	Vijay Shekhar Sharma	Noida
4	NSDL payments bank	2018	Abhijit Kamalapurkar	Mumbai
5	Airtel Payments Bank	2017	Anubrata Biswas	New Delhi
6	Jio payments bank	2018	Vinod Easwaran	Mumbai
7	Kotak 811	2017	Uday Kotak	Mumbai
8	RazorPay X	2014	Harshil Mathur	Bengaluru
9	Jupiter	2019	Jitendra Gupta	Mumbai
10	Open	2017	Anish Achuthan	Bengaluru
11	Fi bank	2019	Sujith Narayanan	Bengaluru
12	NiYo	2015	Vinay Bagri	Bengaluru
13	Fampay	2019	Kush Taneja and Sambhav Jain	Bengaluru
14	Flobiz	2019	Rahul Raj	Bengaluru
15	Chqbook	2020	Vipul Sharma	Bengaluru
16	InstantPay	2012	Shailendra Agarwal	New Delhi
17	Junio	2020	Ankit Gera	New Delhi
18	Payzello	2017	Pruthiraj Rath	Hyderabad
19	Finin	2019	Sudheer Maram	Bengaluru
20	Walrus	2019	Bhagaban Behera	Bengaluru
21	Yodaa	2021	Gaurav Sharma	Bengaluru
22	Ocareneo (Health care neobank)	2015	Neeraj Sheth	Mumbai
23	ZikZuk	2020	Avinash Godkhindi	Hyderabad
24	Freo	2021	Kunal Varma	Bengaluru
25	MoneyHop	2020	Mayank Goyal	Bengaluru
26	Revolut	2022	Paroma Chatterjee	Mumbai
27	Tide	2022	Gurjodhpal Singh	Hyderabad and Gurgaon
28	Mahila Money	2021	Siddhika Aggarwal	Remote
29	Mool	2020	Abhinav Nayar	New Delhi
30	Dinero	2022	Kashyap Mahavadi	Hyderabad
31	DGV	2019	Ragavan Venkatesan	Bengaluru
32	Fold	2022	Akash Nimare	Bengaluru
33	Zyro	2021	Vikas K.	Noida
34	Nupay	2017	Neeraj Singh and Alok Arora	Gurugram
35	Indmoney	2019	Ashish Kashyap	Gurugram
36	NEO	2022		

Leaps and bound growth have been palpable in case of almost all six Neo Banks which are actively operational in Indian Financial system, the one which has shown remarkable growth is IPPB (India post payment Bank) with around 300% incremental operating revenue from FY2020 to FY2021, followed by Instant pay with the operating revenue increment of 91%, Razor pay X with 64% and so on, plotted in graph below. The only exception being Niyo with negative growth. With continued innovation and growth in digital infrastructure, neo-banks are positioned to capture a growing share of the global banking market. (Schilling de Carvalho, 2022)

4.7. Revenue Models of Neobanks

Neobanks, operating solely in the digital realm, have devised unique revenue models to generate income while keeping expenses low. Unlike traditional banks, Neobanks focus on leveraging digital platforms, customer-centric services, and efficient operations to drive their revenue. Below are the primary revenue streams for Neobanks:

4.7.1. Interchange Fees

- *Revenue from Card Payments:* Neobanks earn a significant portion of their income from interchange fees, which merchants pay when customers use their debit or credit cards. These fees are typically a percentage of the transaction amount and are split between the issuing bank and the payment processor.
- *Payment Processing Fees:* Neobanks also generate income by offering payment services for businesses and individuals, earning a fee for each transaction processed.

4.7.2. Subscription Fees

- *Premium Account Services:* Neobanks offer premium accounts or subscription-based services that provide additional features, such as higher withdrawal limits, enhanced budgeting tools, or personalized financial advice. Customers pay a recurring fee for these premium offerings.
- *Tiered Pricing:* Some Neobanks use a tiered pricing structure, providing basic services for free while charging for more advanced features, such as higher savings interest rates or expanded loan options.

4.7.3. Lending and Credit Products

- *Interest on Loans:* Neobanks that provide personal loans, credit lines, and overdraft facilities earn revenue by charging interest on the borrowed amount. These rates are often more competitive than those of traditional banks.
- *Pay Later Services:* Neobanks that offer "buy now, pay later" (BNPL) services generate income through interest or fees imposed on customers who opt for deferred payment options. (Patnaik, et.al., 2022)

4.7.4. Transaction Fees for International Transfers

- *Global Payments:* Many Neobanks offer affordable international money transfer services, generating revenue through transaction fees or currency conversion mark-ups. These services are popular with users needing quick and cost-effective cross-border transactions.

4.7.5. Investment and Wealth Management Fees

- *Management Fees:* Neobanks offering investment services such as stocks, ETFs, or robo-advisory services charge management fees, typically a small percentage of the assets managed.
- *Commission from Third-Party Investments:* Neobanks may also earn referral or commission fees from third-party investment platforms when customers engage in investment activities.

4.7.6. Advertising and Partnerships

- *In-App Advertising:* Neobanks sometimes generate revenue through targeted ads displayed within their apps. By analysing user data, they deliver personalized advertisements, earning income from advertisers.
- *Collaborations with External Services:* Neobanks often partner with other fintech services like insurance providers or cryptocurrency platforms, earning commission or referral fees when customers sign up. (Murinde, et al., 2022)

4.7.7. Data Monetization

- *Selling Anonymized Data:* Neobanks collect transactional and behavioural data, which can be anonymized and sold to third parties, such as market research firms or advertisers. This is done while ensuring compliance *with privacy regulations.* (Mogaji, 2023)

4.7.8. Fee-Based Financial Services

- *Currency Conversion:* Neobanks with multi-currency accounts or travel-related services generate revenue through foreign exchange fees when users convert currencies, often at competitive rates compared to traditional banks.
- *ATM Withdrawal Fees:* While many Neobanks offer fee-free ATM withdrawals within their networks, they may charge fees for using out-of-network ATMs, providing another source of income.

4.7.9. Referral Fees

- *Partnerships for Financial Products:* Neobanks often refer customers to partner services such as insurance or loans, earning referral bonuses or commissions in return.

Neobanks generate revenue through various methods tailored to their digital-first model. By focusing on cost-efficient services, transaction fees, premium offerings, and strategic collaborations, Neobanks have diversified their income streams while keeping their services competitively priced. Through innovative digital services like lending, international transfers, and data monetization, Neobanks can generate substantial revenue while offering customers low-cost alternatives to traditional banking.

4.8. SWOC Analysis of Neo Banks vs. Traditional Banks

Neo banks, or digital-only banks, can be compared to traditional banks using a SWOC (Strengths, Weaknesses, Opportunities, and Challenges) analysis to learn about their advantages, disadvantages, and potential. Strengths, Weaknesses, Opportunities, and Challenges of Neo Banks (digital-only banks) and Traditional Banks (brick-and-mortar banks with digital offerings) are highlighted in this comparative analysis (SWOC). Table 1 gives an explanation of the same.

Table 1. Comparative analysis (SWOC)

Category	Neo Banks	Traditional Banks
Strengths	• ***Technology-Driven***: Fully digital operations provide seamless, mobile-first banking. • ***Low Operational Costs***: No physical branches, reducing expenses. • ***Faster On boarding***: Instant account setup and real-time transactions. • ***Personalized Services***: AI-driven insights, budgeting tools, and smart recommendations. • ***Financial Inclusion***: Serves the unbanked/underbanked with minimal documentation.	• ***Established Trust & Brand Reputation***: Decades or centuries of reliability. • ***Comprehensive Financial Services***: Offers loans, credit, investments, and mortgages. • ***Physical Presence & Human Interaction***: Important for complex banking needs. • ***Stable Business Model***: Diversified revenue streams (interest, wealth management, fees). • ***Regulatory Compliance & Risk Management***: Strong frameworks ensure security and trust.
Weaknesses	• ***Limited Product Offerings***: Many lack lending, investments, or insurance products. • ***No Physical Branches***: Some customers prefer in-person banking for major transactions. • ***Trust & Credibility Issues***: No full banking license; relies on partner banks. • ***Profitability Challenges***: Free/low-fee models struggle to generate long-term profits. • ***Regulatory Uncertainty***: Constantly evolving fintech regulations.	• ***High Operational Costs***: Maintaining branches, ATMs, and staff adds expenses. • ***Slow Digital Transformation***: Legacy systems make innovation slower than fintech start-ups. • ***Cumbersome Processes***: Traditional banks often have lengthy KYC, loan approvals, and paperwork. • ***Limited Financial Inclusion***: Higher eligibility criteria and fees restrict access for some customers. • ***Less Personalization***: Lacks AI-driven financial insights and digital-first services.
Opportunities	• ***Growing Digital Adoption***: More people prefer mobile-first banking. • ***Partnerships with Fintechs & Traditional Banks***: Expanding product offerings via collaboration. • ***Open Banking & Embedded Finance***: Neo banks can integrate with third-party platforms (e.g., e-commerce, ride-hailing). • ***AI & Blockchain Innovations***: Improving security, fraud detection, and efficiency. • ***Subscription & Lending Models***: Potential to monetize premium banking services.	• ***Accelerated Digital Transformation***: Upgrading legacy systems with AI, cloud computing, and automation. • ***Collaboration with Fintech's & Neo Banks***: Traditional banks can integrate digital innovations through partnerships. • ***Expansion into Rural & Emerging Markets***: Leveraging digital banking for financial inclusion. • ***Growth in ESG & Sustainable Banking***: Offering green finance and impact investments. • ***Data Analytics & AI Adoption***: Enhancing credit risk assessment and fraud detection.
Challenges	• ***Cybersecurity Risks***: Digital-only presence makes them prime targets for fraud. • ***Customer Retention Issues***: Easy account switching leads to low loyalty. • ***Economic Downturns & Market Volatility***: Dependency on transaction fees can impact sustainability. • ***Tough Competition***: From traditional banks, fintech's, and even tech giants like Google and Apple. • ***Regulatory & Compliance Uncertainty***: Changing laws could impact growth and operations.	• ***Competition from Neo Banks & Fintechs***: Digital disruptors are attracting younger generations. • ***Legacy Systems & Cyber Threats***: Older infrastructure makes security upgrades complex. • ***Regulatory Burden & Compliance Costs***: Stricter rules on capital requirements and AML policies. • ***Shrinking Relevance of Physical Branches***: Digital banking is reducing the need for in-person visits. • ***Changing Customer Expectations***: Younger consumers demand more digital and personalized banking experiences.

Key Insights from the Comparative Analysis: Traditional banks enjoy the advantages of regulatory stability, diversified services, and credibility, but they also face high operating costs and a slow pace of digital adoption. Neo banks, on the other hand, excel in digital innovation and cost efficiency but struggle with profitability, trust, and regulatory issues. Both banking models are merging: In order to increase profitability, neo banks are investigating lending and investment services, while traditional banks are introducing digital-only platforms (such as SBI's YONO and JPMorgan Chase's "Chase Digital Bank"). Hybrid banking models, which blend the agility and innovation of neobanks with the stability of traditional banking, are the way of the future. Neo banks are reshaping the banking industry, but in order to be sustainable over the long run, they must diversify their sources of income and fortify their regulatory frameworks. However, in order to remain competitive, traditional banks need to reduce operational inefficiencies and speed up their digital transformation. A successful banking future will probably combine trusted financial institutions with digital-first banking, utilising the advantages of both approaches. (Manzoor, 2023)

4.9. The Impact of Neobanks on the Financial Ecosystem

Neobanks are transforming the financial sector by offering innovative, tech-driven solutions that challenge conventional banking methods. Their influence spans financial inclusion, customer engagement, operational efficiency, and market competition, fundamentally reshaping the financial ecosystem. Key areas of their impact include:

4.9.1. Expanding Financial Inclusion

Neobanks are instrumental in bringing banking services to underserved populations:

- *Reaching Unbanked Communities:* With low-cost, mobile-first models, Neobanks extend services to individuals in regions lacking traditional banking infrastructure.
- *Affordable Financial Services:* Features such as no-fee accounts and small-scale credit options make banking accessible to low-income groups.
- *Global Reach:* Streamlined international money transfers with reduced costs benefit remote workers, expatriates, and small businesses engaged in cross-border activities.

4.9.2. Fostering Technological Advancement

By utilizing cutting-edge technologies, neobanks are redefining the way financial services are delivered:

- *AI and Advanced Analytics:* These tools enable personalized services, enhanced fraud prevention, and predictive insights.
- *Open Banking Integrations:* APIs allow seamless collaboration with fintech platforms, enhancing service diversity.
- *Blockchain Applications:* Neobanks leverage blockchain for secure, efficient cross-border transactions. (Elsaid, 2023)

4.9.3. Transforming Customer Experiences

Neobanks prioritize customer-centric solutions for seamless interactions:

- *Hassle-Free Onboarding:* Digital, paperless processes enable quick account setup without the need for physical visits.

- *Customized Features:* Expense tracking, budgeting tools, and real-time alerts cater to individual needs.
- *Round-the-Clock Accessibility:* Customers can manage accounts at any time through mobile and online platforms.

4.9.4. Increasing Market Competition

Neobanks are driving competition within the financial industry:

- *Encouraging Innovation Among Legacy Banks:* Traditional banks are adopting digital strategies and forming partnerships with Neobanks to stay relevant.
- *Attracting New Entrants:* The success of Neobanks has prompted tech giants like Google and Apple to explore financial services.

4.9.5. Optimizing Cost Efficiency

Neobanks offer a leaner, more cost-effective approach to banking:

- *Reduced Operational Costs:* Operating without physical branches allows Neobanks to lower expenses and offer more affordable services.
- *Agility and Scalability:* Cloud-based infrastructure enables efficient, scalable operations.

4.9.6. Promoting Financial Literacy

Neobanks empower customers with tools to improve their financial knowledge:

- *Expense Insights:* Real-time tracking helps users better understand their spending habits.
- *Educational Features:* Gamified learning and tailored advice teach users about saving, investing, and budgeting.

4.9.7. Influencing Regulatory Frameworks

The rise of Neobanks has encouraged regulators to adapt:

- *Digital Banking Licenses:* Governments are introducing licenses tailored for Neobanks to ensure compliance and safety.
- *Enhanced Oversight:* Greater emphasis on data security, anti-money laundering (AML), and cybersecurity measures has been implemented.

4.9.8. Supporting Small Businesses and Entrepreneurs

Neobanks cater to the specific needs of start-ups and SMEs:

- *Simplified Financial Management:* Services like invoicing, payroll processing, and expense tracking are designed for small business operations.
- *Quick Access to Credit:* Fast loan approvals and microfinancing options address the financial challenges faced by small enterprises. (Bhatnagr et al., 2024)

4.9.9. Encouraging Collaboration and Ecosystem Integration

Neobanks promote a more interconnected financial ecosystem:

- *Partnerships with Fintechs:* Collaborating with payment processors, cryptocurrency platforms, and insurers enhances their offerings.
- *One-Stop Financial Solutions:* Neobanks often integrate third-party services, such as investment and insurance products, for added convenience.

Neobanks are reshaping the financial landscape by driving technological innovation, enhancing inclusivity, and setting new standards for customer-centric banking. Their emergence has pushed traditional banks to modernize and embrace digital transformation. As the ecosystem continues to evolve, collaboration among Neobanks, traditional institutions, fintechs, and regulators will lead to a more efficient, integrated, and customer-focused financial future.

4.10. Neo Bank Case Studies and Global Trends in Neo Banking

4.10.1. Neo Bank Case Studies

- *Nubank (Brazil):* Nubank has become a prominent financial institution in Latin America by addressing the needs of Brazil's underbanked population. Offering fee-free credit cards, personal loans, and digital accounts, it leverages AI for tailored customer service while reducing banking costs. This approach has significantly promoted financial inclusion in a region known for its high-cost banking landscape.
- *Revolut (United Kingdom):* Revolut has revolutionized digital banking globally, providing features like multi-currency accounts, real-time spending insights, and cryptocurrency trading. Focused on international travelers and expatriates, it offers competitive exchange rates and innovative services, setting new benchmarks for the digital banking experience worldwide.
- *Chime (United States):* Chime has gained traction among millennials and gig economy workers with its fee-free banking model. Features such as no overdraft fees, early paycheck access, and automated savings tools appeal to customers looking for cost-effective and straightforward banking options, solidifying its position as a leading digital bank in the U.S. (Okunevych, et al., 2018)
- *Paytm Payments Bank (India):* Leveraging its popular digital payments platform, Paytm Payments Bank has made significant strides in India's digital banking sector. It offers high-interest savings accounts, seamless bill payment services, and wallet-to-bank transfers, playing a pivotal role in advancing the nation's cashless economy and improving financial accessibility in underserved areas.

4.10.2. Global Trends in Neo Banking

Neobanking is experiencing rapid growth worldwide, driven by advancements in technology, shifting consumer expectations, and favorable regulatory environments. In mature markets like Europe and North America, Neobanks offer a wide range of financial services, including multi-currency accounts, investment options, and budgeting tools, targeting tech-savvy individuals and businesses. In contrast, emerging markets such as Latin America, Africa, and Asia focus on providing accessible, mobile-first solutions to the unbanked and underserved populations. Key trends include the use of AI and machine learning for personalized banking experiences, integration with open banking APIs to enhance service connectivity, and partnerships with fintech companies to expand offerings. Additionally, the rise of blockchain and cryptocurrency is fueling product innovation in certain sectors. (Rogers, 2021) Despite facing regulatory challenges, Neobanks are thriving by addressing specific market demands and disrupting traditional banking models on a global scale. (Lindström, 2023) The recent trends are:

- *Expansion of Offerings:* Neobanks are diversifying by offering services like wealth management, insurance, and credit facilities, and partnering with fintech platforms to create comprehensive ecosystems.
- *Embedded Financial Services:* The integration of banking features into non-financial platforms like e-commerce and ride-hailing apps is being explored to expand their reach. (Temelkov, 2020)
- *Financial Inclusion Focus:* The initiative aims to provide affordable, mobile-first solutions to underserved communities, especially in emerging economies, and provide micro-lending to those exclude d from traditional lending systems. (Kaur,et.al., 2022)
- *Supportive Regulatory Developments:* Governments worldwide are implementing digital banking licenses and data sharing initiatives to promote growth and facilitate seamless integration with fintech services. (Sung, et al, 2029)

4.10.3. Regional Variations in Neobanking

- *North America:* Traditional banks are partnering with neobanks to expand digital offerings, focusing on fee-free accounts, early wage access, and credit-building tools, as seen in Chime and Varo.
- *Europe:* The focus is on multi-currency services, open banking compliance, and investment tools, with strong regulatory backing through frameworks like PSD2 boosting growth.
- *Asia-Pacific:* The focus is on digital wallets, integrated payment solutions, and financial inclusion, driven by rapid adoption of smartphones and government-led digital initiatives.
- *Latin America:* The focus is on providing affordable credit products and inclusive banking services, with examples like Nubank in Argentina, to fill traditional banks' gaps.
- *Africa:* The trend involves leveraging mobile technology to facilitate low-cost cross-border transactions, such as those offered by TymeBank in South Africa and Kuda in Nigeria.

5. FUTURE OUTLOOK AND CHALLENGES FOR NEOBANKS

5.1. Future Outlook

The future of Neobanks is promising as the digital transformation continues to revolutionize the financial services industry. With the integration of advanced technologies such as artificial intelligence, machine learning, and blockchain, Neobanks are set to provide increasingly personalized services, smarter financial management tools, and more efficient payment solutions. Their mobile-first, cost-effective banking models make them particularly well-suited to serve the unbanked and underbanked populations, especially in emerging markets where traditional banking infrastructure is lacking. Neobanks are also expected to expand their service offerings beyond basic banking, potentially including wealth management, insurance, and investment products, allowing them to compete more directly with traditional financial institutions. Their focus on customer experience, lower costs, and operational efficiency is likely to drive continued growth. Moreover, partnerships with fintech companies and deeper integration into broader financial ecosystems will enable them to offer a more comprehensive suite of services. (Rocchi, 2022)

5.2. Challenges

Despite the optimistic outlook, Neobanks face several challenges. Regulatory compliance is a key concern, as they must navigate a rapidly changing regulatory landscape, especially regarding data privacy, cybersecurity, and anti-money laundering practices. Stricter regulations could increase operational costs and affect business models.

- Another challenge comes from fierce competition, with traditional banks accelerating their digital transformations and leveraging their established customer bases, brand trust, and regulatory expertise. Additionally, large technology companies like Apple, Google, and Amazon are entering the financial services industry, intensifying the competitive landscape. (Sutton, 2023)
- Cybersecurity also remains a significant risk for Neobanks. As entirely digital platforms, they are vulnerable to cyberattacks, and any data breach or service disruption could severely damage customer trust and limit growth. Moreover, the absence of physical branches may undermine confidence, particularly in regions where customers value in-person interactions. (Shashidhar, 2020)
- Expanding into new regions also presents difficulties, as Neobanks must adapt to varying cultural, economic, and customer behavior differences across markets. Tailoring services to local preferences will be crucial to their success in global expansion.

In summary, while the potential for Neobanks is vast, they must overcome regulatory, competitive, cybersecurity, and regional adaptation challenges. Those that can innovate and address these obstacles will be well-positioned to succeed in the evolving financial ecosystem.

6. CONCLUSION

Neobanks have revolutionized the financial industry, driven by innovations in technology, evolving customer expectations, and dynamic regulatory changes. Unlike traditional banks, Neobanks operate exclusively online, offering cost-effective, customer-focused, and efficient banking services. With their emphasis on mobile-first platforms, paperless banking, lower fees, and real-time financial management, Neo banks have gained popularity, especially among tech-savvy users and underserved communities in emerging markets. Key features such as quick account setup, seamless payments, and transparent pricing make Neo banks distinct from traditional banks, which often rely on outdated systems and higher operational costs. By integrating cutting-edge technologies like AI, machine learning, and blockchain, Neo banks offer tailored services, automated financial insights, and innovative products, including peer-to-peer lending and international payments.

The rapid rise of Neo banks can be attributed to factors such as widespread smartphone usage, increasing consumer demand for convenience, affordability, and favorable regulatory conditions. Neo banks are also improving financial inclusion by offering banking services to unbanked and underbanked populations, especially in regions with limited access to conventional banking. However, Neo banks also face challenges, including navigating complex regulations, addressing cybersecurity risks, and ensuring data privacy. Additionally, they are in direct competition with traditional banks adopting digital models and large tech companies entering the financial space. Nevertheless, Neo banks have a promising future, with continued innovation and expansion into new markets. Their potential to reshape the financial landscape and transform the way customers interact with banking services is evident.

Looking ahead, Neo banks must manage the delicate balance of building customer trust, adhering to regulatory requirements, ensuring data security, and scaling operations. The Neo banks that succeed will be those that offer exceptional customer experiences while effectively addressing these challenges. In conclusion, Neo banks are set to be key players in the future of banking, driving innovation, fostering competition, and promoting greater financial inclusion in the digital age.

REFERENCES

Arun, T., Markose, S., Murinde, V., Kostov, P., Khan, A., Ari, N., & Sethi, R. (2023). *Impact of Neo-banks (Digital Banks).* UK–India Comparison.

Banga, C., Beena, F., Manchandani, P., & Shukla, V. (2023, March). Growth and Future of Neo Banks–A Survey. In *2023 International Conference on Computational Intelligence and Knowledge Economy (ICCIKE)* (pp. 467-472). IEEE.

Bhatnagr, P., & Rajesh, A. (2024). Neobanking adoption – An integrated UTAUT-3, perceived risk and recommendation model. *South Asian Journal of Marketing*, *5*(2), 93–112. DOI: 10.1108/SAJM-06-2022-0040

Bhatnagr, P., Rajesh, A., & Misra, R. (2024). Neobank adoption: Integrating the information systems effectiveness framework with the innovation resistance model. *Management Decision*, *62*(10), 3315–3352. DOI: 10.1108/MD-06-2023-0977

Chauhan, S., Akhtar, A., & Gupta, A. (2021). Gamification in banking: A review, synthesis and setting research agenda. *Young Consumers*, *22*(3), 456–479. DOI: 10.1108/YC-10-2020-1229

Elia, G., Stefanelli, V., & Ferilli, G. B. (2023). Investigating the role of Fintech in the banking industry: What do we know? *European Journal of Innovation Management*, *26*(5), 1365–1393. DOI: 10.1108/EJIM-12-2021-0608

Elsaid, H. M. (2023). A review of literature directions regarding the impact of fintech firms on the banking industry. *Qualitative Research in Financial Markets*, *15*(5), 693–711. DOI: 10.1108/QRFM-10-2020-0197

Garg, N., & Sahu, G. P. (2024). Modeling the Barriers in Adoption of Neo Banks in India. *IFIP Advances in Information and Communication Technology, 698 AICT*. DOI: 10.1007/978-3-031-50192-0_17

Jaglan, D. (2021). NEO BANKS-The Rise of Banking Industry. In *International Journal of Management and Commerce Innovations*.

Kaur, J., Syan, A. S., Kaur, S., & Sharma, R. R. (2022). *Understanding the Factors Influencing Actual Usage of Payments Banks: An Empirical Investigation Using the Extended Information Systems Success Model*. FIIB Business Review., DOI: 10.1177/23197145221099095

Lindström, V., & Nilsson, O. (2023). The sudden rise of neobanks and the threat it poses upon the traditional banking system.

Mall, S., Panigrahi, T. R., & Kabir Hassan, M. (2024). Neo banking: A bibliometric review of the current research trend and future scope. *International Review of Economics & Finance*, *96*, 103559. DOI: 10.1016/j.iref.2024.103559

Manzoor, A. (2023). Antecedents to Following Brands on Facebook and Instagram with Moderating Role of User Experience. *FIIB Business Review*, *0*(0). Advance online publication. DOI: 10.1177/23197145221151010

Mogaji, E. (2023). Redefining banks in the digital era: A typology of banks and their research, managerial and policy implications. *International Journal of Bank Marketing, 41*(7), 1899–1918. DOI: 10.1108/IJBM-06-2023-0333

Monis, E., & Pai, R. (2023a). Neo Banks: A Paradigm Shift in Banking. *International Journal of Case Studies in Business, IT, and Education*. DOI: 10.47992/IJCSBE.2581.6942.0275

Monis, E., & Pai, R. (2023b). Neo Banks: A Paradigm Shift in Banking. *International Journal of Case Studies in Business, IT, and Education*, 318–332. DOI: 10.47992/IJCSBE.2581.6942.0275

Naresh Sardar Vallabhbhai Patel, R., Ravichandran, R., Muralidhar, D., Naresh, N., & Professor, A. (2022). Neo Banks, Fintech, And Banking-The Changing Landscape-A Perspective-On Dangers, Growth, Opportunities-A Critical Study. In *Peer Reviewed and Refereed Journal* (Issue 6).

Nguyen, Y. T. H., Tapanainen, T., & Nguyen, H. T. T. (2022). Reputation and its consequences in Fintech services: The case of mobile banking. *International Journal of Bank Marketing, 40*(7), 1364–1397. DOI: 10.1108/IJBM-08-2021-0371

Nur Aliftiani, N., Firdaus, M., & Supeni, N. (2024). COMPARATIVE ANALYSIS OF HEALTH LEVELS AT BANK NEO COMMERCE & BANK JAGO. *MBA - Journal of Management and Business Aplication, 6*(2). DOI: 10.31967/mba.v6i2.1026

Patnaik, R., Patra, S. K., Mahapatra, D. M., & Baral, S. K. (2022). *Adoption and Challenges Underlying OTT Platform in India during Pandemic: A Critical Study of Socio-Economic and Technological Issues*. FIIB Business Review., DOI: 10.1177/23197145221101676

Schilling de Carvalho, P. (2022). Retaining Influence in Post-Brexit International Financial Regulation: Lessons from the UK's FinTech Framework. *Journal of Financial Regulation, 8*(1), 104–131. DOI: 10.1093/jfr/fjac004

Shabu, K., & Ramankutty, V. (2022). Neobanking in India: Opportunities and Challenges from Customer Perspective. SSRN *Electronic Journal*. DOI: 10.2139/ssrn.4037656

Shanti, R., Siregar, H., Zulbainarni, N., & Tony, . (2024). Revolutionizing Banking: Neobanks' Digital Transformation for Enhanced Efficiency. *Journal of Risk and Financial Management, 17*(5), 188. DOI: 10.3390/jrfm17050188

Sharma, S. (2024). Digital Disruption in Banking: A Comparative Analysis of Neo Banks and Traditional Institutions. *International Journal of Management and Development Studies, 13*(3), 01–12. DOI: 10.53983/ijmds.v13n3.001

Singh, N., Srivastava, S., & Sinha, N. (2017). Consumer preference and satisfaction of M-wallets: A study on North Indian consumers. *International Journal of Bank Marketing, 35*(6), 944–965. DOI: 10.1108/IJBM-06-2016-0086

Sung, A., Leong, K., Sironi, P., O'Reilly, T., & McMillan, A. (2019). An exploratory study of the FinTech (Financial Technology) education and retraining in UK. *Journal of Work-Applied Management, 11*(2), 187–198. DOI: 10.1108/JWAM-06-2019-0020

Surya Gifari, M., Wibowo Manajemen Pemasyarakatan, P., Ilmu Pemasyarakatan, P., Kunci, K., Berpindah, N., & Bank, N. (2023). Pengaruh Job Insecurityterhadap Turnover Intent Pegawai Bank Neo Jakarta. *Neraca Manajemen, Akuntansi Ekonomi, 1*(8).

Sutton, J. (2023). The rise of the Neobanks in the UK. The Corporate Law Academy, Retrieved from The rise of the Neobanks in the UK | The Corporate Law Academy

Temelkov, Z. (2020) Differences between traditional bank model and fintech based digital bank and neobanks models. SocioBrains, International scientific refereed online journal with impact factor (74). pp. 8-15. ISSN 2367-5721

Vidya, R. (2023). Digital Disruption of Neo Banks with Reference to Indian Banking Landscape. *International Journal For Multidisciplinary Research*, *5*(6). Advance online publication. DOI: 10.36948/ijfmr.2023.v05i06.10561

Ziouache, A., & Bouteraa, M. (2023). Descriptive Approach of Neo-Banking System: Conception, Challenges and Global Practices. *International Journal of Business and Technology Management*, *5*(2), 194–204.

Chapter 12
Perception of Hybrid Learning Platform Self-Efficacy:
Technological Readiness on Student Satisfaction Using Emotional Engagement as Mediator

Ritu Makhija
https://orcid.org/0009-0009-6972-3518
Chandigarh University, India

Shalini Aggarwal
https://orcid.org/0000-0002-7357-9880
Chandigarh University, India

Rajat Gupta
Chandigarh University, India

ABSTRACT

In the rapidly evolving landscape of higher education, hybrid learning platforms have become a central mode of instruction, combining traditional in-person teaching with online learning. . This study investigates the role of hybrid learning platforms, self-efficacy, and technological readiness in shaping student satisfaction, with emotional engagement serving as a mediating factor. Using a quantitative research approach, survey data was collected from students in hybrid learning environments. Structural equation modeling (SEM) was employed to assess the direct and indirect relationships between the constructs. Results indicate that both self-efficacy and technological readiness positively affect emotional engagement, which, in turn, significantly influences student satisfaction.This research underscores the need for educational institutions to focus on enhancing students' emotional engagement, as well as ensuring technological readiness and fostering self-efficacy to maximize student satisfaction in hybrid learning environments.

DOI: 10.4018/979-8-3373-0209-6.ch012

1. INTRODUCTION

The COVID-19 pandemic forced higher education institutions to shift from in-person to online instruction (Anthony et al,2020), transitioning from classroom-based learning to virtual platforms (Bandura,1997). This change was unexpected, catching several educational institutions, faculty, and students unprepared for the shift to online learning (Bokoloet al, 2020; Chenet al., 2024). They were faced with challenges including low motivation, restricted internet access, limited learning materials, and disruptions in studies (Daultani et al, 2021).

This unexpected shift has empowered stakeholders in educational institutions, highlighting the need for extensive use of technology in learning. In fact, online education has proven to be quite successful. According to Soffer and Nachmias (2018), online learning can be as effective, if not more so, than in-person instruction. Tartavulea et al. (2020) argue that the shift to online learning during the pandemic has had beneficial effects that could be leveraged in the future. When pandemic-related challenges are effectively addressed and transformed into opportunities, online learning can thrive (Fornell and Larcker, 1981). Additionally, online learning offers several advantages, such as increased accessibility and flexibility regarding location, content, time, pace, learning style, learning path, and evaluation (Fredrickse al., 2004). Consequently, these modifications may guide the development of new learning styles post-pandemic. Thus, a thorough assessment of the effectiveness of online education during the COVID-19 pandemic is essential.

Several studies have found online learning to be less successful or ineffective during the pandemic (Febrianto et al,2020). Additionally, face-to-face instruction is preferred (Gomez et al, 2023), and online learning often fails to achieve desired outcomes (Hadi and Baskaran 2021). A study found that while online learning can supplement traditional classroom instruction, it cannot fully replace it (Henseleret al., 2015). However, other research suggests that online learning during the COVID-19 pandemic is as effective as offline learning (Jones et al., 2020). Additionally, Allo (2020) and Kalman et al. (2020) indicate that online learning is suitable for the pandemic and has yielded positive results (Imranet al., 2023). Online education is accessible, affordable, and straightforward (Kokkodis & Ransbothamk, 2023). Bączek et al. (2021) find that while online learning effectively enhances knowledge of students, it has a lesser impact on their social skills and abilities.

The COVID-19 pandemic led educational institutions to shift to fully online study, negatively impacting social well-being of students. Hybrid learning has been found to help mitigate these effects (Lenget al., 2023). Existing research on hybrid learning has focused on bachelor's and master's levels but has not assessed its effectiveness across bachelor's, master's, and doctoral levels. This study aims to address that gap.

Despite the growing use of hybrid learning models, there is a lack of comprehensive scholarly evaluations of their effectiveness. Existing research mostly offers general observations rather than identifying specific factors affecting readiness and success. This gap underscores the need for detailed studies on variables influencing successful hybrid learning (Bokolo et al, 2020). Additionally, exploring learner perception, self-efficacy, and technological readiness could provide valuable insights for optimizing these models.

Most research on hybrid learning focuses on countries like the USA, Malaysia, the UK, and Australia, leaving a gap in the Indian context (Anthony et al., 2020). Many studies use small sample sizes, limiting the generalizability of their findings. Larger sample sizes could offer more robust insights into hybrid learning effectiveness. Additionally, the rapid evolution of educational technology calls for innovative models that integrate traditional and distance learning, particularly in business management education (Imran et al., 2023).

2. LITERATURE REVIEW AND HYPOTHESES DEVELOPMENT

2.1. The Constructs

Perception Towards Hybrid Learning

Over time, there have been several modifications and adjustments to educational techniques. One of the main components of the global education system has been the incorporation of technology (Li et al, 2022) .The use of blended learning, often referred to as hybrid learning, has increased in recent years as a result of the rapid advancement of technology (Liu et al, 2024). The term "student perceptions" describes how learners view and understand the things they have seen and experienced during the learning process. Their understanding and behaviour in the classroom are shaped by their senses and emotions.

Self-Efficacy Towards Hybrid Learning

Students' faith in their abilities when utilizing a virtual learning platform is known as self-efficacy (Nguyen et al, 2024). According to Eom and Estelami (2012), self-efficacy is the conviction that one can accomplish a task and achieve perceivably desirable performance levels that are commensurate with one's skill set. People's motivation, interpersonal interactions, and behaviour are all influenced by their level of self-efficacy (Park et al,2023). But in the context of hybrid learning, students' self-efficacy is defined as their capacity to put into practice the skills necessary to effectively use and profit from computers and other information technologies (Parasuraman, 2000)

Technology Readiness Towards Hybrid Learning

Another important factor linked to students' learning in a blended learning environment is their preparedness for technology (Richardson,2005). The development of diverse computer technologies makes it possible to use multimedia communication and content for education (Sitar et al, 2024) and offers access to the learning materials at any time and from any location.

Emotional Engagement Towards Hybrid Learning

Student emotional engagement refers to their emotional reactions to activities, peers, and the teacher, and their sense of belonging to the course e.g.: feelings of interest, sense of belonging, boredom, frustration or enjoyment (Skinner et al, 2009) Fun, excitement, happiness, contentment, and vigor are a few of the good feelings that students can have. Anger, boredom, frustration, anxiety, and sadness are examples of negative emotions. Students' motivation and learning during the learning process are significantly influenced by their emotions (Smith & Jones, 2020).

Hypotheses

This part of the study aims to explore the intricate relationships among various psychological constructs within the context of student engagement and satisfaction in a hybrid learning environment. Specifically, it will investigate how students' perceptions, self-efficacy, and technological readiness influence their emotional engagement and satisfaction levels. The first set of hypotheses proposes direct relationships, suggesting that students' perceptions, self-efficacy, and technological readiness significantly impact their emotional engagement and satisfaction. Additionally, the study will look into the potential mediating role of emotional engagement in the relationships between students' perceptions, self-efficacy, technological readiness, and satisfaction. These hypotheses collectively seek to deepen our understanding of the mechanisms underlying student engagement and satisfaction in the context of hybrid learning. The concerned alternate hypotheses are:

2.2 Perception of Students and Emotional Engagement Towards Hybrid Learning

Emotions play a significant role in the learning process. Positive and negative emotions effects on academic engagement. Stress in the students affected their degree of academic engagement whereas enthusiasm in the students lead to their high degree of engagement (Teng et al, 2024) To nurture student engagement in hybrid learning the guiding role of teacher also effect on emotions of learners (Teo, 2011)

H1: Perception of students is significantly related to emotional engagement

2.3 Perception of Students and Satisfaction Oo Students Towards Hybrid Learning

Hybrid learning strategies raise the degree of students' satisfaction. Hybrid learning not only remove time constraints for communication but also does away with geographic barriers (Wang et al, 2021) Students are motivated to take the responsibility for their own learning process. They are free to choose how and when to use the available resources (Wu et al, 2024)

H2: perception of students is significantly related to satisfaction of students.

2.4 Self Efficacy and Emotional Engagement Towards Hybrid Learning

The students are more engaged in learning behaviour if they are having stronger emotional engagement. Positive emotions such as confidence can enhance self-efficacy on the other hand negative emotions such as anxiety can hamper self -efficacy (Xiong et al, 2022)

H3: Self-efficacy is significantly related to emotional engagement

2.5 Self Efficacy and Satisfaction of Students Towards Hybrid Learning

Jen 2010 identified three factors self-efficacy, technological environment and social environment which impact on learner's satisfaction. Student involvement is a direct result of computer self-efficacy, and student engagement in turn affects group satisfaction (Xue et al, 2023)

H4: Self-efficacy is significantly related to satisfaction of students.

2.6 Technology Readiness and Emotional Engagement Towards Hybrid Learning

The term "technology readiness" describes students' inclination to adopt new technologies in order to meet their learning objectives (Parasuraman, 2000). Higher technology readiness among students is correlated with a more favourable attitude toward innovative communication platforms and technological learning materials. It may take students longer to become proficient users of online learning platforms if they feel uneasy or insecure about utilizing technology (Yoganarasimhan et al, 2023).

H 5: Technological readiness is significantly related to emotional engagement.

2.7 Technological Readiness and Student's Satisfaction Towards Hybrid Learning

Students are inclined towards hybrid learning due to many reasons. Researchers studied the factors that contribute to readiness towards online learning are motivation, self- efficacy, learner's control, on-line communication, technological readiness and motivation (Zheng et al,2023). Covid pandemic period brought a drastic change. Learners are tech-savvy. They are ready to embrace new technologies (Mishra et al,2022. The intention to participate in hybrid learning environment effects on student's satisfaction.

H 6: Technological readiness is significantly related to Student's satisfaction

2.8 Emotional Engagement and Student's Satisfaction Towards Hybrid Learning

Research advocated that the emotions played a prominent role in enhancing learner's attention and interest. Learners with positive mindset embrace new technology. This positive attitude increases student engagement and leads to student satisfaction. Students are inspired because they can choose the place, schedule and speed of their education. Student engagement can be improved through hybrid learning platform. (Zhou et al, 2023)

H 7: Emotional engagement is significantly related to Student's satisfaction.

2.9 Emotional Engagement as a Mediator of Student Perception and Satisfaction

Research has also explored emotional engagement as a mediator between various factors (such as course design, instructor presence, and technological readiness) and student satisfaction. In a hybrid learning setting, where online learning technologies are heavily utilized, emotional engagement can bridge the gap between digital tools and student satisfaction.

The mediating role of emotional engagement in the relationship between student perceptions and satisfaction has been supported by various studies. Pekrun and Linnenbrink-Garcia (2012) argue that emotions shape how students perceive and interact with their learning environments, and these emotional experiences ultimately determine their satisfaction. Students who perceive a supportive and engaging learning environment are more likely to develop positive emotions, which in turn enhance their overall satisfaction. Kahu and Nelson (2018) developed an engagement framework that identifies emotional engagement as a key mediator between institutional factors (such as course design, instructor presence, and learning support) and student outcomes (including satisfaction). Their research emphasizes that emotional engagement can amplify the positive effects of a well-designed learning environment, as students who are emotionally engaged are more likely to stay motivated, persist in their studies, and report greater satisfaction.

H8: Emotional Engagement has a mediating effect on relation of Perception of students and their satisfaction

2.10 Emotional Engagement as a Mediator of Self-Efficacy and Student Satisfaction

Several studies support the notion that emotional engagement plays a mediating role in the self-efficacy-satisfaction relationship. For instance, Joo, Lim, and Kim (2013) found that emotional engagement significantly mediated the effect of self-efficacy on student satisfaction in online learning environments. Students with high self-efficacy were more likely to be emotionally engaged in their studies, which led to higher satisfaction levels. Similarly, Liaw and Huang (2013) showed that emotional engagement acted as a buffer between self-efficacy and student satisfaction, helping students remain satisfied even when they encountered difficulties with technology or course content.

H9: Emotional Engagement has a mediating effect on relation of self-efficacy and students' satisfaction

2.11 Emotional Engagement as a Mediator of Technological Readiness and Student Satisfaction

Several studies support the idea that emotional engagement mediates the relationship between technological readiness and student satisfaction. For example, Joo, Lim, and Kim (2013) found that students who were technologically ready for online learning were more likely to be emotionally engaged in their courses, which in turn led to higher levels of satisfaction. Similarly, Liaw and Huang (2013) demonstrated that emotional engagement served as a buffer against the negative effects of technological challenges, allowing students with high technological readiness to remain satisfied with their learning experiences even when they encountered difficulties.

H10: Emotional Engagement has a mediating effect on relation of technological readiness and students' satisfaction.

Figure 1. Shows the proposed theoretical model

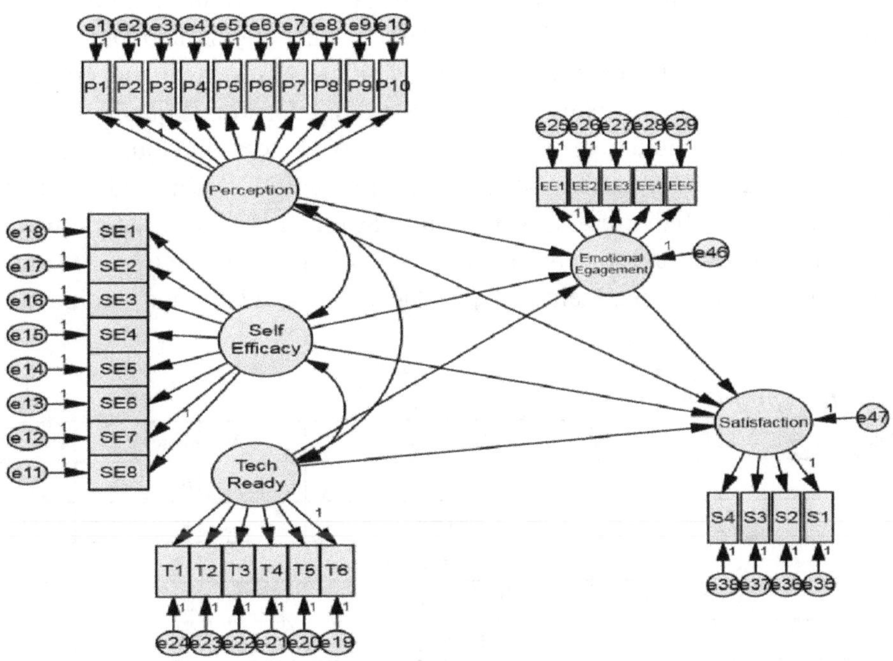

3. METHODS

This section aims to investigate the multifaceted interplay between learners' perception, self-efficacy, and technological readiness, and their collective influence on the shaping of a hybrid learning environment. Autonomous learning and the effective integration of digital technologies have become crucial elements in contemporary higher education, especially in the context of online and blended learning (Pratiwi & Waluyo, 2023). The COVID-19 pandemic has further accelerated this shift, necessitating institutions to rapidly adapt and develop robust hybrid learning models (Stensaker, 2021).

This study will explore the complex dynamics that underpin the learners' experiences and their active engagement within a hybrid learning ecosystem. Specifically, it will examine how learners' perceptions of the hybrid learning environment, their self-efficacy beliefs, and their technological readiness collectively contribute to the successful implementation and sustainability of such learning modalities (Otto et al, 2023).

The study adopts a dual approach, being both exploratory and descriptive in nature, to comprehensively investigate the factors influencing hybrid learning environments, with a specific focus on learner perception, self-efficacy, and technological readiness.

3.1 Sample and Data

The population for this study consists of students enrolled in undergraduate and postgraduate management programs across selected higher educational institutes in the northern region of India. This region includes the states of Haryana, Himachal Pradesh, Punjab, Chandigarh, and Delhi. These institutions have been selected based on their accreditation by the National Assessment and Accreditation Council (NAAC), which ensures that they maintain a high standard of educational quality and relevance.

The scope of the study is limited to the students of the NAAC accredited institutions of North India. The selection of NAAC-accredited institutions is critical because NAAC accreditation is a hallmark of quality in higher education in India. It assesses institutions on various parameters such as curriculum, faculty, infrastructure, research, and student services. Institutions that receive NAAC accreditation have demonstrated their commitment to maintaining high educational standards and continuous improvement.

Table 1. Demographic profile of students

Demographic Measures	Category	Frequency	Percentage
Gender	Male	270	43.5
	Female	350	56.5
Educational Qualification	Undergraduate	310	50.0
	Postgraduate	180	29.0
	Doctoral	90	14.5
	Others	40	6.5

Source(s): Authors

Primary Source

The Table 1 displays demographic profile of students which is a part of primary data. The primary data for this study has been collected through a self-administered questionnaire. This questionnaire is designed in Google Forms, which offers several advantages in terms of distribution and collection efficiency. Google Forms is an accessible and user-friendly tool that allows researchers to create and distribute surveys quickly and efficiently. It supports various types of questions, such as multiple-choice, Likert scales, and open-ended questions, enabling the collection of both quantitative and qualitative data.

The choice of a self-administered questionnaire ensures that respondents can complete the survey at their convenience, which is crucial for obtaining honest and reflective responses. This method also minimizes interviewer bias, as there is no direct interaction between the researcher and the respondent during the data collection process. Furthermore, the digital nature of Google Forms allows for easy tracking and management of responses, as well as automated data compilation, which facilitates efficient data analysis (Creswell & Creswell, 2017).

Secondary Source

Secondary data were sourced from existing research studies, reports, and databases, ensuring that the study is grounded in established knowledge and current trends. This includes utilizing databases from the University Grants Commission (UGC) and the All-India Survey on Higher Education (AISHE) reports. The UGC provides comprehensive data on higher education institutions in India, including accreditation status, program offerings, and enrolment statistics. The AISHE reports offer detailed insights into the state of higher education in India, including data on student demographics, faculty qualifications, and infrastructure.

These secondary sources are invaluable for providing context and background information that supports the primary data collected through the questionnaire. They help to validate the findings and ensure that the study is aligned with broader educational trends and policies. Moreover, secondary data can fill in gaps that the primary data might not cover, offering a more comprehensive understanding of the research problem (Bhattacherjee, 2012).

3.2 Sampling Unit

The sampling unit for this study comprises management students who are enrolled in hybrid learning programs at selected NAAC-accredited universities. This specific demographic is crucial for several reasons.

Firstly, management students are often at the forefront of utilizing innovative learning methodologies, including hybrid learning, which combines traditional classroom experiences with online educational resources. By focusing on this group, the study can gain valuable insights into how hybrid learning models are being perceived and utilized by students who are likely to be future leaders and managers (Bokolo et al., 2020). Secondly, the selection of NAAC-accredited universities ensures that the institutions included in the study adhere to high standards of educational quality. Therefore, students from these accredited universities are more likely to experience well-implemented hybrid learning environments, making them ideal candidates for this research (Anthony et al, 2020).

3.3 Sampling Method

The study employs a combination of cluster sampling and random sampling methods to ensure a diverse and representative sample while maintaining logistical feasibility. This mixed approach leverages the strengths of both sampling techniques to effectively capture data from various subpopulations within the study area.

4. DATA ANALYSIS AND RESULTS

The primary data analysis was done with the help of the Statistical software SPSS. Basic frequency analysis and descriptive assessments were done. Mean, standard deviation, skewness, and kurtosis values were calculated for the individual items and the constructs. The data was found to be normal, and further analysis was undertaken. Basic issues of normality, multicollinearity (VIF < 5), and common method bias were checked in detail. Exploratory and confirmatory factor analyses (EFA and CFA) were done to assess the reliability and validity of the measurement model. Structural equation modelling was used to evaluate the proposed hypotheses with the help of Smart PLS 4 (Ringle et al, 2022).

4.1 Confirmatory Factor Analysis (CFA)

Confirmatory Factor Analysis (CFA) is a sophisticated statistical technique used to verify the factor structure of a set of observed variables. This technique is crucial for testing the hypothesis that the items of a questionnaire are related to specific factors. Reliability analysis ensures that the measurement instruments consistently reflect the construct they are intended to measure.

A higher Cronbach's alpha value (typically above 0.70) suggests that the items measure the same underlying construct (Nunnally & Bernstein, 1994), thus ensuring the reliability of the survey instruments used. Unlike Cronbach's alpha, which assumes equal loadings and inter-item correlations, Composite Reliability takes into account the actual factor loadings of items. CR values of 0.70 or higher are considered acceptable, indicating good reliability (Fornell & Larcker, 1981). Convergent validity & Discriminant validity has been used in the study.

Model Fit Measures

Table 2. Measurement model: reliability and validity of the construct

Measure	Estimate	Result	Criteria
CMIN	1337.75	--	--
DF	485	--	--
CMIN/DF	2.75	Acceptable	>1
CFI	0.904	Acceptable	>0.90
SRMR	0.047	Acceptable	<0.08
RMSEA	0.067	Acceptable	<0.08

Source(s): Authors

The table 2 presents several model fit measures used to evaluate the adequacy of the proposed model. The Chi-square value (CMIN) is 1337.75 with 485 degrees of freedom (DF). The ratio of CMIN to DF is 2.75, which falls within the acceptable range of less than 3, indicating a reasonable fit of the model to the data (Kline, 2015).

The Comparative Fit Index (CFI) is 0.904, which exceeds the commonly accepted threshold of 0.90 (Bentler, 1990), suggesting a good fit. The Standardized Root Mean Square Residual (SRMR) is 0.047, which is below the threshold of 0.08, indicating an acceptable fit (Bentler, 1999). Additionally, the Root Mean Square Error of Approximation (RMSEA) is 0.067, which is below the threshold of 0.08 and within the acceptable range, indicating a good fit (Steiger, 1990).

Overall, these fit indices collectively indicate that the proposed model has a good fit to the data, meeting the established criteria for model adequacy.

Discriminant Validity

Table 3. Discriminant validity-HTMT ratio for model 1

	P	SE	T	EE
P				
SE	0.803307			
T	0.777612	0.817254		
EE	0.775883	0.766338	0.795635	

Personal= Perception; SE = Self Efficacy; TR = Technology Readiness; EE = Emotional Engagement; S = Satisfaction; EF = Effectiveness

Source(s): Authors

In the table 3 the HTMT ratios for the constructs of Perception (P), Self Efficacy (SE), Technology Readiness (T), and Emotional Engagement (EE) indicate good discriminant validity among these constructs. Specifically, The HTMT ratio between Perception and Self Efficacy is 0.803, which is below the 0.85 threshold suggested by Henseler et al. (2015), confirming that these constructs are distinct from each other. Similarly, the HTMT ratio between Perception and Technology Readiness is 0.778, and between Perception and Emotional Engagement is 0.776. Both values are comfortably below the 0.85 threshold, further supporting the discriminant validity of these constructs.

Furthermore, the HTMT ratio between Self Efficacy and Technology Readiness is 0.817, which is also below 0.85, indicating that these constructs do not overlap significantly and are distinct. The ratio between Self Efficacy and Emotional Engagement is 0.766, reinforcing the discriminant validity as it remains under the 0.85 threshold.

Lastly, the HTMT ratio between Technology Readiness and Emotional Engagement is 0.796, which is well within the acceptable limit of 0.85. This indicates that Technology Readiness and Emotional Engagement are distinct constructs, further confirming the discriminant validity.

In summary, the HTMT ratios provided in the table 4 demonstrate that the constructs of Perception, Self-Efficacy, Technology Readiness, and Emotional Engagement exhibit good discriminant validity. Each HTMT ratio is below the 0.85 threshold, suggesting that the constructs are distinct and do not exhibit significant overlap. This discriminant validity is essential for ensuring that the constructs measure different concepts, which enhances the reliability and validity of the study's findings (Henseler et al., 2015).

Table 4. Discriminant Validity-Fornell-Larcker criteria for model 1

	P	SE	TR	EE
P	0.898			
SE	0.778	0.907		
T	0.741	0.779	0.852	
EE	0.850	0.735	0.749	0.902

Personal= Perception; SE = Self Efficacy; TR = Technology Readiness; EE = Emotional Engagement; CE = Cognitive Engagement; S = Satisfaction; EF = Effectiveness

Note: Color Coding Square root of AVE Inter factor correlation

Source(s): Authors

The discriminant validity of the constructs in this study was evaluated using the Fornell-Larcker criterion. According to this criterion, discriminant validity is confirmed if the square root of the Average Variance Extracted (AVE) for each construct is greater than the highest correlation of that construct with any other construct (Zou et al., 2024).

Tthan its correlations with Self Efficacy (0.778), Technology Readiness (0.741), and Emotional Engagement (0.850). This indicates good discriminant validity for the Perception construct, as it is distinct from the other constructs.

For the **Self Efficacy (SE)** construct, the square root of the AVE is 0.907, which exceeds its correlations with Perception (0.778), Technology Readiness (0.779), and Emotional Engagement (0.735). This demonstrates that the Self Efficacy construct has adequate discriminant validity.

The **Technology Readiness (TR)** construct has a square root of AVE of 0.852. This value is greater than its correlations with Perception (0.741), Self Efficacy (0.779), and Emotional Engagement (0.749), confirming its discriminant validity.

Lastly, for the **Emotional Engagement (EE)** construct, the square root of the AVE is 0.902, which is higher than its correlations with Perception (0.850), Self Efficacy (0.735), and Technology Readiness (0.749). This also indicates strong discriminant validity for Emotional Engagement.

Overall, the results confirm that each construct in the study has satisfactory discriminant validity, as the square root of the AVE for each construct is greater than the highest correlation of that construct with any other construct, thereby supporting the distinctiveness of the constructs (Fornell & Larcker, 1981).

Table 5. Path analysis and hypotheses results for direct relationships for model 1

Alternate Hypotheses	Path Relationship	Standardized coefficients	Result
H1	P → EE	0.917*	Supported
H2	P → S	0.340*	Supported
H3	SE → EE	-0.423*	Supported
H4	SE → S	-0.140	Not Supported
H5	T → EE	0.498*	Supported

Alternate Hypotheses	Path Relationship	Standardized coefficients	Result
H6	T → S	0.461*	Supported
H7	EE → S	0.349	Not Supported

* p< 0.05
P= Perception; SE = Self Efficacy; TR = Technology Readiness; EE = Emotional Engagement; S = Satisfaction
Source(s): Authors

The path analysis for this Model evaluates the direct relationships between various constructs: Perception (P), Self-Efficacy (SE), Technology Readiness (TR), Emotional Engagement (EE), and Satisfaction (S). The standardized coefficients and significance levels provide insight into which hypotheses are supported by the data in table 5 as below:

(H1): Perception (P) → Emotional Engagement (EE): The path coefficient for P → EE is 0.917, indicating a strong positive relationship. This result is statistically significant ($p < 0.05$), supporting the hypothesis that perception positively influences emotional engagement.
(H2): Perception (P) → Satisfaction (S): The path coefficient for P → S is 0.340, suggesting a moderate positive relationship. This relationship is statistically significant ($p < 0.05$), supporting the hypothesis that perception positively affects satisfaction.:
(H3): Self-Efficacy (SE) → Emotional Engagement (EE): The path coefficient for SE → EE is -0.423, indicating a significant negative relationship. This result is statistically significant ($p < 0.05$), supporting the hypothesis that self-efficacy negatively influences emotional engagement.
(H4): Self-Efficacy (SE) → Satisfaction (S): The path coefficient for SE → S is -0.140, indicating a weak negative relationship. This relationship is not statistically significant, thus not supporting the hypothesis that self-efficacy influences satisfaction.
(H5): Technology Readiness (T) → Emotional Engagement (EE): The path coefficient for T → EE is 0.498, showing a significant positive relationship. This result is statistically significant ($p < 0.05$), supporting the hypothesis that technology readiness positively affects emotional engagement.
(H6): Technology Readiness (T) → Satisfaction (S): The path coefficient for T → S is 0.461, indicating a significant positive relationship. This relationship is statistically significant ($p < 0.05$), supporting the hypothesis that technology readiness positively influences satisfaction.
(H7): Emotional Engagement (EE) → Satisfaction (S): The path coefficient for EE → S is 0.349, suggesting a moderate positive relationship. However, this relationship is not statistically significant, thus not supporting the hypothesis that emotional engagement influences satisfaction.

Overall, the path analysis indicates that perception and technology readiness play significant roles in influencing both emotional engagement and satisfaction, whereas self-efficacy negatively affects emotional engagement and does not significantly impact satisfaction.

Emotional Engagement as Mediator

Table 6. Direct, indirect & total effects on satisfaction

Alternate Hypotheses	IV	Direct Effect (Mediation Path)	Indirect Effect (LLCI, ULCI) (Mediation Path)	Total Effect	VAF	Mediation	Result
H8	P	0.340* (P → S)	0.320 (-0.214, 0.556) (P → EE → S)	0.659	48.55%	Partial	Supported
H9	SE	-0.140 (SE → S)	-0.148 (-0.303, 0.080) (SE → EE → S)	-0.287	42.7%	Partial	Supported
H10	T	0.461* (T → S)	0.174 (-0.095, 0.355) (T → EE → S)	0.635	27.4%	Partial	Supported

* p< 0.05,
DV = Dependent Variable = Satisfaction, IV = Independent Variables, Mediator = Emotional Engagement
LLCI = Lower level confidence Interval, ULCI = Upper Level Confidence Interval
P= Perception; SE = Self Efficacy; TR = Technology Readiness; EE = Emotional Engagement; S = Satisfaction
Source(s): Authors

Table 6 interprets the direct, indirect, and total effects of perception, self-efficacy, and technological readiness on student satisfaction, with emotional engagement as a mediator. The focus is on understanding how emotional engagement mediates the relationship between these independent variables (IV) and the dependent variable (DV), which is student satisfaction.

(H8): Perception (P) → Emotional Engagement (EE) → Satisfaction (S): The direct effect of perception on satisfaction is significant with a standardized coefficient of 0.340 ($p < 0.05$), indicating a positive relationship. The indirect effect, mediated through emotional engagement, is 0.320, with confidence intervals ranging from -0.214 to 0.556. This implies partial mediation, as the confidence interval includes zero. The total effect of perception on satisfaction is 0.659, with a variance accounted for (VAF) of 48.55%, showing that nearly half of the effect is mediated through emotional engagement. These results support the hypothesis that perception positively affects satisfaction, with emotional engagement partially mediating this relationship.

(H9): Self-Efficacy (SE) → Emotional Engagement (EE) → Satisfaction (S): The direct effect of self-efficacy on satisfaction is negative and not significant (-0.140). The indirect effect, mediated through emotional engagement, is -0.148, with confidence intervals from -0.303 to 0.080. The inclusion of zero in the confidence interval suggests partial mediation. The total effect of self-efficacy on satisfaction is -0.287, with a VAF of 42.7%, indicating that emotional engagement partially mediates this relationship. Although the direct effect is negative and non-significant, the partial mediation suggests that improving self-efficacy could enhance emotional engagement, subsequently increasing satisfaction.

(H10): Technological Readiness (T) → Emotional Engagement (EE) → Satisfaction (S): The direct effect of technological readiness on satisfaction is significant with a coefficient of 0.461 ($p < 0.05$), indicating a strong positive relationship. The indirect effect, mediated through emotional engagement, is 0.174, with confidence intervals from -0.095 to 0.355. The inclusion of zero in the confidence interval indicates partial mediation. The total effect of technological readiness on satisfaction is 0.635, with a VAF of 27.4%, showing that a portion of the effect is mediated by emotional engagement. These results support the hypothesis that technological readiness positively affects satisfaction, with emotional engagement serving as a partial mediator.

Overall, emotional engagement plays a critical role in mediating the relationships between perception, self-efficacy, technological readiness, and student satisfaction. Although the mediation effects are partial, they highlight the importance of fostering emotional engagement to enhance the satisfaction of students in hybrid learning environments. This suggests that initiatives aimed at increasing emotional engagement could amplify the positive effects of perception and technological readiness and potentially mitigate the negative effects of self-efficacy on satisfaction (Babu et al,2022).

5. DISCUSSIONS

The path analysis for Model 1 provides valuable insights into the direct relationships among the constructs of Perception, Self-Efficacy, Technology Readiness, Emotional Engagement, and Satisfaction within the context of hybrid learning. The results indicate several noteworthy patterns and support specific hypotheses based on standardized coefficients and their statistical significance. Firstly, the hypothesis that students' perception positively influences emotional engagement (H1) is strongly supported. This finding aligns with previous studies indicating that positive perceptions of learning environments can enhance emotional engagement, thereby fostering a more immersive and motivating learning experience (Fredricks et al,2004). Similarly, the hypothesis that perception positively affects satisfaction (H2) is also supported, suggesting that students who perceive the learning environment positively are more likely to be satisfied with their learning experience. This is consistent with the literature emphasizing the role of positive perceptions in student satisfaction (Richardson, 2005).

In contrast, the hypothesis that self-efficacy positively influences emotional engagement (H4) is not supported. Surprisingly, the data reveals a significant negative relationship between self-efficacy and emotional engagement, suggesting that higher self-efficacy might lead to lower emotional engagement. This counterintuitive finding could be explored further in the context of hybrid learning, possibly indicating that highly self-efficacious students might engage emotionally less due to overconfidence or disengagement from perceived easier tasks (Bandura, 1997). Additionally, self-efficacy does not significantly impact satisfaction (H5), indicating that students' belief in their capabilities does not necessarily translate to overall satisfaction in a hybrid learning environment. On the other hand, the hypothesis that technology readiness positively influences emotional engagement (H7) is supported, suggesting that students who are more comfortable and prepared to use technology are more likely to be emotionally engaged. This finding is in line with previous research that highlights the importance of technological readiness in enhancing student engagement (Parasuraman, 2000). Similarly, technology readiness positively influences satisfaction (H8), indicating that students who are technologically ready find the hybrid learning environment more satisfying, which is supported by studies emphasizing the role of technology in student satisfaction (Teo, 2011). Lastly, the hypothesis that emotional engagement positively influences satisfaction (H10) is not supported, suggesting that while emotional engagement is important, it may not directly translate into overall satisfaction within a hybrid learning context. This finding invites further exploration into other factors that might mediate the relationship between emotional engagement and satisfaction.

Overall, the path analysis underscores the significant roles of perception and technology readiness in influencing both emotional engagement and satisfaction. In contrast, self-efficacy negatively impacts emotional engagement and does not significantly influence satisfaction. These findings provide a deep understanding of the dynamics at play in hybrid learning environments and suggest areas for further research to optimize student engagement and satisfaction.

Mediation Effect of Emotional Engagement

This section presents the direct, indirect, and total effects of perception, self-efficacy, and technological readiness on student satisfaction, with emotional engagement as a mediator. The results focus on understanding the mediating role of emotional engagement in the relationships between these independent variables (IV) and the dependent variable (DV), which is student satisfaction. For the hypothesis that perception positively affects satisfaction (H3), the direct effect of perception on satisfaction is significant, indicating a positive relationship. The indirect effect, mediated through emotional engagement, suggests partial mediation as the confidence interval includes zero. The total effect shows that nearly half of the effect is mediated through emotional engagement, supporting the hypothesis that perception positively influences satisfaction with emotional engagement partially mediating this relationship. This finding aligns with previous research showing that students' positive perceptions of learning environments can enhance both their engagement and satisfaction (Fredricks et al., 2004). Regarding the hypothesis that self-efficacy influences satisfaction (H6), the direct effect of self-efficacy on satisfaction is negative and not significant. However, the indirect effect through emotional engagement indicates partial mediation. Although the direct effect is negative and non-significant, the partial mediation suggests that enhancing self-efficacy could improve emotional engagement, subsequently increasing satisfaction. This finding reflects the complex nature of self-efficacy's impact on student outcomes, as discussed by (Zou et al., 2024)). For the hypothesis that technological readiness positively affects satisfaction (H9), the direct effect is significant and positive. The indirect effect, mediated through emotional engagement, also indicates partial mediation. The total effect shows that a portion of the effect is mediated by emotional engagement, supporting the hypothesis that technological readiness positively influences satisfaction with emotional engagement serving as a partial mediator. This finding corroborates earlier studies highlighting the importance of technological readiness in enhancing student engagement and satisfaction (Parasuraman, 2000; Teo, 2011).

Overall, emotional engagement plays a crucial role in mediating the relationships between perception, self-efficacy, technological readiness, and student satisfaction. While the mediation effects are partial, they underscore the significance of fostering emotional engagement to enhance student satisfaction in hybrid learning environments. These insights suggest that initiatives aimed at increasing emotional engagement could amplify the positive effects of perception and technological readiness and potentially mitigate the negative effects of self-efficacy on satisfaction.

5.1 Practical Implications

Based on the findings of the study, students can take several steps to enhance their learning experience in hybrid learning environments. Firstly, students should focus on cultivating a positive perception of their learning environment. This can be achieved by actively engaging with the course material, participating in discussions, and utilizing available resources. A positive outlook can significantly boost emotional engagement, making the learning process more immersive and enjoyable. Furthermore, students should strive to improve their technological readiness. Becoming more familiar and comfortable with the technology used in hybrid learning can enhance both engagement and satisfaction (Patnaik et al,2022). This includes taking advantage of tutorials, seeking help when needed, and practicing the use of educational tools. Additionally, while self-efficacy is important, students should be mindful of not letting high self-confidence lead to disengagement. Balancing self-assurance with a continuous desire to learn and engage can prevent the negative impact of overconfidence on emotional engagement. By adopting these strategies, students can maximize their satisfaction and effectiveness in hybrid learning environments.

For Academic Institutions

Academic institutions play a crucial role in shaping the hybrid learning experience and can implement several strategies to enhance student engagement and satisfaction. Firstly, institutions should prioritize creating a positive learning environment. This includes providing supportive and responsive faculty, fostering a collaborative learning culture, and ensuring that the course content is relevant and engaging. Enhancing the technological infrastructure and providing comprehensive training to both students and staff can significantly boost technological readiness. Institutions should offer regular workshops, tutorials, and technical support to help students become proficient with the required technology. Additionally, academic institutions should pay attention to the emotional engagement of students. Programs and initiatives that promote mental well-being, such as counselling services and stress management workshops, can help maintain high levels of emotional engagement. Finally, institutions should conduct regular assessments and feedback sessions to understand student perceptions and experiences better. This ongoing dialogue can help identify areas for improvement and ensure that the hybrid learning environment continues to evolve in ways that enhance student satisfaction and learning outcomes.

The study on the "Role of Learner's Perception, Self-Efficacy, and Technological Readiness in Shaping Hybrid Learning Environments" highlights the intricate interplay between these factors in determining the effectiveness and satisfaction of hybrid learning models. The findings underscore the necessity for both students and academic institutions to actively engage in enhancing their respective roles within this educational paradigm.

5.2 Limitations and Directions of Future Research

Limitations of the Study

1. Sample Size and Diversity: The study may have been limited by the size and diversity of its sample population. If the sample was not sufficiently large or diverse, the findings may not be generalizable to all student populations, particularly those from different cultural or socioeconomic backgrounds.

2. Self-Reported Data: The reliance on self-reported data for measuring perceptions, self-efficacy, and technological readiness can introduce biases. Participants might overestimate or underestimate their abilities and perceptions, which can affect the accuracy of the findings.

Directions for Future Research

1. Longitudinal Studies: Future research should employ longitudinal designs to track changes in students' perceptions, self-efficacy, and technological readiness over time. This approach can provide insights into the long-term effects of these factors on hybrid learning outcomes.
2. Experimental Studies: Conducting experimental studies where specific interventions aimed at improving technological readiness, self-efficacy, and engagement are implemented and assessed can help establish causal relationships and identify effective strategies.

By addressing these limitations and exploring these directions, future research can build on the current findings to develop more varied and effective strategies for enhancing hybrid learning environments.

6. CONCLUSION

Students are pivotal in optimizing their hybrid learning experiences. The study suggests that students should cultivate a positive perception of their learning environments by actively engaging with course materials, participating in discussions, and utilizing available resources. This positive outlook can significantly boost emotional and cognitive engagement, making the learning process more immersive and enjoyable. Additionally, improving technological readiness through tutorials, help-seeking behaviours', and consistent practice with educational tools can enhance engagement and satisfaction. Students should also balance self-efficacy with a continuous desire to learn, avoiding complacency that can result from overconfidence. By setting realistic goals, seeking feedback, and engaging in peer interactions, students can bolster their self-efficacy and emotional investment, ultimately leading to a more fulfilling educational experience.

REFERENCES

Anthony, B., Kamaludin, A., Romli, A., Raffei, A. F. M., Phon, D. N. A. L., Abdullah, A., & Ming, G. L. (2020). Blended learning adoption and implementation in higher education: A theoretical and systematic review. Technology, Knowledge and Learning,25(4) https://link.springer.com/article/10.1007/s10758-020-09477-z

Babu, V., Kumar, A., & Kumar, V. (2022). *Exploring Mindfulness and Leadership Development: Lessons Learnt Using Grounded Theory Through the Study of the Performing Arts*. FIIB Business Review., DOI: 10.1177/23197145221088643

Bandura, A. (1997). Self-Efficacy: The Exercise of Control. New York, NY: Freeman; Pajares, F. (1996). Self-efficacy beliefs in academic settings. *Review of Educational Research*, *66*(4), 543–578.

Bokolo, A. J., De Reuver, M., & Marijn Janssen, M. (2020). A coordinated model for identifying and managing the risk and cost drivers of hybrid cloud adoption in enterprises. Journal of Cloud Computing: Advances. *Systems and Applications*, *9*, 1–20.

Bokolo, A. J., Petersen, S. A., & Lai, R. T. (2020). Examining factors affecting hybrid learning readiness and effectiveness. *Journal of Hybrid Learning and Teaching*, *8*(1), 45–58.

Chen, Y., Farzan, R., Kraut, R., YeckehZaare, I., & Zhang, A. F. (2024). Motivating experts to contribute to digital public goods: A personalized field experiment on Wikipedia. *Management Science*, *70*(5), 3264–3280. DOI: 10.1287/mnsc.2023.4852

Daultani, Y., Goswami, M., Kumar, A., & Pratap, S. (2021). Perceived outcomes of e-learning: Identifying key attributes affecting user satisfaction in higher education institutes. *Measuring Business Excellence*, *25*(2), 216–229. DOI: 10.1108/MBE-07-2020-0110

Fornell, C., & Larcker, D. F. (1981). Evaluating Structural Equation Models with Unobservable Variables and Measurement Error. *JMR, Journal of Marketing Research*, *18*(1), 39–50. DOI: 10.1177/002224378101800104

Fredricks, J. A., Blumenfeld, P. C., & Paris, A. H. (2004). School engagement: Potential of the concept, state of the evidence. *Review of Educational Research*, *74*(1), 59–109. DOI: 10.3102/00346543074001059

Gómez-Morales, A., Coon, D. W., Glinka, A., Stirling, R., Pipe, T., Joseph, R. P., & Garcia-Segura, S. (2023). Training alternatives for Alzheimer's disease and related dementia caregivers: Assessing economic and environmental benefits of internet of health things. *Journal of Cleaner Production*, *418*, 138206. DOI: 10.1016/j.jclepro.2023.138206

Hadi, S., & Baskaran, S. (2021). Examining sustainable business performance determinants in Malaysia upstream petroleum industry. *Journal of Cleaner Production*, *294*, 126231. DOI: 10.1016/j.jclepro.2021.126231

Henseler, J., Ringle, C. M., & Sarstedt, M. (2015). A New Criterion for Assessing Discriminant Validity in Variance-Based Structural Equation Modeling. *Journal of the Academy of Marketing Science*, *43*(1), 115–135. https://link.springer.com/article/10.1007/s11747-014-0403-8. DOI: 10.1007/s11747-014-0403-8

Imran, A., Jian, X., Sulieman, H., & Jin, S. (2023). Evaluating the Impact of Blended Learning on Student Engagement and Performance in Higher Education. *Journal of Educational Technology Development and Exchange, 16*(2), 189–208. https://link.springer.com/article/10.1007/s44217-024-00253-0

Joo, Y. J., Lim, K. Y., & Kim, N. H. (2013). Online university students' satisfaction and persistence: Examining the role of self-efficacy, use of learning management systems, and course satisfaction. *Internet and Higher Education, 16*, 68–7. DOI: 10.1016/j.compedu.2011.02.008

Kahu, E. R., & Nelson, K. (2018). Student engagement in the educational interface: Understanding the mechanisms of student success. Higher Education Research & Development, 37(1), 58-71. ps://DOI: 10.1080/07294360.2017.1344197

Kokkodis, M., & Ransbotham, S. (2023). Learning to successfully hire in online labor markets. *Management Science, 69*(3), 1597–1614. DOI: 10.1287/mnsc.2022.4426

Leng, J., Guo, J., Zhang, H., Xu, K., Qiao, Y., Zheng, P., & Shen, W. (2023). Dual deep reinforcement learning agents-based integrated order acceptance and scheduling of mass individualized prototyping. *Journal of Cleaner Production, 427*, 139249. DOI: 10.1016/j.jclepro.2023.139249

Li, C., He, P., Peng, W., Lü, F., Du, R., & Zhang, H. (2022). Exploring available input variables for machine learning models to predict biogas production in industrial-scale biogas plants treating food waste. *Journal of Cleaner Production, 380*, 135074. DOI: 10.1016/j.jclepro.2022.135074

Liaw, S. S., & Huang, H. M. (2013). Perceived satisfaction, perceived usefulness and interactive learning environments as predictors to self-regulation in e-learning environments. *Computers & Education, 60*(1), 14–24. DOI: 10.1016/j.compedu.2012.07.015

Liu, Q., Gao, J., & Li, S. (2024). The innovation model and upgrade path of digitalization driven tourism industry: Longitudinal case study of OCT. *Technological Forecasting and Social Change, 200*, 123127. DOI: 10.1016/j.techfore.2023.123127

Mishra, V., & Singh, J. (2022). *Health Technology Assessment of Telemedicine Interventions in Diabetes Management: Evidence from UAE.* FIIB Business Review., DOI: 10.1177/23197145221130651

Nguyen, P. N. D., & Nguyen, H. H. (2024). Unveiling the link between digital entrepreneurship education and intention among university students in an emerging economy. *Technological Forecasting and Social Change, 203*, 123330. https://doi.org/ rights and contentDOI: 10.1016/j.techfore.2024.123330Get

Parasuraman, A. (2000). Technology Readiness Index (TRI): A multiple-item scale to measure readiness to embrace new technologies. *Journal of Service Research, 2*(4), 307–320. DOI: 10.1177/109467050024001

Park, J., Son, Y., & Angst, C. M. (2023). The Value of Centralized IT in Building Resilience During Crises: Evidence from US Higher Education's Transition to Emergency Remote Teaching. *Management Information Systems Quarterly, 47*(1), 451–482. DOI: 10.25300/MISQ/2022/17265

Patnaik, R., Patra, S. K., Mahapatra, D. M., & Baral, S. K. (2022). *Adoption and Challenges Underlying OTT Platform in India during Pandemic: A Critical Study of Socio-Economic and Technological Issues.* FIIB Business Review., DOI: 10.1177/23197145221101676

Pekrun, R., & Linnenbrink-Garcia, L. (2012). Academic emotions and student engagement. In Christenson, S. L. (Eds.), *Handbook of research on student engagement* (pp. 259–282). Springer. DOI: 10.1007/978-1-4614-2018-7_12

Richardson, J. T. E. (2005). Students' perceptions of academic quality and approaches to studying in distance education. *British Educational Research Journal, 31*(1), 7–27. DOI: 10.1080/0141192052000310001

Sitar-Tăut, D. A., Mican, D., & Moisescu, O. I. (2024). To be (online) or not to be? The antecedents of online study propensity and e-learning-dependent dropout intention in higher education. *Technological Forecasting and Social Change, 207*, 123566. DOI: 10.1016/j.techfore.2024.123566

Skinner, E. A., Kindermann, T. A., & Furrer, C. J. (2009). A motivational perspective on engagement and disaffection: Conceptualization and assessment of children's behavioral and emotional participation in academic activities in the classroom. *Educational and Psychological Measurement, 69*(3), 493–525. DOI: 10.1177/0013164408323233

Smith, A., & Jones, B. (2020). Understanding the role of job satisfaction in employee performance. *International Journal of Human Resource Management, 31*(4), 567–589.

Teng, Y., Zheng, J., Li, Y., & Wu, D. (2024). Optimizing digital transformation paths for industrial clusters: Insights from a simulation. *Technological Forecasting and Social Change, 200*, 123170. DOI: 10.1016/j.techfore.2023.123170

Teo, T. (2011). Factors influencing teachers' intention to use technology: Model development and test. *Computers & Education, 57*(4), 2432–2440. DOI: 10.1016/j.compedu.2011.06.008

Wang, G., Chen, G., Zhao, H., Zhang, F., Yang, S., & Lu, T. (2021). Leveraging Multisource Heterogeneous Data for Financial Risk Prediction: A Novel Hybrid-Strategy-Based Self-Adaptive Method. *Management Information Systems Quarterly, 45*(4), 1949–1998. DOI: 10.25300/MISQ/2021/16118

Wu, F. S., Tsai, C. C., Wu, C. H., & Lo, T. H. (2024). An exploratory study of breakthrough innovations in digital businesses: The case of the Perfect Corporation. *Technological Forecasting and Social Change, 201*, 123233. DOI: 10.1016/j.techfore.2024.123233

Xiong, L., Ning, J., & Dong, Y. (2022). Pollution reduction effect of the digital transformation of heavy metal enterprises under the agglomeration effect. *Journal of Cleaner Production, 330*, 129864. DOI: 10.1016/j.jclepro.2021.129864

Xue, Q., Li, J., Xiao, Y., Chai, Z., Liu, Z., & Chen, J. (2023). A Flexible deep convolutional neural network coupled with progressive training framework for online capacity estimation of lithium-ion batteries. *Journal of Cleaner Production, 397*, 136575. DOI: 10.1016/j.jclepro.2023.136575

Yoganarasimhan, H., Barzegary, E., & Pani, A. (2023). Design and evaluation of optimal free trials. *Management Science, 69*(6), 3220–3240. DOI: 10.1287/mnsc.2022.4507

Zheng, Y. H., Shi, G., Zhong, H., Liu, M. T., & Lin, Z. (2023). Motivating strategic front-line employees for innovative sales in the digital transformation era: The mediating role of salesperson learning. *Technological Forecasting and Social Change, 193*, 122593. DOI: 10.1016/j.techfore.2023.122593

Zhou, J., Zhang, Q., Zhou, S., Li, X., & Zhang, X. M. (2023). Unintended emotional effects of online health communities: A text mining-supported empirical study. *Management Information Systems Quarterly*, *47*(1), 195–226. DOI: 10.25300/MISQ/2022/17018

Zou, Y., Zhong, N., Chen, Z., & Zhao, W. (2024). Bridging digitalization and sustainability in universities: A Chinese green university initiative in the digital era. *Journal of Cleaner Production*, *469*, 143181. DOI: 10.1016/j.jclepro.2024.143181

Chapter 13
Reimagining Compliance:
Explainable AI Models for Financial Regulatory Audits

Hrishikesh Desai
https://orcid.org/0000-0002-7945-3744
Arkansas State University, USA

ABSTRACT

This chapter develops an analytical model for Explainable AI (XAI) designed to support major types of banking regulatory compliance audits. Financial institutions increasingly rely on AI for efficiency in compliance tasks, but the opacity of complex models creates challenges in meeting regulatory transparency requirements. The proposed mathematical framework incorporates explainability as a quantifiable constraint in the optimization of AI models across five critical audit categories: CAMELS examinations, BSA/AML compliance, Consumer Compliance, IT Audits, and Internal Audits. By quantifying explainability through information-theoretic measures and Shapley values, the model balances predictive performance with regulatory requirements. The methodology is validated through a numerical example demonstrating significant improvement in the objective function while satisfying all regulatory constraints. The chapter addresses implementation challenges across different regulatory jurisdictions, human-AI collaboration considerations, and resource requirements for institutions of varying sizes.

1. INTRODUCTION

Banks operate under rigorous regulatory scrutiny, with compliance audits serving as important mechanisms to ensure sound practices (Ghosh et al., 2024). Traditional compliance methods, while effective, are increasingly supplemented by AI-driven systems for transaction monitoring, risk scoring, and data analysis (Doumpos et al., 2023). The increasing reliance on artificial intelligence (AI) to increase efficiency and decision-making introduces a key challenge: explainability. AI models, particularly complex ones like deep neural networks, often function as "black boxes," making it difficult to understand or justify their decisions, which is a significant limitation in the context of regulatory compliance (Hassija et al., 2024). Thus, the opacity of these systems poses challenges in satisfying the explainability and transparency requirements demanded by regulators (Fernández, 2024; Torrie & Payette, 2023). In this chapter, I develop an analytical model for Explainable AI (XAI) designed to support major types of

DOI: 10.4018/979-8-3373-0209-6.ch013

regulatory compliance audits. Thus, this study addresses the fundamental question: *how can financial institutions balance AI's efficiency gains with regulatory requirements for explainability?*

Prior research has explored various aspects of AI explainability in financial services. Information-theoretic measures have been proposed to quantify relationships between model inputs and outputs (Islam et al., 2021; Piras et al., 2023), while Shapley values from cooperative game theory have been used to attribute importance to individual features (Holzinger et al., 2022). However, existing frameworks often lack integration of domain-specific regulatory constraints into model design (Longo et al., 2024). Current approaches tend to prioritize either accuracy or explainability but seldom balance these objectives within compliance audit contexts (Hosain et al., 2024).

This study contributes to the literature by developing an analytical model for Explainable AI (XAI) designed to support major types of regulatory compliance audits. The model incorporates constraints for five critical audit categories: Safety and Soundness Examinations (CAMELS System), Bank Secrecy Act/Anti-Money Laundering (BSA/AML) Compliance, Consumer Compliance (TILA, ECOA, CRA), Information Technology Audits, and Internal Audits. The model aims to provide a structured approach to balance predictive performance with regulatory transparency requirements. The methodology employs an optimization framework that maximizes model accuracy while incorporating explainability as a quantifiable constraint. The framework is validated through a numerical example using synthetic data, which demonstrates improvement in the objective function from -5.63 to 1.12 while satisfying all regulatory constraints.

2. THEORY

2.1 Major Types of Bank Compliance Audits

I focus on the following five main bank regulatory compliance audits, namely, (i) Safety and Soundness Examinations (CAMELS System), (ii) Bank Secrecy Act/Anti-Money Laundering (BSA/AML) Compliance, (iii) Consumer Compliance (TILA, ECOA, CRA), (iv) Information Technology (Cybersecurity, Data Protection), and (v) Internal Audits (Internal Control Reviews). Each compliance domain imposes unique constraints on explainability, which the model incorporates into its optimization framework.

2.1.1 Safety and Soundness Examinations (CAMELS System)

Safety and Soundness Examinations assess the ability of banks to withstand financial shocks, manage operational risks, and comply with regulatory mandates. Central to this process is the CAMELS rating system, a comprehensive framework used by regulatory agencies such as the Federal Reserve, Office of the Comptroller of the Currency (OCC), and the Federal Deposit Insurance Corporation (FDIC). The CAMELS system evaluates six critical dimensions of a bank's operations: Capital Adequacy, Asset Quality, Management Quality, Earnings, Liquidity, and Sensitivity to Market Risk (Kočenda & Iwasaki, 2022). Each component provides a lens through which regulators gauge a bank's overall health, assign risk ratings, and determine necessary supervisory actions.

The Capital adequacy component evaluates whether the bank maintains sufficient capital reserves to support its risk-weighted assets, as defined by international regulatory frameworks such as Basel III (Li et al., 2016). Regulators assess metrics like the Common Equity Tier 1 (CET1) capital ratio, Total

Capital Ratio, and Leverage Ratio (Le et al., 2023). The asset quality component focuses on the bank's loan and investment portfolios and evaluates their soundness and vulnerability to potential losses. Poor asset quality is a significant indicator of credit risk, often stemming from non-performing loans (NPLs) or investments in volatile or low-quality securities. Examiners may assess the level of delinquent or defaulted loans, the adequacy of loan loss reserves, and the concentration risk posed by sectoral or geographic dependencies (Badunenko et al., 2022). Management quality is a determinant of a bank's ability to identify, measure, and control risks effectively. Examiners assess the competence, experience, and strategic vision of the bank's leadership team, along with their responsiveness to emerging risks and regulatory requirements (Quoc Trung, 2021). Earnings stability and sustainability are essential for supporting a bank's operations, capital accumulation, and future growth. Examiners analyze financial performance metrics such as Net Interest Margin (NIM), Return on Assets (ROA), and Return on Equity (ROE). They also assess the quality of earnings, i.e., whether they arise from core banking operations or are reliant on one-time gains or volatile market activities (Al-Najjar & Assous, 2021).

Liquidity indicates a bank's ability to meet its financial obligations as they come due, without incurring significant losses (Akhtar et al.,2024). Examiners evaluate liquid asset holdings, the maturity profile of liabilities, and access to reliable funding sources. Metrics such as the Liquidity Coverage Ratio (LCR) and Net Stable Funding Ratio (NSFR), mandated under Basel III, play a key role in this assessment (Ben Lahouel et al., 2024). The Sensitivity to Market Risk component assesses the bank's exposure to market fluctuations, including changes in interest rates, foreign exchange rates, and commodity prices (Elyasiani, & Mansur, 2005; Handorf, 2016).

The CAMELS examination process is comprehensive, involving both quantitative and qualitative evaluations (Baer, 2024). The steps typically include:

1. *Data Collection:* Examiners gather extensive financial and operational data, including call reports, stress test results, and internal audit findings (Office of the Comptroller of the Currency (2022).
2. *Risk Assessments:* AI and machine learning models are increasingly used to identify emerging risks, such as deteriorating asset quality or liquidity mismatches, through predictive analytics (Leo et al., 2019; Guerra & Castelli, 2021).
3. *Component Ratings:* Each CAMELS component is rated on a scale from 1 (strong performance) to 5 (critically deficient). The individual ratings are then combined to produce an overall composite score.
4. *Supervisory Actions:* Based on the composite rating, regulators determine whether the institution requires increased oversight, corrective action, or enforcement measures.

CAMELS ratings are confidential to encourage transparency during examinations and to maintain depositor confidence (Klein, 2020). Banks with strong ratings (1 or 2) are deemed to operate safely, while those with lower ratings (4 or 5) may face supervisory interventions, such as restrictions on growth, mandated capital injections, or even resolution proceedings in extreme cases (Stackhouse, 2018).

2.1.2 Bank Secrecy Act/Anti-Money Laundering (BSA/AML) Compliance Audits

The Bank Secrecy Act (BSA) of 1970, and subsequent anti-money laundering (AML) regulations form the centerpiece of the United States' financial crime prevention framework. These regulations are designed to prevent, detect, and report money laundering, terrorist financing, and other illicit financial activities. BSA/AML compliance is an important obligation for financial institutions, and it requires them to implement robust systems and processes to monitor transactions, identify suspicious activities, and report them to regulatory authorities (FIFEC, 2021). Compliance audits for BSA/AML are conducted to ensure that financial institutions adhere to these regulatory requirements (FFIEC, 2021; Lessambo, 2023).

BSA/AML compliance audits are designed to (Miller & Kohr, 2017) (i) evaluate the effectiveness of a financial institution's anti-money laundering program; (ii) ensure adherence to recordkeeping and reporting requirements mandated under the BSA; (iii) detect gaps in customer due diligence (CDD), suspicious activity monitoring, and transaction reporting; (iv) mitigate risks associated with exposure to high-risk customers, jurisdictions, or products; and (v) assess the institution's ability to adapt to evolving financial crime tactics and regulatory expectations.

The core components of a BSA/AML compliance audit typically include the following:

1) *Customer Identification Program (CIP) and Customer Due Diligence (CDD):* Financial institutions are required to verify the identity of their customers and assess their risk profile as part of their CIP and CDD processes (FFIEC, 2021).
2) *Suspicious Activity Monitoring and Reporting (SAR):* Financial institutions are required to file Suspicious Activity Reports (SARs) when red flags are identified. Auditors evaluate (a) the effectiveness of the institution's transaction monitoring systems in identifying unusual patterns, such as structuring, rapid movement of funds, or transactions involving high-risk jurisdictions; (b) the timeliness and accuracy of SAR filings, which must be submitted to Financial Crimes Enforcement Network (FinCEN) within 30 calendar days of detecting suspicious activity; and (c) whether flagged activities are sufficiently documented and supported with evidence in the SAR (FFIEC, 2021).
3) *Currency Transaction Reporting (CTR):* Financial institutions must file Currency Transaction Reports (CTRs) for cash transactions exceeding $10,000 in a single day (FFIEC, 2021).
4) *Recordkeeping Requirements:* Under the BSA, financial institutions must retain records of customer transactions for at least five years (FFIEC, 2021). Auditors review (a) the completeness and accuracy of transaction logs, including wire transfers, deposits, and withdrawals, and (b) the institution's ability to retrieve records promptly upon request by regulators or law enforcement agencies.
5) *Independent Testing and Internal Audits:* The BSA requires financial institutions to conduct independent testing of their AML programs (FFIEC, 2021).
6) Training Programs: A robust BSA/AML program relies on ongoing training for employees and ensures they are equipped to identify and report suspicious activities (Howard, 2017; FFIEC, 2021). Auditors evaluate (a) the comprehensiveness of the training program, including content tailored to different roles (e.g., frontline staff, compliance officers); and (b) documentation of training attendance and frequency.

Modern financial institutions increasingly rely on AI and machine learning models to enhance BSA/AML compliance (Gupta et al., 2023). These tools analyze vast volumes of transactional data to detect anomalies indicative of financial crime. However, the "black box" nature of many AI models poses challenges in regulatory audits. Examiners focus on (a) Explainability (the ability of the institution to explain how the AI system identifies suspicious transactions or assigns risk ratings), (b) False Positives (the system's efficiency in reducing false positives, which can overwhelm compliance teams and divert resources from genuine threats), and (c) Scalability (the institution's ability to adapt monitoring systems to changes in transaction volumes, customer profiles, or emerging threats) (Estrada, 2020; Kute et al., 2021).

2.1.3 Consumer Compliance (TILA, ECOA, CRA) Audits

Consumer compliance audits are an important component of the regulatory framework that ensures financial institutions operate in a fair, transparent, and non-discriminatory manner when providing services to individuals and communities. These audits evaluate adherence to consumer protection laws such as the Truth in Lending Act (TILA), Equal Credit Opportunity Act (ECOA), and Community Reinvestment Act (CRA) (Nicoletti & Zhu, 2023). As regulators such as the Consumer Financial Protection Bureau (CFPB) and other federal banking agencies enforce these laws, consumer compliance audits serve as a mechanism for identifying violations, assessing systemic risks, and protecting consumer rights.

Examiners analyze credit applications, underwriting decisions, and pricing policies to detect disparities. Advanced analytical tools, including AI, are often employed to identify patterns of discrimination in credit approvals or terms (Griffith, 2023; Langenbucher, 2020; Ratzan & Rahman, 2023). Non-compliance with these laws can result in severe consequences, including substantial civil penalties, loss of public trust, and reputational harm. For example, the CRA aims to reduce the practice of "redlining" (i.e., denying credit to LMI communities) and promote equitable access to credit. CRA compliance audits assess a bank's record of meeting community credit needs (Cyree & Winters, 2023). Examiners review lending data, community development activities, and outreach efforts (Avramidis et al., 2022; An et al., 2024). Poor CRA performance can result in restrictions on mergers, acquisitions, and branch expansions. It can also lead to reputational harm, as CRA ratings are publicly disclosed.

Consumer compliance audits for TILA, ECOA, and CRA typically involve the following steps (CFPB, 2015, 2023; FDIC, 2024a):

1) Examiners collect documentation such as loan applications, credit reports, and disclosures. Statistical models are used to analyze trends in lending decisions, pricing, and geographic distribution.
2) High-risk areas, such as subprime lending or redlining practices, are prioritized. AI and machine learning tools are increasingly used to identify anomalies or patterns indicative of non-compliance (Mostaghim, 2021).
3) Auditors conduct interviews with bank management and staff to understand policies and procedures. A review of internal compliance programs, including training and internal audit findings, is conducted.
4) Examiners provide a detailed report outlining findings, including any violations or deficiencies. Recommendations for corrective actions, such as policy revisions or enhanced employee training, are issued.

2.1.4 Information Technology (IT) Audits

With the financial sector increasingly targeted by cyberattacks and data breaches, regulatory bodies have established stringent requirements for cybersecurity, data protection, and IT governance (D'Onza et al., 2015). IT audits assess a financial institution's adherence to these standards and focus on the adequacy of controls, risk management practices, and disaster recovery capabilities (Van Greuning & Bratanovic, 2020). Regulatory frameworks, such as the Federal Financial Institutions Examination Council (FFIEC) IT Examination Handbook, Gramm-Leach-Bliley Act (GLBA), and state-specific data protection laws, form the foundation of these audits (FFIEC, 2024; Nzeako et al., 2024).

IT audits aim to (FFIEC, 2024):

1. Assess the effectiveness of a bank's cybersecurity measures in safeguarding systems, networks, and data from unauthorized access and attacks.
2. Evaluate compliance with regulatory mandates for data privacy, protection, and secure processing.
3. Ensure the institution has robust disaster recovery and business continuity plans to minimize disruptions during crises.
4. Identify vulnerabilities in IT infrastructure and recommend corrective actions to mitigate risks.

IT compliance audits utilize advanced tools for threat detection, log analysis, and anomaly identification (FFIEC, 2024; KPMG, 2024). Examiners rely on standards and best practices from frameworks like International Organization for Standardization or ISO 27001, National Institute of Standards and Technology or NIST, and Control Objectives for Information and Related Technologies or COBIT to benchmark IT governance and security practices (Al Hadad & Maulana, 2023). They also review banks' adherence to privacy laws, such as the GLBA, California Consumer Privacy Act (CCPA), and European Union's General Data Protection Regulation (GDPR), if applicable (Davis, 2020).

2.1.5 Internal Audits

Internal audits are an integral component of a bank's governance framework, which ensure the effectiveness of internal controls, risk management practices, and overall compliance with regulatory requirements (Jarah et al., 2022). These audits, conducted by the bank's internal audit department or outsourced to third-party firms, are mandated by regulatory agencies such as the Federal Reserve, the Office of the Comptroller of the Currency (OCC), and the Federal Deposit Insurance Corporation (FDIC) (FDIC, 2024b). They primarily report findings to internal stakeholders like the audit committee and management with a focus on improving internal processes. Internal audits serve as a first line of defense in identifying and mitigating risks across operational, financial, and technological domains.

The primary objectives of internal audits in the banking sector include (FDIC, 2024c):

1) Assess whether the bank's internal control systems adequately mitigate risks related to fraud, financial misstatements, and operational inefficiencies.
2) Verify adherence to laws and regulations such as the Sarbanes-Oxley Act (SOX), the Gramm-Leach-Bliley Act (GLBA), and anti-money laundering (AML) provisions.
3) Identify gaps in risk management frameworks and recommend corrective actions.
4) Highlight inefficiencies in processes and recommend enhancements to improve productivity and cost-effectiveness.
5) Provide insights to the board of directors and audit committees to support strategic decision-making and oversight.

There are several overlaps in the steps for doing internal audits and the steps for doing the compliance audits described in the earlier sections, particularly in terms of planning, risk assessment, data collection, reviewing documentation, testing controls, analyzing findings, reporting results and recommending corrective actions. However, internal audits are broader in scope and focus on the bank's internal control systems, governance frameworks, and operational efficiency. Other compliance audits, such as BSA/AML, TILA, or CAMELS examinations, are more targeted and address specific areas like financial stability, anti-money laundering, or consumer protection.

2.2 Explainable AI in Financial Services

Artificial intelligence (AI) in financial services has enabled automation, efficiency, and precision in decision-making processes such as credit scoring, fraud detection, and compliance audits (Černevičienė & Kabašinskas, 2024). However, the opaque nature of many AI models, particularly deep learning algorithms, has raised significant concerns about their interpretability and accountability. This has led to an increasing focus on Explainable AI (XAI) to address the need for transparency in financial applications. AI models used in financial services often operate as "black boxes" and produce outputs without providing intuitive explanations for their decisions (Fernández, 2024). This lack of transparency is particularly problematic in highly regulated sectors such as banking, where decisions must be explainable to auditors, regulators, and affected stakeholders. For example, anti-money laundering (AML) systems require the ability to justify flagged transactions, and credit scoring models must provide fair and interpretable evaluations to avoid biases against protected groups (Giudici & Raffinetti, 2021).

The European Union's General Data Protection Regulation (GDPR) has been particularly influential, with Articles 13-15 establishing a "right to explanation" for automated decisions affecting individuals (Kaminski, 2019). This regulatory requirement has accelerated the development of post-hoc explainability methods for black-box models. Similarly, the United States' Fair Credit Reporting Act (FCRA) and Equal Credit Opportunity Act (ECOA) require that adverse credit decisions provide specific reasons, which indirectly mandates some degree of explainability in lending algorithms (Selbst & Barocas, 2018). The historical evolution of XAI in banking compliance reflects the tension between technological advancement and regulatory oversight. Early approaches to explainable financial models in the 1990s and 2000s emphasized rule-based systems and decision trees, which offered transparency at the expense of predictive power (Arrieta et al., 2020).

Cross-jurisdictional challenges further complicate the implementation of XAI in global banking operations. Financial institutions operating across multiple regions must reconcile differing standards for explainability, from the principles-based approach of the EU to the more rules-based frameworks in the United States and Singapore (Floridi et al., 2018). The Basel Committee on Banking Supervision has recognized this challenge and indicated the need for "explainability by design" in its principles for operational resilience, though concrete standards remain underdeveloped (BIS, 2021).

Explainable AI seeks to bridge this gap by providing techniques and frameworks to make AI decisions interpretable. Two prominent approaches include:

1. *Information-Theoretic Measures:* Metrics like mutual information quantify the relationship between input features and outputs. They provide insights into the importance of specific variables in a model's predictions (Islam et al., 2021; Piras et al., 2023). In financial applications, mutual information can be used to determine how features like credit history or transaction patterns contribute to loan approvals or fraud detection.
2. *Shapley Values:* Derived from cooperative game theory, Shapley values attribute contributions to individual input features by analyzing their marginal impact on a model's output (Holzinger et al., 2022). This method is particularly effective in identifying feature importance and ensuring fairness in credit scoring and lending decisions (Giudici et al., 2024).

Traditional AI models often struggle to meet these requirements, which leads to a gap between operational performance and regulatory compliance. Existing approaches to XAI in financial compliance have several notable limitations. First, many frameworks treat explainability as a post-hoc consideration rather than an intrinsic design parameter, which leads to models that may satisfy technical transparency requirements without providing meaningful insights to non-technical stakeholders like regulators or customers (Carvalho et al., 2019). Second, current methodologies often fail to address the trade-off between global and local explainability. A model may provide accurate explanations for individual decisions while obscuring systemic patterns that could indicate discriminatory practices or other compliance risks (Rudin, 2019). Third, the computational complexity of calculating certain explainability metrics, such as Shapley values for high-dimensional data, creates practical challenges for real-time compliance monitoring and reporting (Molnar, 2020). Current approaches prioritize either accuracy or explainability but seldom balance these objectives within the context of compliance audits (Longo et al., 2024). This highlights the need for a mathematical framework that explicitly incorporates explainability as a constraint within the optimization process and balances predictive performance, regulatory compliance, and interpretability.

3. MATHEMATICAL MODEL

The absence of explainability in many AI-driven systems poses significant risks in satisfying the stringent requirements of regulatory bodies. To address this, I propose a mathematical model that incorporates explainability as a quantifiable constraint within the optimization framework of AI models, which can ensure compliance with regulatory mandates while maintaining operational efficiency. The model is tailored for the five major categories of bank compliance audits discussed in the prior section. Each category imposes unique constraints and requirements, which the model accommodates.

3.1 Model Framework

The objective is to maximize the predictive accuracy A of AI models used in compliance tasks while incorporating explainability E and ensuring regulatory compliance. The optimization problem is expressed as:

$$\max_{M} A(M) - \lambda \cdot C(M) + \gamma \cdot E(M)$$

Where M indicate the AI model parameters; $A(M)$ indicates predictive accuracy of the model; $C(M)$ indicates complexity of the model; $E(M)$ indicates explainability score; λ is the weighting factor for model complexity; and γ is the weighting factor for model explainability. The AI model parameters (M) are the adjustable variables or weights within a machine learning or artificial intelligence model (e.g., weights in a neural network) that are learned from training data during the model's training phase. These parameters govern the behavior of the model and determine how it processes input data and produces predictions or outputs. Thus, this objective function balances accuracy and explainability while penalizing excessive complexity, which may reduce interpretability.

The explainability score $E(M)$ is quantified using information-theoretic measures, such as mutual information and Shapley values. The constraint below ensures that the model meets a minimum explainability threshold E_{min} required by regulators.

$$E(M) \geq E_{min}$$

Mutual Information (MI) is metric that quantifies the amount of information shared between two random variables, i.e., it measures how much knowing one variable reduces the uncertainty about the other (Islam et al., 2021; Piras et al., 2023). For an AI model, MI can be used to evaluate how much the input features (e.g., loan amount, credit score) explain or contribute to the output (e.g., loan approval). MI thus helps identify which input features contribute the most to the model's predictions by quantifying the relationship between features and outputs (Li et al., 2020; Nauta et al., 2023). Features with higher MI scores provide more information about the output, which makes the model's decisions more interpretable. On the other hand, Shapley values come from cooperative game theory and are used to fairly distribute the "payout" (in this case, the model's output) among all input features based on their contribution to the prediction (Holzinger et al., 2022). They assign each feature an importance score by considering all possible combinations of feature contributions (Giudici & Raffinetti, 2021). Shapley values thus provide a way to determine each feature's contribution to a specific prediction and ensure fairness by considering every possible interaction between features.

Now, each compliance audit category imposes specific constraints as follows:

1) *CAMELS:* Ensure interpretability of risk weight assignments, stress-test outcomes, and CAMELS ratings.
2) *BSA/AML:* Minimize false positives in suspicious activity detection while maintaining explainable transaction monitoring models.
3) *Consumer Compliance:* Ensure bias mitigation in AI-driven credit scoring models, with clear feature attributions for decisions.
4) *IT Audits:* Guarantee transparency in cybersecurity anomaly detection and system risk assessments.
5) *Internal Audits:* Provide detailed justifications for flagged control deficiencies.

These constraints are incorporated into the optimization framework as additional terms or bounds. These constraints enforce adherence to regulatory requirements while maintaining explainability and model performance.

The mathematical representation of the CAMELS Compliance constraint is given below:

$$I(X;Y) \geq I_{min}$$

Where, $I(X;Y)$ indicates mutual information between features X (e.g., risk weights, liquidity ratios) and outputs Y (e.g., CAMELS ratings); and I_{min} indicates the minimum mutual information threshold that ensures adequate interpretability. This ensures that the features used in the model (e.g., capital adequacy, asset quality) provide sufficient explanatory power for the assigned ratings. Thus, the CAMELS constraint ensures that the model's outputs (e.g., CAMELS ratings, stress-test results) are interpretable in terms of feature contributions.

The mathematical representation of the BSA/AML Compliance constraint is given below:

$$FP \leq FP_{max} \text{ and } E(M) \geq E_{min}$$

Where FP indicates the number of false positives in flagged suspicious transactions; FP_{max} indicates the maximum allowable false positives; $E(M)$ indicates the explainability score of the model (e.g., based on Shapley values or feature importance); and E_{min} is the minimum explainability threshold. This dual BSA/AML constraint ensures the model minimizes false positives, which overwhelm compliance teams, while remaining interpretable enough to justify flagged transactions. Thus, the BSA/ AML constraint balances the trade-off between reducing false positives and ensuring explainability in flagged transactions.

The mathematical representation of the Consumer Compliance constraint is given below:

$$\Delta\text{Approval} \leq \epsilon \text{and } \phi_i \geq \phi_{min}$$

Where, ΔApproval is the difference in approval rates between protected and unprotected groups; ϵ indicates the acceptable threshold for disparity; ϕ_i indicates the Shapley value for feature i, which represents its contribution to the model's decisions; and ϕ_{min} is the minimum attribution threshold or the minimum acceptable contribution or importance assigned to key input features (e.g., income, credit history). ϕ_{min} is thus the minimum value that a key feature's Shapley attribution score must meet or exceed to ensure it is adequately considered by the model in its decision-making process. This threshold ensures that important features are not underrepresented in the decision-making process in regulated applications such as lending. Thus, this constraint helps check that credit decisions are fair (low disparity) and interpretable (clear feature contributions). It ensures fairness in these decisions by eliminating bias against protected groups while providing clear feature attributions.

The mathematical representation of the IT Audit constraint is given below:

$$P_{\text{critical}} \geq P_{\text{min}} \text{ and } H(X) - H(X|Y) \geq T_{\text{min}}$$

Where, P_{critical} is the probability of correctly detecting a critical anomaly; P_{min} is the minimum detection probability required by regulators; $H(X) - H(X|Y)$ indicates mutual information between input features X and model outputs Y; and T_{min} is the mutual information required to satisfy transparency standards. This ensures the cybersecurity system is both effective and explainable, which allows auditors to understand why specific anomalies were flagged.

Here, X would represent input features (e.g., login time, IP address, data volume) and Y model outputs (e.g., anomaly flag). Mutual information, $I(X; Y)$, quantifies the amount of information that the input features X provide about the output Y, i.e., it measures how much knowing X reduces uncertainty about Y (Ayoub et al., 2022). It is derived from the difference between $H(X)$, the entropy of X, which represents the uncertainty or randomness in the input features, and $H(X|Y)$, the conditional entropy of X given Y, which represents the remaining uncertainty in X after knowing Y (Ayoub et al., 2022). T_{min} is the minimum information threshold, which ensures that there is a sufficient relationship between the inputs and outputs for the model to be considered interpretable.

The equation $H(X) - H(X|Y) \geq T_{\text{min}}$ ensures that the amount of information X provides about Y is above a predefined minimum threshold T_{min}, which would indicate that the model is sufficiently transparent. This also builds confidence that the model does not rely on opaque or arbitrary relationships but instead uses clear, quantifiable dependencies between the inputs and outputs. A high value of $I(X; Y)$ or $H(X) - H(X|Y)$ indicates that the model's output Y can be well-explained by the input features X. If $I(X; Y)$ is too low, the model might be relying on hidden patterns or noise, which makes it difficult to justify its decisions. Thus, this constraint guarantees transparency in anomaly detection while ensuring the system identifies risks effectively.

The mathematical representation of the Internal Audit constraint is given below:

$$\text{Coverage}(D) \geq C_{min} \text{ and } E(M) \geq E_{min}$$

Where, Coverage(D) is the proportion of flagged deficiencies D for which clear justifications are provided; C_{min} is the minimum required proportion of flagged issues that must have explanations; $E(M)$ is the explainability score of the model's output; and E_{min} represents the minimum explainability threshold required for an AI model M to satisfy transparency and interpretability standards in regulatory compliance settings, i.e., it is a predefined benchmark that ensures the model's decisions can be adequately explained, either to internal stakeholders or external regulators.

Here, Coverage(D) could indicate issues in internal controls or anomalies that are accompanied by clear justifications or explanations. The equation Coverage(D) $\geq C_{min}$ constraint ensures that most, if not all, flagged deficiencies are justified with clear, auditable explanations. $E(M)$ quantifies how well the model's decisions can be understood in terms of input features and outputs. The equation $E(M) \geq E_{min}$ ensures that these attributions meet the minimum transparency standard. Together, these constraints build confidence that flagged deficiencies in internal audits are well-justified and clearly explained to stakeholders.

To sum it up, the regulatory constraints are incorporated into the overall optimization problem as either hard constraints or penalty terms as follows:

$$\max_{M} A(M) - \lambda \cdot C(M) + \gamma \cdot E(M)$$

Subject to:

$$I(X;Y) \geq I_{min} \text{ (CAMELS Compliance)}$$

$$FP \leq FP_{max} \text{ and } E(M) \geq E_{min} \text{ (BSA/AML Compliance)}$$

$$\Delta\text{Approval} \leq \epsilon \text{and } \phi_i \geq \phi_{min} \text{ (Consumer Compliance)}$$

$$P_{\text{critical}} \geq P_{\text{min}} \text{ and } H(X) - H(X|Y) \geq T_{\text{min}} \text{ (IT Audits)}$$

$$\text{Coverage}(D) \geq C_{min} \text{ and } E(M) \geq E_{min} \text{ (Internal Audits)}$$

3.2 Practical Integration into Compliance Workflows

While the mathematical formulation establishes a theoretical foundation for explainable AI in banking compliance, successful implementation requires integration into existing compliance workflows. Explainability should be considered at each stage of the compliance process. Table 1 illustrates how the analytical framework translates into practical workflows at each stage of the compliance process across different compliance domains.

Table 1. End-to-end XAI integration in banking compliance workflows

Compliance Domain	Input	Processing	Explanation Generation	Compliance Documentation	Regulatory Defense/ Engagement
BSA/AML Transaction Monitoring	Customer transaction data	Model flags suspicious activities while maintaining false positive rate below threshold	Calculates Shapley values to quantify contribution of each feature (transaction amount, frequency, customer risk score, etc.)	Automatically generates SAR narratives incorporating key factors from explainability analysis	Demonstrates that flagged transactions meet both detection accuracy and explainability requirements during examinations
Consumer Compliance Fair Lending	Loan application data	Evaluates creditworthiness while applying fairness constraint and feature attribution requirements	Generates counterfactual explanations identifying minimum changes needed for approval	Translates explanations into compliant adverse action notices with clear reasons for denial	Uses aggregated explanation data for comparative analyses across demographic groups
CAMELS Financial Stability Assessment	Financial performance metrics, risk measures, governance data	Generates component scores while maintaining required mutual information between inputs and outputs	Produces hierarchical explanations showing how specific financial metrics influence each CAMELS component	Provides supporting documentation for rating determinations	Enables officials to discuss rating determinants with examiners and develop targeted improvement plans for lower-rated components

4. NUMERICAL EXAMPLE

In this section, I provide a numerical example for the optimization problem with explainability and compliance constraints. Let's consider a bank deploying an AI-based system for anomaly detection in transaction monitoring. The system aims to optimize detection performance while satisfying regulatory explainability requirements. The optimization problem incorporates constraints for different compliance audits: CAMELS (safety and soundness), BSA/AML (anti-money laundering), Consumer Compliance (fair lending practices), IT Audits (cybersecurity), and Internal Audits (internal control justifications). This example demonstrates the model's application, using synthetic data to evaluate how the constraints affect the optimization process. The goal is to maximize the model's predictive accuracy $A(M)$, which is balanced with complexity $C(M)$ and explainability $E(M)$.

For CAMELS Compliance, mutual information $I(X;Y)$ between input features X (e.g., risk weights, asset quality) and model outputs Y (e.g., CAMELS rating) must meet the minimum threshold as follows:

$$I(X;Y) \geq I_{min} = 1.5 \; bits$$

A bit is the basic unit of information in information theory, and bits are used to measure the amount of uncertainty, information, or entropy in a system (Witten, 2020). Higher mutual information (in bits) typically means the model's decisions are more explainable.

For BSA/AML Compliance, false positives in suspicious transaction detection must be below a maximum allowable rate, and the explainability score $E(M)$ must meet a minimum threshold as follows:

$FP \leq FP_{max} = 5\%$ and $E(M) \geq E_{min} = 0.8$

For Consumer Compliance, the disparity in loan approval rates between protected and unprotected groups must not exceed a certain threshold rate, and key feature attribution scores ϕ_i must meet a minimum threshold as follows:

$\Delta\text{Approval} \leq \epsilon = 0.05$ and $\phi_i \geq \phi_{min} = 0.2$

For IT Audits, anomaly detection must meet a minimum detection probability, and mutual information between inputs X (e.g., login time, IP address) and outputs Y (anomaly flags) must meet a transparency threshold as follows:

$P_{\text{critical}} \geq 90\%$ and $H(X) - H(X|Y) \geq T_{\min} = 1.0\ bit$

For Internal Audits, proportion of flagged deficiencies D with justifications must be above a threshold, and explainability $E(M)$ must meet a minimum level as follows:

$\text{Coverage}(D) \geq C_{min} = 95\%$ and $E(M) \geq E_{min} = 0.8\%$

Thus, the optimization problem in this illustrative scenario with the synthetic data values is as follows:

$$\max_{M} A(M) - \lambda \cdot C(M) + \gamma \cdot E(M)$$

Subject to: $I(X;Y) \geq 1.5$ bits; $FP \leq 5\%$; $E(M) \geq 0.8$; $\Delta\text{Approval} \leq 0.05$;$\phi_i \geq 0.2$;$P_{\text{critical}} \geq 90\%$;$H(X) - H(X|Y) \geq 1.0$ bits; and $\text{Coverage}(D) \geq 95\%$.

The optimization problem is transformed into a constrained optimization problem by incorporating penalties for any violations of constraints directly into the objective function. This helps to solve the problem as an unconstrained optimization, where penalties discourage the solution from violating the constraints. Each constraint is thus represented as a penalty term. If a constraint is violated, the penalty increases the cost, reducing the overall objective value. Let α_i represent the weight (penalty factor) associated with each constraint. Then,

For CAMELS Compliance,

Penalty: $-\alpha_1 \cdot max(0,\ 1.5 - I(X;Y))$

For BSA/AML Compliance,

Penalties: $-\alpha_2 \cdot max(0,\ FP - 0.05)$ and $-\alpha_3 \cdot max(0,\ 0.8 - E(M))$

For Consumer Compliance,

Penalties: $-\alpha_4 \cdot max(0, \Delta\text{Approval} - 0.05)$ and $-\alpha_5 \cdot \sum_i max(0, 0.2 - \phi_i)$, which is summed for all critical features i.

For IT Audits,

Penalties: $-\alpha_6 \cdot max(0, 0.9 - P_{\text{critical}})$ and $-\alpha_7 \cdot max(0,\ 1.0 - (H(X) - H(X|Y)))$.

For Internal Audits,

Penalty: $-\alpha_8 \cdot max(0, 0.95 - \text{Coverage}(D))$

Thus, the final transformed or the full penalized objective function, becomes:

$$L(M) = A(M) - \lambda \cdot C(M) + \gamma \cdot E(M) \ - \alpha_1 \cdot max(0,\ 1.5 - I(X;Y)) - \alpha_2 \cdot max(0,\ FP - 0.05)$$

$$-\alpha_3 \cdot \max(0,\ 0.8 - E(M)) - \alpha_4 \cdot \max(0, \Delta\text{Approval} - 0.05) - \alpha_5 \cdot \sum_i max(0, 0.2 - \phi_i)$$

$$-\alpha_6 \cdot max(0,\ 0.9 - P_{\text{critical}}) - \alpha_7 \cdot max(0,\ 1.0 - (H(X) - H(X|Y))) - \alpha_8 \cdot max(0,\ 0.95 - Coverage(D))$$

To reiterate, all the penalty terms ($\alpha_i \cdot max$) reduce the objective value when constraints are violated.

Now, to solve the optimization problem further, a combination of gradient-based methods and sub-gradient approaches can be used. For differentiable components, such as the objective function terms $A(M)$, $C(M)$, and $E(M)$, stochastic gradient descent (SGD) could be employed to iteratively refine the model parameters M. Non-differentiable penalty terms, such as $max(0, \cdot)$, can be handled using sub-gradient methods or smooth approximations to ensure convergence. The optimization would begin with initial parameters M_0, where the objective function $L(M)$ is evaluated, and gradients or sub-gradients are calculated at each iteration. Through iterative refinement, the model parameters would need to be adjusted to maximize $L(M)$ so that accuracy and explainability is improved while reducing penalties associated with constraint violations. For example, adjustments might aim to reduce the false-positive rate (FP) and improve the explainability score ($E(M)$), which brings the model into compliance with requirements like $FP \leq 5\%$ and $E(M) \geq 0.8$. After the optimization process converges, the final model is validated by verifying that all constraints are satisfied.

For the purpose of this illustrative scenario, let's assume the following initial metric values of the AI model:

Accuracy - $A(M) = 94\%$; Complexity - $C(M) = 0.4$; Explainability - $E(M) = 0.7$; Mutual Information - $I(X;Y) = 1.2 bits$; False-Positive Rate - $FP = 7\%$; Approval Disparity - $\Delta\text{Approval} = 0.08$; Feature Attribution - $\phi_i = 0.15$ (critical features like income, credit history); Critical Detection Probability - $P_{\text{critical}} = 88\%$; Transparency (IT) - $H(X) - H(X|Y) = 0.9 bits$; and Justification Coverage - Coverage $(D) = 90\%$.

The weights for penalties are as follows: $\lambda = 0.2, \gamma = 0.3$, and $\alpha_1, \ldots\ldots, \alpha_8$. Substituting these values into the full penalized objective function,

$$L(M) = 0.94 - 0.2 \cdot 0.4 + 0.3 \cdot 0.7 - 10 \cdot max(0,\ 1.5 - 1.2) - 10 \cdot max(0,\ 0.07 - 0.05) - 10 \cdot$$

$$max(0,\ 0.8 - 0.7) - 10 \cdot max(0,\ 0.08 - 0.05) - 10 \cdot \sum_i max(0,\ 0.2 - 0.15) - 10 \cdot max(0,\ 0.9$$

$$-0.88) - 10 \cdot max(0,\ 1.0 - 0.9) - 10 \cdot max(0,\ 0.95 - 0.9)$$

Thus, $L(M) = 0.94 - 0.08 + 0.21 - 3 - 0.2 - 1 - 0.3 - 0.5 - 0.2 - 1 - 0.5 = -5.63$.

After the optimization process, the AI model parameters M are adjusted to balance accuracy, complexity, and explainability while satisfying all regulatory constraints. This involves iterative refinement to improve the model's compliance performance and minimize penalties associated with constraint violations. Key outcomes after optimization include:

1) Accuracy ($A(M)$) may slightly decrease due to trade-offs required for enhancing transparency and fairness.
2) The complexity penalty ($C(M)$) is reduced to align with regulatory expectations while maintaining model performance.
3) The explainability score ($E(M)$) is improved to meet or exceed the minimum required threshold (E_{min}).

Also, all regulatory constraints are verified to be satisfied. For example:

1) The false-positive rate (FP) is reduced to within acceptable limits.
2) Mutual information ($I(X;Y)$) meets the CAMELS transparency requirement.
3) Approval disparities and feature attribution thresholds in Consumer Compliance are within permissible bounds.
4) Critical anomaly detection probability (P_{critical}) and IT transparency measures are improved.
5) Internal audit coverage (Coverage(D)) exceeds the required minimum.

Thus, after optimization, the refined metrics are as follows:

Accuracy - $A(M) = 93\%$; Complexity - $C(M) = 0.35$; Explainability - $E(M) = 0.85$; Mutual Information - $I(X;Y) = 1.6 bits$; False-Positive Rate - $FP = 4.5\%$; Approval Disparity - $\Delta\text{Approval} = 0.04$; Feature Attribution - $\phi_i = 0.2$; Critical Detection Probability - $P_{\text{critical}} = 91\%$; Transparency (IT) - $H(X) - H(X|Y) = 1.1 bits$; and Justification Coverage - Coverage$(D) = 96\%$.

Recalculating $L(M)$,

$$L(M) = 0.93 - 0.2 \cdot 0.35 + 0.3 \cdot 0.85 - 10 \cdot max(0,\ 1.5 - 1.6) - 10 \cdot max(0,\ 0.045 - 0.05) - 10 \cdot max(0,\ 0.8 - 0.85) - 10 \cdot max(0,\ 0.04 - 0.05) - 10 \cdot \sum_i max(0,\ 0.2 - 0.2) - 10 \cdot max(0,\ 0.9 - 0.91) - 10 \cdot max(0,\ 1.0 - 1.1) - 10 \cdot max(0,\ 0.95 - 0.96)$$

Thus, $L(M) = 0.93 - 0.07 + 0.255 - 0 - 0 - 0 - 0 - 0 - 0 - 0 - 0 = 1.12$.

To sum it up, after optimization, the objective function $L(M)$ improves from -5.63 to 1.12, and all constraints are satisfied. The increase in the refined objective function indicates an optimal balance between accuracy, explainability, and regulatory compliance. The optimized model is practical for real world implementation so that effective performance is achieved while adhering to stringent regulatory requirements.

5. LIMITATIONS

Despite its practical applications and ability to integrate explainability into regulatory compliance frameworks, the proposed mathematical model has several limitations that warrant consideration.

First, the model quantifies explainability using mutual information and Shapley values. Mutual Information assumes that input-output relationships can be fully captured through probabilistic measures. This may oversimplify complex dependencies, particularly in high-dimensional datasets. Shapley Values attribute importance to individual features but can be computationally prohibitive for models with numerous input features or complex interdependencies.

Second, the optimization framework inherently involves trade-offs, where increasing explainability or reducing complexity may decrease predictive accuracy. While this is necessary to meet regulatory standards, it may limit the model's utility in scenarios where maximum predictive performance is important, such as fraud detection or high-frequency trading. Incorporating multiple regulatory constraints, each with its own penalty terms, significantly increases the computational burden of solving the optimization problem. For example, calculating Shapley values involves examining all possible combinations of input features, which grows exponentially with the number of features.

Third, a significant limitation of this study is the reliance on synthetic data rather than empirical validation with real-world financial datasets. Empirical validation would require access to proprietary banking data containing sensitive compliance information, transaction patterns, and historical regulatory outcomes. Such data is subject to stringent privacy regulations, confidentiality requirements, and competitive considerations that make it exceptionally difficult to obtain for research purposes. Financial institutions are generally unable to share transaction monitoring data, CAMELS ratings, or regulatory examination findings due to both legal restrictions and reputational risk concerns.

Fourth, the implementation of explainable AI models in banking compliance faces varying challenges across different regulatory jurisdictions. In the United States, principles-based approaches from agencies like the Federal Reserve and OCC emphasize outcomes and risk management rather than prescribing specific technical solutions (American Bankers Association, 2020). This contrasts with the European Union's more prescriptive approach under the AI Act, which categorizes AI systems for banking compliance as "high-risk" applications requiring robust transparency, documentation, and human oversight (European Commission, 2021). These divergent approaches create implementation challenges for global financial institutions. For example, a model that meets the explainability standards for BSA/AML compliance in the U.S. may not satisfy the "right to explanation" provisions under the EU's GDPR.

Fifth, the practical application of explainable AI in compliance audits depends critically on how human auditors interpret and act upon model outputs. While the mathematical model in this chapter quantifies explainability through metrics like mutual information and Shapley values, translating these technical measures into actionable insights for auditors remains challenging (Bhatt et al., 2020). Effective human-AI collaboration in compliance audits requires consideration of both the technical accuracy of explanations and their cognitive accessibility to users with varying technical backgrounds.

Finally, regulatory environments are dynamic, with frequent updates to compliance standards and expectations. The model's static constraints may require continuous re-calibration to remain compliant, which may necessitate additional resources and expertise. Banking regulations evolve in response to emerging risks, technological innovations, and changing market conditions. Future iterations of the framework should incorporate mechanisms for dynamically updating explainability constraints based on regulatory changes without requiring complete model retraining. One promising approach is to develop meta-learning frameworks that can rapidly adapt to new regulatory contexts by leveraging knowledge from previously encountered compliance scenarios (Finn et al., 2017). Additionally, incorporating formal verification techniques could provide stronger guarantees about model behavior under changing regulatory conditions (Katz et al., 2017).

Case studies from different banking environments illustrate these challenges. For example, a large multinational bank implementing AI-based transaction monitoring systems across its global operations must navigate not only technical challenges in model explainability but also variations in how regulators across different jurisdictions interpret and evaluate those explanations. Similarly, a community bank adopting AI for credit scoring must ensure that explanations are accessible to both internal compliance teams and external examiners who may have limited technical expertise in machine learning. These practical considerations highlight the importance of designing explainability frameworks that are both technically robust and operationally feasible across diverse regulatory and organizational contexts.

6. REAL WORLD COMPLEXITIES IN COMPLIANCE

While the numerical example above demonstrates the model's application in a simplified setting, real-world banking compliance scenarios introduce additional complexities that merit consideration. In practice, financial institutions face multidimensional compliance requirements across heterogeneous datasets that vary in size, structure, and quality.

For example, a large bank's BSA/AML monitoring system may process millions of transactions daily across diverse channels (wire transfers, ACH, card payments, etc.), each with different risk profiles and data attributes. The transaction monitoring algorithm must synthesize this heterogeneous data while maintaining explainability across multiple compliance dimensions simultaneously. A suspicious transaction might trigger both BSA/AML and consumer compliance considerations. This may require coordinated explanations that satisfy different regulatory frameworks.

Also, in the real world, the BSA/AML monitoring system would ingest data from core banking systems, customer information files (CIF), watch lists, and external sources like Financial Intelligence Units (FIUs). Each source contributes different features with varying reliability and completeness. The explainability constraints would need to account for this variation through confidence intervals around metrics like mutual information ($I(X; Y)$) and feature attribution scores (ϕ_i). A transaction flagged as suspicious for BSA/AML purposes might simultaneously raise consumer compliance concerns if it relates to a credit decision affecting a protected class. The feasible solution space narrows considerably when multiple compliance frameworks must be satisfied simultaneously, which often requires more sophisticated model architectures or ensemble approaches.

The optimization outcomes can also vary significantly based on data quality and organizational context. Banks with more mature data governance frameworks would likely achieve higher post-optimization objective function values compared to those with fragmented data infrastructures. This indicates that data quality serves as a limiting factor for explainability performance. Explainability performance could also significantly vary across different regulatory domains. The BSA/AML models may achieve post-optimization objective function values that are different from consumer compliance models, which suggests domain-specific challenges in balancing accuracy and explainability.

The application of the proposed mathematical framework at enterprise scale also introduces significant computational and operational challenges. Many large financial institutions process billions of transactions annually across thousands of features, which makes direct calculation of metrics like Shapley values computationally prohibitive. Most banks also have substantial investments in legacy compliance systems that cannot be replaced wholesale. The optimization framework would need to interface with existing transaction monitoring, case management, and regulatory reporting systems. This integration typically requires (a) a layered architecture that applies the explainability constraints without disrupting core transaction processing; (b) API-based interfaces to existing compliance workflows; and (c) governance mechanisms to track and document model changes as explainability constraints evolve.

Financial institutions implementing such frameworks should adopt a phased approach, beginning with specific high-risk compliance domains before expanding to enterprise-wide deployment. They should also establish continuous monitoring mechanisms to detect potential degradation in explainability metrics over time as data distributions or regulatory expectations change.

The computational and expertise requirements for implementing the proposed mathematical framework present significant challenges, especially for smaller financial institutions with limited resources. Financial institutions vary dramatically in their capacity to implement sophisticated AI explainability frameworks. Large multinational banks typically possess dedicated data science teams, substantial computing infrastructure, and specialized compliance technology personnel. In contrast, community banks and smaller credit unions often rely on third-party vendors for compliance solutions and may lack specialized AI expertise (Turksen et al., 2024). This resource disparity creates implementation barriers that could exacerbate technological inequality in the financial sector. For institutions with limited in-house expertise, the calculation of complex explainability metrics like Shapley values and mutual information measures may be prohibitively difficult without external support. The Federal Financial Institutions Examination Council (FFIEC) has also recognized these resource disparities and issued guidance encouraging tailored approaches to model risk management based on an institution's size, complexity, and risk profile (FFIEC, 2023).

To address this issue, financial institutions can adopt a risk-based approach where explainability requirements are calibrated to both the complexity of the AI systems and the institution's size and risk profile. For smaller institutions with less complex models, simplified explainability metrics focused on feature importance and decision rules may be sufficient to satisfy regulatory requirements while remaining computationally tractable. Industry consortia or regulatory technology (RegTech) providers could develop shared platforms that implement the proposed framework as a service. Technologies like Apache Spark, Ray, or Dask enable distributed computation of explainability metrics across computing clusters and may make previously intractable calculations feasible even for smaller institutions by leveraging cloud resources on demand rather than maintaining expensive infrastructure. This would spread development and operational costs across multiple institutions. These platforms could provide standardized explainability metrics and optimization capabilities that smaller banks could use without building in-house expertise.

7. CONCLUSION

This study addressed the critical challenge of incorporating explainability into AI models used for banking regulatory compliance audits. The research focused on developing a mathematical framework that balances predictive accuracy with regulatory transparency requirements across five major types of compliance audits: CAMELS examinations, BSA/AML compliance, consumer compliance, IT audits, and internal audits. The proposed mathematical model successfully integrates explainability as a quantifiable constraint within the optimization framework through two key mechanisms: information-theoretic measures and Shapley values.

The model's formulation demonstrates how predictive accuracy can be optimized while maintaining regulatory compliance and model interpretability. The numerical example validated the model's effectiveness by showing improvement in the objective function from -5.63 to 1.12 while satisfying all regulatory constraints. This research contributes significantly to the intersection of AI and banking regulation by (a) providing a structured approach to quantify and optimize explainability in compliance AI systems; (b) incorporating domain-specific regulatory requirements into the mathematical framework; (c) demonstrating practical implementation through detailed constraints for each audit type; and (d) establishing a balanced approach between model performance and regulatory transparency.

The study's limitations include computational complexity in calculating Shapley values, potential oversimplification of input-output relationships through mutual information metrics, and the need for continuous recalibration as regulatory requirements evolve. Additionally, the static nature of the constraints may not fully capture the dynamic regulatory environment. Also, there is a huge computational challenge because calculating Shapley values requires examining all possible feature combinations, and the combinations grow exponentially with feature count (2^n for n features as each feature can either be included or excluded in a combination). For 50 features, that could be over a quadrillion combinations. Features such as transaction amount, frequency, location, customer risk score, merchant type, and device ID can easily add up to 50 or more. Variables like income, credit history, debt-to-income ratio, employment status, and number of credit inquiries can surpass 100. Aggregated behavioral data, such as browsing habits, transaction patterns, geolocation, and social media activity, might involve 1000+ data points. More efficient computational methods could be required, such as, sampling-based approximations of Shapley values, dimension reduction techniques, parallel computing algorithms, and feature selection to focus on most important variables (Kumar et al., 2020; Wang et al., 2024).

Future research directions should explore:

1) Dynamic optimization frameworks that adapt to evolving regulatory requirements
2) Integration of alternative explainability metrics beyond mutual information and Shapley values
3) Application of the model to specific use cases within each audit category
4) Development of more efficient computational methods for handling high-dimensional feature spaces (i.e., datasets with many variables or features)
5) Investigation of the model's effectiveness across different banking jurisdictions and regulatory frameworks

This research provides a foundation for developing more transparent and accountable AI systems in banking compliance. It addresses the growing need for explainable AI in regulated industries while maintaining operational efficiency.

Note: Use of Generative AI tools

During the preparation of this work, the author used Anthropic's Claude AI in order to check for spelling and grammar errors in the write-up and make corrections and to solve/check the numerical math faster. After using this tool/service, the author reviewed and edited the content as needed and take full responsibility for the content of the publication.

REFERENCES

Akhtar, S., Azmi, S. N., Khan, P. A., Jan, A. A., & Ansari, Z. (2024). Unveiling the financial landscape: Analyzing profitability, productivity, and efficiency of banks in an emerging economy using the CAMELS framework and panel analysis. *Cogent Business & Management, 11*(1), 2399747. DOI: 10.1080/23311975.2024.2399747

Al Hadad, R. S., & Maulana, H. (2023, December). A Comprehensive Review of COBIT and ISO 27001: Approaches to Auditing Credit Bureau Automation System (CBAS) at PT XYZ. In *2023 9th International Conference on Signal Processing and Intelligent Systems (ICSPIS)* (pp. 1-8). IEEE. https://doi.org/DOI: 10.1109/ICSPIS59665.2023.10402713

Al-Najjar, D., & Assous, H. F. (2021). Key determinants of deposits volume using CAMEL rating system: The case of Saudi banks. *PLoS One, 16*(12), e0261184. DOI: 10.1371/journal.pone.0261184 PMID: 34910785

American Bankers Association. (2020, March 13). *ABA letter to OMB on principles for the regulation of artificial intelligence*. Retrieved from Link.

An, B., Bushman, R., Kleymenova, A., & Tomy, R. E. (2024). Bank Supervision and Organizational Capital: The Case of Minority Lending. *Journal of Accounting Research, 62*(2), 505–549. DOI: 10.1111/1475-679X.12529

Arrieta, A. B., Díaz-Rodríguez, N., Del Ser, J., Bennetot, A., Tabik, S., Barbado, A., Garcia, S., Gil-Lopez, S., Molina, D., Benjamins, R., Chatila, R., & Herrera, F. (2020). Explainable Artificial Intelligence (XAI): Concepts, taxonomies, opportunities and challenges toward responsible AI. *Information Fusion, 58*, 82–115. DOI: 10.1016/j.inffus.2019.12.012

Avramidis, P., Pennacchi, G., Serfes, K., & Wu, K. (2022). The role of regulation and bank competition in small firm financing: Evidence from the Community Reinvestment Act. *Journal of Money, Credit and Banking, 54*(8), 2301–2340. DOI: 10.1111/jmcb.12938

Ayoub, O., Di Cicco, N., Ezzeddine, F., Bruschetta, F., Rubino, R., Nardecchia, M., Milano, M., Musumeci, F., Passera, C., & Tornatore, M. (2022). Explainable Artificial Intelligence in communication networks: A use case for failure identification in microwave networks. *Computer Networks, 219*, 109466. DOI: 10.1016/j.comnet.2022.109466

Badunenko, O., Dadoukis, A., Fusi, G., & Simper, R. (2022). The impact of efficiency on asset quality in banking. *European Journal of Finance, 28*(6), 596–620. DOI: 10.1080/1351847X.2021.1946117

Baer, G. (2024, July 17). *The Bank Examination Problem, and How to Fix It.* Bank Policy Institute. Retrieved from https://bpi.com/wp-content/uploads/2024/07/The-Bank-Examination-Problem__and-How-to-Fix-It.pdf

Ben Lahouel, B., Taleb, L., Ben Zaied, Y., & Managi, S. (2024). Financial stability, liquidity risk and income diversification: Evidence from European banks using the CAMELS–DEA approach. *Annals of Operations Research, 334*(1), 391–422. DOI: 10.1007/s10479-022-04805-1

Bhatt, U., Xiang, A., Sharma, S., Weller, A., Taly, A., Jia, Y., Ghosh, J., Puri, R., Moura, J. M. F., & Eckersley, P. (2020). Explainable machine learning in deployment. *Proceedings of the 2020 Conference on Fairness, Accountability, and Transparency,* 648-657. https://doi.org/DOI: 10.1145/3351095.3375624

BIS or Bank for International Settlements. (2021). *Principles for operational resilience.* Basel Committee on Banking Supervision. https://www.bis.org/bcbs/publ/d516.pdf

Carvalho, D. V., Pereira, E. M., & Cardoso, J. S. (2019). Machine learning interpretability: A survey on methods and metrics. *Electronics (Basel)*, *8*(8), 832. DOI: 10.3390/electronics8080832

Černevičienė, J., & Kabašinskas, A. (2024). Explainable artificial intelligence (XAI) in finance: A systematic literature review. *Artificial Intelligence Review*, *57*(8), 216. DOI: 10.1007/s10462-024-10854-8

Consumer Financial Protection Bureau or CFPB. (2015). *Equal Credit Opportunity Act (ECOA) examination procedures*. Retrieved from Link.

Consumer Financial Protection Bureau or CFPB. (2023). *Supervision and Examination Manual*. Retrieved from Link.

Cyree, K. B., & Winters, D. B. (2023). Investigating bank lending discrimination in the US using CRA-rated banks' HMDA loan data. *Public Choice*, *197*(3), 371–395. DOI: 10.1007/s11127-023-01078-5

D'Onza, G., Lamboglia, R., & Verona, R. (2015). Do IT audits satisfy senior manager expectations? A qualitative study based on Italian banks. *Managerial Auditing Journal*, *30*(4/5), 413–434. DOI: 10.1108/MAJ-07-2014-1051

Davis, L. (2020). The impact of the California consumer privacy act on financial institutions across the nation. [Retrieved from Link.]. *North Carolina Banking Institute Journal*, *24*, 499.

Doumpos, M., Zopounidis, C., Gounopoulos, D., Platanakis, E., & Zhang, W. (2023). Operational research and artificial intelligence methods in banking. *European Journal of Operational Research*, *306*(1), 1–16. DOI: 10.1016/j.ejor.2022.04.027 PMID: 35874494

Elyasiani, E., & Mansur, I. (2005). The association between market and exchange rate risks and accounting variables: A GARCH model of the Japanese banking institutions. *Review of Quantitative Finance and Accounting*, *25*(2), 183–206. DOI: 10.1007/s11156-005-4248-6

Estrada, J. C. (2020). The AML Arms Race: How Artificial Intelligence and Machine Learning Will Combat Money Laundering. [Retrieved from Link.]. *Rutgers Business Law Journal*, *16*, 383.

European Commission. (2021). *Proposal for a regulation laying down harmonized rules on artificial intelligence.*https://digital-strategy.ec.europa.eu/en/library/proposal-regulation-laying-down-harmonised-rules-artificial-intelligence

FDIC. (2024a). *Consumer Compliance Examination Manual.* Federal Deposit Insurance Corporation. Retrieved from https://www.fdic.gov/consumer-compliance-examination-manual

FDIC. (2024b). *Corporate Governance and Auditing Programs.* Banker Resource Center - Federal Deposit Insurance Corporation. Retrieved from https://www.fdic.gov/corporate-governance-and-auditing-programs

FDIC. (2024c). Section 4.2 Internal Routine and Controls. *In Risk Management Manual of Examination Policies.* Federal Deposit Insurance Corporation. Retrieved from Link.

Fernández, A. (2024). Opacity, Machine Learning and Explainable AI. In *Ethics of Artificial Intelligence* (pp. 39–58). Springer Nature Switzerland., DOI: 10.1007/978-3-031-48135-2_3

FFIEC (2021). *Bank secrecy act anti-money laundering examination manual.* Federal Financial Institutions Examination Council. Retrieved from Link.

FFIEC. (2023). *Annual Report.* Retrieved from https://www.ffiec.gov/PDF/annrpt23.pdf

FFIEC. (2024). IT Examination Handbook InfoBase. https://ithandbook.ffiec.gov/ Accessed November 03, 2024.

Finn, C., Abbeel, P., & Levine, S. (2017, July). Model-agnostic meta-learning for fast adaptation of deep networks. In *International conference on machine learning* (pp. 1126-1135). PMLR. Retrieved from https://proceedings.mlr.press/v70/finn17a/finn17a.pdf

Floridi, L., Cowls, J., Beltrametti, M., Chatila, R., Chazerand, P., Dignum, V., Luetge, C., Madelin, R., Pagallo, U., Rossi, F., Schafer, B., Valcke, P., & Vayena, E. (2018). AI4People—an ethical framework for a good AI society: Opportunities, risks, principles, and recommendations. *Minds and Machines*, *28*(4), 689–707. DOI: 10.1007/s11023-018-9482-5 PMID: 30930541

Ghosh, A., Jarva, H., & Ryan, S. G. (2024). Bank regulation/supervision and bank auditing. *European Accounting Review*, •••, 1–26. DOI: 10.1080/09638180.2024.2373207

Giudici, P., & Raffinetti, E. (2021). Shapley-Lorenz eXplainable artificial intelligence. *Expert Systems with Applications*, *167*, 114104. DOI: 10.1016/j.eswa.2020.114104

Griffith, M. A. (2023). AI Lending and the ECOA: Avoiding Accidental Discrimination. [Retrieved from Link.]. *North Carolina Banking Institute Journal*, *27*, 349.

Guerra, P., & Castelli, M. (2021). Machine learning applied to banking supervision a literature review. *Risks*, *9*(7), 136. DOI: 10.3390/risks9070136

Gupta, A., Dwivedi, D. N., & Shah, J. (2023). *Artificial Intelligence Applications in Banking and Financial Services*. SpringerNature., DOI: 10.1007/978-981-99-2571-1

Handorf, W. C. (2016). CAMEL to CAMELS: The risk of sensitivity. *Journal of Banking Regulation*, *17*(4), 273–287. DOI: 10.1057/jbr.2015.24

Hassija, V., Chamola, V., Mahapatra, A., Singal, A., Goel, D., Huang, K., Scardapane, S., Spinelli, I., Mahmud, M., & Hussain, A. (2024). Interpreting black-box models: A review on explainable artificial intelligence. *Cognitive Computation*, *16*(1), 45–74. DOI: 10.1007/s12559-023-10179-8

Holzinger, A., Saranti, A., Molnar, C., Biecek, P., & Samek, W. (2022). Explainable AI methods-a brief overview. In *International workshop on extending explainable AI beyond deep models and classifiers* (pp. 13-38). Springer, Cham. https://doi.org/DOI: 10.1007/978-3-031-04083-2_2

Hosain, M. T., Jim, J. R., Mridha, M. F., & Kabir, M. M. (2024). Explainable AI approaches in deep learning: Advancements, applications and challenges. *Computers & Electrical Engineering, 117*, 109246. DOI: 10.1016/j.compeleceng.2024.109246

Islam, S. R., Eberle, W., Ghafoor, S. K., & Ahmed, M. (2021). Explainable artificial intelligence approaches: A survey. *arXiv preprint arXiv:2101.09429*. https://doi.org//arXiv.2101.09429DOI: 10.48550

Jarah, B. A. F., Al Jarrah, M. A., Al-Zaqeba, M. A. A., & Al-Jarrah, M. F. M. (2022). The role of internal audit to reduce the effects of creative accounting on the reliability of financial statements in the Jordanian islamic banks. *International Journal of Financial Studies, 10*(3), 60. DOI: 10.3390/ijfs10030060

Kaminski, M. E. (2019). The right to explanation, explained. *Berkeley Technology Law Journal, 34*(1), 189–218. DOI: 10.15779/Z38TD9N83H

Katz, G., Barrett, C., Dill, D. L., Julian, K., & Kochenderfer, M. J. (2017). Reluplex: An efficient SMT solver for verifying deep neural networks. In *Computer Aided Verification:29th International Conference, CAV 2017,Heidelberg, Germany,July 24-28, 2017, Proceedings, Part I 30* (pp. 97-117). Springer International Publishing. https://doi.org/DOI: 10.1007/978-3-319-63387-9_5

Klein, A. (2020, February 27). *Why bank regulators should make their secret ratings public.* The Brookings Institution Research. Retrieved from https://www.brookings.edu/articles/why-bank-regulators-should-make-their-secret-ratings-public/

Kočenda, E., & Iwasaki, I. (2022). Bank survival around the World: A meta-analytic review. *Journal of Economic Surveys, 36*(1), 108–156. DOI: 10.1111/joes.12451

KPMG. (2024). *AI in financial reporting and audit: Navigating the new era.* Retrieved from https://assets.kpmg.com/content/dam/kpmgsites/ch/pdf/kpmg-ch-report-global-ai-audit-study-trusted-ai-framework.pdf.coredownload.inline.pdf

Kumar, I. E., Venkatasubramanian, S., Scheidegger, C., & Friedler, S. (2020, November). Problems with Shapley-value-based explanations as feature importance measures. In *International conference on machine learning* (pp. 5491-5500). PMLR. Retrieved from Link.

Kute, D. V., Pradhan, B., Shukla, N., & Alamri, A. (2021). Deep learning and explainable artificial intelligence techniques applied for detecting money laundering–a critical review. *IEEE Access : Practical Innovations, Open Solutions, 9*, 82300–82317. DOI: 10.1109/ACCESS.2021.3086230

Le, T. N. L., Nasir, M. A., & Huynh, T. L. D. (2023). Capital requirements and banks performance under Basel-III: A comparative analysis of Australian and British banks. *The Quarterly Review of Economics and Finance, 87*, 146–157. DOI: 10.1016/j.qref.2020.06.001

Leo, M., Sharma, S., & Maddulety, K. (2019). Machine Learning in Banking Risk Management: A Literature Review. *Risks, 7*(1), 29. DOI: 10.3390/risks7010029

Lessambo, F. I. (2023). AML/CFT Compliance and Audit. In *Anti-Money Laundering, Counter Financing Terrorism and Cybersecurity in the Banking Industry: A Comparative Study within the G-20* (pp. 205-214). Cham: Springer Nature Switzerland. https://doi.org/DOI: 10.1007/978-3-031-23484-2_27

Li, X. H., Cao, C. C., Shi, Y., Bai, W., Gao, H., Qiu, L., Wang, C., Gao, Y., Zhang, S., Xue, X., & Chen, L. (2020). A survey of data-driven and knowledge-aware explainable ai. *IEEE Transactions on Knowledge and Data Engineering*, *34*(1), 29–49. DOI: 10.1109/TKDE.2020.2983930

Li, Y., Chen, Y. K., Chien, F. S., Lee, W. C., & Hsu, Y. C. (2016). Study of optimal capital adequacy ratios. *Journal of Productivity Analysis*, *45*(3), 261–274. DOI: 10.1007/s11123-016-0469-z

Longo, L., Brcic, M., Cabitza, F., Choi, J., Confalonieri, R., Del Ser, J., & Stumpf, S. (2024). Explainable Artificial Intelligence (XAI) 2.0: A manifesto of open challenges and interdisciplinary research directions. *Information Fusion*, *106*, 102301. DOI: 10.1016/j.inffus.2024.102301

Miller, Z. C., & Kohr, L. (2017). Senior management training, accountability and oversight for anti-money laundering compliance. [Retrieved from Link.]. *Journal of Financial Compliance*, *1*(1), 81–88. DOI: 10.69554/SGMS2903

Molnar, C. (2020). *Interpretable machine learning*. Lulu. com.

Mostaghim, C. (2021). Constructing the yellow brick road: Preventing discrimination in financial services against the LGBTQ+ community. [Retrieved from Link.]. *Michigan Business & Entrepreneurial Law Review*, *11*(11.1), 63. DOI: 10.36639/mbelr.11.1.constructing

Nauta, M., Trienes, J., Pathak, S., Nguyen, E., Peters, M., Schmitt, Y., Schlötterer, J., van Keulen, M., & Seifert, C. (2023). From anecdotal evidence to quantitative evaluation methods: A systematic review on evaluating explainable ai. *ACM Computing Surveys*, *55*(13s), 1–42. DOI: 10.1145/3583558

Nicoletti, A., & Zhu, C. (2023). Economic Consequences of Transparency Regulation: Evidence from Bank Mortgage Lending. *Journal of Accounting Research*, *61*(5), 1827–1871. DOI: 10.1111/1475-679X.12498

Nzeako, G., Akinsanya, M. O., Popoola, O. A., Chukwurah, E. G., Okeke, C. D., & Akpukorji, I. S. (2024). Theoretical insights into IT governance and compliance in banking: Perspectives from African and US regulatory environments. *International Journal of Management & Entrepreneurship Research*, *6*(5), 1457–1466. DOI: 10.51594/ijmer.v6i5.1094

Office of the Comptroller of the Currency. (2022, March). Large bank supervision. In *Comptroller's Handbook: Examination Process*. U.S. Department of the Treasury. Retrieved from https://www.occ.gov/publications-and-resources/publications/comptrollers-handbook/files/large-bank-supervision/pub-ch-large-bank-supervision.pdf

Piras, D., Peiris, H. V., Pontzen, A., Lucie-Smith, L., Guo, N., & Nord, B. (2023). A robust estimator of mutual information for deep learning interpretability. *Machine Learning: Science and Technology*, *4*(2), 025006. DOI: 10.1088/2632-2153/acc444

Quoc Trung, N. K. (2021). Determinants of bank performance in Vietnamese commercial banks: An application of the camels model. *Cogent Business & Management*, *8*(1), 1979443. DOI: 10.1080/23311975.2021.1979443

Ratzan, J., & Rahman, N. (2023). Measuring responsible artificial intelligence (RAI) in banking: A valid and reliable instrument. *AI and Ethics*, •••, 1–19. DOI: 10.1007/s43681-023-00321-5

Rudin, C. (2019). Stop explaining black box machine learning models for high stakes decisions and use interpretable models instead. *Nature Machine Intelligence, 1*(5), 206–215. DOI: 10.1038/s42256-019-0048-x PMID: 35603010

Selbst, A. D., & Barocas, S. (2018). The intuitive appeal of explainable machines. *Fordham Law Review, 87*, 1085. https://ir.lawnet.fordham.edu/flr/vol87/iss3/11/

Stackhouse, J. L. (2018, July 23). The ABCs of CAMELS. Federal Reserve Bank of St. Louis. Retrieved from https://www.stlouisfed.org/on-the-economy/2018/july/abcs-camels

Torrie, V., & Payette, D. (2023). AI governance frameworks for the banking sector. In *Artificial Intelligence in Finance* (pp. 114–141). Edward Elgar Publishing., DOI: 10.4337/9781803926179.00014

Turksen, U., Benson, V., & Adamyk, B. (2024). Legal implications of automated suspicious transaction monitoring: Enhancing integrity of AI. *Journal of Banking Regulation, 25*(4), 359–377. DOI: 10.1057/s41261-024-00233-2

Van Greuning, H., & Bratanovic, S. B. (2020). *Analyzing banking risk: a framework for assessing corporate governance and risk management*. World Bank Publications. Retrieved from Link.

Wang, H., Liang, Q., Hancock, J. T., & Khoshgoftaar, T. M. (2024). Feature selection strategies: A comparative analysis of SHAP-value and importance-based methods. *Journal of Big Data, 11*(1), 44. DOI: 10.1186/s40537-024-00905-w

Witten, E. (2020). A mini-introduction to information theory. *La Rivista del Nuovo Cimento della Società Italiana di Fisica, 43*(4), 187–227. DOI: 10.1007/s40766-020-00004-5

Chapter 14
Strategic Significance of Machine Learning in Financial Services

Shamrao Parashram Ghodake
https://orcid.org/0000-0003-3017-1364
Sanjivani College of Engineering, Kopargaon, India

Jaya Saxena
https://orcid.org/0000-0001-5365-046X
Indira School of Business Studies PGDM, India

Nitesh Behare
https://orcid.org/0000-0002-9338-8563
Balaji Institute of International Business, Sri Balaji University, Pune, India

Tabrej Mulla
Arihant Institute of Business Management, India

Shrikant Waghulkar
https://orcid.org/0000-0002-3767-3765
Ramchandran Institute of Management Studies, India

Pritesh Somani
https://orcid.org/0000-0002-0039-0358
Balaji Institute of International Business, Sri Balaji University, Pune, India

Vishwanathan Iyer
https://orcid.org/0009-0007-1469-2369
Balaji Institute of International Business, Sri Balaji University, Pune, India

Rashmi D. Mahajan
https://orcid.org/0000-0001-9082-6874
Balaji Institute of International Business, Sri Balaji University, Pune, India

ABSTRACT

Machine learning (ML) is transforming the financial services industry by driving innovation in fraud detection, risk management, customer personalization, and more. This chapter explores the strategic significance of ML, its key applications, and future trends shaping its adoption. Integration with blockchain technology enhances security and automation, while advancements in quantum computing promise faster, more accurate financial models. However, challenges such as data privacy, algorithmic bias, and regulatory compliance persist. The evolution of regulatory frameworks and the growing importance of explainable AI (XAI) are critical for ensuring transparency and fairness. As financial institutions embrace these trends, they stand to enhance operational efficiency, decision-making accuracy, and customer trust while navigating the complexities of modern financial landscapes.

DOI: 10.4018/979-8-3373-0209-6.ch014

1. INTRODUCTION

The financial services industry is a cornerstone of the global economy, encompassing a broad spectrum of services, including banking, insurance, wealth management, and financial advisory. This sector serves as a crucial intermediary between individuals, businesses, and governments, facilitating transactions, managing risks, and driving economic growth. As the financial landscape becomes increasingly complex and competitive, institutions face the challenge of delivering more efficient, personalized, and secure services (Walker et al., 2020). The demand for innovation, coupled with evolving customer expectations and regulatory requirements, is reshaping the industry. In response, financial institutions are embracing technological advancements to maintain their competitive edge and ensure operational resilience. One of the most transformative technologies in this evolution is machine learning (ML) (Pereira et al., 2024).

Machine learning refers to the ability of systems to learn from data and improve their performance over time without explicit programming. This technology is driven by algorithms that identify patterns, predict outcomes, and make decisions based on vast amounts of historical and real-time data (Cruz, 2017). Machine learning's importance lies in its capacity to process large and complex datasets at unprecedented speeds, offering financial institutions the ability to gain actionable insights and optimize various processes. In today's data-driven world, financial institutions generate and manage enormous amounts of information. The ability to effectively analyze and derive meaning from this data has become critical, and machine learning plays a pivotal role in unlocking the potential of this vast resource (Islam & Pandow, 2024).

In the financial services sector, the strategic significance of machine learning extends across multiple areas. One of its primary applications is in risk management, where it helps institutions enhance credit scoring, detect fraud, and assess market risks with greater precision (Raji et al., 2024). By leveraging historical data, ML models can predict borrower defaults, identify suspicious transactions, and assess market volatility in real time, enabling institutions to take preemptive measures (Espinoza Alvarado et al., 2024). Machine learning also drives automation in customer service through chatbots and virtual assistants, which provide personalized recommendations and streamline operations. In portfolio management and trading, ML algorithms analyze market trends and sentiment to make more informed investment decisions, thus improving financial outcomes.

Moreover, machine learning is instrumental in regulatory compliance. Financial institutions operate in a highly regulated environment, and the ability to swiftly adapt to changing regulations is essential (Pasrija et al., 2022). ML systems can monitor transactions for compliance issues, automate reporting, and identify potential risks, helping institutions avoid costly penalties. In addition, the technology's capacity to enhance customer experience by providing tailored products and services further strengthens its strategic value in the sector (Samanthapudi et al., 2024).

Despite its growing relevance, a key gap exists in understanding the strategic role of machine learning in achieving sustainable growth within financial services. While numerous studies have explored individual applications of ML, few have offered a comprehensive view of its integration across core operational areas (Mahalakshmi et al., 2022). This paper aims to address this gap by examining how ML is being strategically leveraged to drive innovation, manage risk, enhance compliance, and personalize customer experience in the financial services industry.

Therefore, the objectives of this study are threefold:

- To explore the significance of ML in transforming financial services,

- To identify key functional areas where ML is making a strategic impact, and
- To evaluate how ML adoption contributes to resilience, efficiency, and sustainable growth.

By articulating these objectives, the chapter highlights the significance of investigating ML not just as a technological trend, but as a strategic importance for the future of financial institutions

2. METHODOLOGY AND CHAPTER STRUCTURE

This chapter is based on conceptual analysis approach, drawing upon a wide range of academic literature, industry reports and case-based insights to explore the strategic role of ML in financial services. It does not rely on empirical data collection or systematic review protocols, but rather synthesizes secondary sources to examine how ML technologies are reshaping key dimensions of the financial sector, including risk management, customer engagement, regulatory compliance, and ESG investing. The chapter is structured to first establish a foundational understanding of ML in the financial domain, followed by an exploration of its strategic applications, implementation challenges, and sectoral use cases. The concluding sections address future directions and emerging trends, with emphasis on responsible AI deployment and sustainability.

3. KEY AREAS OF MACHINE LEARNING APPLICATION

Machine learning (ML) is revolutionizing the financial services industry by transforming how institutions approach challenges and opportunities. With its ability to process vast amounts of data, uncover patterns, and make accurate predictions, ML has become an indispensable tool in various domains (Kour, Revolutionizing Finance: Unleashing Machine Learning's Potential for a New Financial Era, 2024). Following are the key areas of machine learning application within the financial sector, including fraud detection and prevention, risk management, customer relationship management (CRM), investment and portfolio management, algorithmic trading, and credit scoring and lending.

3.1 Fraud Detection and Prevention

Fraud detection and prevention stand as crucial and well-established applications of machine learning within the realm of sustainable financing. With financial institutions handling an enormous volume of transactions daily, safeguarding the security and integrity of these transactions is of utmost importance (Ding, 2023). While traditional rule-based systems provide a degree of effectiveness, they often fall short when confronted with sophisticated and continually evolving fraudulent activities. In contrast, machine learning models excel at identifying anomalies and detecting suspicious behaviors in real-time, offering a more robust solution to these challenges (Miao, 2024).

ML algorithms analyze historical transaction data to create baseline patterns of normal behavior for individual customers. Any deviation from these patterns, such as an unusually large purchase or transactions from foreign locations, triggers alerts (Cunningham & Delany, 2021). Unlike rule-based systems, ML models continuously learn from new data and can adapt to new forms of fraud as they emerge, enhancing detection accuracy. Moreover, ML's capacity to reduce false positives—incorrectly flagging legitimate transactions as fraud—improves the customer experience by minimizing disruptions (Dash et al., 2023).

One prominent example of machine learning in fraud detection is the use of deep learning techniques in analyzing unstructured data such as emails, social media posts, and even voice calls (Dere, 2025). These techniques allow institutions to monitor for signs of identity theft, phishing attacks, or other fraud-related activities, providing a multi-layered approach to fraud prevention (Harisha & Bhat, 2024).

3.2 Risk Management

In sustainable financing, managing risk is critical to ensuring stability and minimizing losses. Machine learning plays a crucial role in improving the accuracy and efficiency of risk management processes by offering predictive insights and real-time monitoring of various risk factors (Saha et al., 2023). Whether it is credit risk, market risk, or operational risk, ML algorithms can process vast datasets to assess and predict potential threats more accurately than traditional statistical models (Saha et al., 2023).

For credit risk, machine learning models can analyze not only traditional financial indicators like income and credit history but also non-traditional data sources such as social media activity or online behavior. This results in a more comprehensive assessment of a borrower's creditworthiness (Özcan, 2023). In market risk, ML can predict the likelihood of price movements or market volatility by analyzing historical data and identifying subtle patterns that human analysts might overlook. Operational risks, such as system failures or internal errors, can also be monitored using ML to detect early warning signs of system breakdowns (Bejjar & Siala, 2024).

Additionally, machine learning enhances risk management by automating the monitoring of regulatory compliance. Financial institutions must continuously ensure that they adhere to evolving regulatory standards, and ML-driven systems can flag potential compliance breaches, reducing the risk of costly fines and reputational damage (Silva et al., 2021).

3.3 Customer Relationship Management (CRM)

CRM is another area where machine learning significantly impacts financial services. In an era where customer expectations are constantly evolving, financial institutions must prioritize delivering personalized and seamless experiences (Hamdoun & Rguibi, 2019). Machine learning enables institutions to better understand customer behavior, preferences, and needs by analyzing both structured and unstructured data from various sources, including transactional data, social media activity, and interaction history (Rodrigues Chagas et al., 2019).

By leveraging ML, financial institutions can segment their customer base more effectively, allowing them to offer tailored products and services. For example, a bank can use ML to analyse spending patterns and recommend personalized financial products, such as investment options or loan products, based on the customer's financial goals and risk tolerance (Balamohan & Khanaa, 2024). Moreover, ML-powered chatbots and virtual assistants can handle routine customer inquiries, improving response times and freeing up human agents to handle more complex tasks (Lampropoulos et al., 2022).

In customer retention, predictive analytics plays a significant role by identifying customers who are likely to churn. By understanding early signs of dissatisfaction or disengagement, financial institutions can proactively address concerns, improving customer loyalty and reducing attrition rates (Pahul Preet et al., 2024).

3.4 Investment and Portfolio Management

Machine learning is reshaping investment and portfolio management by providing more data-driven and accurate insights for decision-making. ML algorithms can analyze vast amounts of financial data, market trends, and even social sentiment to identify profitable investment opportunities and optimize portfolio allocations. One key application of ML in portfolio management is the development of robo-advisors (Islam & Pandow, 2024). These automated platforms use machine learning to offer personalized investment advice based on an individual's financial goals, risk tolerance, and time horizon. Robo-advisors not only provide a cost-effective solution for retail investors but also reduce the barriers to entry for investment services. By continuously learning from market data and client feedback, these platforms can adjust their recommendations in real time to optimize investment outcomes (Bonelli & Dongul, 2023). In addition to robo-advisors, hedge funds and institutional investors increasingly rely on machine learning to develop more sophisticated models for portfolio optimization. ML algorithms can factor in a multitude of variables, including asset correlations, historical returns, and market volatility, to create diversified portfolios that minimize risk and maximize returns (Park et al., 2017).

3.5 Algorithmic Trading

Algorithmic trading, also known as algo-trading, has been one of the most prominent applications of machine learning in financial markets. ML-driven algorithms execute trades automatically based on predefined criteria such as price movements, volume, and other market conditions. What sets machine learning apart in this domain is its ability to adapt to changing market conditions in real time (Czuba, 2024). Machine learning models can process large volumes of historical and real-time data to identify trading opportunities and predict price movements. These algorithms can react to market changes faster than human traders, executing trades at optimal times to capitalize on short-term price fluctuations. This high-frequency trading (HFT) approach relies heavily on machine learning for speed and precision, offering a significant competitive advantage to financial institutions (Islam & Pandow, 2024).

Moreover, machine learning enhances algo-trading by incorporating sentiment analysis from news articles, social media posts, and other sources of market-moving information. By analyzing unstructured data in addition to traditional market indicators, ML models can make more informed trading decisions and avoid potential losses caused by unforeseen market events (Sowmya et al., 2024).

3.6 Credit Scoring and Lending

Credit scoring and lending have traditionally relied on rigid frameworks and limited data sets to assess the creditworthiness of borrowers. Machine learning is transforming this space by offering more nuanced and accurate assessments based on a broader range of data. In traditional credit scoring, financial institutions typically use variables such as income, debt-to-income ratio, and credit history. However, ML models can incorporate additional data sources, including transactional behavior, online activity, and even social network analysis, to create a more holistic view of a borrower's financial health (Raji et al., 2024).

ML-driven credit scoring models can assess non-traditional borrowers, such as those with limited credit histories or those operating in emerging markets, who may be underserved by conventional models. These systems can more accurately predict the likelihood of repayment, reducing the risk of default and enabling institutions to extend credit to a wider range of individuals and businesses (Blanco et al., 2013). In lending, machine learning automates and optimizes the loan approval process. By analyzing historical lending data and borrower profiles, ML models can approve or reject loan applications in real time, reducing the time required for underwriting. This streamlining not only enhances operational efficiency but also improves the customer experience by offering faster approvals and more personalized loan products.

4. MACHINE LEARNING TECHNIQUES IN FINANCIAL SERVICES

ML is a transformative force in the financial services, offer innovative solutions for crucial challenges in the field of risk management, fraud detection, trading and customer experience. Various machine learning techniques, each with unique methodologies and applications, enable financial institutions to analyze massive amounts of data, identify patterns, and make data-driven decisions (Kour, 2023). Following are key machine learning techniques applied in financial services, including supervised learning, unsupervised learning, reinforcement learning and deep learning, along with specific methods like regression analysis, classification, clustering, anomaly detection and neural networks (Belanche et al., 2019).

4.1 Supervised Learning

Supervised learning is a cornerstone of machine learning in financial services, where models are trained on labeled datasets to make accurate predictions. Techniques like regression and classification are widely used for tasks such as forecasting asset prices, assessing credit risk, and detecting fraud (Makadia et al., 2023). Regression analysis, including linear and logistic regression, helps establish relationships between financial indicators—for instance, predicting stock prices using historical trends or determining the likelihood of loan default (Hwang et al., 2022). Classification techniques, such as decision trees, SVMs, and KNN, categorize data into predefined labels (Pistoia et al., 2021). These are instrumental in credit scoring, fraud detection, and customer segmentation, enabling financial institutions to automate decisions, enhance security, and personalize services (Cunningham & Delany, 2021).

4.2 Unsupervised Learning

Unsupervised learning addresses unlabeled data to uncover hidden structures, making it vital for tasks like market analysis, anomaly detection, and customer segmentation. Clustering, a key technique, groups similar data points—commonly applied in segmenting customers by behavior or demographics (Hwang et al., 2022). Banks use this to tailor offerings for different client clusters, enhancing service personalization (Guoxun et al., 2009). Anomaly detection, another powerful tool, identifies outliers in financial data that may signal fraud, market manipulation, or operational risk. For example, sudden transaction spikes or trading anomalies trigger alerts for investigation, thus improving risk management and decision-making in real-time financial environments (Tao & Chao, 2023).

4.3 Reinforcement Learning

Reinforcement learning is a type of machine learning where an agent learns to make decisions by interacting with an environment and receiving feedback in the form of rewards or penalties. This trial-and-error approach allows the agent to learn optimal strategies over time. Reinforcement learning is particularly useful in dynamic environments where decisions must be made sequentially, making it well-suited for applications in trading and investment (Czuba, 2024). Reinforcement learning algorithm analyses stock price movements and determine the best times to execute trades to maximize profits. Over time, the algorithm can adapt to changing market conditions, identifying patterns that lead to profitable trades. Reinforcement learning can also be applied to portfolio management, where the goal is to optimize asset allocation based on market fluctuations and the investor's risk tolerance (Rodrigues Chagas et al., 2019).

4.4 Deep Learning

Deep learning, a powerful subset of machine learning, uses artificial neural networks (ANNs) with multiple layers to process large and complex datasets. These deep networks excel at recognizing intricate patterns, making them ideal for applications such as time series forecasting, credit scoring, and sentiment analysis in financial services (Li & Ma, 2010). Neural networks, inspired by the human brain, adjust the connections between nodes (neurons) to learn from data. In finance, they are used to predict stock prices, interest rates, and market volatility, uncovering non-linear relationships that traditional models may overlook (Samanthapudi et al., 2024). They also enhance credit scoring by accurately assessing borrower risk based on diverse input variables. Another critical deep learning application is natural language processing (NLP), particularly for sentiment analysis (Ling et al., 2024). NLP algorithms analyze unstructured text from news articles, social media, or financial reports to evaluate market sentiment. This insight helps firms refine trading strategies, as positive or negative sentiment often influences investor behavior and market trends (Sowmya et al., 2024).

5. BENEFITS OF MACHINE LEARNING IN FINANCIAL SERVICES

ML is driving profound changes in modern financial services by enabling institutions to harness the power of data, improve decision-making processes, and create innovative products and services. Financial institutions, from traditional banks to fintech startups, are increasingly incorporating machine learning into their systems to optimize efficiency, reduce costs, and improve the overall customer experience (Bonelli & Dongul, 2023). Following are the key benefits of machine learning in financial services, focusing on improved accuracy and efficiency, real-time data processing, enhanced customer experience, cost reduction, and predictive analytics for better forecasting.

5.1 Improved Accuracy and Efficiency

One of the most significant advantages of machine learning in financial services is its ability to improve the accuracy and efficiency of various operations. Traditional financial models often rely on historical data and static assumptions, which may not account for the complexities of rapidly changing markets. Machine learning algorithms, however, can process vast amounts of data from multiple sources and identify intricate patterns and trends that are difficult for humans to detect (Zhu et al., 2023).

5.1.1 Fraud Detection and Prevention:

In areas like fraud detection, machine learning algorithms offer superior accuracy by analyzing historical transaction data and learning to detect anomalous behaviors that may indicate fraudulent activities. These algorithms continuously refine themselves as they are exposed to new data, making them highly adaptive and effective in identifying complex fraud patterns. This improves accuracy and reduces the number of false positives, ensuring that legitimate transactions are not unnecessarily flagged, which would otherwise inconvenience customers (Pasrija et al., 2022).

5.1.2 Risk Management:

Similarly, in risk management, machine learning improves the precision of credit risk assessments and market forecasts. ML models analyze financial history and market indicators to predict loan defaults and downturns (Huang, 2024). This enables financial institutions to take preemptive actions, mitigating losses and improving their financial resilience.

5.2 Real-time Data Processing and Decision Making

The ability to process data in real time is critical for financial services, particularly in areas like trading, investment management, and fraud detection. Traditional methods of data analysis often involve significant delays due to the time required for data collection, processing, and analysis. Machine learning, on the other hand, enables financial institutions to analyze real-time data streams and make decisions almost instantaneously.

5.2.1 Algorithmic Trading:

In algorithmic trading, where milliseconds can make the difference between profit and loss, ML algorithms can analyze market data, news reports, and social media sentiment in real time to identify trading opportunities and execute trades at optimal prices. High-frequency trading platforms rely heavily on machine learning to execute thousands of trades within a second, maximizing profitability by reacting faster than human traders (Regulagadda et al., 2024).

5.2.2 Fraud Detection and Prevention:

Real-time fraud detection systems powered by machine learning can analyze ongoing transactions as they happen, instantly flagging suspicious activities such as unusual spending patterns or transactions from unexpected locations. This capability enables financial institutions to respond to fraud attempts as they occur, preventing potential losses and enhancing customer trust (Tarambale et al., 2024).

5.3 Enhanced Customer Experience

The rise of customer-centric approaches in financial services has made enhancing the customer experience a top priority for institutions. Machine learning plays a pivotal role in achieving this by enabling personalization, improving customer interactions, and providing timely and relevant financial advice.

5.3.1 Personalization:

Machine learning allows financial institutions to offer personalized products and services based on individual customer behavior and preferences. For example, by analyzing transaction history, spending patterns, and lifestyle data, ML algorithms can recommend tailored financial products, such as investment portfolios, savings accounts, or credit card offers. This level of personalization improves customer satisfaction by ensuring that they receive services that align with their specific needs and financial goals (Corral de La Mata et al., 2024).

5.3.2 Chatbots and Virtual Assistants:

Another area where machine learning enhances the customer experience is through AI-powered chatbots and virtual assistants. These tools use NLP to understand and respond to customer queries in real time. They can handle a wide range of customer service tasks, such as answering frequently asked questions, assisting with account management, and even offering financial advice. This reduces wait times for customers and provides them with 24/7 service, improving overall engagement and satisfaction (Belanche et al., 2019).

5.3.3 Customer Retention:

Predictive analytics, driven by machine learning, helps institutions identify customers at risk of churn. By analysing behavioural patterns and interaction history, machine learning models can detect early warning signs of customer dissatisfaction (Irfan et al., 2023). Institutions can then take proactive measures, such as offering special incentives or resolving service issues, to retain these customers and reduce attrition rates.

5.4 Cost Reduction and Operational Efficiency

Cost reduction and operational efficiency are key benefits of machine learning for financial institutions. By automating repetitive tasks and improving decision-making processes, machine learning reduces the reliance on human labor and minimizes errors, leading to significant cost savings.

5.4.1 Automation of Routine Tasks:

Many financial institutions are using machine learning to automate routine tasks that were traditionally performed by humans, such as processing loan applications, verifying customer information, and handling compliance checks. For instance, ML algorithms can automate the document verification process in customer onboarding, significantly reducing the time and resources required. This automation improves operational efficiency, reduces human error, and frees up employees to focus on more strategic tasks (Hamdoun & Rguibi, 2019).

5.4.2 Risk Management:

In risk management, machine learning models automate the analysis of vast datasets to identify potential risks, such as market fluctuations or credit defaults. By automating these processes, financial institutions can reduce the time spent on manual data analysis and improve the accuracy of risk assessments (Hamdoun & Rguibi, 2019). This not only reduces operational costs but also enhances decision-making capabilities, enabling institutions to respond to risks more swiftly.

5.4.3 Fraud Prevention and Compliance:

Machine learning also helps financial institutions cut costs by improving fraud detection and compliance processes. Fraudulent transactions and regulatory fines can result in significant financial losses for banks and other institutions (Huang, 2024). Machine learning models reduce these costs by detecting fraud in real time and ensuring that institutions adhere to regulatory standards. By minimizing fraud-related losses and compliance penalties, machine learning contributes to overall cost reduction (Ding, 2023).

5.5 Predictive Analytics for Better Forecasting

Predictive analytics is one of the most powerful applications of machine learning in financial services. By analyzing historical data and identifying patterns, machine learning models can provide accurate forecasts for a variety of financial activities, ranging from stock prices to credit risks and consumer behavior (Irfan et al., 2023).

5.5.1 Investment and Market Predictions:

In the investment space, machine learning models can analyze historical market data, economic indicators, and news sentiment to predict future stock prices or market trends. Investors and asset managers rely on these predictive models to make more informed investment decisions and optimize their portfolios (Hamdoun & Rguibi, 2019). Predictive analytics can also help identify market trends before they become apparent to the broader market, offering a competitive advantage to investors who can act early.

5.5.2 Credit Risk Forecasting:

Machine learning also plays a key role in credit risk forecasting. Traditional credit scoring models often rely on static data points, such as income, credit history, and debt levels, to assess borrower risk. Machine learning, however, can incorporate a wider range of data, including behavioral data and social media activity, to provide a more holistic view of an individual's creditworthiness. By improving the accuracy of credit risk predictions, financial institutions can reduce defaults and make better lending decisions (Khandani et al., 2010).

5.5.3 Consumer Behavior Insights:

Machine learning-driven predictive analytics can also provide insights into consumer behavior, helping financial institutions anticipate customer needs and preferences (Kumar et al., 2023). For example, banks can use predictive models to identify customers who may be interested in refinancing a loan or purchasing a new financial product based on their spending patterns and financial history. This enables institutions to offer targeted marketing and promotions, improving customer engagement and increasing revenue.

6 CHALLENGES AND RISKS

While machine learning (ML) offers vast potential for financial services, it introduces significant challenges and risks that institutions must address. Key issues include data privacy, algorithmic bias, regulatory compliance, and the complexities of integrating ML with legacy systems. In addition, interpretability and transparency, scalability, and the constant evolution of technology create hurdles that can impact the successful deployment of ML models.

6.1 Data Privacy and Security Issues

Machine learning relies on vast amounts of data, much of which is sensitive financial or personal information. Financial institutions face major risks related to data breaches, cyberattacks, and non-compliance with stringent data privacy regulations like GDPR and CCPA. Hackers may exploit ML models, potentially exposing customer data or manipulating algorithms for fraud (Moreira et al., 2022). Ensuring robust data governance and cybersecurity measures is critical for mitigating these risks (Asmar & Tuqan, 2024).

6.2 Ethical Considerations and Bias in Algorithms

Algorithmic bias is a significant concern in machine learning. If the data used to train ML models contains historical biases, these biases can be perpetuated, leading to unfair outcomes in areas like lending, credit scoring, and hiring. Discriminatory decisions can damage reputations and result in legal challenges. Financial institutions must ensure fairness, regularly audit their models, and improve the transparency of their algorithms to minimize bias and prevent ethical issues (Cunningham & Delany, 2021).

6.3 Bias in AI Models

Despite the potential, ML models can unconsciously disseminate or intensify societal biases present in historical data. In financial services, this is particularly concerning in areas such as credit scoring, where biased training data can lead to discriminatory outcomes based on race, gender, or socioeconomic status (Alelyani, 2021). For instance, applicants from marginalized communities may be unfairly denied credit due to historical inequalities embedded in data. These biases undermine trust in AI systems and call for transparent model development, robust auditing mechanisms, and inclusive data representation to ensure fairness and accountability (Corliss, 2024).

6.4 Privacy Concerns with Real-Time Data Processing

The integration of ML into financial services often involves real-time analysis of vast amounts of personal and transactional data. While this enables faster decision-making and improved customer experiences, it also raises serious privacy concerns. Continuous data monitoring may encroach on user consent and data minimization principles, exclusively if individuals are unaware of how their information is being used (Kour, 2024). Financial institutions must strike a balance between innovation and user privacy by ensuring data encryption, clear consent protocols, and strict governance frameworks to protect sensitive information in real-time environments (Corral de La Mata et al., 2024).

6.5 Regulatory Compliance

Machine learning poses challenges in adhering to financial regulations, as many laws were designed before the widespread adoption of AI. Regulatory frameworks often demand transparency in decision-making, which can be difficult with complex ML models (Kour, 2023). Financial institutions must stay updated on evolving regulations and ensure their models comply with standards related to data privacy, fairness, and accountability (Thakur & Kaur, 2025).

6.6 Regulatory Risks

ML applications in finance must navigate an evolving regulatory landscape, with stringent requirements around the data protection and algorithmic transparency. Regulations such as the General Data Protection Regulation (GDPR) impose strict obligations on financial institutions, particularly concerning automated decision-making and the 'right to explanation' (Veale et al., 2018). Non-compliance can lead to severe penalties and reputational damage. Moreover, global inconsistencies in AI governance further complicate cross-border operations (Giudici & Raffinetti, 2023). Consequently, businesses must entrench regulatory compliance into their AI strategies, ensuring that their models are explainable, auditable, and aligned with both local and international legal frameworks (Al-Moman et al., 2021).

6.7 Integration with Legacy Systems

Many financial institutions rely on outdated legacy systems that are not compatible with modern machine learning technologies. Integrating ML models with these systems is often costly, time-consuming, and technically challenging. Data silos and fragmented databases further complicate this process, making it difficult for ML models to access the data needed for accurate predictions (Irfan et al., 2023).

6.8 Interpretability and Transparency of ML Models

The "black box" nature of some machine learning models, especially deep learning algorithms, makes it hard for financial institutions to explain how decisions are made. This lack of transparency can lead to issues with regulators, who require institutions to provide clear reasoning behind decisions, especially those affecting customers. Explainable AI (XAI) is being developed to address these issues, but balancing model performance with interpretability remains a challenge (Dhar et al., 2024).

6.9 Scalability and Operational Costs

As machine learning models grow more complex, so do their computational and data storage demands. For large-scale operations, scaling these models can lead to increased infrastructure and operational costs. Additionally, the need for continuous model retraining and refinement, as new data becomes available, adds to the complexity of managing ML systems effectively. Institutions must carefully plan their infrastructure to scale ML solutions efficiently without escalating costs (Rendle et al., 2016).

6.10 Model Drift and Maintenance

ML models require ongoing updates to remain effective, as market conditions and customer behaviors evolve. Model drift—where a model's accuracy declines over time due to changes in underlying data—can lead to poor predictions and financial losses. Institutions must regularly monitor and retrain their models to avoid drift and ensure their decisions remain accurate and relevant.

6.11 Talent Gap

Developing, deploying, and maintaining advanced ML models requires specialized expertise in data science, machine learning, and financial services. The scarcity of skilled professionals can hinder the adoption of ML technologies. Financial institutions need to invest in talent acquisition and training to build the necessary capabilities for implementing machine learning effectively (Cruz, 2017).

7 REAL-WORLD APPLICATIONS

Machine learning (ML) has transformed financial services, driving innovation across various domains. Below are three real-world case studies that highlight the impact of ML on fraud detection, risk management, and customer personalization.

7.1 Case Study 1: Fraud Detection in Banking

Bank of America's AI-driven Fraud Detection System

Fraud detection is one of the most critical applications of machine learning in banking. Banks like Bank of America have implemented advanced ML algorithms to detect fraudulent transactions in real-time.

Traditionally, fraud detection relied on rule-based systems, which often failed to adapt to new patterns of fraudulent activity. Machine learning, however, learns from both historical and real-time data, identifying unusual patterns that could indicate fraud, such as abnormal spending behavior or transactions from unfamiliar locations (Nasser, 2024).

The Solution:

Bank of America's fraud detection system leverages supervised learning techniques, particularly classification algorithms, to flag suspicious transactions. By analyzing massive datasets of legitimate and fraudulent transactions, the model can accurately classify which transactions are likely to be fraudulent (Nasser, 2024). For example, the model might flag a transaction where a cardholder who typically shops in California suddenly makes a high-value purchase in a foreign country.

To enhance accuracy, the system continuously retrains itself using the latest data, ensuring that it stays up to date with evolving fraud tactics. Additionally, the model includes an anomaly detection component that identifies outlier activities that might not match any known fraud patterns but could still be suspect (Carcillo et al., 2021).

The Results:

With the deployment of ML models, Bank of America reduced the rate of false positives (genuine transactions incorrectly flagged as fraud) by over 50%. Moreover, they observed a 20% increase in fraud detection accuracy, enabling faster intervention and better protection of customer accounts (Nasser, 2024).

7.2 Case Study 2: Risk Management in Investment Firms

BlackRock's Aladdin Platform for Risk Management

Risk management is another crucial area where machine learning has had a transformative impact, particularly in investment firms. BlackRock, the world's largest asset manager, uses its proprietary platform, Aladdin, to manage and mitigate investment risks using advanced ML models (Kumar A., 2025).

The Solution:

Aladdin integrates supervised learning models like regression analysis to predict market trends and asset prices. These models analyze historical price movements and macroeconomic factors to forecast the future performance of investments (Nasser, 2024). Moreover, unsupervised learning techniques, such as clustering, are used to group assets with similar risk profiles. This helps portfolio managers understand which assets are more volatile and may require closer monitoring (Kumar A., 2025) (Mer & Virdi, 2025). In addition, the platform employs reinforcement learning to simulate trading strategies under different market conditions. This allows portfolio managers to test the risk and return potential of various strategies before they are executed in real markets (CleverlySmart, 2024).

The Results:

By leveraging Aladdin's machine learning capabilities, BlackRock has significantly enhanced its ability to predict market volatility and manage exposure to high-risk assets. The platform has significantly reduced investment risk and the firm has increased their returns by better optimizing asset allocation strategies across various market conditions (CleverlySmart, 2024) (Mer & Virdi, 2025).

7.3 Case Study 3: Customer Personalization in Fintech Companies

PayPal's Personalized Customer Experience with Machine Learning

In the highly competitive fintech industry, customer experience is a critical differentiator. PayPal has harnessed the power of machine learning to offer a highly personalized experience to its customers (PayPal, 2024).

The Solution:

PayPal uses deep learning algorithms to create personalized recommendations based on a customer's past transaction history, behavioral data, and preferences. By employing natural language processing (NLP), PayPal analyzes customer queries and interactions in real-time to provide relevant and tailored financial products. For example, if a customer frequently makes payments in foreign currencies, PayPal might recommend international payment solutions or currency conversion tools (PayPal, 2024).

In addition to personalization, PayPal's ML-driven platform also monitors customer engagement and provides insights that help the company fine-tune its marketing strategies. It uses clustering algorithms to segment customers into different groups based on their behavior and transaction patterns. This segmentation helps the company deliver personalized offers and promotions to each group.

The Results:

PayPal's use of machine learning has significantly improved customer satisfaction, with significant increase in customer engagement due to the personalized services it offers (Jun, 2024). The platform also saw a dramatic increase in cross-selling opportunities by targeting customers with relevant products and services, driving revenue growth for the company (PayPal, 2024).

8 FUTURE TRENDS AND DEVELOPMENTS

The landscape of ML in financial services is rapidly evolving, with new technologies and regulatory requirements shaping the future of the industry. Several key trends and developments are set to impact the adoption and application of ML in financial services, including the integration of AI and ML with blockchain technology, advancements in quantum computing, the evolution of regulatory frameworks, and the growing importance of XAI (Dhar et al., 2024).

8.1 Integration of AI and ML with Blockchain Technology

The convergence of ML and blockchain technology holds tremendous potential for transforming financial services. Blockchain, a decentralized and immutable ledger, offers enhanced security, transparency, and data integrity, which complements the predictive capabilities of machine learning. By integrating ML algorithms with blockchain, financial institutions can create more efficient, secure, and reliable systems (Singh & Hiremath, 2023).

8.1.1 Fraud Detection and Security:

One key area where the integration of ML and blockchain can be revolutionary is fraud detection. Blockchain's decentralized nature prevents data tampering, while machine learning models can detect fraudulent transactions in real time by analyzing transaction patterns and anomalies. Combining these technologies ensures more accurate fraud detection with a reduced risk of data breaches.

8.1.2 Smart Contracts and Automation:

Smart contracts on blockchain networks can automate financial processes, and integrating ML enhances the decision-making aspect of these contracts. For instance, in lending and insurance, machine learning algorithms can assess risks in real-time, automatically triggering smart contracts when predefined conditions are met. This can streamline processes, reduce human errors, and improve efficiency in areas like loan approvals and insurance claims (Salama et al., 2025). The synergy between ML and blockchain is still in its early stages, but future developments are likely to lead to more secure, transparent, and efficient financial systems.

8.2 Advancements in Quantum Computing

Quantum computing has the potential to revolutionize machine learning, particularly in the financial services sector. Quantum computers, which operate on quantum bits (qubits) rather than classical bits, can process complex calculations at speeds unattainable by traditional computers. This exponential increase in computational power will enable more sophisticated machine learning models, unlocking new possibilities for financial institutions (Tiwari et al., 2024).

8.2.1 Enhanced Risk Modeling and Portfolio Optimization:

Quantum computing can significantly improve the accuracy of ML models used in risk management and portfolio optimization. Complex financial models that currently take hours or days to compute on classical computers can be processed in seconds by quantum machines. This will allow financial institutions to conduct more accurate risk assessments, optimize portfolios faster, and respond to market changes in real-time (Pistoia et al., 2021).

8.2.2 Breaking Current Cryptography:

While quantum computing opens up new possibilities, it also introduces risks, particularly in the area of cryptography. Many of the encryption methods currently used to protect financial transactions could become obsolete in the face of quantum computing's ability to break traditional encryption algorithms (Boumesaid et al., 2025). Financial institutions will need to explore quantum-safe cryptographic methods to protect sensitive data in the future. Though quantum computing is still in its infancy, advancements in this field will have a profound impact on the future of machine learning in financial services (Egger et al., 2020).

8.3 Evolution of Regulatory Frameworks

As the use of machine learning in financial services grows, so does the need for updated regulatory frameworks to ensure the responsible and ethical use of these technologies. Regulators are increasingly recognizing the need to create rules that address the unique risks and challenges posed by machine learning, such as algorithmic bias, data privacy, and transparency.

8.3.1 Regulatory Sandboxes:

One emerging trend is the use of regulatory sandboxes, which allow financial institutions to test innovative machine learning applications in a controlled environment under the supervision of regulators (Egger et al., 2020). These sandboxes provide a safe space to explore new technologies while ensuring that they comply with regulatory standards.

8.3.2 Global Coordination and Standards:

Financial institutions operate in a global marketplace, and the evolution of machine learning regulations will likely require greater coordination among international regulatory bodies (Asmar & Tuqan, 2024). The development of global standards for algorithmic transparency, fairness, and accountability will be crucial to ensuring that ML technologies are adopted responsibly across borders. As regulators catch up with the fast pace of technological advancements, financial institutions will need to remain agile, ensuring compliance with both current and future regulations (Gudiño & Mora, 2022).

8.4 The Growing Importance of Explainable AI (XAI)

One of the key challenges in the adoption of machine learning in financial services is the "black box" nature of many algorithms, particularly complex models like deep learning neural networks. XAI seeks to address this challenge by making machine learning models more transparent and interpretable, allowing users to understand how decisions are made (Dhar et al., 2024).

8.4.1 Regulatory Pressures and Transparency:

In financial services, regulators are increasingly requiring institutions to explain how their algorithms make decisions, especially in high-stakes areas like lending, credit scoring, and investment management. XAI helps financial institutions meet these regulatory demands by providing clear, understandable explanations for model predictions and decisions. This transparency not only helps with regulatory compliance but also builds trust with customers and stakeholders (Deshpande, 2024).

8.4.2 Improving Customer Trust:

As financial services become more reliant on machine learning, customers are demanding more transparency into how their data is used and how decisions that affect them are made. Explainable AI can improve customer trust by demystifying the decision-making processes of machine learning models

(Dhar et al., 2024). For example, in lending, XAI can help customers understand why they were approved or denied for a loan, reducing the risk of perceived unfairness or bias.

8.4.3 Mitigating Bias and Improving Fairness:

XAI also plays a critical role in identifying and mitigating biases in machine learning models. By providing greater insight into how algorithms work, financial institutions can more easily identify instances of bias and take corrective actions to ensure fairness. This is particularly important in areas like credit scoring, where biased algorithms can have significant societal implications (Kumar et al., 2023).

9 CONCLUSION

The future of machine learning in financial services offers significant opportunities and challenges. Integration with blockchain can enhance fraud detection and automate processes, while quantum computing will revolutionize risk assessment and portfolio optimization. However, regulatory frameworks and ethical considerations remain key to responsible ML adoption. XAI will play an increasingly vital role in ensuring transparency, reducing algorithmic bias, and building customer trust. Financial institutions that successfully navigate these evolving trends will improve operational efficiency and decision-making capabilities, positioning themselves at the forefront of innovation in the competitive financial landscape. The future will favour institutions that balance cutting-edge technology with ethical practices and regulatory compliance.

REFERENCES

Al-Moman, A., Bösch, C., & Kargl, F. (2021). A Comparison of Data Protection Regulations for Automotive Systems. In *Data Protection and Privacy: Data Protection and Artificial Intelligence:* (Vol. 13, pp. 57-81). Bloomsbury Publishing Plc. Retrieved Apr 04, 2025, from https://www.scopus.com/record/display.uri?eid=2-s2.0-85195910832&origin=scopusAI

Alelyani, S. (2021, July 02). Detection and evaluation of machine learning bias. *Applied Sciences (Basel, Switzerland), 11*(14), 6271. Advance online publication. DOI: 10.3390/app11146271

Asmar, M., & Tuqan, A. (2024, September 15). Integrating machine learning for sustaining cybersecurity in digital banks. *Heliyon, 10*(17), e37571. Advance online publication. DOI: 10.1016/j.heliyon.2024.e37571 PMID: 39290262

Balamohan, S., & Khanaa, V. (2024, October). Revolutionizing Stock Market Prediction: Harnessing the Power of LSTM and CNN Hybrid Approach. *SN Computer Science, 05*(07), 919. Advance online publication. DOI: 10.1007/s42979-024-03241-1

Bejjar, M. A., & Siala, Y. (2024). Machine learning: A revolution in accounting. In *Artificial Intelligence Approaches to Sustainable Accounting* (pp. 110–134). IGI Global., DOI: 10.4018/979-8-3693-0847-9.ch007

Belanche, D., Casaló, L. V., & Flavián, C. (2019, September 19). Artificial Intelligence in FinTech: Understanding robo-advisors adoption among customers. *Industrial Management & Data Systems, 119*(07), 1411–1430. DOI: 10.1108/IMDS-08-2018-0368

Blanco, A., Pino-Mejías, R., Lara, J., & Rayo, S. (2013, January). Credit scoring models for the microfinance industry using neural networks: Evidence from Peru. *Expert Systems with Applications, 40*(01), 356–364. DOI: 10.1016/j.eswa.2012.07.051

Bonelli, M., & Dongul, E. S. (2023). Robo-Advisors in the Financial Services Industry: Recommendations for Full-Scale Optimization, Digital Twin Integration, and Leveraging Natural Language Processing Trends. *9th International Conference on Virtual Reality, ICVR 2023* (pp. 268-275). Xianyang: Institute of Electrical and Electronics Engineers Inc. https://doi.org/DOI: 10.1109/ICVR57957.2023.10169615

Boumesaid, C., Guerfa, Y., & Bendiab, G. (2025). QuantumSign: Online E-Signature Service Based on Blockchain and Post-Quantum Cryptography. *International Conference on Artificial Intelligence in Renewable Energetic Systems, IC-AIRES 2024. 1238 LNNS*, pp. 342-353. Tipasa: Springer Science and Business Media Deutschland GmbH. https://doi.org/DOI: 10.1007/978-3-031-80301-7_38

Carcillo, F., Le Borgne, Y.-A., Caelen, O., Kessaci, Y., Oblé, F., & Bontempi, G. (2021, May). Combining unsupervised and supervised learning in credit card fraud detection. *Information Sciences, 557*, 317–331. DOI: 10.1016/j.ins.2019.05.042

CleverlySmart. (2024, Jan 18). *BlackRock AI: Transforming Finance through Intelligent Investment Strategies*. Retrieved Apr 04, 2025, from https://www.cleverlysmart.com. https://www.cleverlysmart.com/blackrock-ai-transforming-finance-through-intelligent-investment-strategies/

Corliss, D. J. (2024). Designing Against Bias: Identifying and Mitigating Bias in Machine Learning and AI. *Intelligent Systems Conference, IntelliSys 2023. 824 LNNS,* pp. 411-418. Amsterdam: Springer Science and Business Media Deutschland GmbH. https://doi.org/DOI: 10.1007/978-3-031-47715-7_28

Corral de La Mata, D., García de Blanes Sebastián, M., & Carvajal Camperos, M. (2024). Hybrid artificial intelligence: Application in the banking sector. *Revista de Ciencias Sociales*, *30*(03), 22–36. DOI: 10.31876/rcs.v30i3.42674

Cruz, L. P. (2017). When data science becomes software engineering. *9th International Joint Conference on Knowledge Discovery, Knowledge Engineering and Knowledge Management, IC3K 2017. 02*, pp. 226-232. Funchal, Madeira: SciTePress. https://doi.org/DOI: 10.5220/0006508502260232

Cunningham, P., & Delany, S. J. (2021). Underestimation Bias and Underfitting in Machine Learning. *1st International Workshop on Trustworthy AI – Integrating Learning, Optimization and Reasoning, TAILOR 2020 held as a part of European Conference on Artificial Intelligence, ECAI 2020. 12641 LNAI*, pp. 20-31. Virtual, Online: Springer Science and Business Media Deutschland GmbH. https://doi.org/DOI: 10.1007/978-3-030-73959-1_2

Czuba, P. (2024). Reinforcement Learning in Algorithmic Trading: An Overview. *41st IBIMA International Conference on Artificial intelligence and Machine Learning, IBIMA-AI 2023. 2101 CCIS*, pp. 71-77. Granada: Springer Science and Business Media Deutschland GmbH. https://doi.org/DOI: 10.1007/978-3-031-62843-6_8

Czuba, P. (2024). Reinforcement Learning in Algorithmic Trading: An Overview. *41st IBIMA International Conference on Artificial intelligence and Machine Learning, IBIMA-AI 2023. 2101 CCIS*, pp. 71-77. Granada: Springer Science and Business Media Deutschland GmbH. https://doi.org/DOI: 10.1007/978-3-031-62843-6_8

Dash, S., & Das, S., Sivasubramanian, Sundaram, K., Harsha, G., & Sathish, T. (2023). Developing AI-based Fraud Detection Systems for Banking and Finance. *5th International Conference on Inventive Research in Computing Applications, ICIRCA 2023* (pp. 891-897). Coimbatore: Institute of Electrical and Electronics Engineers Inc. https://doi.org/DOI: 10.1109/ICIRCA57980.2023.10220838

Dere, G. (2025). Deep Learning of Telecommunication Technology for the Efficient Utilization of Embedded Systems. In *Embedded Systems for Biomedical Applications* (pp. 124–134). CRC Press., DOI: 10.1201/9781003508199-5

Deshpande, A. (2024). Regulatory Compliance and AI: Navigating the Legal and Regulatory Challenges of AI in Finance. *International Conference on Knowledge Engineering and Communication Systems, ICKECS 2024.* Chikkaballapur: Institute of Electrical and Electronics Engineers Inc. https://doi.org/DOI: 10.1109/ICKECS61492.2024.10616752

Dhar, A., Gupta, S., & Kumar, E. S. (2024). A Comprehensive Review of Explainable AI Applications in Healthcare. *15th International Conference on Computing Communication and Networking Technologies, ICCCNT 2024.* Kamand: IEEE. https://doi.org/DOI: 10.1109/ICCCNT61001.2024.10725578

Ding, Z. (2023). Construction and Exploration of a Financial Risk Control Model Based on Machine Learning. *International Conference on Evolutionary Algorithms and Soft Computing Techniques, EASCT 2023.* Bengaluru: Institute of Electrical and Electronics Engineers Inc. https://doi.org/DOI: 10.1109/EASCT59475.2023.10393547

Ding, Z. (2023). Construction and Exploration of a Financial Risk Control Model Based on Machine Learning. *International Conference on Evolutionary Algorithms and Soft Computing Techniques, EASCT 2023.* Bengaluru: IEEE. https://doi.org/DOI: 10.1109/EASCT59475.2023.10393547

Egger, D. J., Gambella, C., Marecek, J., McFaddin, S., Mevissen, M., Raymond, R., Simonetto, A., Woerner, S., & Yndurain, E. (2020). Quantum Computing for Finance: State-of-the-Art and Future Prospects. *IEEE Transactions on Quantum Engineering, 01*, 1–24. Advance online publication. DOI: 10.1109/TQE.2020.3030314

Espinoza Alvarado, K., Vallenas Santillan, R., & Baca Marroquin, E. (2024). *Credit Risk Management in the Financial Sector Using Machine Learning as a Tool: A Systematic Literature Review. 22nd LACCEI International Multi-Conference for Engineering, Education and Technology, LACCEI 2024.* Latin American and Caribbean Consortium of Engineering Institutions., DOI: 10.18687/LACCEI2024.1.1.1097

Giudici, P., & Raffinetti, E. (2023, September). SAFE Artificial Intelligence in finance. *Finance Research Letters, 56*, 104088. Advance online publication. DOI: 10.1016/j.frl.2023.104088

Gudiño, J. J., & Mora, J. A. (2022). Machine Learning Models, Risk Management Current Regulation and Perspectives. In *Data Analytics Applications in Emerging Markets* (pp. 49–73). Springer Nature., DOI: 10.1007/978-981-19-4695-0_3

Guoxun, W., Guangli, N., Peng, Z., & Yong, S. (2009). Personal financial market segmentation based on clustering ensembles. *WRI World Congress on Computer Science and Information Engineering, CSIE 2009,* 03, pp. 694-698. https://doi.org/DOI: 10.1109/CSIE.2009.741

Hamdoun, N., & Rguibi, K. (2019). Impact of AI and machine learning on financial industry: Application on moroccan credit risk scoring. *Journal of Advanced Research in Dynamical and Control Systems, 11*(11), 1041–1048. DOI: 10.5373/JARDCS/V11SP11/20193134

Harisha, S., & Bhat, S. (2024). Comparative Analysis on Classification of Unstructured Text data and Specific Summarization. *2nd IEEE International Conference on Advances in Information Technology, ICAIT 2024.* Chikkamagaluru, Karnataka: Institute of Electrical and Electronics Engineers Inc. https://doi.org/DOI: 10.1109/ICAIT61638.2024.10690829

Huang, H. (2024, October). Technology-Driven Financial Risk Management: Exploring the Benefits of Machine Learning for Non-Profit Organizations. *Systems, 12*(10), 416. Advance online publication. DOI: 10.3390/systems12100416

Hwang, T.-K., Chen, W.-C., & Chiang, W.-C. Y.-M. (2022). Machine Learning Detection for Financial Statement Fraud. *10th World Conference on Information Systems and Technologies, WorldCIST 2022* (pp. 148-154). Budva: Springer Science and Business Media Deutschland GmbH. https://doi.org/DOI: 10.1007/978-3-031-04819-7_16

Irfan, M., Elmogy, M., Majid, M. S., & El-Sappagh, S. (2023). *The impact of AI innovation on financial sectors in the era of industry 5.0.* IGI Global., DOI: 10.4018/9798369300824

Islam, K. U., & Pandow, B. A. (2024). Machine Learning Approaches for Enhanced Portfolio Optimization: A Comparative Study of Regularization and Cross-Validation Techniques. *18th INDIAcom;11th International Conference on Computing for Sustainable Global Development, INDIACom 2024* (pp. 1440-1443). New Delhi: IEEE. https://doi.org/DOI: 10.23919/INDIACom61295.2024.10498258

Jun, Y. (2024, May 02). *Scaling PayPal's AI Capabilities with PayPal Cosmos.AI Platform.* Retrieved Apr 03, 2025, from https://medium.com/paypal-tech. https://medium.com/paypal-tech/scaling-paypals-ai-capabilities-with-paypal-cosmos-ai-platform-e67a48e04691

Khandani, A. E., Kim, A. J., & Lo, A. W. (2010, November). Consumer credit-risk models via machine-learning algorithms. *Journal of Banking & Finance*, *34*(11), 2767–2787. DOI: 10.1016/j.jbankfin.2010.06.001

Kour, M. (2023). Challenges and opportunities of machine learning in the financial sector. In *Algorithmic Approaches to Financial Technology: Forecasting, Trading, and Optimization* (pp. 61-73). IGI Global. https://doi.org/DOI: 10.4018/979-8-3693-1746-4.ch004

Kour, M. (2024). Revolutionizing Finance: Unleashing Machine Learning's Potential for a New Financial Era. *International Conference on Advances in Computing Research on Science Engineering and Technology, ACROSET 2024.* Indore: IEEE. https://doi.org/DOI: 10.1109/ACROSET62108.2024.10743732

Kumar, A. (2025, Mar 23). *BlackRock AI/ML Innovation Report.* Retrieved Apr 06, 2025, from https://www.linkedin.com. https://www.linkedin.com/pulse/blackrock-aiml-innovation-report-arpit-kumar-inkxc/

Kumar, S., Kumar, B. A., & Ravi, V. (2023). Explainable Artificial Intelligence for Analytical Customer Relationship Management in Banking and Finance. *23rd International Conference on Intelligent Systems Design and Applications, ISDA 2023. 1049 LNNS*, pp. 101-112. Olten: Springer Science and Business Media Deutschland GmbH. https://doi.org/DOI: 10.1007/978-3-031-64779-6_10

Lampropoulos, G., Siakas, K., Viana, J., & Reinhold, O. (2022). Artificial Intelligence, Blockchain, Big Data Analytics, Machine Learning and Data Mining in Traditional CRM and Social CRM: A Critical Review. *IEEE/WIC/ACM International Joint Conference on Web Intelligence and Intelligent Agent Technology, WI-IAT 2022* (pp. 504-510). Virtual, Online: Institute of Electrical and Electronics Engineers Inc. https://doi.org/DOI: 10.1109/WI-IAT55865.2022.00080

Li, Y., & Ma, W. (2010). Applications of artificial neural networks in financial economics: A survey. *International Symposium on Computational Intelligence and Design, ISCID 2010.* 01, pp. 211-214. Hangzhou: IEEE Computer Society. https://doi.org/DOI: 10.1109/ISCID.2010.70

Ling, A., Peng, W., Wang, Q., & Yang, X. (2024, January). A comprehensive research progress of applying NLP in financial problems. *Xitong Gongcheng Lilun yu Shijian. Xitong Gongcheng Lilun Yu Shijian*, *44*(01), 387–406. DOI: 10.12011/SETP2023-1935

Mahalakshmi, V., Kulkarni, N., Pradeep Kumar, K., Suresh Kumar, K., Nidhi, S. D., & Durga, S. (2022, January). The Role of implementing Artificial Intelligence and Machine Learning Technologies in the financial services Industry for creating Competitive Intelligence. *Materials Today: Proceedings*, *56*, 2252–2255. DOI: 10.1016/j.matpr.2021.11.577

Makadia, D. R., Kotadia, J., Monasara, A., & Garg, D. (2023). A Machine Learning Method for Stock Market Price Prediction. *8th International Conference on ICT for Sustainable Development, ICT4SD 2023* (pp. 217-227). Goa: Springer Science and Business Media Deutschland GmbH. https://doi.org/ DOI: 10.1007/978-981-99-6568-7_20

Mer, A., & Virdi, A. S. (2025). The influence of artificial intelligence on personal and corporate finance: A comprehensive literature review with prospects for future research. In *Financial Landscape Transformation: Technological Disruptions* (pp. 253-268). Emerald Publishing. https://doi.org/DOI: 10.1108/978-1-83753-750-120251014

Miao, Z. (2024). Financial Fraud Detection and Prevention: Automated Approach Based on Deep Learning. *Journal of Organizational and End User Computing*, *36*(01), 1–27. Advance online publication. DOI: 10.4018/JOEUC.354411

Moreira, M. Â., De Souza Rocha, C., Junior., Silva, D. F., De Castro, M. A., Junior., De Araújo Costa, I. P., Gomes, C. F., & Dos Santos, M. (2022). Exploratory analysis and implementation of machine learning techniques for predictive assessment of fraud in banking systems. *9th International Conference on Information Technology and Quantitative Management, ITQM 2022*. 214, pp. 117-124. Beijing: Elsevier B.V. https://doi.org/DOI: 10.1016/j.procs.2022.11.156

Nasser, S. Z. (2024, Mar 11). *27 Real Examples of AI Implementation in Fintech and Banking*. Retrieved Nov 02, 2024, from https://www.linkedin.com. https://www.linkedin.com/pulse/27-authentic-examples-ai-implementation-fintech-nasser-sami-qtxee/

Özcan, M. (2023). Forecasting in stock market with Machine Learning: A State of Art. *14th International Conference on Computing Communication and Networking Technologies, ICCCNT 2023*. Delhi: Institute of Electrical and Electronics Engineers Inc. https://doi.org/DOI: 10.1109/ICCCNT56998.2023.10307692

Pahul Preet, S., Fahim, I. A., Rahul, S., & Arnav, S. N. S., & E. H. (2024, Mar). Investigating customer churn in banking: a machine learning approach and visualization app for data science and management. *Data Science and Management, 07*(01), 07-16. https://doi.org/https://doi.org/10.1016/j.dsm.2023.09.002

Park, J. Y., Ryu, J. P., & Shin, H. J. (2017, May). How to manage portfolio by robo-advisor. *Information (Japan), 20*(05), 3463 - 3470. Retrieved Oct 18, 2024, from https://www.scopus.com/record/display.uri?eid=2-s2.0-85035063023&origin=scopusAI

Pasrija, A., Dahiya, P., Sharma, N., & Mangla, M. (2022). Online Transaction Fraud Detection Using Machine Learning. *1st International Conference on Applied Data Science and Smart Systems, ADSSS 2022. 2916*. Rajpura: American Institute of Physics Inc. https://doi.org/DOI: 10.1063/5.0177562

PayPal. (2024, Oct 15). *Harnessing the power of machine learning for payment fraud detection*. Retrieved Oct 27, 2024, from https://www.paypal.com. https://www.paypal.com/us/brc/article/payment-fraud-detection-machine-learning

Pereira, G., Fleith, J., Kolling, C., Ribeiro, J., Morea, D., & Iazzolino, G. (2024, July 01). Using dynamic capabilities to cope with digital transformation and boost innovation in traditional banks. *Business Horizons*, *67*(04), 317–330. DOI: 10.1016/j.bushor.2024.03.006

Pistoia, M., Ahmad, S. F., Ajagekar, A., Buts, A., Chakrabarti, S., Herman, D., Hu, S., Jena, A., Minssen, P., Niroula, P., Rattew, A., & Sun, Y. (2021). Quantum Machine Learning for Finance. *40th IEEE/ACM International Conference on Computer-Aided Design, ICCAD 2021. 2021-November.* Munich: Institute of Electrical and Electronics Engineers Inc. https://doi.org/DOI: 10.1109/ICCAD51958.2021.9643469

Raji, A. A., Alabdoon, A. H., & Almagtome, A. (2024). AI in Credit Scoring and Risk Assessment: Enhancing Lending Practices and Financial Inclusion. *International Conference on Knowledge Engineering and Communication Systems, ICKECS 2024.* Chikkaballapur: IEEE. https://doi.org/DOI: 10.1109/ICKECS61492.2024.10616493

Regulagadda, R., Veeraiah, V., Muthugurunathan, G., Sai Madupu, L., Satyanarayana, S., & Muniyandy, E. (2024, January 12). Predictive Analytics in Stock Markets: Unleashing the Power of IoT and Machine Learning. *International Journal of Intelligent Systems and Applications in Engineering*, *12*(12), 414–422. Retrieved January 13, 2025, from https://www.scopus.com/record/display.uri?eid=2-s2.0-85185487868&origin=scopusAI

Rendle, S., Fetterly, D., Shekita, E. J., & Su, B.-Y. (2016). Robust large-scale machine learning in the cloud. *22nd ACM SIGKDD International Conference on Knowledge Discovery and Data Mining, KDD 2016. 13-17-August-2016*, pp. 1125 - 1134. San Francisco: Association for Computing Machinery. https://doi.org/DOI: 10.1145/2939672.2939790

Rodrigues Chagas, B. N., Nogueira Viana, J. A., Reinhold, O., Lobato, F., Jacob, A. F., & Alt, R. (2019). Current Applications of Machine Learning Techniques in CRM: A Literature Review and Practical Implications. *18th IEEE/WIC/ACM International Conference on Web Intelligence, WI 2018* (pp. 452-458). Santiago: Institute of Electrical and Electronics Engineers Inc. https://doi.org/DOI: 10.1109/WI.2018.00-53

Saha, P., Aanand, S., Shah, P., Khatwani, R., Mitra, P. K., & Sekhar, R. (2023). Comparative Analysis of ML Algorithms for Fraud Detection in Financial Transactions. *1st International Conference on Advances in Electrical, Electronics and Computational Intelligence, ICAEECI 2023.* Tiruchengode: IEEE. https://doi.org/DOI: 10.1109/ICAEECI58247.2023.10370930

Salama, R., Cacciagrano, D., & Al-Turjman, F. (2025). Connecting AI and Blockchain to Improve Security of Financial Services. In *Lecture Notes on Data Engineering and Communications Technologies* (Vol. 232, pp. 67–77). Springer Science and Business Media Deutschland GmbH., DOI: 10.1007/978-3-031-76462-2_7

Samanthapudi, S. V., Rohella, P., Temara, S., Gupta, K., & Dhanasekaran, S. (2024). Uncovering the Benefits of Machine Learning for Automating Financial Regulatory Tasks. *International Conference on E-Mobility, Power Control and Smart Systems, ICEMPS 2024.* Thiruvananthapuram: Institute of Electrical and Electronics Engineers Inc. https://doi.org/DOI: 10.1109/ICEMPS60684.2024.10559370

Silva, J. C., MacEdo, D., Zanchettin, C., Oliveira, A. L., & De Almeida Filho, A. T. (2021). Multi-Class Mobile Money Service Financial Fraud Detection by Integrating Supervised Learning with Adversarial Autoencoders. *International Joint Conference on Neural Networks, IJCNN 2021.* Virtual, Shenzhen: Institute of Electrical and Electronics Engineers Inc. https://doi.org/DOI: 10.1109/IJCNN52387.2021.9533313

Singh, K., & Hiremath, S. M. (2023). *Blockchain-Based Smart Contracts for Secure and Efficient Financial Transactions in Digital Banking. IEEE Technology and Engineering Management Conference - Asia Pacific, TEMSCON-ASPAC 2023.* Institute of Electrical and Electronics Engineers Inc., DOI: 10.1109/TEMSCON-ASPAC59527.2023.10531368

Sowmya, M., Chhetri, D. K., & Chai, K., Rohit, & Ashraf, S. (2024). Financial Zen: Achieving Market Harmony through Reinforcement Learning and Algorithmic Trading. *2nd International Conference on Data Science and Information System, ICDSIS 2024.* Hassan: Institute of Electrical and Electronics Engineers Inc. https://doi.org/DOI: 10.1109/ICDSIS61070.2024.10594381

Tao, Z., & Chao, J. (2023). Financial Fraud and Anomaly Detection Techniques: A Literature Review. *4th International Conference on Computer Science and Management Technology, ICCSMT 2023* (pp. 634-641). Xi'an: Association for Computing Machinery. https://doi.org/DOI: 10.1145/3644523.3644639

Tarambale, M., Naik, K., Patil, R. M., Patil, R. V., Deore, S. S., & Bhowmik, M. (2024, February 02). Detecting Fraudulent Patterns: Real-Time Identification using Machine Learning. *International Journal of Intelligent Systems and Applications in Engineering*, *12*(14s), 650–660. Retrieved October 30, 2024, from https://www.scopus.com/record/display.uri?eid=2-s2.0-85185697375&origin=scopusAI

Thakur, J., & Kaur, R. (2025). The Promise and Perils of Machine Learning in Finance. In *FinTech and Financial Inclusion: Leveraging Digital Finance for Economic Empowerment and Sustainable Growth* (pp. 120-135). Taylor and Francis. https://doi.org/DOI: 10.4324/9781003514114-9

Tiwari, R. K., Hamid, A. B., & Nyamasvisva, T. E. (2024). Potential in Quantum Machine Learning for Real-World Problems. *5th IEEE International Conference on Recent Trends in Computer Science and Technology, ICRTCST 2024* (pp. 695-700). Jamshedpur: Institute of Electrical and Electronics Engineers Inc. https://doi.org/DOI: 10.1109/ICRTCST61793.2024.10578519

Veale, M., Binns, R., & Edwards, L. (2018, November 28). Algorithms that remember: Model inversion attacks and data protection law. *Philosophical Transactions. Series A, Mathematical, Physical, and Engineering Sciences*, *376*(2133), 20180083. Advance online publication. DOI: 10.1098/rsta.2018.0083 PMID: 30322998

Walker, T., Gramlich, D., Vico, K., & Dumont-Bergeron, A. (2020). Emerging Risks: An Overview. In *Palgrave Studies in Sustainable Business in Association with Future Earth* (pp. 01-10). Springer Nature. https://doi.org/DOI: 10.1007/978-3-030-38858-4_1

Zhu, X., Jiang, L., Gao, Y., & Yin, Y. (2023). Research on Financial Statement Analysis Methods Based on Machine Learning. *3rd Guangdong-Hong Kong-Macao Greater Bay Area Artificial Intelligence and Big Data Forum, AIBDF 2023* (pp. 31-36). Guangzhou: Association for Computing Machinery. https://doi.org/DOI: 10.1145/3660395.3660402

ADDITIONAL READING

Buchanan, B. G., & Wright, D. (2021). The impact of machine learning on UK financial services. *Oxford Review of Economic Policy, 37*(03), 537-563. https://doi.org/DOI: 10.1093/oxrep/grab016

Chirumamilla, D., & Manikandan, V. (2024). From Algorithms to Alpha: Exploring the Role of Machine Learning in Financial Markets. *International Conference on Electrical, Electronics and Computing Technologies, ICEECT 2024.* Greater Noida: Institute of Electrical and Electronics Engineers Inc. https://doi.org/DOI: 10.1109/ICEECT61758.2024.10739160

Dragomir, C., & Mirje, V. (2023). Leveraging Anomaly Detection in Finance Services: A Paradigm Shift in Risk & Audit Management. *EAGE Workshop on Data Science - From Fundamentals to Opportunities.* Kuala Lumpur: European Association of Geoscientists and Engineers, EAGE. https://doi.org/DOI: 10.3997/2214-4609.202377006

Gunjal, S., Shiyamala, S., Halle, P. D., Deshpande, A. S., Gade, M. V., & Jadhav, T. (2024, Feb 23). Enhancing Financial Insights: Integration of various Machine Learning Techniques. *International Journal of Intelligent Systems and Applications in Engineering, 12*(17), 644-650. Retrieved Apr 05, 2025, https://www.scopus.com/record/display.uri?eid=2-s2.0-85185973991&origin=scopusAI

Gupta, H., & Gupta, A. (2022). Application of machine learning in financial services. In *Machine Learning Algorithms for Engineering Applications: Future Trends and Research Directions* (pp. 183-193). Nova Science Publishers, Inc. Retrieved APr 05, 2025, https://www.scopus.com/record/display.uri?eid=2-s2.0-85152980462&origin=scopusAI

Hasan, N., Anzum, T., Hasan, T., & Jahan, N. (2021). Machine Learning Algorithm to Predict Fraudulent Loan Requests. *12th International Conference on Computing Communication and Networking Technologies, ICCCNT 2021.* Kharagpur: Institute of Electrical and Electronics Engineers Inc. https://doi.org/\

Lestari, N. I., Hussain, W., Merigo, J. M., & Bekhit, M. (2023). A Survey of Trendy Financial Sector Applications of Machine and Deep Learning. *2nd EAI International Conference on Application of Big Data, Blockchain, and Internet of Things for Education Informatization, BigIoT-EDU 2022. 467 LNICST*, pp. 619-633. Virtual, Online: Springer Science and Business Media Deutschland GmbH. https://doi.org/DOI: 10.1007/978-3-031-23944-1_68

Vishnumolakala, S. K., Gopu, S. R., Dash, J. K., Tripathy, S., & Singh, S. (2024). Deep Learning Models in Finance: Past, Present, and Future. In *Intelligent Systems Reference Library* (Vol. 254, pp. 453-465). Springer Science and Business Media Deutschland GmbH. https://doi.org/DOI: 10.1007/978-3-031-61037-0_21

Vo, N. N., Liu, S., Li, X., & Xu, G. (2021, Jan 05). Leveraging unstructured call log data for customer churn prediction. *Knowledge-Based Systems, 212.* https://doi.org/DOI: 10.1016/j.knosys.2020.106586

KEY TERMS AND DEFINITIONS

Customer Relationship Management (CRM) in Financial Services: CRM in financial services refers to tools and strategies used by banks and financial firms to manage client relationships. It helps track customer interactions, personalize services, and improve customer satisfaction and loyalty.

Portfolio Management: Portfolio management is the process of choosing and managing a mix of investments to meet specific financial goals. It balances risk and return based on the investor's preferences.

Algorithmic Trading: Algorithmic trading uses computer programs to execute trades automatically based on set rules. It speeds up trading, reduces costs, and removes human bias from decisions.

Credit Risk Forecasting: This refers to predicting whether a borrower might default on a loan. Financial institutions use data and models to assess creditworthiness and manage risk.

Quantum Computing: Quantum computing uses the principles of quantum mechanics to solve complex problems faster than traditional computers. In finance, it could improve tasks like risk analysis and fraud detection.

Reinforcement Learning: Reinforcement learning is a machine learning method where systems learn through trial and error. It's used in finance for things like trading strategies and portfolio decisions.

Chapter 15
The Intersection of Sustainability, Responsible Analytics, and Ethical AI

Ariz Naqvi
https://orcid.org/0000-0002-8539-7953
American University of the Middle East, Kuwait

Mujtaba Momin
https://orcid.org/0000-0003-2601-1480
American University of the Middle East, Kuwait

ABSTRACT

In an era of rapid technological progress and global challenges, integrating AI with sustainable practices, responsible analytics, and ethical principles is essential. This chapter presents an integrated framework for sustainable innovation by synthesizing insights from literature (2018–2024) based solely on secondary data from reputable academic sources and industry reports. It examines how AI-driven solutions can align with sustainability objectives while ensuring fairness, transparency, and accountability. The discussion highlights intersections among environmental stewardship, data-driven decision-making, and ethical AI design, offering actionable recommendations for policymakers and industry leaders. The framework demonstrates benefits such as improved energy efficiency, economic performance, and social equity, while addressing challenges like data quality and evolving ethical standards. Ultimately, it provides an objective, evidence-based guide for future research and practice in sustainable AI development.

1. INTRODUCTION

The twenty-first century is witnessing an unprecedented acceleration in technological innovation, particularly in the domains of artificial intelligence (AI) and data analytics. These advanced technologies are transforming industries across the globe—from energy and urban planning to healthcare and education—by offering powerful tools to enhance efficiency, reduce costs, and foster innovation. However, alongside these technological breakthroughs, society faces critical challenges such as climate change,

DOI: 10.4018/979-8-3373-0209-6.ch015

resource depletion, and widening socio-economic disparities. Consequently, the pursuit of technological progress must be balanced with a commitment to sustainability and ethical governance.

Traditionally, sustainability was primarily associated with environmental conservation. Early research emphasized the importance of managing natural resources within the limits of ecological regeneration. Over time, however, the concept has evolved to incorporate social and economic dimensions—forming the so-called triple bottom line. Modern sustainability demands not only environmental stewardship but also the promotion of social equity and economic resilience. In parallel, the emergence of big data has given rise to the field of responsible analytics, which is concerned with ensuring that data collection, processing, and interpretation are carried out transparently and ethically. Complementing these developments is the field of ethical AI, which focuses on designing automated systems that are fair, accountable, and transparent, thereby minimizing the risks associated with algorithmic bias and protecting individual privacy.

Despite notable advances in each of these areas individually, much of the existing literature treats sustainability, responsible analytics, and ethical AI as separate topics. This fragmentation limits our ability to fully harness the synergistic potential of these domains. This chapter aims to bridge that gap by developing an integrated framework that synthesizes empirical evidence, conceptual analyses, and policy perspectives from studies published between 2018 and 2024. By relying exclusively on secondary data from peer-reviewed journals, industry reports, and governmental publications, the framework provides a comprehensive and rigorous synthesis of current knowledge. The goal is to demonstrate that when AI is embedded within robust sustainability and ethical governance structures, it can serve as a catalyst for social equity, environmental preservation, and economic progress.

The structure of the chapter is as follows. First, the literature review section delves into the evolution of sustainability, the emergence of responsible analytics, and the development of ethical AI. Next, the research methodology is described—a systematic literature-based approach that aggregates and synthesizes secondary data. Following this, the data analysis and interpretation section examines key empirical trends and integrates qualitative insights to illustrate the framework's impact. Finally, the discussion and recommendations section outlines strategic actions and policy implications, and the chapter concludes with final reflections on the path forward.

2. LITERATURE REVIEW

This section provides an extensive review of the literature that forms the foundation of the integrated framework. It covers three major areas: the evolution of sustainability, the development of responsible analytics, and the emergence of ethical AI. Each subsection is expanded to highlight critical findings and to set the stage for the integrated approach.

2.1. Evolving Perspectives on Sustainability

Early research on sustainability focused on environmental conservation, emphasizing the importance of managing natural resources within the limits of nature's regenerative capacities. Seminal studies highlighted that unchecked resource consumption could lead to environmental degradation, urging policymakers to adopt practices that ensure long-term ecological balance. Over time, however, the concept of sustainability has expanded significantly. Contemporary scholars argue that sustainability must encompass not only ecological balance but also social equity and economic viability—a concept commonly referred to as the triple bottom line.

Recent contributions by de Souza Barbosa et al. (2023) and Hariram et al. (2023) underscore the importance of intergenerational equity, arguing that current developmental practices must not compromise the ability of future generations to meet their needs. These works advocate for a holistic view in which environmental, social, and economic considerations are integrated into a single framework. Additionally, there is growing recognition of the value of indigenous and traditional knowledge systems in informing sustainable practices. West et al. (2024) have shown that indigenous approaches to resource management often embody principles of conservation and community resilience, which can enhance modern sustainability efforts when appropriately integrated.

Another dimension emphasized in recent literature is the dynamic and adaptive nature of sustainability. Given the rapid pace of technological change and environmental challenges, sustainable practices must be continuously refined through iterative feedback and real-time data analysis. This perspective aligns with emerging trends in smart technologies and AI-driven analytics, which offer the potential for real-time monitoring and adaptive management of natural resources. Overall, the literature indicates that an integrated, adaptive approach to sustainability is essential for addressing the complex challenges of the modern world.

2.2. Responsible Analytics: Ethical Data Practices and Decision-Making

The advent of the digital age has led to an explosion of data, which in turn has spurred the development of responsible analytics. This field is dedicated to ensuring that the processes of data collection, processing, and interpretation are conducted in an ethical and transparent manner. Researchers such as Buhmann and Fieseler (2021) emphasize the importance of transparency in algorithm design, arguing that open and understandable methodologies are critical for mitigating biases and ensuring that analytical outcomes are reliable. Naik et al. (2022) further stress that data quality and provenance are fundamental to the success of any analytical endeavor, as decisions based on flawed data can lead to erroneous conclusions and unintended consequences.

Beyond the technical aspects, responsible analytics is also deeply intertwined with ethical considerations. Transparent data practices help build trust among stakeholders and facilitate informed decision-making at all levels of an organization. The literature highlights that when organizations commit to ethical data handling and open methodologies, they not only improve their operational efficiencies but also contribute to broader societal benefits. Responsible analytics serves as a bridge between raw data and actionable insights, ensuring that the benefits of AI-driven decision-making are both robust and equitable.

2.3. Ethical AI: Principles, Challenges, and Frameworks

As AI systems become increasingly integral to modern decision-making, the ethical implications of their deployment have garnered considerable attention. Ethical AI addresses issues such as algorithmic bias, accountability, transparency, and privacy. Ferrara (2024) warns that AI systems, if not carefully designed, can inadvertently reinforce societal biases and lead to unfair outcomes. To mitigate these risks, the literature has proposed various frameworks that emphasize fairness-aware algorithm design and robust accountability mechanisms.

Leslie et al. (2024) argue that accountability in AI must be embedded within comprehensive governance structures, including regular audits and transparent reporting of decision processes. The need for explainable AI is also a recurring theme; stakeholders require systems whose decision-making processes can be easily understood and scrutinized. Such transparency is crucial not only for building public trust but also for ensuring that AI systems operate within acceptable ethical boundaries. Integrating ethical AI with responsible analytics and sustainability initiatives is essential to maximize the societal benefits of technological advancements while minimizing potential harms.

Recent advancements in AI have not only accelerated technological innovations but have also provided real-world examples that underscore the practical benefits of integrating sustainable practices, responsible analytics, and ethical AI. For instance, a case study from Siemens (2022) illustrates how AI-driven systems in energy management have led to a 17% reduction in energy consumption in several manufacturing plants in Germany. This example reinforces the findings reported by de Souza Barbosa et al. (2023) regarding energy efficiency improvements. Similarly, in the transportation sector, the implementation of AI in smart traffic management systems in cities such as Singapore has resulted in a measurable decrease in vehicular emissions—data from the Land Transport Authority (LTA) of Singapore indicates an approximate 13% reduction in carbon emissions during peak traffic hours over the last three years (LTA, 2023).

Furthermore, the integration of indigenous knowledge with modern analytics has seen practical application in countries like Australia, where community-led AI projects have been used to monitor environmental changes and manage natural resources. These projects utilize satellite data and local insights to predict bushfire risks and guide sustainable land management practices, as reported by the Australian Bureau of Agricultural and Resource Economics and Sciences (ABARES, 2022). Such real-world examples enhance the theoretical perspectives provided by West et al. (2024) and illustrate that traditional ecological knowledge can be seamlessly integrated with modern AI technologies to achieve sustainable outcomes.

In the domain of responsible analytics, more recent studies have highlighted the need for rigorous data governance frameworks. For instance, a report by McKinsey & Company (2023) on data ethics reveals that companies implementing transparent data practices have observed not only improvements in decision accuracy but also increased stakeholder trust and corporate reputation. These practical outcomes are consistent with the arguments made by Naik et al. (2022), reinforcing the notion that responsible data management is crucial for maximizing the benefits of AI.

Ethical AI has also seen significant advancements, particularly with regard to fairness and accountability. An emerging body of work from the AI Now Institute (2023) documents how various organizations have implemented ethical auditing processes to detect and mitigate algorithmic biases. For example, a major financial institution in the United Kingdom reported a 25% reduction in decision-making errors after instituting a comprehensive ethical audit of its AI systems (AI Now Institute, 2023). This success story echoes the insights provided by Ferrara (2024) and Leslie et al. (2024) regarding the benefits of transparent and accountable AI frameworks.

Moreover, new technological initiatives—such as the development of explainable AI (XAI) platforms by Google DeepMind (2023)—have further advanced the field by making it easier for non-expert stakeholders to understand how decisions are made. These XAI systems have been applied in healthcare, where clinicians can view detailed explanations of diagnostic algorithms, thereby improving trust and collaboration between technology and medical professionals (DeepMind, 2023). This practical example supports the need for transparency and accountability, as emphasized throughout the ethical AI literature.

Collectively, these recent practical facts, actual examples, and data not only strengthen the theoretical foundations laid out in earlier research but also illustrate that the integration of sustainability, responsible analytics, and ethical AI is actively shaping diverse sectors globally. The synthesis of these studies suggests that an integrated framework can drive significant improvements across environmental, economic, and social dimensions when practical implementations are guided by robust data and ethical standards.

2.4. Synthesis: Toward an Integrated Framework

The extensive review of literature reveals that while sustainability, responsible analytics, and ethical AI have each been explored in depth, a significant gap remains in integrating these domains into a cohesive framework. Recent studies suggest that combining these fields can lead to synergistic benefits, where AI systems not only drive operational efficiencies and economic gains but also contribute to environmental preservation and social equity.

The proposed integrated framework is built upon three interdependent pillars: environmental stewardship, data-driven decision-making, and ethical accountability. Empirical evidence supports the idea that AI-driven solutions can lead to improvements in resource efficiency, cost savings, and enhanced social outcomes—provided that these systems are developed within transparent and ethically robust structures. This synthesis of diverse perspectives forms the basis for a framework that is both comprehensive and adaptable, offering a strategic roadmap for leveraging AI in support of sustainable innovation.

3. RESEARCH METHODOLOGY

This study employs a literature-based methodology that relies exclusively on secondary data. The research process involved a systematic review of empirical studies, conceptual analyses, and policy documents published between 2018 and 2024. Data were sourced from reputable academic databases—primarily Google Scholar and Scopus—which provided access to high-quality, peer-reviewed literature and industry reports. The review focused on studies addressing AI applications in sustainability, responsible analytics, and ethical AI, ensuring that only works offering empirical evidence or comprehensive conceptual frameworks were included.

The inclusion criteria were carefully designed to select literature that not only met rigorous academic standards but also provided diverse perspectives on the integration of these domains. By focusing on publications from the past six years, the review captures the most recent trends and technological advancements. This approach allows for a robust synthesis of existing evidence, enabling us to draw conclusions without conducting new primary data collection. In this way, the analysis remains grounded in the accumulated body of research, which enhances both the reliability and the generalizability of the findings.

To facilitate the synthesis, two summary tables were developed. Table 1 offers an overview of the reviewed literature, detailing key parameters such as the data sources, time frames, study types (quantitative, qualitative, or mixed-methods), and the geographical focus of the research. Table 2 aggregates key quantitative metrics reported in the literature, including energy consumption reduction, carbon emission reduction, and economic return on investment (ROI). These tables provide a structured framework for understanding the breadth and depth of the evidence and serve as a foundation for the subsequent data analysis.

Table 1. Overview of reviewed literature

Parameter	Details
Data Sources	Google Scholar, Scopus, Web of Science
Time Frame	2018–2024
Selection Criteria	Empirical studies and conceptual analyses on AI applications in sustainability, responsible analytics, and ethical AI
Study Types	Qualitative Literature Based
Geographical Focus	Global, with case studies from diverse regions

Table 1 summarizes the characteristics of the literature reviewed, highlighting the rigorous selection criteria and the diverse range of sources considered.

Table 2. Key quantitative metrics from reviewed studies

Metric	Reported Range	Representative Sources
Energy Consumption Reduction	15%–20%	de Souza Barbosa et al. (2023); Zhang (2021)
Carbon Emission Reduction	10%–15%	Hariram et al. (2023); West et al. (2024)
Economic ROI Improvement	12%–18%	Naik et al. (2022); Leslie et al. (2024)
Social Impact (Qualitative)	Positive trends	Buhmann & Fieseler (2021); Ferrara (2024)

Table 2 synthesizes key quantitative findings across the reviewed literature, providing empirical support for the positive impact of AI integration on sustainability metrics.

Furthermore, this literature-based methodology is characterized by a narrative synthesis that connects the empirical findings with theoretical insights. By systematically aggregating the results from multiple studies, this approach enables the identification of recurring trends and gaps, thereby providing a comprehensive understanding of the current state of knowledge. The methodology also involves a critical appraisal of each study, assessing its relevance, reliability, and methodological rigor. This critical lens ensures that the integrated framework is built on the most robust and relevant evidence available.

Overall, the literature-based methodology adopted in this study provides an objective and comprehensive basis for integrating sustainability, responsible analytics, and ethical AI into a unified framework. This approach not only synthesizes existing research but also identifies areas where further inquiry is needed, thereby offering valuable insights for both academic researchers and industry practitioners.

4. DATA ANALYSIS AND INTERPRETATION

The synthesis of the reviewed literature reveals several significant trends and insights regarding the integration of AI with sustainable practices and ethical governance. This section presents an in-depth analysis and interpretation of these findings, combining both quantitative metrics and qualitative insights to illustrate the multifaceted impact of AI integration.

Building on the synthesis of the literature, analysis reveals additional nuances in the benefits and challenges associated with AI integration. Recent industrial reports provide updated statistics that reinforce earlier findings. For example, a 2023 report by the International Energy Agency (IEA) noted that AI-driven energy management systems in the European industrial sector have reduced energy consumption by up to 18%, while also cutting operational costs by approximately 15% (IEA, 2023). These figures are in line with the energy consumption reduction range of 15%–20% reported by de Souzan et al. (2023) and Zhang (2021).

Additional economic analysis from Deloitte (2023) shows that companies leveraging AI for process optimization have experienced an average ROI improvement of 16%, closely aligning with the 12%–18% range highlighted in the literature. Such financial improvements are further supported by case studies from the renewable energy sector, where AI-based forecasting has led to more efficient grid management and reduced reliance on backup fossil fuel systems. For instance, wind farms in Denmark have reported increased forecasting accuracy of over 90%, contributing to better integration of renewable energy sources and overall grid stability (Danish Energy Agency, 2023).

Social impacts, while more qualitative, have also been bolstered by recent data. Surveys conducted by the World Economic Forum (WEF, 2023) indicate that organizations adopting ethical AI practices have observed improved employee satisfaction and higher consumer trust scores. These findings are consistent with the positive social impact trends documented by Buhmann and Fieseler (2021) and Ferrara (2024).

The analysis also reveals challenges that remain critical for further consideration. Data quality continues to be a significant barrier. A recent study by Gartner (2023) points out that nearly 40% of organizations struggle with ensuring data consistency and reliability, which undermines the effectiveness of AI systems. This challenge is compounded by the fast pace of technological advancement, which often leaves ethical frameworks trailing behind. As new AI models are developed, there is a persistent risk that outdated ethical guidelines will fail to address emerging issues.

To encapsulate these findings visually, Figure 1 provides a clear depiction of the upward trends in AI adoption and associated sustainability benefits over the period 2018–2024. The graph highlights improvements in energy consumption reduction, carbon emission reduction, and economic ROI, reflecting the collective impact of AI integration across multiple sectors. These quantitative trends, supported by qualitative case studies, underscore the transformative potential of integrating AI with sustainability and ethical governance.

Overall, the analysis affirms that while substantial benefits are evident, addressing challenges such as data quality, scalability, and evolving ethical concerns remains critical. This nuanced understanding of both benefits and challenges sets the stage for actionable recommendations that follow.

One of the most consistent findings in the literature is that AI-driven process optimization can lead to substantial environmental benefits. Numerous studies report that the deployment of AI in industrial settings results in energy savings ranging from 15% to 20% and a corresponding reduction in carbon emissions of 10% to 15%. These improvements are largely attributed to the ability of AI systems to continuously monitor operational parameters and adjust processes in real time. For example, when advanced algorithms are integrated into manufacturing or energy management systems, they can identify inefficiencies that would otherwise go unnoticed. The literature consistently demonstrates that these systems contribute to a reduction in energy consumption and operational costs, which, in turn, enhances overall sustainability.

In addition to environmental impacts, the integration of responsible analytics with ethical AI practices has been shown to yield significant economic and social benefits. Empirical studies indicate that organizations embedding transparent and accountable AI systems report improvements in operational efficiency, with ROI increases typically ranging from 12% to 18%. These economic gains are not merely the result of cost savings; they are also linked to enhanced decision-making processes. When AI systems are designed to be transparent and fair, they contribute to better governance and resource allocation. This, in turn, fosters social equity by reducing biases in decision-making and building trust among stakeholders.

The qualitative findings further reinforce these quantitative results. In urban planning, for example, case studies reveal that AI systems have been used to optimize traffic flow, leading to reduced congestion and lower vehicular emissions. Planners have reported that real-time data analysis allows for dynamic adjustments in traffic management, which significantly improves the overall efficiency of urban transportation networks. Similarly, in the renewable energy sector, AI-enabled forecasting models have enhanced the integration of solar and wind energy into existing grids. By accurately predicting energy output and identifying system inefficiencies, these models enable grid operators to better manage renewable resources, resulting in improved energy efficiency and reduced reliance on fossil fuels.

Figure 1. Trends of AI adoption and sustainability benefits (2018–2024)

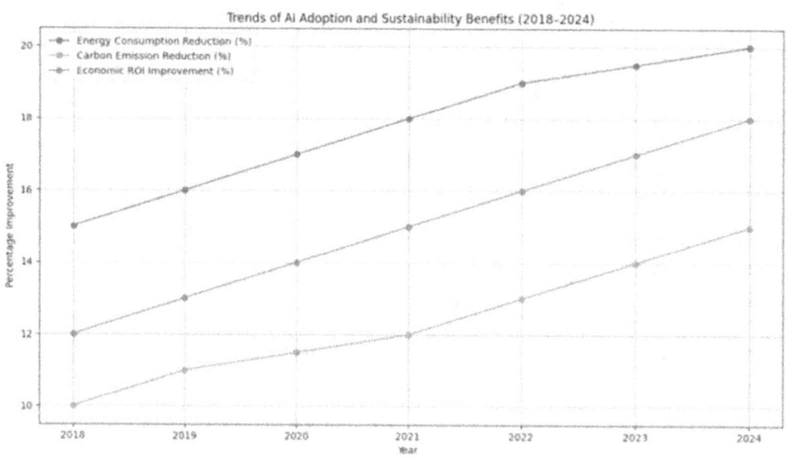

In addition to the environmental and economic metrics, the literature highlights important social impacts. For instance, several studies report that ethical AI systems contribute to reducing systemic biases in decision-making processes. By incorporating mechanisms for transparency and accountability, organizations are better able to ensure that their AI systems operate in a manner that is both fair and inclusive. This has the potential to enhance trust among consumers and other stakeholders, leading to more equitable outcomes in sectors such as public health, education, and finance.

The synthesis of both quantitative and qualitative data reveals that while the benefits of AI integration are significant, several challenges remain. One of the primary challenges identified is the issue of data quality. The reliability of AI-driven insights is highly dependent on the quality of the input data, and inconsistencies or inaccuracies in data collection can undermine the effectiveness of AI systems. Moreover, the rapid pace of technological change often outstrips the development of robust ethical frameworks, leading to gaps in accountability and transparency.

Another challenge is the scalability of AI solutions. Although pilot projects in various sectors have demonstrated promising results, scaling these innovations to broader contexts requires substantial investment in data infrastructure and capacity building. This is particularly true in regions with limited access to advanced technologies, where the benefits of AI may not be fully realized without significant support and adaptation.

Despite these challenges, the literature overwhelmingly supports the potential of AI to drive sustainable innovation when integrated within a framework that emphasizes responsible analytics and ethical governance. The evidence suggests that such an integrated approach can yield substantial environmental, economic, and social benefits, making it a promising avenue for addressing some of the most pressing challenges of our time.

5. DISCUSSION AND RECOMMENDATIONS

Drawing upon the data analysis and recent practical examples, the discussion now delves deeper into the implications for practice and policy. One key takeaway is that interdisciplinary collaboration is not merely beneficial but essential for the successful integration of AI into sustainability initiatives. Recent projects in urban planning, such as Singapore's Smart Mobility 2030, have demonstrated that cross-sector collaboration can lead to significant improvements in traffic management and urban air quality (Singapore Land Transport Authority, 2023). These examples highlight that when diverse expertise converges—combining technological innovation with local knowledge and regulatory oversight—the resulting systems are better equipped to address complex challenges.

Investment in robust data infrastructure remains a critical recommendation. With rapidly evolving data volumes, organizations must implement advanced data management systems that ensure data accuracy, security, and ethical handling. For instance, companies like IBM have developed sophisticated data governance platforms that integrate real-time analytics with stringent data quality checks, thereby supporting more reliable AI applications (IBM, 2023). Such investments not only enhance operational performance but also provide a solid foundation for scaling AI solutions across larger contexts.

Scalability is another area where strategic actions are required. Although pilot projects show promising results, transitioning these innovations to a broader scale involves overcoming significant hurdles related to technology adoption and infrastructure investment. Regulatory support is crucial in this regard. Governments need to establish clear, adaptive regulatory frameworks that incentivize the adoption of ethical AI practices while providing guidelines for scalability. In this context, public-private partnerships play a pivotal role; collaborations between government agencies, technology companies, and academic institutions can pool resources and expertise to drive large-scale implementation.

Aligning AI initiatives with specific sustainability targets is equally important. Organizations should set measurable benchmarks for environmental, economic, and social outcomes, as these metrics provide a basis for continuous improvement. For example, setting a target to reduce energy consumption by 20%

over a defined period, coupled with real-time monitoring and feedback mechanisms, enables organizations to adjust their strategies dynamically. This approach not only ensures that AI applications are aligned with sustainability goals but also promotes accountability and transparency.

Ethical considerations must be embedded throughout the entire lifecycle of AI systems. This involves developing fairness-aware algorithms, conducting regular bias audits, and establishing clear accountability structures. Recent initiatives such as the EU's Ethics Guidelines for Trustworthy AI (European Commission, 2021) provide valuable frameworks that can be adapted and implemented by organizations worldwide. These guidelines emphasize the need for explainable AI models, which are essential for building stakeholder trust and ensuring that automated decisions are understandable and contestable.

The findings from the literature synthesis provide a compelling case for the integration of AI with sustainability and ethical governance. However, the realization of these benefits requires addressing several key issues and adopting strategic actions. This section discusses the implications of the findings and offers recommendations for both practitioners and policymakers.

One of the most critical factors highlighted by the literature is the importance of interdisciplinary collaboration. The success of AI integration in sustainable initiatives is significantly enhanced when there is active collaboration among policymakers, industry experts, and academic researchers. For example, urban planning projects that implemented AI for traffic management reported greater success when local authorities and community stakeholders were involved in the design and implementation process. Such collaborative efforts ensure that AI systems are tailored to the specific needs of diverse communities and are capable of addressing localized challenges effectively.

Transparency in data handling and algorithmic design is another cornerstone of successful integration. Empirical evidence shows that organizations that adopt transparent methodologies—such as conducting regular bias audits and openly reporting algorithmic processes—experience higher levels of stakeholder trust and better performance outcomes. Therefore, it is recommended that organizations invest in robust data management systems and adopt standardized reporting protocols. These measures will not only enhance the reliability of AI-driven insights but also establish a clear framework for accountability.

Scalability remains a significant challenge that must be addressed to maximize the impact of AI solutions. While pilot projects have demonstrated promising results, scaling these innovations to broader contexts requires significant investments in technology, infrastructure, and workforce training. Policymakers have a crucial role to play in creating regulatory environments that facilitate the scaling of AI solutions without compromising ethical standards. Public-private partnerships can be instrumental in providing the necessary resources and support to expand successful initiatives across different regions and sectors.

Moreover, aligning AI initiatives with clearly defined sustainability targets is essential. The literature indicates that organizations that set specific benchmarks for environmental, economic, and social outcomes are better able to track progress and adjust their strategies accordingly. Continuous monitoring of key performance indicators—such as energy consumption, carbon emissions, and economic ROI—enables organizations to fine-tune their AI systems to deliver optimal results. Integrating these performance metrics into the operational framework creates a feedback loop that fosters continuous improvement and innovation.

Based on these insights, the following strategic recommendations are proposed:

1. **Enhance Interdisciplinary Collaboration:** Foster partnerships among government agencies, industry stakeholders, and academic institutions to co-create AI systems that are not only technologically advanced but also socially responsive. Collaborative research initiatives and cross-sectoral partnerships

are key to ensuring that AI solutions are contextually relevant and capable of addressing complex societal challenges.

2. **Invest in Robust Data Infrastructure:** Prioritize the development of advanced data management systems that ensure high-quality, reliable data. Transparent data practices, including regular audits and standardized reporting, are essential for building trust and enhancing the effectiveness of AI-driven decision-making.
3. **Promote Scalability Through Supportive Regulation:** Develop regulatory frameworks that encourage the scaling of ethical AI solutions. Policies should support public-private partnerships and incentivize investments in technology infrastructure and workforce training, particularly in under-resourced regions.
4. **Align AI Initiatives with Sustainability Targets:** Establish clear, measurable sustainability benchmarks and integrate them into AI systems. Continuous monitoring and evaluation of these metrics will enable organizations to make data-driven adjustments, ensuring that AI applications contribute meaningfully to environmental and social objectives.
5. **Embed Ethical Principles Throughout the AI Lifecycle:** Implement rigorous ethical guidelines at every stage of AI development. This includes the adoption of fairness-aware algorithms, regular bias audits, and the creation of transparent accountability structures. Explainable AI models are crucial for ensuring that stakeholders understand and trust the decisions made by these systems.

Overall, these recommendations provide a strategic roadmap for integrating AI with sustainability and ethical governance. By addressing challenges such as data quality, scalability, and transparency, organizations and policymakers can unlock the full potential of AI to drive sustainable innovation and achieve long-term societal benefits.

In addition to the earlier recommendations, recent practical experiences underscore the need for a holistic approach that integrates technological innovation with robust governance and ethical oversight. For example, in the context of smart cities, initiatives such as the Smart City Project in Barcelona have demonstrated that integrating AI with sustainability goals can transform urban environments. The project employs a range of AI-driven solutions—from intelligent street lighting to real-time waste management systems—that have collectively reduced energy usage by over 20% and improved public services significantly (Ajuntament de Barcelona, 2023). Such real-world examples provide strong evidence that a data-driven, ethically aligned approach to urban management not only improves environmental outcomes but also enhances the quality of life for residents.

Furthermore, in the energy sector, companies like Siemens and General Electric have been at the forefront of deploying AI-enabled energy management systems. Siemens, for instance, has reported that its AI systems have enabled industrial facilities in Europe to achieve energy consumption reductions of up to 18%, with corresponding decreases in greenhouse gas emissions (Siemens, 2022). These advancements are bolstered by comprehensive data analytics that monitor performance in real time and adjust operational parameters to optimize efficiency. In a similar vein, General Electric has integrated AI within its renewable energy operations to predict equipment failures and optimize maintenance schedules, resulting in significant cost savings and improved system reliability (General Electric, 2023).

Another area where the integrated framework is proving beneficial is in the financial sector. With the increasing reliance on AI for risk assessment and decision-making, ethical concerns have become paramount. Financial institutions are now adopting explainable AI models to ensure that their automated systems can be audited and understood by human experts. A notable example is a leading UK bank that implemented a transparent AI system for loan approvals, resulting in a 25% reduction in error rates and improved customer satisfaction scores (AI Now Institute, 2023). These outcomes align closely with the recommendations put forth by Leslie et al. (2024), emphasizing that transparency and accountability are key to building trust and ensuring equitable outcomes in AI applications.

The discussion also highlights the crucial role of regulatory frameworks in fostering scalable and ethically sound AI solutions. Governments worldwide are beginning to recognize that a proactive regulatory approach is essential to address the rapid pace of AI advancements. For example, the European Commission's Ethics Guidelines for Trustworthy AI (European Commission, 2021) serve as a benchmark for ensuring that AI systems are designed and implemented in a manner that upholds ethical standards. These guidelines call for regular ethical audits, comprehensive documentation, and robust accountability mechanisms, which together provide a blueprint for organizations aiming to scale their AI initiatives responsibly. Similar regulatory initiatives are emerging in North America and Asia, reflecting a global trend toward stricter oversight of AI technologies.

Moreover, interdisciplinary collaboration remains a recurring theme in both the literature and practical applications. The integration of expertise from fields such as data science, environmental engineering, social sciences, and ethics is critical for developing AI systems that are both innovative and socially responsible. Collaborative research initiatives, such as those facilitated by the World Economic Forum (WEF, 2023), have proven effective in bridging the gap between theory and practice. These initiatives bring together diverse stakeholders to share insights, identify common challenges, and develop unified solutions that are applicable across different sectors.

In practice, the alignment of AI initiatives with sustainability targets has proven to be a catalyst for innovation. Organizations that adopt a holistic view of sustainability are able to leverage AI not only to optimize their internal processes but also to drive broader environmental and social benefits. For example, a global manufacturing firm recently reported that by integrating AI with its sustainability strategy, it was able to reduce its overall carbon footprint by 16% over a three-year period while simultaneously increasing operational efficiency (Deloitte, 2023). Such case studies serve as powerful examples of how clear, measurable benchmarks can drive continuous improvement and ensure that technological advancements translate into tangible benefits.

7. FUTURE RESEARCH DIRECTIONS AND POLICY IMPLICATIONS

While the integrated framework presented in this chapter is grounded in a robust synthesis of literature, its dynamic nature underscores the need for continued investigation. Future research must prioritize longitudinal studies that can track the long-term impacts of AI integration on sustainability outcomes. Although current studies consistently report improvements in energy efficiency and reductions in carbon emissions, it is important to determine whether these gains are sustained over time as AI systems evolve and are scaled to larger, more complex environments.

Another important area for future inquiry is the exploration of emerging ethical challenges as AI technologies become increasingly autonomous. As these systems learn from ever-growing datasets, the potential for unintended biases and adverse societal impacts may increase. Future research should focus on developing adaptive ethical frameworks that can respond to rapid technological advancements. Such frameworks might include dynamic audit mechanisms and iterative feedback loops that allow organizations to continuously refine their AI systems in light of new data and evolving societal norms.

In addition, there is a clear need to better understand the interplay between technological innovation and policy. As governments and regulatory bodies attempt to keep pace with rapid AI developments, adaptive and forward-thinking policy frameworks are required. Policymakers must work in tandem with industry experts, academic researchers, and community stakeholders to create regulations that support innovation while ensuring ethical accountability. This collaboration should foster environments where transparent data practices, accountability mechanisms, and explainable AI are not only encouraged but mandated.

The policy implications of the integrated framework are far-reaching. First, regulators should establish clear guidelines for data management, ensuring that the quality and integrity of data underpinning AI systems are maintained. This could include mandatory reporting standards and periodic audits, which would help mitigate risks associated with poor data quality. Second, policies that incentivize the adoption of transparency measures—such as the publication of algorithmic decision processes—can promote accountability and build public trust in AI systems. Third, given the challenges associated with scaling pilot projects, public-private partnerships should be encouraged. Such collaborations can provide the necessary financial and technological support to expand successful AI initiatives, particularly in regions where infrastructure may be lacking.

The integrated framework also highlights the importance of aligning AI initiatives with well-defined sustainability targets. For instance, organizations should set explicit benchmarks for environmental outcomes—such as specific reductions in energy consumption or carbon emissions—and incorporate these targets into their AI-driven decision-making processes. Continuous monitoring of these key performance indicators (KPIs) will allow for iterative improvements and ensure that AI systems contribute meaningfully to sustainable development.

In summary, future research should:

- Conduct longitudinal studies to evaluate the enduring impact of AI on sustainability.
- Develop adaptive ethical frameworks that can evolve with technological advancements.
- Investigate the effectiveness of interdisciplinary collaborations in fostering successful AI integration.
- Explore scalable models and public-private partnerships that support the widespread adoption of ethical AI solutions.
- Analyze the role of regulatory frameworks in promoting transparency, accountability, and equitable outcomes in AI applications.

From a policy perspective, it is essential to balance the imperatives of innovation with the need for robust ethical governance. Policymakers must embrace a proactive approach, engaging with experts across various fields to develop flexible, forward-thinking regulations. These regulatory efforts should ensure that the benefits of AI are maximized while minimizing potential risks to society and the environment.

8. CONCLUSION

The integration of sustainability, responsible analytics, and ethical AI represents a transformative approach to addressing the complex challenges of our time. Through a comprehensive review of literature published between 2018 and 2024, this chapter has developed an integrated framework that synthesizes empirical evidence, conceptual analyses, and policy insights. The findings indicate that AI-driven solutions—when implemented within robust, transparent, and ethically grounded systems—can lead to significant improvements in energy efficiency, economic performance, and social equity.

Environmental benefits are achieved through the optimization of processes that reduce energy consumption and minimize carbon emissions. Economic gains emerge from improved operational efficiencies and increased return on investment, while social benefits are realized through enhanced transparency, reduced biases, and greater stakeholder trust. However, the integration of these dimensions is not without its challenges. Issues such as data quality, scalability, and the evolving nature of ethical considerations require ongoing attention and adaptive strategies.

The integrated framework developed in this chapter serves as a strategic roadmap for harnessing the transformative power of AI. It underscores that technological innovation should not be pursued in isolation but must be aligned with broader societal goals that prioritize sustainability and ethical accountability. The framework calls for interdisciplinary collaboration, robust data infrastructures, and adaptive regulatory frameworks that together create an environment in which AI can drive sustainable innovation.

Ultimately, the future of AI lies in its ability to support sustainable development without compromising ethical principles. As global communities confront the pressing issues of climate change, social inequity, and economic instability, the integrated framework offers a compelling vision for how technology can be leveraged to create a more equitable, efficient, and sustainable world. By continuously refining AI systems, engaging in interdisciplinary research, and fostering collaborative policy efforts, stakeholders can ensure that technological progress serves as a force for positive, lasting change.

In conclusion, this chapter highlights that the convergence of sustainability, responsible analytics, and ethical AI is not only necessary but also achievable. The integrated framework provides actionable insights for both practitioners and policymakers, laying the groundwork for future research and real-world applications that can drive holistic, sustainable innovation. The journey toward a sustainable future is complex and multifaceted, but with a commitment to transparency, accountability, and interdisciplinary collaboration, AI can be transformed from a mere tool of efficiency into a catalyst for societal and environmental well-being.

REFERENCES

Aggarwal, S., Dsouza, S., Joshi, M., Antoun, R., & Phan, D. H. T. (2025). Environmental, social and governance investing: Systematic literature review using ADO model. *Journal of Accounting Literature*. Advance online publication. DOI: 10.1108/JAL-11-2024-0319

Al-kfairy, M., Mustafa, D., Kshetri, N., Insiew, M., & Alfandi, O. (2024). Ethical challenges and solutions of generative AI: An interdisciplinary perspective. *Informatics (MDPI)*, *11*(3), 58. DOI: 10.3390/informatics11030058

Alam, A., & Mohanty, A. (2022, November). Business models, business strategies, and innovations in EdTech companies: Integration of learning analytics and artificial intelligence in higher education. In *2022 IEEE 6th Conference on Information and Communication Technology (CICT)* (pp. 1–6). IEEE.

Alam, A., & Mohanty, A. (2023). Educational technology: Exploring the convergence of technology and pedagogy through mobility, interactivity, AI, and learning tools. *Cogent Engineering*, *10*(2), 2283282. DOI: 10.1080/23311916.2023.2283282

Antil, A., Saini, N., Sehgal, S., Aggarwal, S., & Shahzad, U. Effectiveness of Metaphorical Communication in Government Campaign on Digitization. *FIIB Business Review*. https://doi.org/DOI: 10.1177/23197145231166746

Aslaksen, H. M., Hildebrandt, C., & Johnsen, H. C. (2021). The long-term transformation of the concept of CSR: Towards a more comprehensive emphasis on sustainability. *International Journal of Corporate Social Responsibility*, *6*(1), 1–14. DOI: 10.1186/s40991-021-00063-9

Balasubramanian, V., Niksan, O., Jain, M. C., Golovin, K., & Zarifi, M. H. (2023). Non-destructive erosive wear monitoring of multi-layer coatings using AI-enabled differential split ring resonator based system. *Nature Communications*, *14*(1), 1–12. DOI: 10.1038/s41467-023-40636-9 PMID: 37582844

Balsalobre-Lorente, D., Abbas, J., He, C., Pilař, L., & Shah, S. A. R. (2023). Tourism, urbanization and natural resources rents matter for environmental sustainability: The leading role of AI and ICT on sustainable development goals in the digital era. *Resources Policy*, *82*, 103445. DOI: 10.1016/j.resourpol.2023.103445

Bekbolatova, M., Mayer, J., Ong, C. W., & Toma, M. (2024). Transformative Potential of AI in Healthcare: Definitions, Applications, and Navigating the Ethical Landscape and Public Perspectives. *Health Care*, *12*(2), 125. PMID: 38255014

Bin-Nashwan, S. A., Sadallah, M., & Bouteraa, M. (2023). Use of ChatGPT in academia: Academic integrity hangs in the balance. *Technology in Society*, *75*, 102370. DOI: 10.1016/j.techsoc.2023.102370

Bozkurt, A. (2023). Generative artificial intelligence (AI) powered conversational educational agents: The inevitable paradigm shift. *Asian Journal of Distance Education*, *18*, 198–204.

Buhmann, A., & Fieseler, C. (2021). Towards a deliberative framework for responsible innovation in artificial intelligence. *Technology in Society*, *64*, 101475. DOI: 10.1016/j.techsoc.2020.101475

Chau, K. Y., Moslehpour, M., Tu, Y. T., Tai, N. T., Tien, N. H., & Huy, P. Q. (2022). Exploring the impact of green energy and consumption on the sustainability of natural resources: Empirical evidence from G7 countries. *Renewable Energy*, *196*, 1241–1249. DOI: 10.1016/j.renene.2022.07.085

Da Silva, M. C., Da Silva, L. B., Morioka, S. N., & De Souza, V. F. (2023). Integration of Environmental, Social, and Governance (ESG) criteria: Their impacts on corporate sustainability performance. *Humanities & Social Sciences Communications*, *10*(1), 1–18.

Di Vaio, A., Hasan, S., Palladino, R., & Hassan, R. (2023). The transition towards circular economy and waste within accounting and accountability models: A systematic literature review and conceptual framework. *Environment, Development and Sustainability*, *25*(1), 734–810. DOI: 10.1007/s10668-021-02078-5 PMID: 35035274

Díaz-Rodríguez, N., Del Ser, J., Coeckelbergh, M., López de Prado, M., Herrera-Viedma, E., & Herrera, F. (2023). Connecting the dots in trustworthy Artificial Intelligence: From AI principles, ethics, and key requirements to responsible AI systems and regulation. *Information Fusion*, *99*, 101896. DOI: 10.1016/j.inffus.2023.101896

Elendu, C. M., Amaechi, D. C., Elendu, T. C., Jingwa, K. A., Okoye, O. K., Okah, M., Ladele, J. A., Farah, A. H., & Alimi, H. A. (2023). Ethical implications of AI and robotics in healthcare. *Revista de Medicina (São Paulo)*, *102*(50), e36671. PMID: 38115340

Ezeudu, O. B. (2024). Harnessing the drivers and barriers to implementation of extended producer responsibility for circular economy in Nigeria. *Circular Economy and Sustainability*, *4*(2), 1461–1486. DOI: 10.1007/s43615-023-00340-8

Faibil, D., Asante, R., Agyemang, M., Addaney, M., & Baah, C. (2023). Extended producer responsibility in developing economies: Assessment of promoting factors through retail electronic firms for sustainable e-waste management. *Waste Management & Research*, *41*(1), 117–142. DOI: 10.1177/0734242X221105433 PMID: 35892190

Farghali, M., Osman, A. I., Chen, Z., Abdelhaleem, A., Ihara, I., Mohamed, I. M., Yap, P.-S., & Rooney, D. W. (2023). Social, environmental, and economic consequences of integrating renewable energies in the electricity sector: A review. *Environmental Chemistry Letters*, *21*(3), 1381–1418. DOI: 10.1007/s10311-023-01587-1

Farkic, J., Cai, W., & Isailovic, G. (2024). Tourist re-enchantment: Cultivating planetary wellbeing through more-than-human entanglements in the forest. *Journal of Sustainable Tourism*, *33*(3), 457–473. DOI: 10.1080/09669582.2024.2350651

Ferrara, E. (2024). The butterfly effect in artificial intelligence systems: Implications for AI bias and fairness. *Machine Learning with Applications*, *7*, 100245. DOI: 10.1016/j.mlwa.2024.100525

Gupta, S., Aga, D., Pruden, A., Zhang, L., & Vikesland, P. (2021). Data analytics for environmental science and engineering research. *Environmental Science & Technology*, *55*(16), 10895–10907. DOI: 10.1021/acs.est.1c01026 PMID: 34338518

Hariram, N. P., Mekha, K. B., Suganthan, V., & Sudhakar, K. (2023). Sustainalism: An integrated socio-economic-environmental model to address sustainable development and sustainability. *Sustainability (Basel), 15*(4), 2301. DOI: 10.3390/su151310682

Hautala, J., & Ahlqvist, T. (2024). Integrating futures imaginaries, expectations and anticipatory practices: Practitioners of artificial intelligence between now and future. *Technology Analysis and Strategic Management, 36*(9), 2100–2112. DOI: 10.1080/09537325.2022.2130041

Hernández, E. G. (2024). *Towards an Ethical and Inclusive Implementation of Artificial Intelligence in Organizations: A Multidimensional Framework.* ArXiv.

Hoffmann, S. (2022). Challenges and opportunities of area-based conservation in reaching biodiversity and sustainability goals. *Biodiversity and Conservation, 31*(2), 325–352. DOI: 10.1007/s10531-021-02340-2

Jones, M. W., Abatzoglou, J. T., Veraverbeke, S., Andela, N., Lasslop, G., Forkel, M., ... & Le Quéré, C. (2022). Global and regional trends and drivers of fire under climate change. Reviews of Geophysics, 60(3), e2020RG000726.

Khan, S. (2025). *AI in Wonderland: Engineering in the age of overpromised technology* (SAE EDGE Research Reports). SAE International. ISBN: 1468609238, 9781468609233.

Koundal, P., Bhalla, M., & Bandna. (2025). The role of AIS in enhancing small business agility and sustainability in Industry 5.0. In *The Future of Small Business in Industry 5.0* (pp. 1–30). https://doi.org/ DOI: 10.4018/979-8-3693-7362-0.ch012

Kulkov, I., Kulkova, J., Rohrbeck, R., Menvielle, L., Kaartemo, V., & Makkonen, H. (2024). Artificial intelligence-driven sustainable development: Examining organizational, technical, and processing approaches to achieving global goals. *Sustainable Development (Bradford), 32*(3), 2253–2267. DOI: 10.1002/sd.2773

Laasch, O., Moosmayer, D. C., & Antonacopoulou, E. P. (2023). The interdisciplinary responsible management competence framework: An integrative review of ethics, responsibility, and sustainability competences. *Journal of Business Ethics, 187*(4), 733–757. DOI: 10.1007/s10551-022-05261-4

Leiss, W. (2023). *The domination of nature: New edition.* McGill-Queen's University Press., DOI: 10.1515/9780228017264

Leslie, D., Rincon, C., Briggs, M., Perini, A., Jayadeva, S., Borda, A., Bennett, S., Burr, C., Aitken, M., Katell, M., Fischer, C., Wong, J., & Garcia, I. K. (2024). AI Sustainability in Practice Part One: Foundations for Sustainable AI Projects. ArXiv. https://doi.org/DOI: 10.2139/ssrn.4731832

Mahalik, M. K., Pal, S., Le, T. H., & Mishra, S. (2024). Does environmental policy stringency improve nature's health in BRICS economies? *Environmental Science and Pollution Research International, 31*(1), 509–528. DOI: 10.1007/s11356-023-31134-y PMID: 38015395

Malan, K. M. (2021). A Survey of Advances in Landscape Analysis for Optimisation. *Algorithms, 14*(2), 40. DOI: 10.3390/a14020040

Mann, M., Hosman, C. M. H., Schaalma, H. P., & de Vries, N. K. (2004). Self-esteem in a broad-spectrum approach for mental health promotion. *Health Education Research, 19*(4), 357–372. DOI: 10.1093/her/cyg041 PMID: 15199011

Mohsin Khan, M., Shah, N., Shaikh, N., Thabet, A., Alrabayah, T., & Belkhair, S. (2025). Towards secure and trusted AI in healthcare: A systematic review of emerging innovations and ethical challenges. *International Journal of Medical Informatics, 195*, 105780. DOI: 10.1016/j.ijmedinf.2024.105780 PMID: 39753062

Mökander, J., Morley, J., Taddeo, M., & Floridi, L. (2021). Ethics-based auditing of automated decision-making systems: Nature, scope, and limitations. *Science and Engineering Ethics, 27*(4), 44. DOI: 10.1007/s11948-021-00319-4 PMID: 34231029

Mourtzis, D., Angelopoulos, J., & Panopoulos, N. (2022). A literature review of the challenges and opportunities of the transition from Industry 4.0 to Society 5.0. *Energies, 15*(17), 6276. DOI: 10.3390/en15176276

Muhmad, K., Wan Mohd Jaafar, W. S., Mohd Said, M. N., Saad, S. N. M., & Mohan, M. (2023). UAV implementations in urban planning and related sectors of rapidly developing nations: A review and future perspectives for Malaysia. *Remote Sensing (Basel), 15*(11), 2845. DOI: 10.3390/rs15112845

Naik, N., Hameed, B. M. Z., Shetty, D. K., Swain, D., Shah, M., Paul, R., Aggarwal, K., Ibrahim, S., Patil, V., Smriti, K., Shetty, S., Rai, B. P., Chlosta, P., & Somani, B. K. (2022). Legal and ethical consideration in artificial intelligence in healthcare: Who takes responsibility? *Frontiers in Surgery, 9*, 862322. DOI: 10.3389/fsurg.2022.862322 PMID: 35360424

Năstasă, A., Dumitra, T., & Grigorescu, A. (2024). Artificial intelligence and sustainable development during the pandemic: An overview of the scientific debates. *Heliyon, 10*(9), e30412. DOI: 10.1016/j.heliyon.2024.e30412 PMID: 38711639

Nazaretsky, T., Bar, C., Walter, M., & Alexandron, G. (2022). Empowering teachers with AI: Co-designing a learning analytics tool for personalized instruction in the science classroom. In *LAK22: 12th International Learning Analytics and Knowledge Conference* (pp. 1–12). Association for Computing Machinery. https://doi.org/DOI: 10.1145/3506860.3506861

Olorunfemi, O. L., Amoo, O. O., Atadoga, A., Fayayola, O. A., Abrahams, T. O., & Shoetan, P. O. (2024). Towards a conceptual framework for ethical AI development in IT systems. *Computer Science & IT Research Journal, 5*(3), 616–627. DOI: 10.51594/csitrj.v5i3.910

Owolabi, O. S., Uche, P. C., Adeniken, N. T., Ihejirika, C., Islam, R. B., Chhetri, B. J. T., & Jung, B. (2024). Ethical implication of artificial intelligence (AI) adoption in financial decision making. *Comput. Inf. Sci, 17*(1), 49–56. DOI: 10.5539/cis.v17n1p49

Radanliev, P., Santos, O., Brandon-Jones, A., & Joinson, A. (2024). Ethics and responsible AI deployment. *Frontiers in Artificial Intelligence, 7*, 1377011. DOI: 10.3389/frai.2024.1377011 PMID: 38601110

Regona, M., Yigitcanlar, T., Hon, C., & Teo, M. (2024). Artificial intelligence and sustainable development goals: Systematic literature review of the construction industry. *Sustainable Cities and Society, 108*, 105499. DOI: 10.1016/j.scs.2024.105499

Scannapieco, M., & Virgillito, A. (2021). How to be responsible in all the steps of a data science pipeline: The case of the Italian public sector. *Patterns (New York, N.Y.)*, *2*(12), 100393. DOI: 10.1016/j.patter.2021.100393 PMID: 34950908

Sharifi, A. (2021). Urban sustainability assessment: An overview and bibliometric analysis. *Ecological Indicators*, *121*, 107102. DOI: 10.1016/j.ecolind.2020.107102

Swope, C. B., Hernández, D., & Cushing, L. J. (2022). The relationship of historical redlining with present-day neighborhood environmental and health outcomes: A scoping review and conceptual model. *Journal of Urban Health*, *99*(6), 959–983. DOI: 10.1007/s11524-022-00665-z PMID: 35915192

Tantia, V., & Sukanya, R. (2024). Reinventing the business model to navigate the evolving business landscape. In *ESG and ecosystem services for sustainability* (pp. 1–24). IGI Global. DOI: 10.4018/979-8-3693-3771-4.ch010

Twyford, E. J., Musundwa, S., Tanima, F. A., & George, S. (2024). Bridging the gap: Sustainable development goals as catalysts for change in accounting education and society. *Meditari Accountancy Research*, *32*(5), 1758–1786. DOI: 10.1108/MEDAR-02-2024-2375

Uralovich, K. S., Toshmamatovich, T. U., Kubayevich, K. F., Sapaev, I. B., Saylaubaevna, S. S., Beknazarova, Z. F., & Khurramov, A. (2023). A primary factor in sustainable development and environmental sustainability is environmental education. *Caspian Journal of Environmental Sciences*, *21*(4), 965–975.

Venkatesh, V., & Bala, H. (2008). Technology Acceptance Model 3 and a Research Agenda on Interventions. *Decision Sciences*, *39*(2), 273–315. DOI: 10.1111/j.1540-5915.2008.00192.x

West, S., Haider, L. J., Hertz, T., Mancilla Garcia, M., & Moore, M. L. (2024). Relational approaches to sustainability transformations: Walking together in a world of many worlds. *Ecosystems and People (Abingdon, England)*, *20*(1), 2370539. DOI: 10.1080/26395916.2024.2370539

Xu, J. (2024, February 29). AI in ESG for financial institutions: An industrial survey. *SSRN*. http://dx.doi.org/DOI: 10.2139/ssrn.4949354

Zhang, Y. (2021). Measuring progress toward sustainable development goals through legal integration and policy guidance. *Journal of Energy and Environmental Policy Options*, *7*(2), 145–162.

Chapter 16
Transforming Financial Services in India:
Impact of Blockchain Technology and Decentralized Finance (DeFi)

Ram Singh
https://orcid.org/0000-0002-6565-3091
Symbiosis University of Applied Sciences, Indore, India

Babudhan Tripura
https://orcid.org/0000-0002-0283-1946
AMBS Mahavidyalaya, India

Vikram Manchanda
https://orcid.org/0009-0002-1391-9588
MVN University, Haryana, India

Chandra Shekhar Pandey
https://orcid.org/0000-0002-3660-1858
Mahatma Gandhi International Hindi University, Wardha, India

Madhu Totla
https://orcid.org/0000-0001-9665-097X
University of Delhi, India

Manish Sharma
https://orcid.org/0000-0002-0964-3366
Maharaja Agrasen Institute of Management Studies, India

Ishan Atrey
https://orcid.org/0009-0006-1619-6425
Indian Institute of Management, Rohtak, India

Saurabh Mittal
https://orcid.org/0000-0003-2377-8627
Maharishi Markandeshwar University, India

ABSTRACT

The rapid evolution of blockchain technology and decentralized finance (DeFi) has significantly disrupted traditional financial services globally. DeFi, by leveraging blockchain, enables financial services without relying on traditional intermediaries such as banks, creating a more inclusive, efficient, and transparent financial ecosystem. The chapter explores blockchain and DeFi's impact on the Indian financial services sector. The purpose is to identify how these technologies are transforming financial products, services, and regulations in India while addressing key issues like financial inclusion, security, and scalability. The research methodology involves a qualitative approach, including an analysis of secondary data, case studies of Indian blockchain startups. The study will also provide insights into the regulatory and institutional changes required to support this transformation. In conclusion, while blockchain and DeFi offer significant promise for the Indian financial sector, their adoption requires overcoming technological,

DOI: 10.4018/979-8-3373-0209-6.ch016

regulatory, and cultural barriers.

1. INTRODUCTION

India's financial services sector has been a cornerstone of the country's economic development, evolving significantly over the decades. From the nationalization of banks in the 20th century to the fintech revolution of the 21st century, the industry has embraced technological advancements to cater to the diverse needs of its population. However, despite these strides, several systemic challenges persist, including financial exclusion, inefficiencies in service delivery, and high costs associated with traditional banking systems (Reserve Bank of India [RBI], 2023). Blockchain technology and Decentralized Finance (DeFi) represent a paradigm shift in addressing these challenges. By introducing a decentralized and transparent ecosystem, these innovations promise to revolutionize how financial services are delivered and consumed. This chapter explores the transformative potential of blockchain and DeFi within the Indian financial landscape, emphasizing their implications for efficiency, accessibility, and inclusivity.

1.1 Evolution of Financial Services in India

The Indian financial sector has undergone significant changes over the past decades, transitioning from a heavily regulated and centralized system to a more open, technology-driven ecosystem. Despite these advancements, challenges such as financial exclusion, inefficiencies in operations, and high transaction costs persist, particularly in rural and semi-urban areas. According to the Reserve Bank of India (RBI), over 190 million Indian adults remain unbanked, emphasizing the need for innovative solutions to bridge this gap (RBI, 2023). Emerging technologies, particularly blockchain and decentralized finance (DeFi), offer the potential to address these systemic challenges. These technologies promise greater transparency, efficiency, and inclusivity, essential for transforming financial services in India. The introduction of the Unified Payments Interface (UPI) demonstrated the potential of digital solutions to enhance accessibility, but it operates within a centralized framework, leaving room for further innovation (Dasgupta & Mehta, 2022). The financial services sector in India has undergone a significant transformation, reflecting the nation's journey from a regulated economy to one of the fastest-growing emerging markets. This evolution can be broadly categorized into three phases: the pre-liberalization era, the post-liberalization reforms, and the current digital revolution driven by financial technology (fintech) innovations (Table 1).

Table 1. Evolution of financial services in India: pre- and post-liberalization

Era	Year	Major Developments	Description	Impact
Pre-Liberalization (Before 1991)	1955	Establishment of State Bank of India (SBI)	Nationalization of the Imperial Bank of India to improve banking access.	Strengthened rural banking and financial infrastructure.
	1969	Nationalization of 14 major banks	Government took control of major private banks to increase financial inclusion.	Expanded banking services to rural and semi-urban areas.
	1972	Establishment of Credit Guarantee Corporation of India (CGCI)	Introduced to support credit availability for small-scale industries.	Encouraged lending to MSMEs and entrepreneurs.
	1975	Establishment of Regional Rural Banks (RRBs)	Created to serve banking needs of rural areas and agriculture.	Improved access to credit for farmers and small businesses.
	1980	Nationalization of 6 more banks	Further increased government control over banking.	Strengthened public sector dominance in banking.
	1982	Establishment of NABARD (National Bank for Agriculture and Rural Development)	Specialized financial institution for rural credit.	Boosted agricultural finance and rural development.
	1985	Introduction of Lead Bank Scheme	Banks were assigned districts to promote credit and economic development.	Improved regional banking coverage and rural economic growth.
	1990	Weak financial sector with high NPAs, inefficiency, and lack of competition	Public sector banks faced issues of low profitability and poor customer service.	Need for economic reforms to revive banking efficiency.
Post-Liberalization (After 1991)	1991	Economic Liberalization & Banking Reforms	Allowed private and foreign banks, deregulated interest rates, and improved efficiency.	Increased competition, banking efficiency, and financial stability.
	1992	Establishment of SEBI (Securities and Exchange Board of India)	Introduced to regulate capital markets and protect investors.	Improved transparency and investor confidence.
	1993	Introduction of National Stock Exchange (NSE)	Enabled electronic trading, replacing open outcry systems.	Boosted stock market efficiency and participation.
	1999	Implementation of KYC (Know Your Customer) Guidelines	Strengthened regulations to prevent money laundering.	Improved transparency and security in banking transactions.
	2000	Launch of Demat Accounts	Allowed electronic holding of shares, reducing paperwork.	Increased retail investor participation in stock markets.
	2004	Introduction of RTGS (Real-Time Gross Settlement)	Enabled instant settlement of high-value transactions.	Improved efficiency and security in banking transactions.
	2005	Introduction of NEFT (National Electronic Funds Transfer)	Facilitated nationwide digital money transfers.	Enhanced banking convenience and financial inclusion.
	2010	Launch of IMPS (Immediate Payment Service)	Enabled 24/7 instant interbank money transfers.	Promoted digital banking and reduced dependency on cash.
	2014	Launch of Pradhan Mantri Jan Dhan Yojana (PMJDY)	Aimed at financial inclusion by providing banking access to all.	Opened millions of new bank accounts, improving financial accessibility.
	2016	Demonetization & Digital Payments Drive	Rs. 500 and Rs. 1000 notes withdrawn to curb black money and promote digital transactions.	Boosted adoption of UPI, mobile wallets, and fintech innovation.
	2017	Implementation of Goods and Services Tax (GST)	Introduced a unified indirect tax system.	Simplified taxation and improved ease of doing business.
	2018	Rise of Fintech & UPI Payments	Growth of digital wallets, UPI-based payments, and fintech startups.	Increased digital financial transactions and reduced cash dependency.
	2021	RBI's Central Bank Digital Currency (CBDC) Initiative	Exploration of digital rupee for a more efficient monetary system.	Enhanced monetary policy execution and financial inclusion.
	2023	Integration of AI & Blockchain in Financial Services	Adoption of AI, machine learning, and blockchain in banking.	Strengthened security, automation, and financial transparency.

Sources: Authors' Compilation

This structured timeline presents how India's financial services evolved before and after the 1991 economic reforms, highlighting the transition from a government-controlled banking system to a digitally-driven and competitive financial ecosystem.

1.1.1 Pre-Liberalization Era: Foundation and Early Challenges:

During the pre-liberalization period (1947–1991), India's financial services sector was heavily regulated and dominated by government-controlled institutions. Key milestones included the nationalization of major commercial banks in 1969 and 1980, aimed at ensuring greater public control and financial inclusion. These efforts prioritized rural development, agricultural financing, and the promotion of small industries. However, despite these initiatives, inefficiencies such as bureaucratic delays, limited accessibility, and a lack of customer-centric services plagued the system (Chakraborty, 2022). The establishment of the Reserve Bank of India (RBI) in 1935 played a critical role in stabilizing the financial framework and supervising banking operations. By the late 1980s, however, the system was struggling to meet the demands of a growing economy. Limited private sector participation, stringent regulations, and outdated technology further constrained the sector's growth (Nayyar, 2021).

1.1.2 Post-Liberalization Reforms: Opening the Market:

The economic reforms initiated in 1991 marked a turning point in the evolution of financial services in India. The liberalization policies introduced under the leadership of Dr. Manmohan Singh focused on deregulation, competition, and modernization. Key reforms included:

- ***Privatization of Banks:*** Allowing private and foreign banks to operate increased competition and efficiency.
- ***Expansion of Capital Markets:*** Establishment of the Securities and Exchange Board of India (SEBI) in 1992 strengthened the regulatory framework for stock markets.
- ***Technology Integration:*** Adoption of core banking solutions (CBS) and automated teller machines (ATMs) improved service delivery (Sharma & Singh, 2023).

The reforms not only enhanced operational efficiency but also attracted foreign investments, laying the groundwork for a more robust financial ecosystem. Banks like HDFC and ICICI emerged as leaders in innovation and customer service, setting benchmarks for the sector.

1.1.3 Digital Revolution and the Rise of Fintech:

The advent of technology in the early 2000s initiated a new phase in the financial sector's evolution. With increased internet penetration and smartphone usage, India witnessed a surge in digital financial services. Initiatives such as the Unified Payments Interface (UPI), launched by the National Payments Corporation of India (NPCI) in 2016, revolutionized real-time payments, making India a global leader in digital transactions (NPCI, 2023). Government-led initiatives like Pradhan Mantri Jan Dhan Yojana (PMJDY) facilitated financial inclusion by opening over 500 million bank accounts for the unbanked population (Ministry of Finance, 2023). Additionally, the integration of Aadhaar with financial services enabled streamlined Know Your Customer (KYC) processes and direct benefit transfers (DBT). The emergence of fintech companies like Paytm, PhonePe, and Razorpay further disrupted traditional banking models. These firms leveraged artificial intelligence (AI), blockchain, and big data analytics to provide innovative solutions for payments, lending, and wealth management. The fintech boom not only increased accessibility but also addressed gaps in underserved rural and semi-urban markets (Goyal et al., 2024).

1.1.4 Trends and Challenges:

Today, the financial services sector in India stands as a global example of technological adoption and scalability. However, challenges such as cybersecurity risks, digital illiteracy, and regulatory ambiguities persist. Furthermore, while urban areas have embraced digital solutions, rural regions still face barriers due to inadequate infrastructure and limited awareness. The evolution of financial services in India demonstrates the sector's resilience and adaptability. From traditional banking models to cutting-edge fintech innovations, the journey reflects a continuous effort to align financial services with the needs of a diverse and dynamic population. As blockchain and decentralized finance (DeFi) technologies gain traction, the sector is poised for further transformation, ensuring greater transparency, inclusivity, and efficiency.

1.2 Global Evolution of Financial Services

The evolution of financial services globally has been marked by significant milestones, from the early establishment of financial institutions to the rise of digital finance. In the pre-20th century, financial systems were shaped by the creation of stock exchanges, central banks, and the formalization of economic principles. The Amsterdam Stock Exchange (1602) and the New York Stock Exchange (1792) laid the foundation for global capital markets, while the establishment of the Bank of England (1694) and the Federal Reserve System (1913) introduced structured monetary policies. The Bretton Woods Agreement (1944) played a crucial role in shaping post-war global financial cooperation, leading to the establishment of institutions like the IMF and World Bank. However, by the late 20th century, deregulation and financial liberalization gained momentum, bringing innovation but also increased risks, as seen in events like Black Monday (1987) and the global financial crisis of 2008. In the 21st century, financial services underwent a digital transformation, with fintech, blockchain, and artificial intelligence driving innovation. The launch of Bitcoin (2009) introduced decentralized finance (DeFi), disrupting traditional banking systems, while the growth of mobile banking and digital wallets (2010s) improved financial inclusion worldwide. The introduction of open banking (2016) encouraged competition by allowing third-party developers to access banking data securely. The COVID-19 pandemic (2020) further accelerated the shift towards digital transactions, boosting fintech adoption. More recently, the emergence of Central Bank Digital Currencies (CBDCs, 2022) and AI-driven financial services (2023) has enhanced efficiency and security in financial transactions. This rapid transformation highlights the growing role of technology in reshaping financial services, making them more accessible, efficient, and secure on a global scale. Here is the Evolution of Financial Services at the Global Level in a well-structured (Table 2)

Table 2. Global evolution of financial services

Year	Major Development	Description	Impact
Pre-20th Century: Foundations of Modern Finance			
1602	Establishment of the Amsterdam Stock Exchange	First modern stock exchange in the Netherlands.	Laid the foundation for global capital markets.
1694	Creation of the Bank of England	Established to manage public debt and monetary policy.	Influenced central banking worldwide.
1776	Publication of *The Wealth of Nations* (Adam Smith)	Introduced principles of free markets and capitalism.	Shaped modern economic and financial policies.
1792	Formation of the New York Stock Exchange (NYSE)	Created under the Buttonwood Agreement for securities trading.	Became the world's largest stock exchange.
1867	First Wire Transfer System (Western Union)	Enabled electronic money transfer using telegraphs.	Revolutionized global remittance and transactions.
20th Century: Industrialization & Banking Modernization			
1913	Establishment of the Federal Reserve System (USA)	Created to regulate U.S. monetary policy and ensure financial stability.	Influenced central banking systems globally.
1944	Bretton Woods Agreement	Established the IMF and World Bank, pegging currencies to the U.S. dollar.	Created a framework for international financial cooperation.
1950	Introduction of Credit Cards (Diners Club)	First universal credit card for cashless transactions.	Paved the way for global digital payments.
1971	End of Bretton Woods System	The U.S. abandoned the gold standard, shifting to fiat currency.	Increased exchange rate volatility but allowed monetary policy flexibility.
1973	Establishment of SWIFT (Society for Worldwide Interbank Financial Telecommunication)	Introduced a global interbank messaging system for secure transactions.	Improved the security and efficiency of international transactions.
1980s	Deregulation & Financial Liberalization	Countries relaxed financial controls, allowing private sector growth.	Led to financial innovation but also increased risks.
1987	Black Monday Stock Market Crash	A sudden global market crash due to computerized trading.	Triggered regulatory reforms to control market volatility.
21st Century: Digital Transformation & Fintech Revolution			
1999	Gramm-Leach-Bliley Act (USA)	Allowed banks to offer investment and insurance services.	Increased financial consolidation and complexity.
2008	Global Financial Crisis	Collapse of Lehman Brothers led to a worldwide recession.	Triggered Basel III regulations to ensure banking stability.
2009	Introduction of Bitcoin & Blockchain	Bitcoin, the first cryptocurrency, was introduced by Satoshi Nakamoto.	Revolutionized digital payments and decentralized finance (DeFi).
2010	Rise of Mobile Banking & Digital Wallets	Banks and fintech firms launched mobile banking apps.	Increased financial inclusion, especially in emerging markets.
2015	Expansion of Fintech Startups	Companies like Stripe, PayPal, and Revolut disrupted traditional banking.	Enhanced digital payments, lending, and robo-advisory services.
2016	Introduction of Open Banking & APIs	Banks started sharing customer data securely with third-party providers.	Increased competition and innovation in financial services.
2020	COVID-19 & Acceleration of Digital Finance	Shift to digital payments, contactless transactions, and remote banking.	Boosted fintech adoption and online financial services.

continued on following page

Table 2. Continued

Pre-20th Century: Foundations of Modern Finance			
Year	**Major Development**	**Description**	**Impact**
2022	Growth of Central Bank Digital Currencies (CBDCs)	Central banks like China's PBOC and the ECB explored digital currencies.	Aimed at modernizing monetary systems and reducing dependency on cash.
2023	Expansion of AI & Blockchain in Finance	AI-driven financial services and blockchain-based decentralized finance (DeFi).	Improved automation, security, and transparency in financial transactions.

Sources: Authors' Compilation

This structured table presents key milestones in the global evolution of financial services, from the establishment of stock exchanges and central banks to the rise of fintech, cryptocurrencies, and artificial intelligence in finance.

1.3. Blockchain Technology: A Catalyst for Financial Transformation

Blockchain technology, defined as a decentralized and immutable ledger, is the backbone of many transformative financial innovations. Its applications in financial services include real-time settlements, fraud prevention, and streamlined operations. Blockchain eliminates intermediaries, significantly reducing transaction costs and time, making it particularly suitable for India's financial ecosystem, where high costs often deter users from accessing formal financial services (NASSCOM, 2023). In India, blockchain has been applied in areas like remittances, trade finance, and digital identity management. For example, the State Bank of India (SBI) has explored blockchain for trade financing, reducing operational complexities and improving transparency in supply chain finance (Chakraborty et al., 2022). Similarly, the Reserve Bank of India's pilot project on Central Bank Digital Currency (CBDC) highlights blockchain's potential to enhance secure and efficient payment systems (RBI, 2023). These developments showcase how blockchain is beginning to disrupt traditional financial systems, although its full potential is yet to be realized. Blockchain technology, a decentralized and immutable ledger system, has emerged as a transformative force across various industries, with financial services being a primary beneficiary. Its potential to revolutionize the financial ecosystem lies in its ability to enhance transparency, improve efficiency, and eliminate intermediaries. In the Indian context, blockchain offers solutions to long-standing challenges in financial services, ranging from high transaction costs to financial inclusion gaps.

Blockchain operates as a distributed ledger where transactions are recorded across a network of computers in a secure and tamper-proof manner. Each transaction is grouped into blocks and linked to the previous one using cryptographic hashes, creating a chain of records. The decentralized nature of blockchain ensures that no single entity has control over the data, making it resilient against fraud and manipulation (Nakamoto, 2008). Key features of blockchain that make it suitable for financial services include:

- ***Decentralization:*** Removes the need for centralized intermediaries, reducing costs and increasing transaction speed.
- ***Transparency:*** All participants in the network have access to the same information, fostering trust and accountability.

- ***Immutability:*** Once recorded, transactions cannot be altered, ensuring data integrity.

These attributes make blockchain particularly relevant for India's financial sector, where inefficiencies and lack of trust have historically hindered progress.

1.3.1 Applications of Blockchain in Financial Services

1.3.1.1 Payment Systems and Cross-Border Transactions:

Traditional payment systems, especially for cross-border transactions, involve intermediaries such as correspondent banks, leading to delays and high costs. Blockchain-enabled payment systems like Ripple and Stellar offer real-time settlement and reduced transaction fees, making international remittances faster and more affordable. This is especially significant for India, the world's largest recipient of remittances, which received $111 billion in 2022 (World Bank, 2023).

1.3.1.2 Smart Contracts and Automated Transactions:

Smart contracts are self-executing contracts with predefined rules coded into the blockchain. They enable automated and trustless transactions without the need for intermediaries. In the Indian financial sector, smart contracts have the potential to streamline processes such as loan disbursement, insurance claims, and trade finance. For example, ICICI Bank has utilized blockchain to facilitate automated trade finance transactions, reducing operational complexities (Chakraborty et al., 2022).

1.3.1.3 Fraud Prevention and Identity Verification:

Fraud and identity theft are persistent issues in the Indian financial ecosystem. Blockchain-based solutions can mitigate these risks by creating a secure and verifiable digital identity for users. Aadhaar, India's biometric identification system, could integrate blockchain to enhance data security and prevent unauthorized access (NASSCOM, 2023).

1.3.1.4 Tokenization of Assets:

Blockchain enables the tokenization of real-world assets, such as real estate and commodities, allowing fractional ownership and easier liquidity. Tokenized assets can democratize investment opportunities in India, especially for retail investors, by reducing entry barriers and increasing transparency (Sharma & Verma, 2023).

1.4 Decentralized Finance (DeFi): Redefining Financial Services

Decentralized Finance (DeFi) extends the utility of blockchain by creating financial services and products that operate without traditional intermediaries like banks. DeFi platforms use smart contracts to automate transactions, providing services such as lending, borrowing, and asset management. These solutions have the potential to democratize access to financial services, particularly in a country like India, where underserved populations often face barriers to accessing formal credit systems (Kumar & Singh, 2023). For example, DeFi can enable peer-to-peer lending platforms that offer microloans to small businesses and individuals in rural areas, bypassing traditional credit systems. Furthermore, DeFi's role in facilitating low-cost remittances is particularly relevant for India, the world's largest recipient of remittances (World Bank, 2023). However, challenges such as limited digital literacy, regulatory uncertainty, and volatility in crypto-assets remain significant barriers to DeFi's widespread adoption in the Indian context.

2. REVIEW OF LITERATURE

In the vast and dynamic realm of financial services, blockchain technology has emerged as a revolutionary force. As researchers and innovators explore its potential, a compelling story unfolds one that charts a journey through evolving paradigms, groundbreaking discoveries, and unresolved challenges. Here, we embark on a narrative journey of literature reviews, weaving insights into a coherent tale. The story begins with Nakamoto's (2008) seminal whitepaper, introducing blockchain as the underlying technology of Bitcoin. This decentralized ledger system promised transparency, security, and immutability, laying the foundation for blockchain's foray into financial services. Its potential to disrupt traditional models was quickly recognized by Tapscott and Tapscott (2016), who envisioned blockchain as the cornerstone of a new financial order. The initial chapters were dominated by cryptocurrencies, with Bitcoin and Ethereum taking center stage. Antonopoulos (2017) highlighted how cryptocurrencies could bypass intermediaries, reducing costs and delays. However, Swan (2015) expanded the narrative by proposing blockchain's application beyond digital currencies, including smart contracts, decentralized finance (DeFi), and tokenized assets. In a country like India, where financial exclusion remains a challenge, scholars like Narula and Vasudevan (2020) found blockchain-powered microfinance platforms to be game-changers. They illustrated how decentralized platforms could enable peer-to-peer lending, reaching underserved rural areas. Similarly, Goyal et al. (2021) argued that blockchain could support low-cost, secure payment systems, critical for emerging economies. Their case studies on mobile-based blockchain applications in rural India showcased the technology's transformative potential for financial inclusion. But the plot thickens with the rise of DeFi. Hayes et al. (2019) depicted DeFi as a "parallel financial ecosystem," free from the constraints of traditional banking. Through protocols like Compound and Aave, DeFi introduced lending, borrowing, and trading without intermediaries. This evolution fascinated Gupta et al. (2022), who analyzed DeFi's adoption in India. Their findings underscored its ability to democratize access to credit and investment opportunities, albeit highlighting concerns about regulatory ambiguities. One of blockchain's most impactful applications, as underscored by Zohar (2015), is in cross-border transactions. Traditional remittance systems are slow and expensive, but Ripple and similar platforms showcased blockchain's ability to revolutionize this domain.

For India, the world's largest remittance receiver, D'Silva et al. (2020) noted blockchain's potential to cut transaction costs by 50%, making it invaluable for migrant workers and their families. Turning the lens to trust, Kumar and Rajan (2023) narrated how blockchain's immutable ledger could reduce fraud in India's financial system. From counterfeit securities to loan misappropriation, the transparency offered by blockchain is heralded as a solution to entrenched issues. This theme is echoed by Mohanty et al. (2022), who explored blockchain's role in secure digital identities. They found that integrating Aadhaar with blockchain could prevent identity theft and streamline Know Your Customer (KYC) processes. A fascinating subplot involves the tokenization of real-world assets. According to Sharma and Verma (2023), blockchain enables fractional ownership of high-value assets like real estate and art. Their study on Indian real estate markets revealed how tokenization could attract retail investors, transforming a traditionally illiquid market. An equally captivating narrative unfolds with smart contracts, as detailed by Szabo (1997). These self-executing contracts automate complex transactions, minimizing human intervention. Singh et al. (2022) explored their application in India's insurance sector, where smart contracts could simplify claim settlements and enhance customer satisfaction.

The plot is not without hurdles. Regulatory uncertainty, highlighted by Bose and Dutta (2023), remains a major barrier in India. While the Reserve Bank of India (RBI) has taken a cautious stance, initiatives like the Central Bank Digital Currency (CBDC) pilot project reflect growing acceptance of blockchain's potential. Digital literacy, or the lack thereof, is another antagonist. According to Chaudhary et al. (2023), rural India's limited understanding of blockchain poses significant adoption challenges. Their recommendations include government-led awareness programs and simplified user interfaces. Adding complexity to the tale, environmental concerns emerge as a subplot. Bhattacharya et al. (2021) criticized blockchain's high energy consumption, particularly in proof-of-work systems like Bitcoin. In response, Jain and Malhotra (2022) advocated for proof-of-stake and other energy-efficient consensus mechanisms. The story of blockchain in financial transformation is far from over. Researchers like Das et al. (2024) envision a future where blockchain seamlessly integrates with AI and IoT, creating smart financial ecosystems. They emphasize the need for collaborative efforts among policymakers, technologists, and financial institutions to overcome existing challenges. The blockchain journey began with Nakamoto (2008), whose invention of Bitcoin introduced the world to a decentralized, tamper-proof ledger. This breakthrough laid the foundation for broader applications beyond cryptocurrencies, as noted by Tapscott and Tapscott (2016), who envisioned blockchain reshaping industries through trust and transparency.

The inefficiencies of traditional banking, particularly for international transactions, have been extensively critiqued by Zohar (2015). Ripple's blockchain-based payment solution emerged as a disruptor, drastically reducing costs and processing times. D'Silva et al. (2020) highlighted the potential of blockchain to revolutionize remittances in India, where migrant workers send billions annually. Inclusion forms the heart of India's financial narrative. Goyal et al. (2021) explored blockchain's role in extending financial services to unbanked populations. Das et al. (2024) noted how decentralized microfinance systems in India, powered by blockchain, enabled small-scale lending, fostering economic resilience in rural areas. Szabo's (1997) concept of smart contracts gained traction with Ethereum's launch in 2015. Singh et al. (2022) examined their application in Indian insurance, demonstrating reduced claim settlement times and improved customer satisfaction. Gupta et al. (2022) found similar benefits in trade finance, where smart contracts streamlined documentation and payment processes.

DeFi protocols, as explored by Hayes et al. (2019), eliminated intermediaries in lending, borrowing, and trading. In India, Gupta et al. (2022) analyzed DeFi's growing popularity, emphasizing its role in democratizing investment opportunities for retail users. Sharma and Verma (2023) introduced tokenization as a means to fractionalize high-value assets, such as real estate. They argued that this innovation democratized access to investment, allowing retail investors in India to participate in traditionally exclusive markets. Kumar and Rajan (2023) illustrated how blockchain reduced fraud in Indian banking by ensuring immutable transaction records. Mohanty et al. (2022) discussed the integration of Aadhaar with blockchain, which could enhance identity verification processes and prevent identity theft. Banks often face challenges in meeting KYC and anti-money laundering (AML) requirements. Gatteschi et al. (2018) explored how blockchain's transparent and traceable architecture simplifies compliance, a theme echoed in Singh and Sharma's (2021) study on Indian financial institutions. Chen et al. (2020) focused on blockchain's application in supply chain finance, ensuring transparency and reducing payment disputes. Their findings align with Chakraborty et al.'s (2022) case studies on Indian SMEs benefiting from blockchain-based invoice financing. High energy consumption in blockchain systems remains a contentious issue. Bhattacharya et al. (2021) critiqued proof-of-work mechanisms, while Jain and Malhotra (2022) advocated for energy-efficient alternatives like proof-of-stake. The Reserve Bank of India's (RBI) Digital Rupee initiative, as detailed by RBI (2023), underscores blockchain's role in central bank digital currencies (CBDCs). Bose and Dutta (2023) examined its potential to complement India's robust digital payment ecosystem. Mobile blockchain solutions, as studied by Narula and Vasudevan (2020), have shown promise in extending low-cost financial services to rural areas. Their research highlighted pilot projects enabling secure peer-to-peer transactions. Tapscott and Tapscott (2018) discussed blockchain's potential to eliminate inefficiencies in capital markets. In India, Chaudhary et al. (2022) analyzed blockchain-powered equity settlement systems, reducing delays and costs.

In India's insurance sector, blockchain has proven effective in fraud prevention. Mohanty et al. (2022) detailed pilot projects using blockchain for transparent claim histories, benefiting both insurers and policyholders. Peer-to-peer lending platforms, as explored by Goyal et al. (2021), leverage blockchain to facilitate direct loans between individuals. This reduces intermediary costs, a significant advantage for borrowers and lenders alike. Crowdfunding platforms using blockchain, as described by Ji et al. (2019), enhance trust through transparency. Singh et al. (2022) noted the rising popularity of such platforms in India, especially for social impact projects. Chakraborty et al. (2022) highlighted blockchain's role in streamlining trade finance. The technology reduced documentation delays and minimized the risk of fraud in India's cross-border trade. Narayanan et al. (2020) explored the role of blockchain in creating secure digital identities. Their research aligns with Aadhaar's potential integration, as proposed by Mohanty et al. (2022). Education is key to adoption. Das et al. (2024) proposed blockchain-powered platforms for financial literacy, ensuring accessible and affordable learning modules for rural populations. Chaudhary et al. (2022) examined collaborations between blockchain startups and financial institutions in India. These partnerships are pivotal for scaling innovations and overcoming adoption barriers. Bose and Dutta (2023) critiqued India's cautious regulatory stance on blockchain, emphasizing the need for clarity to encourage innovation. Jain and Malhotra (2022) argued for proactive policy frameworks to balance innovation and security. Narula and Vasudevan (2020) detailed the success of blockchain in microfinance platforms, enabling transparent fund allocation and reduced operational costs. Blockchain's application in e-commerce, as highlighted by Gupta et al. (2022), ensures faster payment settlements, benefiting India's burgeoning online retail sector.

Chen et al. (2020) emphasized the need for scalable blockchain solutions. Their research included Layer 2 protocols, which are being tested in Indian financial systems. Sharma and Verma (2023) examined blockchain's role in crowdfunding and venture capital, enabling transparent fund tracking and democratizing access to investment opportunities. Chaudhary et al. (2023) identified digital literacy as a barrier in India. Their recommendations include user-friendly platforms and government-backed awareness campaigns. Kumar and Rajan (2023) argued that blockchain could enhance transparency in public financial management, curbing corruption in welfare schemes. Ji et al. (2019) discussed blockchain's potential to streamline tax collection and refunds, reducing errors and delays in India's tax administration. Gupta et al. (2022) emphasized the need for interoperability between blockchain networks to ensure seamless integration with existing financial systems. The narrative concludes with Das et al. (2024), who predicted blockchain's integration with AI and IoT, creating smart financial ecosystems that could redefine India's financial landscape.

2.1 Research Gap

Despite the extensive exploration of blockchain technology's potential to transform financial services, significant research gaps remain. While existing studies highlight blockchain's applications in areas such as payments, lending, smart contracts, and decentralized finance (DeFi), limited research has addressed the challenges specific to large-scale adoption in India, particularly in rural and semi-urban regions. The issues of regulatory ambiguity, digital literacy, and scalability have been acknowledged but not thoroughly investigated with context-specific solutions. Additionally, the environmental implications of blockchain in India's energy-constrained economy and the integration of blockchain with existing financial technologies, such as UPI and Aadhaar, require deeper examination. Moreover, while tokenization and smart contracts have been explored, their impact on asset democratization and operational efficiency in India's financial ecosystem is under-researched. Addressing these gaps is critical to unlocking blockchain's full potential for inclusive and sustainable financial transformation in India.

3. OBJECTIVES AND METHODOLOGY

This chapter aims to explore the impact of blockchain and DeFi on the Indian financial services sector. The purpose is to identify how these technologies are transforming financial products, services, and regulations in India, while addressing key issues like financial inclusion, security, and scalability. The research methodology involves a qualitative approach, including an analysis of secondary data, case studies of Indian blockchain startups.

4. IMPACT OF BLOCKCHAIN & DeFi ON THE INDIAN FINANCIAL SERVICES SECTOR

The Indian financial services sector, characterized by its complex regulatory environment and a large unbanked population, is undergoing significant transformation with the integration of blockchain and decentralized finance (DeFi). These technologies offer immense potential to enhance efficiency, transparency, and financial inclusion across various subsectors.

4.1 Banking and Payments Sector:

Blockchain technology has brought about a radical shift in India's banking and payments ecosystem, particularly in improving cross-border payments and remittance services. Traditional banking systems are plagued by slow transaction times, high fees, and reliance on intermediaries, which often delay settlement processes and increase costs for both businesses and consumers. Blockchain-based solutions such as Ripple have helped address these inefficiencies by enabling faster, cheaper, and more secure transactions (Zohar, 2015). In India, the State Bank of India (SBI) and other public-sector banks have begun to pilot blockchain projects aimed at streamlining payments and improving the security of financial transactions (Chaudhary et al., 2022). Additionally, DeFi protocols, which eliminate the need for traditional financial intermediaries, have gained significant traction in India. These platforms allow individuals to access financial services such as loans, savings, and insurance through decentralized networks, bypassing banks and other financial institutions. According to Gupta et al. (2022), India's growing adoption of DeFi platforms, especially for international remittances, has the potential to revolutionize cross-border transactions, reducing both the cost and time of transfers. This development is especially crucial in India, which is one of the largest recipients of remittances globally, with millions of migrant workers sending money home. The efficiency of blockchain in facilitating these transfers has been transformative, allowing users to access decentralized exchange platforms and lending solutions that provide greater financial autonomy and inclusivity.

4.2 Lending and Credit:

The blockchain and DeFi revolution has also had a profound impact on the lending and credit sectors in India. Traditional lending systems in India are often characterized by high-interest rates, stringent credit assessments, and limited access for the underbanked population, particularly in rural and semi-urban areas. Blockchain has emerged as a solution to democratize access to credit, particularly through peer-to-peer (P2P) lending platforms. Blockchain-based platforms like LenDen Club leverage smart contracts and decentralized ledgers to facilitate secure, transparent, and fast loans between individuals without the need for traditional financial intermediaries (Singh & Sharma, 2021). These platforms use blockchain's immutable nature to ensure transparency in transactions, reducing the risk of fraud and enhancing trust among users. P2P lending has proven to be particularly valuable in India's financial landscape, where small and medium enterprises (SMEs) and rural entrepreneurs often face difficulty obtaining loans due to a lack of credit history or collateral. Furthermore, DeFi protocols offer micro-lending and borrowing solutions, where individuals can access credit by collateralizing their digital assets, which has been a game changer for small borrowers who would otherwise be excluded from traditional credit systems. Gupta et al. (2022) note that these innovations have the potential to significantly improve financial inclusion, offering affordable credit solutions to underserved populations in rural areas. By offering lower interest rates and more flexible repayment terms, these decentralized solutions have the power to disrupt the traditional banking system and foster greater economic participation.

4.3 Insurance Sector:

Blockchain's potential to improve efficiency and transparency in the Indian insurance sector has been widely recognized. In traditional insurance systems, claims processing is often slow and cumbersome, involving multiple intermediaries and resulting in inefficiencies, fraud, and customer dissatisfaction. Blockchain's immutable ledger and smart contracts offer a solution by automating and securing insurance processes. According to Mohanty et al. (2022), blockchain-based insurance platforms in India are now being developed to streamline claim settlements and reduce fraud. These platforms utilize smart contracts to automatically execute claims payments when predefined conditions are met, ensuring faster settlements and reducing human errors. For example, in crop insurance, where farmers face delays in claim settlements after natural disasters, blockchain systems can enable real-time data processing and automatic payouts based on pre-agreed criteria, which would significantly reduce the burden on farmers. Furthermore, blockchain's ability to create transparent and auditable transaction records improves trust between insurers and policyholders, a critical issue in India's insurance market. The use of blockchain also simplifies the management of policies by creating a single source of truth for all involved parties, enhancing operational efficiency and ensuring that there is no duplication of claims. DeFi protocols, on the other hand, offer decentralized insurance solutions where risk-sharing can occur directly between users, bypassing traditional insurers, which could lower costs and increase accessibility for underserved populations.

4.4 Capital Markets:

Blockchain technology is playing a pivotal role in transforming capital markets by increasing the transparency, security, and efficiency of securities trading, clearing, and settlement processes. In India, where the Securities and Exchange Board of India (SEBI) has been exploring the use of blockchain for stock trading and clearing, blockchain's decentralized nature ensures that trading records are tamper-proof and instantly verifiable by all participants, thereby reducing fraud and the risk of settlement failures. Tapscott and Tapscott (2018) highlighted how blockchain's distributed ledger allows for real-time settlement, eliminating the need for intermediaries such as clearinghouses, which often delay settlements and add costs. In India, the Bombay Stock Exchange (BSE) has explored blockchain for equity settlement systems, showing that it can significantly reduce transaction times from T+2 to near-instantaneous settlement (Chaudhary et al., 2022). By reducing settlement delays, blockchain enhances market liquidity and lowers the cost of capital for businesses. Additionally, tokenization of assets via blockchain enables fractional ownership of securities, allowing retail investors to participate in markets traditionally reserved for institutional investors. This democratization of asset ownership, as discussed by Sharma and Verma (2023), is particularly promising in India, where access to high-value assets such as real estate and shares is often restricted by high entry barriers. DeFi protocols also enable decentralized trading of assets through automated market makers (AMMs) and decentralized exchanges (DEXs), further lowering entry barriers and increasing financial inclusion in the capital markets.

4.5 Regulatory and Compliance Landscape:

One of the most significant impacts of blockchain technology in India's financial services sector is its potential to transform regulatory compliance. Blockchain's transparency and immutability address several issues related to anti-money laundering (AML) and know-your-customer (KYC) regulations, which have been challenging for Indian banks and financial institutions. Gatteschi et al. (2018) explored how blockchain's distributed ledger can ensure that financial transactions are fully auditable, providing regulators with a real-time view of transactions and reducing the likelihood of fraud or financial crimes. In India, where financial fraud remains a significant issue, the integration of blockchain with KYC systems can simplify and expedite the verification process. The Indian government's Digital India initiative, along with the Reserve Bank of India's (RBI) digital currency project, aims to leverage blockchain to create a secure and efficient digital financial infrastructure. By using blockchain to verify identities and transactions, financial institutions can enhance compliance with AML and KYC regulations while reducing the risk of data breaches (Bose & Dutta, 2023). Furthermore, the decentralized nature of DeFi protocols inherently offers more robust privacy and data security, ensuring that users have greater control over their financial data and transactions. As the regulatory environment in India matures, blockchain's role in enhancing transparency and ensuring compliance will be a key driver in reshaping the country's financial sector.

5. CHALLENGES IN BLOCKCHAIN & DeFi ADOPTION: FINANCIAL INCLUSION, SECURITY, & SCALABILITY

While blockchain technology and decentralized finance (DeFi) offer significant benefits to India's financial services sector, there are several challenges that must be addressed to fully realize their potential. Key issues include financial inclusion, security, and scalability. These concerns are critical to the successful integration of blockchain and DeFi, especially in a diverse and developing country like India.

5.1 Financial Inclusion:

One of the primary promises of blockchain and DeFi is the potential to foster financial inclusion, particularly for underserved and unbanked populations in India. India is home to a large proportion of individuals without access to traditional banking services, especially in rural areas. Blockchain has the potential to bridge this gap by providing secure, low-cost alternatives to traditional financial services, such as lending, payments, and insurance (Gupta et al., 2022). DeFi platforms further enhance accessibility by allowing individuals to access financial products directly, without the need for intermediaries. However, the lack of digital literacy and access to the internet remains a significant barrier to financial inclusion. According to Chaudhary et al. (2022), while blockchain-based solutions like decentralized lending and microfinance can offer significant benefits, the adoption rate in rural India remains low due to insufficient awareness and technological infrastructure. Financial inclusion will only be achieved if efforts are made to educate and equip the population with the necessary skills and resources, including internet connectivity and smartphone access, to use blockchain-based services effectively. Additionally, while DeFi platforms offer access to financial products, many still require participants to have a basic understanding of cryptocurrency and blockchain operations, which limits their reach in rural areas.

5.2 Security Concerns:

Despite its reputation for enhancing security, blockchain technology presents certain risks. Blockchain's decentralized nature makes it inherently resistant to tampering and fraud, but the security of the underlying infrastructure is still a concern. In India, where cybercrime and financial fraud are growing issues, ensuring the security of blockchain systems is paramount (Bose & Dutta, 2023). For example, the risk of hacking and security breaches in decentralized exchanges (DEXs) has been a concern. In 2020, the Indian DeFi project "Value DeFi" faced a hack where millions of dollars in assets were stolen due to vulnerabilities in its code (Narula & Vasudevan, 2020). Furthermore, the security of digital assets, particularly cryptocurrencies, is a significant concern. If private keys are lost or stolen, users can lose access to their assets permanently, which presents a challenge for less tech-savvy individuals. This issue is particularly relevant in India, where a large portion of the population is still new to digital currencies and may not fully understand the security measures required to protect their assets. Additionally, the immutability of blockchain, while providing security, also means that once a fraudulent transaction has been executed, it is difficult to reverse. This creates new challenges in fraud detection and rectification, as well as regulatory oversight, which needs to be carefully addressed by both developers and regulators (Chaudhary et al., 2022).

5.3 Scalability Issues:

Scalability is another major challenge for the widespread adoption of blockchain and DeFi platforms in India. While blockchain provides a secure and transparent infrastructure, it faces limitations in terms of processing large volumes of transactions quickly. As the number of users and transactions on a blockchain network grows, the system can become congested, leading to slower transaction speeds and higher fees. This is particularly problematic for real-time financial applications such as cross-border payments, micropayments, and high-frequency trading, which are critical for financial services (Tapscott & Tapscott, 2018). The Bitcoin and Ethereum blockchains, for example, are often criticized for their inability to handle a large number of transactions simultaneously without delays. In India, where there is an increasing demand for digital payment solutions due to the push for a cashless economy, scalability becomes an urgent issue (Chaudhary et al., 2022). The adoption of blockchain for mainstream financial applications will be constrained unless solutions such as the implementation of layer-2 scaling protocols (e.g., the Lightning Network for Bitcoin) or more efficient consensus mechanisms (e.g., Proof of Stake) are widely adopted. Without these improvements, the operational efficiency of blockchain and DeFi platforms in India will remain limited, especially in sectors such as banking, lending, and capital markets, where large transaction volumes are the norm. While blockchain and DeFi technologies hold great promise for transforming India's financial services landscape, addressing the challenges related to financial inclusion, security, and scalability is crucial for their successful implementation. To ensure that blockchain can reach underserved populations, efforts must be made to improve digital literacy and provide adequate infrastructure. Security concerns also need to be addressed through rigorous testing, regular audits, and the development of user-friendly security protocols to protect digital assets. Finally, scalability issues must be tackled through the development of more efficient blockchain solutions and the implementation of innovative technologies that can support high transaction volumes. As these challenges are overcome, India's financial sector can fully benefit from the efficiencies and inclusivity offered by blockchain and DeFi.

6. TRANSFORMING FINANCIAL PRODUCTS, SERVICES, AND REGULATIONS

Blockchain technology and decentralized finance (DeFi) have introduced transformative changes in financial products, services, and regulatory frameworks in India. These technologies are not only reshaping traditional financial systems but are also creating new opportunities for innovation and financial inclusion. This transformation is particularly significant in India, where there is a growing demand for more accessible, secure, and efficient financial solutions, especially for underserved and unbanked populations.

6.1 Transformation of Financial Products:

Blockchain and DeFi have significantly impacted financial products in India by offering more personalized, secure, and efficient alternatives to traditional offerings. In the lending space, blockchain enables decentralized platforms where peer-to-peer (P2P) lending is facilitated without the need for intermediaries. Platforms like LenDenClub and Faircent, which leverage blockchain's transparency and security features, have seen rapid adoption across India. These platforms are able to offer competitive interest rates while reducing the barriers for borrowers, especially from underbanked sectors, by relying on blockchain to verify the authenticity of credit scores and collateral without intermediaries (Singh & Sharma, 2021). Similarly, blockchain's ability to tokenize assets has made it possible to create fractional ownership of traditionally illiquid assets like real estate and gold. Tokenization allows smaller investors to participate in high-value assets, democratizing access to investment opportunities. In India, this has the potential to transform investment products, as people in rural or low-income areas gain access to previously inaccessible financial markets (Sharma & Verma, 2023). Additionally, DeFi protocols are offering innovative financial products, including synthetic assets, decentralized exchanges (DEXs), and automated lending, which operate on blockchain-based smart contracts. These products offer increased transparency, greater security, and faster execution times compared to traditional financial products. For example, platforms such as Maker DAO and Compound enable Indian investors to earn interest on their cryptocurrency holdings by lending them on decentralized platforms.

6.2 Transformation of Financial Services:

Blockchain technology is transforming the way financial services are delivered in India, particularly in payments, insurance, and wealth management. One of the most significant impacts is in the area of cross-border payments. Traditional remittance systems in India are costly, slow, and heavily reliant on intermediaries. Blockchain-based payment systems, such as Ripple, have revolutionized this process by enabling faster and cheaper international money transfers. Ripple's distributed ledger technology allows users to make cross-border payments in real time, with significantly reduced transaction fees compared to traditional banking systems (Chaudhary et al., 2022). This is particularly important for India, where remittances from the Indian diaspora contribute significantly to the economy. By reducing the cost and improving the speed of international transactions, blockchain has the potential to enhance financial inclusion, especially for low-income families relying on remittances. Blockchain is also transforming the insurance sector in India, where challenges such as fraud, claim delays, and inefficient administrative processes are rampant. The use of blockchain to create decentralized insurance platforms is helping solve these issues. For instance, the use of smart contracts in crop insurance enables automatic payouts when predefined conditions are met, such as verifying damage through satellite data. This innovation is critical for Indian farmers who often struggle with delayed claim payments and complex documentation procedures (Mohanty et al., 2022). Additionally, blockchain is enabling peer-to-peer (P2P) insurance models, where groups of individuals can pool their resources to cover each other's risks in a decentralized manner, reducing the cost of premiums and improving accessibility. DeFi platforms also provide innovative financial services, including decentralized lending, borrowing, and yield farming, which allow individuals to earn interest on their cryptocurrency holdings or collateralize their digital assets for loans, all without needing a bank as an intermediary.

6.3 Transformation of Financial Regulations:

The regulatory landscape in India is evolving to accommodate the disruptive potential of blockchain and DeFi. Blockchain's ability to offer a transparent, immutable ledger has made it easier for regulators to monitor and verify transactions. In India, this has led to the exploration of blockchain for enhancing regulatory compliance in sectors such as banking and capital markets. For instance, the Securities and Exchange Board of India (SEBI) has been investigating the use of blockchain technology for streamlining the clearing and settlement of securities, ensuring transparency and reducing settlement risks (Tapscott & Tapscott, 2018). Blockchain's immutability ensures that all transactions are recorded and auditable, providing regulators with a real-time, tamper-proof record of financial activities. This is particularly important in preventing market manipulation, insider trading, and other forms of financial fraud. Blockchain's transparency and security features also provide a framework for improving know-your-customer (KYC) and anti-money laundering (AML) procedures. The integration of blockchain with the Aadhaar system in India holds promise for creating a secure, tamper-proof digital identity for Indian citizens, which could be used for KYC verification in a more efficient manner. This could drastically reduce fraud and enhance the security of financial transactions. However, while blockchain offers these advantages, there are still regulatory challenges to address, such as how to ensure consumer protection in the decentralized world of DeFi. The Reserve Bank of India (RBI) and other regulatory bodies are currently working on frameworks to integrate blockchain into the existing financial system while addressing risks related to privacy, security, and volatility in digital assets (Bose & Dutta, 2023). Furthermore, the government has expressed concerns about the use of cryptocurrencies in illegal activities, leading to debates on the need for regulations that balance innovation with risk mitigation.

DeFi's decentralized nature, which bypasses traditional intermediaries such as banks, poses a regulatory challenge as it operates outside the reach of conventional financial authorities. In response, Indian regulators are considering the development of a comprehensive regulatory framework for cryptocurrencies and DeFi to address potential risks associated with market manipulation, fraud, and money laundering. While DeFi platforms operate globally and are not restricted by geographical boundaries, India's regulatory bodies are exploring ways to regulate these platforms without stifling innovation. The introduction of the Digital Rupee (Central Bank Digital Currency) by the RBI is also an important step toward creating a regulated digital currency infrastructure that can coexist with decentralized finance.

7. FINDINGS AND SUGGESTIONS

7.1 Findings

7.1.1 Enhanced Financial Inclusion:

Blockchain and decentralized finance (DeFi) have the potential to significantly improve financial inclusion in India. By eliminating intermediaries, these technologies can offer financial products and services to underserved populations, especially in rural areas. Blockchain's ability to offer secure, low-cost, and transparent alternatives to traditional financial services makes it an attractive solution for enhancing access to banking, lending, and insurance (Singh & Sharma, 2021). DeFi platforms, which are based on blockchain, enable access to financial services without the need for a bank account, making it easier for individuals in remote areas to access loans, savings, and investments.

7.1.2 Security and Transparency Benefits:

Blockchain's inherent features of immutability and decentralization provide enhanced security and transparency in financial transactions. This is particularly important for India, where concerns over fraud, corruption, and inefficiency in the financial system have been persistent. Blockchain enables secure and verifiable transactions, reducing the potential for fraud and ensuring trust among users (Chaudhary et al., 2022). Additionally, the transparent nature of blockchain can help regulators and financial institutions track transactions in real time, ensuring accountability in the financial system.

7.1.3 Revolutionizing Traditional Financial Services:

Blockchain and DeFi are revolutionizing traditional financial services such as lending, payments, insurance, and wealth management. In lending, blockchain enables peer-to-peer (P2P) lending platforms that offer faster and cheaper alternatives to traditional bank loans. Platforms like LenDenClub are already providing loans to individuals without the need for intermediaries, while simultaneously reducing the cost of borrowing for underserved populations. Similarly, DeFi has introduced innovative financial products such as decentralized exchanges (DEXs), synthetic assets, and yield farming, offering new investment avenues that were previously inaccessible to the majority of the population (Sharma & Verma, 2023).

7.1.4 Regulatory Challenges and Opportunities:

The Indian regulatory landscape is still evolving to accommodate the disruptive nature of blockchain and DeFi. While there is recognition of the potential benefits, there are concerns about the lack of consumer protection, market volatility, and the risk of money laundering and fraud. The Reserve Bank of India (RBI) and the Securities and Exchange Board of India (SEBI) are exploring frameworks for integrating blockchain into the existing financial system, but the lack of clear regulations around cryptocurrencies and DeFi is a significant challenge. The government's stance on cryptocurrencies and digital assets will play a crucial role in determining the pace of blockchain and DeFi adoption in India (Bose & Dutta, 2023).

7.1.5 Scalability Issues:

Despite the advantages of blockchain and DeFi, scalability remains a key challenge, particularly for large-scale applications such as payments, high-frequency trading, and cross-border transactions. Blockchain networks, particularly those based on Proof of Work (PoW), such as Bitcoin, face scalability issues due to slow transaction speeds and high fees. Although newer blockchain networks and layer-2 solutions, such as Ethereum 2.0 and the Lightning Network, offer promising scalability improvements, their widespread adoption in India remains limited (Tapscott & Tapscott, 2018).

7.1.6 Technological and Digital Infrastructure Gaps:

For blockchain and DeFi to succeed in India, there is a need to improve the country's digital infrastructure, particularly in rural and underserved areas. Many potential users lack access to smartphones, internet connectivity, or the technical knowledge required to engage with blockchain-based platforms. Initiatives to promote digital literacy, provide affordable internet access, and create infrastructure for blockchain adoption will be essential for overcoming these barriers (Gupta et al., 2022).

7.2 Suggestions

7.2.1 Promote Digital Literacy and Awareness:

To unlock the full potential of blockchain and DeFi, it is crucial to promote digital literacy across all segments of the population. Educational programs should focus on explaining the basics of blockchain, cryptocurrencies, and decentralized financial systems. Government agencies, educational institutions, and private-sector players can collaborate to design programs that target both urban and rural populations. This will help bridge the knowledge gap and increase the adoption of blockchain-based financial services (Chaudhary et al., 2022).

7.2.2 Develop a Comprehensive Regulatory Framework:

One of the most critical steps for fostering the growth of blockchain and DeFi in India is the creation of a clear, transparent regulatory framework. The government and financial regulators should work together to address concerns around consumer protection, fraud prevention, and market stability. The framework should outline how decentralized financial systems will be integrated into India's existing legal structure and define clear guidelines for cryptocurrencies, smart contracts, and decentralized exchanges. Regulators should also focus on creating mechanisms for real-time surveillance and monitoring of DeFi platforms to ensure compliance with legal standards (Bose & Dutta, 2023).

7.2.3 Enhance Scalability Solutions:

For blockchain and DeFi to scale effectively in India, there is a need for the development and adoption of more scalable blockchain solutions. Layer-2 scaling protocols, such as the Lightning Network for Bitcoin and Ethereum 2.0, should be promoted as they offer the ability to handle higher transaction volumes with lower costs. Additionally, blockchain developers and researchers should collaborate with Indian fintech companies to create customized blockchain solutions that are optimized for the local market's needs, ensuring that scalability does not come at the expense of security or decentralization.

7.2.4 Strengthen Infrastructure for Rural and Underserved Areas:

As the adoption of blockchain and DeFi relies heavily on internet connectivity and digital devices, it is essential to strengthen infrastructure, especially in rural areas. The government should prioritize initiatives aimed at expanding broadband access and ensuring affordable smartphones are available to the underserved population. Additionally, integrating blockchain with existing identity systems, such as Aadhaar, could streamline KYC processes and enable individuals in rural India to access financial services seamlessly (Mohanty et al., 2022).

7.2.5 Encourage Public-Private Partnerships:

Public-private partnerships (PPPs) can play a crucial role in advancing the adoption of blockchain and DeFi in India. Collaborations between government agencies, financial institutions, blockchain startups, and technology firms can help create a conducive environment for innovation. Such partnerships can facilitate the development of pilot projects, regulatory sandboxes, and blockchain-based solutions for specific sectors such as agriculture, insurance, and micro-lending. These collaborations can also help address critical challenges like cybersecurity, scalability, and regulatory compliance while ensuring that blockchain adoption remains inclusive and equitable (Sharma & Verma, 2023).

7.2.6 Introduce a National Blockchain Policy:

India should consider introducing a national blockchain policy that sets a strategic direction for blockchain adoption across various sectors, including finance, healthcare, and logistics. This policy should provide clarity on how blockchain can be integrated into the country's economic and technological landscape. It should also define the roles and responsibilities of various stakeholders, including government bodies, financial institutions, and technology providers, in fostering a secure and efficient blockchain ecosystem.

8. CONCLUSION

Blockchain technology and decentralized finance (DeFi) are poised to drive significant transformation in India's financial services sector. These technologies offer the potential to address long-standing issues such as financial inclusion, transparency, and efficiency in financial products and services. By enabling decentralized, secure, and transparent transactions, blockchain and DeFi have already begun reshaping lending, payments, insurance, and wealth management, offering innovative solutions that were once unattainable for large sections of the population. The promise of blockchain's immutable ledger and DeFi's decentralized nature holds the key to democratizing access to financial services, particularly for underserved and rural populations, which have traditionally faced barriers to accessing banking and credit. However, the widespread adoption and integration of these technologies in India will require addressing several challenges, including regulatory uncertainties, technological scalability, and digital literacy. While the Indian government and financial regulators are taking steps toward creating a conducive environment, such as exploring frameworks for cryptocurrencies and integrating blockchain with existing financial systems, a comprehensive and clear regulatory framework is still needed. Furthermore, overcoming infrastructure gaps, particularly in rural areas, and educating the public on the benefits and risks of blockchain and DeFi will be crucial for ensuring these innovations achieve their full potential. With continued collaboration between the public and private sectors, India can harness the power of blockchain and DeFi to drive financial sector growth, inclusivity, and innovation, positioning itself as a global leader in digital finance.

9. REFERENCES

Antonopoulos, A. M. (2017). *Mastering Bitcoin: Unlocking Digital Cryptocurrencies*. O'Reilly Media.

Bhattacharya, R., Kapoor, P., & Mehta, S. (2021). Blockchain and sustainability: A critical analysis. *Energy Policy Journal*, *45*(6), 89–104.

Bose, P., & Dutta, R. (2023). Blockchain regulation in India: Challenges and prospects. *Economic and Political Weekly*, *58*(4), 22–27.

Chakraborty, R. (2022). Banking reforms in India: A historical perspective. *Journal of Financial Studies*, *12*(3), 45–60.

Chakraborty, R., Bhattacharya, A., & Mukherjee, S. (2022). Blockchain applications in Indian banking sector: Case studies and prospects. *International Journal of Financial Innovation*, *14*(3), 121–138.

Chaudhary, P., Kapoor, S., & Malik, R. (2023). Digital literacy and blockchain adoption in rural India: Challenges and solutions. *Journal of Emerging Technologies*, *11*(2), 45–59.

Chaudhary, P., Singh, V., & Sharma, T. (2022). Blockchain in trade finance: An Indian perspective. *Guoji Maoyi Wenti*, *17*(3), 112–127.

Chaudhary, R., Singh, M., & Patel, V. (2023). Blockchain literacy in rural India: Challenges and strategies. *Indian Journal of Digital Transformation*, *8*(1), 34–50.

D'Silva, D., Filkova, M., & Singh, R. (2020). *Cross-border remittances and blockchain: A case study of India*. World Bank Policy Paper.

Das, A., Verma, S., & Mehta, P. (2024). Blockchain and AI: Future financial ecosystems. *Journal of Emerging Technologies*, *10*(2), 102–118.

Das, A., Verma, S., & Mehta, P. (2024). Blockchain for financial inclusion in India. *Journal of Fintech Innovation*, *10*(1), 89–102.

Dasgupta, S., & Mehta, R. (2022). Digital payment ecosystem in India: Challenges and opportunities. *Economic and Political Weekly*, *57*(4), 32–39.

Economic Times. (2024). India's crypto regulation debate: Implications for blockchain and DeFi.

Goyal, A., Bhardwaj, R., & Kapoor, V. (2021). Financial inclusion through blockchain. *International Journal of Development Studies*, *13*(3), 45–65.

Goyal, A., Verma, S., & Mehta, P. (2024). *India's fintech revolution: Trends, challenges, and opportunities*. Springer.

Gupta, S., Kumar, A., & Patel, D. (2022). DeFi and financial transformation in India. *Fintech Review*, *5*(2), 87–100.

Hayes, A., Anderson, P., & Zhao, W. (2019). Decentralized finance and financial markets: An overview. *Journal of Financial Innovation*, *6*(1), 32–48.

Kumar, A., & Singh, P. (2023). Decentralized finance (DeFi) and financial inclusion: Perspectives from India. *Journal of Fintech and Policy Research*, *5*(1), 98–110.

Kumar, S., & Rajan, P. (2023). Blockchain for fraud prevention in Indian banking. *Journal of Financial Integrity*, *9*(4), 67–79.

Ministry of Finance. (2023). *Jan Dhan Yojana: 10-year progress report*. Government of India.

Mohanty, P., Sharma, K., & Sen, A. (2022). Blockchain and Aadhaar integration: Opportunities and risks. *India Digital Journal*, *7*(3), 54–73.

Narula, S., & Vasudevan, R. (2020). Blockchain-based microfinance in rural India. *Journal of Social Entrepreneurship*, *12*(3), 210–226.

NASSCOM. (2023). *State of blockchain adoption in India: Opportunities and challenges*. National Association of Software and Service Companies.

National Payments Corporation of India (NPCI). (2023). Unified Payments Interface: Growth and global leadership. Retrieved from https://www.npci.org.in

Nayyar, R. (2021). Economic reforms and financial sector liberalization in India. *Economic and Political Weekly*, *56*(2), 12–24.

Reserve Bank of India (RBI). (2023). Central bank digital currency pilot projects: Progress report. Retrieved from https://www.rbi.org.in

Sharma, V., & Singh, P. (2023). Financial services transformation in India: A study of liberalization and digital integration. *Journal of Emerging Markets*, *9*(4), 98–110.

Sharma, V., & Verma, N. (2023). Tokenization of assets: Blockchain use cases in India. *Journal of Blockchain Applications*, *8*(1), 98–114.

Singh, D., & Sharma, R. (2021). Blockchain-based KYC systems for Indian banks. *Asian Banking Journal*, *5*(3), 65–89.

Singh, T., & Verma, R. (2024). *Blockchain and financial inclusion in emerging economies: The Indian experience*. Springer.

Swan, M. (2015). *Blockchain: Blueprint for a New Economy*. O'Reilly Media.

Szabo, N. (1997). *Smart contracts: Building blocks for digital markets*. Extropy Journal.

Tapscott, D., & Tapscott, A. (2018). Blockchain for capital markets: A vision for the future. *Capital Markets Review*, *11*(2), 39–57.

World Bank. (2023). Remittances trends: India's global leadership. Retrieved from https://www.worldbank.org

Zohar, A. (2015). Bitcoin and blockchain: Economic and technological challenges. *Journal of Financial Innovation*, *3*(2), 27–35.

Chapter 17
Unlocking Financial Performance of Commercial Banks:
The Role of Liquidity and Return on Average Equity

Samreen Tunio
University of Milan, Italy

ABSTRACT

This study aims to examine the impact of liquidity on the return on average equity (ROAE) and overall financial performance of Pakistan's commercial banking sector. The analysis is based on audited financial data from 20 commercial banks covering the period from 2006 to 2022. Using the Generalized Method of Moment (GMM), the research explores how liquidity, along with the other factors such as credit risk, the efficiency ratio, equity ratio, and bank size, influences profitability. The findings revealed that liquidity has a positive and significant effect on ROAE. Additionally, external macroeconomic factors such as Gross Domestic Product (GDP) and Consumer Price Index (CPI), indirectly affect profitability due to their high volatility and challenges in predicting these indicators. The study recommends developing stable policies to strengthen the banking sector by diversifying and optimizing liquidity management strategies.

1. INTRODUCTION

Financial sector plays a significant role in the economic development of Pakistan, serving as a backbone for the country's growth and stability. Among its various components, commercial banks are essential players, facilitating a wide range of financial services that include investments, savings, and spending (Asteriou et al., 2024). Their operational effectiveness not only affects the health of the banking system but also has a border implication for the economy, as a robust and efficient banking sector fosters confidence among consumers and investors, promoting economic activities across various industries. A well-functioning banking system is essential for mobilizing savings, allocating resources efficiently, and enhancing overall economic productivity (Ofoeda et al., 2024). One of the biggest issues facing the

DOI: 10.4018/979-8-3373-0209-6.ch017

banking sector globally, and the banking sector in Pakistan specifically, these days is liquidity risk. It is now a significant danger in banking operations, and regulators and policymakers are quite concerned about it. Liquidity emerges as one of the most critical factors influencing the performance and profitability of banks. It acts as a lifeline enabling banks to meet their short-term obligations manage unforeseen financial demands, and support ongoing financial activities (Rashaduzzaman, 2024). The relationship between liquidity and profitability, particularly in terms of Return on Average Equity (ROAE), has been the subject of extensive research within the field of finance and banking (Tanwar, 2024). While numerous studies suggest a positive correlation between liquidity levels and profitability outcomes, others indicate varying outcomes based on the specific economic context in which banks operate. For instance, Rahman and Nasr (2007) observed that financial accessibility is frequently linked to late payments which not only increases operational costs but also compels firms to rely on more expensive financing sources. Consequently, the implementation of an optimal liquidity management strategy becomes vital for enhancing firm value and achieving efficient returns (Abu Khalaf et al., 2024).

In Pakistan, the banking sector is confronted with a multitude of challenges, that can significantly impact its liquidity and consequently its profitability (Hassan et al., 2022). Macroeconomic factors such as inflation rates, and interest rate fluctuations, introduce considerable volatility that complicates effective liquidity management. Furthermore, internal factors including credit risk management and assets composition play significant roles in determining a bank's overall financial performance and stability (Ridwan, 2022). Research conducted by Prem Bahadur Budhathoki (2024) in Nepal emphasizes the positive impact of trading volume a key indicator of liquidity on stock return in commercial banks, suggesting that higher liquidity levels can substantially influence market performance. In contrast, Mehmood & Kaewsaeng-on (2024), underscores the importance of working capital management for enhancing profitability, illustrating how cash conversion cycles and effective cash flow strategies can significantly influence earning outcomes (Sawarni et al., 2023).

Despite the significant importance of liquidity on ROAE, the relationship has historically carried mixed results for economic performance in distinct economies. There is often a positive and clear relationship between liquidity and ROAE in the developed markets, contrary to the findings in the emerging markets like Pakistan having a peculiar economic class of conditions and regulatory environment. In order to fill this gap in the literature, this study examines the empirical relationship between ROAE and liquidity in the context of Pakistan's commercial banking industry between 2006 and 2022. In particular, it seeks to determine the relationship between liquidity and external factors, such as macroeconomic indicators like the GDP and the CPI, and internal bank factors, such as credit risk, asset management effectiveness, and internal bank work.

This investigation's main research question is: How does liquidity empirically impact return on average equity in Pakistani commercial banks?

This study also looks at how Pakistan's commercial banks' effective liquidity management strategies differ from those in other developing nations and how they can affect the financial system and the business cycle as a whole. This study aims to achieve two main objectives: In order to determine the internal and external factors that impact this crucial relationship, the primary objective was to empirically investigate the relationship between liquidity and ROAE in the context of Pakistan's commercial banking sector. Thus, this study expands the body of knowledge in the field of ROAE, by exploring how effective liquidity management can impact profitability, ultimately contributing to the understanding of how banks can leverage resources to create value for their society, the environment, and the economy. The remainder of this study is structured as follows; Section 2 provides the literature. Part 3 talks about methodology.

Section 4 discusses the results and findings, Finally, Section 5 concludes the chapter, Section 6 provides Limitations and recommendations and finally, Section 7 provides managerial implications

2. LITERATURE REVIEW

The concept of liquidity arises from numerous economic perspectives. One way to describe liquidity is the ease with which a security can be sold and the ease with which financing can be obtained to trade it. According to Khan et al. (2022), the first is known as market liquidity, and the second is known as liquidity financing. Bank liquidity is a measure of the bank's ability to meet its financial obligations on time. Commercial banks' ability to fund, when necessary, all of their contractual commitments, including lending, investing, and withdrawing deposits as well as the maturity of liabilities in the regular course of banking operations, is referred to as liquidity (Hacini et al., 2021). Arniati et al. (2024), Liquidity management is the planning and oversight required to guarantee that the business has sufficient liquid assets, either as a requirement to meet the demands of incidental lenders or as a step to implement the monetary authorities' needs. The main objective of managing liquidity is to make sure that a bank's cash inflows and outflows are equal. A healthy and stable banking industry is encouraged by this equilibrium, if it is maintained across all banks. This is a prerequisite for the effective operation of banking intermediation. An overview of bank liquidity management's goals is as follows: Fulfilling all cash outflow commitments consistently and regularly (both on and off the balance sheet), avoiding the acquisition of money through the forced sale of assets or at market premiums, and adhering to statutory reserve requirements and specified liquidity constraints (Nguyen & Dao, 2022). Several studies have extensively examined the effect of liquidity on a bank profitability and other financial sectors of the economy. These analyses explore the role of liquidity in maintaining stable and consistent earnings within the financial system.

2.1 Hypothesis Development

2.1.1 Impact of Liquidity on Performance

Liquidity is the capacity to produce enough cash to cover financial obligations, but in the banking industry, it mostly relates to the capacity to honor maturing deposits. Given that a significant amount of their liabilities are receivable on demand (deposits), banks do in fact need liquidity; yet, the more liquid an asset is, the lower its yield. Therefore, choosing one asset combination over another while accounting for a bank's obligation size would have a significant impact on risk, profitability, and liquidity management (Jabbouri et al., 2022). Bank performance is the efficacy and efficiency of a bank's operations as demonstrated by metrics including management performance, profitability, and efficiency assessments. Both the overall stability of the banking industry and the probability of bank collapses are significantly impacted by it (Kweh et al., 2024a).

The relationship between liquidity and firm performance has been a significant focus of financial research, which wearying perspectives offered by different studies. Ededjo (2023), investigated the link between working capital and firm value using data from 2005 to 2010 and found no positive working capital firm performance, however, Shahchera (2012) uses GMM analysis to explain the indirect working capital earnings respectively. On the other hand, Franklin Patrick et al. (2024) found that corporate performance has a significant impact on Return on Equity (ROE) for Indonesian listed companies and showed how liquidity is important in developing countries. Drawing on Sharma et al. (2024) analysis, effective liquidity management is critical for the operational success of Indian textile firms. Likewise, Bordeleau et al. (2010) demonstrate that banks maximize profitability by keeping liquidty at optimal levels. However, studies like Abba Mohammad et al. (2023) showed that there is a negative relationship between liquidity and earnings in Nigerian banks which implies excess liquidity carries with it risk. Further study by Periokaitė and Dobrovolskienė (2021) during the same COVID-19 pandemic highlights how liquidity plays an important role in robustness while other studies like AlShethiri (2021) showed that liquidity is critical in determining how firms survive. Others such as Berger (1995), have pointed out that strategic liquidity management results in profitability and stability, and still others, Brink and Jan (2002), have indicated that excess liquidity can be considered an opportunity cost. But taken together, these findings point to how management of liquidity impacts performance and how external factors influence liquidity matter.

2.1.2 Impact of Credit Risk on Performance

Sustainable business growth and high profitability in financial institutions greatly depend on credit expansion and its associated return (M. N. Tunio & Tunio, 2024). credit risk, one of the most crucial factors influencing business performance (Kweh et al., 2024a). According to Charles and Kenneth et al (2013), credit risk fosters loan growth, which not only impacts the banking sector but also has far-reaching effects on the overall economy. Hosna et al. (2009), examined data from four listed firms in Sweden between 2000 to 2008, and revealed that non-performing loans(NPLs) and equity ratios significantly influence equity return in Swedish banks. Olalekan & Pamp; Adeyinka (2013), analyzing data from 2007 to 2011, found that credit risk adversely affects earnings in conventional banks in Indonesia. Furthermore, Smaoui et al. (2024), observed no positive impact of non-performing loans(NLPs) on a firm's value, underscoring the detrimental effect of credit risk.

2.1.3 Impact of Equity on Performance

Bank equity plays a crucial role in addressing financial crises and other challenges. During times of crises, equity serves as a safeguard against unexpected losses and poor management ensuring the survival of the business. By holding more equity, banks can reduce their reliance on borrowing, which lower borrowing cost and increases returns (Gupta et al., 2024). (Filomeni (2024), highlighted the positive impact of capital on a bank's performance, recommending that holding more capital can reduce operating and financing costs, which in turn increases profitability. Additionally, lower business costs protect firms from bankruptcy and enhance expected profits. Eshwari & Baby (2023), emphasized the importance of maintaining a certain level of invested capital, which is associated with lower costs and higher earnings. The results revealed a direct correlation between capital and profitability. Furthermore, sufficient Capital not only reduces costs but also protects businesses from losses due to credit risk.

2.1.4 Impact of Size on Performance

The attainment of high profit is a concern to large-sized businesses which shows its strength to cover costs and efficiently uplift the performance. The execution of strength to attract depositors and enhance lending activities is considered a large-scale financial entity that affects positively on firm's performance while many studies researched contradictory results and reveal having a large-sized business implies high costs and expenses to bear. The reason is defined as adopting an aggressive approach of diversification inclined high business cost to capture efficiently also it maximizes the risk for business to expand with low return and affect performance. De Silva et al (2019) concluded the same results. Also suggested large large-sized banks captured more opportunities compared to small-scale businesses due to injecting more capital and finance at a low cost. While on the other side, Rehman et al (2018) revealed a comparative study between small and large-scale businesses and concluded holding high total assets entails low returns. Betten & Pamp; Vo (2019) and Rahman et al (2020).

2.1.5 Impact of Gross Domestic Product on Performance

The efficient economy implies growth in trade and financial business performance. Operating activities become high when the financial structure entails a consistent approach with a high demand for services. Fluctuations in the economy bring shock to every business entity and shake the investor's confidence in investment and diversification. Volatility hurts the sustainable market approach towards development and growth in efficiency and performance. According to De Leon (2020) researched the negative association between gross domestic product (GDP) and profitability. Investing and spending activities depend on economic growth and stability. When these practices are at their peak; represent the development in the financial system where credit facilities are enhanced and as a result, banks earn efficient earnings.

2.1.6 Impact of Consumer Price Index on Performance

According to Kweh et al. (2024), instant bank earnings are a sign of low financing costs indicating a positive association with the inflation rate while Almaqtari et al. (2022), revealed no direct influence of the inflation rate on earnings. Mohammad (2022), found no positive influence of the inflation rate on a firm's value due to the inability to anticipate the macroeconomic. Rathnasiri (2024), revealed the same impact on net interest margin. High profitability is expected when banks can anticipate the consumer price index in time to adjust interest rates to generate more earnings.

3. METHODOLOGY

3.1 Data Collection

The study's population consists of Pakistani local banks. Each selected bank has a registration and operates in accordance with the State Bank of Pakistan's normal operating procedures. The sample consists of 20 commercial banks. In this research annual data has been collected and examined for the period from 2006 to 2022. The data has been gathered from the Publications of the State Bank of Pakistan and the World Bank.

3.2 Econometric Technique

Clear and transparent assumptions must be analysed to ensure unbiased results (Asghar et al., 2024). Outcomes may become biased when issues such as multicollinearity, autocorrelation, and heteroscedasticity are present. To address these problems, various techniques are employed. For resolving multicollinearity and heteroscedasticity issues random and fixed effect models are often appropriate for obtaining consistent parameter estimates (Hamza & Nechchad, 2024). However, if an endogeneity problem exists these models may still produce biased results. To address this, the study aims to predict the true values of parameters while resolving endogeneity, multicollinearity, autocorrelation, and heteroscedasticity effectively.

3.3 Generalized Method of Moments

One of the estimation techniques used to resolve issues such as endogeneity, multicollinearity, autocorrelation, serial correlation, and heteroscedasticity is the Generalized Method of Moments (GMM). This method was introduced by Arellano and Bond (1991) to address all these challenges effectively. GMM resolves endogeneity in the model, whereas applying Multiple Ordinary Least Square (OLS) and Least Square Dummy Variables (LSDV) estimators often results in inconsistent parameters, leading to biased estimators.

4. RESULTS AND DISCUSSION

The relationship between liquidity on return of average equity and the financial performance of commercial banks has shown varying results across different regions and timeframes. In the context of the Pakistani commercial banking sector, it is important to analyze the impact of liquidity to develop tailored policies for this region. The analysis in this study follows a systematic approach. The following is the methodology used for the analysis. Initially, descriptive data are examined to obtain a summary of the banking statistics relevant to this research. Second, the relationship between these variables is demonstrated using correlation analysis. Thirdly, the impact of liquidity on bank performance is examined by regression analysis. Finally, a risk analysis of liquidity is carried out and the liquidity position is examined.

Table 1. Determinants of liquidity management and bank profitability

Variable	Abbreviation	Formula
Return on Average Equity	ROAE	Net Income/Total Equity
Liquidity Risk	ADVTA	Advances/Total Assets
Equity Ratio	ER	Equity/Total Assets
Size	SIZE	Total Assets
Credit Risk	CR	Loan Loss Provision/Loans
Efficiency	EFF	Efficiency/Income

continued on following page

Table 1. Continued

Variable	Abbreviation	Formula
Loan Growth	LG	Loan (t)-Loan (t-1)/Loan (t-1)
Asset Growth	AG	Assets (t)-Assets (t-1)/Assets (t-1)
Interest Expense	INTEXP	-
Gross Domestic Product	GDP	-
Inflation Rate	CPI	-

Table 2 presents the descriptive statistics, which include 320 observations, along with the average values, standard deviation, and minimum and maximum values for each variable. These statics provide an overview of the key variables under study, such as liquidity ratio, return on average equity (ROAE), credit risk, efficiency ratio, equity ratio, GDP growth, and CPI. The results indicate significant variation in the liquidity ratio across banks, reflecting the diverse liquidity management strategies used by different institutions. Similarly, the range of ROAE highlights the variability in profitability performance within the sector, pointing to differences in operational strategies, level of risk exposure, and external conditions that influence financial outcomes across banks.

Table 2. Descriptive analysis

Variables	Observations	Mean	Std. Deviation	Minimum	Maximum
ROAE	321	0.112	0.238	-1.77	0.68
ADVTA	321	0.570	2.378	0.13	50.37
ER	321	0.084	0.069	-0.17	0.5
EFF	321	0.317	0.137	0.1	1.28
INTEXP	321	2.27	2.60	1554	1.68
LG	321	0.378	6.612	-1	118
SIZE	321	6.77	8.06	4024674	5.24
CR	321	0.104	0.102	0	0.09
GDP	321	0.035	0.019	0.01	0.06
CPI	321	0.027	0.034	0.05	0.08

Table 3: provides a correlation matrix between liquidity, return on average equity (ROAE) other independent variables, confirming that the values are free from multicollinearity. The correlation analysis shows important relationships between liquidity and other variables. Results suggest a positive correlation between ROAE and liquidity, demonstrating that higher liquidity gives a higher positive impact on profitability. On the other hand, liquidity demonstrates a negative relation with the efficiency ratio and credit risk, which implies that increased liquidity levels will reduce risk exposure and facilitate better operational efficiency. These results highlight how crucial efficient liquidity management is to overall financial stability.

Table 3. Correlation matrix

	ROAE	LIQ	ER	EFF	INTEXP	LG	SIZE	CR	GDP	CPI
ROAE	1									
ADVTA	0.007	1								
ER	-0.079	-0.004	1							
EFF	-0.043	-0.022	0.066	1						
INTEXP	0.175	0.013	-0.208	-0.272	1					
LG	-0.018	-0.001	0.090	-0.026	-0.034	1				
SIZE	0.240	-0.052	-0.225	-0.225	0.306		1			
CR	-0.427	0.011	0.032	-0.049	-0.049	0.012	-0.917	1		
GDP	0.070	0.016	0.112	0.008	-0.057	0.044	-0.217	-0.126	1	
CPI	0.037	-0.118	-0.003	0.023	-0.042	0.020	-0.393	-0.047	0.521	1

Table 4: summarises the regression analysis findings, highlighting liquidity as critical factor in financial markets due to its significant impact on firm performance. Regression analysis examines how liquidity affects ROAE while controlling for macroeconomic variables like GDP growth and CPI as well as variables like the equity ratio and credit risk efficiency ratio. The findings show that liquidity positively affects ROAE in a statistically significant way, proving its crucial role in raising profitability. However, the credit risk and efficiency ratio has a negative impact on ROAE, underscoring the importance of effective risk management strategies. Conversely, the equity ratio favourably affects profitability and emphasizes the significance of maintaining enough capitalization.

Table 4. Impact of liquidity on average equity return (2006-2022)

Variables	(1)	(2)	(3)	(4)	(5)
ROAE	0.353 0.000	0.417 0.000	0.406 0.000	0.402 0.000	0.503 0.003
INTEXP	0.244 0.390	0.560 0.033	2.16 0.534	7.89 0.101	1.02 0.484
ER	1.326 0.033	1.336 0.152	1.240 0.089	1.686 0.052	1.23 0.284
EFF	-0.195 0.127	-0.252 0.198	-0.185 0.157	-0.188 0.314	0.017 0.905
CR	-0.427 0.005	0.704 0.034	-0.591 0.073	-	-
ADVTA	0.007 0.034	0.008 0.055	0.005 0.247	0.006 0.370	0.001 0.902
GDP	-	-0.865 0.460	-1.12 0.088	0.146 0.469	0.045 0.805
CPI	-	0.070 0.744	-	-0.158 0.466	-0.125 0.691
SIZE	-	-	-4.07 0.000	5.53 0.000	5.13 0.004

continued on following page

Table 4. Continued

Variables	(1)	(2)	(3)	(4)	(5)
LG	-	-	-	-	0.002 0.234
CONSTANT	0.044 0.550	0.127 0.356	0.043 0.578	-0.112 0.235	-0.137 0.336
OBSERVATIONS	284	284	284	284	284
INSTRUMENTS	318	320	320	300	324
AR (1)	0.001	0.005	0.050	0.040	0.022
AR (2)	0.123	0.159	0.166	0.191	0.152
SARGAN	12.095	10.955	11.023	9.481	11.475

The analysis of liquidity risk reveals that liquidity buffers are effective among banks. Medium and small banks have lower liquid buffers because they have less access to a wider range of sources of funding, and they are less compliant with regulations than larger banks. This draws attention to the larger institutions' contributions to systemic stability while simultaneously highlighting any weaknesses in smaller banks that might call for regulatory action.

The results of this study indicate that bank earnings are positively influenced by liquidity, consistent with earlier research conducted by (Prem Bahadur et al, 2024). Similarly, a study by Ratnasari et al. (2021) examined the effect of liquidity on bank performance and found that liquidity enhances profitability. However, contrary to these findings, Ichsan (2013) reported no significant correlation between earnings and liquidity.

5. CONCLUSION

This paper aimed to examine the impact of liquidity on return of average equity and financial performance of commercial banks in Pakistan. Additionally, it explores how internal and external factors influenced the stability of Pakistani banks during the financial years 2006–2022. The dynamic Two Steps (GMM) explores the efficient estimators. Findings revealed that there is a negative and empirically significant influence of liquidity on profitability. It indicates holding more liquidity entails a reduction in profitability and vice versa. Balance and optimal approach entail stable performance in operating activities and business survival while depending on excess or shortage on current measures implies shock to future sustainability. Credit risk has an inverse association with profitability while it is statistically insignificant. When banks poorly manage and monitor the loans, this risk becomes high. The capital positively and significantly impacts profitability. It indicates banks declare dividends to their shareholders from retained earnings which implies the bank's capital is small and medium and vice versa. Assets indirectly effect on bank's profitability on account of maintenance costs. Large-sized banks demonstrate high internal costs and risks which lead to threats in order to make business expansive small-sized financial businesses imply low-cost costs with high expected future earnings and performance (S. Tunio et al., 2024). Gross domestic product and consumer price index are both external determinants that inversely impact performance due to inconsistent environment and the inability to anticipate economic indicators.

6. LIMITATIONS AND FUTURE RESEARCH DIRECTION

The current research has achieved its objectives but there are several limitations associated with it. First, the data for this research was obtained solely from commercial banks in Pakistan, which limits the generalizability of the findings. Future research could include banks from other regions or countries to provide a comparative perspective and border insights. Second, this research focused on the impact of liquidity on the return of average equity (ROAE) and overall financial performance. Further future research can be extended across additional variables such as operational efficiency, capital adequacy and competition in the market in order to achieve a more comprehensive explanation on bank performance. Third, the analysis is carried out using audited financials of 20 banks in the period 2006 to 2022, which can be extended by future researchers by adding more recent data to enhance data analysis. The sample size for this research was taken of 20 commercial banks, future researchers may increase the sample and add more banks from other parts of Pakistan to get more realistic results. Moreover, this research investigates the relation between profitability and liquidity, other variables like bank size, efficiency ratio, equity ratio, and credit risk, and uses the Generalized Method of Moment (GMM) method. Future researchers can extend the scope by developing variables of bank performance in terms of operational efficiency, capital adequacy or market competition to a more complete understanding of a bank performance.

7. MANAGERIAL IMPLICATIONS

Keeping the earlier discussion in view, this section deals with managerial implications for effective liquidity management and minimum credit risk and to increase bank's financial performance in Pakistan. First, managers need to develop an effective liquidity management system to reduce credit risk and increase profitability. Secondly, the banking sector should prioritize executing new projects within their equity framework to foster growth in both the banking sector and the overall financial market. Developing the ability to anticipate changes in the external environment can help reduce financing costs, thereby enhancing profitability and improving return on average on equity. Additionally, adopting a balanced liquidity approach is crucial for maintaining a stable, risk-free environment, and ensuring the financial stability of the bank while safeguarding the interest of stakeholders and clients.

REFERENCES

Abu Khalaf, B., Awad, A. B., & Ellis, S. (2024). The Impact of Non-Interest Income on Commercial Bank Profitability in the Middle East and North Africa (MENA) Region. *Journal of Risk and Financial Management, 17*(3), 103. DOI: 10.3390/jrfm17030103

Almaqtari, F. A., Hashid, A., Farhan, N. H. S., Tabash, M. I., & Al-ahdal, W. M. (2022). An empirical examination of the impact of country-level corporate governance on profitability of Indian banks. *International Journal of Finance & Economics, 27*(2), 1912–1932. DOI: 10.1002/ijfe.2250

Arniati, T., Muslichah, M., & Utami, N. N. (2024). The Effect Of Liquidity And Business Volume On Cooperative Performance. *International Journal of Scientific Research, 1*(03), 03. Advance online publication. DOI: 10.62894/6brqs150

Asghar, M., Ali, S., Hanif, M., & Ullah, S. (2024). Energy transition in newly industrialized countries: A policy paradigm in the perspective of technological innovation and urbanization. *Sustainable Futures : An Applied Journal of Technology, Environment and Society, 7*, 100163. DOI: 10.1016/j.sftr.2024.100163

Asteriou, D., Spanos, K., & Trachanas, E. (2024). Financial development, economic growth and the role of fiscal policy during normal and stress times: Evidence for 26 EU countries. *International Journal of Finance & Economics, 29*(2), 2495–2514. DOI: 10.1002/ijfe.2793

Ededjo, F. (2023). *Determinants of banks performance before and after the financial crisis of 2007-2009: A study of global systemically important banks in the United Kingdom* [Thesis, Anglia Ruskin Research Online (ARRO)]. https://aru.figshare.com/articles/thesis/Determinants_of_banks_performance_before_and_after_the_financial_crisis_of_2007-2009_a_study_of_global_systemically_important_banks_in_the_United_Kingdom/24512380/1

Eshwari, D., & Baby, M. K. (2023). The Effect of Capital Structure on the Profitability of FMCG Companies. In Aloysius Edward, J., Jaheer Mukthar, K. P., Asis, E. R., & Sivasubramanian, K. (Eds.), *Current Trends in Economics, Business and Sustainability* (pp. 313–320). Springer Nature., DOI: 10.1007/978-981-99-3366-2_37

Filomeni, S. (2024). The impact of the Paycheck Protection Program on the risk-taking behaviour of US banks. *Review of Quantitative Finance and Accounting, 62*(4), 1329–1353. DOI: 10.1007/s11156-023-01223-7

Gupta, S. K., Nagar, N., Srivastava, S., Somvanshi, P., & Akimova, L. (2024). An Application of Structure Equation Modelling in Determinants of Customer-Based Brand Equity (CBBE) in the Banking Area. In Khoury, R. E., & Nasrallah, N. (Eds.), *Intelligent Systems, Business, and Innovation Research* (pp. 399–411). Springer Nature Switzerland., DOI: 10.1007/978-3-031-36895-0_32

Hacini, I., Boulenfad, A., & Dahou, K. (2021). The Impact of Liquidity Risk Management on the Financial Performance of Saudi Arabian Banks. *EMAJ: Emerging Markets Journal, 11*(1), 1. Advance online publication. DOI: 10.5195/emaj.2021.221

Hamza, A., & Nechchad, F. (2024). An Econometric & Systematic Analysis of Thailand's Economic Output, Exports and Imports; Utilizing Vector Error Correction Methodology. *Journal of Business Technology and Economics*, *1*(3), 3.

Hassan, K. H. U., Sheikh, S. M., & Rahman, S. U. (2022). The Determinants of Non-Performing Loans (NPLs); Evidence from the Banking Sector of Pakistan. *ANNALS OF SOCIAL SCIENCES AND PERSPECTIVE, 3*(1), Article 1.

Jabbouri, I., Satt, H., Azzouzi, O. E., & Naili, M. (2022). Working capital management and firm performance nexus in emerging markets: Do financial constraints matter? *Journal of Economic and Administrative Sciences*, *40*(5), 1020–1030. DOI: 10.1108/JEAS-01-2022-0010

Khan, M. A., Hussain, A., Ali, M. M., & Tajummul, M. A. (2022). Assessing the impact of liquidity on the value of assets return. [GBMR]. *Global Business and Management Research*, *14*(1), 1. Advance online publication. DOI: 10.32890/gbmr2022.14.1.4

Kweh, Q. L., Lu, W.-M., Tone, K., & Liu, H.-M. (2024a). Evaluating the resource management and profitability efficiencies of US commercial banks from a dynamic network perspective. *Financial Innovation*, *10*(1), 19. DOI: 10.1186/s40854-023-00531-0

Kweh, Q. L., Lu, W.-M., Tone, K., & Liu, H.-M. (2024b). Evaluating the resource management and profitability efficiencies of US commercial banks from a dynamic network perspective. *Financial Innovation*, *10*(1), 19. DOI: 10.1186/s40854-023-00531-0

Mehmood, S., & Kaewsaeng-on, R. (2024). Charting an Economic Sustainability Path: Quantile Regression Analysis of Green Finance and Financial Development in Newly Industrialized Economies. *Global Business Review*, *09721509231224019*, 09721509231224019. Advance online publication. DOI: 10.1177/09721509231224019

Mohammad, H. Q. (2022). *THE IMPACT OF MONETARY POLICY ON PROFITABILITY OF BANKING INDUSTRY IN IRAQ*.

Nguyen, N. P. A., & Dao, T. T. B. (2022). Liquidity, corporate governance and firm performance: A meta-analysis. *Cogent Business & Management*, *9*(1), 2137960. DOI: 10.1080/23311975.2022.2137960

Ofoeda, I., Amoah, L., Anarfo, E. B., & Abor, J. Y. (2024). Financial inclusion and economic growth: What roles do institutions and financial regulation play? *International Journal of Finance & Economics*, *29*(1), 832–848. DOI: 10.1002/ijfe.2709

Rashaduzzaman, M. (2024). *Risk Management in Banks: It's Relationship with the Financial Performance of Commercial Banks in Bangladesh* [Thesis, ©University of Dhaka]. http://reposit.library.du.ac.bd:8080/xmlui/xmlui/handle/123456789/3078

Rathnasiri, R. A. (2024). The Impact of Macroeconomic Stability on Commercial Bank Profitability: A Study of Sri Lanka. *The International Journal of Accounting*, *4*(1). Advance online publication. DOI: 10.4038/ija.v4i1.61

Ratnasari, T., Surwanti, A., & Pribadi, F. (2021). Implementation of Green Banking and Financial Performance on Commercial Banks in Indonesia. In *Recent Developments in Asian Economics International Symposia in Economic Theory and Econometrics* (world; Vol. 28, pp. 323–336). Emerald Publishing Limited. DOI: 10.1108/S1571-038620210000028018

Ridwan, M. (2022). DETERMINANTS OF INFLATION: Monetary and Macroeconomic Perspectives. *KINERJA: Jurnal Manajemen Organisasi Dan Industri*, *1*(1), 1. Advance online publication. DOI: 10.34005/kinerja.v2i02.793

Sawarni, K. S., Narayanasamy, S., & Padhan, P. C. (2023). Impact of earnings management on working capital management efficiency. *Finance Research Letters*, *54*, 103778. DOI: 10.1016/j.frl.2023.103778

Smaoui, H., Jatmiko, W., & Miniaoui, H. (2024). *Bank Size and Systemic Risk: Evidence from Dual Banking Systems* (SSRN Scholarly Paper No. 5034653). Social Science Research Network. DOI: 10.2139/ssrn.5034653

Tanwar, A. (2024). An Empirical Analysis of the Interactional Relationship Between Liquidity Risk, Credit Risk, and Profitability of Banks in India. In Taneja, S., Kumar, P., Sood, K., Özen, E., & Grima, S. (Eds.), *Finance Analytics in Business* (pp. 267–292). Emerald Publishing Limited., DOI: 10.1108/978-1-83753-572-920241014

Tunio, M. N., & Tunio, S. (2024). Green Entrepreneurship Craving for the Green Finance. In Hunjra, A. I., & Goodell, J. W. (Eds.), *The Palgrave Handbook of Green Finance for Sustainable Development* (pp. 237–262). Springer International Publishing., DOI: 10.1007/978-3-031-65756-6_9

Tunio, S., Ihsanullah, , Parveen, F., & Ishaq, K. (2024). Resilience Approaches and Comparative Evaluation of Classical Time Series Models in Modeling and Forecasting Wheat Production. *Pakistan Journal of Humanities and Social Sciences*, *12*(2), 2. Advance online publication. DOI: 10.52131/pjhss.2024.v12i2.2287

Compilation of References

Abhilash, S., Shenoy, S. S., Shetty, D. K., Lobo, L. S., & N, S. K. (2023). Green bond as an innovative financial instrument in the Indian financial market: Insights from systematic literature review approach. *SAGE Open*, *13*(2), 21582440231178783. Advance online publication. DOI: 10.1177/21582440231178783

Abu Khalaf, B., Awad, A. B., & Ellis, S. (2024). The Impact of Non-Interest Income on Commercial Bank Profitability in the Middle East and North Africa (MENA) Region. *Journal of Risk and Financial Management*, *17*(3), 103. DOI: 10.3390/jrfm17030103

Acharya, N. (2023, October 11). India looks to boost domestic green bond market with longer-dated deal. Responsible Investor. https://www.responsible-investor.com/india-looks-to-boost-domestic-greenbond-market-with-longer-dated-deal/

Adams, D., Adams, K., Ullah, S., & Ullah, F. (2019). Globalisation, governance, accountability and the natural resource 'curse': Implications for socio-economic growth of oil-rich developing countries. *Resources Policy*, *61*, 128–140. DOI: 10.1016/j.resourpol.2019.02.009

Addula, S. R., Meduri, K., Nadella, G. S., & Gonaygunta, H. (2024). AI, and Blockchain in Finance: Opportunities and Challenges for the Banking Sector. *International Journal of Advanced Research in Computer and Communication Engineering*, *13*(2), 184–190. DOI: 10.17148/IJARCCE.2024.13231

Agarwal, S., & Singh, T. (2018). Unlocking The Green Bond Potential in India. TERI. https://www.teriin.org/projects/nfa/files/Green-Bond-Working-Paper.pdf

Aggarwal, S., Dsouza, S., Joshi, M., Antoun, R., & Phan, D. H. T. (2025). Environmental, social and governance investing: Systematic literature review using ADO model. *Journal of Accounting Literature*. Advance online publication. DOI: 10.1108/JAL-11-2024-0319

Aggarwal, S., Garg, V., & Pathak, S. (2021). Green Bonds: A Catalyst for Sustainable Development. *Journal of Contemporary Issues in Business and Government*, *27*(1), 2633–2651. https://cibg.org.au/article_9378.html

Agudelo, M. A. L., Johannsdottir, L., & Davidsdottir, B. (2020). Drivers that motivate energy companies to be responsible. A systematic literature review of Corporate Social Responsibility in the energy sector. *Journal of Cleaner Production*, *247*, 119094. DOI: 10.1016/j.jclepro.2019.119094

Aker, J. C., Boumnijel, R., McClelland, A., & Tierney, N. (2016). Payment mechanisms and mobile money adoption in Niger. *Journal of Development Economics*, *118*, 148–159. DOI: 10.1016/j.jdeveco.2015.12.003

Aker, J. C., & Mbiti, I. M. (2010). Mobile phones and economic development in Africa. *The Journal of Economic Perspectives*, *24*(3), 207–232. DOI: 10.1257/jep.24.3.207

Akhtar, S., Azmi, S. N., Khan, P. A., Jan, A. A., & Ansari, Z. (2024). Unveiling the financial landscape: Analyzing profitability, productivity, and efficiency of banks in an emerging economy using the CAMELS framework and panel analysis. *Cogent Business & Management*, *11*(1), 2399747. DOI: 10.1080/23311975.2024.2399747

Akinyomi, O. J., & Olagunju, A. (2013). Determinants of capital structure in Nigeria.

Al Hadad, R. S., & Maulana, H. (2023, December). A Comprehensive Review of COBIT and ISO 27001: Approaches to Auditing Credit Bureau Automation System (CBAS) at PT XYZ. In *2023 9th International Conference on Signal Processing and Intelligent Systems (ICSPIS)* (pp. 1-8). IEEE. https://doi.org/DOI: 10.1109/ICSPIS59665.2023.10402713

Alam, A., & Mohanty, A. (2022, November). Business models, business strategies, and innovations in EdTech companies: Integration of learning analytics and artificial intelligence in higher education. In *2022 IEEE 6th Conference on Information and Communication Technology (CICT)* (pp. 1–6). IEEE.

Alam, S., & Umar, F. (2019). PENGARUH GOOD COORPORATE GOVERNANCE, RISIKO PERBANKAN TERHADAP KINERJA PERBANKAN PADA BANK UMUM SWASTA DEVISA.

Alam, A., & Mohanty, A. (2023). Educational technology: Exploring the convergence of technology and pedagogy through mobility, interactivity, AI, and learning tools. *Cogent Engineering*, *10*(2), 2283282. DOI: 10.1080/23311916.2023.2283282

Alegre, J., Callahan, J., & Iszatt-White, M. (2023). Innovative conceptual contributions—Raising the game for theory-driven reviews. *International Journal of Management Reviews*, *25*(2), 233–239. DOI: 10.1111/ijmr.12333

Alelyani, S. (2021, July 02). Detection and evaluation of machine learning bias. *Applied Sciences (Basel, Switzerland)*, *11*(14), 6271. Advance online publication. DOI: 10.3390/app11146271

Alfawareh, F. S., & Al-Kofahi, M. (2024). Analysis of global research trends on FinTech: A bibliometric study. *Journal of Internet and Digital Economics*, *4*(1), 30–49. DOI: 10.1108/JIDE-06-2023-0014

Alghadi, M. Y. (2024). The influence of some fintech service on the performance of Islamic bank in Jordan. *International Journal of Data and Network Science*, *8*(1), 393–400. DOI: 10.5267/j.ijdns.2023.9.015

Ali, I. (2011). Determinants of Capital Structure: Empirical Evidence from Pakistan. SSRN Electronic Journal. DOI: 10.2139/ssrn.1977024

Alipour, M., Mohammadi, M. F. S., & Derakhshan, H. (2015). Determinants of capital structure: An empirical study of firms in Iran. *International Journal of Law and Management*, *57*(1), 53–83. DOI: 10.1108/IJLMA-01-2013-0004

Al-kfairy, M., Mustafa, D., Kshetri, N., Insiew, M., & Alfandi, O. (2024). Ethical challenges and solutions of generative AI: An interdisciplinary perspective. *Informatics (MDPI)*, *11*(3), 58. DOI: 10.3390/informatics11030058

Almaqtari, F. A., Hashid, A., Farhan, N. H. S., Tabash, M. I., & Al-ahdal, W. M. (2022). An empirical examination of the impact of country-level corporate governance on profitability of Indian banks. *International Journal of Finance & Economics*, *27*(2), 1912–1932. DOI: 10.1002/ijfe.2250

Al-Moman, A., Bösch, C., & Kargl, F. (2021). A Comparison of Data Protection Regulations for Automotive Systems. In *Data Protection and Privacy: Data Protection and Artificial Intelligence:* (Vol. 13, pp. 57-81). Bloomsbury Publishing Plc. Retrieved Apr 04, 2025, from https://www.scopus.com/record/display.uri?eid=2-s2.0-85195910832&origin=scopusAI

Al-Najjar, D., & Assous, H. F. (2021). Key determinants of deposits volume using CAMEL rating system: The case of Saudi banks. *PLoS One*, *16*(12), e0261184. DOI: 10.1371/journal.pone.0261184 PMID: 34910785

Alonso-Garcia, J., Pablo-Martí, F., & Nunez-Barriopedro, E. (2021). Omnichannel Management in a B2B context: Concept, research agenda and bibliometric review. *International Journal of Industrial Engineering and Management*, *12*(1), 37–48. DOI: 10.24867/IJIEM-2021-1-275

Alper, K., Binici, M., Demiralp, S., Kara, H., & Özlü, P. (2018). Reserve requirements, liquidity risk, and bank lending behavior. *Journal of Money, Credit and Banking*, *50*(4), 817–827. DOI: 10.1111/jmcb.12475

Alshbili, I., Elamer, A. A., & Beddewela, E. (2020). Ownership types, corporate governance and corporate social responsibility disclosures: Empirical evidence from a developing country. *Accounting Research Journal*, *33*(1), 148–166. DOI: 10.1108/ARJ-03-2018-0060

Aluchna, M., & Roszkowska-Menkes, M. (2019). Integrating corporate social responsibility and corporate governance at the company level. Towards a conceptual model. *The Engineering Economist*, *30*(3), 349–361. DOI: 10.5755/j01.ee.30.3.17511

Alzaidi, A. A. (2018). Impact of artificial intelligence on performance of banking industry in Middle East. *International Journal of Computer Science and Network Security*, *18*(10), 140–148.

Alzaidi, A. A. (2018). Impact of use of big data in decision making in banking sector of Saudi Arabia. *International Journal of Computer Science and Network Security*, *18*(12), 72–80.

Ambadkar, S. Rupali, (2010), Determinants of Capital Structure – A Study of FDI Companies in India, The Maharaja Sayajirao University of Baroda's thesis, retrieved from https://shodhganga.inflibnet.ac.in/handle/10603/59571

American Bankers Association. (2020, March 13). *ABA letter to OMB on principles for the regulation of artificial intelligence*. Retrieved from Link.

Anarfo, E. B., Abor, J. Y., Osei, K. A., & Gyeke-Dako, A. (2019). Financial inclusion and financial sector development in Sub-Saharan Africa: A panel VAR approach. *International Journal of Managerial Finance*, *15*(4), 444–463. DOI: 10.1108/IJMF-07-2018-0205

An, B., Bushman, R., Kleymenova, A., & Tomy, R. E. (2024). Bank Supervision and Organizational Capital: The Case of Minority Lending. *Journal of Accounting Research*, *62*(2), 505–549. DOI: 10.1111/1475-679X.12529

Andersen, N. (2021). Mapping the expatriate literature: A bibliometric review of the field from 1998 to 2017 and identification of current research fronts. *International Journal of Human Resource Management, 32*(22), 4687–4724. DOI: 10.1080/09585192.2019.1661267

Anggraeni, A. (2020). dkk. 2020. Prediction Models for Bank Failure: ASEAN Countries. *JurnalEkonomi Malaysia, 54*(2), 41–51.

Anthony, B., Kamaludin, A., Romli, A., Raffei, A. F. M., Phon, D. N. A. L., Abdullah, A., & Ming, G. L. (2020). Blended learning adoption and implementation in higher education: A theoretical and systematic review. Technology, Knowledge and Learning,25(4) https://link.springer.com/article/10.1007/s10758-020-09477-z

Antil, A., Saini, N., Sehgal, S., Aggarwal, S., & Shahzad, U. Effectiveness of Metaphorical Communication in Government Campaign on Digitization. *FIIB Business Review*. https://doi.org/DOI: 10.1177/23197145231166746

Antonopoulos, A. M. (2017). *Mastering Bitcoin: Unlocking Digital Cryptocurrencies*. O'Reilly Media.

Aria, M., & Cuccurullo, C. (2017). bibliometrix: An R-tool for comprehensive science mapping analysis. *Journal of Informetrics, 11*(4), 959–975. DOI: 10.1016/j.joi.2017.08.007

Arif, M., Naeem, M. A., Farid, S., Nepal, R., & Jamasb, T. (2021). Diversifier or more? Hedge and safe haven properties of green bonds during COVID-19. SSRN *Electronic Journal*. DOI: 10.2139/ssrn.3782126

Arjun, R., Abhisek, K., & Suprabha, K. R. (2021). Developing banking intelligence in emerging markets: Systematic review and agenda. *International Journal of Information Management Data Insights, 1*(2), 1–11.

Arner, D. W., Barberis, J., & Buckley, R. P. (2017). FinTech, regtech, and the reconceptualization of financial regulation. *Northwestern Journal of International Law & Business, 37*(3), 371-413. https://scholarlycommons.law.northwestern.edu/njilb/vol37/iss3/2

Arniati, T., Muslichah, M., & Utami, N. N. (2024). The Effect Of Liquidity And Business Volume On Cooperative Performance. *International Journal of Scientific Research, 1*(03), 03. Advance online publication. DOI: 10.62894/6brqs150

Arno, A. K. (2018). Failure Bank dan Resiko Sistemik Perbankan (Sebuah Konsep Penanganan). Journal Of Institution And Sharia Fiance, 1.

Arora, S., & Madan, P. (2023). Conceptual Framework Depicting the Drivers for the Fintech Growth: An Outlook for India. In *Contemporary Studies of Risks in Emerging Technology, Part A* (pp. 197–220). Emerald Publishing Limited. DOI: 10.1108/978-1-80455-562-020231014

Arrieta, A. B., Díaz-Rodríguez, N., Del Ser, J., Bennetot, A., Tabik, S., Barbado, A., Garcia, S., Gil-Lopez, S., Molina, D., Benjamins, R., Chatila, R., & Herrera, F. (2020). Explainable Artificial Intelligence (XAI): Concepts, taxonomies, opportunities and challenges toward responsible AI. *Information Fusion, 58*, 82–115. DOI: 10.1016/j.inffus.2019.12.012

Arshad, A., Shahzad, F., Rehman, I. U., & Sergi, B. S. (2023). A systematic literature review of blockchain technology and environmental sustainability: Status quo and future research. *International Review of Economics & Finance*, *88*, 1602–1622. DOI: 10.1016/j.iref.2023.07.044

Arun, T., Markose, S., Murinde, V., Kostov, P., Khan, A., Ari, N., & Sethi, R. (2023). *Impact of Neobanks (Digital Banks)*. UK–India Comparison.

Ascarya, P. (2011). The persistence of low profit and loss sharing financing in Islamic banking: The case of Indonesia. Review of Indonesian Economic and Business Studies, 1.

Asghar, M., Ali, S., Hanif, M., & Ullah, S. (2024). Energy transition in newly industrialized countries: A policy paradigm in the perspective of technological innovation and urbanization. *Sustainable Futures : An Applied Journal of Technology, Environment and Society*, *7*, 100163. DOI: 10.1016/j.sftr.2024.100163

Aslaksen, H. M., Hildebrandt, C., & Johnsen, H. C. (2021). The long-term transformation of the concept of CSR: Towards a more comprehensive emphasis on sustainability. *International Journal of Corporate Social Responsibility*, *6*(1), 1–14. DOI: 10.1186/s40991-021-00063-9

Asmar, M., & Tuqan, A. (2024, September 15). Integrating machine learning for sustaining cybersecurity in digital banks. *Heliyon*, *10*(17), e37571. Advance online publication. DOI: 10.1016/j.heliyon.2024.e37571 PMID: 39290262

Asteriou, D., Spanos, K., & Trachanas, E. (2024). Financial development, economic growth and the role of fiscal policy during normal and stress times: Evidence for 26 EU countries. *International Journal of Finance & Economics*, *29*(2), 2495–2514. DOI: 10.1002/ijfe.2793

Athanasoglou, P. P., Daniilidis, I., & Delis, M. D. (2014). Bank procyclicality and output: Issues and policies. *Journal of Economics and Business*, *72*, 58–83. DOI: 10.1016/j.jeconbus.2013.10.003

Avramidis, P., Pennacchi, G., Serfes, K., & Wu, K. (2022). The role of regulation and bank competition in small firm financing: Evidence from the Community Reinvestment Act. *Journal of Money, Credit and Banking*, *54*(8), 2301–2340. DOI: 10.1111/jmcb.12938

Ayomi, S., &Hermanto, B. (2013). Mengukur Risiko Sistemik Dan Keterkaitan Finansial Perbankan Di Indonesia. *Buletin Ekonomi Moneter dan Perbankan, 16*(2), 103-125.

Ayoub, O., Di Cicco, N., Ezzeddine, F., Bruschetta, F., Rubino, R., Nardecchia, M., Milano, M., Musumeci, F., Passera, C., & Tornatore, M. (2022). Explainable Artificial Intelligence in communication networks: A use case for failure identification in microwave networks. *Computer Networks*, *219*, 109466. DOI: 10.1016/j.comnet.2022.109466

Azhgaliyeva, D., Kapoor, A., & Liu, Y. (2020). Green bonds for financing renewable energy and energy efficiency in South-East Asia: A review of policies. *Journal of Sustainable Finance & Investment*, *10*(2), 113–140. DOI: 10.1080/20430795.2019.1704160

Babu, V., Kumar, A., & Kumar, V. (2022). *Exploring Mindfulness and Leadership Development: Lessons Learnt Using Grounded Theory Through the Study of the Performing Arts*. FIIB Business Review., DOI: 10.1177/23197145221088643

Badunenko, O., Dadoukis, A., Fusi, G., & Simper, R. (2022). The impact of efficiency on asset quality in banking. *European Journal of Finance*, *28*(6), 596–620. DOI: 10.1080/1351847X.2021.1946117

Baer, G. (2024, July 17). *The Bank Examination Problem, and How to Fix It.* Bank Policy Institute. Retrieved from https://bpi.com/wp-content/uploads/2024/07/The-Bank-Examination-Problem__and-How-to-Fix-It.pdf

Baffour Gyau, E., Appiah, M., Gyamfi, B. A., Achie, T., & Naeem, M. A. (2024). Transforming banking: Examining the role of AI technology innovation in boosting banks financial performance. *International Review of Financial Analysis*, *96*, 103700. Advance online publication. DOI: 10.1016/j.irfa.2024.103700

Bagozzi, R. P. (1992). The self-regulation of attitudes, intentions, and behavior. *Social Psychology Quarterly*, *55*(2), 178–204. DOI: 10.2307/2786945

Balamohan, S., & Khanaa, V. (2024, October). Revolutionizing Stock Market Prediction: Harnessing the Power of LSTM and CNN Hybrid Approach. *SN Computer Science*, *05*(07), 919. Advance online publication. DOI: 10.1007/s42979-024-03241-1

Balasubramanian, V., Niksan, O., Jain, M. C., Golovin, K., & Zarifi, M. H. (2023). Non-destructive erosive wear monitoring of multi-layer coatings using AI-enabled differential split ring resonator based system. *Nature Communications*, *14*(1), 1–12. DOI: 10.1038/s41467-023-40636-9 PMID: 37582844

Balsalobre-Lorente, D., Abbas, J., He, C., Pilař, L., & Shah, S. A. R. (2023). Tourism, urbanization and natural resources rents matter for environmental sustainability: The leading role of AI and ICT on sustainable development goals in the digital era. *Resources Policy*, *82*, 103445. DOI: 10.1016/j.resourpol.2023.103445

Bandura, A. (1997). Self-Efficacy: The Exercise of Control. New York, NY: Freeman; Pajares, F. (1996). Self-efficacy beliefs in academic settings. *Review of Educational Research*, *66*(4), 543–578.

Banga, C., Beena, F., Manchandani, P., & Shukla, V. (2023, March). Growth and Future of Neo Banks–A Survey. In *2023 International Conference on Computational Intelligence and Knowledge Economy (ICCIKE)* (pp. 467-472). IEEE.

Bank Indonesia (BI). (2021). Kebijakan Makroprudensial. https://www.bi.go.id/id/fungsi-utama/stabilitas-sistem-keuangan/ikhtisar/Default.aspx#floating-2 (diakses pada 13 juli 2021)

Baral, K. J. (2004). Determinants of capital structure: A case study of listed companies of Nepal. *Journal of Nepalese Business Studies*, *7*(1), 1–13.

Baruah, A. (2020). *AI applications in the Top 4 Indian Banks.* EMERJ.

Basu, K., & Rajeev, M. (2013), "Determinants of capital structure of Indian corporate sector: Evidence of regulatory impact," Working Papers 306, Institute for Social and Economic Change, Bangalore.

Beck, T., Demirgüç-Kunt, A., & Levine, R. (2007). Finance, inequality, and the poor. *Journal of Economic Growth*, *12*(1), 27–49. DOI: 10.1007/s10887-007-9010-6

Bejjar, M. A., & Siala, Y. (2024). Machine learning: A revolution in accounting. In *Artificial Intelligence Approaches to Sustainable Accounting* (pp. 110–134). IGI Global., DOI: 10.4018/979-8-3693-0847-9.ch007

Bekbolatova, M., Mayer, J., Ong, C. W., & Toma, M. (2024). Transformative Potential of AI in Healthcare: Definitions, Applications, and Navigating the Ethical Landscape and Public Perspectives. *Health Care*, *12*(2), 125. PMID: 38255014

Belanche, D., Casaló, L. V., & Flavián, C. (2019, September 19). Artificial Intelligence in FinTech: Understanding robo-advisors adoption among customers. *Industrial Management & Data Systems*, *119*(07), 1411–1430. DOI: 10.1108/IMDS-08-2018-0368

Ben Lahouel, B., Taleb, L., Ben Zaied, Y., & Managi, S. (2024). Financial stability, liquidity risk and income diversification: Evidence from European banks using the CAMELS–DEA approach. *Annals of Operations Research*, *334*(1), 391–422. DOI: 10.1007/s10479-022-04805-1

Bevan, A. A., & Danbolt, J. Dynamics in the Determinants of Capital Structure in the UK (May 2000). Capital Structure Dynamics Working Paper No. 2000-9, Available at SSRN: https://ssrn.com/abstract=233551 or DOI: 10.2139/ssrn.233551

Bhagat, C., & Reddy, S. (2019). Overcoming digital literacy barriers in fintech adoption. *International Journal of Financial Studies*, *7*(3), 45–58. DOI: 10.3390/ijfs7030045

Bhatnagr, P., & Rajesh, A. (2024). Neobanking adoption – An integrated UTAUT-3, perceived risk and recommendation model. *South Asian Journal of Marketing*, *5*(2), 93–112. DOI: 10.1108/SAJM-06-2022-0040

Bhatnagr, P., Rajesh, A., & Misra, R. (2024). Neobank adoption: Integrating the information systems effectiveness framework with the innovation resistance model. *Management Decision*, *62*(10), 3315–3352. DOI: 10.1108/MD-06-2023-0977

Bhattacharjee, B. J. (2010). Determinants of capital structure of Indian industries. The Indian Journal of Commerce, Vol. 63, Issue No. 3, Pp 14-25.

Bhattacharjee, A., & Dash, M. (2015). Determinants of capital structure in the Indian sugar sector. *Sky Journal of Business Administration and Management*, *3*(6), 63–69.

Bhattacharya, C., & Sinha, M. (2022). The role of artificial intelligence in banking for leveraging customer experience. Australasian Accounting, Business and Finance Journal, 16(5).

Bhattacharya, R., Kapoor, P., & Mehta, S. (2021). Blockchain and sustainability: A critical analysis. *Energy Policy Journal*, *45*(6), 89–104.

Bhatt, U., Xiang, A., Sharma, S., Weller, A., Taly, A., Jia, Y., Ghosh, J., Puri, R., Moura, J. M. F., & Eckersley, P. (2020). Explainable machine learning in deployment. *Proceedings of the 2020 Conference on Fairness, Accountability, and Transparency*, 648-657. https://doi.org/DOI: 10.1145/3351095.3375624

Bhuvana, M., Thirumagal, P. G., & Vasantha, S. (2016). Big data analytics-a leveraging technology for Indian commercial banks. *Indian Journal of Science and Technology*, *9*(32), 98643. DOI: 10.17485/ijst/2016/v9i32/98643

Bin-Nashwan, S. A., Sadallah, M., & Bouteraa, M. (2023). Use of ChatGPT in academia: Academic integrity hangs in the balance. *Technology in Society*, *75*, 102370. DOI: 10.1016/j.techsoc.2023.102370

BIS or Bank for International Settlements. (2021). *Principles for operational resilience.* Basel Committee on Banking Supervision. https://www.bis.org/bcbs/publ/d516.pdf

Blanco, A., Pino-Mejías, R., Lara, J., & Rayo, S. (2013, January). Credit scoring models for the microfinance industry using neural networks: Evidence from Peru. *Expert Systems with Applications*, *40*(01), 356–364. DOI: 10.1016/j.eswa.2012.07.051

Blazquez, J., Dale, S., Jefferiss, P., Heffron, R. J., Herbertson, J., West, R., & Hegland, J. (2020). Decarbonization pathways for oil and gas. In *Oxford Energy Forum (Vol. 121, pp. 1-40).*

Blondeel, M., & Bradshaw, M. (2022). Managing transition risk: Toward an interdisciplinary understanding of strategies in the oil industry. *Energy Research & Social Science*, *91*, 102696. DOI: 10.1016/j.erss.2022.102696

Bloomberg, N. E. F. (2023). *New Energy Outlook India* accessed on 2 October, 2024 from https://assets.bbhub.io/professional/sites/24/BNEF_New-Energy-Outlook-India-2023.pdf

Bokolo, A. J., De Reuver, M., & Marijn Janssen, M. (2020). A coordinated model for identifying and managing the risk and cost drivers of hybrid cloud adoption in enterprises. Journal of Cloud Computing: Advances. *Systems and Applications*, *9*, 1–20.

Bokolo, A. J., Petersen, S. A., & Lai, R. T. (2020). Examining factors affecting hybrid learning readiness and effectiveness. *Journal of Hybrid Learning and Teaching*, *8*(1), 45–58.

Bonelli, M., & Dongul, E. S. (2023). Robo-Advisors in the Financial Services Industry: Recommendations for Full-Scale Optimization, Digital Twin Integration, and Leveraging Natural Language Processing Trends. *9th International Conference on Virtual Reality, ICVR 2023* (pp. 268-275). Xianyang: Institute of Electrical and Electronics Engineers Inc. https://doi.org/DOI: 10.1109/ICVR57957.2023.10169615

Booth, L., Aivazian, V., Demirguc-Kunt, A., & Maksimovic, V. (2001). Capital Structures in Developing Countries. *The Journal of Finance*, *56*(1), 87–130. DOI: 10.1111/0022-1082.00320

Bose, P., & Dutta, R. (2023). Blockchain regulation in India: Challenges and prospects. *Economic and Political Weekly*, *58*(4), 22–27.

Boumesaid, C., Guerfa, Y., & Bendiab, G. (2025). QuantumSign: Online E-Signature Service Based on Blockchain and Post-Quantum Cryptography. *International Conference on Artificial Intelligence in Renewable Energetic Systems, IC-AIRES 2024. 1238 LNNS*, pp. 342-353. Tipasa: Springer Science and Business Media Deutschland GmbH. https://doi.org/DOI: 10.1007/978-3-031-80301-7_38

Bozkurt, A. (2023). Generative artificial intelligence (AI) powered conversational educational agents: The inevitable paradigm shift. *Asian Journal of Distance Education*, *18*, 198–204.

Brei, M., Mohan, P., & Strobl, E. (2019). The impact of natural disasters on the banking sector: Evidence from hurricane strikes in the Caribbean. *The Quarterly Review of Economics and Finance*, *72*, 232–239. DOI: 10.1016/j.qref.2018.12.004

Brennan, N. M., Subramaniam, N., & Van Staden, C. J. (2019). Corporate governance implications of disruptive technology: An overview. *The British Accounting Review*, *51*(6), 100860. DOI: 10.1016/j.bar.2019.100860

Breslin, D., & Gatrell, C. (2023). Theorizing through literature reviews: The miner-prospector continuum. *Organizational Research Methods*, *26*(1), 139–167. DOI: 10.1177/1094428120943288

Briones de Araluze, G., & Cassinello Plaza, N. (2023). The relevance of initial trust and social influence in the intention to use open banking-based services: An empirical study. *SAGE Open*, *13*(3), 21582440231187607. Advance online publication. DOI: 10.1177/21582440231187607

Brown, C. O., & Dinc, I. S. (2005). The politics of bank failures: Evidence from emerging markets. *The Quarterly Journal of Economics*, *120*(4), 1413–1444. DOI: 10.1162/003355305775097506

Buferna, F. M., Bangassa, K., & Hodgkinson, L. (2005), Determinants of Capital Structure: Evidence from Libya, WP2005/08, ISSN:1744-0718.

Buhmann, A., & Fieseler, C. (2021). Towards a deliberative framework for responsible innovation in artificial intelligence. *Technology in Society*, *64*, 101475. DOI: 10.1016/j.techsoc.2020.101475

Burgess, R., & Pande, R. (2005). Do rural banks matter? Evidence from the Indian social banking experiment. *The American Economic Review*, *95*(3), 780–795. DOI: 10.1257/0002828054201242

Cámara, N., & Tuesta, D. (2014). Measuring financial inclusion: A multidimensional index. *BBVA Research Working Paper*, No. 14/26. Retrieved from https://www.bbvaresearch.com

Carcillo, F., Le Borgne, Y.-A., Caelen, O., Kessaci, Y., Oblé, F., & Bontempi, G. (2021, May). Combining unsupervised and supervised learning in credit card fraud detection. *Information Sciences*, *557*, 317–331. DOI: 10.1016/j.ins.2019.05.042

Carvalho, D. V., Pereira, E. M., & Cardoso, J. S. (2019). Machine learning interpretability: A survey on methods and metrics. *Electronics (Basel)*, *8*(8), 832. DOI: 10.3390/electronics8080832

Černevičienė, J., & Kabašinskas, A. (2024). Explainable artificial intelligence (XAI) in finance: A systematic literature review. *Artificial Intelligence Review*, *57*(8), 216. DOI: 10.1007/s10462-024-10854-8

Cevheroglu-Acar, M. (2018). Determinants of Capital Structure: Empirical Evidence from Turkey. *Journal of Management and Sustainability*, *8*(1), 31. DOI: 10.5539/jms.v8n1p31

Chadha, S., & Sharma, A. K. (2015), Determinants of capital structure: An empirical evaluation from India, Journal of Advances in Management Research, Vol.12, Issue No.1, Pp 3-14.

Chakrabarty, K. C. (2012). Financial inclusion: Issues in measurement and analysis. *Reserve Bank of India Bulletin*, May 2012, 75-81. Retrieved from https://www.rbi.org.in

Chakraborty, I. (2010). Capital structure in an emerging stock market: The case of India. Research in International Business and Finance, Vol. 24, Issue No.3, Pp 295-314. ISSN 0275-5319, DOI: 10.1016/j.ribaf.2010.02.001

Chakraborty, R. (2022). Banking reforms in India: A historical perspective. *Journal of Financial Studies*, *12*(3), 45–60.

Chakraborty, R., Bhattacharya, A., & Mukherjee, S. (2022). Blockchain applications in Indian banking sector: Case studies and prospects. *International Journal of Financial Innovation, 14*(3), 121–138.

Chattopadhyay, S. (2019). Regulatory sandboxes for financial inclusion. *Economic and Political Weekly, 54*(32), 32–37. https://www.epw.in/

Chaudhary, P., Kapoor, S., & Malik, R. (2023). Digital literacy and blockchain adoption in rural India: Challenges and solutions. *Journal of Emerging Technologies, 11*(2), 45–59.

Chaudhary, P., Singh, V., & Sharma, T. (2022). Blockchain in trade finance: An Indian perspective. *Guoji Maoyi Wenti, 17*(3), 112–127.

Chaudhary, R., Singh, M., & Patel, V. (2023). Blockchain literacy in rural India: Challenges and strategies. *Indian Journal of Digital Transformation, 8*(1), 34–50.

Chauhan, S., Akhtar, A., & Gupta, A. (2021). Gamification in banking: A review, synthesis and setting research agenda. *Young Consumers, 22*(3), 456–479. DOI: 10.1108/YC-10-2020-1229

Chau, K. Y., Moslehpour, M., Tu, Y. T., Tai, N. T., Tien, N. H., & Huy, P. Q. (2022). Exploring the impact of green energy and consumption on the sustainability of natural resources: Empirical evidence from G7 countries. *Renewable Energy, 196*, 1241–1249. DOI: 10.1016/j.renene.2022.07.085

Chen, J., Meng, W., Chen, Y., & Zhou, W. (2024). To be an eco-and tech-friendly society: Impact research of green finance on AI innovation. *Journal of Cleaner Production, 466*, 142900. DOI: 10.1016/j.jclepro.2024.142900

Chen, L., Zhang, Y., & Huang, R. (2020). The impact of AI-driven recommendation systems on retail: A customer perspective. *Journal of Retailing and Consumer Services, 55*, 102109. DOI: 10.1016/j.jretconser.2020.102109

Chen, Y., Farzan, R., Kraut, R., YeckehZaare, I., & Zhang, A. F. (2024). Motivating experts to contribute to digital public goods: A personalized field experiment on Wikipedia. *Management Science, 70*(5), 3264–3280. DOI: 10.1287/mnsc.2023.4852

Chirwa, T. G., & Odhiambo, N. M. (2016). Macroeconomic determinants of economic growth: A review of international literature. The South East European Journal of Economics and Business, 11(2).

Cho, H. J., & Pucik, V. (2005). Relationship between innovativeness, quality, growth, profitability, and market value. *Strategic Management Journal, 26*(6), 555–575. DOI: 10.1002/smj.461

Chowdhury, R. H., Choi, S., Ennis, S., and Chung, D. (2019). Which dimension of corporate social responsibility is a value driver in the oil and gas industry? *Canadian Journal of Administrative Sciences/ Revue Canadienne des Sciences de l'Administration, 36*(2), 260-272.

CleverlySmart. (2024, Jan 18). *BlackRock AI: Transforming Finance through Intelligent Investment Strategies*. Retrieved Apr 04, 2025, from https://www.cleverlysmart.com. https://www.cleverlysmart.com/blackrock-ai-transforming-finance-through-intelligent-investment-strategies/

Climate Bonds Initiative. (2017). Green Bonds Highlights accessed on 2 October, 2024 from https://www.climatebonds.net/files/files/2016%20GB%20Market%20Roundup

Climate Bonds Initiative. (2023). *India's debut in the sovereign green bond market: First deal landed a greenium!*https://www.climatebonds.net/2023/03/india%E2%80%99s-debut-sovereign-greenbond-market-first-deal-landed-greenium

Consumer Financial Protection Bureau or CFPB. (2015). *Equal Credit Opportunity Act (ECOA) examination procedures*. Retrieved from Link.

Consumer Financial Protection Bureau or CFPB. (2023). *Supervision and Examination Manual*. Retrieved from Link.

Corliss, D. J. (2024). Designing Against Bias: Identifying and Mitigating Bias in Machine Learning and AI. *Intelligent Systems Conference, IntelliSys 2023. 824 LNNS,* pp. 411-418. Amsterdam: Springer Science and Business Media Deutschland GmbH. https://doi.org/DOI: 10.1007/978-3-031-47715-7_28

Corral de La Mata, D., García de Blanes Sebastián, M., & Carvajal Camperos, M. (2024). Hybrid artificial intelligence: Application in the banking sector. *Revista de Ciencias Sociales*, *30*(03), 22–36. DOI: 10.31876/rcs.v30i3.42674

Crifo, P., Escrig-Olmedo, E., & Mottis, N. (2019). Corporate governance as a key driver of corporate sustainability in France: The role of board members and investor relations. *Journal of Business Ethics*, *159*(4), 1127–1146. DOI: 10.1007/s10551-018-3866-6

Cruz, L. P. (2017). When data science becomes software engineering. *9th International Joint Conference on Knowledge Discovery, Knowledge Engineering and Knowledge Management, IC3K 2017. 02*, pp. 226-232. Funchal, Madeira: SciTePress. https://doi.org/DOI: 10.5220/0006508502260232

Cull, R., Demirgüç-Kunt, A., & Morduch, J. (2014). Banks and microfinance: Institutions, stability, and growth. *World Bank Policy Research Working Paper No. 7136*. https://doi.org/DOI: 10.1596/1813-9450-7136

Cunningham, P., & Delany, S. J. (2021). Underestimation Bias and Underfitting in Machine Learning. *1st International Workshop on Trustworthy AI – Integrating Learning, Optimization and Reasoning, TAILOR 2020 held as a part of European Conference on Artificial Intelligence, ECAI 2020. 12641 LNAI*, pp. 20-31. Virtual, Online: Springer Science and Business Media Deutschland GmbH. https://doi.org/DOI: 10.1007/978-3-030-73959-1_2

Cyree, K. B., & Winters, D. B. (2023). Investigating bank lending discrimination in the US using CRA-rated banks' HMDA loan data. *Public Choice*, *197*(3), 371–395. DOI: 10.1007/s11127-023-01078-5

Czuba, P. (2024). Reinforcement Learning in Algorithmic Trading: An Overview. *41st IBIMA International Conference on Artificial intelligence and Machine Learning, IBIMA-AI 2023. 2101 CCIS*, pp. 71-77. Granada: Springer Science and Business Media Deutschland GmbH. https://doi.org/DOI: 10.1007/978-3-031-62843-6_8

D'Onza, G., Lamboglia, R., & Verona, R. (2015). Do IT audits satisfy senior manager expectations? A qualitative study based on Italian banks. *Managerial Auditing Journal*, *30*(4/5), 413–434. DOI: 10.1108/MAJ-07-2014-1051

D'Silva, D., Filkova, M., & Singh, R. (2020). *Cross-border remittances and blockchain: A case study of India*. World Bank Policy Paper.

Da Silva, M. C., Da Silva, L. B., Morioka, S. N., & De Souza, V. F. (2023). Integration of Environmental, Social, and Governance (ESG) criteria: Their impacts on corporate sustainability performance. *Humanities & Social Sciences Communications*, *10*(1), 1–18.

Dar, B. I., Badwan, N., & Kumar, J. (2024). Investigating the role of Fintech innovations and green finance toward sustainable economic development: A bibliometric analysis. *International Journal of Islamic and Middle Eastern Finance and Management*, *17*(6), 1175–1195. DOI: 10.1108/IMEFM-01-2024-0018

Das, A., Verma, S., & Mehta, P. (2024). Blockchain and AI: Future financial ecosystems. *Journal of Emerging Technologies*, *10*(2), 102–118.

Das, A., Verma, S., & Mehta, P. (2024). Blockchain for financial inclusion in India. *Journal of Fintech Innovation*, *10*(1), 89–102.

Dasgupta, S., & Mehta, R. (2022). Digital payment ecosystem in India: Challenges and opportunities. *Economic and Political Weekly*, *57*(4), 32–39.

Dash, S., & Das, S., Sivasubramanian, Sundaram, K., Harsha, G., & Sathish, T. (2023). Developing AI-based Fraud Detection Systems for Banking and Finance. *5th International Conference on Inventive Research in Computing Applications, ICIRCA 2023* (pp. 891-897). Coimbatore: Institute of Electrical and Electronics Engineers Inc. https://doi.org/DOI: 10.1109/ICIRCA57980.2023.10220838

Daultani, Y., Goswami, M., Kumar, A., & Pratap, S. (2021). Perceived outcomes of e-learning: Identifying key attributes affecting user satisfaction in higher education institutes. *Measuring Business Excellence*, *25*(2), 216–229. DOI: 10.1108/MBE-07-2020-0110

Davis, L. (2020). The impact of the California consumer privacy act on financial institutions across the nation. [Retrieved from Link.]. *North Carolina Banking Institute Journal*, *24*, 499.

DeAngelo, H., & Masulis, R. W. (1980). Optimal Capital Structure Under Corporate and Personal Taxation. *Journal of Financial Economics*, *8*(1), 3–29. DOI: 10.1016/0304-405X(80)90019-7

Deepa, R. (2011), A Study on the Determinants of Capital Structure and Profitability with Special Reference to Food Industry in India, Pondicherry University's thesis, retrieved from https://shodhganga.inflibnet.ac.in/handle/10603/5253

Demirgüç-Kunt, A., Klapper, L., Singer, D., Ansar, S., & Hess, J. (2021). *The Global Findex Database 2021: Financial Inclusion, Digital Payments, and Resilience in the Age of COVID-19*. World Bank. https://doi.org/DOI: 10.1596/978-1-4648-1751-1

Demirgüç-Kunt, A., Klapper, L. F., Singer, D., & Van Oudheusden, P. (2018). *The Global Findex Database 2017: Measuring financial inclusion and the fintech revolution*. World Bank., DOI: 10.1596/978-1-4648-1259-0

Dere, G. (2025). Deep Learning of Telecommunication Technology for the Efficient Utilization of Embedded Systems. In *Embedded Systems for Biomedical Applications* (pp. 124–134). CRC Press., DOI: 10.1201/9781003508199-5

Deshpande, A. (2024). Regulatory Compliance and AI: Navigating the Legal and Regulatory Challenges of AI in Finance. *International Conference on Knowledge Engineering and Communication Systems, ICKECS 2024.* Chikkaballapur: Institute of Electrical and Electronics Engineers Inc. https://doi.org/DOI: 10.1109/ICKECS61492.2024.10616752

Dhar, A., Gupta, S., & Kumar, E. S. (2024). A Comprehensive Review of Explainable AI Applications in Healthcare. *15th International Conference on Computing Communication and Networking Technologies, ICCCNT 2024.* Kamand: IEEE. https://doi.org/DOI: 10.1109/ICCCNT61001.2024.10725578

Di Vaio, A., Hasan, S., Palladino, R., & Hassan, R. (2023). The transition towards circular economy and waste within accounting and accountability models: A systematic literature review and conceptual framework. *Environment, Development and Sustainability*, *25*(1), 734–810. DOI: 10.1007/s10668-021-02078-5 PMID: 35035274

Díaz-Rodríguez, N., Del Ser, J., Coeckelbergh, M., López de Prado, M., Herrera-Viedma, E., & Herrera, F. (2023). Connecting the dots in trustworthy Artificial Intelligence: From AI principles, ethics, and key requirements to responsible AI systems and regulation. *Information Fusion*, *99*, 101896. DOI: 10.1016/j.inffus.2023.101896

Dicuonzo, G., Donofrio, F., Iannuzzi, A. P., & Dell'Atti, V. (2022). The integration of sustainability in corporate governance systems: An innovative framework applied to the European systematically important banks. *International Journal of Disclosure and Governance*, *19*(3), 249–263. DOI: 10.1057/s41310-021-00140-2

Dimitrova, I., Öhman, P., & Yazdanfar, D. (2022). Barriers to bank customers' intention to fully adopt digital payment methods. *International Journal of Quality and Service Sciences*, *14*(5), 16–36. DOI: 10.1108/IJQSS-03-2021-0045

Ding, Z. (2023). Construction and Exploration of a Financial Risk Control Model Based on Machine Learning. *International Conference on Evolutionary Algorithms and Soft Computing Techniques, EASCT 2023.* Bengaluru: Institute of Electrical and Electronics Engineers Inc. https://doi.org/DOI: 10.1109/EASCT59475.2023.10393547

Donthu, N., Kumar, S., Mukherjee, D., Pandey, N., & Lim, W. M. (2021). How to conduct a bibliometric analysis: An overview and guidelines. *Journal of Business Research*, *133*, 285–296. DOI: 10.1016/j.jbusres.2021.04.070

Doumpos, M., Zopounidis, C., Gounopoulos, D., Platanakis, E., & Zhang, W. (2023). Operational research and artificial intelligence methods in banking. *European Journal of Operational Research*, *306*(1), 1–16. DOI: 10.1016/j.ejor.2022.04.027 PMID: 35874494

Drobetz, W., & Fix, R. (2005). What are the Determinants of the Capital Structure? Evidence from Switzerland, Swiss Journal of Economics and Statistics (SJES) [SSES]. *Swiss Society of Economics and Statistics*, *141*(I), 71–113.

Dudin, M. N., Frolova, E. E., Protopopova, O. V., Mamedov, O., & Odintsov, S. V. (2019). Study of innovative technologies in the energy industry: Nontraditional and renewable energy sources. *Entrepreneurship and Sustainability Issues*, *6*(4), 1704–1713. DOI: 10.9770/jesi.2019.6.4(11)

Duflo, E., Kremer, M., & Robinson, J. (2013). Nudging in education. *Brookings Papers on Economic Activity, 2013*(2), 1–56. https://www.brookings.edu/bpea-articles/nudging-in-education/

Dumičić, M. (2019). Linkages Between Fiscal Policy and Financial (In) Stability. *Journal of central banking theory and practice, 8*(1), 97-109.

Economic Times. (2024). India's crypto regulation debate: Implications for blockchain and DeFi.

Ededjo, F. (2023). *Determinants of banks performance before and after the financial crisis of 2007-2009: A study of global systemically important banks in the United Kingdom* [Thesis, Anglia Ruskin Research Online (ARRO)]. https://aru.figshare.com/articles/thesis/Determinants_of_banks_performance_before_and_after_the_financial_crisis_of_2007-2009_a_study_of_global_systemically_important_banks_in_the_United_Kingdom/24512380/1

Egger, D. J., Gambella, C., Marecek, J., McFaddin, S., Mevissen, M., Raymond, R., Simonetto, A., Woerner, S., & Yndurain, E. (2020). Quantum Computing for Finance: State-of-the-Art and Future Prospects. *IEEE Transactions on Quantum Engineering, 01*, 1–24. Advance online publication. DOI: 10.1109/TQE.2020.3030314

Eichler, S., & Sobański, K. (2016). National politics and bank default risk in the eurozone. *Journal of Financial Stability, 26*, 247–256. DOI: 10.1016/j.jfs.2016.07.008

El-Bassiouny, D., & El-Bassiouny, N. (2019). Diversity, corporate governance and CSR reporting: A comparative analysis between top-listed firms in Egypt, Germany and the USA. *Management of Environmental Quality, 30*(1), 116–136. DOI: 10.1108/MEQ-12-2017-0150

Elendu, C. M., Amaechi, D. C., Elendu, T. C., Jingwa, K. A., Okoye, O. K., Okah, M., Ladele, J. A., Farah, A. H., & Alimi, H. A. (2023). Ethical implications of AI and robotics in healthcare. *Revista de Medicina (São Paulo), 102*(50), e36671. PMID: 38115340

Elia, G., Stefanelli, V., & Ferilli, G. B. (2023). Investigating the role of Fintech in the banking industry: What do we know? *European Journal of Innovation Management, 26*(5), 1365–1393. DOI: 10.1108/EJIM-12-2021-0608

Ellitan, L. (2020). The information technology industrial revolution and its role in building business strategy of global retail. *Jurnal Manajemen Maranatha, 19*(2), 151–158. DOI: 10.28932/jmm.v19i2.2408

Elsaid, H. M. (2023). A review of literature directions regarding the impact of fintech firms on the banking industry. *Qualitative Research in Financial Markets, 15*(5), 693–711. DOI: 10.1108/QRFM-10-2020-0197

Elyasiani, E., & Mansur, I. (2005). The association between market and exchange rate risks and accounting variables: A GARCH model of the Japanese banking institutions. *Review of Quantitative Finance and Accounting, 25*(2), 183–206. DOI: 10.1007/s11156-005-4248-6

Eshwari, D., & Baby, M. K. (2023). The Effect of Capital Structure on the Profitability of FMCG Companies. In Aloysius Edward, J., Jaheer Mukthar, K. P., Asis, E. R., & Sivasubramanian, K. (Eds.), *Current Trends in Economics, Business and Sustainability* (pp. 313–320). Springer Nature., DOI: 10.1007/978-981-99-3366-2_37

Espinoza Alvarado, K., Vallenas Santillan, R., & Baca Marroquin, E. (2024). *Credit Risk Management in the Financial Sector Using Machine Learning as a Tool: A Systematic Literature Review. 22nd LACCEI International Multi-Conference for Engineering, Education and Technology, LACCEI 2024.* Latin American and Caribbean Consortium of Engineering Institutions., DOI: 10.18687/LACCEI2024.1.1.1097

Estrada, J. C. (2020). The AML Arms Race: How Artificial Intelligence and Machine Learning Will Combat Money Laundering. [Retrieved from Link.]. *Rutgers Business Law Journal, 16*, 383.

European Commission. (2021). *Proposal for a regulation laying down harmonized rules on artificial intelligence.*https://digital-strategy.ec.europa.eu/en/library/proposal-regulation-laying-down-harmonised-rules-artificial-intelligence

Ezeudu, O. B. (2024). Harnessing the drivers and barriers to implementation of extended producer responsibility for circular economy in Nigeria. *Circular Economy and Sustainability, 4*(2), 1461–1486. DOI: 10.1007/s43615-023-00340-8

Fahimnia, B., Sarkis, J., & Davarzani, H. (2015). Green supply chain management: A review and bibliometric analysis. *International Journal of Production Economics, 162*, 101–114. DOI: 10.1016/j.ijpe.2015.01.003

Faibil, D., Asante, R., Agyemang, M., Addaney, M., & Baah, C. (2023). Extended producer responsibility in developing economies: Assessment of promoting factors through retail electronic firms for sustainable e-waste management. *Waste Management & Research, 41*(1), 117–142. DOI: 10.1177/0734242X221105433 PMID: 35892190

Fan, D., Breslin, D., Callahan, J. L., & Iszatt-White, M. (2022). Advancing literature review methodology through rigour, generativity, scope and transparency. *International Journal of Management Reviews, 24*(2), 171–180. DOI: 10.1111/ijmr.12291

Farghali, M., Osman, A. I., Chen, Z., Abdelhaleem, A., Ihara, I., Mohamed, I. M., Yap, P.-S., & Rooney, D. W. (2023). Social, environmental, and economic consequences of integrating renewable energies in the electricity sector: A review. *Environmental Chemistry Letters, 21*(3), 1381–1418. DOI: 10.1007/s10311-023-01587-1

Farkic, J., Cai, W., & Isailovic, G. (2024). Tourist re-enchantment: Cultivating planetary wellbeing through more-than-human entanglements in the forest. *Journal of Sustainable Tourism, 33*(3), 457–473. DOI: 10.1080/09669582.2024.2350651

Fatahullah, F. (2019). Eksistensi Wakaf Dengan Uang Dalam Sistem Hukum Indonesia. *Jatiswara, 34*(2), 117–130. DOI: 10.29303/jtsw.v34i2.202

Fatima, T., & Elbanna, S. (2023). Corporate social responsibility (CSR) implementation: A review and a research agenda towards an integrative framework. *Journal of Business Ethics, 183*(1), 105–121. DOI: 10.1007/s10551-022-05047-8 PMID: 35125567

Fazio, D. M., Silva, T. C., Tabak, B. M., & Cajueiro, D. O. (2018). Inflation targeting and financial stability: Does the quality of institutions matter? *Economic Modelling, 71*, 1–15. DOI: 10.1016/j.econmod.2017.09.011

FDIC. (2024a). *Consumer Compliance Examination Manual.* Federal Deposit Insurance Corporation. Retrieved from https://www.fdic.gov/consumer-compliance-examination-manual

FDIC. (2024b). *Corporate Governance and Auditing Programs.* Banker Resource Center - Federal Deposit Insurance Corporation. Retrieved from https://www.fdic.gov/corporate-governance-and-auditing-programs

FDIC. (2024c). Section 4.2 Internal Routine and Controls. *In Risk Management Manual of Examination Policies.* Federal Deposit Insurance Corporation. Retrieved from Link.

Fernández, A. (2024). Opacity, Machine Learning and Explainable AI. In *Ethics of Artificial Intelligence* (pp. 39–58). Springer Nature Switzerland., DOI: 10.1007/978-3-031-48135-2_3

Fernández-Temprano, M. A., & Tejerina-Gaite, F. (2020). Types of director, board diversity and firm performance. *Corporate Governance (Bradford), 20*(2), 324–342. DOI: 10.1108/CG-03-2019-0096

Ferrara, E. (2024). The butterfly effect in artificial intelligence systems: Implications for AI bias and fairness. *Machine Learning with Applications, 7*, 100245. DOI: 10.1016/j.mlwa.2024.100525

FFIEC (2021). *Bank secrecy act anti-money laundering examination manual.* Federal Financial Institutions Examination Council. Retrieved from Link.

FFIEC. (2023). *Annual Report.* Retrieved from https://www.ffiec.gov/PDF/annrpt23.pdf

FFIEC. (2024). IT Examination Handbook InfoBase. https://ithandbook.ffiec.gov/ Accessed November 03, 2024.

Filomeni, S. (2024). The impact of the Paycheck Protection Program on the risk-taking behaviour of US banks. *Review of Quantitative Finance and Accounting, 62*(4), 1329–1353. DOI: 10.1007/s11156-023-01223-7

Finlay, R. (2017). Building trust in fintech: Solutions for overcoming digital finance's barriers. *Journal of Financial Services Marketing, 22*(1), 39–52. DOI: 10.1057/s41264-017-0032-0

Finn, C., Abbeel, P., & Levine, S. (2017, July). Model-agnostic meta-learning for fast adaptation of deep networks. In *International conference on machine learning* (pp. 1126-1135). PMLR. Retrieved from https://proceedings.mlr.press/v70/finn17a/finn17a.pdf

Floridi, L., Cowls, J., Beltrametti, M., Chatila, R., Chazerand, P., Dignum, V., Luetge, C., Madelin, R., Pagallo, U., Rossi, F., Schafer, B., Valcke, P., & Vayena, E. (2018). AI4People—an ethical framework for a good AI society: Opportunities, risks, principles, and recommendations. *Minds and Machines, 28*(4), 689–707. DOI: 10.1007/s11023-018-9482-5 PMID: 30930541

Flyverbom, M., Deibert, R., & Matten, D. (2019). The governance of digital technology, big data, and the internet: New roles and responsibilities for business. *Business & Society, 58*(1), 3–19. DOI: 10.1177/0007650317727540

Fornell, C., & Larcker, D. F. (1981). Evaluating Structural Equation Models with Unobservable Variables and Measurement Error. *JMR, Journal of Marketing Research, 18*(1), 39–50. DOI: 10.1177/002224378101800104

Frederik Klus, M., Stefan Lohwasser, T., Holotiuk, F., Moormann, J., Frederik, M., & Stefan, T. (2019). Strategic alliances between banks and fintechs for digital innovation: Motives to collaborate and types of interaction. *The Journal of Entrepreneurial Finance*, *21*(1).

Fredricks, J. A., Blumenfeld, P. C., & Paris, A. H. (2004). School engagement: Potential of the concept, state of the evidence. *Review of Educational Research*, *74*(1), 59–109. DOI: 10.3102/00346543074001059

Garg, N., & Sahu, G. P. (2024). Modeling the Barriers in Adoption of Neo Banks in India. *IFIP Advances in Information and Communication Technology, 698 AICT*. DOI: 10.1007/978-3-031-50192-0_17

Garg, P., Srivastava, T., Goel, A., & Gupta, N. (2024). Accelerating Financial Inclusion in Developing Economies (India) Through Digital Financial Technology. In AI-Driven Decentralized Finance and the Future of Finance (pp. 201-224). IGI Global.

Garg, N., & Jain, N. (2023). An Empirical Analysis on Facilitators and Inhibitors of Bankers' Intention to Use Artificial Intelligence Applications in Delhi/NCR. *International Management Review*, *19*(2), 64–94.

Garima Dalal (2013), Capital Structure Decisions, Journal of Business Management Social Sciences Research (JBM&SSR) ISSN No: 2319-5614.

Ghayas, A., & Khan, T. (2020). A Study on the Determinants of Capital Structure: Evidence from India. *The IUP Journal of Applied Finance.*, *26*, 47–59.

Ghosh, A., Jarva, H., & Ryan, S. G. (2024). Bank regulation/supervision and bank auditing. *European Accounting Review*, •••, 1–26. DOI: 10.1080/09638180.2024.2373207

Ghosh, S. (2017). How financial literacy and awareness drive fintech adoption. *Economic and Political Weekly*, *52*(9), 23–26. https://www.epw.in/

Giri, G., Nivedhitha, K. S., & Manohar, H. L. (2024). Can blockchain enabled green bond issuance lead to intent to invest? A moderated mediation model. *Applied Economics*, *56*(18), 2191–2208. DOI: 10.1080/00036846.2023.2186360

Giudici, P., & Raffinetti, E. (2021). Shapley-Lorenz eXplainable artificial intelligence. *Expert Systems with Applications*, *167*, 114104. DOI: 10.1016/j.eswa.2020.114104

Giudici, P., & Raffinetti, E. (2023, September). SAFE Artificial Intelligence in finance. *Finance Research Letters*, *56*, 104088. Advance online publication. DOI: 10.1016/j.frl.2023.104088

Global Partnership for Financial Inclusion (GPFI). (2020). *Fintech for financial inclusion: A framework for digital financial services*. https://www.gpfi.org/publications

Gómez-Morales, A., Coon, D. W., Glinka, A., Stirling, R., Pipe, T., Joseph, R. P., & Garcia-Segura, S. (2023). Training alternatives for Alzheimer's disease and related dementia caregivers: Assessing economic and environmental benefits of internet of health things. *Journal of Cleaner Production*, *418*, 138206. DOI: 10.1016/j.jclepro.2023.138206

Gonenc, H. (2005). comparison of debt financing between international and domestic firms: Evidence from Turkey, Germany and UK. *International Journal of Managerial Finance*, *1*(1), 49–68. DOI: 10.1108/17439130510584883

Government of India. (2022). *India's Updated First Nationally Determined Contribution Under Paris Agreement (2021-2030).* UNFCCC. https://unfccc.int/sites/default/files/NDC/2022-08/India%20Updated %20 First% 20 Nationally %20Determined%20Contrib.pdf

Goyal, A., Bhardwaj, R., & Kapoor, V. (2021). Financial inclusion through blockchain. *International Journal of Development Studies*, *13*(3), 45–65.

Goyal, A., Verma, S., & Mehta, P. (2024). *India's fintech revolution: Trends, challenges, and opportunities*. Springer.

Grewal, D., Roggeveen, A. L., & Nordfält, J. (2021). AI in retail: A strategic review and research agenda. *Journal of Retailing*, *97*(1), 6–22. DOI: 10.1016/j.jretai.2021.02.004

Griffith, M. A. (2023). AI Lending and the ECOA: Avoiding Accidental Discrimination. [Retrieved from Link.]. *North Carolina Banking Institute Journal*, *27*, 349.

Grigorescu, A., Oprisan, O., Lincaru, C., & Pirciog, C. S. (2023). E-banking convergence and the adopter's behavior changing across EU countries. *SAGE Open*, *13*(4), 21582440231220455. Advance online publication. DOI: 10.1177/21582440231220455

Gudiño, J. J., & Mora, J. A. (2022). Machine Learning Models, Risk Management Current Regulation and Perspectives. In *Data Analytics Applications in Emerging Markets* (pp. 49–73). Springer Nature., DOI: 10.1007/978-981-19-4695-0_3

Guerra, P., & Castelli, M. (2021). Machine learning applied to banking supervision a literature review. *Risks*, *9*(7), 136. DOI: 10.3390/risks9070136

Gunday, G., Ulusoy, G., Kilic, K., & Alpkan, L. (2011). Effects of innovation types on firm performance. *International Journal of Production Economics*, *133*(2), 662–676. DOI: 10.1016/j.ijpe.2011.05.014

Guoxun, W., Guangli, N., Peng, Z., & Yong, S. (2009). Personal financial market segmentation based on clustering ensembles. *WRI World Congress on Computer Science and Information Engineering, CSIE 2009,* 03, pp. 694-698. https://doi.org/DOI: 10.1109/CSIE.2009.741

Gupta, A., Dwivedi, D. N., & Shah, J. (2023). *Artificial Intelligence Applications in Banking and Financial Services*. SpringerNature., DOI: 10.1007/978-981-99-2571-1

Gupta, S. K., Nagar, N., Srivastava, S., Somvanshi, P., & Akimova, L. (2024). An Application of Structure Equation Modelling in Determinants of Customer-Based Brand Equity (CBBE) in the Banking Area. In Khoury, R. E., & Nasrallah, N. (Eds.), *Intelligent Systems, Business, and Innovation Research* (pp. 399–411). Springer Nature Switzerland., DOI: 10.1007/978-3-031-36895-0_32

Gupta, S., Aga, D., Pruden, A., Zhang, L., & Vikesland, P. (2021). Data analytics for environmental science and engineering research. *Environmental Science & Technology*, *55*(16), 10895–10907. DOI: 10.1021/acs.est.1c01026 PMID: 34338518

Gupta, S., Kumar, A., & Patel, D. (2022). DeFi and financial transformation in India. *Fintech Review*, *5*(2), 87–100.

Hacini, I., Boulenfad, A., & Dahou, K. (2021). The Impact of Liquidity Risk Management on the Financial Performance of Saudi Arabian Banks. *EMAJ: Emerging Markets Journal, 11*(1), 1. Advance online publication. DOI: 10.5195/emaj.2021.221

Hadi, S., & Baskaran, S. (2021). Examining sustainable business performance determinants in Malaysia upstream petroleum industry. *Journal of Cleaner Production, 294*, 126231. DOI: 10.1016/j.jclepro.2021.126231

Hall, G., Hutchinson, P., & Michaelas, N. (2004). Determinants of the capital structures of European SMEs. *Journal of Business Finance & Accounting, 31*(5-6), 711–728. DOI: 10.1111/j.0306-686X.2004.00554.x

Hamdoun, N., & Rguibi, K. (2019). Impact of AI and machine learning on financial industry: Application on moroccan credit risk scoring. *Journal of Advanced Research in Dynamical and Control Systems, 11*(11), 1041–1048. DOI: 10.5373/JARDCS/V11SP11/20193134

Hampton, J. J. (1992). *Financial decision making: concepts, problems and cases*. Prentice-Hall of India.

Hamza, A., & Nechchad, F. (2024). An Econometric & Systematic Analysis of Thailand's Economic Output, Exports and Imports; Utilizing Vector Error Correction Methodology. *Journal of Business Technology and Economics, 1*(3), 3.

Handoo, A., & Sharma, K. (2014). A study on determinants of capital structure in India. IIMB Management Review. Volume 26. Issue 3. Pp 170-182, ISSN 0970-3896, DOI: 10.1016/j.iimb.2014.07.009

Handorf, W. C. (2016). CAMEL to CAMELS: The risk of sensitivity. *Journal of Banking Regulation, 17*(4), 273–287. DOI: 10.1057/jbr.2015.24

Hariram, N. P., Mekha, K. B., Suganthan, V., & Sudhakar, K. (2023). Sustainalism: An integrated socio-economic-environmental model to address sustainable development and sustainability. *Sustainability (Basel), 15*(4), 2301. DOI: 10.3390/su151310682

Harisha, S., & Bhat, S. (2024). Comparative Analysis on Classification of Unstructured Text data and Specific Summarization. *2nd IEEE International Conference on Advances in Information Technology, ICAIT 2024*. Chikkamagaluru, Karnataka: Institute of Electrical and Electronics Engineers Inc. https://doi.org/DOI: 10.1109/ICAIT61638.2024.10690829

Harrison, T. (2000). *Financial services marketing*. Prentice Hall.

Hassan, K. H. U., Sheikh, S. M., & Rahman, S. U. (2022). The Determinants of Non-Performing Loans (NPLs); Evidence from the Banking Sector of Pakistan. *ANNALS OF SOCIAL SCIENCES AND PERSPECTIVE, 3*(1), Article 1.

Hassija, V., Chamola, V., Mahapatra, A., Singal, A., Goel, D., Huang, K., Scardapane, S., Spinelli, I., Mahmud, M., & Hussain, A. (2024). Interpreting black-box models: A review on explainable artificial intelligence. *Cognitive Computation, 16*(1), 45–74. DOI: 10.1007/s12559-023-10179-8

Hautala, J., & Ahlqvist, T. (2024). Integrating futures imaginaries, expectations and anticipatory practices: Practitioners of artificial intelligence between now and future. *Technology Analysis and Strategic Management, 36*(9), 2100–2112. DOI: 10.1080/09537325.2022.2130041

Hayes, A., Anderson, P., & Zhao, W. (2019). Decentralized finance and financial markets: An overview. *Journal of Financial Innovation*, *6*(1), 32–48.

Henseler, J., Ringle, C. M., & Sarstedt, M. (2015). A New Criterion for Assessing Discriminant Validity in Variance-Based Structural Equation Modeling. *Journal of the Academy of Marketing Science*, *43*(1), 115–135. https://link.springer.com/article/10.1007/s11747-014-0403-8. DOI: 10.1007/s11747-014-0403-8

Hepsiba, M. M. S., & Yamuna, S. M. (2022). Thriving With Artificial Intelligence In Banking Industry. *GEDRAG & ORGANISATIE REVIEW*, *35*(2), 194–199.

Hernández, E. G. (2024). *Towards an Ethical and Inclusive Implementation of Artificial Intelligence in Organizations: A Multidimensional Framework*. ArXiv.

Heryanah, H. (2017). Kesenjangan Pendapatan Di Indonesia: Berdasarkan Susenas 2008, 2011 Dan 2013. *Jurnal BPPK: Badan Pendidikan Dan Pelatihan Keuangan*, *10*(2), 43–58.

Heshmatisafa, S., & Seppänen, M. (2023). Exploring API-driven business models: Lessons learned from Amadeus's digital transformation. *Digital Business*, *3*(1), 100055. Advance online publication. DOI: 10.1016/j.digbus.2023.100055

Hidajat, T. (2020). Rural banks fraud: A story from Indonesia. *Journal of Financial Crime*, *27*(3), 933–943. DOI: 10.1108/JFC-01-2020-0010

Hidayat-ur-Rehman, I. (2024). The role of financial literacy in enhancing firm's sustainable performance through Fintech adoption: A moderated mediation analysis. *International Journal of Innovation Science*. Advance online publication. DOI: 10.1108/IJIS-03-2024-0056

Hoffmann, S. (2022). Challenges and opportunities of area-based conservation in reaching biodiversity and sustainability goals. *Biodiversity and Conservation*, *31*(2), 325–352. DOI: 10.1007/s10531-021-02340-2

Holzinger, A., Saranti, A., Molnar, C., Biecek, P., & Samek, W. (2022). Explainable AI methods-a brief overview. In *International workshop on extending explainable AI beyond deep models and classifiers* (pp. 13-38). Springer, Cham. https://doi.org/DOI: 10.1007/978-3-031-04083-2_2

Hong, J., Wang, N., & Zhou, T. (2024). The effects of FinTech adoption on bank loan spreads. *Managerial Finance*. Advance online publication. DOI: 10.1108/MF-03-2024-0238

Hornuf, L., Safari, K., & Voshaar, J. (2025). Mobile fintech adoption in Sub-Saharan Africa: A systematic literature review and meta-analysis. *Research in International Business and Finance*, *73*, 102529. Advance online publication. DOI: 10.1016/j.ribaf.2024.102529

Hosain, M. T., Jim, J. R., Mridha, M. F., & Kabir, M. M. (2024). Explainable AI approaches in deep learning: Advancements, applications and challenges. *Computers & Electrical Engineering*, *117*, 109246. DOI: 10.1016/j.compeleceng.2024.109246

Hossain, F., & Ali, A. (2012). Impact of firm specific factors on capital structure decision: An empirical study of Bangladeshi Companies. *International Journal of Business Research and Management*, *3*(4), 163–182.

Huang, G., & Song, F. (2002). The Determinants of Capital Structure: Evidence from China. *China Economic Review*, *17*(1), 14–36. DOI: 10.1016/j.chieco.2005.02.007

Huang, H. (2024, October). Technology-Driven Financial Risk Management: Exploring the Benefits of Machine Learning for Non-Profit Organizations. *Systems*, *12*(10), 416. Advance online publication. DOI: 10.3390/systems12100416

Huang, M. H., & Rust, R. T. (2020). Engaged to a robot? The role of AI in service. *Journal of Service Research*, *23*(2), 155–168. DOI: 10.1177/1094670517752459

Husain, A. R. A. M., Hamdan, A., & Fadhul, S. M. (2022). The impact of artificial intelligence on the banking industry performance. *Future of organizations and work after the 4th industrial revolution: The role of artificial intelligence, big data, automation, and robotics*, 145-156.

Hwang, T.-K., Chen, W.-C., & Chiang, W.-C. Y.-M. (2022). Machine Learning Detection for Financial Statement Fraud. *10th World Conference on Information Systems and Technologies, WorldCIST 2022* (pp. 148-154). Budva: Springer Science and Business Media Deutschland GmbH. https://doi.org/DOI: 10.1007/978-3-031-04819-7_16

Imran, A., Jian, X., Sulieman, H., & Jin, S. (2023). Evaluating the Impact of Blended Learning on Student Engagement and Performance in Higher Education. *Journal of Educational Technology Development and Exchange*, *16*(2), 189–208. https://link.springer.com/article/10.1007/s44217-024-00253-0

Irfan, M., Elmogy, M., Majid, M. S., & El-Sappagh, S. (2023). *The impact of AI innovation on financial sectors in the era of industry 5.0.* IGI Global., DOI: 10.4018/9798369300824

Islam, S. R., Eberle, W., Ghafoor, S. K., & Ahmed, M. (2021). Explainable artificial intelligence approaches: A survey. *arXiv preprint arXiv:2101.09429*. https://doi.org//arXiv.2101.09429DOI: 10.48550

Islam, K. U., & Pandow, B. A. (2024). Machine Learning Approaches for Enhanced Portfolio Optimization: A Comparative Study of Regularization and Cross-Validation Techniques. *18th INDIAcom; 11th International Conference on Computing for Sustainable Global Development, INDIACom 2024* (pp. 1440-1443). New Delhi: IEEE. https://doi.org/DOI: 10.23919/INDIACom61295.2024.10498258

Jabbouri, I., Satt, H., Azzouzi, O. E., & Naili, M. (2022). Working capital management and firm performance nexus in emerging markets: Do financial constraints matter? *Journal of Economic and Administrative Sciences*, *40*(5), 1020–1030. DOI: 10.1108/JEAS-01-2022-0010

Jack, W., & Suri, T. (2014). Risk sharing and transactions costs: Evidence from Kenya's mobile money revolution. *The American Economic Review*, *104*(1), 183–223. DOI: 10.1257/aer.104.1.183

Jagannathan, U., & Narayanarao, S. (2017), The Nature and Determinants of Capital Structure in Indian Service Firms (November 1, 2017). Indian Journal of Finance, Available at SSRN: https://ssrn.com/abstract=3078393 DOI: 10.17010/ijf/2017/v11i11/119340

Jagirdar, S. S., & Gupta, P. K. (2023). Value and contrarian investment strategies: Evidence from Indian stock market. *Journal of Risk and Financial Management*, *16*(2), 113. DOI: 10.3390/jrfm16020113

Jagirdar, S. S., & Gupta, P. K. (2024). Charting the financial odyssey: A literature review on history and evolution of investment strategies in the stock market (1900–2022). *China Accounting and Finance Review*, *26*(3), 277–307. DOI: 10.1108/CAFR-10-2023-0124

Jaglan, D. (2021). NEO BANKS-The Rise of Banking Industry. In *International Journal of Management and Commerce Innovations*.

Jaiwani, M., & Gopalkrishnan, S. (2022). Adoption of RPA and AI to Enhance the Productivity of Employees and Overall Efficiency of Indian Private Banks: An Inquiry. *In 2022 International Seminar on Application for Technology of Information and Communication (iSemantic)* (pp. 191-197). IEEE.

Jarah, B. A. F., Al Jarrah, M. A., Al-Zaqeba, M. A. A., & Al-Jarrah, M. F. M. (2022). The role of internal audit to reduce the effects of creative accounting on the reliability of financial statements in the Jordanian islamic banks. *International Journal of Financial Studies*, *10*(3), 60. DOI: 10.3390/ijfs10030060

Jayawarsa, A. K., Saputra, K. A. K., Jayanti, L. G. P. S. E., Kawisana, P. G. W. P., & Aryawan, G. (2021). WITHDRAWN: A comprehensive overview on intelligent mechanical systems and its applications of mobile banking technology.

Jean, C. J. (2003). Determinants of capital structure of Chinese-listed companies. *Journal of Business Research*, *57*, 1341–1351.

Jewandah, S. (2018). How artificial intelligence is changing the banking sector–A case study of top four commercial Indian banks. International Journal of Management. *Technology And Engineering*, *8*(7), 525–530.

Jha, S., & Dangwal, R. C. (2024). Fintech services and financial inclusion: a systematic literature review of developing nations. *Journal of Science and Technology Policy Management*. DOI: 10.1108/JSTPM-03-2023-0034

Jones, M. W., Abatzoglou, J. T., Veraverbeke, S., Andela, N., Lasslop, G., Forkel, M., ... & Le Quéré, C. (2022). Global and regional trends and drivers of fire under climate change. Reviews of Geophysics, 60(3), e2020RG000726.

Joo, Y. J., Lim, K. Y., & Kim, N. H. (2013). Online university students' satisfaction and persistence: Examining the role of self-efficacy, use of learning management systems, and course satisfaction. *Internet and Higher Education*, *16*, 68–7. DOI: 10.1016/j.compedu.2011.02.008

Jun, Y. (2024, May 02). *Scaling PayPal's AI Capabilities with PayPal Cosmos.AI Platform*. Retrieved Apr 03, 2025, from https://medium.com/paypal-tech. https://medium.com/paypal-tech/scaling-paypals-ai-capabilities-with-paypal-cosmos-ai-platform-e67a48e04691

Kahu, E. R., & Nelson, K. (2018). Student engagement in the educational interface: Understanding the mechanisms of student success. Higher Education Research & Development, 37(1), 58-71. ps://DOI: 10.1080/07294360.2017.1344197

Kalatie, S., Laakkonen, H., & Tölö, E. (2015). Indicators used in setting the countercyclical capital buffer. Bank of Finland Research Discussion Paper(8).

Kaminski, M. E. (2019). The right to explanation, explained. *Berkeley Technology Law Journal, 34*(1), 189–218. DOI: 10.15779/Z38TD9N83H

Kaplan, A., & Haenlein, M. (2019). Siri, Siri, in my hand: Who's the fairest in the land? *Business Horizons, 62*(1), 15–25. DOI: 10.1016/j.bushor.2018.08.004

Kara, G., & Vojtech, C. M. (2020). Bank Failures, Capital Buffers, and Exposure to the Housing Market Bubble. Capital Buffers, and Exposure to the Housing Market Bubble (July 20, 2020).

Karlan, D., Ratan, A. L., & Zinman, J. (2014). Savings by and for the poor: A research review and agenda. *Review of Income and Wealth, 60*(1), 36–78. DOI: 10.1111/roiw.12101 PMID: 25792764

Katz, G., Barrett, C., Dill, D. L., Julian, K., & Kochenderfer, M. J. (2017). Reluplex: An efficient SMT solver for verifying deep neural networks. In *Computer Aided Verification:29th International Conference, CAV 2017,Heidelberg, Germany,July 24-28, 2017, Proceedings, Part I 30* (pp. 97-117). Springer International Publishing. https://doi.org/DOI: 10.1007/978-3-319-63387-9_5

Kaur, R., Chattopadhyay, A. K., & Rakshit, D. (2020). Determinants of Capital Structure with Reference to Select Indian Companies: A Panel Data Regression Analysis. Asia-Pacific Journal of Management Research and Innovation, 2319510X2091345. DOI: 10.1177/2319510X20913454

Kaur, D. N., Sahdev, S. L., Sharma, D. M., & Siddiqui, L. (2020). Banking 4.0:'the influence of artificial intelligence on the banking industry & how ai is changing the face of modern day banks'. *International Journal of Management, 11*(6). Advance online publication. DOI: 10.34218/IJM.11.6.2020.049

Kaur, J., Syan, A. S., Kaur, S., & Sharma, R. R. (2022). *Understanding the factors influencing actual usage of payments banks: An empirical investigation using the extended information systems success model*. FIIB Business Review., DOI: 10.1177/23197145221099095

Kavitha, S. (2014), Determinants of Corporate Capital Structure among Selected Manufacturing Industries in India, Avinashilingam Institute for Home Scienceand Higher Education for Women Thesis, Retrieved from, https://shodhganga.inflibnet.ac.in/handle/10603/40672

Khan, S. (2025). *AI in Wonderland: Engineering in the age of overpromised technology* (SAE EDGE Research Reports). SAE International. ISBN: 1468609238, 9781468609233.

Khandani, A. E., Kim, A. J., & Lo, A. W. (2010, November). Consumer credit-risk models via machine-learning algorithms. *Journal of Banking & Finance, 34*(11), 2767–2787. DOI: 10.1016/j.jbankfin.2010.06.001

Khan, M. A., Hussain, A., Ali, M. M., & Tajummul, M. A. (2022). Assessing the impact of liquidity on the value of assets return. [GBMR]. *Global Business and Management Research, 14*(1), 1. Advance online publication. DOI: 10.32890/gbmr2022.14.1.4

Kharb, R., Suneja, V., Aggarwal, S., Singh, P., Shahzzad, U., Saini, N., & Kumar, D. (2024). The Relationship between investment determinants and environmental sustainability: Evidence through meta-analysis. *The Quarterly Review of Economics and Finance, 94*(April), 267–280. DOI: 10.1016/j.qref.2024.02.001

Kim, L., Jindabot, T., & Yeo, S. F. (2024). Understanding customer loyalty in banking industry: A systematic review and meta-analysis. *Heliyon, 10*(17), e36619. Advance online publication. DOI: 10.1016/j.heliyon.2024.e36619 PMID: 39281651

Klein, A. (2020, February 27). *Why bank regulators should make their secret ratings public.* The Brookings Institution Research. Retrieved from https://www.brookings.edu/articles/why-bank-regulators-should-make-their-secret-ratings-public/

Klein, P. G., Mahoney, J. T., McGahan, A. M., & Pitelis, C. N. (2019). Organizational governance adaptation: Who is in, who is out, and who gets what. *Academy of Management Review, 44*(1), 6–27. DOI: 10.5465/amr.2014.0459

Kočenda, E., & Iwasaki, I. (2022). Bank survival around the World: A meta-analytic review. *Journal of Economic Surveys, 36*(1), 108–156. DOI: 10.1111/joes.12451

Kokkodis, M., & Ransbotham, S. (2023). Learning to successfully hire in online labor markets. *Management Science, 69*(3), 1597–1614. DOI: 10.1287/mnsc.2022.4426

Koolwal, N., & Khandelwal, S. (2019, February). Corporate social responsibility (CSR) implementation in oil and gas industry: Challenges and solutions. In *Proceedings of International Conference on Sustainable Computing in Science, Technology and Management (SUSCOM), Amity University Rajasthan, Jaipur-India.* DOI: 10.2139/ssrn.3358059

Koundal, P., Bhalla, M., & Bandna. (2025). The role of AIS in enhancing small business agility and sustainability in Industry 5.0. In *The Future of Small Business in Industry 5.0* (pp. 1–30). https://doi.org/DOI: 10.4018/979-8-3693-7362-0.ch012

Kour, M. (2023). Challenges and opportunities of machine learning in the financial sector. In *Algorithmic Approaches to Financial Technology: Forecasting, Trading, and Optimization* (pp. 61-73). IGI Global. https://doi.org/DOI: 10.4018/979-8-3693-1746-4.ch004

Kour, M. (2024). Revolutionizing Finance: Unleashing Machine Learning's Potential for a New Financial Era. *International Conference on Advances in Computing Research on Science Engineering and Technology, ACROSET 2024.* Indore: IEEE. https://doi.org/DOI: 10.1109/ACROSET62108.2024.10743732

KPMG. (2020). The future of blockchain in financial inclusion. *KPMG Insights.* https://home.kpmg/xx/en/home/insights.html

KPMG. (2024). *AI in financial reporting and audit: Navigating the new era.* Retrieved from https://assets.kpmg.com/content/dam/kpmgsites/ch/pdf/kpmg-ch-report-global-ai-audit-study-trusted-ai-framework.pdf.coredownload.inline.pdf

Kraus, A., & Litzenberger, R. H. (1973). A State-Preference Model of Optimal Financial Leverage. *The Journal of Finance, 28*(4), 911–922.

Kuang, M., Kuang, D., Rasool, Z., Saleem, H. M. N., & Ullah, M. I. (2024). *From bytes to sustainability: Asymmetric nexus between industrial artificial intelligence and green finance in advanced industrial AI nations.* Borsa Istanbul Review.

Kulkov, I., Kulkova, J., Rohrbeck, R., Menvielle, L., Kaartemo, V., & Makkonen, H. (2024). Artificial intelligence-driven sustainable development: Examining organizational, technical, and processing approaches to achieving global goals. *Sustainable Development (Bradford), 32*(3), 2253–2267. DOI: 10.1002/sd.2773

Kumar, A. (2025, Mar 23). *BlackRock AI/ML Innovation Report*. Retrieved Apr 06, 2025, from https://www.linkedin.com. https://www.linkedin.com/pulse/blackrock-aiml-innovation-report-arpit-kumar-inkxc/

Kumar, N., Vaze, P., & Kidney, S. (2019). Moving from Growth to Development: Financing Green Investment in India. ORF. https://www.orfonline.org/wp-content/uploads/2019/02/pg-98-115.pdf

Kumar, S., & Kundalia, L. (2023). Green Bonds - Role and scope in India's financial and fiscal landscape The Journal of Indian Institute of Banking & Finance accessed on 1 October, 2024 from https://www.iibf.org.in/documents/BankQuest/6.%20.pdf

Kumar, S., Kumar, B. A., & Ravi, V. (2023). Explainable Artificial Intelligence for Analytical Customer Relationship Management in Banking and Finance. *23rd International Conference on Intelligent Systems Design and Applications, ISDA 2023. 1049 LNNS*, pp. 101-112. Olten: Springer Science and Business Media Deutschland GmbH. https://doi.org/DOI: 10.1007/978-3-031-64779-6_10

Kumar, A., & Singh, P. (2023). Decentralized finance (DeFi) and financial inclusion: Perspectives from India. *Journal of Fintech and Policy Research*, *5*(1), 98–110.

Kumar, I. E., Venkatasubramanian, S., Scheidegger, C., & Friedler, S. (2020, November). Problems with Shapley-value-based explanations as feature importance measures. In *International conference on machine learning* (pp. 5491-5500). PMLR. Retrieved from Link.

Kumar, J., & Gupta, S. S. (2023). Impact of artificial intelligence towards customer relationship in Indian banking industry. *Gyan Manag. J*, *17*(1), 105–115. DOI: 10.48165/gmj.2022.17.1.12

Kumar, R., & Bhattacharya, P. (2020). Gender-sensitive fintech innovations for rural women. *Journal of Gender Studies*, *29*(4), 510–523. DOI: 10.1080/09589236.2020.1744611

Kumar, S. (2022). Critical Assessment Of Green Financing Initiatives In Emerging Market: A Review Of India's Green Bond Issuances. *Academy of Marketing Studies Journal*, *26*(5).

Kumar, S., & Rajan, P. (2023). Blockchain for fraud prevention in Indian banking. *Journal of Financial Integrity*, *9*(4), 67–79.

Kumra, R., & Arora, S. (2022). Digital Sensory Marketing Factors Affecting Customers' Intentions to Continue Organic Online Purchases during COVID in India. *FIIB Business Review*, *0*(0), 23197145221105674. Advance online publication. DOI: 10.1177/23197145221105674

Kunisch, S., Denyer, D., Bartunek, J. M., Menz, M., & Cardinal, L. B. (2023). Review research as scientific inquiry. *Organizational Research Methods*, *26*(1), 3–45. DOI: 10.1177/10944281221127292

Kute, D. V., Pradhan, B., Shukla, N., & Alamri, A. (2021). Deep learning and explainable artificial intelligence techniques applied for detecting money laundering–a critical review. *IEEE Access : Practical Innovations, Open Solutions*, *9*, 82300–82317. DOI: 10.1109/ACCESS.2021.3086230

Kweh, Q. L., Lu, W.-M., Tone, K., & Liu, H.-M. (2024a). Evaluating the resource management and profitability efficiencies of US commercial banks from a dynamic network perspective. *Financial Innovation*, *10*(1), 19. DOI: 10.1186/s40854-023-00531-0

Laasch, O., Moosmayer, D. C., & Antonacopoulou, E. P. (2023). The interdisciplinary responsible management competence framework: An integrative review of ethics, responsibility, and sustainability competences. *Journal of Business Ethics*, *187*(4), 733–757. DOI: 10.1007/s10551-022-05261-4

Lampropoulos, G., Siakas, K., Viana, J., & Reinhold, O. (2022). Artificial Intelligence, Blockchain, Big Data Analytics, Machine Learning and Data Mining in Traditional CRM and Social CRM: A Critical Review. *IEEE/WIC/ACM International Joint Conference on Web Intelligence and Intelligent Agent Technology, WI-IAT 2022* (pp. 504-510). Virtual, Online: Institute of Electrical and Electronics Engineers Inc. https://doi.org/DOI: 10.1109/WI-IAT55865.2022.00080

Larcker, D., & Tayan, B. (2020). *Corporate governance matters*. FT Press.

Lee, M.-C. (2010). The analytic hierarchy and the network process in multicriteria decision making: Performance evaluation and selecting key performance indicators based on ANP model. Convergence and Hybrid Information Technologies, 426.

Leiss, W. (2023). *The domination of nature: New edition*. McGill-Queen's University Press., DOI: 10.1515/9780228017264

Lembaga Penjamin Simpanan (LPS). 2020. Banyak Dana Korporasi Berpindah Ke bank-bank kecil, LPS ;Tanda Meningkatnya Kepercayaan Pada Sistem Perbankan. Siaran Pers Nomor: PRESS-42 /SEKL/2020

Lembaga Penjamin Simpanan (LPS). 2020. Kondisi Perbankan Stabil, Tidak Ada Bank Umum Yang Ditangani LPS. Siaran Pers Nomor: 35/X/2020

Leng, J., Guo, J., Zhang, H., Xu, K., Qiao, Y., Zheng, P., & Shen, W. (2023). Dual deep reinforcement learning agents-based integrated order acceptance and scheduling of mass individualized prototyping. *Journal of Cleaner Production*, *427*, 139249. DOI: 10.1016/j.jclepro.2023.139249

Leo, M., Sharma, S., & Maddulety, K. (2019). Machine Learning in Banking Risk Management: A Literature Review. *Risks*, *7*(1), 29. DOI: 10.3390/risks7010029

Leslie, D., Rincon, C., Briggs, M., Perini, A., Jayadeva, S., Borda, A., Bennett, S., Burr, C., Aitken, M., Katell, M., Fischer, C., Wong, J., & Garcia, I. K. (2024). AI Sustainability in Practice Part One: Foundations for Sustainable AI Projects. ArXiv. https://doi.org/DOI: 10.2139/ssrn.4731832

Lessambo, F. I. (2023). AML/CFT Compliance and Audit. In *Anti-Money Laundering, Counter Financing Terrorism and Cybersecurity in the Banking Industry: A Comparative Study within the G-20* (pp. 205-214). Cham: Springer Nature Switzerland. https://doi.org/DOI: 10.1007/978-3-031-23484-2_27

Le, T. N. L., Nasir, M. A., & Huynh, T. L. D. (2023). Capital requirements and banks performance under Basel-III: A comparative analysis of Australian and British banks. *The Quarterly Review of Economics and Finance*, *87*, 146–157. DOI: 10.1016/j.qref.2020.06.001

Liaw, S. S., & Huang, H. M. (2013). Perceived satisfaction, perceived usefulness and interactive learning environments as predictors to self-regulation in e-learning environments. *Computers & Education*, *60*(1), 14–24. DOI: 10.1016/j.compedu.2012.07.015

Li, C., He, P., Peng, W., Lü, F., Du, R., & Zhang, H. (2022). Exploring available input variables for machine learning models to predict biogas production in industrial-scale biogas plants treating food waste. *Journal of Cleaner Production*, *380*, 135074. DOI: 10.1016/j.jclepro.2022.135074

Lim, J. S., & Zhang, J. (2022). Adoption of AI-driven personalization in digital news platforms: An integrative model of technology acceptance and perceived contingency. *Technology in Society*, *69*, 1–10. DOI: 10.1016/j.techsoc.2022.101965

Lim, T. (2024). Environmental, social, and governance (ESG) and artificial intelligence in finance: State-of-the-art and research takeaways. *Artificial Intelligence Review*, *57*(4), 76. DOI: 10.1007/s10462-024-10708-3

Li, N., Huang, J., & Feng, Y. (2020). Construction and confirmatory factor analysis of the core cognitive ability index system of ship C2 system operators. *PLoS One*, *15*(8), e0237339. DOI: 10.1371/journal.pone.0237339 PMID: 32833969

Lindström, V., & Nilsson, O. (2023). The sudden rise of neobanks and the threat it poses upon the traditional banking system.

Ling, A., Peng, W., Wang, Q., & Yang, X. (2024, January). A comprehensive research progress of applying NLP in financial problems. *Xitong Gongcheng Lilun yu Shijian. Xitong Gongcheng Lilun Yu Shijian*, *44*(01), 387–406. DOI: 10.12011/SETP2023-1935

Ling, X., & Wang, H. (2024). Green Behavior Strategies in the Green Credit Market: Analysis of the Impacts of Enterprises' Greenwashing and Blockchain Technology. *Sustainability (Basel)*, *16*(11), 4858. DOI: 10.3390/su16114858

Li, R., Sun, F., & Zhao, J. (2020). Ethical implications of AI in retail. *Computers in Human Behavior*, *124*, 106909. DOI: 10.1016/j.chb.2020.106909

Litvinenko, V. (2020). The role of hydrocarbons in the global energy agenda: The focus on liquefied natural gas. *Resources*, *9*(5), 59. DOI: 10.3390/resources9050059

Liu, D., Fang, H., Tang, Y., Mohd Isa, S., & Tang, J. (2023). Intelligent technology solutions and banking efficiency: The impacts of institutional innovation and consumer participation. *SAGE Open*, *13*(2), 21582440231184205. Advance online publication. DOI: 10.1177/21582440231184205

Liu, Q., Gao, J., & Li, S. (2024). The innovation model and upgrade path of digitalization driven tourism industry: Longitudinal case study of OCT. *Technological Forecasting and Social Change*, *200*, 123127. DOI: 10.1016/j.techfore.2023.123127

Li, X. H., Cao, C. C., Shi, Y., Bai, W., Gao, H., Qiu, L., Wang, C., Gao, Y., Zhang, S., Xue, X., & Chen, L. (2020). A survey of data-driven and knowledge-aware explainable ai. *IEEE Transactions on Knowledge and Data Engineering*, *34*(1), 29–49. DOI: 10.1109/TKDE.2020.2983930

Li, Y., Chen, Y. K., Chien, F. S., Lee, W. C., & Hsu, Y. C. (2016). Study of optimal capital adequacy ratios. *Journal of Productivity Analysis*, *45*(3), 261–274. DOI: 10.1007/s11123-016-0469-z

Li, Y., & Ma, W. (2010). Applications of artificial neural networks in financial economics: A survey. *International Symposium on Computational Intelligence and Design, ISCID 2010.* 01, pp. 211-214. Hangzhou: IEEE Computer Society. https://doi.org/DOI: 10.1109/ISCID.2010.70

Lone, F., Aggarwal, S. & Jain, S. (2024). Retail Investors' Perception towards Green Bonds in Advancing Sustainability: Evidence from India. accepted for publication in Asia pacific Financial markets

Lone, F., Aggarwal, S., & Gupta, S. (2024). Green Bonds Sustainable Development and Economic Benefits for Investors and Pharmaceutical Companies. IGI Global. https://www.igi-global.com/gateway/chapter/353812

Longo, L., Brcic, M., Cabitza, F., Choi, J., Confalonieri, R., Del Ser, J., & Stumpf, S. (2024). Explainable Artificial Intelligence (XAI) 2.0: A manifesto of open challenges and interdisciplinary research directions. *Information Fusion*, *106*, 102301. DOI: 10.1016/j.inffus.2024.102301

Lopes, J. M., Sousa, A., Calçada, E., & Oliveira, J. (2021). A citation and co-citation bibliometric analysis of omnichannel marketing research. *Management Review Quarterly*, 1-34

LPS. (2020). Lembaga Penjamin Simpanan - Banyak dana korporasi berpindah ke bank-bank kecil, LPS; Tanda meningkatnya kepercayaan pada sistem perbankan - Siaran Pers [Press release]. Retrieved from https://lps.go.id/web/guest/siaran-pers/-/asset_publisher/1T0a/content/banyak-dana-koorporasi-berpindah-ke-bank-bank-kecil-lps-tanda-meningkatnya-kepercayaan-pada-sistem-perbankan?inheritRedirect=false&redirect=https%3A%2F%2Flps.go.id%2Fweb%2Fguest%2Fsiaran-pers%3Fp_p_id%3D101_INSTANCE_1T0a%26p_p_lifecycle%3D0%26p_p_state%3Dnormal%26p_p_mode%3Dview%26p_p_col_id%3Dcolumn-2%26p_p_col_count%3D1

Lu, Z., Wan, X., Yang, J., Wu, J., Zhang, C., Hung, P. C. K., & Huang, S.-C. (2019). BIS: A novel blockchain-based bank-tax interaction system in smart city. *2019 IEEE Intl Conf on Dependable, Autonomic and Secure Computing, Intl Conf on Pervasive Intelligence and Computing, Intl Conf on Cloud and Big Data Computing, Intl Conf on Cyber Science and Technology Congress (DASC/PiCom/CBDCom/CyberSciTech)*, 1008–1014. https://doi.org/DOI: 10.1109/DASC/PiCom/CBDCom/CyberSciTech.2019.00183

Maček, A., Murg, M., & Čič, Ž. V. (2020). How robotic process automation is revolutionizing the banking sector. In *Managing customer experiences in an omnichannel world: Melody of online and offline environments in the customer journey* (pp. 271–286). Emerald Publishing Limited. DOI: 10.1108/978-1-80043-388-520201020

Mahalakshmi, V., Kulkarni, N., Pradeep Kumar, K., Suresh Kumar, K., Nidhi, S. D., & Durga, S. (2022, January). The Role of implementing Artificial Intelligence and Machine Learning Technologies in the financial services Industry for creating Competitive Intelligence. *Materials Today: Proceedings*, *56*, 2252–2255. DOI: 10.1016/j.matpr.2021.11.577

Mahalik, M. K., Pal, S., Le, T. H., & Mishra, S. (2024). Does environmental policy stringency improve nature's health in BRICS economies? *Environmental Science and Pollution Research International*, *31*(1), 509–528. DOI: 10.1007/s11356-023-31134-y PMID: 38015395

Makadia, D. R., Kotadia, J., Monasara, A., & Garg, D. (2023). A Machine Learning Method for Stock Market Price Prediction. *8th International Conference on ICT for Sustainable Development, ICT4SD 2023* (pp. 217-227). Goa: Springer Science and Business Media Deutschland GmbH. https://doi.org/ DOI: 10.1007/978-981-99-6568-7_20

Makrides, A., Kvasova, O., Thrassou, A., Hadjielias, E., & Ferraris, A. (2021). Consumer cosmopolitanism in international marketing research: A systematic review and future research agenda. *International Marketing Review*. Advance online publication. DOI: 10.1108/IMR-12-2020-0304

Makudza, F. (2021). Augmenting customer loyalty through customer experience management in the banking industry. *Journal of Asian Business and Economic Studies*, *28*(3), 191–203. DOI: 10.1108/JABES-01-2020-0007

Malan, K. M. (2021). A Survey of Advances in Landscape Analysis for Optimisation. *Algorithms*, *14*(2), 40. DOI: 10.3390/a14020040

Mallikarjunappa T and Carmelita Goveas (2007), "Factors determining the capital structure of pharmaceutical companies in India," The ICFAI journal of applied finance, Vol.13 (11), Pp.56-72.

Mall, S., Panigrahi, T. R., & Kabir Hassan, M. (2024). Neo banking: A bibliometric review of the current research trend and future scope. *International Review of Economics & Finance*, *96*, 103559. DOI: 10.1016/j.iref.2024.103559

Mancuso, I., Petruzzelli, A. M., Panniello, U., & Vaia, G. (2025). Business model innovation in the banking sector: How digital technologies transform innovation drivers in value mechanisms innovations. *Journal of Engineering and Technology Management - JET-M, 75*. https://doi.org/DOI: 10.1016/j.jengtecman.2024.101858

Manita, R., Elommal, N., Baudier, P., & Hikkerova, L. (2020). The digital transformation of external audit and its impact on corporate governance. *Technological Forecasting and Social Change*, *150*, 119751. DOI: 10.1016/j.techfore.2019.119751

Manning, B., Braam, G., & Reimsbach, D. (2019). Corporate governance and sustainable business conduct—Effects of board monitoring effectiveness and stakeholder engagement on corporate sustainability performance and disclosure choices. *Corporate Social Responsibility and Environmental Management*, *26*(2), 351–366. DOI: 10.1002/csr.1687

Mann, M., Hosman, C. M. H., Schaalma, H. P., & de Vries, N. K. (2004). Self-esteem in a broad-spectrum approach for mental health promotion. *Health Education Research*, *19*(4), 357–372. DOI: 10.1093/her/cyg041 PMID: 15199011

Manyika, J., Lund, S., Chui, M., Bughin, J., Woetzel, J., Batra, P., & Sanghvi, S. (2017). *What the future of work will mean for jobs, skills, and wages*. McKinsey Global Institute. https://www.mckinsey.com/featured-insights/future-of-work/what-the-future-of-work-will-mean-for-jobs-skills-and-wages

Manzoor, A. (2023). Antecedents to following brands on Facebook and Instagram with moderating role of user experience. *FIIB Business Review*, *0*(0). Advance online publication. DOI: 10.1177/23197145221151010

Margaretha, F., & Aditya, K. (2013). Pengaruh Resiko Likuiditas Terhadap Profitabilitas Bank Konvensional di Indonesia. *Journal of Accounting and Investment*, *14*(2), 96–105.

Martiskainen, M., Axon, S., Sovacool, B. K., Sareen, S., Del Rio, D. F., & Axon, K. (2020). Contextualizing climate justice activism: Knowledge, emotions, motivations, and actions among climate strikers in six cities. *Global Environmental Change*, *65*, 102180. DOI: 10.1016/j.gloenvcha.2020.102180

McCarthy, J., & Wright, P. (2021). The role of AI in customer service. *Journal of Service Management*, *31*(4), 789–808. DOI: 10.1108/JSM-2020-0187

McDonald, J., & Johnson, S. M. (2010). Tax Policies To Improve The Stability Of Financial Markets. *Bank Of Italy Occasional Paper*.

McKinsey Global Institute. (2016). Digital finance for all: Powering inclusive growth in emerging economies. https://www.mckinsey.com/mgi

Mehmood, S., & Kaewsaeng-on, R. (2024). Charting an Economic Sustainability Path: Quantile Regression Analysis of Green Finance and Financial Development in Newly Industrialized Economies. *Global Business Review*, *09721509231224019*, 09721509231224019. Advance online publication. DOI: 10.1177/09721509231224019

Mehrotra, A., & Yetman, J. (2015). Financial inclusion and optimal monetary policy. *Bank for International Settlements Working Paper No. 482*. https://doi.org/DOI: 10.2139/ssrn.2582911

Mer, A., & Virdi, A. S. (2025). The influence of artificial intelligence on personal and corporate finance: A comprehensive literature review with prospects for future research. In *Financial Landscape Transformation: Technological Disruptions* (pp. 253-268). Emerald Publishing. https://doi.org/DOI: 10.1108/978-1-83753-750-120251014

Meyer, C., & Schwager, A. (2021). How AI is reshaping customer service in retail. *Journal of Retailing and Marketing*, *92*(4), 42–53. DOI: 10.1007/s10729-021-09541-9

Miao, Z. (2024). Financial Fraud Detection and Prevention: Automated Approach Based on Deep Learning. *Journal of Organizational and End User Computing*, *36*(01), 1–27. Advance online publication. DOI: 10.4018/JOEUC.354411

Miller, Z. C., & Kohr, L. (2017). Senior management training, accountability and oversight for anti-money laundering compliance. [Retrieved from Link.]. *Journal of Financial Compliance*, *1*(1), 81–88. DOI: 10.69554/SGMS2903

Minchin, T. J. (2021). 'The factory of the future' Historical continuity and labor rights at Tesla. *Labor History*, *62*(4), 434–453. DOI: 10.1080/0023656X.2021.1940115

Ministry of Finance. (2023). *Jan Dhan Yojana: 10-year progress report*. Government of India.

Mishra, V., & Singh, J. (2022). *Health Technology Assessment of Telemedicine Interventions in Diabetes Management: Evidence from UAE*. FIIB Business Review., DOI: 10.1177/23197145221130651

Miskak, S. (2020). Kegagalan Analisis Laporan Keuangan Dalam Memprediksi Kebangkrutan BPR/BPRS di Indonesia. *Kajian Ekonomi Dan Keuangan*, *3*(3), 161–181.

Mitrega, M., Spacil, V., & Pfajfar, G. (2021). Co-creating value in post-communists contexts: Capability perspective. *Journal of Services Marketing*, *35*(2), 169–181. DOI: 10.1108/JSM-03-2019-0114

Mogaji, E. (2023). Redefining banks in the digital era: A typology of banks and their research, managerial and policy implications. *International Journal of Bank Marketing*, *41*(7), 1899–1918. DOI: 10.1108/IJBM-06-2023-0333

Mohammad, H. Q. (2022). *THE IMPACT OF MONETARY POLICY ON PROFITABILITY OF BANKING INDUSTRY IN IRAQ*.

Mohanty, P., Sharma, K., & Sen, A. (2022). Blockchain and Aadhaar integration: Opportunities and risks. *India Digital Journal*, *7*(3), 54–73.

Mohapatra, S., Plaza, S., & Ratha, D. (2019). *Remittance markets in Africa: Prospects and challenges*. World Bank Publications., DOI: 10.1596/978-0-8213-8256-6

Mohr, P. (2001). The governors and deputy governors of the South African Reserve Bank 1921-2001. *South African Journal of Economic History*, 16(1_2), 101-138.

Mohsin Khan, M., Shah, N., Shaikh, N., Thabet, A., Alrabayah, T., & Belkhair, S. (2025). Towards secure and trusted AI in healthcare: A systematic review of emerging innovations and ethical challenges. *International Journal of Medical Informatics*, *195*, 105780. DOI: 10.1016/j.ijmedinf.2024.105780 PMID: 39753062

Mökander, J., Morley, J., Taddeo, M., & Floridi, L. (2021). Ethics-based auditing of automated decision-making systems: Nature, scope, and limitations. *Science and Engineering Ethics*, *27*(4), 44. DOI: 10.1007/s11948-021-00319-4 PMID: 34231029

Molnar, C. (2020). *Interpretable machine learning*. Lulu. com.

Monis, E., & Pai, R. (2023a). Neo Banks: A Paradigm Shift in Banking. *International Journal of Case Studies in Business, IT, and Education*. DOI: 10.47992/IJCSBE.2581.6942.0275

Moreira, M. Â., De Souza Rocha, C., Junior., Silva, D. F., De Castro, M. A., Junior., De Araújo Costa, I. P., Gomes, C. F., & Dos Santos, M. (2022). Exploratory analysis and implementation of machine learning techniques for predictive assessment of fraud in banking systems. *9th International Conference on Information Technology and Quantitative Management, ITQM 2022*. 214, pp. 117-124. Beijing: Elsevier B.V. https://doi.org/DOI: 10.1016/j.procs.2022.11.156

Morgan, P. J., Regis, P. J., & Salike, N. (2019). LTV policy as a macroprudential tool and its effects on residential mortgage loans. *Journal of Financial Intermediation*, *37*, 89–103. DOI: 10.1016/j.jfi.2018.10.001

Mostaghim, C. (2021). Constructing the yellow brick road: Preventing discrimination in financial services against the LGBTQ+ community. [Retrieved from Link.]. *Michigan Business & Entrepreneurial Law Review*, *11*(11.1), 63. DOI: 10.36639/mbelr.11.1.constructing

Mourtzis, D., Angelopoulos, J., & Panopoulos, N. (2022). A literature review of the challenges and opportunities of the transition from Industry 4.0 to Society 5.0. *Energies*, *15*(17), 6276. DOI: 10.3390/en15176276

Muduli, A., & Choudhury, A. (2024). Digital technology adoption, workforce agility and digital technology outcomes in the context of the banking industry of India. Journal of Science and Technology Policy Management.

Muhmad, K., Wan Mohd Jaafar, W. S., Mohd Said, M. N., Saad, S. N. M., & Mohan, M. (2023). UAV implementations in urban planning and related sectors of rapidly developing nations: A review and future perspectives for Malaysia. *Remote Sensing (Basel)*, *15*(11), 2845. DOI: 10.3390/rs15112845

Mukherjee, D., Lim, W. M., Kumar, S., & Donthu, N. (2022). Guidelines for advancing theory and practice through bibliometric research. *Journal of Business Research*, *148*, 101–115. DOI: 10.1016/j.jbusres.2022.04.042

Mukherjee, S., & Mahakud, J. (2012). Are trade-off and pecking order theories of capital structure mutually exclusive?: Evidence from Indian manufacturing companies. *Journal of Management Research*, *12*(1), 41–55.

Mushtaq, R., Dastane, O., Rafiq, M., & Başar, B. D. (2023). Women financial inclusion research: A bibliometric and network analysis. *International Journal of Social Economics*, *50*(8), 1169–1185. DOI: 10.1108/IJSE-06-2022-0438

Myers, S. C. (1984). The capital structure puzzle. *The Journal of Finance*, *39*(3), 574–592. DOI: 10.1111/j.1540-6261.1984.tb03646.x

Mzoughi, H., Amar, A. B., Guesmi, K., & Benkraiem, R. (2024). Blockchain markets, green finance investments, and environmental impacts. *Research in International Business and Finance*, *69*, 102249. DOI: 10.1016/j.ribaf.2024.102249

Naeem, H. M., & di Maria, E. (2020). Customer participation in new product development: An Industry 4.0 perspective. *European Journal of Innovation Management*, *25*(6), 637–655. DOI: 10.1108/EJIM-01-2021-0036

Naik, N., Hameed, B. M. Z., Shetty, D. K., Swain, D., Shah, M., Paul, R., Aggarwal, K., Ibrahim, S., Patil, V., Smriti, K., Shetty, S., Rai, B. P., Chlosta, P., & Somani, B. K. (2022). Legal and ethical consideration in artificial intelligence in healthcare: Who takes responsibility? *Frontiers in Surgery*, *9*, 862322. DOI: 10.3389/fsurg.2022.862322 PMID: 35360424

Naili, M., Jabbouri, I., & Helmi, I. (2023). Financial inclusion and the financial and economic development: Review of the literature, evidence gaps and the road ahead. *Qualitative Market Research*, *26*(5), 632–662. DOI: 10.1108/QMR-02-2023-0017

Narain, R. (2019). Financial inclusion through fintech: A study of financial access in India. *Indian Journal of Economics and Development*, *7*(4), 448–457. DOI: 10.5958/2322-0430.2019.00072.1

Naresh Sardar Vallabhbhai Patel, R., Ravichandran, R., Muralidhar, D., Naresh, N., & Professor, A. (2022). Neo Banks, Fintech, And Banking-The Changing Landscape-A Perspective-On Dangers, Growth, Opportunities-A Critical Study. In *Peer Reviewed and Refereed Journal* (Issue 6).

Narula, R. (2020). Blockchain and the future of financial inclusion. *Journal of International Business and Economy*, *21*(2), 113–126. DOI: 10.5102/jibe.2020.01.07

Narula, S., & Vasudevan, R. (2020). Blockchain-based microfinance in rural India. *Journal of Social Entrepreneurship, 12*(3), 210–226.

NASSCOM. (2023). *State of blockchain adoption in India: Opportunities and challenges*. National Association of Software and Service Companies.

Nasser, S. Z. (2024, Mar 11). *27 Real Examples of AI Implementation in Fintech and Banking*. Retrieved Nov 02, 2024, from https://www.linkedin.com. https://www.linkedin.com/pulse/27-authentic-examples-ai-implementation-fintech-nasser-sami-qtxee/

Năstasă, A., Dumitra, T., & Grigorescu, A. (2024). Artificial intelligence and sustainable development during the pandemic: An overview of the scientific debates. *Heliyon, 10*(9), e30412. DOI: 10.1016/j.heliyon.2024.e30412 PMID: 38711639

National Payments Corporation of India (NPCI). (2023). Unified Payments Interface: Growth and global leadership. Retrieved from https://www.npci.org.in

National Payments Corporation of India (NPCI). (2023). UPI monthly report. Retrieved from https://www.npci.org.in

Nauta, M., Trienes, J., Pathak, S., Nguyen, E., Peters, M., Schmitt, Y., Schlötterer, J., van Keulen, M., & Seifert, C. (2023). From anecdotal evidence to quantitative evaluation methods: A systematic review on evaluating explainable ai. *ACM Computing Surveys, 55*(13s), 1–42. DOI: 10.1145/3583558

Nave, A., & Ferreira, J. (2019). Corporate social responsibility strategies: Past research and future challenges. *Corporate Social Responsibility and Environmental Management, 26*(4), 885–901. DOI: 10.1002/csr.1729

Nayyar, R. (2021). Economic reforms and financial sector liberalization in India. *Economic and Political Weekly, 56*(2), 12–24.

Nazaretsky, T., Bar, C., Walter, M., & Alexandron, G. (2022). Empowering teachers with AI: Co-designing a learning analytics tool for personalized instruction in the science classroom. In *LAK22: 12th International Learning Analytics and Knowledge Conference* (pp. 1–12). Association for Computing Machinery. https://doi.org/DOI: 10.1145/3506860.3506861

Neri, S. (2021). Environmental, Social and Governance (ESG) and Integrated Reporting. In *Global Challenges to CSR and Sustainable Development: Root Causes and Evidence from Case Studies*, 293-302.

Nguyen, P. N. D., & Nguyen, H. H. (2024). Unveiling the link between digital entrepreneurship education and intention among university students in an emerging economy. *Technological Forecasting and Social Change, 203*, 123330. https://doi.org/ rights and contentDOI: 10.1016/j.techfore.2024.123330Get

Nguyen, N. P. A., & Dao, T. T. B. (2022). Liquidity, corporate governance and firm performance: A meta-analysis. *Cogent Business & Management, 9*(1), 2137960. DOI: 10.1080/23311975.2022.2137960

Nguyen, Y. T. H., Tapanainen, T., & Nguyen, H. T. T. (2022). Reputation and its consequences in Fintech services: The case of mobile banking. *International Journal of Bank Marketing, 40*(7), 1364–1397. DOI: 10.1108/IJBM-08-2021-0371

Nicoletti, A., & Zhu, C. (2023). Economic Consequences of Transparency Regulation: Evidence from Bank Mortgage Lending. *Journal of Accounting Research, 61*(5), 1827–1871. DOI: 10.1111/1475-679X.12498

Nobanee, H., Ellili, N. O. D., Chakraborty, D., & Shanti, H. Z. (2024). Mapping the fintech revolution: How technology is transforming credit risk management. *Global Knowledge, Memory and Communication*. Advance online publication. DOI: 10.1108/GKMC-12-2023-0492

Nosrati, L., Bidgoli, A. M., & Javadi, H. H. S. (2024). Identifying people's faces in smart banking systems using artificial neural networks. *International Journal of Computational Intelligence Systems, 17*(1), 9. Advance online publication. DOI: 10.1007/s44196-023-00383-7

Noth, F., & Schüwer, U. (2018). Natural disaster and bank stability: Evidence from the US financial system.

Nugrohowati, R. N. I., & Bimo, S. (2019). Analisis pengaruh faktor internal bank dan eksternal terhadap Non-Performing Financing (NPF) pada Bank Perkreditan Rakyat Syariah di Indonesia. Jurnal Ekonomi & Keuangan Islam, 42-49.

Nur Aliftiani, N., Firdaus, M., & Supeni, N. (2024). COMPARATIVE ANALYSIS OF HEALTH LEVELS AT BANK NEO COMMERCE & BANK JAGO. *MBA - Journal of Management and Business Aplication, 6*(2). DOI: 10.31967/mba.v6i2.1026

Nzeako, G., Akinsanya, M. O., Popoola, O. A., Chukwurah, E. G., Okeke, C. D., & Akpukorji, I. S. (2024). Theoretical insights into IT governance and compliance in banking: Perspectives from African and US regulatory environments. *International Journal of Management & Entrepreneurship Research, 6*(5), 1457–1466. DOI: 10.51594/ijmer.v6i5.1094

Office of the Comptroller of the Currency. (2022, March). Large bank supervision. In *Comptroller's Handbook: Examination Process*. U.S. Department of the Treasury. Retrieved from https://www.occ.gov/publications-and-resources/publications/comptrollers-handbook/files/large-bank-supervision/pub-ch-large-bank-supervision.pdf

Ofoeda, I., Amoah, L., Anarfo, E. B., & Abor, J. Y. (2024). Financial inclusion and economic growth: What roles do institutions and financial regulation play? *International Journal of Finance & Economics, 29*(1), 832–848. DOI: 10.1002/ijfe.2709

Oguejiofor, B. B., Omotosho, A., Abioye, K. M., Alabi, A. M., Oguntoyinbo, F. N., Daraojimba, A. I., & Daraojimba, C. (2023). A review on data-driven regulatory compliance in Nigeria. *International Journal of Applied Research in Social Sciences, 5*(8), 231–243. DOI: 10.51594/ijarss.v5i8.571

Ojha, S. (2023, July 21). *Pension funds to invest in green bonds: How it will impact retail investors?* Mint. https://www.livemint.com/money/personal-finance/pension-funds-to-invest-in-sovereign-greenbonds-sgrbs-how-it-will-impact-retail-investors-11689920200494.html

Okello Candiya Bongomin, G., Akol Malinga, C., Manzi Amani, A., & Balinda, R. (2024). Recalibrating the scope of financial inclusion through financial technologies in the digital age: The role of digital literacy as a moderator in rural Uganda. *Information Technology & People*. Advance online publication. DOI: 10.1108/ITP-09-2022-0732

Olanipekun, A. O., Oshodi, O. S., Darko, A., & Omotayo, T. (2020). The state of corporate social responsibility practice in the construction sector. *Smart and Sustainable Built Environment*, *9*(2), 91–111. DOI: 10.1108/SASBE-11-2018-0056

Olilingo, F. Z., & Putra, A. H. P. K. (2020). How Indonesia economics works: Correlation analysis of macroeconomics in 2010-2019. *The Journal of Asian Finance, Economics and Business*, *7*(8), 117–130. DOI: 10.13106/jafeb.2020.vol7.no8.117

Oliveira, A., Martins, F. V., & Brandao, E. (2015). Bank failure and the financial crisis: An econometric analysis of US banks. *Available atSSRN* 2698881. DOI: 10.2139/ssrn.2698881

Olorunfemi, O. L., Amoo, O. O., Atadoga, A., Fayayola, O. A., Abrahams, T. O., & Shoetan, P. O. (2024). Towards a conceptual framework for ethical AI development in IT systems. *Computer Science & IT Research Journal*, *5*(3), 616–627. DOI: 10.51594/csitrj.v5i3.910

Omol, E. J. (2024). Organizational digital transformation: From evolution to future trends. In *Digital Transformation and Society* (Vol. 3, Issue 3, pp. 240–256). Emerald Publishing. https://doi.org/DOI: 10.1108/DTS-08-2023-0061

Oshri, I., & Plugge, A. (2022). Introducing RPA and automation in the financial sector: Lessons from KAS Bank. *Journal of Information Technology Teaching Cases*, *12*(1), 88–95. DOI: 10.1177/2043886921994828

Otoritas Jasa Keuangan (OJK). (2019). *Buku I – OJK dan Pengawasan Makroprudensial*. Otoritas Jasa Keuangan.

Owolabi, O. S., Uche, P. C., Adeniken, N. T., Ihejirika, C., Islam, R. B., Chhetri, B. J. T., & Jung, B. (2024). Ethical implication of artificial intelligence (AI) adoption in financial decision making. *Comput. Inf. Sci*, *17*(1), 49–56. DOI: 10.5539/cis.v17n1p49

Özcan, M. (2023). Forecasting in stock market with Machine Learning: A State of Art. *14th International Conference on Computing Communication and Networking Technologies, ICCCNT 2023*. Delhi: Institute of Electrical and Electronics Engineers Inc. https://doi.org/DOI: 10.1109/ICCCNT56998.2023.10307692

Ozili, P. K. (2020). Financial inclusion and fintech during COVID-19 crisis: Policy solutions. *Journal of Financial Regulation and Compliance*, *28*(4), 565–573. DOI: 10.1108/JFRC-06-2020-0046

Ozili, P. K. (2020). Financial inclusion research around the world: A review. *The Forum for Social Economics*, *49*(4), 457–478. DOI: 10.1080/07360932.2020.1715238

Ozili, P. K. (2020). Theories of Financial Inclusion. In *Uncertainty and Challenges in Contemporary Economic Behaviour* (pp. 89–115). Emerald Publishing Limited., DOI: 10.1108/978-1-80043-095-220201008

Ozili, P. K., Ademiju, A., & Rachid, S. (2023). Impact of financial inclusion on economic growth: Review of existing literature and directions for future research. *International Journal of Social Economics*, *50*(8), 1105–1122. DOI: 10.1108/IJSE-05-2022-0339

Pahari, S., Polisetty, A., Sharma, S., Jha, R., & Chakraborty, D. (2023). Adoption of AI in the banking industry: A case study on Indian banks. *Indian Journal of Marketing*, *53*(3), 26–41. DOI: 10.17010/ijom/2023/v53/i3/172654

Pahul Preet, S., Fahim, I. A., Rahul, S., & Arnav, S. N. S., & E. H. (2024, Mar). Investigating customer churn in banking: a machine learning approach and visualization app for data science and management. *Data Science and Management, 07*(01), 07-16. https://doi.org/https://doi.org/10.1016/j.dsm.2023.09.002

Pandey, I.M. (2004). Capital structure, Profitability and market structure: Evidence from Malaysia, Asia Pacific Journal of Economics and Business, Vol.8, Issue No.2, Pp 78-91.

Parasuraman, A. (2000). Technology Readiness Index (TRI): A multiple-item scale to measure readiness to embrace new technologies. *Journal of Service Research*, *2*(4), 307–320. DOI: 10.1177/109467050024001

Park, J. Y., Ryu, J. P., & Shin, H. J. (2017, May). How to manage portfolio by robo-advisor. *Information (Japan), 20*(05), 3463 - 3470. Retrieved Oct 18, 2024, from https://www.scopus.com/record/display.uri?eid=2-s2.0-85035063023&origin=scopusAI

Park, J., Cuervo-Cazurra, A., & Montiel, I. (2023). The evolution of sustainability concerns over business activities: from local to cross-national to global. In *Research Handbook on International Corporate Social Responsibility* (pp. 7–24). Edward Elgar Publishing. DOI: 10.4337/9781802207040.00007

Park, J., Son, Y., & Angst, C. M. (2023). The Value of Centralized IT in Building Resilience During Crises: Evidence from US Higher Education's Transition to Emergency Remote Teaching. *Management Information Systems Quarterly*, *47*(1), 451–482. DOI: 10.25300/MISQ/2022/17265

Pasrija, A., Dahiya, P., Sharma, N., & Mangla, M. (2022). Online Transaction Fraud Detection Using Machine Learning. *1st International Conference on Applied Data Science and Smart Systems, ADSSS 2022. 2916.* Rajpura: American Institute of Physics Inc. https://doi.org/DOI: 10.1063/5.0177562

Pathria, M., Saini, R., & Manchanda, M. (2022). Examining Consumer Attitude towards AI-powered M-banking Chatbots: A Study on Elderly Users in an Emerging Market. *Bank Parikrama, XLVII*(3 & 4), 74–108.

Patnaik, R., Patra, S. K., Mahapatra, D. M., & Baral, S. K. (2022). *Adoption and Challenges Underlying OTT Platform in India during Pandemic: A Critical Study of Socio-Economic and Technological Issues.* FIIB Business Review., DOI: 10.1177/23197145221101676

Patnaik, R., Patra, S. K., Mahapatra, D. M., & Baral, S. K. (2024). Adoption and challenges underlying OTT platform in India during pandemic: A critical study of socio-economic and technological issues. *FIIB Business Review*, *13*(3), 356–363.

Paul, J., & Criado, A. R. (2020). The art of writing literature review: What do we know and what do we need to know? *International Business Review*, *29*(4), 101717. DOI: 10.1016/j.ibusrev.2020.101717

Paul, J., Lim, W. M., O'Cass, A., Hao, A. W., & Bresciani, S. (2021). Scientific Procedures and Rationales for Systematic Literature Reviews (SPAR-4-SLR). *International Journal of Consumer Studies*, *45*(4), O1–O16. DOI: 10.1111/ijcs.12695

PayPal. (2024, Oct 15). *Harnessing the power of machine learning for payment fraud detection.* Retrieved Oct 27, 2024, from https://www.paypal.com. https://www.paypal.com/us/brc/article/payment-fraud-detection-machine-learning

Pekrun, R., & Linnenbrink-Garcia, L. (2012). Academic emotions and student engagement. In Christenson, S. L. (Eds.), *Handbook of research on student engagement* (pp. 259–282). Springer. DOI: 10.1007/978-1-4614-2018-7_12

Pereira, G., Fleith, J., Kolling, C., Ribeiro, J., Morea, D., & Iazzolino, G. (2024, July 01). Using dynamic capabilities to cope with digital transformation and boost innovation in traditional banks. *Business Horizons*, *67*(04), 317–330. DOI: 10.1016/j.bushor.2024.03.006

Peruchini, M., da Silva, G. M., & Teixeira, J. M. (2024). Between artificial intelligence and customer experience: A literature review on the intersection. *Discover Artificial Intelligence*, *4*(1), 4. Advance online publication. DOI: 10.1007/s44163-024-00105-8

Piras, D., Peiris, H. V., Pontzen, A., Lucie-Smith, L., Guo, N., & Nord, B. (2023). A robust estimator of mutual information for deep learning interpretability. *Machine Learning: Science and Technology*, *4*(2), 025006. DOI: 10.1088/2632-2153/acc444

Pistoia, M., Ahmad, S. F., Ajagekar, A., Buts, A., Chakrabarti, S., Herman, D., Hu, S., Jena, A., Minssen, P., Niroula, P., Rattew, A., & Sun, Y. (2021). Quantum Machine Learning for Finance. *40th IEEE/ACM International Conference on Computer-Aided Design, ICCAD 2021. 2021-November.* Munich: Institute of Electrical and Electronics Engineers Inc. https://doi.org/DOI: 10.1109/ICCAD51958.2021.9643469

Popescu, C. R. G. (2019). Corporate social responsibility, corporate governance and business performance: Limits and challenges imposed by the implementation of directive 2013/34/EU in Romania. *Sustainability (Basel)*, *11*(19), 5146. DOI: 10.3390/su11195146

Prahalad, C. K., & Hammond, A. (2002). Serving the world's poor, profitably. *Harvard Business Review*, *80*(9), 48–57. https://hbr.org/2002/09/serving-the-worlds-poor-profitably PMID: 12227146

Prakash, B. K. (2023). Adoption, Applications and Challenges of Artificial Intelligence in Indian Banking Sector. *Journal of Management and Entrepreneurship*, *17*(2).

Pramod, D. (2021). Robotic process automation for industry: Adoption status, benefits, challenges and research agenda. *Benchmarking*, *29*(5), 1562–1586. DOI: 10.1108/BIJ-01-2021-0033

Prastowo, P. (2018). Analisis regional keuangan inklusi perbankan syariah terhadap ketimpangan pendapatan di Indonesia. Jurnal Ekonomi & Keuangan Islam, 51-57.

Pujadas, R., Valderrama, E., & Venters, W. (2024). The value and structuring role of web APIs in digital innovation ecosystems: The case of the online travel ecosystem. *Research Policy*, *53*(2), 104931. Advance online publication. DOI: 10.1016/j.respol.2023.104931

Puni, A., & Anlesinya, A. (2020). Corporate governance mechanisms and firm performance in a developing country. *International Journal of Law and Management*, *62*(2), 147–169. DOI: 10.1108/IJLMA-03-2019-0076

Purohit, H., & Khanna, S. (2012). Determinants of Capital Structure in Indian Manufacturing Sector. *Asia-Pacific Journal of Management Research and Innovation*, *8*(3), 265–269. DOI: 10.1177/2319510X1200800306

Purwono, R., & Dimayanti, A. U. R. (2020). The effect of internal banking and macroeconomic variables on systemic risk. Polish Journal of Management Studies, 21.

Quoc Trung, N. K. (2021). Determinants of bank performance in Vietnamese commercial banks: An application of the camels model. *Cogent Business & Management*, *8*(1), 1979443. DOI: 10.1080/23311975.2021.1979443

Radanliev, P., Santos, O., Brandon-Jones, A., & Joinson, A. (2024). Ethics and responsible AI deployment. *Frontiers in Artificial Intelligence*, *7*, 1377011. DOI: 10.3389/frai.2024.1377011 PMID: 38601110

Rai, S., & Choudhary, M. (2018). Fintech in India: Role of financial inclusion in driving economic growth. *International Journal of Economics and Financial Issues*, *8*(6), 59–66. https://www.econjournals.com/index.php/ijefi/article/view/7032

Rajan, R., & Zingales, L. (1995). What do we know about capital structure? Some evidence from international data. *The Journal of Finance*, *50*(5), 1421–1460. DOI: 10.1111/j.1540-6261.1995.tb05184.x

Raji, A. A., Alabdoon, A. H., & Almagtome, A. (2024). AI in Credit Scoring and Risk Assessment: Enhancing Lending Practices and Financial Inclusion. *International Conference on Knowledge Engineering and Communication Systems, ICKECS 2024.* Chikkaballapur: IEEE. https://doi.org/DOI: 10.1109/ICKECS61492.2024.10616493

Raju, P., Joshi, J., & Nannapaneni, P. (2022, September 19). *Green Bonds - Environmental Law - India.* Mondaq. https://www.mondaq.com/india/environmental-law/1231314/green-bonds

Ram, K. K. (1999). The Determinants of Capital Structure- An Econometric Analysis. *Finance India*, *XIII*(1), 51–69.

Rangaswamy, E., Nawaz, N., Mohamed, S. B. S., & Joy, G. V. (2024). A study on entrepreneurial innovation among entities in Singapore. *Journal of Innovation and Entrepreneurship*, *13*(1), 10. Advance online publication. DOI: 10.1186/s13731-024-00362-y

Ransbotham, S., Kiron, D., Gerbert, P., & Reeves, M. (2020). Artificial intelligence in business gets real. *MIT Sloan Management Review*. https://sloanreview.mit.edu/article/artificial-intelligence-in-business-gets-real

Rashaduzzaman, M. (2024). *Risk Management in Banks: It's Relationship with the Financial Performance of Commercial Banks in Bangladesh* [Thesis, ©University of Dhaka]. http://reposit.library.du.ac.bd:8080/xmlui/xmlui/handle/123456789/3078

Rashed, A., Alchuban, M., Hamdan, A., & Alareeni, B. (2021). The Impact of Robotic Process Automation (RPA) Technology in Banking Sector in Bahrain. *InInternational Conference on Business and Technology(pp.* 273-281*)*. Cham*:* Springer International Publishing.

Rashmi, R., & Nirmal, R. V. (2021). A study on the implementation and the impact of artificial intelligence in banking processes. *Asian Journal of Management*, *12*(1), 47–54.

Rasoolpur, G. S. (2012). An empirical analysis of capital Structure determinants: Evidence from the Indian corporate sector. International Journal of Management & Information Technology, Vol. 1, Issue No.3, Pp 1-12.

Ratha, D., Mohapatra, S., & Plaza, S. (2011). *Leveraging migration for Africa: Remittances, skills, and investments*. World Bank., DOI: 10.1596/978-0-8213-8257-8

Rathee, P. (2023, January 09). Governing Behaviours of Impact Investors in India: A Path to Balance Double Bottom Line. *Global Business Review*, 09721509221141200. Advance online publication. DOI: 10.1177/09721509221141200

Rathee, P., & Aggarwal, S. (2022a). Understanding Impact Investment Intention Using the Extended Theory of Planned Behaviour. *Global Business Review*, 09721509221115001. Advance online publication. DOI: 10.1177/09721509221115001

Rathee, P., & Aggarwal, S. (2022b). Investors' Preference for Creating Impact:(A study to understand impact investors' preference while making investment in India). *Vision (Basel)*, •••, 09722629221131110.

Rathnasiri, R. A. (2024). The Impact of Macroeconomic Stability on Commercial Bank Profitability: A Study of Sri Lanka. *The International Journal of Accounting*, *4*(1). Advance online publication. DOI: 10.4038/ija.v4i1.61

Ratnasari, T., Surwanti, A., & Pribadi, F. (2021). Implementation of Green Banking and Financial Performance on Commercial Banks in Indonesia. In *Recent Developments in Asian Economics International Symposia in Economic Theory and Econometrics* (world; Vol. 28, pp. 323–336). Emerald Publishing Limited. DOI: 10.1108/S1571-038620210000028018

Ratzan, J., & Rahman, N. (2023). Measuring responsible artificial intelligence (RAI) in banking: A valid and reliable instrument. *AI and Ethics*, •••, 1–19. DOI: 10.1007/s43681-023-00321-5

Ravi, H. (2021). Innovation in banking: Fusion of artificial intelligence and blockchain. *Asia Pacific Journal of Innovation and Entrepreneurship*, *15*(1), 51–61.

Rawas, S. (2024). AI: The future of humanity. In *Discover Artificial Intelligence* (Vol. 4, Issue 1). Springer Nature. https://doi.org/DOI: 10.1007/s44163-024-00118-3

Regona, M., Yigitcanlar, T., Hon, C., & Teo, M. (2024). Artificial intelligence and sustainable development goals: Systematic literature review of the construction industry. *Sustainable Cities and Society*, *108*, 105499. DOI: 10.1016/j.scs.2024.105499

Regulagadda, R., Veeraiah, V., Muthugurunathan, G., Sai Madupu, L., Satyanarayana, S., & Muniyandy, E. (2024, January 12). Predictive Analytics in Stock Markets: Unleashing the Power of IoT and Machine Learning. *International Journal of Intelligent Systems and Applications in Engineering*, *12*(12), 414–422. Retrieved January 13, 2025, from https://www.scopus.com/record/display.uri?eid=2-s2.0-85185487868&origin=scopusAI

Remmers, L., Stonehill, A., Wright, R., & Beekhuisen, T. (1974). Industry and Size as Debt Ratio Determinants in Manufacturing Internationally. *Financial Management*, *3*(2), 24–32. DOI: 10.2307/3665286

Rendle, S., Fetterly, D., Shekita, E. J., & Su, B.-Y. (2016). Robust large-scale machine learning in the cloud. *22nd ACM SIGKDD International Conference on Knowledge Discovery and Data Mining, KDD 2016. 13-17-August-2016*, pp. 1125 - 1134. San Francisco: Association for Computing Machinery. https://doi.org/DOI: 10.1145/2939672.2939790

Reserve Bank of India (RBI). (2023). Central bank digital currency pilot projects: Progress report. Retrieved from https://www.rbi.org.in

Reserve Bank of India. (2023). Annual Report 2022-2023. https://www.rbi.org.in/Scripts/AnnualReportPublications.aspx

Rhyne, E., & Otero, M. (2006). Microfinance through the next decade: Visioning the who, what, where, when and how. *Accion International Report*. https://www.accion.org/resource/microfinance-through-the-next-decade

Richardson, J. T. E. (2005). Students' perceptions of academic quality and approaches to studying in distance education. *British Educational Research Journal, 31*(1), 7–27. DOI: 10.1080/0141192052000310001

Ridwan, M. (2022). DETERMINANTS OF INFLATION: Monetary and Macroeconomic Perspectives. *KINERJA: Jurnal Manajemen Organisasi Dan Industri, 1*(1), 1. Advance online publication. DOI: 10.34005/kinerja.v2i02.793

Rodrigues Chagas, B. N., Nogueira Viana, J. A., Reinhold, O., Lobato, F., Jacob, A. F., & Alt, R. (2019). Current Applications of Machine Learning Techniques in CRM: A Literature Review and Practical Implications. *18th IEEE/WIC/ACM International Conference on Web Intelligence, WI 2018* (pp. 452-458). Santiago: Institute of Electrical and Electronics Engineers Inc. https://doi.org/DOI: 10.1109/WI.2018.00-53

Rousseau, D. M., Manning, J., & Denyer, D. (2008). 11 Evidence in management and organizational science: Assembling the field's full weight of scientific knowledge through syntheses. *The Academy of Management Annals, 2*(1), 475–515. DOI: 10.5465/19416520802211651

Roy, S. (2025). AI Adoption and Central Banks in Emerging Markets: Challenges and Strategies. Available at *SSRN* 5121231. DOI: 10.2139/ssrn.5121231

Rudin, C. (2019). Stop explaining black box machine learning models for high stakes decisions and use interpretable models instead. *Nature Machine Intelligence, 1*(5), 206–215. DOI: 10.1038/s42256-019-0048-x PMID: 35603010

Rustiarini, N. W., Suryandari, N. N. A., & Nova, I. K. S. (2016). Red flags and fraud prevention on rural banks. BuletinEkonomiMoneter dan Perbankan, 19(2), 177-206.

Rusydiana, A. S. (2016). Analisismasalahpengembanganperbankan syariah di Indonesia: Aplikasi Metode analytic network process. Esensi: Jurnal Bisnis dan Manajemen, 6(2), 237-246.

Rusydiana, A. S., & Devi, A. (2018). Elaborating cash waqf development in Indonesia using analytic network. International Journal of Islamic Business and Economics (IJIBEC), 1-13.

Rusydiana, A. S., Rani, L. N., & Hasib, F. F. (2019). Manakah indikator terpenting stabilitas sistem keuangan?: Perspektif makroprudensial. Jurnal Ekonomi dan Pembangunan, 27(1), 25-42.

Sachdeva, K., & Sivakumar, P. (2022). Performance of commercial banks in India: A non-parametric Malmquist index-based DEA approach. *International Journal of Business and Globalisation, 32*(4), 392–413. DOI: 10.1504/IJBG.2022.128175

Saha, P., Aanand, S., Shah, P., Khatwani, R., Mitra, P. K., & Sekhar, R. (2023). Comparative Analysis of ML Algorithms for Fraud Detection in Financial Transactions. *1st International Conference on Advances in Electrical, Electronics and Computational Intelligence, ICAEECI 2023.* Tiruchengode: IEEE. https://doi.org/DOI: 10.1109/ICAEECI58247.2023.10370930

Sahay, R., Čihák, M., N'Diaye, P., & Barajas, A. (2015). *Financial inclusion: Can it meet multiple macroeconomic goals?* IMF Staff Discussion Notes., DOI: 10.5089/9781513542683.006

Sahi, G. K., Modi, P., & Mantok, S. (2023). New product innovations in times of crisis: How did women entrepreneurs survive the COVID-19 crisis? *Industrial Marketing Management*, *111*, 19–29. DOI: 10.1016/j.indmarman.2023.03.004

Salama, R., Cacciagrano, D., & Al-Turjman, F. (2025). Connecting AI and Blockchain to Improve Security of Financial Services. In *Lecture Notes on Data Engineering and Communications Technologies* (Vol. 232, pp. 67–77). Springer Science and Business Media Deutschland GmbH., DOI: 10.1007/978-3-031-76462-2_7

Samanthapudi, S. V., Rohella, P., Temara, S., Gupta, K., & Dhanasekaran, S. (2024). Uncovering the Benefits of Machine Learning for Automating Financial Regulatory Tasks. *International Conference on E-Mobility, Power Control and Smart Systems, ICEMPS 2024.* Thiruvananthapuram: Institute of Electrical and Electronics Engineers Inc. https://doi.org/DOI: 10.1109/ICEMPS60684.2024.10559370

Sanga, B., & Aziakpono, M. (2024). FinTech developments and their heterogeneous effect on digital finance for SMEs and entrepreneurship: Evidence from 47 African countries. *Journal of Entrepreneurship in Emerging Economies*. https://doi.org/DOI: 10.1108/JEEE-09-2023-0379

Santosa, P. W., Setianingrum, A., & Huda, N. (2020). The Relationship of Macro-risk Indicators, Internal Factors, and Risk Profile of Islamic Banking in Indonesia. *ETIKONOMI*, *19*(2), 221–236. DOI: 10.15408/etk.v19i2.15528

Santos, S. C., Liguori, E. W., & Garvey, E. (2023). How digitalization reinvented entrepreneurial resilience during COVID-19. *Technological Forecasting and Social Change*, *189*, 122398. Advance online publication. DOI: 10.1016/j.techfore.2023.122398 PMID: 36778643

Saraswat, P., Chouhan, V., & Goswami, S. (2024). Application of Robotic Process Automation (RPA) in Accounting: A Study of User's Perception At Delhi-NCR and Gujarat. *Finance India*, *38*(3), 589.

Sarhan, A. A., Ntim, C. G., & Al-Najjar, B. (2019). Board diversity, corporate governance, corporate performance, and executive pay. *International Journal of Finance & Economics*, *24*(2), 761–786. DOI: 10.1002/ijfe.1690

Saumitra, B. N. (2002). Determinants of Corporate Borrowings: Some Evidence from the Indian Corporate Sector. *Journal of Economics and Finance*, *26*(2), 200–215. DOI: 10.1007/BF02755986

Sawarni, K. S., Narayanasamy, S., & Padhan, P. C. (2023). Impact of earnings management on working capital management efficiency. *Finance Research Letters*, *54*, 103778. DOI: 10.1016/j.frl.2023.103778

Scannapieco, M., & Virgillito, A. (2021). How to be responsible in all the steps of a data science pipeline: The case of the Italian public sector. *Patterns (New York, N.Y.)*, *2*(12), 100393. DOI: 10.1016/j.patter.2021.100393 PMID: 34950908

Schilling de Carvalho, P. (2022). Retaining Influence in Post-Brexit International Financial Regulation: Lessons from the UK's FinTech Framework. *Journal of Financial Regulation*, *8*(1), 104–131. DOI: 10.1093/jfr/fjac004

Schoenmaker, D. (2020). The impact economy: Balancing profit and impact. In *The Impact Economy: Balancing Profit and Impact*, Working Paper, 4.

Schreieck, M., Huang, Y., Kupfer, A., & Krcmar, H. (2024). The effect of digital platform strategies on firm value in the banking industry. *Journal of Management Information Systems*, *41*(2), 394–421. DOI: 10.1080/07421222.2024.2340825 PMID: 38974483

Schuetz, S., & Venkatesh, V. (2020). Blockchain, adoption, and financial inclusion in India: Research opportunities. *International Journal of Information Management*, *52*, 101936. DOI: 10.1016/j.ijinfomgt.2019.04.009

Selbst, A. D., & Barocas, S. (2018). The intuitive appeal of explainable machines. *Fordham Law Review*, *87*, 1085. https://ir.lawnet.fordham.edu/flr/vol87/iss3/11/

Setiawaty, A. (2016). Pengaruh mekanisme good corporate governance terhadap kinerja perbankan dengan manajemen risiko sebagai variabel intervening. Kinerja. *Jurnal Ekonomi Dan Manajemen*, *13*(1), 13–24.

Shabir, S., & Ali, J. (2022). Determinants of financial inclusion across gender in Saudi Arabia: Evidence from the World Bank's Global Financial Inclusion survey. *International Journal of Social Economics*, *49*(5), 780–800. DOI: 10.1108/IJSE-07-2021-0384

Shabu, K., & Ramankutty, V. (2022). Neobanking in India: Opportunities and Challenges from Customer Perspective. SSRN *Electronic Journal*. DOI: 10.2139/ssrn.4037656

Shahid, S., Islam, J. U., Malik, S., & Hasan, U. (2022). Examining consumer experience in using m-banking apps: A study of its antecedents and outcomes. *Journal of Retailing and Consumer Services*, *65*, 102870. Advance online publication. DOI: 10.1016/j.jretconser.2021.102870

Shah, S. Q. A., Lai, F. W., Shad, M. K., & Jan, A. A. (2022). Developing a green governance framework for the performance enhancement of the oil and gas industry. *Sustainability (Basel)*, *14*(7), 3735. DOI: 10.3390/su14073735

Shanti, R., Siregar, H., Zulbainarni, N., & Tony, . (2024). Revolutionizing Banking: Neobanks' Digital Transformation for Enhanced Efficiency. *Journal of Risk and Financial Management*, *17*(5), 188. DOI: 10.3390/jrfm17050188

Sharifi, A. (2021). Urban sustainability assessment: An overview and bibliometric analysis. *Ecological Indicators*, *121*, 107102. DOI: 10.1016/j.ecolind.2020.107102

Sharma, S. (2024). Digital Disruption in Banking: A Comparative Analysis of Neo Banks and Traditional Institutions. *International Journal of Management and Development Studies, 13*(3), 01–12. DOI: 10.53983/ijmds.v13n3.001

Sharma, M., & Choubey, A. (2024). Impact of information technology on Indian banking sector. *Journal of Financial Services Marketing*, *29*(4), 1609–1622. DOI: 10.1057/s41264-024-00287-3

Sharma, M., & Choubey, A. A. (2021). Qualitative Study on Role of Information Technology in Indian Banking Sector. *AIMA Journal of Management & Research*, *15*(3/4), 1–24.

Sharma, V., & Singh, P. (2023). Financial services transformation in India: A study of liberalization and digital integration. *Journal of Emerging Markets*, *9*(4), 98–110.

Sharma, V., & Verma, N. (2023). Tokenization of assets: Blockchain use cases in India. *Journal of Blockchain Applications*, *8*(1), 98–114.

Shen, Y., Agyekum, F., Reddy, K., & Wallace, D. (2024). The welfare impact of financial inclusion: A research agenda. *Journal of Accounting Literature*. Advance online publication. DOI: 10.1108/JAL-10-2023-0190

Shi, W., Ali, M., & Leong, C.-M. (2024). Dynamics of personal financial management: A bibliometric and systematic review on financial literacy, financial capability and financial behavior. *International Journal of Bank Marketing*. Advance online publication. DOI: 10.1108/IJBM-06-2023-0359

Silalahi, E. S. B. (2018). *Analisis Keterkaitan Kebijakan Mikroprudensial Dengan Kebijakan Makroprudensial Di Indonesia. Fakultas Ekonomi dan Bisnis*. Universitas Brawijaya Malang.

Silva, J. C., MacEdo, D., Zanchettin, C., Oliveira, A. L., & De Almeida Filho, A. T. (2021). Multi-Class Mobile Money Service Financial Fraud Detection by Integrating Supervised Learning with Adversarial Autoencoders. *International Joint Conference on Neural Networks, IJCNN 2021*. Virtual, Shenzhen: Institute of Electrical and Electronics Engineers Inc. https://doi.org/DOI: 10.1109/IJCNN52387.2021.9533313

Simorangkir, I. (2011). Penyebab Bank Runs di Indonesia: Bad Luck atau Fundamental?.Buletin Ekonomi Moneter dan Perbankan, 14(1), 51-78.

Singh, A. (1995), Corporate financial patterns in industrializing economies, International Finance Corporation Technical Paper 2.

Singh, R., & Singh, V. P. (2025). Global Mobility and Economic Incentives in Prenatal Tourism. In, Exploration of Prenatal Tourism and Birthright Citizenship (pp. 77-104). IGI Global Scientific Publishing. https://doi.org/ Available on: https://www.igi-global.com/gateway/chapter/365545DOI: 10.4018/979-8-3693-8206-6.ch005

Singh, R., Singh, V. P., Rabby, F., Bansal, R., & Gupta, N. K. (2025). The Road to Sustainable Tourism: Financial Mechanisms for Green Project Development. In B. Sousa, L. Arantes, & S. Bhartiya (Eds.), Regenerative Tourism for Social Development (pp. 235-254). IGI Global Scientific Publishing. Available on: https://doi.org/DOI: 10.4018/979-8-3373-0235-5.ch010

Singh, U. V., & Shrivastava, M. K. (2024). Accelerating the Growth of Green Bonds in India. New Delhi:The Energy and Resources Institute accessed on 1 October, 2024 from https://teriin.org/sites/default/files/files/Accelerating_the_Growth_of_Green_Bonds_Policy_Brief.pdf

Singh, D., & Sharma, R. (2021). Blockchain-based KYC systems for Indian banks. *Asian Banking Journal*, *5*(3), 65–89.

Singh, K., & Hiremath, S. M. (2023). *Blockchain-Based Smart Contracts for Secure and Efficient Financial Transactions in Digital Banking. IEEE Technology and Engineering Management Conference - Asia Pacific, TEMSCON-ASPAC 2023*. Institute of Electrical and Electronics Engineers Inc., DOI: 10.1109/TEMSCON-ASPAC59527.2023.10531368

Singh, N., Srivastava, S., & Sinha, N. (2017). Consumer preference and satisfaction of M-wallets: A study on North Indian consumers. *International Journal of Bank Marketing*, *35*(6), 944–965. DOI: 10.1108/IJBM-06-2016-0086

Singh, T., & Verma, R. (2024). *Blockchain and financial inclusion in emerging economies: The Indian experience*. Springer.

Sipahi, S., & Timor, M. (2010). The analytic hierarchy process and analytic network process: An overview of applications. *Management Decision*, *48*(5), 775–808. DOI: 10.1108/00251741011043920

Siregar, P. A., Supitriyani, S., Parinduri, L., Astuti, A., Azwar, K., Simarmata, H. M. P., . . . Sudarmanto, E. (2021). Bank dan Lembaga Keuangan Lainnya: Yayasan Kita Menulis.

Sitar-Tăut, D. A., Mican, D., & Moisescu, O. I. (2024). To be (online) or not to be? The antecedents of online study propensity and e-learning-dependent dropout intention in higher education. *Technological Forecasting and Social Change*, *207*, 123566. DOI: 10.1016/j.techfore.2024.123566

Skinner, E. A., Kindermann, T. A., & Furrer, C. J. (2009). A motivational perspective on engagement and disaffection: Conceptualization and assessment of children's behavioral and emotional participation in academic activities in the classroom. *Educational and Psychological Measurement*, *69*(3), 493–525. DOI: 10.1177/0013164408323233

Smaoui, H., Jatmiko, W., & Miniaoui, H. (2024). *Bank Size and Systemic Risk: Evidence from Dual Banking Systems* (SSRN Scholarly Paper No. 5034653). Social Science Research Network. DOI: 10.2139/ssrn.5034653

Smith, A., & Jones, B. (2020). Understanding the role of job satisfaction in employee performance. *International Journal of Human Resource Management*, *31*(4), 567–589.

Smith, K., & Anderson, J. (2022). Consumer preferences for AI-driven personalization. *Retail Analytics Quarterly*, *15*(2), 32–45. DOI: 10.1016/raq.2022.103245

Smith, K., Johnson, P., & Lee, D. (2020). Transparency and trust in AI: Consumer perspectives in digital environments. *Journal of Business Ethics*, *164*(3), 605–623. DOI: 10.1007/s10551-018-4067-3

Sofat, R., & Singh, S. (2017). Determinants of capital structure: An empirical study of manufacturing firms in India. *International Journal of Law and Management*, *59*(6), 1029–1045. DOI: 10.1108/IJLMA-05-2016-0051

Solomon, J. (2020). *Corporate governance and accountability*. John Wiley and Sons.

Song, J., & Philippatos, G. (2004). Have we resolved some critical issues related to international capital structure? Empirical evidence from the 30 OECD countries. Working Paper, University of Tennessee

Sowmya, M., Chhetri, D. K., & Chai, K., Rohit, & Ashraf, S. (2024). Financial Zen: Achieving Market Harmony through Reinforcement Learning and Algorithmic Trading. *2nd International Conference on Data Science and Information System, ICDSIS 2024.* Hassan: Institute of Electrical and Electronics Engineers Inc. https://doi.org/DOI: 10.1109/ICDSIS61070.2024.10594381

Sreenivasan, A., & Suresh, M. (2024). A comparative analysis of lean start-up and design thinking and its integration. *Asia Pacific Journal of Innovation and Entrepreneurship*, *18*(2), 172–194. DOI: 10.1108/APJIE-09-2023-0181

Stackhouse, J. L. (2018, July 23). The ABCs of CAMELS. Federal Reserve Bank of St. Louis. Retrieved from https://www.stlouisfed.org/on-the-economy/2018/july/abcs-camels

Stojčić, N., Dabić, M., & Kraus, S. (2024). Customisation and co-creation revisited: Do user types and engagement strategies matter for product innovation success? *Technovation*, *134*, 103045. Advance online publication. DOI: 10.1016/j.technovation.2024.103045

Subudhi, S. (2019). Banking on artificial intelligence: Opportunities & challenges for banks in India. *International Journal of Research in Commerce, Economics and Management*, *9*(7).

Sung, A., Leong, K., Sironi, P., O'Reilly, T., & McMillan, A. (2019). An exploratory study of the FinTech (Financial Technology) education and retraining in UK. *Journal of Work-Applied Management*, *11*(2), 187–198. DOI: 10.1108/JWAM-06-2019-0020

Suri, T., & Jack, W. (2016). The long-run poverty and gender impacts of mobile money. *Science*, *354*(6317), 1288–1292. DOI: 10.1126/science.aah5309 PMID: 27940873

Surya Gifari, M., Wibowo Manajemen Pemasyarakatan, P., Ilmu Pemasyarakatan, P., Kunci, K., Berpindah, N., & Bank, N. (2023). Pengaruh Job Insecurityterhadap Turnover Intent Pegawai Bank Neo Jakarta. *Neraca Manajemen, Akuntansi Ekonomi*, *1*(8).

Susan, M., Winarto, J., & Gunawan, I. (2023). *Financial Literacy of Micro, Small, and Medium Enterprises: Empirical Study During the Pandemic Period* (pp. 113–122). DOI: 10.1108/S1571-038620230000031014

Suska, M. (2021). Environmental Corporate Social Responsibility (ECSR) on the Example of Polish Champion Oil, Gas and Mining Companies. *Sustainability (Basel)*, *13*(11), 6179. DOI: 10.3390/su13116179

Sutton, J. (2023). The rise of the Neobanks in the UK. The Corporate Law Academy, Retrieved from The rise of the Neobanks in the UK | The Corporate Law Academy

Swan, M. (2015). *Blockchain: Blueprint for a New Economy*. O'Reilly Media.

Swope, C. B., Hernández, D., & Cushing, L. J. (2022). The relationship of historical redlining with present-day neighborhood environmental and health outcomes: A scoping review and conceptual model. *Journal of Urban Health*, *99*(6), 959–983. DOI: 10.1007/s11524-022-00665-z PMID: 35915192

Syaputra, A. A., & Tohirin, A. (2019). Pengaruh kebijakan Financing to Value dan faktor ekonomi terhadap pembiayaan pemilikan rumah di bank syariah. In *Proceeding of Conference on Islamic Management, Accounting, and Economics* (pp. 190-199).

Szabo, N. (1997). *Smart contracts: Building blocks for digital markets*. Extropy Journal.

Sze, J. (2020). *Environmental justice in a moment of danger* (Vol. 11). University of California Press.

Talreja, P., Shrivastava, A., Mishra, A., & Gupta, N. (2023). A Critical Study of ICT Oriented Innovations based on Artificial Intelligence (AI) Applications towards BFSI Sector. In 2023 IEEE International Conference on ICT in Business Industry & Government (ICTBIG) (pp. 1-5). IEEE.

Tantia, V., & Sukanya, R. (2024). Reinventing the business model to navigate the evolving business landscape. In *ESG and ecosystem services for sustainability* (pp. 1–24). IGI Global. DOI: 10.4018/979-8-3693-3771-4.ch010

Tanwar, A. (2024). An Empirical Analysis of the Interactional Relationship Between Liquidity Risk, Credit Risk, and Profitability of Banks in India. In Taneja, S., Kumar, P., Sood, K., Özen, E., & Grima, S. (Eds.), *Finance Analytics in Business* (pp. 267–292). Emerald Publishing Limited., DOI: 10.1108/978-1-83753-572-920241014

Tan, Y., He, M., & Xu, Z. (2019). AI applications in retail: From inventory management to demand forecasting. *Operations Research Perspectives*, *7*, 100127. DOI: 10.1016/j.orp.2019.100127

Tao, Z., & Chao, J. (2023). Financial Fraud and Anomaly Detection Techniques: A Literature Review. *4th International Conference on Computer Science and Management Technology, ICCSMT 2023* (pp. 634-641). Xi'an: Association for Computing Machinery. https://doi.org/DOI: 10.1145/3644523.3644639

Tapscott, D., & Tapscott, A. (2018). Blockchain for capital markets: A vision for the future. *Capital Markets Review*, *11*(2), 39–57.

Tarambale, M., Naik, K., Patil, R. M., Patil, R. V., Deore, S. S., & Bhowmik, M. (2024, February 02). Detecting Fraudulent Patterns: Real-Time Identification using Machine Learning. *International Journal of Intelligent Systems and Applications in Engineering*, *12*(14s), 650–660. Retrieved October 30, 2024, from https://www.scopus.com/record/display.uri?eid=2-s2.0-85185697375&origin=scopusAI

Temelkov, Z. (2020) Differences between traditional bank model and fintech based digital bank and neobanks models. SocioBrains, International scientific refereed online journal with impact factor (74). pp. 8-15. ISSN 2367-5721

Teng, Y., Zheng, J., Li, Y., & Wu, D. (2024). Optimizing digital transformation paths for industrial clusters: Insights from a simulation. *Technological Forecasting and Social Change*, *200*, 123170. DOI: 10.1016/j.techfore.2023.123170

Tente, N., Stein, I., Silbermann, L., & Deckers, T. (2015). *The countercyclical capital buffer in Germany. Analytical framework for the assessment of an appropriate domestic buffer rate*. Deutsche Bundesbank.

Teo, T. (2011). Factors influencing teachers' intention to use technology: Model development and test. *Computers & Education*, *57*(4), 2432–2440. DOI: 10.1016/j.compedu.2011.06.008

Thakur, J., & Kaur, R. (2025). The Promise and Perils of Machine Learning in Finance. In *FinTech and Financial Inclusion: Leveraging Digital Finance for Economic Empowerment and Sustainable Growth* (pp. 120-135). Taylor and Francis. https://doi.org/DOI: 10.4324/9781003514114-9

The Economic Times. (2023, February 10). *India's green bond issuances just 3.8 PC of overall domestic corporatebond market: Report.*https://economictimes.indiatimes.com/markets/bonds/indias-green-bondissuances-just-3-8-pc-of-overall-domestic-corporate-bond-market-report/articleshow/97806148.Cms

Thelwall, M., & Sud, P. (2022). Scopus 1900–2020: Growth in articles, abstracts, countries, fields, and journals. *Quantitative Science Studies, 3*(1), 37–50. DOI: 10.1162/qss_a_00177

Thomas, A., & Gupta, V. (2022). Tacit knowledge in organizations: Bibliometrics and a framework-based systematic review of antecedents, outcomes, theories, methods and future directions. *Journal of Knowledge Management, 26*(4), 1014–1041. DOI: 10.1108/JKM-01-2021-0026

Thomas, N. M., Mendiratta, P., & Kashiramka, S. (2023). FinTech credit: Uncovering knowledge base, intellectual structure and research front. *International Journal of Bank Marketing, 41*(7), 1769–1802. DOI: 10.1108/IJBM-01-2023-0039

Thottoli, M. M. (2024). The tactician role of FinTech in the accounting and auditing field: A bibliometric analysis. *Qualitative Research in Financial Markets, 16*(2), 213–238. DOI: 10.1108/QRFM-11-2021-0196

Thottoli, M. M., Islam, M. A., Yusof, M. F., Hassan, M. S., & Hassan, M. A. (2023). Embracing digital transformation in financial services: From past to future. *SAGE Open, 13*(4), 21582440231214590. Advance online publication. DOI: 10.1177/21582440231214590

Titman, S., & Wessels, R. (1988). The determinants of capital structure choice. *The Journal of Finance, 43*(1), 1–19.

Tiwari, R. K., Hamid, A. B., & Nyamasvisva, T. E. (2024). Potential in Quantum Machine Learning for Real-World Problems. *5th IEEE International Conference on Recent Trends in Computer Science and Technology, ICRTCST 2024* (pp. 695-700). Jamshedpur: Institute of Electrical and Electronics Engineers Inc. https://doi.org/DOI: 10.1109/ICRTCST61793.2024.10578519

Tomfort, A. (2023). Making Green Bonds Greener: Proposals to Increase the Efficiency of Green Bonds. *Journal of Applied Finance & Banking, 13*(1), 5. DOI: 10.47260/jafb/1315

Tong, G., & Green, C. J. (2005), "Pecking Order or Trade-Off Hypothesis? Evidence on the Capital Structure of Chinese Companies", Journal of Applied Economics, Vol 37, Issue 19, Pp.2179-2189, ISSN 0003-6846.

Tongkong, S. (2012). Key factors influencing capital structure decision and its speed of adjustment of Thai listed real estate companies. *Procedia: Social and Behavioral Sciences, 40*, 716–720.

Torrie, V., & Payette, D. (2023). AI governance frameworks for the banking sector. In *Artificial Intelligence in Finance* (pp. 114–141). Edward Elgar Publishing., DOI: 10.4337/9781803926179.00014

Tripathi, V. D. K. (2018), An Analysis of Capital Structure of Leading Automobile Companies in India, Gujarat University's thesis, retrieved from https://shodhganga.inflibnet.ac.in/handle/10603/208737

Tunio, M. N., & Tunio, S. (2024). Green Entrepreneurship Craving for the Green Finance. In Hunjra, A. I., & Goodell, J. W. (Eds.), *The Palgrave Handbook of Green Finance for Sustainable Development* (pp. 237–262). Springer International Publishing., DOI: 10.1007/978-3-031-65756-6_9

Tunio, S., Ihsanullah, , Parveen, F., & Ishaq, K. (2024). Resilience Approaches and Comparative Evaluation of Classical Time Series Models in Modeling and Forecasting Wheat Production. *Pakistan Journal of Humanities and Social Sciences, 12*(2), 2. Advance online publication. DOI: 10.52131/pjhss.2024.v12i2.2287

Turksen, U., Benson, V., & Adamyk, B. (2024). Legal implications of automated suspicious transaction monitoring: Enhancing integrity of AI. *Journal of Banking Regulation, 25*(4), 359–377. DOI: 10.1057/s41261-024-00233-2

Twyford, E. J., Musundwa, S., Tanima, F. A., & George, S. (2024). Bridging the gap: Sustainable development goals as catalysts for change in accounting education and society. *Meditari Accountancy Research, 32*(5), 1758–1786. DOI: 10.1108/MEDAR-02-2024-2375

Tyagi, A. (2024). Risk Management in Fintech. In *The Emerald Handbook of Fintech* (pp. 157–175). Emerald Publishing Limited., DOI: 10.1108/978-1-83753-608-520241015

UNESCO. (2022) UNESCO recommendation on open science. Available from: DOI: 10.54677/MNMH8546

Uralovich, K. S., Toshmamatovich, T. U., Kubayevich, K. F., Sapaev, I. B., Saylaubaevna, S. S., Beknazarova, Z. F., & Khurramov, A. (2023). A primary factor in sustainable development and environmental sustainability is environmental education. *Caspian Journal of Environmental Sciences, 21*(4), 965–975.

Van der Zwan, N., Gersonius, B., & Tilmans, P. (2020). Barriers to financial inclusion: A socio-economic perspective. *The Journal of Development Studies, 56*(9), 1683–1700. DOI: 10.1080/00220388.2019.1643388

Van Eck, N., & Waltman, L. (2010). Software survey: VOSviewer, a computer program for bibliometric mapping. *scientometrics, 84*(2), 523-538.

Van Greuning, H., & Bratanovic, S. B. (2020). *Analyzing banking risk: a framework for assessing corporate governance and risk management.* World Bank Publications. Retrieved from Link.

Veale, M., Binns, R., & Edwards, L. (2018, November 28). Algorithms that remember: Model inversion attacks and data protection law. *Philosophical Transactions. Series A, Mathematical, Physical, and Engineering Sciences, 376*(2133), 20180083. Advance online publication. DOI: 10.1098/rsta.2018.0083 PMID: 30322998

Venkatesh, V., & Bala, H. (2008). Technology Acceptance Model 3 and a Research Agenda on Interventions. *Decision Sciences, 39*(2), 273–315. DOI: 10.1111/j.1540-5915.2008.00192.x

Vergas, N., Cerqueira, A., & Brandão, E. (2015), "The determinants of the capital structure of listed on stock market non-financial firms: Evidence for Portugal", FEP-UP, School of Economics and Management, University of Porto, Retrieved from https://wps.fep.up.pt/wps/wp555.pdf

Vidya, R. (2023). Digital Disruption of Neo Banks with Reference to Indian Banking Landscape. *International Journal For Multidisciplinary Research, 5*(6). Advance online publication. DOI: 10.36948/ijfmr.2023.v05i06.10561

Vijai, C., Suriyalakshmi, S. M., & Elayaraja, M. (2020). The future of robotic process automation (RPA) in the banking sector for better customer experience. *Shanlax International Journal of Commerce*, *8*(2), 61–65. DOI: 10.34293/commerce.v8i2.1709

Vijayalakshmi, D., & Manoharan, P. (2014). Corporate Leverage and its Impact on Profitability and Shareholder Value Creation in the Indian Textile Sector. *Indian Journal of Finance*, *8*(12), 21. Advance online publication. DOI: 10.17010/ijf/2014/v8i12/71689

Wahab, A. (2024). Impact of Artificial Intelligence on Indian Banking Sector-A Study of Banks. [IR-JAEM]. *International Research Journal on Advanced Engineering and Management*, *2*(05), 1261–1268.

Walker, T., Gramlich, D., Vico, K., & Dumont-Bergeron, A. (2020). Emerging Risks: An Overview. In *Palgrave Studies in Sustainable Business in Association with Future Earth* (pp. 01-10). Springer Nature. https://doi.org/DOI: 10.1007/978-3-030-38858-4_1

Wang, G., Chen, G., Zhao, H., Zhang, F., Yang, S., & Lu, T. (2021). Leveraging Multisource Heterogeneous Data for Financial Risk Prediction: A Novel Hybrid-Strategy-Based Self-Adaptive Method. *Management Information Systems Quarterly*, *45*(4), 1949–1998. DOI: 10.25300/MISQ/2021/16118

Wang, H., Liang, Q., Hancock, J. T., & Khoshgoftaar, T. M. (2024). Feature selection strategies: A comparative analysis of SHAP-value and importance-based methods. *Journal of Big Data*, *11*(1), 44. DOI: 10.1186/s40537-024-00905-w

Warjiyo, P. (2017). Indonesia: The Macroprudential Framework and the Central Bank's Policy Mix. BIS Paper, (94n).

Weber, O., & Saravade, V. (2019). Green Bonds: Current Development and Their Future. DOI: 10.13140/RG.2.2.10059.82722

Wenten, I. K., & Nadi, L. (2021). ANALISIS PENGARUH KEBIJAKAN LOAN TO VALUE, NON PERFORMING LOAN, LOAN TO DEPOSIT RATIO DAN SUKU BUNGA KREDIT TERHADAP SUPPLY KREDIT KEPEMILIKAN RUMAH PADA BANK TABUNGAN NEGARA. Jurnal Riset Akuntansi dan Keuangan, 9(1).

West, S., Haider, L. J., Hertz, T., Mancilla Garcia, M., & Moore, M. L. (2024). Relational approaches to sustainability transformations: Walking together in a world of many worlds. *Ecosystems and People (Abingdon, England)*, *20*(1), 2370539. DOI: 10.1080/26395916.2024.2370539

White, J. V., & Borgholthaus, C. J. (2022). Who's in charge here? A bibliometric analysis of upper echelons research. *Journal of Business Research*, *139*, 1012–1025. DOI: 10.1016/j.jbusres.2021.10.028

Witten, E. (2020). A mini-introduction to information theory. *La Rivista del Nuovo Cimento della Società Italiana di Fisica*, *43*(4), 187–227. DOI: 10.1007/s40766-020-00004-5

World Bank. (2023). *India incorporates green bonds into its climate finance strategy*. https://blogs.worldbank.org/climatechange/india-incorporates-green-bonds-its-climate-finance-strategy

World Bank. (2023). Remittances trends: India's global leadership. Retrieved from https://www.worldbank.org

Wu, D., Zhang, H., Feng, Y., & Dong, Z. (2024). MITU: Locating relevant tutorial fragments of APIs with multi-source API knowledge. *Journal of Systems and Software, 112296*. Advance online publication. DOI: 10.1016/j.jss.2024.112296

Wu, F. S., Tsai, C. C., Wu, C. H., & Lo, T. H. (2024). An exploratory study of breakthrough innovations in digital businesses: The case of the Perfect Corporation. *Technological Forecasting and Social Change, 201*, 123233. DOI: 10.1016/j.techfore.2024.123233

Xiong, L., Ning, J., & Dong, Y. (2022). Pollution reduction effect of the digital transformation of heavy metal enterprises under the agglomeration effect. *Journal of Cleaner Production, 330*, 129864. DOI: 10.1016/j.jclepro.2021.129864

Xue, Q., Li, J., Xiao, Y., Chai, Z., Liu, Z., & Chen, J. (2023). A Flexible deep convolutional neural network coupled with progressive training framework for online capacity estimation of lithium-ion batteries. *Journal of Cleaner Production, 397*, 136575. DOI: 10.1016/j.jclepro.2023.136575

Xu, J. (2024, February 29). AI in ESG for financial institutions: An industrial survey. *SSRN*. http://dx.doi.org/DOI: 10.2139/ssrn.4949354

Yadav, N., Singh, A. B., & Tandon, P. (2023). Volatility Spillover Effects between Indian Stock Market and Global Stock Markets: A DCC-GARCH Model. *FIIB Business Review, 0*(0), 23197145221141186. Advance online publication. DOI: 10.1177/23197145221141186

Yang, Q., & Lee, Y. C. (2024). Enhancing financial advisory services with GenAI: Consumer perceptions and attitudes through service-dominant logic and artificial intelligence device use acceptance perspectives. *Journal of Risk and Financial Management, 17*(10), 470. Advance online publication. DOI: 10.3390/jrfm17100470

Yeh, C. H., Lin, H. H., Wang, Y. M., Wang, Y. S., & Lo, C. W. (2021). Investigating the relationships between entrepreneurial education and self-efficacy and performance in the context of internet entrepreneurship. *International Journal of Management Education, 19*(3), 100565. Advance online publication. DOI: 10.1016/j.ijme.2021.100565

Yoel, E. M. T. (2016). Pengaruh kebijakan makroprudensial terhadap siklus kredit: Sebuah studi atas penggunaan instrumen CAR dan GWM perbankan Indonesia 2006-2013. *Bina Ekonomi, 20*(1), 77–96.

Yoganarasimhan, H., Barzegary, E., & Pani, A. (2023). Design and evaluation of optimal free trials. *Management Science, 69*(6), 3220–3240. DOI: 10.1287/mnsc.2022.4507

Yunita, P. (2020). The Future of Indonesia Islamic Banking Industry: Bankruptcy Analyzing the Second Wave of Global Financial Crisis. [IJIEF]. *International Journal of Islamic Economics and Finance, 3*(2), 199–226. DOI: 10.18196/ijief.3227

Yusron, M. (2020). Kondisi Perbankan Stabil, Tidak Ada Bank Umum Yang Ditangani LPS [Press release]. Retrieved from https://lps.go.id/web/guest/siaran-pers/-/asset_publisher/1T0a/content/banyak-dana-koorporasi-berpindah-ke-bank-bank-kecil-lps-tanda-meningkatnya-kepercayaan-pada-sistem-perbankan?inheritRedirect=false&redirect=https%3A%2F%2Flps.go.id%2Fweb%2Fguest%2Fsiaran-pers%3Fp_p_id%3D101_INSTANCE_1T0a%26p_p_lifecycle%3D0%26p_p_state%3Dnormal%26p_p_mode%3Dview%26p_p_col_id%3Dcolumn-2%26p_p_col_count%3D1

Zámborský, P., Ingršt, I., & Bhandari, K. R. (2023). Knowledge creation capability under different innovation-investment motives abroad: The knowledge-based view of international innovation management. *Technovation, 127*, 102829. Advance online publication. DOI: 10.1016/j.technovation.2023.102829

Zhang, Y. (2021). Measuring progress toward sustainable development goals through legal integration and policy guidance. *Journal of Energy and Environmental Policy Options*, *7*(2), 145–162.

Zheng, Y. H., Shi, G., Zhong, H., Liu, M. T., & Lin, Z. (2023). Motivating strategic front-line employees for innovative sales in the digital transformation era: The mediating role of salesperson learning. *Technological Forecasting and Social Change*, *193*, 122593. DOI: 10.1016/j.techfore.2023.122593

Zhou, J., Zhang, Q., Zhou, S., Li, X., & Zhang, X. M. (2023). Unintended emotional effects of online health communities: A text mining-supported empirical study. *Management Information Systems Quarterly*, *47*(1), 195–226. DOI: 10.25300/MISQ/2022/17018

Zhou, S. (2021). Research on Banking Process Optimization Based on RPA in Financial Sharing Mode. [). IOP Publishing.]. *Journal of Physics: Conference Series*, *1865*(2), 022069. DOI: 10.1088/1742-6596/1865/2/022069

Zhu, X., Jiang, L., Gao, Y., & Yin, Y. (2023). Research on Financial Statement Analysis Methods Based on Machine Learning. *3rd Guangdong-Hong Kong-Macao Greater Bay Area Artificial Intelligence and Big Data Forum, AIBDF 2023* (pp. 31-36). Guangzhou: Association for Computing Machinery. https://doi.org/DOI: 10.1145/3660395.3660402

Zhu, L., Li, X., & Wang, Y. (2021). Algorithmic bias in AI-driven retail systems: Implications for ethical AI adoption. *Computers in Human Behavior*, *124*, 106909. DOI: 10.1016/j.chb.2021.106909

Ziouache, A., & Bouteraa, M. (2023). Descriptive Approach of Neo-Banking System: Conception, Challenges and Global Practices. *International Journal of Business and Technology Management*, *5*(2), 194–204.

Zohar, A. (2015). Bitcoin and blockchain: Economic and technological challenges. *Journal of Financial Innovation*, *3*(2), 27–35.

Zou, Y., Zhong, N., Chen, Z., & Zhao, W. (2024). Bridging digitalization and sustainability in universities: A Chinese green university initiative in the digital era. *Journal of Cleaner Production*, *469*, 143181. DOI: 10.1016/j.jclepro.2024.143181

Zupic, I., & Čater, T. (2015). Bibliometric methods in management and organization. *Organizational Research Methods*, *18*(3), 429–472. DOI: 10.1177/1094428114562629

About the Contributors

Sudhir Rana Gulf Medical University, UAE Sudhir Rana is Program Director and Associate Professor at the College of Healthcare Management and Economics, Gulf Medical University, UAE. He has academic associations with Fortune Institute of International Business, India, Paris School of Business, France and Indian Institute of Management, Nagpur, India. He has established FIIB Business Review (Scopus Q1 and Published by Sage Publishing) which is a fast growing multi-disciplinary journal as Editor-in-Chief. He is also co-editor-in-chief of South Asian Journal of Marketing (Emerald) and Senior Editor of International Journal of Emerging Markets (Emerald). He is Editor of two series Review of Management Literature (Scoous by Emerald Publishing) and Advances in Emerging Markets and Business Operations (Taylor and Francis). His area of research is consumer behavior, emerging markets and business education.

Shalini Aggarwal, an alumnus of the Indian Institute of Management (IIM) Ahmedabad is a Professor of Finance at Chandigarh University, Mohali. She has a total work experience of 18 years of industry and teaching. She is MBA with specialisation in Finance and PhD in the area of Risk Management Practices in banking sector of India. She has more than 40 research papers published in SCI, Q1, Q2, Scopus and ABDC- A, B and C listed journal. Her case studies are published in IIM Ahmedabad case centre. She has also authored 2 edited books published by Taylor and Francis. She has completed three funded research projects (two with IIM, Ahmedabad) and one by IMS Ghaziabad. She has conducted more than 100 workshops on data analysis using time series data in SPSS, E-views, finding variables and model building, SLR, Bibliometric analysis, Quantitative study, Qualitative study and R-Studio and has delivered guest lectures at national and international level like South Africa, Bangladesh, Afghanistan, Thailand, Indonesia and Brazil. She has delivered guest lectures at renowned institutes like NITTTR Chandigarh, NIFM, Faridabad (30 lectures), NITTR Chandigarh (5 lectures), GLS School of doctoral research and innovation, Gujarat, VIT Vellor. Further, she has chaired session at national and International conferences in the countries Thailand, Indonesia, Brazil, Muscat, Africa. She has chaired a session at NICMAR, Pune. She has 8 copyrights and 1 patent in her name and acts as reviewer for emerald, inderscience and sage publications. Four students have completed their Ph.D with her. She has floated one special issue with the Journal of Sustainable finance and investment of Taylor and francis entitled "International Finance and Sustainability". She is the associate editor of the journal "Journal of Sustainable finance and investment" and "Asia pacific financial market".

Sharneet Singh Jagirdar, FRM, is a distinguished financial professional with 19 years of diverse experience across ICICI Bank Ltd, Spice Communications Pvt Ltd, Idea Cellular, and TATA DOCOMO. With a PhD in Finance and certification as a Financial Risk Manager (FRM) by US GARP, Dr. Jagirdar excels in driving performance enhancement, implementing best practices, and fostering talent development. His extensive industry expertise is complemented by significant academic contributions, including research publications in top-tier ABDC and Scopus Indexed Q1 journals and presentations at prestigious global conferences such as the Academy of Management (USA) and the European Academy of Management. Dr. Jagirdar is renowned for his success in both industry and academia. His passion for teaching and mentoring future leaders, combined with a deep understanding of financial intricacies, underscores his commitment to excellence. Outside of his professional pursuits, he is an avid runner, reader, and traveler, bringing a well-rounded perspective to his endeavours.

Sanjeev Jain, a distinguished senior executive and thought leader, brings over 30 years of versatile experience to his roles. Armed with a Post Graduate Diploma in Management from the prestigious Indian Institute of Management Ahmedabad and a Bachelor's degree in Engineering with a Gold Medal from Swami Bikaner University, Rajasthan he stands out as a seasoned professional. Mr. Jain has excelled in strategy development, target setting, and plan execution throughout his career, having held key positions in business development, sales, marketing, project management, contract administration, and operations management. His expertise extends to managing profit and loss accounts, showcasing a profound understanding of revenue and cost management. Currently serving as the Director of the Centre of Excellence for Data Analytics and Digital Transformation, as well as heading the AIT Management department at Chandigarh University, Mr. Jain has played pivotal roles in shaping academic and industry landscapes. His earlier assignment at Nirma University reflects his commitment to excellence. In his distinguished career, Mr. Sanjeev Jain has contributed significantly to various fields through his research endeavors. His scholarly works include seminal papers such as "Probabilistic Paradigms for Employee Performance Prognostication: Unveiling Influential Factors via Bayesian Networks," shedding light on innovative approaches to forecasting employee performance. Additionally, his research on "Intrusion Detection Systems for Cybersecurity using Machine Learning" addresses critical challenges in cybersecurity, demonstrating his commitment to advancing technological solutions in safeguarding digital environments. Mr. Jain's expertise extends to "IoT Smart Communication Technologies for Narrow Band IoT," where he explores the intricate realm of Internet of Things, paving the way for efficient communication technologies in IoT networks. Furthermore, his insights into "The Architecture and Design of The Hadoop Distributed File System" underscore his profound understanding of distributed computing systems, contributing to the development of robust data storage solutions. Alongside his research pursuits, Mr. Jain has also secured copyrights, notably for the innovative "NEURODECISION MATRIX OF CONSUMER CHOICE (NDMCC)," showcasing his dedication to pioneering approaches in consumer decision-making. Through his scholarly endeavors and copyright achievements, Mr. Jain exemplifies a commitment to excellence and innovation, leaving a lasting impact on academia and industry alike. Mr.Sanjeev Jain has successfully registered copyright on SOSTAC model recently (A structured strategic planning framework) with the Copyright Office, Government of India.

***

Nitesh Behare is an accomplished author with a wealth of knowledge and 16 years of experience in the academic field. He currently holds the position of Associate Professor at the Balaji Institute of International Business (BIIB), Sri Balaji University Pune (SBUP). Throughout his career, Dr. Behare has made significant contributions to the academic world through the publication of numerous research papers and book chapters, establishing himself as a recognized authority in his field.

Jyoti Bhoj working as an assistant professor in the department RICS School of Built Environment at Amity University, Noida, Uttar Pradesh. She is a distinguished academic and professional in the field of Management and Commerce, with a specialization in behavioral finance. She completed her B.Com (Hons) and M.Com from the University of Delhi, and further pursued a PhD from the University of Rajasthan, focusing on regret aversion and false reference points in residential real estate. Before joining RICS School of built environment she worked at SRM University. She is an Assistant Professor, actively involved in academic teaching, research, and student outreach. Dr. Bhoj has a robust research portfolio, having published numerous articles in reputable journals and presented papers at various national and international conferences.

Sulagna Das is an Associate Professor at JIS University Kolkata with over 18 years of experience in Corporate and Academics. Her research areas cover Management and Social Science. She has papers on Banking, Microfinance, Digital Finance and Marketing, Blockchain and Finance, Cybersecurity aspects of the Finance Sector, Women Empowerment etc. She has done her MBA and PhD from KIIT School of Management, KIIT University, Bhubaneswar. Dr. Das has her articles published in National and International, peer reviewed / Scopus indexed journals and participated in conferences organized by IIMs and IITs. She has achieved Best Paper Awards in conferences of National and International repute and received, JIS Puraskar and Innovation Award in 2020-21 & 2021-22, 2022-23 from her University, for her contribution towards research. Currently, she has five scholars under her guidance. She is a reviewer for Scopus indexed, ABDC-A ranked journals of Springer, Emerald and IGI Global. She is also an external thesis evaluator for Foreign and Central Universities of India.

Aarti Suryavanshi is associated with MRIIRS, Haryana. She is having 17 years of experience in corporate and in academia. She has a number of publications in national and international journals.

Hrishikesh Desai is an accomplished accounting professor who holds several professional designations, such as CA, CFA, CMA and EA. He is also the Director of the Master of Accountancy with Data Analytics Program at the university. His work on emerging technologies has also been published in leading journals, including Issues in Accounting Education, The CPA Journal, The International Journal of Digital Accounting Research, Bloomberg BNA Tax Management Memorandum, and the Enrolled Agent Journal. He has also authored several book chapters in on the topic of Artificial Intelligence (AI) systems. He has also been invited to deliver numerous educational presentations on emerging technologies impacting accountants by the Arkansas Society of Certified Public Accountants (ARCPA).

Suzan Dsouza is an Associate Professor of Accounting at the American University of the Middle East, Kuwait and teaches accounting courses in the BS Accounting and MBA program. She has received her PhD in Accounting and Finance, M com and PGDFM from India. She is a certified CMA from Australia and an Accounting Technician from Institute of Chartered Accountants India. With 7 years of corporate and 16 years of academic work experience across three countries, she has authored 35 research papers, 2 book chapters,1 edited book and presented at various conferences throughout Asia and Europe. One of her recent studies related to the impact of COVID-19, was selected by W.H.O. to be a part of their database. She is an active reviewer with various international journals, as well as an editorial board member with 4 international journals. She has served as a research advisor with the Institute of Management Accountants USA.

Ghodake Shamrao Parashram brings over 14 years of experience in higher education within the field of Management. He currently serves as an Assistant Professor in the Department of MBA at Sanjivani College of Engineering, Kopargaon, an autonomous institute affiliated with Savitribai Phule Pune University. Dr. Ghodake holds a Master of Commerce with a specialization in Advanced Accounting & Business Taxation, a Diploma in Taxation Laws, and a Master of Business Administration with dual specializations in Financial Management and Human Resource Management. He has successfully cleared the SET examination in Commerce and the NET examination in Management. He earned his Ph.D. in Financial Management from Dr. D.Y. Patil School of Management, Pune, under the same university. A seasoned academician, Dr. Ghodake has participated in numerous national and international conferences and has published 15 research papers in prestigious journals. His contributions include 3 research articles in Scopus-indexed journals and 3 case studies published at The Case Centre, UK. He possesses a deep understanding of accreditation processes and compliance with major administrative bodies such as NAAC, NBA, UGC, and AICTE.

Rajat Gupta has been working as Professor in Chandigarh University since 5th sep 2022 .He has done Btech from Govt Engg College in 1995 and Mtech from NIT/RECK, Kurukshetra . He won the gold medal in Mtech in 1999 and Phd in Advance Filter design for good quality image reproduction in 2012. He has 24 years of experience in the field of academics in various universities and Engg.colleges as Professor,Dean, Director.-Principal. He has done the first project in north india in SAP (implementation in real estate BPTP). He has many research papers and patents.

Pradeep Kumar Gupta presently holds the faculty position of Associate Professor in Accounting and Finance area at LM Thapar School of Management, Thapar Institute of Engineering and Technology, Patiala. He has more than eighteen years of teaching, research, consulting, and industry experience in the field of accounting, auditing, financial management and commodity market. His research interests are in value relevance, leverage analysis, investment strategies, corporate social responsibility, and corporate governance. His research is published in the peer-reviewed national and international journals and world's top-rated conferences. He is a trained professional for leading national and international rankings and accreditation.

Shweta Harish I am a dynamic professional with over two decades of experience in the field of banking with specialization in services, operations, portfolio management, Client on-boarding, Client due diligence along with Client Relationship management, Project Management and Business Analysis. Proven track record of driving operational improvement & developing plans to build consumer preference; achieving pre-set service targets by implementing competent business strategies to market using my unique analytical skills, driving automation by simplifying existing end to end processes. Adroit in building and maintaining healthy business relations in the corporate world. I am passionate about bringing value added innovations and high quality client experience. Having Strategy, innovation and management in my DNA which I can use in any field or industry. Currently, I am pursuing PhD in Management to gain the theoretical knowledge and to implement the best practices in the real world. Apart from above, I have post graduation diploma in Data Science and Business Analytical program from University of Texas through Great Learning and post graduation in Business Administration from Symbiosis, India.

Mohammad Irfan is presently working as an Associate Professor at School of Business and Management, Christ University, Bengaluru, India. Dr. Irfan has done his Ph.D. from the Central University of Haryana. He is MBA (Finance), M.Com (Account and Law), and MA (Economics). He has qualified UGC-JRF/SRF/NET in Management and Commerce. Dr. Irfan certified NSEs (NCFM) and BSEs certification. He has experience of more than sixteen years in the area of SAPM, Artificial Intelligence, Machine Learning, Blockchain, Cryptocurrency, Financial Engineering, Fintech, Green Finance, and Alternative Finance. He has to his credit more than 62+ Scopus Indexed articles, includes The Journal of Economic Cooperation and Development (Q2), International Journal of Business Excellence (IJBEX), International Journal of Economics and Management (IJEM), Montenegrin Journal of Economics (Q2), Cogent Business & Management (Taylor & Francis) (Q2), Indian Journal of Finance (IJF) and Journal of Islamic Monetary Economics and Finance (JIMF). His citations reached 406+ along with 13 H-index. Dr. Irfan has published 10 books in Springer, IGI Global Publication (Scopus indexed).

Vishwanathan Iyer is a research enthusiast who is exploring finance, accounting, marketing, HR, and every other field of academics to the best of his abilities. His research is based on primary data as well as secondary data. Being consistent at research and providing quality research work is the ultimate aim of Dr Iyer. Collaborating with authors across spectrum is one of his strengths. Publishing articles and writing chapters are motivating factors for Dr Iyer to pursue his dream of becoming a Researcher to be recokned with.

Pawan Kumar is a Marketing graduate with and Doctorate in Business Management from Haryana School of Business, GJUS&T, Hisar, Dr Pawan Kumar, has a strong inclination towards academics and research. He has about 4 years of teaching experience to his credit. He has published more than 15 research articles in various International and National journals of repute. He has participated in and presented research papers at more than 25 international and national conferences at IIM, IIT, and Internationally, etc. His areas of interest include Marketing Management, Rural Marketing, Computer Applications in Business, and Business Research Methods.

Prashant Kumar Assistant Professor Study Hall College, Lucknow Affiliated to University of Lucknow prshntkumar6@gmail.com ORCID: 0009-0006-0760-268X Dr Prashant Kumar is an assistant professor with more than 8 years of Experience in Academics. He is Doctorate in Business Administration from University of Lucknow, Lucknow, A++ NAAC Accredited. He has qualified NET- JRF in Management and NET in Commerce. His area of Interest includes Financial Management, Portfolio Analysis, International Business, Entrepreneurship, Research Methodology, Production and Operation Management, Logistic and Supply Chain Management, Business Ethics and Corporate Governance, Business Communication. He has publication in refereed journals and chapters in edited Books. He has participated and presented more than 30 papers in various reputed National and International Seminars & Conferences and participated in various FDP, workshops and ICSSR sponsored Research Methodology workshops. He has guided the MBA, MTech. and PhD Course work students in writing the Research report and Research Proposal. Dr Prashant Kumar is Life Member of Indian Accounting Association and All India Commerce Association.

Farhat Lone is a research scholar at Chandigarh university. She has attended many conferences. Her papers are published in scopus indexed journal and ABDC journals.

Mujtaba M. Momin is an Associate Professor of Human Resource Management (HRM) at the American University of the Middle East (AUM), Kuwait, affiliated with Purdue University, Indiana, USA. Previously, he held academic roles at Prince Salman Bin Abdulaziz University, in the Kingdom of Saudi Arabia. Dr. Momin's research focuses on ethics and sustainability, as well as technology in HRM, including the impact of AI and HR analytics on modern HR practices. He also explores organizational behavior (OB), with an emphasis on employee well-being and leadership, and works on employability skills enhancement, developing strategies to better prepare students for the job market. His expertise extends to entrepreneurship, where he promotes innovation and business creation, and corporate social responsibility (CSR), highlighting the importance of ethical business practices. Dr. Momin is passionate about building strong industry-academia partnerships and improving interpersonal communication skills within professional environments.

Ritu Makhija is a Post Graduate Teacher in S. A Jain Senior Model School, Ambala City affilated to CBSE. She has a total experience of 27 Years of teaching . She is M Com., BEd and Pursuing PhD in Management from Chandigarh University. She Is HOD of Commerce and Academic Coordinator . She is Head Examiner of Business Studies and monitor the evaluation process of Business Studies Subject, Exam conducted by CBSE. Recently She has selected as Resource Person chosen By CBSE.

Tabrej Mulla is an experienced academic and researcher specializing in marketing, consumer behavior, and digital transformation. In her academic tenure, she published her research work extensively in reputed journals and actively engages in consulting and training. She is passionate about bridging industry-academia through research and innovation.

Ariz Naqvi is an accomplished associate professor and learning and development expert at the American University of the Middle East in Kuwait, boasting over 17 years of professional experience in academic administration, business development, and training. He holds a PhD in Commerce and a PGCAP from Lancaster University, a Master's in Psychology, and multiple certifications including SHRM, HRCI, CIPD, and AACSB. Dr. Naqvi designs and implements innovative learning programs that ensure academic excellence, drive income through knowledge commercialization, and foster sustainable relationships with external stakeholders. His expertise in digital LMS, blended learning, and evidence-based problem-solving underpins his commitment to enhancing education and research impact.

Manisha Paliwal, Ph.D., M.Phil, MIB, DIPL, B.Sc. with top honors and a Gold Medal, is an accomplished academic researcher with over two decades of experience. She is a Professor, Head of the Entrepreneurship Center, and Deputy Head of the Research and Development Cell at Sri Balaji University, Pune. She has a strong track record of leading national-level research projects and training programs in collaboration with various Ministries in the Government of India. As an accomplished person, she has authored multiple books on subjects including international business, strategic management, international marketing, and business ethics. She has published numerous research papers in reputed Scopus, and ABDC-indexed journals. She is also a PhD guide and reviewer of many international research journals. Her work is characterized by a commitment to ethical values and a dedication to advancing knowledge in strategy, marketing entrepreneurship, ethics, and governance.

Madhu Ruhil is an Assistant Professor at a renowned college IITM Delhi, affiliated with GGSIPU. She has completed her Ph.D in finance in 2023. She has various accolades in her name and published a number of articles in national and international journals.

Jaya Saxena is a seasoned academician with over many years of experience in teaching, research, and administration. Her areas of expertise include financial management, financial services, strategic management, and emerging technologies. She has published numerous research papers and actively contributes to academic conferences and editorial boards.

Manish Sharma is a Certified Project Management Professional (PMP®) with 15 years of extensive experience in Project Management, Business Development, Consultancy, and Strategic Planning. He has a proven track record of coordinating and monitoring operations across various departments, ensuring streamlined processes for increased efficiency and cost reduction. Manish excels in team leadership, operations management, and client relationship building. His expertise includes liaising with government and private agencies, developing business plans, and driving business growth. Dedicated to problem-solving and operational excellence, Manish has successfully managed projects in diverse sectors, including renewable energy, infrastructure, and technology.

Sushma Sharma a HR graduate and Doctorate in Business Management from IMSAR, Rohtak, Dr. Sushma Sharma, is having a strong inclination towards academics. She is M.Phil., M.Ed., and HTET qualified professional. She has about 10 year of teaching experience in GGSIPU affiliated colleges and 2 years in corporate sector. She has published more than 10 research paper in various International and National journals which are UGC listed, EBSCO, Indian Citation indexed journals. She has participated in more than 25 international and national conferences and presented research papers. She has attended more than 20 webinars and 15 Faculty Development Programme. She has also participated in 5 workshops and 2 Management Development Programme. Her areas of interest include Human Resource Management, Strategic Management, Principles of Management & Business Ethics & CSR.

Ram Singh, a forward-thinking educator, serves as a Professor at School of BFSI, Symbiosis University of Applied Sciences, Indore, India. With over 15 years of extensive experience in teaching, research, and administration, Dr. Singh is a prominent figure in academia. His diverse roles include membership on the Editorial Boards of esteemed journals focusing on Accounting, Finance, and Management. Dr. Singh is actively involved in eight national and international academic organizations, contributing significantly to the field. His scholarly work comprises 16 books, 30 research papers, 32 book chapters, and 10 conference proceedings at both national and international levels.

Pritesh Somani is working as an assistant professor at the Balaji Institute of International Business, Sri Balaji University, Pune with a widespread teaching experience of more than 11 years teaching subjects spread across general management and research. He specializes in research methodology and has good experience in operating SPSS. He has conducted sessions through faculty development programs on statistical analysis as an integral part of research methodology. He has published chapters across different disciples that are Scopus-indexed. Also, a few papers are published in ABDC-indexed journals.

Samreen Tunio is currently serving as an Assistant Professor and Head of the Department of Commerce at Gulzar-e-Hijri Girls College in Karachi. Before this role, she worked as a Lecturer of Commerce at Khatoon-e-Pakistan College, Karachi, Sindh, Pakistan. Additionally, she is recognized as an Ambassador for Peace Leader. Ms. Tunio holds a Master of Science degree in Human Resource Management and Organizational Psychology from Bahria University, Karachi Campus, and a Master's in Commerce (Finance). She actively participates in various international conferences, where she has presented numerous papers and won Best Presentation Awards at various platforms. In addition to her conference presentations, Ms. Tunio has published several book chapters, further contributing to her field of expertise. Her research interests are diverse and include Intellectual Capital, Organizational Resilience, Digital Leadership, Innovation, HR Analytics, Ethical AI in HRM, Green HRM, Artificial Intelligence (AI), Machine Learning, Knowledge Management, Entrepreneurship, and Sustainability. Samreen Tunio Department of Political, Economic and Social Sciences, University of Milan, Italy.

Gagan Vibhu brings 28 years of experience in corporate and academic sectors to Apex Institute of Management. He has successfully headed Supply Chain Operations at Vodafone India Services Pvt Ltd and has significant expertise in the financial industry. Holding an MBA, he also has certifications in Logistics and Supply Management from IIM, NISM VA, and International Wealth Management from Moody's. As the head of the Centre of Excellence, Mr. Vibhu fosters innovation and excellence in business education. His visionary leadership shapes future leaders and drives impactful academia-industry collaborations. Committed to mentoring, he empowers students with the knowledge and skills needed in a global marketplace.

Shrikant Waghulkar is a dedicated educator with over 10 years of experience in management education. He holds a Doctorate in Management from Savitribai Phule Pune University, Pune, reflecting his academic rigor and achievements. His teaching and research interests include Research Methodology, Personal Management, Rural Marketing, and Digital Marketing. Beyond academia, Dr. Waghulkar is deeply committed to social welfare and leads a charitable trust focused on improving the educational prospects of farmers' children. Through this initiative, he strives to uplift underserved communities by providing better learning opportunities, contributing to their social and economic empowerment. With a strong passion for both education and marketing research, Dr. Waghulkar's work exemplifies a holistic dedication to advancing knowledge and fostering societal progress.

Index

A

B

C

D

E

F

G

H

I

L

M

N

O

P

R

S

T

U

www.ingramcontent.com/pod-product-compliance
Lightning Source LLC
LaVergne TN
LVHW060359300926
849162LV00006B/1304
* 9 7 9 8 3 3 7 3 0 2 0 9 6 *